Communications
in Computer and Information Science   **1696**

Wei Quan (Ed.)

Emerging Networking Architecture and Technologies

First International Conference, ICENAT 2022
Shenzhen, China, November 15–17, 2022
Proceedings

Springer

Editor
Wei Quan
Beijing Jiaotong University
Beijing, China

ISSN 1865-0929 ISSN 1865-0937 (electronic)
Communications in Computer and Information Science
ISBN 978-981-19-9696-2 ISBN 978-981-19-9697-9 (eBook)
https://doi.org/10.1007/978-981-19-9697-9

This Springer imprint is published by the registered company Springer Nature Singapore Pte Ltd.
The registered company address is: 152 Beach Road, #21-01/04 Gateway East, Singapore 189721, Singapore

Preface

We welcome you to the proceedings of the 2022 International Conference on Emerging Networking Architecture and Technologies (ICENAT 2022), which was due to take place in Shenzhen, China, and was then held online during November 16–17, 2022.

ICENAT 2022 was sponsored by the Peng Cheng Laboratory, and supported by the National Natural Science Foundation of China (NSFC), the Chinese Institute of Electronics, the China Institute of Communications, Beijing Jiaotong University, Beijing University of Posts and Telecommunications, and China Academy of Information and Communications Technology (CAICT).

Although network technology has achieved great success, it also faces new demands and challenges. This drives continuous innovation of network systems and technology to achieve enhanced intelligence, integration, security and mobility. In this context, networking architectures and technologies has become a focus for research from across the world, and distinctive achievements and applications have emerged. The International Conference on Emerging Networking Architecture and Technologies (ICENAT) focuses on the latest achievements in the field of emerging network technologies, covering the topics of emerging networking architectures, network frontier technologies, and industry network applications. ICENAT invites experts to exchange the latest research progress and application experience, so as to jointly explore the development trends and hot topics of emerging networking, and to strengthen cooperation between academia and industry in the field of emerging networking.

We wish to express our sincere appreciation to all the individuals who contributed to the conference. Special thanks are extended to our colleagues in the program committee for their thorough review of all the submissions, which is vital to the success of the conference, and also to the members of the organizing committee and the volunteers who dedicated their time and efforts in planning, promoting, organizing, and helping the conference.

The conference received 106 submissions and this proceedings collects 50 accepted papers submitted by authors from universities, research institutes, and industry, presenting the latest research findings and results of most related topics. Each accepted paper was handled using a strict single-blind peer-review process, with reviews by at least 3 reviewers selected from the technical program committee.

We hope the conference participants had good experiences during the two days of conference sessions.

January 2023

Weizhe Zhang
Ke Xu
Gaogang Xie
Zhiyong Feng
Ping Dong
Li Ao
Fan Shi
Shuai Gao
Changqiao Xu
Hongbin Luo
Hongfang Yu
Jiayuan Chen
Jiguang Cao

Organization

Conference Committee

Conference Chairs

Wen Gao	PengCheng Laboratory, China
Binxing Fang	PengCheng Laboratory, China

Conference Co-chairs

Jianhua Lu	National Natural Science Foundation of China, Tsinghua University, China
Feng Zhang	Chinese Institute of Electronics, China
Yanchuan Zhang	China Institute of Communications, China

Executive Chair

Hongke Zhang	Beijing Jiaotong University, PengCheng Laboratory, China

Technical Steering Committee Chairs

Jiangxing Wu	Information Engineering University, China
Xuemin Shen	University of Waterloo, Canada
Nei Kato	Tohoku University, Japan

Technical Program Chairs

Weizhe Zhang	PengCheng Laboratory, China
Ke Xu	Tsinghua University, China
Gaogang Xie	Chinese Academy of Sciences, China
Zhiyong Feng	Beijing University of Posts and Telecommunications, China
Ping Dong	Beijing Jiaotong University, China
Li Ao	CAICT, China
Fan Shi	China Telecom, China

Conference General Secretary

Jia Chen	Beijing Jiaotong University, China

Program Committee Chairs

Shuai Gao	Beijing Jiaotong University, China
Changqiao Xu	Beijing University of Posts and Telecommunications, China
Hongbin Luo	Beihang University, China
Hongfang Yu	University of Electronic Science and Technology of China, China
Jiayuan Chen	China Mobile Research Institute, Network and IT Technology Research Institute, China
Jiguang Cao	CAICT, China

Publicity Chairs

Dong Yang	Beijing Jiaotong University, China
Fei Song	Beijing Jiaotong University, China

Publication Chairs

Wei Quan	Beijing Jiaotong University, China

Local Chairs

Kai Lei	Peking University Shenzhen Graduate School, China
Binqiang Wang	PengCheng Laboratory, China

Finance Chair

Wei Su	Beijing Jiaotong University, China

Technical Committee Members

Yu Zhang	Harbin Institute of Technology, China
Chunxiao Jiang	Tsinghua University, China
Zhenyu Li	Chinese Academy of Sciences, China
Jianfeng Guan	Beijing University of Posts and Telecommunications, China
Shangguang Wang	Beijing University of Posts and Telecommunications, China
Su Yao	Tsinghua University, China
Fei Qin	University of Chinese Academy of Sciences, China
Bohao Feng	Beijing Jiaotong University, China
Tao Zheng	Beijing Jiaotong University, China
Yuyang Zhang	Beijing Jiaotong University, China

Weiting Zhang	Beijing Jiaotong University, China
Mingchuan Zhang	Henan University of Science and Technology, China
Shan Zhang	Beihang University, China
Long Luo	University of Electronic Science and Technology of China, China
Liang Guo	CAICT, China
Junfeng Ma	CAICT, China

Additional Reviewers

Ao Wang	liangjun Song	Xiang Ji
Changqiao Xu	Ningchun Liu	Xiaohan Qiu
Chenxi Liao	Ping Dong	Xiaoya Zhang
Han Xiao	Qinghua Zhang	Xindi Hou
Haoxiang Luo	Qingkai Meng	Xishuo Li
Hongbin Luo	Qingqing Cai	Xu Huang
Hongfang Yu	Qiwei Zhang	Yuchen Zhang
Jia Chen	Shang Liu	Yucong Xiao
Jianbing Wu	Shuai Gao	Yunxiao Ma
Jing Chen	Tao Zhang	Zhiyuan Wang
Kuo Guo	Wenxuan Qiao	

Contents

Information Centric Networking (ICN)

Networking and the Metaverse:
Challenges and Opportunities

An In-Network Computing Service Placement Mechanism for NUMA-based Software Router

Bowen Liang, Jianye Tian, and Yi Zhu[✉]

School of Computer Science and Communication Engineering, JiangSu University,
Zhenjiang 212013, China
zhuyi@ujs.edu.cn

Abstract. With the development of network computing integration technology, deploying the computing services as Virtual Machines (VMs) on software router is emerging for achieving flexible in-network computing recently. But for current widely used x86 software router, to maximize the throughput of computing service VMs placed on it, how to optimize the placement scheme based on its non-uniform memory access (NUMA) architecture is still a challenge. Facing this problem, we propose a NUMA-oriented in-network computing service placement mechanism (NUMA-ISP). In our mechanism, the computing service VMs to be deployed are selected by their popularity. Through monitoring the memory bandwidth usage inside NUMA node and interconnect bandwidth usage between two NUMA nodes, NUMA-ISP tries to allocate CPU-memory resources to the selected VM from the nodes with enough remaining resources and low bandwidth contention, while closing to the VM of virtual routing function as possible. Experimental results show that, comparing with traditional FF and WF placement mechanisms, NUMA-ISP can increase about 10% total throughput of deployed computing service VMs.

Keywords: In-Network computing · NUMA · Software router · Placement mechanism

1 Introduction

As the era of intelligence approaching, invoking computing services from Internet become more and more frequent for Internet users. Facing this trend, how to improve current network to effectively support the computing service supply has been a hot research topic. Conventional solutions always focus on the design of computing-aware routing or intelligent forwarding [1]. But benefiting from the rapid development of virtualization technology, today, integrating the computing services as VMs with software router to enable flexible in-network computing has emerged as a potential solution.

Due to named addressing is more convenient for VMs migration, since 2014, some researches of in-network computing under Named Data Networking (NDN) [2] are proposed, such as Named Function Networking (NFN) [3] and Named

W. Quan (Ed.): ICENAT 2022, CCIS 1696, pp. 3–12, 2023.
https://doi.org/10.1007/978-981-19-9697-9_1

Function as a Service (NFaaS) [4], etc. NFaaS is a typical framework which extends the NDN router to support in-network function execution by loading lightweight VMs on NDN router. For TCP/IP architecture, most of the traditional in-network computing models are based on programable network devices [5]. Recently, some researchers begin to introduce virtualization and container technology to integrate virtualized network functions and virtualized in-network computing into a general computing platform, instead of delegating computing tasks to network devices [6].

Obviously, loading computing service VMs on router side can shorten the invoking delay while decreasing the network traffic. But facing current widely used NUMA-based software router, how to optimally place computing service VMs on it is still a challenge.

Today, NUMA is a common micro architecture of software router due to most software routers are equipped with x86 Processor [7]. Figure 1 shows an example of integrating Virtual Routing Function (VRF) and computing service VM to a NUMA-based software router, where the router owns two NUMA nodes, named Node0 and Node1 respectively. The VM of VRF is always placed on Node0 and the NIC is also connected to Node0, the computing service VMs will be placed on Node0 or Node1 according to their remaining resources situations. But different placement location will affect the communication efficiency between the VM of VRF and computing service VMs.

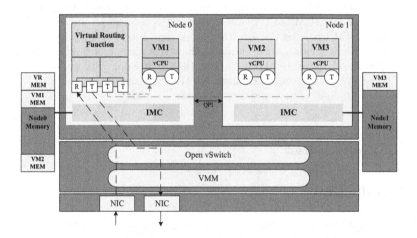

Fig. 1. An example of integrating VRF and computing service VM.

As shown in Fig. 1, now computing service VM1 is placed on Node0, it can directly communicate with the VM of VRF through local memory replication. But computing service VM3 is placed on Node1, so the communication between VM3 and the VM of VRF needs to execute cross-node operations via the interconnect link of two nodes (e.g., Intel QPI link shown in Fig. 1), then leading more transmission delay [8]. On the other hand, for a computing service VM, if its memory is bound on Node0, it will also face the internal memory bandwidth contention with the VM of VRF [9]. For VM2 in Fig. 1, its CPU is bound on Node1 and its memory is bound on Node0, if the VM of VRF is processing very heavy traffic, its performance will seriously degraded due to that most of internal memory bandwidth will be occupied by VRF.

Facing the computing service VMs placement problems for NUMA-based software router, we propose a NUMA-oriented in-network computing service placement mechanism (NUMA-ISP) in this paper. Different from current VMs placement mechanisms mainly consider external affecting factors, e.g., service popularity or free resources [10], NUMA-ISP both considers external computing service popularity and internal resource contention under NUMA architecture. In NUMA-ISP, each CPU-memory allocation scheme is regarded as a bin [11,12], all bins will be periodically sorted according to two factors, one is the VRF's deployment location, another is the bandwidth usage inside single node or between two nodes. Meanwhile, the computing service VMs to be deployed will be also sorted by their popularity. Then, through traversing the sorted bins, NUMA-ISP will search the optimal bin for placing the selected VM. If the memory bandwidth contention from VRF isn't high, NUMA-ISP will try to place computing service VMs close to the VM of VRF; otherwise, NUMA-ISP will preferentially place computing service VMs on the bin with enough resources and low internal bandwidth contention. Experimental results show that, our mechanism can effectively promote the total throughput of placed computing service VMs on NUMA-based software router.

The main contributions of this paper include two points.

(1) We focus on the virtualization-based in-network computing services, propose NUMA-ISP mechanism to optimize their placement locations from the aspect of the micro-architecture of software router.
(2) Based on two classical stress testing suites of NUMA research field, we design the evaluation experiments for NUMA-ISP, then test the throughput upper bound of network-intensive service and memory-intensive service respectively.

The remainder of the paper is organized as follows. Section 2 gives the system architecture of NUMA-ISP. Its detailed designs are presented in Sect. 3. Section 4 provides the experimental results of NUMA-ISP. In Sect. 5, we summarize this paper.

2   System Architecture

In this section, we will introduce the system architecture of a software router for running NUMA-ISP. Figure 2 shows a typical NUMA-based software router, including four nodes, where Node0 has allocated part of its resources (CPU and memory) to the VM of VRF. The NUMA-ISP is built within the Virtual Machine Monitor (VMM) which consists of two main modules, the performance monitor module and the VM placement manager module.

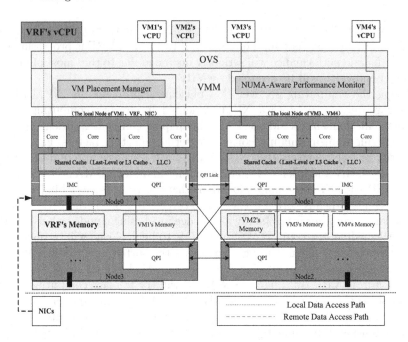

Fig. 2. Internal architecture of a software router for NUMA-ISP.

(1) **Performance Monitor module.** This module collects the running data of software router and provides the statistics to VM placement manager module. First, it records the numbers of historical invoking requests of all computing services, then calculates the popularity of each computing services. Second, through a hardware performance monitoring unit (PMU), it also monitors the free resources (CPU and memory) of each NUMA node and the bandwidth usage, including the internal memory bandwidth usage within each NUMA node and the interconnect bandwidth usage between two NUMA nodes.

(2) **VM Placement Manager module.** When a new computing service VM needs to be deployed on the router, this module runs NUMA-ISP to determine the placement location for target VM according to the statistical data from the performance monitor module.

In addition, on top of VMM layer, the system uses Open vSwitch (OVS) to interconnect the VMs inside the software router and create a mapping between the physical NIC and the virtual NIC (vNIC) of the VMs. When a computing service invoking request reaches the physical NIC, OVS firstly forwards the request to the VM of VRF through the vNIC, and then performs the routing function of VRF to obtain the next-hop virtual outgoing port. Finally, OVS looks up the flow table to decide the destination VM or the next-hop physical output port of software router.

3   Design of NUMA-ISP

In order to clearly illustrate the proposed mechanism of this paper, we first give the following settings.

(1) When a NUMA-based software router runs, the VM placement manager will maintain a list of all possible CPU-memory allocation relationships, **now we use "bins" to denote these allocation schemes**. For example, if the software router owns three NUMA nodes, there will be nine possible CPU-memory allocation schemes, including

$$\left\{ \begin{array}{l} (C_0 M_0)\ (C_0 M_1)\ (C_0 M_2) \\ (C_1 M_0)\ (C_1 M_1)\ (C_1 M_2) \\ (C_2 M_0)\ (C_2 M_1)\ (C_2 M_2) \end{array} \right\}$$

where $C_i M_j$ means that the bin is allocated Node i's CPU and Node j's memory.

(2) If the CPU and memory of a bin are allocated from the same node, this bin is called as a single-node bin; if the CPU and memory of a bin are allocated from different node, this bin is called as a hybrid bin.

(3) The total physical resources of software router are denoted as the set $\{R_C, R_M\}$, where R_C represents CPU Cores and R_M represents memory size.

(4) The software router contains K NUMA nodes, the initial two-dimensional resources of each NUMA node are the same, and the free resources of node k are denoted by $\{R_C(k), R_M(k)\}$, $k = 1, \cdots, K$.

(5) Assuming that all physical NICs are connected to Node0 and the virtual routing function also runs on Node0. Meanwhile, the resources occupied by the VRF are defined as $\{vR_C, vR_M\}$.

(6) Assuming that there are P classes of computing services in the network, and we use VM_p to represent the pth computing service. The resources required by VM_p are defined as $\{vM_C(p), vM_M(p)\}$, $p = 1, \cdots, P$.

Under the aforementioned settings, the workflow of NUMA-ISP consists of three steps. Note that, most in-network computing services are satisfied the features of network-intensive task, so NUMA-ISP is designed for optimizing the network-intensive computing services.

Step 1. Sort all bins

According to the VRF's deployment location, the bandwidth usage and the remaining resources of each NUMA node, NUMA-ISP sorts all bins using the following ordering rules.

Rule 1. Classifying all bins into two groups, the first one names VR group, the second one names non-VR group. All bins containing the resources of Node0 will be assigned to VR group due to that the VM of VRF runs on Node0. Other bins will be assigned to non-VR group.

Rule 2. Within VR group, all bins are sorted in ascending order by the bandwidth usage. For a single-node bin, the bandwidth usage is the ratio of occupied internal memory bandwidth to total internal memory bandwidth. For a hybrid bin, the bandwidth usage is the ratio of occupied interconnect bandwidth to total interconnect bandwidth. When there are two bins with the same bandwidth usage, the bin with the greater sum of remaining resources is prioritized.

Rule 3. Within non-VR group, the single-node bin has priority over the hybrid bin. Next, the single-node bins and hybrid bins will execute internal sorting respectively in ascending order by their bandwidth usage.

Step 2. Sort all Computing Service VMs

After sorting the bins, NUMA-ISP sorts all computing service VM according to their popularity from high to low, then output a sorted set $V = \{VM_1, VM_2, \cdots, VM_P\}$

Step 3. Computing Service VMs Placement

Completing all sorting works, NUMA-ISP selects the computing service VM from set V in order, then search the optimal bin from the sorted bins for selected VM.

To avoid the remaining resources of software router are not enough to deploy the selected VM, NUMA-ISP first checks the resources margin. For pth computing service VM, if its resource requirements are satisfied with Eqs. (1) and (2), NUMA-ISP will be further searched the suitable bin for it, otherwise, it will be ignored.

$$
\begin{cases}
vM_C(p) + vR_C < R_C & , p = 1 \\
\sum_{i=1}^{p-1} vM_C(i) * a(i) + vM_C(p) + vR_C < R_C & , p \geq 2
\end{cases}
\tag{1}
$$

$$
\begin{cases}
vM_M(p) + vR_M < R_M & , p = 1 \\
\sum_{i=1}^{p-1} vM_M(i) * a(i) + vM_M(p) + vR_M < R_M & , p \geq 2
\end{cases}
\tag{2}
$$

where $a(i) = 1$ or 0 represents whether VM_i has been successfully placed on the software router or not.

Next, NUMA-ISP will traverse the sorted bin set, search the first bin satisfying the following condition for selected VM, then place the VM on the target bin. If all bins don't meet the following condition, the placement process of this VM stops immediately. Then, the next one in the set V will be selected and run Step 3 again, until finishing the set V.

Condition: The remaining CPU and memory of the bin are both greater than the requirements of selected VM.

4   Experimental Results

In this section, we evaluate the performance of NUMA-ISP through implementing our mechanism on a software router. Our experiment device is a DELL PowerEdge T110 II server with 2 NUMA nodes and an Intel 10 GigE NIC, each node is equipped with 4 cores CPU (Intel Xeon E5-4610 v2 @2.3 GHz) and 16 GB memory. In this server, we install the vSphere 6.7 hypervisor as VMM, and on the top of VMM, a VM with pre-allocation of 2 cores CPU and 8 GB memory is created for running an IPv4-based virtual routing function, which is implemented using Vector Packet Processing (VPP) [13].

To implement in-network computing service, we select three benchmarks from two classical NUMA stress test suites, and each benchmark application will be loaded on a VM with one core CPU and 4 GB memory during the experiments.

(1) TCP STREAM, a network-intensive application from stress test suite Netperf [14], works in bulk data transmission mode over a TCP connection.
(2) TCP RR, another network-intensive application from stress test suite Netperf [14], will execute multiple requests/responses over a TCP connection.
(3) Memcached, a memory-intensive application from stress test suite Memtiter [15], is a NoSQL key-value databases or memory cached system which can response to remote inquiry from its client.

The comparison placement mechanisms of our experiments are FF (First Fit) [16] and WF (Worst Fit) [17]. The FF mechanism tries to find the first NUMA node that meets the CPU and Memory resource requirements of selected VM. The WF mechanism will select the node that both meets the resource requirements of selected VM and owns the maximum amounts of remaining resources.

To ensure the comparison fairness, for three mechanisms, the computing services VMs to be placed are all selected according to their popularity in our experiments. And we design three scenarios to observe the relationship between VM's popularity and their deployed location.

Scenario I. The popularity level of three benchmark applications is TCP STREAM (high), TCP RR (medium) and Memcached (low).
Scenario II. The popularity level of three benchmark applications is TCP RR (high), Memcached (medium) and TCP STREAM (low).
Scenario III. The popularity level of three benchmark applications is Memcached (high), TCP STREAM (medium) and TCP RR (low).

In experiments, the popularity of each service is simulated through pre-configuring the request frequency on VM placement manager, where the ratio of three level is set as $(0.5, 0.3, 0.2)$.

The experiment running time is 30 s, we repeat the experiment 10 times, record the normalized output throughputs of three benchmark applications (the throughput under FF is normalized to 1). The average experimental results are shown in Fig. 3.

Figure 3 gives the service VMs throughput of three mechanisms under scenario I, II and III respectively. It can be seen that, for the most popular service, such as TCP STREAM in Fig. 3 (a) and TCP RR in Fig. 3 (b), the throughput of NUMA-ISP only has a slight advantage over that of FF and WF, but for the service with less popularity, NUMA-ISP can achieve obvious performance superiority. The reason is that NUMA-ISP utilizes the bandwidth usage to search the optimal resources for service VMs while trying to place service VM close to the VM of VRF.

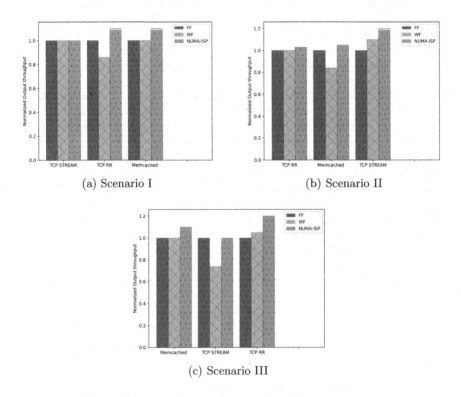

(a) Scenario I   (b) Scenario II

(c) Scenario III

Fig. 3. Normalized throughputs under different scenarios

Obviously, under three mechanisms, the most popular service is usually placed to similar deployment location, but for other services with less popularity, different mechanisms will lead to different deployment locations. In NUMA-ISP, if the resources occupied by VRF on Node0 are not considerable, NUMA-ISP will first search single-node bin from Node0 to place VMs, then shortening the transmission delay. If VRF is facing heavy traffic and the internal memory bandwidth of Node0 is significantly occupied by VRF, NUMA-ISP will preferentially search the hybrid bins from other nodes with enough free internal or interconnect bandwidth, then avoiding resources contention. Benefiting from this design, the throughput of medium and low popularity services are all markedly improved. Comparing with FF, the total throughput of NUMA-ISP increases 12.3%; Comparing with WF, the total throughput of NUMA-ISP increases 10%.

5   Conclusion

In this paper, we propose a NUMA-oriented in-network computing service placement mechanism, named as NUMA-ISP in short. In our mechanism, all possible CPU-memory allocation combinations are defined as bins. Through monitoring the free resources of each NUMA node, internal memory bandwidth usage and interconnect bandwidth usage, NUMA-ISP sorts the bins based on the location of VM of VRF and the monitoring data, then providing optimal placement location for selected computing service VM. The experimental results reveal that, considering the micro-architecture of software router, the deployed in-network computing services can achieve higher throughput and obtain more powerful local processing capability.

Acknowledgement. This paper is supported by Future Network Scientific Research Fund Project of Jiangsu Province (FNSRFP-2021-YB-49).

References

1. Tang, X., et al.: Computing power network: the architecture of convergence of computing and networking towards 6G requirement. China Commun. **18**(2), 175–185 (2021)
2. Zhang, L., et al.: Named data networking. ACM SIGCOMM Comput. Commun. Rev. **44**(3), 66–73 (2014)
3. Tschudin, C., Sifalakis, M.: Named functions and cached computations. In: 2014 IEEE 11th Consumer Communications and Networking Conference (CCNC), pp. 851–857. IEEE (2014)
4. Król, M., Psaras, I.: Nfaas: named function as a service. In: Proceedings of the 4th ACM Conference on Information-Centric Networking, pp. 134–144 (2017)
5. Yang, F., Wang, Z., Ma, X., Yuan, G., An, X.: Switchagg: a further step towards in-network computation. In: Proceedings of the 2019 ACM/SIGDA International Symposium on Field-Programmable Gate Arrays, pp. 185–185 (2019)
6. Hu, N., Tian, Z., Du, X., Guizani, M.: An energy-efficient in-network computing paradigm for 6g. IEEE Trans. Green Commun. Netw. **5**(4), 1722–1733 (2021)
7. Tan, H., Guan, H.: Applications of NFV technology in CENI and the network of telecom carries. Inf. Commun. Technol. Policy **47**(01), 90–96 (2021)
8. Rao, J., Wang, K., Zhou, X., Xu, C.Z.: Optimizing virtual machine scheduling in NUMA multicore systems. In: 2013 IEEE 19th International Symposium on High Performance Computer Architecture (HPCA), pp. 306–317. IEEE (2013)
9. Kim, C., Park, K.H.: Credit-based runtime placement of virtual machines on a single NUMA system for QOS of data access performance. IEEE Trans. Comput. **64**(6), 1633–1646 (2014)

10. Pietri, I., Sakellariou, R.: Mapping virtual machines onto physical machines in cloud computing: a survey. ACM Comput. Surv. (CSUR) **49**(3), 1–30 (2016)
11. Bin packing problem. http://en.wikipedia.org/wiki/Bin_packing_problem (2022)
12. Cheng, Y., Chen, W., Wang, Z., Yu, X.: Performance-monitoring-based traffic-aware virtual machine deployment on NUMA systems. IEEE Syst. J. **11**(2), 973–982 (2015)
13. Themefisher: Vpp (2022). https://fd.io/
14. Brebner, G.: Netperf benchmark (2021). https://github.com/HewlettPackard/netperf
15. Oliveira, F.: Memtier benchmark (2022). https://github.com/RedisLabs/memtier_benchmark
16. Johnson, D.S.: Near-optimal bin packing algorithms. Ph.D. thesis, Massachusetts Institute of Technology (1973)
17. Boyar, J., Epstein, L., Levin, A.: Tight results for next fit and worst fit with resource augmentation. Theoret. Comput. Sci. **411**(26–28), 2572–2580 (2010)

Implementation and Deployment of Digital Twin in Cloud-Native Network

Yuchen Zhan[1], Xiaobin Tan[1,2(✉)], Mingyang Wang[2,3], Tao Wang[1], Quan Zheng[1,2], and Qianbao Shi[2]

[1] Department of Automation, University of Science and Technology of China, Hefei, China
{zyc233,wangtao}@mail.ustc.edu.cn, {xbtan,qzheng}@ustc.edu.cn

[2] Institute of Artificial Intelligence, Hefei Comprehensive National Science Center, Hefei, China
shiqianbao@iai.ustc.edu.cn

[3] Institute of Advanced Technology, University of Science and Technology of China, Hefei, China
wmy903@mail.ustc.edu.cn

Abstract. Virtual-reality fusion is becoming increasingly important for innovative applications such as intelligent manufacturing. Digital twin (DT) is a promising method of realizing virtual-reality fusion by creating high-fidelity digital models of physical objects and interacting with them in real time. However, there is currently a lack of solutions for the implementationand deployment of digital twins on the network, which hinders the in-depth application of digital twins in related fields. In this paper, we propose a scheme for implementing and deploying digital twins in cloud-native networks, with the goal of supporting innovative virtual-reality fusion-based applications. We propose an adaptive organizational form of digital twin components that enables the distributed deployment and execution of digital twins in cloud-native networks and design a digital twin representation method based on the idea of objectoriented programming (OOP). In this scheme, we also design the naming and operation mechanisms for digital twins, and present the trust mechanism among the components of a digital twin using the Merkle tree. Furthermore, we propose an optimization strategy for deploying digital twin components in a cloud-native network. The results of the experiments show that the proposed scheme is both feasible and effective.

Keywords: Digital twin · Virtual-reality fusion · Cloud-native network

1 Introduction

Nowadays, in the application of many scenarios and models, people need to control more and more physical entities. It is very important to manage and calculate entities through the network, which can help administrator to make better decisions. That is virtual-reality fusion, a method which can make communication between cyber space and physical space.

W. Quan (Ed.): ICENAT 2022, CCIS 1696, pp. 13–25, 2023.
https://doi.org/10.1007/978-981-19-9697-9_2

Digital twin (DT) is a digital model of physical objects, which can evolve in real time by receiving data from physical objects, thus keeping consistent with the physical objects in life cycle [6]. Based on the digital twin, it can analyze, predict, diagnose, train, and feedback the simulation results to the physical object to help the optimization and decision-making of the physical object. Digital twin facilitate the means to monitor, understand, and optimize the functions of all physical entities and for humans provide continuous feedback to improve quality of life and well-being [4]. We consider that digital twin is the key technology to implement virtual-real fusion. In order to support new application which have the ability of virtual-real fusion, implementing a digital twin scene on network is exactly what we want to do. Digital Twin has been widely used in modeling and simulation, especially Industry 4.0 [8]. There have a design of digital twin modeling and deployment for Industry 4.0 [9]. But there are still some deficiencies in network management. How to manage the life cycle of digital twin and process control instructions on the network is an urgent problem to be considered [3]. In view of this, this paper proposes a scheme to implement and manage the digital twin on the network.

Cloud-native network is a design methodology that utilizes cloud services to allow dynamic and agile application development techniques that take a modular approach to building, running, and updating software through a suite of cloud-based microservices versus a monolithic application infrastructure. It is helpful for us to contruct digital twin in network.

K. Fu have proposed a deploy strategy of microservices based on QoS-Aware [5]. They find that microservices on the same node competing for resource allocation can affect the QoS of the system instead. So they propose an idea to adjust the deployment strategy based on the node load situation to reduce the impact of resource contention on QoS.

The scheme which can implement and deploy digital twins in cloud-native network proposed in this paper is helpful to support task execution and scheduling and entity information processing in specific scenarios requiring real-time entity control, such as in intelligent manufacturing or intelligent driving scenarios. Base on the idea of OOP, we represent digital tiwn in a hierarchical way. And we distribute and deploy digital twin in the cloud-native network by using container technology so that can improve the resource utilization efficiency and reliability of the system. The contributions of this paper can be summarized as follows:

- We innovatively uses the OOP idea and Merkle tree structure to define the representation of digital twins in network. It enables the digital twin to be defined with a clear structure, integrity protection capability and error correction capability.
- We propose a naming scheme of digital twins in network, makes invoking easier.
- We propose an implementation, deployment and invocation method for the digital twins in the cloud-native network. The digital twin components are implementing by microservices in his paper. It supports distributed deployment, which is suitable for the flexible form of existence in the network and facilitates the storage of the digital twin in the network.

- In order to improve the performance of task executing in cloud-native network invocating digital twins, we design an adaptive algorithm about the deployment strategy of microservices from digital twins. And we verify the effectiveness of the adaptive algorithm through simulation experiments and comparison.

In Sect. 1, we introduce our research scheme, including the definition, implementation, and management of digital twin. In Sect. 2, we analyze the performance impact factors of our solution and consider the optimal solution to improve the performance. In Sect. 3, we compare strategies to show the performance of our adaptive algorithm. And in Sect. 4, we give the conclusion and prospects.

2   Implementation of Digital Twin

2.1   Motivation and Goal

In order to implement new applications such as unmanned driving and intelligent manufacturing, it is necessary to interact and merge the physical space and the network space. Digital twin is a multi-disciplinary, multi-physical, multi-scale and multi-probability simulation process, which makes full use of physical model, sensor update and running history, and completes mapping in virtual space, thus, the whole life cycle process of the corresponding entity equipment is reflected [10].

By constructing an interactive loop between physical space and digital space, the digital twin can reproduce and interact with the physical space entity in the virtual space. Digital twin technology can greatly improve the efficiency of information transfer between physical space and network space, and realize the efficient integration, organization and scheduling of various resources in different scenarios [2].

We consider that digital twin can be seen as a combination of data and services, learning from the idea of edge computing or fog computing, distributed deployment of data and services in the network, and change the network from the process-oriented organization mode to the object-oriented organization mode. In this paper, we use microservices in cloud-native network to implement services in digital twin. Thus, drawing on the Object-oriented programming paradigm, the digital twin is represented as a combination of Class and Object.

In Fig. 1, we consider that a car is composed by several data and microservices. In the later part of this paper, we will discribe how to create a digital twin of this car.

Our research goal is to support digital twin in cloud-native network, including the process of deployment and usage, and consider the performance optimization scheme, suppose a new type of information service which supports the physical system driven by information space such as intelligent manufacturing and intelligent driving.

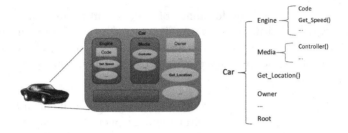

Fig. 1. A car and its interal conponents and its digital twin.

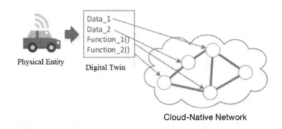

Fig. 2. A digital twin of a car deploy in cloud-native network.

2.2   The Definition and Representation of Digital Twin

The Definition of Class and Object. We draw from the Object-oriented programming paradigm that the digital twin is represented as a combination of Class and Object as we introduced above. Specifically, a class corresponds to a category of digital twin, is the concept of a physical entity. And an object is a concrete digital twin of a class, corresponding to a specific physical entity. Each object has different elements depending on how the physical object is modeled.

In the case of the digital twin Car of a vehicle entity, the data belonging to the vehicle may be static, such as the size data of the vehicle $Car.Length.Data$, $Car.Width.Data$. For dynamic data, such as the real-time location of a vehicle, due to design requirements, it can not be stored in a frequently modified data form$Car.Location$, but instead by function $Car.Get\_Location.funtion()$, to obtain dynamic data with static functions.

For each element to which the twin belongs, a unique component ID is computed as the name, such as $Car.Length.Hash$, $Car.Get\_Location.Hash$. These hash values are computed to establish Merkle tree and the root node values are stored in $Car.Root$. Each digital twin has a Root element. The naming scheme and Merkle tree will be introduced in next paragraph.

Considering the relationship of physical objects, we classify component attributes in digital twin data structures as Private, Public, and Protected to describe the nature of each attribute. It helps to protect privacy and security. The private attributes is decided by the specific type of the digital twin, which mainly contains the exclusive information description of the individual. All digital twin must have public attributes, mainly contains the using information of the digital twin in the network [11]. Anyone can access these data. These are the identity informaiton of digital twin that could be showed to all the visitors, including a description of the digital twin access interface. Protected attributes serve the inheritance relationship, allowing access to the owner or other inheritance digital twins in addition to the digital twins themselves, making it easier for the digital twins to iterate.

Naming System and Organization. On the whole, the naming of digital twin is based on the traditional hierarchical naming of the data structure itself, that the name is set directly at the time of creation. As shown in Fig. 1, we named the component of a digital twin of a car as *Car.Engine.Code*, *Car.Owner*, etc.

On the other hand, considering the requirement of integrity and security service, in order to support the flexible query and modification of twin data content, it is necessary to design and build a distributed, secure and traceable digital twin individual storage structure. Therefore, the Merkle tree structure is selected to construct the digital twin storage structure. The Merkle tree is constructed with the named keyword. The hash value of the leaf node is the check code corresponding to each component of the digital twin, support for distributed storage and integrity checking.

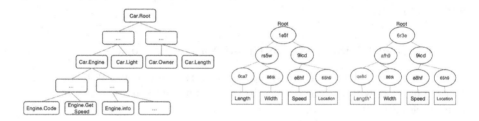

Fig. 3. Merkle Tree of a digital twin of a car and its error-correcting mechanism.

When the contents in a digital twin is updated actively, the Merkle tree-based mechanism needs to update and verify the hash value from the leaf node to the root node layer by layer. In this process, the hash value is recalculated but not authenticated when something is accidentally or maliciously modified, and the error location can be easily checked [7]. In Fig. 3, the components from digital twin of a car are leaf nodes of the Merkle tree. The security protection mechanism will be described in the next paragraph.

2.3   Implementation and Deployment of Digital Wwins in Network

Distributed Deployment of Digital Twin. The elements of digital twins can be stored in different locations in the network and can be deployed and moved as needed. The functions which belonging to the digital twins have two states of representation, which can be stored in static code and run when needed. When awakened, they usually run in memory, provides an interface so that visitors can call functions to get return results.

Mechanism for Maintaining Distributed Deployment. In distributed deployment, when the hash value on a leaf node changes unexpectedly, it will trigger a series of hash value changes to the root node. The security check module can find the unexpected change of the hash value of the root node. Then the system can find the error point layer by layer, recover data through backup or other means.

For active add, modify, delete operations, after maintaining the name, data and the content of the Merkle tree, the system should pass the root node verification.

Create Process from Physical Entity to Digital Twins. Through the pre-established transmission channel, the internet obtain the logical relation information between the physical entity and the data of physical entity components. This channel makes the digital twin update synchronously with the physical entity, and also makes physical entity update synchronously with the digital twin. Next, we deploy the component on distributed nodes in a proper way, create name, routing table, merkle tree and others to make a digital twin individual ready.

2.4   Usage of Digital Twins in Cloud-Native Network

After deploy digital twin in cloud-native network, we can use it to deal with tasks. This part will discribe how digital twin runs and some features of digital twin in cloud-native network.

The Life Cycle of Digital Twins. The life cycle of digital twin includes construction, evolution, evaluation, management and use. We describe the process of building digital twins in the digital twin network designed by the scheme in this paragraph. First, we need to collect the data of the physical object and connect the channel of the real-time sensing synchronous data. On the server node, the data and microservices are deployed while the logical data structure is established, then the digital twin is constructed. After construction, the maintenance and management of digital twins is performed according to the synchronous data change and the return of data and service. The Merkle tree needs to be maintained and integrity checked whenever static data changes.

When an application needs to be executed cooperatively by multiple digital twins, trust relationships need to be constructed to ensure call security. This trust relationship can be implemented by blockchain form or considered with centralized CA, depending on the actual scenario. This is a necessary consideration in practical deployment scenarios in the future.

Invocation of Microservices from Digital Twins. In the new application based on digital twin network, the application runs object-oriented, and the network organizes and runs in the way of object-oriented. In particular, when the visitor needs to access some data belongs to the digital twin, the content can be obtained by the data address, or the return value of the data can be obtained by the corresponding function. So when a function of the digital twin has a call demand, you can directly call it through the function interface.

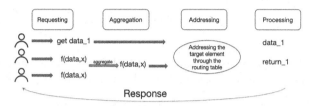

Fig. 4. Process of call for digital twins.

3   Optimal Deployment of Digital Twin in Cloud-Native Network

After the implementation of digital twin network, we should not only be satisfied with the ability to use, but also consider the performance of the network. According to client requirements, when running the new service on the digital twin network, the main difficulties are security, stability and network performance. The most obvious influence on the system function is the network performance. When users make a request to the digital twin network, they expect to get a response as soon as possible. The network performance is better, response time is shorter, then the user experience can be improved.

3.1   System Model and Optimization Problem Formulation

We consider a scenario in which users raise requests with a Poisson distribution of $U = \{U_1, U_2, ...\} \sim Poisson(\lambda)$. Every request is one of K known task types $Task_i \in \{M_1, M_2, ..., M_K\}$. Each task type has a matrix shown relations of microservices that will be called when this task executing.

We consider the global response time under a certain requests distribution as an indicator of network performance. So we can define:

$$T_{ave} = \frac{1}{N} \sum_{i=1}^{N} T_i. \tag{1}$$

T_{ave} is the average of the total response time of N tasks. We consider it can represent global performance of a certain deployment. T_i is the response time of the task Num.i. Furthur, We divide T_i as:

$$T_i = T_{trans,i} + T_{exec,i}. \tag{2}$$

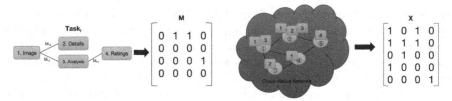

(a) A task type model and its matrix.   (b) A deployment scheme and its matrix.

Fig. 5. Model and its matrix.

$T_{trans,i}$ means the total transmission time of task Num.i. The transmission time is related to the data package size and the channel bandwidth.

$$T_{trans,i} = \sum_{x,y \in Task_i, M_{xy}=1} \mathscr{T}_{trans}(x,y) \tag{3}$$

$$\mathscr{T}_{trans}(x,y) = \frac{1}{|x||y|} \sum_{X_{ix}=1, X_{jy}=1} \mathscr{T}_{trans}(i,j) \tag{4}$$

Let the amount of nodes be R and the amount of microservices be S, we have a $S \times S$ matrix M and a $R \times S$ matrix X shown in Fig. 5. If $M_{ij} = 1$, there have a $i \rightarrow j$ relationship between microservices i and j. If $X_{ij} = 1$, it means the node i has microservice j deploy on it. $|x|$ is the number of how many the microservice x deployed in whole network. $\mathscr{T}_{trans}(i,j)$ is a function to get the transmission time between node i and j.

$$T_{exec,i} = \sum_{x \in Task_i} \mathscr{T}_{exec}(x). \tag{5}$$

$$\mathscr{T}_{exec}(x) = \frac{1}{|x|} \sum_{X_{ix}=1} \mathscr{T}_{exec}(i). \tag{6}$$

$T_{exec,i}$ means the total execution time of task Num.i. $\mathscr{T}_{exec}(i)$ is a function to get the execute time of microservice x in node i.

Thus, the optimization objective of digital twin deployment on the network is: $\min_X T_{ave}$.

Obviously, each node has a finite amount of data storage capacity and computing capacity. That means a single node can not cache an infinite number of data or microservices. So we have some constraint condition when deploy elements in network nodes:

$$\sum_{i \text{ in } x} D_i \leq D_x. \tag{7}$$

D_i is the size of Data i in Node x.
D_x is the storage capacity of node x.

$$\sum_{i \text{ in } x} E_i \leq E_x. \tag{8}$$

E_x is the computing capacity of node x.

So we have the optimization problem of digital twin deployment on the network:

$$\min_{X} \quad T_{ave} = \frac{1}{N} \sum_{i=1}^{N} T_{trans,i} + T_{exec,i} \tag{9}$$

$$s.t. \quad \sum_{i \ in \ x} D_i \le D_x \\ \sum_{i \ in \ x} E_i \le E_x \tag{10}$$

3.2 Adaptive Deployment Algorithm of Digital Twins in Cloud-Native Network

In (4) and (6), we found X is the variable that can affect T_i directly. The $R \times S$ matrix X shows the deployment scheme of microservices in cloud-native network. When X change, there will have new executed scheme for certain $Task_i$ type. Every step we change only one X_{ij} in matrix X and conduct one experiment for results under certain task model and arrival model. Since we do not care about the time complexity of the algorithm, we can traverse and search for the deployment that has best performance. As known as we can find the best deployment scheme while comparing T_{ave} from different X. The search process needs to be carried out under constraints in (10). Since the range of possible optimal solutions is difficult to predict, we choose the genetic algorithm to search for the optimal deployment solution X. Without considering the time complexity, when the number of iterations of the algorithm is large enough, we can assume that what we find will be the optimal solution.

4 Evaluation

4.1 Scenario and Experimental Settings

The microservices in cloud-native network are managed by Kubernetes, which is an open-source container orchestration engine. The cloud-native network in our experiment is comprised of a small-scale cloud platform with VMs. Different VM instances are divided into master node and worker nodes. Master node manages and controls the entire cluster and is responsible for service discovery, service management, service deployment, etc. And worker nodes receive the workload allocated by the master and are responsible for running the containers. The master node deploys the microservices according to the default scheduling strategy or a user-defined strategy. In experiment, as shown in Fig. 5, we have a 5 work nodes network topology with 4 types of microservices. In order to simplify experiment scenario, M is the only type of tasks, as well as $K = 1$. And the parameter of Poisson distribution are set as a variable to get more experiment results. We compute the average response time for 1000 tasks as experimental result.

Because there is few research about this scenario, we have to choose some simple algorithm for comparision. In this paper, to verify the advantage of our adaptive deployment scheme, we use our algorithm (hereinafter abbreviated as ADAPTIVE), greedy deployment strategy (hereinafter abbreviated as GREEDY) and Kebernetes default strategy (hereinafter abbreviated as DEFAULT) to deploy four microservices respectively. Here, GREEDY focuses on reducing the communication overhead among microservices as much as possible. After deployment, we send requests of tasks and monitor the response time, the memory occupancies of each node, etc. to verify the task execution performance of different strategies. These experiments are carried out with the support of China Environment for Network Innovations (CENI-HeFei) [1]. CENI can simulate VMs running microservices in cloud-native network.

4.2   Performance Metrics

- **Task response time:** In a service-based system, task response time is considered as the most important metric. The user's Quality of Service (QoS) also uses tasks' response time as a key performance metric. However, response time is defined as the time required to solve a task request. It is measured from the point in time when a user request is received until the user receives the corresponding response.
- **Storage occupancy:** Storage occupancy is a ratio that indicates the amount of storage capacity used on a node. Since different nodes have different processing capabilities, it may affect the global task execution efficiency when too much content is deployed on a single node.
- **Microservice reuse ratio:** Microservice reuse ratio is defined by the number of a microservice's copies invoked. Without incurring significant queuing delays, the more times a certain microservice's copies is invoked, the better this deployment scheme performs well. This represents a deployment scheme at this point that minimizes deployment redundancy while ensuring mission execution capability.

4.3   Experimental Results and Analysis

Comparison of Task Response Time. In the context of microservices, the response time of the application is the response time of the microservices. In addition, the processing of each microservice request may include a sequence of calls to other microservice components. In this case, the microservice response time includes the sum of the response times of all the invoked microservices. And the response time can be divided as transmission time, execution time and queue time respectively. Microservice-based applications may sometimes experience higher response times comparing with monolithic applications. However, this increase can be addressed by coordinating the microservices belonging to an application.

Fig. 6.(a) shows the comparison of response times of three strategies. We set the rate of arrival model λ as 1, 5, 10 to get response time of three strategies with dynamic λ respectively. Overall, the response times all increase with the increase of λ. The reason is the limited number of nodes in the experimental scenario so that the queuing delay is inevitable when the task arrival interval is short. However, we find that GREEDY performs well than other two strategies with low λ but becomes significantly worse as λ increases. This is because GREEDY tend to deploy microservices more centrally. When the task density increases, it will generate more queuing delays easily while the task arrival interval decreases. But ADAPTIVE has well performance for high λ. This shows that our ADAPTIVE algorithm can handle scenarios that are more likely to generate request queues.

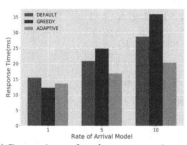
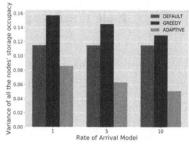

(a) Comparison of task response time of 3 deployment schemes.

(b) Comparision of variance of all the nodes' storage occupacy of 3 schemes.

Fig. 6. Comparison of experimental results.

Storage Occupancy and Load Balancing. For microservices, in addition to the aforementioned, the time spent in communication between the different microservices can also be affected by different deployment. For these reasons, the variance of storage occupancy of all the nodes can be considered one of the most important metrics for assessing the fairness of a deployment strategy. We use variance to show the balance of storage occupancy on the overall nodes in experiments. We define variance of all the nodes' storage overhead as V_{usage} to represent the load balance of a certain deployment scheme from deployment strategy.

$$V_{usage} = \frac{1}{R} \sum_{i}^{R} (u_i - \bar{u})^2 \tag{11}$$

u_i is the storage occupancy of node i, while $\bar{u}$ is the average of all the u_i. Fig. 6.(b) shows the V_{usage} of three strategies. We believe that low variance means well load balancing. Obviously, ADAPTIVE performs well at load balancing because our algorithm tend to deploy microservices more evenly. GREEDY performs very bad in variance because of centralizing strategy. This is the price of simplicity in deploying.

Microservice Reuse Ratio. We calculate reuse ratio in following experiments by the number of reuse times and the number of total tasks. We consider to compare the reuse ratio of microservice 1 in node 1 under different rate λ. Table 1 shows reuse ratio of a certain microservice decreases with increasing λ. This is because ADAPTIVE will deploy more copies of microservice for decreasing queuing delay. In expecting, when the task density in arrival model goes higher, the ADAPTIVE algorithm tends to deploy copies of microservices on each node, while the reuse time of a certain microservice tends to be constant $N \div R = 200$. In Table 1, reuse ratio is still higher than 0.2 when $\lambda = 10$. We can believe that our ADAPTIVE algorithm is effective in minimizing replica deployment and increasing reuse.

Table 1. Reuse ratio of microservice 1 in Node 1

Rate	1	2	3	5	10
Adaptive	0.964	0.832	0.705	0.497	0.412
Greedy	0.958	0.960	0.955	0.947	0.949
Default	0.955	0.746	0.496	0.358	0.240

By comparising the three strategies of deployment, we can find that the performance of adaptive algorithm deployment(ADAPTIVE) is better than other deployment strategies on response time and load balancing. Our algorithm decreases response time by more than 30%. This is because our algorithm generate the deployment scheme to make the data distribution in the network more consistent with the network topology and the task model. We can determine that our deployment algorithm is efficient to reduce response delay when tasks occured.

4.4 Summary

By experiment, we find that the ADAPTIVE algorithm performs well. Under the condition of high reliability of prior knowledge of task model, the algorithm can keep excellent performance in all kinds of environments, which helps to improve the performance of the digital twin in cloud-native network.

5 Conclusion

In this paper, we propose a digital twin network implementation scheme. After analyzing the advantages and disadvantages of the scheme, we propose a feasible optimization idea for deployment strategy of digital twin in cloud-native network, committed to real-time synchronization with objects. Not only for intelligent driving and intelligent manufacturing scenarios but also for more scenarios where there are upper-level task scheduling and control requirements, as a better service for the underlying architecture.

Acknowledgments. This work was supported in part by the National Key R&D Program of China under Grant 2020YFA0711400, in part of Key Science and Technology Project of Anhui under Grant202103a05020007, in part by the key R&D Program of Anhui Province in 2020 under Grant 202004a05020078, in part by the China Environment for Network Innovations under Grant 2016-000052-73-01-000515.

References

1. China environment for network innovations (hefei) (2022). https://ceni.ustc.edu.cn/
2. Bole, M., Powell, G., Rousseau, E.: Taking control of the digital twin. In: SNAME Maritime Convention. OnePetro (2017)
3. Datta, S.P.A.: Emergence of digital twins. arXiv preprint arXiv:1610.06467 (2016)
4. El Saddik, A.: Digital twins: the convergence of multimedia technologies. IEEE Multimedia 25(2), 87–92 (2018)
5. Fu, K., et al.: Qos-aware and resource efficient microservice deployment in cloud-edge continuum. In: 2021 IEEE International Parallel and Distributed Processing Symposium (IPDPS), pp. 932–941. IEEE (2021)
6. Grieves, M.W.: Virtually Intelligent Product Systems: Digital and Physical Twins (2019)
7. Osterland, T., Lemme, G., Rose, T.: Discrepancy detection in merkle tree-based hash aggregation. In: 2021 IEEE International Conference on Blockchain and Cryptocurrency (ICBC), pp. 1–9. IEEE (2021)
8. Rosen, R., Von Wichert, G., Lo, G., Bettenhausen, K.D.: About the importance of autonomy and digital twins for the future of manufacturing. Ifac-papersonline 48(3), 567–572 (2015)
9. Schroeder, G.N., Steinmetz, C., Rodrigues, R.N., Henriques, R.V.B., Rettberg, A., Pereira, C.E.: A methodology for digital twin modeling and deployment for industry 4.0. Proc. IEEE 109(4), 556–567 (2020)
10. Stark, R., Fresemann, C., Lindow, K.: Development and operation of digital twins for technical systems and services. CIRP Ann. 68(1), 129–132 (2019)
11. Tao, F., Qi, Q., Wang, L., Nee, A.: Digital twins and cyber-physical systems toward smart manufacturing and industry 4.0: correlation and comparison. Engineering 5(4), 653–661 (2019)

Domain-Specific Programming Router Model

Zhongpei Liu[✉], Gaofeng Lv, Jichang Wang, and Xiangrui Yang

National University of Defense Technology, Changsha, China
747541120@qq.com

Abstract. Router architecture continues to innovate, performance continues to upgrade and functionality continues to expand, but it still can't support operators to customize network services. On the other hand, the performance and functions of "white box" switches such as Server-Switch based on software defined architecture are better to meet the service requirements of operators. Using DSA (Domain Specific Architecture) as reference, the self-developed programmable switching chip is used as the core of router data plane for innovation. A new programmable data processing unit (dpDPU) based on Reconfigurable Match Tables (RMT) pipeline is designed and implemented to optimize protocol processing and break through heterogeneous accelerated programmable data forwarding plane, software/hardware cooperative protocol control plane, and advanced programming method based on domain language. DPRouter has the advantages of simple structure implementation, high performance switching chip, data processor domain language programming, software defined control and so on. It can simplify the development of network services by operators and lay the foundation for the integration of traditional router and switch devices.

Keywords: White-box switch · Data processor unit · Domain-specific programming · Software defined

1 Introduction

As the core device of the Internet, a router forwards network packets and realizes the interconnection of user networks and enterprise networks. Router has the characteristics of standard protocol, programmable chip, and closed operation environment, which makes its protocol open mechanism opaque and has been monopolized by equipment manufacturers such as Cisco and Huawei for a long time, which not only increases equipment investment, but also slows down iteration and upgrade, hindering network innovation. It is difficult for carriers to design new routing and forwarding processes based on their own service requirements. Router and switch model structures are shown in Fig. 1.

Driven by multiple demands such as device function expansion, performance upgrade and network operation and maintenance simplification. The router architecture has developed from the earliest centralized and distributed forwarding architecture, ForCES (Forwarding and Control Element Separation) architecture separating forwarding and control, reconfigurable component-based router architecture, and servitization router

© The Author(s), under exclusive license to Springer Nature Singapore Pte Ltd. 2023
W. Quan (Ed.): ICENAT 2022, CCIS 1696, pp. 26–37, 2023.
https://doi.org/10.1007/978-981-19-9697-9_3

architecture oriented to function extension, to the current software-defined router architecture based on programmable network chips, etc.Innovations in router architecture have focused on extending functionality, but have not provided developers with feasible programming methods, especially easy programming methods for carriers.

On the basis of standard switching chip, the Server-Switch architecture mainly introduces network accelerator for function expansion [1]. The accelerator mainly uses programmable chips, such as network processor NP, programmable hardware FPGA, data processor DPU, etc. It has powerful network processing ability and advanced programming ability, which greatly simplifies the development difficulty of operators, so as to get the introduction and deployment of operators.

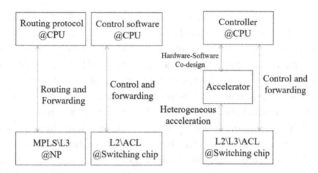

Fig. 1. Router and switch model structures

John Hennessy and David Patterson proposed in their Turing Award speech in 2017 that the main solution after the end of Moore's law is to introduce and enable Domain Specific Architecture (DSA). Carrier-oriented domain programming router has become a new direction of router development. Server-Switch architecture provides a new idea for router architecture innovation and programming [2]. However, there are three major challenges to directly applying Server-Switch architecture in routers: (1) The router data plane needs programming ability and advanced customization ability in router network field to simplify carrier-level programming, which can not be met by the Server-Switch based on the existing network switching chip. (2) Routers are at the core of the network. Under the Server-Switch architecture, accelerators mainly accelerate auxiliary functions such as network management, which cannot meet the requirements of customized service function expansion and performance optimization of carriers in routers. (3) Data plane programming is faced with the legitimacy verification of dynamic reconfiguration and security issues such as shared resource competition management. The existing Server-Switch architecture is not fully open and is not considered.

Aiming at the above challenges, we first propose DPRouter, a domain programming router model based on Server-Switch architecture. The main works include:

The data processor dpDPU based on RMT is designed and implemented, which supports network domain language programming and enables router domain programming ability. The design and implementation of centralized and distributed routing control method, support multi-route optimization, support data plane flow table unified management.

A DPRouter prototype system is designed and implemented to support multi-slot dpDPU based on domestic programmable FPGA, which greatly enhances the performance of router custom service processing. The principle and feasibility of DPRouter model are verified by Segment Routing over UDP (SRoU), NDN, flow detection and other network functions, which lays a foundation for the development of domain programming router and provides a technical guide for the future integration of router and switch platform.

2   Related Work

2.1   White-Box Switch

At present, from the domestic and global data center network equipment market, network software and hardware white-box has become a trend, carrier network, 5G cloud white-box has become an important evolution trend of the future carrier network [3]. The "white box" switch adopts the open device architecture and the idea of decoupling hardware and software to improve the programmability and flexibility of the device. White box switch hardware equipment, such as Server-Switch equipment, adopts commercial programmable chips, unified chip interface, and open source switching operating system under the standardized structure, forming the initial industrialization capacity.

An important component of the "white box" switch operating system is the basic software platform layer, which provides the basic installation environment, driver and other software. Representative open source achievements include SONiC, Stratum, DENT and so on. At the 2016 Open Computing Project OCP Summit, Microsoft officially launched SONiC, a network Switch operating system based on Debian GNU/Linux, which decoupled data control surface from forwarding surface through SAI (Switch Abstract Interface) Interface [4].

2.2   White-Box Router

The four major European operators Vodafone, Telefonica, Orange and TIM also worked together to develop "white box" router specifications, such as Odyssey-DCSG (Disaggregated Cell Site Gateway).

Orion, a second-generation SDN network control plane developed by Google, manages the configuration and real-time control of all data centers Jupiter, campus, and dedicated wide area network B4 [5]. Orion is designed around standalone microservices that coordinate all states through an extensible network information base. The main function of Orion is the routing engine RE, which provides common routing mechanisms, such as L3 multi-route forwarding, load balancing and tunnel encapsulation.

In 2001, the IETF established the ForCES Working Group with the goal of "using a standardized set of mechanisms to connect these components, providing better scalability, and allowing separate upgrades of the control and forwarding planes to facilitate faster device innovation."

In terms of router function reconfiguration, under the advocacy of PLA Information Engineering University, Zhejiang University, National University of Defense Technology, Zhejiang Gongshang University and many other units, a new network technology research group aiming at reconfiguration has been formed in China. In this paper, an open reconfigurable router platform is proposed, which takes the network bearer service as the core and the reconfigurable routing and switching platform as the key supporting technology, and designs a service-oriented network architecture: Universal Carrying Network (UCN) model [6].

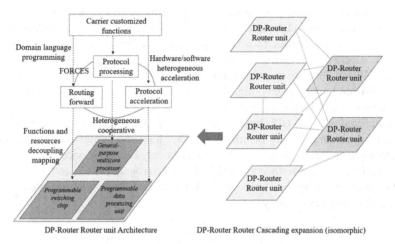

Fig. 2. DPRouter router model

2.3 Network Domain High-Level Language Programming

Nick Mckeown of Stanford University and Jennifer Rexford of Princeton University proposed the domain Programming language P4 (Programming Protocol-Independent Packet Processor) [7]. P4 can not only control the data flow for forwarding, but also define the data processing process of switches and other forwarding devices by software programming, so as to achieve complete SDN in a true sense. Compared with Openflow switch's fixed parsing logic, P4 can customize the data parsing process and perform parallel and serial Match and Action operations. Openflow only supports serial operations and does not support protocol-independent forwarding.

Xilinx launched SDNet toolchain for network packet processing scenarios in 2014 to support FPGA logic development based on high-level languages on Xilinx FPGA. SDNet allows users to program various data packet processing functions, from simple packet classification to complex packet editing.

3 Domain Programming Router Model

3.1 Domain Programming Router DPRouter Architecture

To meet the upgrade requirements of functional services of carriers, the software defined network architecture of separating routing and forwarding and control is adopted to decouple the network protocol and packet processing function from the underlying hardware resources. Based on Server-Switch programmable switching chip SW and programmable data processing unit DPU, DPRouter supports carrier-oriented router domain programming, and constructs a domain programming router with controllable routing and forwarding and programmable network function. DPRouter router model is shown in Fig. 2.

The general router data plane is mainly responsible for network packet routing and forwarding processing, and the functions of high performance route searching and queue scheduling are mainly realized by network processor NP, while the DPRouter data plane is mainly composed of programmable switching chip SW and programmable data processor DPU. SW and DPU are connected through high-speed network interface. Compared with NP, SW has larger capacity, higher port density, open look-up table control, and is managed by software definition. It supports Layer 2 and layer 3 network operations, and ACL. Compared with NP, DPU has the same capacity, more comprehensive computing, storage, network, and security functions, supports high-level programming languages, and supports high-speed storage interfaces to effectively support service function expansion. The DPRouter data surface SW and DPU are heterogeneous and collaborative, and undertake user-oriented general network packet processing and carrier-oriented network service processing, respectively.

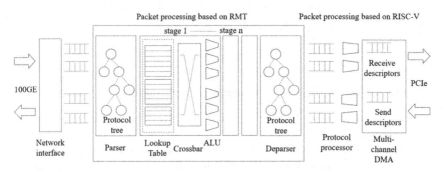

Fig. 3. DPU and its RMT pipeline architecture

The general router control plane is mainly responsible for network protocol processing, and the general multi-core processor CPU provides the running platform for protocol stack processing. The DPRouter control plane also uses a general-purpose multicore processor that connects the SW and DPU via a high-speed system bus. Compared with the traditional router control plane implementation, the routing protocol processing tasks in the CPU of DPRouter control plane can be unloaded to DPU for processing, thus accelerating the convergence speed of network protocols. The DPRouter can implement the frame-type Switch to realize system expansion and router performance upgrade by stacking cascades.

3.2 Domain Programming Data Processor DpDPU Based on RMT

In order to meet the requirements of domain high-level language programming, this paper proposes dpDPU, which is a data processor for domain programming. The reconfigurable RMT + pipeline is designed and implemented in dpDPU [8]. DPU and its RMT pipeline architecture is shown in Fig. 3. The RMT + pipeline is mainly composed of a programmable parser, a multi-level match-action execution unit and a deparser. The programmable parser generates a state transition table according to the target protocol tree, supports packet option operations based on offsets, and realizes the extraction of Packet Header Vector (PHV). Table lookup unit supports exact search based on Hash and fuzzy match search based on CAM. The action execution unit is a customized ALU, extended to support 48bits and 63bits instructions, and support operations such as reading, writing, addition and subtraction of PHV registers. The specific operation of packet options can be realized by writing instruction sequences [9].

To enhance the flexibility of the RMT + pipeline, you need to support the mapping between any PHV packet option and any ALU in the current stage. The fully connected pathway faces problems such as resource limitation and fan-out delay. Therefore, a configurable Crossbar architecture is introduced to interconnect PHV with the local ALU cluster. When the domain-level language program is mapped to the local ALU, the program instructions are assigned to the specific ALU. Based on the target packet options and PHV processed by the instructions, the mapping relationship is established and the Crossbar connection relationship is configured.

DpDPU not only implements RMT + pipeline, but also implements the acceleration of network protocol stack, such as fragment reassembly and verification.

3.3 Domain Programming Languages and Compilation Methods

[{"table":"STAGE2_TABLE_0","Stage":2,"vlanID":3,
"keys":
[{"key":"eth_src"}],
"Actions":[
{"action":"forward","ins":[{"ins":"FW","port":"806000
0000000A58","RO":true}]},
{"action":"discard_1","ins":[{"ins":"DR","discard":"A0
10000000000D70","RO":true}]},
{"action":"set_tport_src","ins":[{"ins":"GE","tport_src":
"tport_src","RO":false}]},
{"action":"set_tport_dst","ins":[{"ins":"GE","tport_dst"
:"tport_dst","RO":false}]},
{"action":"test_AB","ins":[{"ins":"AI","ip_dst":"310000
0000000C68","RO":true}]},
{"action":"test_ABC","ins":[{"ins":"GE","ip_dst":"D000
020000000950","RO":true},
{"ins":"GE","ip_src":"D100030000000478","RO":true}
,{"ins":"FW","port":"8060000000000EB8","RO":true}]
]}

Fig. 4. FPGA-oriented domain language program back-end representation

Based on P4c design, the mapping and configuration of domain language to RMT pipeline are realized. P4c is the reference compiler for the P4 programming language and can support both P4–14 and P4–16 languages. The compiler has a highly modular design, and its core consists of three parts: a standard front-end, a mid-end, and an adaptive back-end.

Intermediate Representation (IR) is used to transfer objects and logical relations between modules. Front-end compilation is independent of the hardware architecture and only validates, type-checks, and optimizes programs for the domain language. Intermediate compilation is independent of the goal, creating tables, actions, handling predicate logic, optimizing, etc., from front-end IR objects. Back-end compilation is related to hardware implementation, allocating resources such as tables, registers, operation instructions and control flow, and generating target-specific execution code or configuration data.

Finally, the resources, control flow and instructions of the mid-end of FPGA back-end compiler based on RMT pipeline architecture are mapped to the hardware architecture of FPGA implementation Figs. 4, 5 and 9.

3.4 Centralized and Distributed Control Plane

The DPRouter control plane supports distributed routing protocols, such as BGP. Server-Switch router Peer nodes can directly establish BGP sessions, advertise routing information, calculate routing tables, generate local forwarding tables, and download them to the layer-3 forwarding tables on the switch chip.

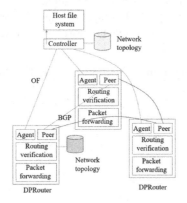

Fig. 5. A combination of centralized and distributed control structure

The DPRouter data plane is based on a programmable switching chip (SW). In this case, the domain programming routers are interconnected to form a large-scale Local Area Network (LAN) and support software defined network management. The centralized network controller floods LDP packets through the Server-Switch router nodes, discovers the network topology, calculates the routing table, generates the forwarding table of the node, and delivers it to the flow table of the switch chip.

The main problem facing the centralized and distributed control model is the selection of routing entries, that is, whether the entries in the switching chip are configured by the routing protocol or by the centralized controller. Usually, the switching chip is selected according to the priority configured by the administrator. This method mainly suffers from suboptimal problems. To this end, a routing table verifier is set up on the DPRouter control plane to establish the local network topology based on LDP and LSA packets. Based on the policies configured by the administrator, such as link cost, the routing entries generated by routing protocols or controllers are compared and selected.

3.5 DPRouter Packet Co-processing

The SW handles the network processing functions of the DPRouter. The SW supports multilevel flow table forwarding, Layer 2 and Layer 3 router operations, and ACL processing.

Domain programming router DPRouter not only supports typical network packet processing, but also supports special route forwarding under the heterogeneous cooperation between SW and dpDPU, such as SR over UDP forwarding. Because SRoU source routing information is carried in packet payloads, traditional routers cannot resolve UDP payloads and cannot support SRoU forwarding. For DPRouter, after receiving the SRoU packet, the data plane SW forwards the packet whose destination address is local to the dpDPU according to the forwarding rules. DpDPU supports Layer 4 processing. It extracts SRH from the UDP payload, replaces the outer destination IP address, and returns the packet to the SW. The SW searches the table again based on the new destination IP address and forwards the packet.

The SW and the dpDPU are heterogeneous. In addition to the packets whose destination IP addresses are local, the SW forwards or mirrors the packets to the dpDPU based on the flow table rules. The SW also forwards the unmatched packets to the dpDPU for additional network services. In this process, the link between the SW and dpDPU may become a bottleneck, and only part of the traffic can be supported by new services. On the other hand, you can add dpDPU configurations based on service traffic requirements.

4 Domain Programming Router Function Extension Method

Domain programming router supports operators to develop customized network functions based on domain high-level languages and dynamically extend router functions.

4.1 On-Stream Detection for Carrier Management Control

In the DPRouter architecture, in addition to SW, independent dpDPU is also introduced into the data plane. Operators can implement measurement and other functions based on the platform, such as on-stream detection. When the router receives a packet and the packet matches the on-stream detection object, the SW sends the incoming timestamp ts0 and outgoing timestamp ts1 of the packet to the dpDPU, which calculates and records the packet processing delay. Based on the traffic path planning, the controller collects the hop-by-hop processing delay on the packet forwarding path from the dpDPU to calculate the path delay, which provides decision-making basis for load balancing and route selection.On-stream detection can not only provide packet routing and forwarding processing delay, but also provide high-precision traffic statistics based on this framework.

4.2   Name Routing and Forwarding for New Carrier Services

Similar to SRoU routing and forwarding, name-based routing and forwarding is proposed in Named-Data Network (NDN) [10]. SRoU Packet format and processing flow is shown in Fig. 6. Regardless of the Layer-2 Ethernet packet format or Layer-3 IP packet format, DPRouter data plane SW does not have the function of name resolution and content storage, and does not support NDN packet addressing and forwarding. In this case, the data plane dpDPU is responsible for performing name-based route forwarding.

Fig. 6. SRoU Packet format and processing flow

In dpDPU, it is mainly completed based on the instruction in RMT pipeline. First, it extracts the name keyword to look up the Content Store (CS) Table. After a match, it directly writes the result into the packet. If no match is found, a new PIT entry is created for this name.

For the above NDN packet processing flow, it is necessary to describe the NDN packet structure, CS table structure, PIT table structure, and packet processing control flow based on domain-level language. After compiling the high-level language code directly, it can be dynamically downloaded to dpDPU for NDN routing and forwarding, which simplifies the development of additional network functions of operators and effectively supports the rapid iteration of network functions.

4.3   Zero-Trust Access Control for Carrier Security

Zero-trust security is a new security concept and architecture, which mainly defines the user identity as the main body of refined access control, and dynamically adjusts based on the trust assessment of the request context. It is an endogenous security mechanism to deal with unknown threats. Attribute-based Access Control (ABAC) is used in the DPRouter Control plane to realize the minimal and dynamic authorization for users [11]. At the same time, based on the user identity attribute information, the control surface trust evaluation engine determines the risk of the access context, identifies the abnormal behavior of the access request, and adjusts the evaluation results to adjust the user's authority.

The DPRouter data plane mainly implements transmission encryption and decryption, traffic detection, port hiding for software defined boundary SDP based on dpDPU, and implements trusted agent to dynamically determine user rights, so as to access applications, data or packets on the data plane.

Zero-trust secure access control dynamically adjusts the authority of the subject according to the context, effectively deals with the unknown threats caused by the third-party user program when processing unexpected packets in the DPRouter dynamic environment, and enhances the security and reliability of DPRouter.

5 Implementation and Performance Analysis of DPRouter Prototype

5.1 Design and Implementation of DPRouter Prototype

The DPRouter prototype is mainly oriented to operators' customized service function expansion. In order to ensure the multi-service processing performance, the SW board and multi-slot dpDPU interconnection architecture are adopted. The system can support a maximum of 10 dpDPU, as shown in the Fig. 7. The SW uses commercial switching chips and provides 18 100GE service ports and 10 100GE ports for connecting to the dpDPU. DpDPU uses domestic high-performance programmable hardware FPGA to realize network packet processing such as RMT + and provides two 100GE service ports, one of which is connected to SW. The DPRouter prototype achieves a maximum throughput of 1.8Tbps and supports additional network service processing of 1Tbps traffic.

In the prototype verification stage, dpDPU is implemented by FPGA, which has dynamic programming ability, supports continuous iteration of functions, has partition reconstruction ability, supports multi-user resource sharing, has heterogeneous fusion SoC, supports collaborative optimization of computing, storage and network, and can meet the functional expansion requirements of DPRouter data surface. With the optimization of functions, when performance becomes the bottleneck, the key IP cores in dpDPU can be solidified.

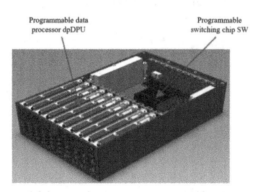

Fig. 7. DPRouter prototype system

5.2 Performance Testing and Analysis

Based on the 100Gbps network tester, the DPRouter prototype is tested. Table 1 shows the DpDPU FPGA prototype resource usage. The network tester generates full-rate SRoU

Table 1. DpDPU FPGA prototype resource usage.

Prototype system	LUT	BRAM
Corundum	65801(5.57%)	349(16.2%)
Corundum + RMT	153104(12.95%)	447(20.69%)
Corundum + RMT that supports tenant isolation	154451(13.06%)	447(20.69%)

packet test excitation, which is processed by SW and dpDPU, and then returned to the network tester. The number of packets forwarded by the router and the forwarding delay are counted under different test packet lengths. It can be seen from the test results, as shown in the Fig. 8, that dpDPU can process 100Gbps traffic at line speed, ensuring the new service processing performance.

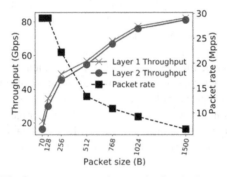

Fig. 8. Performance of RMT pipeline in dpDPU

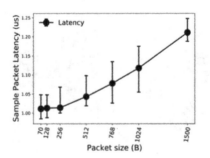

Fig. 9. RMT pipeline processing delay in dpDPU

The commercial switch chip in the DPRouter prototype system implements 1.8TBps non-blocking switching and supports most of the traffic line speed processing such as L2, L3 and ACL. DpDPU based on FPGA, limited by FPGA resources and frequency, realizes RMT + which supports limited instruction set and packet option modification and other program execution. Complex payload processing and other program execution will degrade the performance of pipelined packet processing. RMT + expansion and strong enhancement are the next research focus.

6 Conclusion and Outlook

Router architecture continues to innovate, performance continues to upgrade and functions continue to expand, but it still cannot meet the needs of operators for personalized network services. Taking the self-developed programmable switching chip as the core of router data plane, a domain programming data process unit (dpDPU) based on RMT + pipeline is designed and implemented to optimize protocol processing, and a domain programming router model DPRouter with reconfigurable functional programmable system is constructed. It can simplify the development of customized network services of operators and lay the foundation for the unified integration of traditional router and switch devices.

In the future, the RMT + domain customized instruction set can be extended, and the virtual-real network test bed based on DPRouter prototype can be built to demonstrate its function and performance.

References

1. Lu, G., et al.: ServerSwitch: a programmable and high performance platform for data center networks. In 8th USENIX Symposium on Networked Systems Design and Implementation (NSDI 11) (2011)
2. Hauser, F., et al.: A survey on data plane programming with p4: Fundamentals, advances, and applied research. arXiv preprint arXiv:2101.10632 (2021)
3. de Figueiredo, R.D.J.A.: API design and implementation of a management interface for SDN whitebox switches (2018)
4. AlSabeh, A., Kfoury, E., Crichigno, J., Bou-Harb, E.: Leveraging sonic functionalities in disaggregated network switches. In: 2020 43rd International Conference on Telecommunications and Signal Processing (TSP). IEEE, pp. 457–460 (2020)
5. Wang, H.-S., Zhu, X., Peh, L.-S., Malik, S.: Orion: a power performance simulator for interconnection networks. In: 35th Annual IEEE/ACM International Symposium on Microarchitecture, 2002 (MICRO-35). Proceedings. IEEE, pp. 294–305 (2002)
6. Wang, H.-X., Wang, B.-Q., Yu, J., et al.: Research on architecture of universal carrying network. Chinese J. Comput. 32(3), 371–376 (2009)
7. Bosshart, P., et al.: P4: Programming protocol-independent packet processors. ACM SIGCOMM Comput. Commun. Rev. 44(3), 87–95 (2014)
8. Bosshart, P., et al.: Forwarding metamorphosis: fast programmable match-action processing in hardware for SDN. ACM SIGCOMM Comput. Commun. Rev. 43(4), 99–110 (2013)
9. Wang, T., Yang, X., Antichi, G., Sivaraman, A.,Panda, A.: Isolation mechanisms for {High-Speed}{Packet-Processing} pipelines. In: 19th USENIX Symposium on Networked Systems Design and Implementation (NSDI 22), pp. 1289–1305 (2022)
10. Saxena, D., Raychoudhury, V., Suri, N., Becker, C., Cao, J.: Named data networking: a survey. Comput. Sci. Rev. 19, 15–55 (2016)
11. Claise, B.: Cisco systems netflow services export version 9. Tech. Rep. (2004)

Multi-agent Deep Reinforcement Learning-based Incentive Mechanism For Computing Power Network

Xiaoyao Huang[1]([⊠]), Bo Lei[1], Guoliang Ji[2], Min Wei[1], Yan Zhang[3], and Qinghua Shen[3]

[1] Research Institute China Telecom, Beijing 102209, China
huangxy32@chinatelecom.cn
[2] No. 208 Research Institute of China Ordnance Industries, Beijing 102202, China
[3] China Telecom Co. Ltd Beijing branch, Beijing 102202, China

Abstract. The computing power network is an attractive technology that integrates computing resources and the network to provide converged service and has attracted a great deal of attention. In this paper, we study the problem of task assignment and incentive design in CPN. We first formulate the optimization problem as a multistage Stackelberg game with one leader and multiple followers. In the first stage, the platform determines the optimal assignment of tasks (resource purchase) by solving the problem of utility maximization based on the prices submitted by the resource providers. In the second stage, a multi-agent deep reinforcement learning based algorithm is proposed for each resource provider to optimize its pricing strategy based on the environment information. Finally, extensive simulations have been performed to demonstrate the excellent performance of the proposed algorithm.

Keywords: Computing power network · Multi-agent reinforcement learning · Stackelberg game

1 Introduction

In recent years, with the growth of the amount of data in the network and the development of cloud computing, edge computing and other technologies, how to integrate the computing resources of each node and the network to achieve the coordination of decentralized computing resources has become an important research direction for future network development [1–3]. To solve the above problem, the computing power network (CPN) is proposed. The CPN distributes the computing, storage, network, and other resource information of the service nodes through the network control plane (such as the central controller and the distributed routing protocol). Based on the context of the network and user requirements, the CPN provides optimal allocation, association, transaction, and scheduling of computing, storage, and network resources.

Supported by National Key Research and Development Program 2021YFB2900200.

W. Quan (Ed.): ICENAT 2022, CCIS 1696, pp. 38–49, 2023.
https://doi.org/10.1007/978-981-19-9697-9_4

The key characteristic of CPN is that it consists of a huge amount of heterogeneous computing resource equipment, which can generate great power if such resource can be exploited efficiently. Therefore, it is of great significance to incentivize such distributed computing resource nodes to join CPN and assign tasks among them. However, due to the distribution of CPN, it is important to design algorithms to solve the utility optimization problems without leaking the privacy of participants.

In this paper, we study the problem of task assignment and incentive design in CPN. We first formulate the optimization problem as a multistage Stackelberg game with one leader and multiple followers. In the first stage, the platform determines the optimal assignment of tasks (resource purchasing) by solving the problem of maximization of the utility based on the prices submitted by resource providers. In the second stage, a multi-agent deep reinforcement leaning based algorithm is proposed for each resource provider to optimize its pricing strategy based on the environment information. Finally, extensive simulations have been performed to demonstrate the excellent performance of the proposed algorithm.

2   Related Work

With the rise of edge computing and cloud computing, more and more researchers are focusing on the management and arrangement of computing resources. In [4], a micro-service-based edge computing device is designed in the field of intelligent distribution transformer, and a computing resource allocation method based on a micro-service-based edge computing device is proposed. Xiaoyu Xia et al. made the first attempt to study the data, user and power allocation (DUPA3) problem in the multi-access edge computing (MEC) environment, which tackles the edge data caching problem in MEC environments [5,6] investigated dynamic communication, computation, and energy resource management in computation-limited and energy-limited Wireless powered mobile edge computing (WP-MEC) systems and proposed dynamic throughput maximum (DTM) based on perturbed Lyapunov optimization to jointly optimize the allocation of communication, computation, and energy resources. In [7], Zhipeng Cheng et al. studied the problem of joint task partitioning and power control in a fog computing network with multiple mobile devices (MDs) and fog devices, where each MD has to complete a periodic computation task under the constraints of delay and energy consumption.

Meanwhile, researchers hope to efficiently allocate computing, storage, and other basic resources among the cloud, edge, and terminal through the network. In [8], Liang Tian et al. introduce a solution based on cloud, network, and edge deep fusion, CFN, to meet the requirements of on-demand deployment and flexible computing scheduling between multilevel computing nodes. In 2021, Recommendation ITU-T Y.2501 describes the framework and architecture of the computing power network (CPN) [9]. Since then, the research of CPN has been concerned [10] discusses the development trend of network from cloud and network integration to computing and network integration, and analyzes the computing power network in the 6G era. Through demonstration, it can be concluded that the computing power network technology solution can effectively meet the multi-layer deployment and flexible scheduling requirements of 6G services for computing, storage, and network in the future. Bo Lei et al. propose a computing power network based on IP extended computing and network interconnection architecture [11]. It is a new type of network that realizes the best resource allocation by distributing computing, storage, algorithm, and other resource information of service nodes through network control plane (such as centralized controller, distributed routing protocol, etc.) [12] implements the Kubernetes-based prototype CPN testbed with micro-service architecture, realizing key enabling technologies of CPN, including computing modeling, computing awareness, computing announcement, and computing offloading.

3   System Model

As shown in Fig. 1, the computing power network studied in this paper is composed of a set of users $\mathcal{N} = \{1, 2, ...N\}$, a set of heterogeneous computing power resource devices $\mathcal{M} = \{1, 2, ...M\}$ and a control platform s. The system works by a time-slotted manner. Users with tasks submit offloading request to the platform for task processing. Computing power resource devices, also called resource providers, provide computing service by joining the platform while asking for a certain monetary payment. The platform works to determine the amount of resources to purchase from each resource provider on behalf of the users, and then the tasks of the users can be accordingly assigned to the resource providers. Note that we consider a general "many-to-many" scenario where each task can be assigned to multiple resource providers, and each resource provider can take multiple tasks. In addition, tasks are one-to-one corresponding with the users (virtual user nodes can be made for users with multiple tasks); thus, we use users and tasks interchangeably in the following sections. The interactions between the platform and the resource providers are summarized as follows.

(1) A resource provider $m \in \mathcal{M}$ willing to participate in the platform to provide computing service first registers with the platform with the information of its maximum amount of available resource F_m and its desired reward per unit of resource p_m;

(2) Given the participation information of the resource providers, the platform determines the amount of resource to purchase from each resource provider and assign the tasks according to user request;

(3) The platform informs the users of the result of the assignment and users offload tasks to the corresponding resource providers for processing.

(4) Resource providers process the tasks and return the computation results to users.

3.1   Utility of Users

The users submit task offloading requests to the platform for task processing. A task r_n of the user $n \in \mathcal{N}$ can be denoted by a triple $< D_n, C_n, \tau_n >$ where

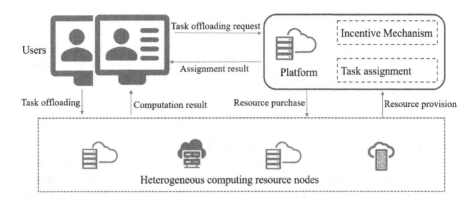

Fig. 1. Illustration of the architecture of the computing power network under study.

D_n is the data size of the task, C_n is the task computation workload, and τ_n is the maximum task delay requirement desired. The utility of a task r_n from user $n \in \mathcal{N}$ is determined by the value of the task and the payment to the resource providers for task processing. Let $x_{n,m}$ denote the amount of resources purchased by user $n \in \mathcal{N}$ from the resource provider $m \in \mathcal{M}$. Users offload tasks to the computing power network for desired quality of service (QoS), and delay is a key metric to characterize QoS in the computing power network. Therefore, we calculate the valuation of a task r_n offloaded to the service provider m (denoted V_n) as follows.

$$V_{n,m} = \frac{2}{1 + e^{(\gamma(Td_{n,m} - \tau_n))}} v_n, \forall n \in \mathcal{N}, m \in \mathcal{M}, \tag{1}$$

where $Td_{n,m}$ is the experienced task delay of the user n, v_n is the basic value of the task r_n and γ is a parameter that controls the degree of valuation drop. We use the sigmoid function here for the reason that the value of a task decreases with the task delay increasing. The delay $Td_{n,m}$ of a task r_n assigned to the resource provider m includes the transmission delay $Tr_{n,m}$ and processing delay $Tp_{n,m}$ which can be calculated as follows respectively.

$$Tr_{n,m} = \frac{D_m}{s_{n,m}} + \frac{L_{n,m}}{V}, \tag{2}$$

where $s_{n,m}$ is the link transmission rate and $L_{n,m}$ is the transmission distance from user n to destination resource provider m.

$$Tp_{n,m} = \frac{C_m}{x_{n,m}}, x_{n,m} > 0 \tag{3}$$

Thus, the total delay $Td_{n,m}$ of a task r_n is calculated as $Td_{n,m} = Tr_{n,m} + Tp_{n,m}$.
The utility of a user n can then be expressed by

$$\phi_n(x_n, \boldsymbol{p}) = \sum_{m \in \mathcal{M}} (V_{n,m} - p_m x_{n,m}), \forall n \in \mathcal{N}. \tag{4}$$

3.2   Utility of Resource Providers

The utility of a resource provider $m \in \mathcal{M}$ joining the platform consists of the payment from the users and the cost of task processing. The cost for resource provider m of processing task r_n by the amount of the purchased resource can be calculated as

$$I_{n,m} = i_{e,m} \alpha_m C_n x_{n,m}^2 + i_{t,n} \frac{C_n}{x_{n,m}}, \tag{5}$$

where the left part and the right part of the equation represent the energy consumption cost and the cost of time occupation, respectively. Furthermore, $i_{e,m}$ and $i_{t,n}$ are the economic costs per unit of energy consumption and time at n receptively. As a result, the utility of a resource provider m can be expressed as

$$\psi_m(p_m, \boldsymbol{x}_m) = \sum_{n \in \mathcal{N}} (p_m x_{n,m} - I_{n,m}), \forall m \in \mathcal{M}. \tag{6}$$

3.3   Utility of the Platform

The platform works to purchase resource from resource providers on behalf of users and thus assign user tasks to resource providers. Thus, the platform aims to maximize the social welfare of the whole system, taking into account the utility of both users and resource providers, which can be expressed as

$$\phi(\boldsymbol{x}, \boldsymbol{p}) = \sum_{n \in \mathcal{N}} \sum_{m \in \mathcal{M}} (V_{n,m} - I_{n,m}). \tag{7}$$

4   Game Analysis

In this section, the optimization of the utilities of the stakeholders in the system is formulated as a two-stage one-leader-multi-follower Stackelberg game.

4.1   Problem Formulation

The platform aims to optimize the resource purchasing decision for each user and thus maximize the social welfare that is formulated as

$$\textbf{P1:} \quad \max_{\boldsymbol{x}} \quad \phi(\boldsymbol{x}, \boldsymbol{p}) \tag{8}$$

$$\text{s.t.} \quad \sum_{m \in \mathcal{M}} x_{n,m} p_m \leq b_n, \ \forall n \in \mathcal{N}; \tag{8a}$$

$$\sum_{n \in \mathcal{N}} x_{m,n} \leq F_m, \ \forall m \in \mathcal{M}; \tag{8b}$$

$$U_n \geq 0, U_m \geq 0, U_s \geq 0, \ \forall n \in \mathcal{N}, m \in \mathcal{M}. \tag{8c}$$

In the above formulation, constraint (8a) is the budget constraint for each user. Constraint (8b) is the resource capacity constraint for each resource provider. Constraint (8c) ensures the individual rationality of each stakeholder.

Each resource provider m aims to maximize its utility by optimizing its unit resource price, and thus the optimization problem is formulated as follows.

$$\textbf{P2:} \quad \max_{p_m} \quad \psi_m(p_m, x_m) \tag{9}$$

$$\text{s.t.} \quad p_m \geq 0. \tag{9a}$$

4.2 Stackelberg Game

The platform plays the role of the leader who chooses a strategy to maximize its utility first. Then each resource provider optimizes its strategy to maximize the utility based on the observation of the strategy adopted by the leader. The Stackelberg leader-follower game is formally defined as follows:

(1) Player: The platform and resource providers are the players in the game, with the platform as the leader and the candidate resource providers as the followers;
(2) Strategy: For each resource provider, the strategy is to determine its unit resource price; for the platform, the strategy is to determine the amount of resource to purchase from each resource provider;
(3) Utility: The utility functions for each resource provider and the platform are given in Eq. (6) and Eq. (7) respectively.

The objective of the game is to find the Stackelberg equilibrium(SE) solutions from which neither the leaders nor the followers have incentive to deviate. The formal definition of the SE is given as follows.

Definition 1. Let $x_m^* = \{x_{n,m}^*\}_{n \in \mathcal{N}}$, $x^* = \{x_{n,m}^*\}_{n \in \mathcal{N}, m \in \mathcal{M}}$ and $p^* = \{p_m^*\}_{m \in \mathcal{M}}$, the point (x^*, p^*) is a Nash equilibrium if it satisfies

$$\psi_m(p_m^*, x_m^*) \geq \psi_m(p_m, x_m^*), \forall p_m \neq p_m^*, \forall m \in \mathcal{M}, \tag{10}$$

and

$$\phi(p^*, x^*) \geq \phi(x, p^*), \forall x \neq x^*. \tag{11}$$

For problem P1, we derive the second derivatives of $\phi(x, p)$ as

$$\phi'' = \frac{2\gamma D\tilde{e}[\gamma D(\tilde{e} - 1) - 2x(1 + \tilde{e})]}{x^4(1 + \tilde{e})^3} - 2i_e\alpha - \frac{2C_n}{x^3}, \tag{12}$$

where $\tilde{e} = e^{(\gamma(Td_{n,m} - \tau_n))}$ and thus $\phi'' <= 0$ so that it is a typical convex optimization problem that can be solved using existing convex optimization tools,e.g. CVX. In this paper, we fully consider the competition among resource providers and propose a Multi-Agent Deep Reinforcement Learning-based(MADRL) algorithm for user utility maximization, which is given in detail in the next section.

5   Proposed MADRL Algorithm for Resource Providers

Each resource provider has to give the strategy based on the strategy given by the platform. We propose a Multi-Agent Deep Reinforcement Learning-based algorithm for resource providers to learn a good strategy by interacting with the environment to optimize its long term reward without requiring any prior knowledge of the actions by the others.

MADRL in this paper is based on a combination of deterministic policy gradient and deep learning, where two deep neural networks are used as approximators for policy and critic [13]. The actor network takes state as input and outputs the deterministic action. Furthermore, the critic network takes the state and action generated by the actor network and outputs the estimated Q-value. Different from traditional multi-agent learning system, which states that the state transition of the environment depends on the joint behavior of the agents, which results in slow policy convergence, we adopt an improved algorithm MADRL with the following two key important techniques.

(1) Centralized training and distributed execution: The training process requires information exchange among agents, while only local observation is needed for each agent during the execution time.
(2) Augmented critic: Critic is augmented by inferring the policies of the other agents [14] .

Next, the functions for the learning process are presented in detail.

State Observation: The state is a vector of environment characteristics that is connected to the objective of the optimization problem defined in Eq. 9. Observations of the previous K time slots are taken into account so that agents have a better chance of tracking changes in the environment. In each time slot t, the observation space of the resource provider i is defined as follows:

$$O_m^t = \{p_m^{t-1}, x_m^{t-1}, ..., p_m^{t-K}, x_i^{t-K}\}, \forall m \in \mathcal{M}. \tag{13}$$

Action: In each time slot t, each resource provider observes the assignment of tasks in the previous K time slots and then determines the unit price of resource p_m^t for the current time slot according to the outputs of the actor network which can be expressed as follows.

$$a_m^t = \mu_m(O_m^t | \theta^{\mu_m}). \tag{14}$$

It should be noted that the action space in this paper is continuous, which meets the requirement of the MADRL.

Reward Function: The reward function is designed for the agents to approach the objective in Eq. 9 and, accordingly, the reward function of the resource provider m including the payment from users and the cost of task processing is defined as

$$r_m^t = \log(1 + p_m^t \sum_{n \in \mathcal{N}} x_{m,n}^t - \sum_{n \in \mathcal{N}} I_{n,m}), \tag{15}$$

We adopt a logarithm function here to ensure a negative reward (also seen as penalty) when the payment received (that is,$p_m^t \sum_{n \in \mathcal{N}} x_{m,n}^t$) is not enough to compensate the task processing cost (that is,$\sum_{n \in \mathcal{N}} I_{n,m}$).

Critic: The loss function of the critic network is defined as

$$\mathcal{L}_m = \frac{1}{T} \sum_t^T (y_m^t - Q_m(o^t, a^t | \theta^{Q_m}))^2, \tag{16}$$

where $a^t = \{a_1^t, ..., a_M^t\}$, $o^t = \{o_1^t, ..., o_M^t\}$ and y_m^t is the target action value defined by

$$y_m^t = r_m^t + \gamma Q_m'(o^{t+1}, o'^{(t+1)} | \theta^{Q_m'}). \tag{17}$$

Furthermore, extensive experiments show that the proposed algorithm achieves the best performance when $\gamma = 0$, which means that the immediate reward can properly reflect the true value of state action.

Actor: The gradient of expected reward with deterministic policies μ^{θ_m} for agent m is expressed as

$$\nabla_{\theta^{\mu_m}} \mathcal{J} \approx \frac{1}{T} a_m \nabla_\theta a_m \nabla_{a_m} Q_m(o^t, a_m, a_{M \setminus m}^t | \theta^{Q_m})|_{a_m = \mu_m(o_m^n | \theta^{\mu_m})}, \tag{18}$$

where $a_{M \setminus m}^t = \{a_1^t, ..., a_{m-1}^t, a_m^t, ..., a_{\mathcal{M}}^t\}$. The detailed process of MADRL is presented in detail in Algorithm 1.

Algorithm 1: Procedure for MADRL Training.

1 Initialize: Randomly initialize critic network $Q_m(o, a | \theta^{Q_m})$ and actor $\mu_m(o | \theta_{\mu_m})$ with weights θ^{Q_m} and θ^{μ_m};

2 Initialize Q_m' and μ_m' of target networks with weights $\theta^{Q_m'} \leftarrow \theta^{Q_m}$ and $\theta^{\mu_m'} \leftarrow \theta^{\mu_m}$;

3 **for** *episode* = 1 *to* I **do**

4   Initialize a random process $\mathcal{M}$ for action exploration;

5   Achieve initial observation state o^1;

6   **for** $t = 1$ *to* T **do**

7   Each agent m selects action $a_m^t = \mu_i^t(o_m^t | \theta^{\mu_m}) + \mathcal{M}_t$ according to the current policy and exploration noise;

8   Execute action $a^t = \{a_1^t, \cdots, a_M^T\}$ and calculate the reward $r^t = \{r_1^t, \cdots, r_M^t\}$ according to Eq. (15) and new state of next time slot o^{t+1} according to Eq. (13) ;

9   Store the transition matrix (o^t, a^t, r^t, o^{t+1}) in $\mathcal{D}$;

10          $o \leftarrow o^{t+1}$;

11   **for** $m = 1$ *to* M **do**

12   Sample a random minibatch of S transitions (o^n, a^n, r^m, o^{n+1}) from $\mathcal{D}$;

13   Update critic by minimizing the loss function in Eq. (16);

14   Update actor using the sampled policy gradient according to Eq. (18)

15   Update the target networks: $\theta^{Q_m'} \leftarrow \tau\theta^{Q_m} + (1 - \tau)\theta^{Q_m'}$;

16          $\theta^{\mu_m'} \leftarrow \tau\theta^{\mu_m} + (1 - \tau)\theta^{\mu_m'}$;

6 Performance Evaluation

In this section, numerical simulations are conducted to evaluate the performance of the proposed algorithm MADRL and the simulator is developed using Python.

6.1 Simulation Setup

We conduct simulations in the CPN based system with multiple users, resource providers and a managing platform. The simulation was carried out on a relatively small network with 2 users and 8 resource providers. The monetary budget of a user is in the range [20, 40]. The resource capacity of each resource provider is in the range [5, 25]. The coefficients for energy consumption cost and time cost are set as 0.01 and 0.5 respectively. For each agent, the actor network and critic network are constructed with one input layer, three hidden layers with 128, 64 and 32 neurons respectively and one output layer. In addition, the ReLU function is adopted by both the actor and the critic networks as activation of hidden layers. Furthermore, the Tanh function is adopted by the actor network as an activation of the output layer to generate policies.

6.2 Simulation Results

We evaluate the performance of MADRL mainly in two aspects, including its convergence and performance compared to other algorithms.

Convergence of MADRL. As shown in Fig. 2, convergence of MADRL is presented as for the unit price and utility of the resource providers (RP). It can be seen that the number of iterations for convergence is about 200 rounds, which is acceptable. As shown in Fig. 2(a), each resource provider first increases its unit price rapidly to achieve more profit and then decreases due to the competition among resource providers with limited budget. The platform prefer resource providers can provide higher QoS with low price. As a result, resource providers dynamically choose unit price to maintain a relatively good benefit, as shown in Fig. 2(b).

Algorithms for Comparison. We compare MADRL with two existing algorithms.

(1) Greedy policy: The platform is assumed to know the global information of the network, which is impossible in practice, and sets the unit prices of the resource providers proportional to the quality offered.
(2) Random policy: Unit prices are chosen at random in the range of (0,1).

As shown in Fig. 3, the proposed algorithm MADRL achieves the best performance in both the utilities of resource providers and social welfare. As shown in Fig. 3(a), the utility of users improves with the improving of budget for the reason that more resource can be purchased to make profit. In Fig. 3(b), the social welfare of MADRL remains stable because it can achieve game equilibrium.

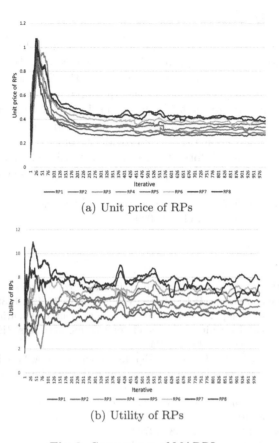

(a) Unit price of RPs

(b) Utility of RPs

Fig. 2. Convergence of MADRL.

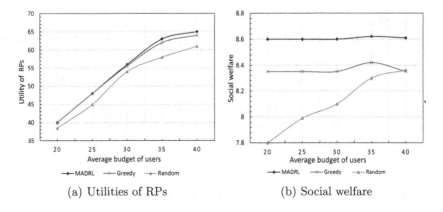

(a) Utilities of RPs

(b) Social welfare

Fig. 3. Comparison of proposed MADRL with benchmark algorithms with different budget.

7   Conclusion

In this paper, we study the problem of task assignment and incentive design in CPN. We first formulate the optimization problem as a multistage Stackelberg game with one leader and multiple followers. In the first stage, the platform determines the optimal assignment of tasks (resource purchasing) by solving the problem of maximization of the utility based on the prices submitted by resource providers. In the second stage, a multi-agent deep reinforcement learning based algorithm is proposed for each resource provider to optimize its pricing strategy based on the environment information. Finally, extensive simulations have been done to demonstrate the excellent performance of the proposed algorithm.

Acknowledgements. This work was supported in part by the National Key Research and Development Program 2021YFB2900200.

References

1. Huang, X., Zhang, B., Li, C.: Platform profit maximization on service provisioning in mobile edge computing. IEEE Trans. Veh. Technol. **70**(12), 13364–13376 (2021)
2. Ma, X., Zhao, J., Gong, Y.: Joint scheduling and resource allocation for efficiency-oriented distributed learning over vehicle platooning networks. IEEE Trans. Veh. Technol. **70**(10), 10894–10908 (2021)
3. Ma, X., Zhao, J., Li, Q., Gong, Y.: Reinforcement learning based task offloading and take-back in vehicle platoon networks. In: 2019 IEEE International Conference on Communications Workshops (ICC Workshops), pp. 1–6. IEEE (2019)
4. Cen, B., et al.: A configuration method of computing resources for microservice-based edge computing apparatus in smart distribution transformer area. Int. J. Electric. Power Energy Syst. **138**, 107935 (2022)
5. Xia, X., et al.: Data, user and power allocations for caching in multi-access edge computing. IEEE Trans. Parallel Distrib. Syst. **33**(5), 1144–1155 (2021)
6. Deng, X., Li, J., Shi, L., Wei, Z., Zhou, X., Yuan, J.: Wireless powered mobile edge computing: dynamic resource allocation and throughput maximization. IEEE Trans. Mob. Comput. (2020)
7. Cheng, Z., Min, M., Liwang, M., Huang, L., Gao, Z.: Multiagent DDPG-based joint task partitioning and power control in fog computing networks. IEEE Internet Things J. **9**(1), 104–116 (2021)
8. Tian, L., Yang, M., Wang, S.: An overview of compute first networking. Int. J. Web Grid Serv. **17**(2), 81–97 (2021)
9. Computing power network - Framework and architecture. Tech. Rep (2021)
10. Tang, X., et al.: Computing power network: The architecture of convergence of computing and networking towards 6G requirement. China Commun. **18**(2), 175–185 (2021)
11. Lei, B., Zhao, Q., Mei, J.: Computing power network: an interworking architecture of computing and network based on IP extension. In: 2021 IEEE 22nd International Conference on High Performance Switching and Routing (HPSR), pp. 1–6. IEEE (2021)

12. Liu, J., et al.: Computing power network: a testbed and applications with edge intelligence. In: IEEE INFOCOM 2022-IEEE Conference on Computer Communications Workshops (INFOCOM WKSHPS), pp. 1–2. IEEE (2022)
13. Lillicrap, T.P., et al.: Continuous control with deep reinforcement learning. arXiv preprint arXiv:1509.02971 (2015)
14. Richter, S., Aberdeen, D., Yu, J.: Natural actor-critic for road traffic optimisation. Adv. Neural Inf. Process. Syst. **19** (2006)

SBR-based User Intent Extraction Mechanism for Intent-Based Network

Jinsuo Jia[1], Xiaochen Liang[1], Peng Xu[1], Weiwei Li[1], Yizhong Hu[2],
and Jianfeng Guan[2(✉)]

[1] China Information Technology Designing and Consulting Institute Co., Ltd.,
Beijing 100048, China
{jiajs5,liangxch,xupeng,liww102}@dimpt.com
[2] Beijing University of Posts and Telecommunications, Beijing 100876, China
{kuai,jfguan}@bupt.edu.cn

Abstract. As an promising technology to improve the network configuration efficiency, IBN (Intent-Based Network) can realize the automatic configuration from users to devices, with the objective to reduce the maintenance costs and improve the stability of system. In the current IBN, the NER (Named Entity Recognition) model is used to extract intents from the natural language information input by the user in form of text or voice. However, traditional intent extraction method requires the user to be familiar with specific network services, which means that users must have certain prior knowledge. It is difficult to completely and clearly extract the true intention of the user in real deployment applications. To this end, this paper proposes the Session based Recommender (SBR) based user intent extraction mechanism for IBN which utilizes the session information between user and system to help users choose the most suitable network configuration scheme. In this way, the proposed model can ensure the integrity and reliability of user intent extraction. Finally, some commonly used SBR models are evaluated on the Diginetica dataset. The results show that these SBR models have good capabilities in the task of session recommendation and illustrate the feasibility of combining IBN with SBR.

Keywords: Intent-based network · Session-based recommender · Network configuration

1 Introduction

With the progress of network technology, users have more diverse and complicated requirements for network services. Thus, to acquire the diverse intentions of users, the traditional networks need to analyze the business requirements from users via off-line communication, which slows down the deployment efficiency of the new network service. For these reasons, it is decided that a simpler architecture can better meet the diversity and complexity of user needs, so as to realize the closed-loop control of the network services. Therefore, IBN (Intent-Based Network) [5] is proposed as a reliable solution for automatic configuration. IBN

© The Author(s), under exclusive license to Springer Nature Singapore Pte Ltd. 2023
W. Quan (Ed.): ICENAT 2022, CCIS 1696, pp. 50–61, 2023.
https://doi.org/10.1007/978-981-19-9697-9_5

can replace the work of technicians and automatically handle system exceptions. Based on these functions, IBN can save labor costs and greatly improve the efficiency of operation and maintenance. However, previous IBN lack of the consideration of client background. In real deployment applications, different users have different requirements, and most users do not have a clear direction for configuration scenarios, and cannot provide complete parameters required in the configuration scenarios. The traditional network may arrange technical personnel to help the user choose a suitable configuration scenario, which will increase the labor costs and reduce the deployment efficiency.

For these reasons, we propose a SBR (Session based Recommender)-based intent extraction mechanism. Based on the proposed mechanism, the system can build user portraits determined by the historical information. SBR depends on the session sequence relationship between user and system to make the prediction. On the contrary, other recommendation depends on the user's long-term static historical data. What we want to achieve is to infer the potential relationship in the user's short-term and dynamic session scenarios, so that SBR is a more suitable model.

The rest of this paper is organized as follows. Section 2 describes the related work. Section 3 explains the process of SBR-based intent extraction. Section 4 presents the experiment results. Section 5 concludes this paper and discusses the future work.

2   Related Work

2.1   Intent-Based Network

IBN architectures are constantly evolving after the concept of intent was proposed. In 2016, ONF published the white paper "Intent NBI-Definition and Principles", which was the first document to describe intent-based northbound interfaces and define the principles, operations and architecture of the Internet NBI. After that, Gartner published "Innovation Insight: Intent-based networkworking systems", which defines the four functions of IBN include translation and verification, automated implementation, network status awareness, assurance and automated optimization. In same year, Cisco [9] published an intent-based network software solution and built an automated network, which can greatly bridge the differences between business departments and IT departments by introducing the four functions: intent, translation, activation, and security to form the closed-loop systems. Based on the above architectures, IBN generally consists of four main components: intent extraction, intent orchestration, intent confirmation, and intent deployment as shown in Fig. 1.

Take the VPN services as an example, IBN realizes the whole automatic process of configuration from users to network. Firstly, when a user needs a new private line, IBN captures the users input information. Then, IBN extracts the configuration entity required by the user. Next, IBN will translate the intent to configuration and verify the integrity. Finally, IBN will deploy configuration to

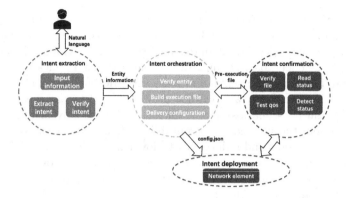

Fig. 1. The process of Intent-Based network

devices and detect network status including allocating resources and generating the configuration strategy.

2.2 Intent Extraction

The intent extraction module needs to collect and process information between user and network, extract the entity information from user's natural language information. Generally, it consists of two sub-modules: semantic parsing, dialogue management.

Semantic Parsing. This module is mainly used to parse unstructured information from users by using NER (Named Entity Recognition), and extract the entity information related to the configuration tasks. In addition, the external interface library limits the function of this module according to the configuration data, so as to ensure the accuracy of intent extraction. Finally, it transmits the extraction information to the dialogue management module.

Dialogue Management. This part mainly completes the dialogue flow with the user. After receiving the entity information, it will verify their integrity and correctness by the historical configuration dataset and the knowledge graph. If all information is verified correctly, it will pass the parsed data to the intent orchestration module, and continue to finish session with the user. Otherwise, it will conduct multiple rounds of dialogue with the user until all entities is correct and complete.

2.3 Intent Orchestration

The main task of this module is to perform intent orchestration. Firstly, it needs to verify the correctness and integrity of the entity information. Therefore, it will first generate pre-execution files and pass them to the intent confirmation module. If they are verified correctly, IBN will generate a directly executable configuration file and send this file to the intent deployment module. Otherwise, this task will be returned to the previous module to confirm the details, or discarded directly to ensure the normal operation of the entire IBN system.

2.4 Intent Confirmation

This module completes intent confirmation and network status detection. Firstly, it is necessary to verify the correctness and integrity of the pre-execution file. In addition, it needs to detect network status, which is beneficial for IBN to monitor the service quality of each service such as private line so that can actively keep the user intent. Therefore, this module needs to implement three functions including intent verification, network status monitoring and path QoS measurement.

2.5 Intent Deployment

This module completes the execution of configuration file to the device. The configuration file is generally in form of JSON format [2], which contains a series of items. Each item consists of key and value in no particular order, but each key is unique. After the file is determined correctly, this module can directly parse the file into a series of action commands and send them to the specific devices one by one, and notify the devices to complete the predetermined actions. In this way, IBN can realize data exchange with devices.

The mutual cooperation of the above four modules constitutes the main framework of the IBN system, which effectively ensures the automatic configuration of the whole process from user to device.

3 SBR-based User Intent Extraction

3.1 Intent Extraction

In the traditional intent extraction module, the main tasks include semantic parsing and dialogue management. Among them, semantic parsing refers to analyzing user semantics, which can be viewed as a sequence labeling task. The usual method is to use BIO (Beginning, Input, Output) to label the natural language information input by the user, and then use NER to extract the entity information required for task configuration.

LSTM (Long Short-Term Memory Network) performs well in sequence labeling tasks and solves the problems of gradient explosion and gradient disappearance. In order to greatly improve the accuracy, contextual text information needs to be considered. Therefore, the BiLSTM (Bi-directional LSTM) is a better choice. Pre-trained model that uses BERT (Bidirectional Encoder Representation from Transformers) [3] can achieve better results on multiple NLP tasks, and has richer semantic information than traditional word vector representations, such as Word2Vec and Glove. The task produces a more suitable feature representation, thereby improves model performance.

Nevertheless, in the actual IBN application, the above models can only ensure the correctness of extracting intent information, cannot complement the user's missing intent information. If the integrity and correctness of intent are guaranteed under only such the models, users must be familiar with the specific network services and have certain prior knowledge, which is obviously not practical for most users. The assistance of technicians may help users finish network configuration. However, it will break the closed-loop process of the IBN system, increase the system cost and slow down the system operation efficiency.

Based on the above reasons, we propose a user intent extraction mechanism based on the SBR, which uses the contextual session information, to recommend the best configuration scenarios for users. For most IBN systems, the recommendation systems are rarely mentioned or just generate recommended items for dialogue module. For example, this system uses IBN to manage the ICT (Information and Communications Technology) [1], which adds a ML (Machine Learning) Recommender to choose the best ML-based algorithms. Thus, we can combine the recommendation system more with IBN. On the one hand, SBR can recommend configuration scenarios for users. On the other hand, SBR can automatically complete configuration parameters for systems.

Therefore, we proposed a session recommendation module to ensure the integrity of user intent extraction.

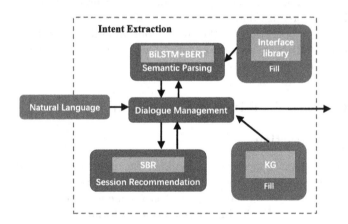

Fig. 2. The process of the proposed intent extraction module

Figure 2 reflects the procedure of proposed intent extraction module. Among them, natural language represents the input information by the user. Semantic parsing, dialogue management and session recommendation represent the three main modules. Other large boxes are auxiliary modules which are used to ensure the integrity of entity information. The little boxes inside them indicate the models or auxiliary information used by the modules. The direction of arrows between boxes point out the flow of work tasks.

Adding the session recommendation in the intent extraction module and adopting SBR, can effectively use the natural language information input by the user, help the user to complete more professional network configuration tasks, and improve the operation efficiency and reliability of the IBN system.

3.2   Procedure of SBR in Intent Extraction

Due to the complexity of current network information, recommender systems play a crucial role to predict user's interests. Recommendation systems are mainly divided into two categories [10]: Session-Based Recommendation and Sequence-Based Recommendation. Sequence recommendation uses a series of past actions from users, such as a list of movies the user has watched. Unlike this recommendation which is based on the user's long-term historical information, we need to predict the user's next action during the short-term dynamic conversation between IBN and user. So SBR is a more suitable choice.

The SBR system can be roughly divided into three categories according to the technology used: traditional methods (Conventional SBR approaches), embedded representation learning (Latent representation-based approaches), neural networks (Deep neural network-based approaches). At first, machine learning methods such as Markov chain and KNN (K-Nearest Neighbor) were used to predict the user's next session. Nowadays, with the development of neural networks such as RNN (Recurrent Neural Network), GNN (Graph Neural Network) and other methods, it has shown better performance in the task of mining the potential relationship of conversations.

The procedure of SBR is based on the entity information extracted by the semantic parsing module, which are the information related to the configuration task parameters mentioned by the user in chronological order. When the intent information is complete enough, the dialogue management module can determine the user's desired network configuration scenario. Otherwise, the SBR module need to use the dialogue management module to complete multiple rounds of dialogue with the user. Fig. 3 shows the user session process of L2VPN VPWS.

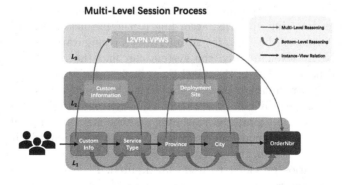

Fig. 3. An example of multi-level session process

Our solution for establishing a SBR-based user intent extraction mechanism is to regard the basic parameters of various configuration services provided as entity information, such as location, time, network speed, network quality, etc. The entity list extracted in time series is handed over to the intent orchestration module, and the configuration scenarios required by the user can be determined through the historical configuration data of other users.

For the configuration requirements of L2VPN VPWS as shown in Table 1, SBR system regards each parameter as an entity information. For example, in Fig. 3, the system has extracted some entity information which is the content of the process box in the L_1 level, that is a list of entity sequences includes Custom Info, Services Type, Province and City. Thus, according to the direction of arrows, session process between IBN and user can be restored.

Table 1. The config data of L2VPN VPWS.

Name	Data type	Required	Description
Custom info	CustomInfo	Yes	Customer information
Service type	String	Yes	Service type required
Province	String	Yes	The number of provinces
City	String	Yes	The number of cities
OrderNbr	String	Yes	Assignment number
svcId	String	Yes	Business code
aSite	AssignedAC	Yes	A-end access port
zSite	AssignedAC	Yes	Z-end access port
qos	qos	Yes	The Qos information of business

Most of the traditional recommender systems read the instance-view relation [12] between entity information. But in a session task, entity information have potential bottom-level reasoning. SBR system should infer the higher-level semantic associations between adjacent entity information, such as Custom Info and Service Type, Province and City in the L_2 level, can be mined to be the associated information of the custom information and the deployment site, respectively. Further inferring upwards, according to the business scenarios to which the entity information belongs, it can infer user's configuration task is L2VPN VPWS in the L_3 level. Finally, the system can find the missing information according to the Table 1, and then feed them back to the user.

Usually, for users in larger trading platforms, the commodities are extremely complex, and it is very difficult to construct a multi-level reasoning view. Because of the complexity of bottom-level reasoning and the lack of entity information, the inferred result may converge to a local optimal solution which is not in line with user expectation. However, in the SBR-based IBN system, the number of business scenarios provided to users are limited, it is possible to infer the user's configuration requirements. In an instance, for the L2VPN and L3VPN configuration tasks provided by the system, although both of them can provide

VPN services for users, there are some differences between them. L3VPN is usually as the core of the national backbone network and used to connect nodes in various regions, and L2VPN is usually used between metropolitan area networks. Therefore, if only one requirement of the user for the area range is known, the system can greatly help the user to reduce the range of alternatives.

3.3 Experiments

Nowadays, there are many SBR system using different methods, such as data mining, machine learning and deep neural network. According to the requirements of recommendation tasks, the performance of each model is different, and choosing a suitable SBR system can greatly improve the accuracy of recommendation. Therefore, the following section will evaluate some commonly used SBR methods to compare their performance and illustrate the feasibility of combining IBN and SBR.

The SBR systems used for evaluation include SKNN (Sequence KNN), STAN (Sequence and time aware neighborhood) [4], and BERT4Rec [8], GCSAN (Graph Contextualized Self-Attention Network) [11], CoSAN (Collaborative Self-Attention Network) [7], and STAMP (Short-Term Attention/Memory Priority) [6]. Then, we calculate three metrics on the Diginetica dataset to compare their recommendation ability. Diginetica data is a recommendation data set published on CIKM-Cup in 2016, which includes anonymous browsing logs of some anonymous users.

SKNN. The model is based on KNN and historical session information, but it does not consider sequence and time information in session tasks.

STAN. The STAN model [4] is also based on KNN, which is derived from SKNN. STAN considers three aspects: the position of item, the impact of previous session, and the adjacent sessions of recommended items. Generally, STAN model outperforms the SKNN model.

BERT4Rec. The BERT4Rec model [8] is a user behavior sequence model based on two-way self-attention and Cloze task. To improve the unidirectional model, it incorporates contexts from both directions to model training on user data.

GCSAN. The GCSAN model [11] is similar to SR-GNN, which maps session information to a graph structure, and transfers the information between entity information through GNN. GCSAN combines the user's long-term and short-term preferences through gate control to predict future session.

CoSAN. The CoSAN model [7] believes the entity information is dynamic, and its embedded position in the session process has a different impact on the context. Thus, CoSAN learns complex dependencies between entity information, not only considering the current session, but also considering collaboration information between sessions. CoSAN also handles the user's long-term and short-term preferences through a self-attention model.

STAMP. The main innovation of STAMP model [6] is the joint recommendation of general interests and current interests. STAMP believes that the general interests extracted by the RNN model is effective, but the traditional RNN model does not consider the user's current interests. So this model uses a short-term memory model to read general interests, and read current interests from current session.

Three metrics including HR, MRR and NDGC are adopted in the performance evaluation. HR@K is an indicator to measure the recommendation recall rate in the Top-K recommendation results. MRR@K is an indicator that will give a score to the items which is successfully recommended. NDCG@K is also an indicator for sequence sorting. The more correct an item appears in the top of the recommendation list, the higher its score will be. The closer their results are to 100%, the better the recommendation results.

4   Results Analysis

Table 2 shows the results of the different models on the Diginetica dataset. The length K of each user recommendation list, which is 1, 5, 10, and 20, respectively. We draw a line graph in the form of evaluation indicators, which makes it easier for us to understand the relationship between the models' recommendation ability and the K value when each model is recommended by TOP-K.

Table 2. Results of main experiments in Diginetica.

Model	HR(%)				MRR(%)				NDCG(%)			
	1	5	10	20	1	5	10	20	1	5	10	20
SKNN	7.8	14.2	15.6	16.5	8.0	25.6	36.6	49.4	8.0	17.0	20.5	23.7
STAN	8.4	14.7	16.1	16.9	8.4	26.3	36.6	48.6	8.4	17.6	20.9	24.0
BERT4Rec	6.4	22.8	34.8	48.7	6.4	12.0	13.6	14.5	6.4	14.7	18.5	22.0
GCSAN	5.1	17.0	25.9	37.0	5.1	9.1	10.3	11.1	5.1	11.1	14.0	16.8
CoSAN	5.2	19.0	29.8	42.6	5.2	9.9	11.3	12.2	5.2	12.1	15.6	18.8
STAMP	6.5	21.7	32.5	45.6	6.5	11.8	13.2	14.2	6.5	14.2	17.7	21.0

From Fig. 4, we can see that all models have enhanced recommendation ability as the K value increases, which means that these models can dig out some items expected by the user, but the evaluation scores for these items in the whole situation are not enough. Thus, it makes that the user's preferred items do not appear at the top of the recommended list, but on the whole, most of the preferred items can be placed at the front of the recommended list. Then, from the evaluation results of HR@K, the four deep learning-based models BERT4Rec,

STAMP, GCSAN, and CoSAN increase with the value of K, and the growth rate of results does not slow down, but the two methods based on KNN, SKNN, STAN starts to level off when K is equal to about 5.

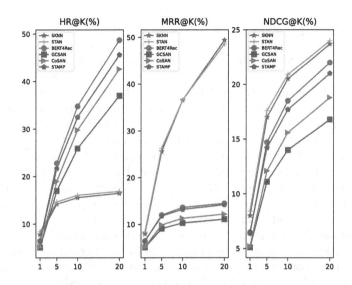

Fig. 4. Evaluation results of several SBR models.

However, this result is opposite in the graph of MRR@K. When the recommendation list length K is about 5, the results of four models based on deep learning tend to grow flat. According to the model results, we can know that the methods based on the deep learning can put most of the user's preference results in the front of recommendation list, but most of them are not in the top of list. Therefore, in the case of sorting the scores according to the sequence, these models have lower evaluation metrics. Both of models based on KNN can better find user preference items based on the similar performance of user data, but the ability to mine potential relationship is weak, so the performance in term of the number of recommendations will be worse.

The NDCG@K evaluation result has a more comprehensive effect. It is more affected by items with strong correlation, and the higher they appear in the list, the higher the score. In these two aspects, both types of models have their own advantages. Therefore, in the evaluation of NDCG@K, they will have a better performance, and the evaluation results will continue to improve with the increase of the K value. In the results of these models, there is little difference between the models, but SKNN and STAN perform better than others, and more specifically, STAN is better than SKNN.

From the above results, we can see these models have different performances in different evaluations. In the appropriate scenario, choosing the appropriate model will bring better results. Usually the TOP-K recall rate can reach $10\% -$

20% is a good result, and these models have a good performance in this regard. The network configuration scenario is relatively simple compared to the above dataset scenarios. Therefore, the combination of IBN and SBR will produce positive feedback for the system's recommendation results.

5   Conclusion

Through the IBN system, the business scenario configuration required by the user can be realized more quickly and stably, which not only improves the operation efficiency of the system, but also reduces the operation and maintenance costs. However, it is difficult for users to give accurate configuration parameters, which may result in incomplete intentions. To solve this problem, the paper proposes a method which combines SBR and IBN based on the contextual dialogue information between the human-machine system and the user, to predict the user's future expected conversation content. By evaluating the TOP-K recommendation results of several current SBR models, it is demonstrated that in the current business scenario, using SBR can effectively predict user configuration requirements. And from the evaluation results, the selection of models in different scenarios will have a greater impact on the recommendation results.

Some further work need to be improved in future. For example, considering that the current configuration data is small, further verification is required for some modules such as intent extraction and deployment. Besides, since many old devices need to be migrated in the network configuration task, it is necessary to consider whether the old and new devices are compatible in the IBN system. Moreover, in the process of device configuration, the management of device environment resources is an important link to ensure the normal operation of the IBN system. Finally, the current IBN system only considers the configuration tasks of network equipment. How to quickly and accurately realize the deployment of cross-domain and cross-professional IBN tasks still need lots of efforts.

Acknowledgment. This research was supported by the National Key Research and Development Program (2018YFE0206800). Jinsuo Jia, Xiaochen Liang, Peng Xu, Weiwei Li and Yizhong Hu contributed equally to this work. Corresponding author is Jianfeng Guan. The authors would like to thank the anonymous reviewers for their valuable comments which helped them to improve the content, organization, and presentation of this paper.

References

1. Bensalem, M., Dizdarevic, J., Jukan, A.: Benchmarking various ML solutions in complex intent-based network management systems. In: 45th Jubilee International Convention on Information, Communication and Electronic Technology, MIPRO 2022, Opatija, Croatia, 23-27 May 2022, pp. 476–481 (2022). https://doi.org/10.23919/MIPRO55190.2022.9803584
2. Bohui, L., Haihong, X., Chenmin, M., et al.: Design and implementation of json-based automated test system. Measure. Control Technol. **36**(04), 120–123+129 (2017). https://doi.org/10.19708/j.ckjs.2017.04.028

3. Devlin, J., Chang, M., Lee, K., Toutanova, K.: BERT: pre-training of deep bidirectional transformers for language understanding. In: Burstein, J., Doran, C., Solorio, T. (eds.) Proceedings of the 2019 Conference of the North American Chapter of the Association for Computational Linguistics: Human Language Technologies, NAACL-HLT 2019, Minneapolis, MN, USA, 2–7 June 2019, Volume 1 (Long and Short Papers), pp. 4171–4186. Association for Computational Linguistics (2019). https://doi.org/10.18653/v1/n19-1423

4. Garg, D., Gupta, P., Malhotra, P., et al.: Sequence and time aware neighborhood for session-based recommendations: STAN. In: Proceedings of the 42nd International ACM SIGIR Conference on Research and Development in Information Retrieval, SIGIR 2019, Paris, France, 21–25 July 2019, pp. 1069–1072 (2019). https://doi.org/10.1145/3331184.3331322

5. Khan, T.A., Abbas, K., Rivera, J.J.D., et al.: Applying routenet and LSTM to achieve network automation: an intent-based networking approach. In: 22nd Asia-Pacific Network Operations and Management Symposium, APNOMS 2021, Tainan, Taiwan, 8–10 September 2021, pp. 254–257 (2021). https://doi.org/10.23919/APNOMS52696.2021.9562499

6. Liu, Q., Zeng, Y., Mokhosi, R., et al.: STAMP: short-term attention/memory priority model for session-based recommendation. In: Proceedings of the 24th ACM SIGKDD International Conference on Knowledge Discovery & Data Mining, KDD 2018, London, UK, 19–23 August 2018. pp. 1831–1839 (2018). https://doi.org/10.1145/3219819.3219950

7. Luo, A., Zhao, P., Liu, Y., et al.: Collaborative self-attention network for session-based recommendation. In: Proceedings of the Twenty-Ninth International Joint Conference on Artificial Intelligence, IJCAI 2020, pp. 2591–2597 (2020). https://doi.org/10.24963/ijcai.2020/359

8. Sun, F., Liu, J., Wu, J., et al.: Bert4rec: sequential recommendation with bidirectional encoder representations from transformer. In: Proceedings of the 28th ACM International Conference on Information and Knowledge Management, CIKM 2019, Beijing, China, 3–7 November 2019. pp. 1441–1450 (2019). https://doi.org/10.1145/3357384.3357895

9. Szigeti, T., Zacks, D., Falkner, M., Arena, S.: Cisco Digital Network Architecture: Intent-based Networking for the Enterprise. Cisco Press (2018)

10. Wang, S., Cao, L., Wang, Y., et al.: A survey on session-based recommender systems. ACM Comput. Surv. **54**(7), 154:1–154:38 (2022). https://doi.org/10.1145/3465401

11. Xu, C., Zhao, P., Liu, Y., et al.: Graph contextualized self-attention network for session-based recommendation. In: Proceedings of the Twenty-Eighth International Joint Conference on Artificial Intelligence, IJCAI 2019, Macao, China, 10–16 August 2019, pp. 3940–3946 (2019). https://doi.org/10.24963/ijcai.2019/547

12. Zhang, P., Guo, J., Li, C., et al.: Efficiently leveraging multi-level user intent for session-based recommendation via atten-mixer network. CoRR abs/2206.12781 (2022). https://doi.org/10.48550/arXiv.2206.12781

Customizable Service Identification Method and System Design for Smart Integration Identifier Network

Shang Liu, Jia Chen$^{(\boxtimes)}$, Shuai Gao, Kuo Guo, and Xu Huang

National Engineering Research Center for Advanced Network Technologies, Beijing Jiaotong University, Beijing, China
chenjia@bjtu.edu.cn

Abstract. Smart Integration Identifier Network (SINET) provides theoretical support for the on-demand supply of customized network services. However, there are still some limitations in the data plane of SINET, such as lacking of flexibility and customizability for providing various network services. Therefore, this paper proposes a customizable service identification method that is compatible with multiple data plane protocols. The method maps the service identifier and family identifier of SINET to the data plane and integrates multiple protocols through identifier to provide users with customizable network services. A prototype system was designed based on the proposed method, and the function and performance of the system are tested.

Keywords: Smart integration identifier network · Programmable network technology · Network packet processing

1 Introduction

The traditional Internet packet processing method has inherent design defects and is difficult to continue to meet the massive growth of users' network service needs [1]. It is widely believed in the industry that the evolution of the existing Internet in an incremental way can no longer fundamentally maintain its sustainable development, and the packet processing method needs to be redesigned [2]. In order to solve this problem, researchers actively carry out research on the future network [3]. Specifically, IPv6 provides massive address space [4]. Named Data Networking (NDN) provides a new content-based packet forwarding method [5]. Software Defined Network (SDN) provides programmable forwarding mode [6]. Polymorphic smart network (PINet) supports the forwarding of packets in multiple modes [7]. To sum up, packet forwarding has shown a trend of "simplification to diversification, solidification to programmability".

The Smart Integration Identifier Network (SINET) is a new network architecture proposed by Academician Zhang Hongke's team to solve the inherent absence of the existing Internet. SINET provides theoretical support for solving the shortcomings of "static rigidity" in traditional networks. Literature [8] proposed a lightweight Service Function Chain (SFC) framework in SINET. The literature uses dockers to implement

W. Quan (Ed.): ICENAT 2022, CCIS 1696, pp. 62–75, 2023.
https://doi.org/10.1007/978-981-19-9697-9_6

virtual network functions, so that SINET can provide richer network services. Literature [9] proposed an intelligent fault monitoring mechanism in SINET. The literature uses BMV2 as the forwarding component and ONOS as the controller to improve the quality of service of SINET. Literature [10] proposed to use identifier to guide routing and forwarding of packets in SINET, which increased network security. However, at the data plane of SINET, users can only make limited choices in the services provided by network providers. SINET cannot provide users with more fine-grained customized and differentiated services. Therefore, this paper proposes a customizable service identification method compatible with multiple data plane protocols, which can provide users with enhancing fine-grained customizable network services.

In order for the data plane to support SINET, programmable characteristics should be in the data plane for making the network more flexible. Secondly, the data plane should be protocol independent and compatible with various network protocols. And these network protocols can be combined on demand to realize the customized service of SINET. Finally, the data plane should have accurate network state awareness capability to provide necessary support for reasonable allocation of network resources.

In order to meet the above requirements of SINET at the data plane, it poses huge challenges to the data processing methods. The data plane needs to have flexible and efficient packet processing capability, and to support the controller to deploy data processing logic in a programmable way. In addition to the basic routing functions, the data plane also needs to support network functions such as congestion control, deterministic services, network measurement, active queue management, security and load balancing. SINET can combine various network functions at the data plane as required by means of family mapping, so as to achieve diversified and customized user service demands.

The main contributions of this paper are as follows:

- A customizable service identification method that can integrate multiple data plane protocols.
- Based on the customizable service identification method proposed in this paper, a prototype system for SINET is designed, which can provide users with customized network services. Customized network services can combine basic network functions on demand and make more efficient use of network resources.
- On the general server, a prototype system based on customizable service identification method is implemented based on bmv2 switch, and the function and performance of the system are tested.

2   Smart Integration Identifier Network Architecture

SINET divides the network into three layers and three domains [11]. The "three layers" are smart service layer, resource adaptation layer and network component layer. The "three domains" are entity domain, behavior domain and knowledge domain. The architecture of the "three layers and three domains" of SINET is shown in Fig. 1.

The smart service layer analyzes the user's demand and maps it to a collection of multiple basic network functions. Different basic network functions can be integrated on demand to generate customized network services that meet user needs. The

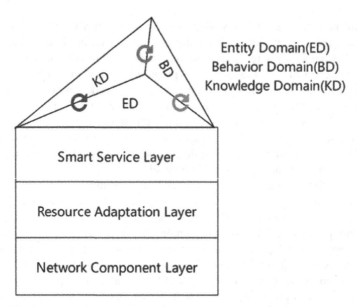

Fig. 1. The architecture of the "three layers and three domains" of SINET

resource adaptation layer dynamically adapts the relationship between network services and network resources, perceives the network status, and constructs network families. The network family is composed of a group of network nodes with the same or similar functions. The network component layer perceives the state of network components and adjusts the behavior of programmable network components. SINET realizes the reasonable scheduling of network resources and the coordination of various services through the vertical tight coupling mapping between the three layers.

Entity domain uniquely identifies a network entity by its identifier; Behavioral domain describing information about the dynamic behavior of network entities; Knowledge domain storage network resource scheduling policy. The behavior domain, entity domain and knowledge domain are interlinked to solve the triple binding problem of "resource and location binding", "control and data binding" and "identity and location binding" in the network [12].

3   Customizable Service Identification Method

In order to meet the demand for customized network services of SINET, this paper proposes an extensible Smart Integration Header (SIH) in data plane. As shown in Fig. 2, the SIH can be expanded infinitely by adding the extended Family Identifier (FID), but the minimum length is 64 bits. In the shortest case, the SIH only contains the Service Identifier (SID), the number of FID and the end mark. When the number of FID is not 0, each extended FID uniquely corresponds to the subsequent extended FID protocol. The extended family protocol is a variable length field. Different extended FID protocols are independent of each other, and they are connected only through the SID and FID. Therefore, the SIH can realize the customization integration of basic network functions.

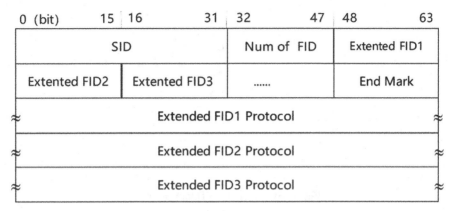

Fig. 2. Smart Integration Header

The SIH is located on the second layer of the packet, which is used to expand the routing function of the network and provide users with more network routing services. The SIH can flexibly determine the range of packet analysis according to user demands, reducing packet processing delay. The following will list the application of SIH in different scenarios.

3.1 Application of SIH in Resource Constrained Scenarios

When facing large-scale Internet of Things scenarios, the network resources are limited, and the shortest application scenario of SIH can be used. As shown in Fig. 3, at this time, the length of the SIH is 8 bytes, in which the number of FID field is 0, the end mark is 0, there is no extended FID, and there is no extended FID protocol.

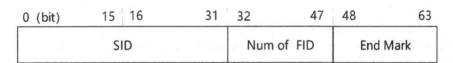

Fig. 3. SIH of resource constrained scenarios

As shown in Fig. 4, when the packet enters the switch of SINET, the switch inserts the SIH according to the five tuples of the packet. The packets containing the SIH are only routed according to the service identity in SINET, and there is no need to analyze the IP and TCP/UDP protocol in the packets. The shortest application scenario in the SIH reduces the packet processing speed and speeds up the routing.

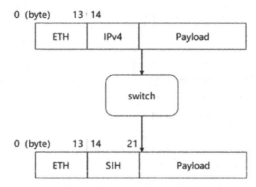

Fig. 4. Switch inserts SIH into packet

3.2 Application of SIH in the Service Function Chain Scenario

When users need to deploy the service function chain, they can use the SFC family identifier field at the SIH. As shown in Fig. 5, the length of the SIH is 22 bytes, including the SFC family identifier, the SFC family identifier protocol, and the number of FID field is 1.

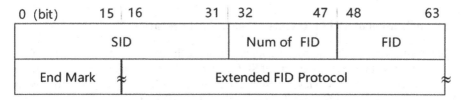

Fig. 5. SIH of service function chain scenario

The SFC family identifier protocol can adopt either the existing NSH protocol or the customized SFC protocol. Users can customize SFC families as required, or reuse existing SFC families to improve the utilization of network resources.

3.3 Application of SIH in Network State Awareness Scenario

When users need In-band Telemetry (INT) services, they can use the INT family identifier at the SIH. The SIH is shown in Fig. 6, where the number of FID is 2.

The INT family and any routing family can jointly form customized network aware services. The family protocol is only associated with the family identifier, and the family protocol are independent of each other. The family identifier is only associated with the service identifier, and the service identifier is independent of each other. Therefore, different network functions can be combined through the FID in the SIH, so as to meet the demand for customized integration of basic network functions of SINET.

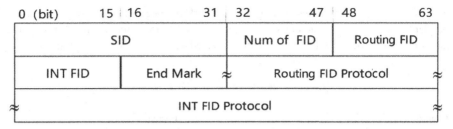

Fig. 6. SIH of network state awareness scenario

4   System Design Based on Customizable Service Identification Method

By introducing artificial intelligence, SINET system realizes real-time adaptation of customizable network services and network resources [13]. Figure 7 shows the architecture of SINET system based on the method proposed in this paper.

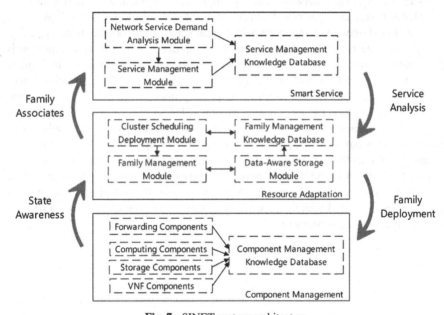

Fig. 7. SINET system architecture

SINET system dispatches basic units in the network by identifiers. The mapping relationships between the identifiers corresponding to the interaction relationships of the basic units in the network. Each time a network service is deployed, the relationship between the identifiers is readjusted based on the scheduling policy. Changes in the relationships between identifiers lead to changes in the interactions of the basic units of the network, which in turn lead to changes in the network structure. And changes in the network structure can cause changes in the performance of the network. Therefore, the identification of the basic units in the network is the key to realize the customizable network services of SINET. All the identifiers in SINET system are shown in Table 1.

Table 1. The identifiers in SINET system

Identifier	Format
Service Identifier (SID)	32-bit integer
Family Identifier (FID)	16-bit integer
Node Identifier (NID)	128-bit string
Service Behavior Identifier (SBD)	JOSN
Family Behavior Identifier (FBD)	JOSN
Node Behavior Identifier (NBD)	JOSN

There is a set of basic network functions in SINET system, and the individual basic network functions can be combined into customizable network services at will. A family is a collection of network components with the same basic network function. Typically, there are multiple network components within a family, and a network component is subordinate to multiple families. Basic network functions are provided within families through family identifiers, and different families form customizable network services through service identifiers. The identifier mapping process of SINET system is shown in Fig. 8. SINET system parses user demands into SDB's service demands information and generates SID according to the service type. The service demands are resolved into network families based on the policy base of the knowledge domain. The knowledge domain determines the FID and NID required for the user's network services, while updating the SBD, FBD and NBD. Finally, based on the data plane identification method designed in this paper, the command information is issued to the network components that have services associated with them. Thus the mapping between identifiers can provide customizable network services to users.

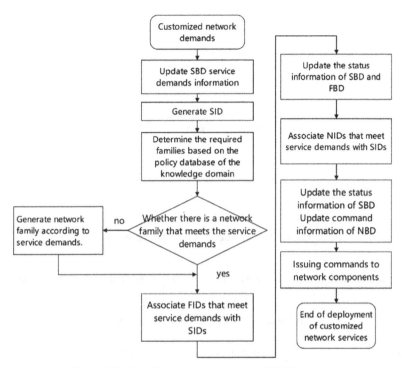

Fig. 8. The identifier mapping process of SINET system

5   Evaluation

The network topology is constructed using standard x86 architecture servers, as shown in Fig. 9. The network topology includes control node and compute nodes, with the node8 server as the control node and the rest of the servers as compute nodes. Docker containers are deployed in the compute nodes to realize the virtual network function and install bmv2 software switches to realize the packet routing and forwarding. Deploy SINET controller in the control node. SINET controller manages docker containers and bmv2 software switches in the network topology through the Kubernetes (K8S) and Open Network Operating System (ONOS).

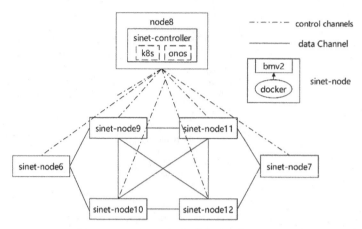

Fig. 9. The topology of the prototype system

The server configuration information and system version are shown in Table 2.

Table 2. Server configuration information

Name	Parameters/Version
CPU	Intel(R) Xeon(R) Silver 4210R CPU @ 2.40GHz
Memory	64GB
OS	Ubuntu18.04.5 LTS
Kubernetes	v1.19.3
ONOS controller	v2.2

5.1 Functional Test Results

This section focuses on function test of customizable service deployments in SINET. The user demand input interface of SINET is shown in Fig. 10. There are multiple parameters for users to select in the service demand description. SINET system analyzes the parameters of the network services and generates customized network services through family mapping.

In the function test, select the demand parameters of the network service: the business scenario is a high security scenario, the source node is host6, the destination node is host7, the network function is firewall and IDS, and INT is required. As shown in Fig. 11, SINET system log demonstrates the service deployment process. SINET system analyzes user demands as SBD and generates SID, and maps network services into SFC family and INT family according to the knowledge database policy. The SFC and INT families are linked to provide customizable network services to users. After the service analysis is

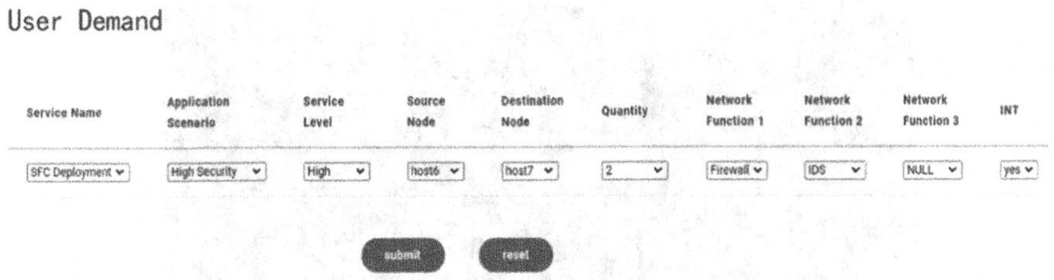

User Demand

Service Name	Application Scenario	Service Level	Source Node	Destination Node	Quantity	Network Function 1	Network Function 2	Network Function 3	INT
SFC Deployment ▾	High Security ▾	High ▾	host6 ▾	host7 ▾	2 ▾	Firewall ▾	IDS ▾	NULL ▾	yes ▾

submit   reset

Fig. 10. The user demand input interface of SINET

completed, the NBD command information is deployed to the corresponding network component.

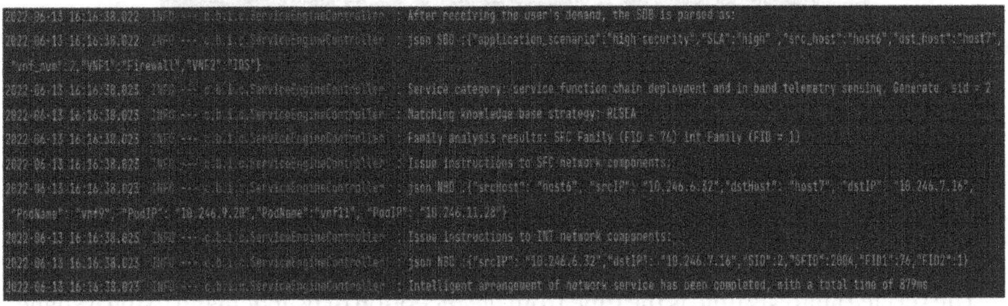

Fig. 11. Service deployment process

After service deployment, verify the deployed functions. The source node of the SFC sends packets to the destination node, and uses Wireshark tools to capture the packets, as shown in Fig. 12. The red part is the SIH, the blue part is the SFC family identifier protocol, and the yellow part is the INT family identifier protocol.

0000	ff ff ff ff ff ff ea 12 f3 6b 8b e1 88 88 00 00	.... .k......
0010	00 02 00 02 00 4c 00 01 00 ff 00 03 4f c2 02 01	.....L.. ....O...
0020	00 00 01 ff 00 00 00 01 ab fa 00 00 00 03 00 00	....
0030	00 00 03 00 00 36 13 0f 1f f4 97 6f da 00 00 00	.....6.. ...o....
0040	00 00 03 ff 00 4f 04 d2 10 e1 00 09 a4 ce 31	.....O.. 1

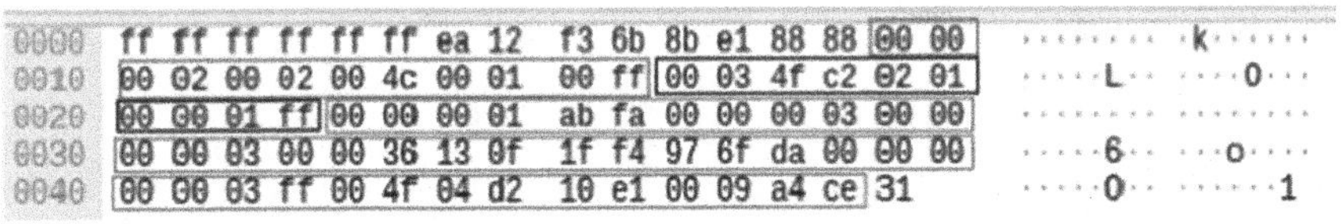

Fig. 12. Packet captured by Wireshark

The state of the network service is aware through INT, as shown in Fig. 13. In the awareness information of INT, sfid represents the service function chain identifier, si represents the network function identifier, and swid represents the passing switch identifier. The INT information shows that the packet goes from the source node is host6 and the destination node is host7, through two network function instances host9 and host11. The experimental results prove that SINET has customizable service deployment capabilities. SINET generates customizable network services through family association, and also flexibly combines each family through customizable service identification method to achieve efficient utilization of network resources.

```
mysql> select * from SFL_INT_DATA;
+----+------+-----+------+--------+------+----------+-----------------+-------------+
| id | sfid | si  | swid | qdepth | port | byte_cnt | cur_time        | hop_latency |
+----+------+-----+------+--------+------+----------+-----------------+-------------+
|  1 | 2004 | 253 |   7  |    0   |   3  | 41864468 | 16528815893036  |          17 |
|  2 | 2004 | 253 |  11  |    0   |   4  |   250670 | 16528815893021  |          10 |
|  3 | 2004 | 254 |  11  |    0   |   5  |   253274 | 16528815893009  |           5 |
|  4 | 2004 | 254 |   9  |    0   |   4  |   249450 | 16528815892995  |          10 |
|  5 | 2004 | 255 |   9  |    0   |   5  |   250234 | 16528815892981  |           7 |
|  6 | 2004 | 255 |   6  |    0   |   1  |   248526 | 16528815892961  |          12 |
|  7 | 2004 | 253 |   7  |    0   |   3  | 41864762 | 16528815903050  |          18 |
|  8 | 2004 | 253 |  11  |    0   |   4  |   250936 | 16528815903036  |          10 |
|  9 | 2004 | 254 |  11  |    0   |   5  |   253540 | 16528815903022  |           7 |
| 10 | 2004 | 254 |   9  |    0   |   4  |   249660 | 16528815903008  |          10 |
| 11 | 2004 | 255 |   9  |    0   |   5  |   250444 | 16528815902994  |           6 |
| 12 | 2004 | 255 |   6  |    0   |   1  |   248680 | 16528815902974  |          13 |
| 13 | 2004 | 253 |   7  |    0   |   3  | 41865306 | 16528815913066  |          18 |
| 14 | 2004 | 253 |  11  |    0   |   4  |   251202 | 16528815913052  |          10 |
| 15 | 2004 | 254 |  11  |    0   |   5  |   253806 | 16528815913039  |           6 |
| 16 | 2004 | 254 |   9  |    0   |   4  |   249870 | 16528815913024  |          11 |
| 17 | 2004 | 255 |   9  |    0   |   5  |   250654 | 16528815913009  |           7 |
| 18 | 2004 | 255 |   6  |    0   |   1  |   248834 | 16528815912988  |          13 |
| 19 | 2004 | 253 |   7  |    0   |   3  | 41865600 | 16528815923087  |          18 |
| 20 | 2004 | 253 |  11  |    0   |   4  |   251468 | 16528815923073  |          10 |
| 21 | 2004 | 254 |  11  |    0   |   5  |   254072 | 16528815923059  |           6 |
| 22 | 2004 | 254 |   9  |    0   |   4  |   250080 | 16528815923046  |           9 |
| 23 | 2004 | 255 |   9  |    0   |   5  |   250864 | 16528815923029  |           9 |
| 24 | 2004 | 255 |   6  |    0   |   1  |   248988 | 16528815923007  |          14 |
+----+------+-----+------+--------+------+----------+-----------------+-------------+
24 rows in set (0.00 sec)
```

Fig. 13. Awareness information of INT

5.2 Performance Results

This section tests and analyzes the performance of SINET system, including service analysis time, command execution time, and packet processing time.

The service analysis time is the time from the reception of user demand to the issuance of command information by SINET system. As shown in Fig. 14, the horizontal axis is the number of tests and the vertical axis is the service analysis time. As can be seen from the figure, the fastest is 836 ms, the slowest is 955 ms, and the average is 880 ms.

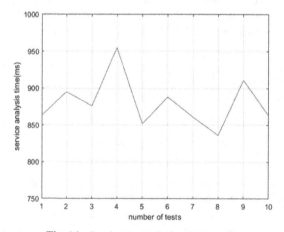

Fig. 14. Service analysis time test results

Instruction execution time is the time from when the system sends instruction information to the network component to when the network component completes the instruction. As shown in Fig. 15, the horizontal axis is the number of tests and the vertical axis is the instruction execution time. From the graph, the fastest is 12 ms, the slowest is 24ms, and the average is 14.9 ms.

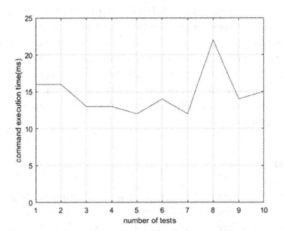

Fig. 15. Instruction execution time test results

The packet processing time is the time for the bmv2 switch to process the packet according to the customizable service identification method designed in this paper. Packet processing time includes first forwarding processing time, in-between forwarding processing time and last forwarding processing time. As shown in Fig. 16, the horizontal axis is the number of tests and the vertical axis is the packet processing time. As can be seen from the figure, the average processing time for first forwarding packets is 1.3 ms, the average processing time for in-between forwarding packets is 0.8ms, and the average processing time for last forwarding packets is 1.8ms.

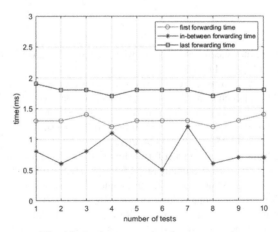

Fig. 16. Packet processing time test results

The service analysis time represents the processing performance of SINET system. When a user initiates a demand, SINET system can finish processing the user's demand in 880ms on average, which has a fast processing speed. The command execution time represents the reaction performance of SINET system. When the controller updates the command, all network components in the system use an average of 14.8ms to complete the response to the command, which has a fast reaction speed. The packet processing time represents the processing efficiency of the customizable service identification method at the data plane. The average packet processing time is in 1 ms, proving that the customizable service identification method has high processing efficiency. To sum up, SINET system can not only complete the customized deployment of network services, but also has good performance.

6 Conclusion

The traditional network architecture relies on special hardware, which is not flexible enough to meet the requirements of diversified network services. The "three layers and three domains" system is introduced into SINET to provide users with customized network services. In terms of improving the flexibility and fine-grained of the customized network services of SINET. This paper designs a customizable service identification method compatible with multiple data plane protocols. However, the customizable service identification method designed in this paper needs to be further improved in terms of packet processing speed and packet processing priority.

Acknowledgement. This research was funded by the fundamental research funds for the central universities under grant no. 2021JBZD003, open research projects of Zhejiang lab under grant no. 2022QA0AB03, nature and science foundation of China under grant no. 61471029, 61972026, 62072030 and 92167204.

References

1. Feldmann, A.: Internet clean-slate design: what and why? ACM SIGCOMM Comput. Commun. Rev. **37**(3), 59–64 (2007)
2. Clark, D., Braden, R., Sollins, K., et al.: New arch: future generation internet architecture. Massachusetts Inst. of Tech Cambridge Lab For Computer Science (2004)
3. White paper on future network development [EB/OL]. https://www.sciping.com/33404.html
4. Wu, P., Cui, Y., Wu, J., et al.: Transition from IPv4 to IPv6: a state-of-the-art survey. IEEE Commun. Surv. Tutorials **15**(3), 1407–1424 (2012)
5. Li, Z., Xu, Y., Zhang, B., et al.: Packet forwarding in named data networking requirements and survey of solutions. IEEE Commun. Surv. Tutorials **21**(2), 1950–1987 (2018)
6. Hu, F., Hao, Q., Bao, K.: A survey on software-defined network and openflow: from concept to implementation. IEEE Commun. Surv. Tutorials **16**(4), 2181–2206 (2014)
7. Yuxiang, H., Peng, Y., Penghao, S., et al.: Research on full dimensional and definable multimodal intelligent network architecture. J. Commun. **40**(8), 1–12 (2019)
8. Chen, J., Cheng, X., Chen, J., et al.: A Lightweight SFC Embedding Framework in SDN/NFV-enabled wireless network based on reinforcement learning. IEEE Syst. J. (2021)

9. Guo, K., Chen, J., Dong, P., et al.: FullSight: a feasible intelligent and collaborative framework for service function chains failure detection. IEEE Trans. Netw. Serv. Manag. (2022)

10. Gang, L.: Research on key technologies of secure packet forwarding of smart finance identification network. Beijing Jiaotong University, Beijing (2021). https://doi.org/10.26944/d.cnki.gbfju.2021.000068

11. Hongke, Z., Hongbin, L.: Basic research on intelligent collaborative network system J. Electron. 41(7), 1249–1252+1254 (2013)

12. Hongke, Z.: Intelligent collaborative network theory and practice. ICT **11**(6), 45–50 (2017)

13. Hongke, Z., Ru, J.: Future internet and its application – smart identity network. Sci. Res. Inf. Technol. Appl. **5**(1), 35–40 (2014)

A Dynamic Live Streaming Service Architecture Integrated Sensing and Control

Qimiao Zeng[✉], Ge Chen, Qi Chen, Yirong Zhuang[✉], Qing Pan, Zhifan Yin, and Jie Liang

China Telecom Research Institute, Guangzhou, China
zengqimiaodyx@163.com, 13316094433@chinatelecom.cn

Abstract. The live streaming of Over-The-Top (OTT) hot events will cause the tidal traffic of the network. As viewership grows, this high network load can lead to network blocking, poor quality of experience for users, high transmission costs for operators, and increased energy consumption. Most OTT lives content providers offer video services with unicast. To save bandwidth, there are some transmission solutions that also use multicast. Transmitting OTT video using the existing Internet Protocol television (IPTV) network is a win-win situation for telecom operators and OTT content providers. However, so far as we know, there is no dynamic service system for live streaming content that is easy to control over the existing IPTV network. As a result, it is more difficult to provide OTT live content on the existing IPTV network. In this paper, we propose a dynamic system architecture for live streaming services with integrated sensing and control. This architecture can leverage existing IPTV networks for real-time smart sensing and control of media services. The client does not need to make modifications and still uses the unicast protocol for video content delivery. We use a MA as a bridge between multicast and unicast. It receives client requests, converts multicast to unicast, and provides services to users. In addition, we design a unicast-multicast convergence method, which first provides unicast services to viewers and then dynamically switches to multicast service, reducing bandwidth and also improving the viewer experience.

Keywords: Multicast · Unicast · OTT Video · Live streaming

1 Introduction

Recently, video on the Internet is growing rapidly, accounting for more than 80% of the overall network bandwidth. In the future, 8K/16K or even higher resolution video will become more and more popular. Meanwhile, OTT live streaming is developing rapidly, and the number of live streaming users in e-commerce, education and games continues to increase [10]. The global OTT services market garnered US$ 2.1 Trillion in 2022. Owing to the increasing advancement in technology, the market is likely to propel to US$ 7.0 Trillion by 2032. The trade is projected at a 12.6% CAGR during the forecast period [1].

© The Author(s), under exclusive license to Springer Nature Singapore Pte Ltd. 2023
W. Quan (Ed.): ICENAT 2022, CCIS 1696, pp. 76–89, 2023.
https://doi.org/10.1007/978-981-19-9697-9_7

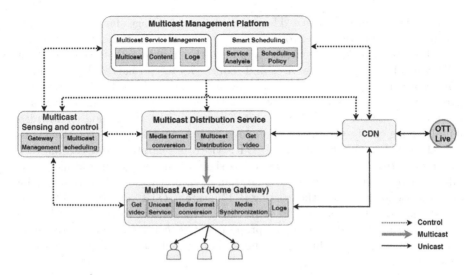

Fig. 1. The architecture of the OTT open-multicast system.

Currently, most OTT live streaming providers provide streaming services using unicast, mainly using HTTP to deliver video content. The client needs to establish a connection with the streaming server to download video playlist files and media files, and the streaming server provides video content to the client with unicast. When the number of OTT live video subscribers increases, the bandwidth consumption is higher and more likely to cause tidal traffic on the network. As a result, telecom operators need to deploy powerful servers to manage large amounts of high-bandwidth traffic simultaneously, which will eventually lead to higher costs for OTT services. At the same time, the large-scale unicast transmission may lead to blocking in the network, which is likely to cause poor quality of user experience [4]. Live OTT experiences have some limitations, including low quality, a latency of more than 30 sec compared with broadcast services [7] and scaling capabilities when millions of viewers want to access content at the same time [3]. Therefore, it is a huge challenge for both OTT content providers and telecom operators to ensure a great user experience without degrading video quality or causing a significant impact on Internet Service Provider (ISP) networks.

Recently, due to the construction of a flexible and interactive network and complete service system, IPTV services of telecom operators are developing rapidly. In providing live IPTV services, telecom operators have built IP-based multicast networks with wide coverage to provide services for various types of live TV. Compared with unicast, the multicast network is characterized by greater savings on server resources and bandwidth resources of the network backbone for live streaming.

Usually, the OTT services use the public Internet to transmit these packets. In contrast, IPTV operators use multicast technology to transmit IP packets over a private network, where security and performance are strictly managed to

enhance the viewer experience. There are several advantages for telecom operators to provide multicast networks to live OTT content providers. (1) The use
of multicast networks can effectively relieve the unpredictable traffic tidal of
OTT video live streaming services and reduce end-to-end bandwidth consumption, especially saving concurrent bandwidth of network peaks. (2) Providing
live streaming services for OTT with multicast, the cost of renting services is
much lower than the cost of the content delivery network (CDN) and bandwidth
rental, saving end-to-end distribution costs and thus making live streaming content cheaper for viewers. (3) When OTT video is migrated from the Internet
to the operator's network, the service has significantly less jitter and more stability. Therefore, telecom operators need an open-multicast system that can be
deployed independently of the existing IPTV system. OTT content providers can
use the open-multicast system to deliver live OTT content to viewers with multicast. Motivated by the above, we propose a sense-control integrated dynamic
live streaming service architecture, and its major contributions are summarized
as follows:

- We propose a novel sense-control integrated real-time dynamic live streaming
  service system over the existing managed IPTV network. Our system contains modules such as a multicast management platform (MMP), multicast
  distribution service (MDS), multicast sensing and control (MSC) module, and
  multicast agent (MA). It can sense and control the service in real time.
- Our system receives requests from clients through a MA and implements the
  function of converting multicast into unicast to provide services to viewers.
  It is not necessary to make changes to the client.
- When viewers first access the live streaming content, the system first provides
  unicast service and then smoothly switches to multicast service. It provides
  dynamic OTT live streaming service using both unicast and multicast.

The reminder of this paper is organized as follows. The related works are
reviewed in Sect. 2. Section 3 presents a novel open-multicast system architecture
and Sect. 4 evaluates the performance of the proposed system. Finally, conclusions are drawn in Sect. 5.

2   Related Works

2.1   OTT Service

OTT service refers to a service that provides various media contents such as
movies, drama series, and educational programs through the internet [14]. OTT
services can be delivered not only over non-managed networks, such as Netflix,
Hulu, and Amazon but also over managed networks, such as IPTV operators [8].
Recently, many optimized OTT service systems have been explored [6,12,15].
Moshe et al. [12] suggest a novel framework for optimizing partial streaming
using the multi-layer cache, which allows storing partial video content in time-
based chunks of data while forwarding these data chunks to the users at various

levels of ISP networks. This framework contributes to solving the OTT bottle-neck caused by video streaming. Tran *et al.* [15] proposed a Temporal-Spatial OTT (TSOTT), a system that varies the bitrate of video content based on the time and geographical location of the requesting client, with a good balance between cost, spent and video quality. To reduce the edge cache load and the total bandwidth consumed by the upstream content server, Dias *et al.* [6] investigated a novel distributed smart caching architecture for OTT content distribution (DSMC). However, their transmission scheme is based entirely on unicast, which cannot significantly reduce the total bandwidth consumed by multiple concurrent user requests.

2.2 Tidal Traffic of Live Streaming

The tidal traffic of live streaming refers to that a large number of users watching live video content at the same time, causing an explosion of network traffic in a short period. In peak traffic areas, network blocking may increase because of a dramatic increase in traffic, while in low traffic areas, network nodes may remain idle with little traffic, wasting a lot of energy [16]. As a result, it is urgent to provide solutions for the tidal traffic problem, which will cause high start-up latency, user viewing latency, and server overload in the service.

Usually, OTT service providers enhance the live streaming experience through optimization of cloud-based live streaming technologies: 1) Optimizing the service logic. For example, the client completes DNS parsing in advance and displays the picture as soon as the first I-frame is acquired. 2) The smoothness of live streaming is ensured by content caching and Adaptive Bit Rate (ABR) Streaming. When the network is blocked, pre-cached data can usually be used to ensure a few seconds of playback, and the client can also choose the appropriate bitrate according to the real-time download rate. 3) Smart scheduling, by calculating the response time of each edge node, schedules live requests to the best service node in real time to alleviate the impact on media servers caused by a large number of users' connections in a short period. However, cloud live streaming technology cannot control the network and passively adapts to the tidal traffic, which cannot fundamentally solve the tidal problem of OTT live streaming.

Another solution to the tidal traffic of OTT live streaming is to deploy the CDN as close to the client as possible. Because this method can reduce the start-up latency and save the bandwidth of the CDN. However, this solution is not the best choice because it requires additional investment in CDN servers.

2.3 OTT Service Over Multicast

Multicast is an efficient one-to-many method for content distribution from a source to all or a large number of destinations [9]. Currently, many multicast-based solutions are proposed to solve the problem of tidal traffic generated by OTT live streaming [5,11,13]. To address the network bottleneck problem that may arise from peaks in OTT video service requests, Bouten *et al.* [5] presented a novel architecture for OTT multimedia services based on HTTP adaptive streaming, which allows for reducing the consumed bandwidth through a combination of caching and multicast streaming. However, in their framework, the delivery server is responsible for receiving multicast messages, and the implementation of multicast to unicast conversion. This module is not deployed closer to the user side of the home gateway to better exploit the capabilities of the multicast system. Okerman *et al.* [13] presented a solution where the High Efficiency Streaming Protocol (typically sent for unicast only) is used to send content over IP multicast. This solution can leverage the existing IPTV network to reduce overall bandwidth consumption while ensuring fast start-up and low-end latency. However, their system simply includes a multicast server module, unicast origin module, and multicast gateway module. Since the solution relies heavily on the gateway to provide key functions, it does not include functions such as management of the gateway and system scheduling. Therefore, it is not possible to update and manage the real-time status of the gateway, and it is difficult to meet the real demand of intelligently handling numerous and complex services. In addition, the client in this solution needs to be changed to support a specific protocol, and such a modification is not appropriate for large-scale users. Koch *et al.* [11] proposed a system for SDN-based multicast system for OTT on-demand video streaming (VoDCast). VoDCast takes into account the costs of multicast group state and group state, user waiting time, and state-of-the-art parameter settings. The proposed SDN-based network system enables ISPs to deliver video content based on efficient network-level multicast. But their solution supports video-on-demand (VOD) rather than live video, making it difficult for the system to meet the needs of live streaming.

Therefore, none of the above solutions solves the problem of how to build an OTT multicast service system for live video content that can be smartly controlled in real-time and utilize the existing multicast network of IPTV efficiently.

3   System Model

The framework of the open-multicast system is shown in Fig. 1, which mainly includes a MMP, MDS module, MSC module, and MA. The flow of a client between first accessing an OTT target video URL and receiving the video content is shown in Fig. 2. The CDN provides the live streaming service. Specifically, the client sends a viewing request, and the CDN request routing (RR) module of the CDN receives the request and returns an HTTP 302 redirect response and the scheduling service address. Then, the client accesses the multicast control module based on the information received, which returns an HTTP 302 redirect response, the MA address, and the MDS address. At the same time, the multicast distribution server pulls videos from the CDN using unicast and converts the unicast streams into multicast streams. The client sends a request to the MA. The MA first pulls the video content from the CDN using unicast, and then sends the media data to the client. Meanwhile, the MA joins the target multicast

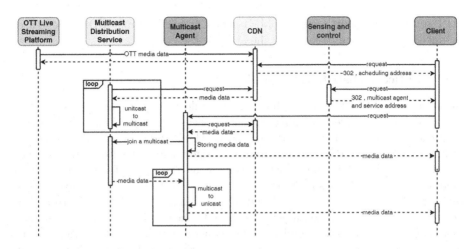

Fig. 2. The flow of OTT open-multicast system.

group, receives the multicast streams and converts them into unicast streams. Finally, the MA sends the converted unicast streams to the client and stops the above unicast pull streams. In this paper, considering the adaptability of a large number of actual users, the multicast protocol and unicast protocol are Real-time Transport Protocol (RTP) and HTTP Live Streaming (HLS) respectively. Besides, all media segments are encapsulated in the MPEG-2 Transport Stream (TS) file format. Next, we will introduce each module in detail.

3.1 Multicast Management Platform

The MMP is the "super brain" of the OTT open-multicast system, which is responsible for the interaction with each module in the system, including the OTT live streaming platform, MDS, MSC, and MA. Firstly, the MMP is responsible for managing the live streaming requests from OTT live streaming platform. When OTT live platform uses the open-multicast system, it sends a request to MMP to create a multicast service and sends metadata of the target media stream. Then, based on this information, the MMP creates a corresponding list of unicast and multicast. In this list, each unicast stream uniquely corresponds to a multicast address. Secondly, the MMP needs to maintain the multicast channel list, such as multicast time and channel information, and send and synchronize the corresponding list of multicast and unicast channels to the MDS. Thirdly, the MMP performs log collection and management. Finally, the MMP also contains the smart scheduling module, which is responsible for service analysis and gateway management after receiving the information uploaded by the sense-control module. The platform counts and analyzes video services and smart scheduling policies. It also monitors whether the gateways support multicast protocols and manages the status of the gateways. In addition, the platform also supports the elastic expansion of MDS. If the current MDS cannot support the traffic burst of

OTT services in a short time, the MMP can schedule multiple MDS to increase the media distribution capacity of the system.

3.2 Multicast Distribution Service

In our open-multicast system, the MDS module is responsible for the multicast distribution of live streaming. Specifically, the multicast server receives the multicast channel list information sent by the MMP and creates multicast channels. The MDS pulls HLS streams from the edge CDN nodes using unicast and converts them into RTP multicast streams using the media format conversion module. Significantly, as shown in Fig. 3, for the MA to be able to convert HLS sequential ts segments from OTT multicast streams, the MDS needs to add a new field for the segment parameter in the RTP header extension of the multicast RTP stream. This field indicates the sequence number in the HLS segment file corresponding to the current video data in the RTP load, representing the value specified by the tag EXT-X-MEDIA-SEQUENCE in the HLS protocol. The EXT-X-MEDIA-SEQUENCE indicates the start sequence number of the segment. Each segment has a unique serial number. To ensure stream continuity, this sequence number is incremented in step of 1. When the client receives playlist files and media segments, it can use the value of this tag as a reference to playing the segment with the corresponding sequence number. Therefore, adding this extent field allows the MA to convert multicast streams to unicast streams successfully in the correct sequence. Subsequently, the MDS sends multicast streams of media content to each MA.

3.3 Multicast Agent

In this architecture, we do not want to make modifications to the client because of the high cost. Therefore, we need a MA to convert multicast streams to unicast streams. Thus, the conversion of the media protocol is not perceptible to the client. Usually, the MA can be deployed in the following places.

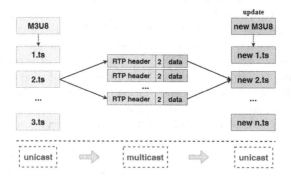

Fig. 3. The detailed conversion process between HLS unicast and RTP multicast.

- **Client**: it can be deployed on end-play devices, such as Set Top Boxes (STBs) and smart TVs. In this case, the client needs to support multicast protocol.
- **Home gateway**: it can be deployed on home gateway devices such as home routers, Optical network terminal (ONT). The multicast gateways need to receive multicast streams and then convert them into unicast streams and send them to multiple home clients.
- **Edge node of network**: it can also be deployed on network edge nodes, such as Optical Line Terminal (OLT), Optical Transport Networking (OTN), or edge CDN. In this case, the MA receives multicast messages and provides multicast-to-unicast conversion for transmission between the network edge node and the home gateway via unicast. This deployment method can be used in the case where the terminal device of the home network do not support IP multicast messages.

The closer the MA is deployed to the viewers, the better it is to utilize the capabilities of the open-multicast system. There will be additional modification costs if it is deployed on the client side. Therefore, in our solution, the MA is deployed on the home gateway.

Compared to unicast and HTTP streams, joining and leaving a multicast network can incur large latency due to the join and leave latency of Internet Group Management Protocol (IGMP). To improve viewers' experience, the MA first accesses the CDN and pulls the HLS unicast stream. At the same time, it joins the multicast group corresponding to the unicast video according to the multicast information. After the MA joins the multicast group successfully, it receives RTP multicast packets and unpacking them. At this point, both unicast and multicast packets exist in the cache of the MA. After the multicast packets are converted to unicast packets, the MA dynamically and seamlessly converges these packets using the media synchronization module. This approach ensures that the client does not lose frames or receive duplicate frames. Subsequently, the MA stops the pulling of HLS unicast streams from CDN. In addition, the number of unicast packets received by the MA is determined by the latency joining the multicast. Thus, it is a dynamic convergence process. In particular, the MA merges all RTP packets with the same segment parameter according to the segment parameter added in the RTP expansion header by the parsing MDS. Then it encapsulates them into the segment file corresponding to the EXT-X-MEDIA-SEQUENCE parameter in HLS by RTP sequence number. By these methods, the HLS unicast stream can be extracted from the RTP multicast stream successfully. Subsequently, the MA transmits the HLS unicast stream to the client, including the M3U8 playlists and the TS segments.

In our open-multicast system, if the MA cannot join the multicast group and receive the multicast stream successfully, it needs to maintain the HLS unicast stream. When viewers join or exit the live streaming, the MA regularly reports the user playing information, the IP address of the live channel, and the IP address of the viewing user to the MSC module. Then the MSC module reports the collected information to the MMP, which performs real-time statistics and analysis of these data.

3.4 Multicast Sensing And Control

Real-time sensing and control of multicast services is very important in the open-multicast system, which makes the system more smart. It contains gateway management module and multicast scheduling module.

Gateway Management Module. As mentioned above, we deploy the MA on the home gateway. Therefore, the gateway management module needs to monitor the status of the home gateway and detect any abnormal cases in time. Specifically, the MA sends a login request to the MMP, and after completing the registration, the heartbeat signaling between the MA and the multicast platform is used to confirm whether the MA is online. Once the module detects that the MA does not support multicast reception, the gateway management module will notify the CDN RR. The HTTP redirect message returned by CDN RR to the client only includes unicast instead of multicast information. Then, the MA directly requests the CDN node to pull the HLS unicast stream and forward the data to the client.

Multicast Scheduling Module. Compared with unicast, the cost of multicast network operation is higher. Therefore, it is unreasonable to transmit unpopular content through multicast, and unicast can be used as another delivery method. The multicast scheduling module receives playback requests from each client and reports this information to the MMP. The smart scheduling module of the MMP evaluates the popularity of videos. If the module determines that the video is popular content, then the MMP generates a scheduling policy. The multicast scheduling module will execute the policy, returning a service redirected reply to the client that also contains the encrypted multicast address. After the client receives the address, the MA sends a request to join the target multicast group. Here, the multicast server address information is encrypted to prevent unauthenticated viewers from joining the multicast group; If the module determines that the video is unpopular content, multicast is not an optimal transmission method. Similarly, the multicast scheduling module returns the CDN address to the client, and the client requests video content using unicast. This method can dynamically adjust the transmission mode of OTT live streaming, so as to minimize the total consumption of resources.

In general, we proposed an open-multicast system architecture, which is a novel sense-control integrated real-time dynamic live streaming service system over the existing managed IPTV network. It can provide the existing multicast network to OTT content providers without modifying the client, thus reducing the impact of the live streaming tidal traffic. In addition, our solution contains a variety of sensing and control methods that allow each module within the system to be flexibly scheduled, thus making the solution more suitable for realistic and complex multi-user situations. Finally, the dynamic convergence of unicast and multicast also increases the flexibility of the system.

4   Experimental Evaluation

This section verifies the function and performance of the open-multicast system proposed in this paper. Based on the existing hardware devices, such as routers, servers, intelligent gateways, and common terminals, we built an open-multicast system in the lab, including the steps of system networking, function module deployment, joint debugging between modules, and finally tested the functions of each module of the system, the interface between modules and the service request process simulating hot content.

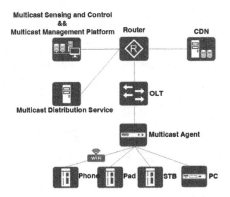

Fig. 4. The networking diagram of the open-multicast system.

4.1   Experimental Networking Diagram and Hardware Configuration

The experimental networking diagram is shown in Fig. 4. It includes a core router, a server to deploy the MSC module and MMP module, a server to deploy the MDS, a CDN cluster servers, including CDN RR server and CDN edge server, an OLT, an intelligent gateway, the function of MA, mobile phones, pads, STBs, PCs and other common terminals. The core router is used to connect the MSC, MMP, MDS and CDN server cluster, and connect the OLT in the down direction. The router needs to be configured with protocols such as Protocol Independent Multicast (PIM), IGMP, Open Shortest Path First (OSPF), etc. to connect the networking link. The MSC can sense the user's request, schedule the user's playback request to the most appropriate MA service, and control the injection, update, user authentication and security management of the content source; MMP mainly includes content injection, content update, multicast authentication management and other functions; The main function of the MDS is to receive the request of the MA to join the multicast group and send the multicast stream to the MA; The MA mainly provides terminal registration, content storage, content services and other functions. It can request multicast from the MDS and unicast from the CDN server. The hardware environment of key modules of open-multicast system is shown in the table 1.

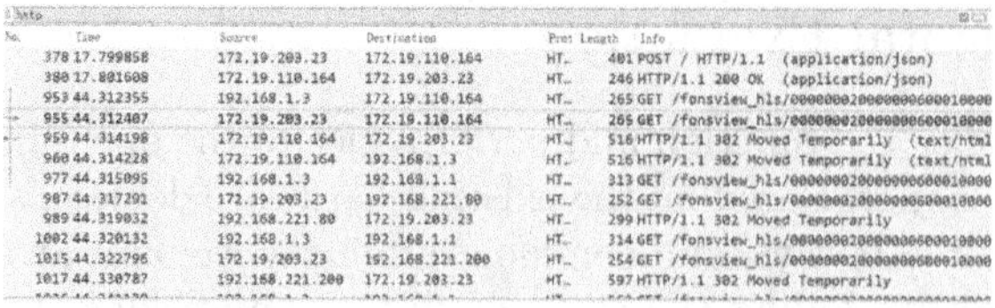

(a) The terminal requests top video link.

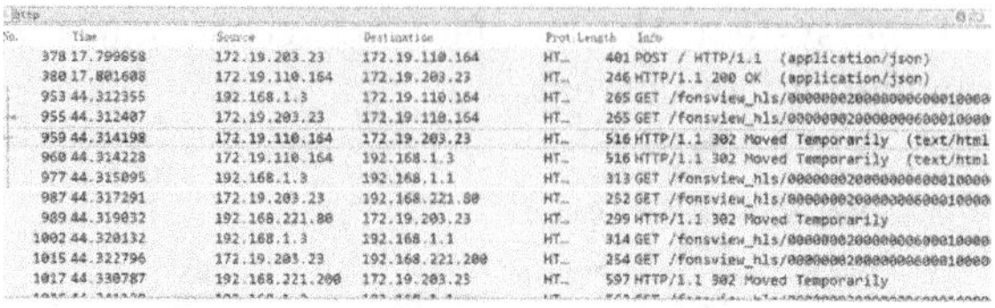

(b) The MSC returns the address of the MA and carries the encrypted multicast group information.

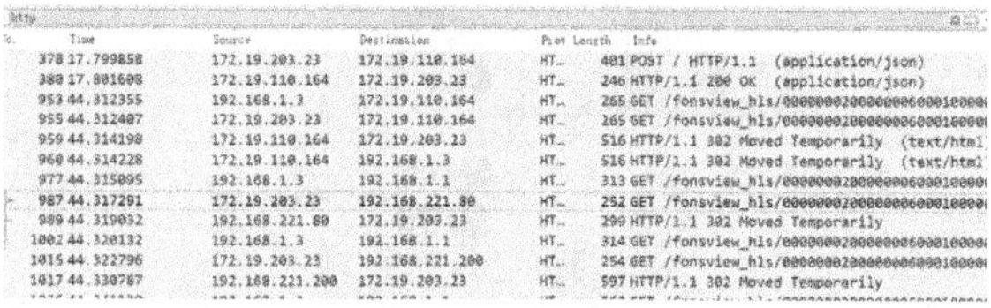

(c) The MA requests service from CDN servers.

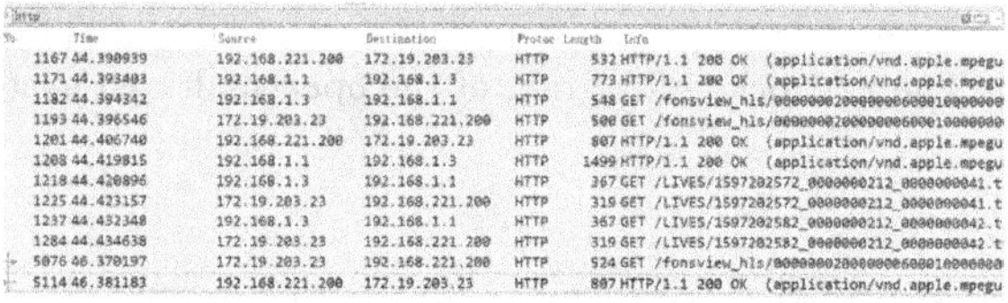

(d) The CDN servers returns unicast content to MA.

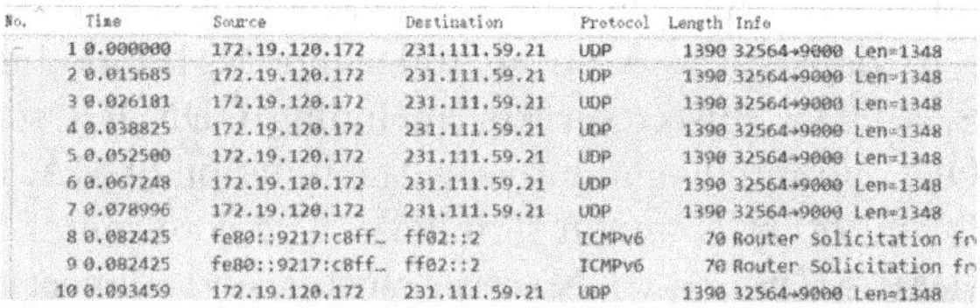

(e) After the MA joins the multicast group, the MDS sends multicast to the MA.

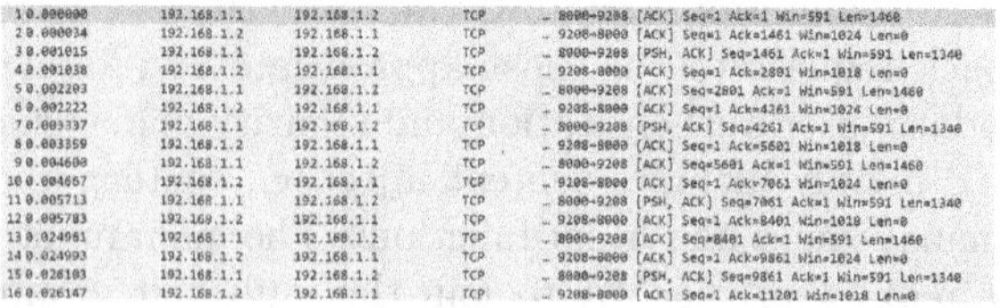

(f) The data message of terminal requesting OTT hot content.

Fig. 5. The data message of terminal requesting OTT hot content.

Table 1. Hardware configuration

System module	Minimum hardware configuration
MSC MMP	CPU: 4 cores Memory: 64 GB System hard disk: 2 × 480 GB SSD Data hard disk: 4 × 4TB SATA Network cards: 2 × 10 GE (SFP+), 2×GE
MDS	The same as above
MA	HG7143D: 10 GE EPON Hi5682T, flash 256 MB Gigabit port×3, ITV port×1, usb×1 Optical port×1, 2.4G & 5G WiFi

4.2   Experimental Procedure

After setting up the open-multicast system in the experimental environment, debug each functional module and the modules, including the management interface between the MA and the MSC, the MSC and the OTT CDN, the data interface of the open-multicast system platform, and the reporting information interface between the MSC and the MDS, and finally, make the open-multicast system work normally. Connecting the network port or WiFi of the MA through multiple terminals, we request the same OTT top video link at the same time and record the access interface packets of each system module, the bandwidth of the MA entrance, and the playback effect of each terminal.

4.3   Experimental Result

Each terminal plays smoothly, and audio and video are synchronized. The data message of the terminal requesting OTT hot content using Wireshark, a popular open source network analysis tool [2], are shown in Fig. 5. By analyzing the data packets captured at the access interface of each system module, we know that after the user requests the OTT link (Fig. 5a), the MSC returns the service address of the MA to the terminal, and the multicast address is encrypted (Fig. 5b). If the MA does not start the recording of the OTT content at this time, the MA requests the CDN RR (Fig. 5c), and the CDN RR schedules the request address to the CDN edge service node. The edge node provides TS segment information to the MA, and then directly provides it to the terminal (Fig. 5d). At the same time, the MA applies to the MDS to join the multicast group. The MDS sends multicast media data to the MA (Fig. 5e). The MA turns on the recording function and saves four fragments information at the same time, to ensure the stability and fluency of HLS playback. Then the MA provides services to the terminal. At this time, the MA takes over the user's request to get the OTT live content later (Fig. 5f). When the number of terminals served by the MA is 4, the bandwidth can be saved by 75% compared with the original unicast.

5   Conclusion

In this paper, to alleviate the tidal traffic of the current popular OTT live streaming on the network, we propose a novel dynamic system of live streaming service with integrated sensing and control. The system includes MMP, MA, sensing and control module, and CDN. The system can sense and control video service in real-time. Besides, it can also transmit OTT video over existing IPTV multicast networks provided by telecom operators without any modification of clients. This approach leverages multicast to reduce the bandwidth consumption of the network and reduce the cost of OTT content distribution, achieving a win-win situation for both telecom operators and OTT content providers. We also cleverly design a dynamic unicast and multicast convergence method to solve the problem of large latency in joining a multicast group at the start-up stage. Finally, we demonstrated the availability of this open-multicast system through a series of experiments.

Acknowledgements. This work is supported by the New morphic network Architecture and Key Technology Research No. CT-P-2022-02.

References

1. Over the top (ott) services market outlook (2022-2032) (2022). https://www.futuremarketinsights.com/reports/over-the-top-ott-services-market
2. Bagyalakshmi, G., et al.: Network vulnerability analysis on brain signal/image databases using nmap and wireshark tools. IEEE Access **6**, 57144–57151 (2018)
3. Biatek, T., Abdoli, M., Burdinat, C., Toullec, E., Gregory, L., Raulet, M.: Live OTT services delivery with ad-insertion using VVC, CMAF-ll and route: an end-to-end chain. In: Proceedings of the 1st Mile-High Video Conference, pp. 79–80 (2022)
4. Biatek, T., François, E., Thienot, C., Hamidouche, W.: Sustainable OTT video distribution powered by 5g-multicast/unicast delivery and versatile video coding. In: Proceedings of the 1st Mile-High Video Conference, pp. 81–82 (2022)
5. Bouten, N., et al.: A multicast-enabled delivery framework for QOE assurance of over-the-top services in multimedia access networks. J. Netw. Syst. Manag. **21**(4), 677–706 (2013)
6. Dias, R., Fiorese, A., Guardalben, L., Sargento, S.: A distributed caching architecture for over-the-top content distribution. In: 2018 14th Annual Conference on Wireless On-demand Network Systems and Services (WONS), pp. 9–16. IEEE (2018)
7. Fautier, T.: How OTT services can match the quality of broadcast. SMPTE Motion Imaging J. **129**(3), 16–25 (2020)
8. Fautier, T.: Can UHD OTT be complementary to terrestrial UHD broadcast? SMPTE Motion Imaging J. **130**(5), 12–19 (2021)
9. Karaata, M.H., Dabees, A., Alazemi, F.: A reliable concurrent multicast algorithm for content distribution. J. Supercomput. 1–33 (2022). https://doi.org/10.1007/s11227-021-04291-5
10. Kim, S., Baek, H., Kim, D.H.: Ott and live streaming services: past, present future. Telecommun. Policy **45**(9), 102244 (2021)

11. Koch, C., Hacker, S., Hausheer, D.: Vodcast: efficient SDN-based multicast for video on demand. In: 2017 IEEE 18th International Symposium on a World of Wireless, Mobile and Multimedia Networks (WoWMoM), pp. 1–6. IEEE (2017)
12. Moshe, B.B., Dvir, A., Solomon, A.: Analysis and optimization of live streaming for over the top video. In: 2011 IEEE Consumer Communications and Networking Conference (CCNC), pp. 60–64. IEEE (2011)
13. Okerman, E., Vounckx, J.: Fast startup multicast streaming on operator IPTV networks using HESP. In: 2021 IEEE International Symposium on Multimedia (ISM), pp. 79–86. IEEE (2021)
14. Seo, B.G., Park, D.H.: Effective strategies for contents recommendation based on psychological ownership of over the top services in cyberspace. J. Theor. Appl. Electron. Comm. Res. **16**(4), 976–991 (2021)
15. Tran, S., Tran, T., Le, H., Truong, T., Nguyen, T.: Temporal-spatial bitrate-adaptivity for OTT service. In: 2021 International Conference on System Science and Engineering (ICSSE), pp. 346–351. IEEE (2021)
16. Zhong, Z., et al.: Energy efficiency and blocking reduction for tidal traffic via stateful grooming in IP-over-optical networks. J. Opt. Commun. Netw. **8**(3), 175–189 (2016)

Network Intelligence Theory
and Technology

Detection of SDN Flow Rule Conflicts Based on Knowledge Graph

Siyun Liang and Jian Su[✉]

National Key Laboratory of Science and Technology on Communications,
University of Electronic Science and Technology of China, Chengdu 611731, China
jsu@uestc.edu.cn

Abstract. Software-Defined Network (SDN) separates the control plane and data plane to provide a more flexible network. In that case, switches only need to follow the flow rules that controllers send. However, when conflicts between policies in applications happen, the flow rules they send may conflict too, then the behavior of switches may not be as expected. Moreover, the process of pipeline with multiple tables has made the match of flow rules more flexible but complicated. Therefore, precisely and easily detecting flow rule conflicts in one table and among multiple tables is crucial. Nowadays, knowledge graph has become a hot spot, with a good representation on entities and complex network relations. Besides, it has a reasoning ability, which can discover new relations between entities. So, we construct an SDN flow rule conflicts detection knowledge graph to store the network information including flow rules, then set up production rules according to the definition of flow rule conflicts with conflicts in one table and conflicts among multiple tables. The production rules are easy to read and modify. The result shows that the conflicts can be detected correctly with a clear reasoning process by production rules.

Keywords: Software-Defined Network · Flow Rule Conflicts · Knowledge Graph

1 Introduction

Software-Defined Network (SDN) separates the control plane and data plane to realize centralized control and simplify the data plane (See Fig. 1). The breakthrough separation makes the network more flexible to adapt to users' demands on network resources, and plays an important role in emerging scenarios such as big data, cloud computing, and the Internet of Things [1].

The control plane connects to the data plane by OpenFlow protocol [2]. It converts the policies from the application plane into flow rules and sends them to the data plane. The data plane forwards or drops the packets according to the action set of flow rules. In that case, network applications control the network easily by only changing the flow rules instead of the underlying facilities.

Generally, these planes cooperate well to make SDN work. But as demand increases, applications make policies based on their own needs. Due to the complexity of the

© The Author(s), under exclusive license to Springer Nature Singapore Pte Ltd. 2023
W. Quan (Ed.): ICENAT 2022, CCIS 1696, pp. 93–104, 2023.
https://doi.org/10.1007/978-981-19-9697-9_8

software and the dependencies between flow rules, these policies may have conflicts because the flow rules are unchecked. When the wrong flow rules are executed, a series of exceptions such as blackhole or forwarding loop will occur. Moreover, the security policy may be missed, making the network vulnerable, which can bring economic losses [1].

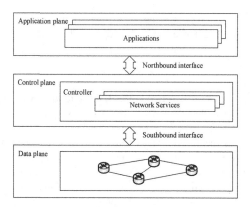

Fig. 1. The architecture of SDN

Each flow rule contains match fields, actions, and priority. Conflict happens when the match fields overlap and their actions have conflicts. Considering the priority, some flow rules may be shadowed or generalized, then packets will match the wrong rules. Moreover, the process of pipeline with multiple tables has made the match of flow rules more flexible but complicated. Brew [3] is a security policy analysis framework for SDN implemented on an OpenDaylight SDN controller, that can classify and resolve the conflicts. Veriflow [4] utilizes a date structure of prefix tree to store the flow rules and simplify the comparison of match fields. FireWell [5], which also presents relations between addresses with tree structure, is a firewall policy analyzer. There are also methods based on machine learning such as Support Vector Machine (SVM) [6]. The above methods are efficient, but the process of reasoning is not easy to read, and they neglect the conflicts that happen among multiple tables.

Meanwhile, knowledge graph [7], as a research topic of artificial intelligence (AI), also called semantic network, has been put into use in the fields of medicine [8] and e-commerce [9] with its excellent knowledge representation and reasoning ability [10]. It uses the form of triples (e.g. (entity, relation, entity)) to describe the entities in the real world and the relations between them, and processes reasoning according to the rules we set. The network carries network entities with complex relations, hence knowledge graph can be a suitable model for network topology. Recently, knowledge graph has been used to solve some network problems. Xu et al. [11] propose a semantic ontology, combined with user-defined rules to perceive the security situation of the IoT network. Chen et al. [12] built an IoT system with semantic ontology to realize automatic classification of resources and behaviors, then diagnose the abnormal status. Souza et al. [13] import the Network Markup Language (NML) model into Neo4j (a graph database for knowledge graph) to augment SDN network state. Li et al. [14] construct an alarm knowledge graph to locate faults in software-defined optical networks.

Since SDN collects network information by controllers, the knowledge graph can easily collect network information to build a semantic model between SDN elements, then resolve flow rule conflicts by production rules of conflict definitions. The form of rules is easy to understand, and the reasoning path is clear so that the administrators can analyze and modify them with no effort.

Our contributions are summarized as follows.

1. We build a knowledge graph for SDN flow conflicts detection, and use the real-time topology information of SDN network as instances. The knowledge graph connects network entities such as devices, ports, and flow tables with complex relations, and presents a unified description of the network situation, which helps to manage and analyze the situation of SDN.
2. We construct a flow rule conflicts detection method by transforming the multi-branch classification of matching relations into the form of binary production rules. With the presentation and reasoning of knowledge graph, we can detect the conflicts both in one flow table and among multiple tables.

2   Introduction of Flow Rule Conflicts

In a switch, the flow rule conflicts happen in one flow table or among multiple tables. In Fig. 2, the policy of application A shows that data packets should output directly on port 1 with the shortest path algorithm, but application B wants to balance the traffic and makes the data packets output on port 2. Under the circumstance, a conflict occurs.

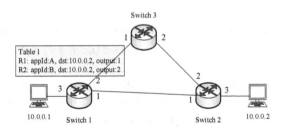

Fig. 2. Conflict in one flow table

Other situations happen in pipeline processing of multiple tables. Figure 3 shows that first the data packets sent to 10.0.0.2 will be matched in Table 1, the actions modify the destination address to 1.1.1.2, go to Table 2, and output on port 1. When matching in Table 2, since the modification has been performed, the flow rule whose match field is *dst:10.0.0.3* will be matched, but the action is output on port 2, which conflicts with rule 1 in Table 1.

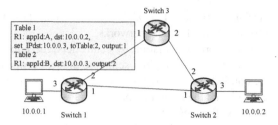

Fig. 3. Conflict among multiple tables

2.1 Conflicts in One Flow Table

When packets match multiple flow rules in one table, the actions can be different, resulting in redundancy or conflict, and it is possible that the correct flow rules cannot be matched due to the wrong priority setting, which affects the implementation of the policy. To classify flow rule conflicts, we first introduce the relations between flow rules.

A flow rule is defined as $F_i = \{M_i, A_i, P_i\}$, M_i, A_i, P_i are the match fields, actions, and priority of the i th flow rule. Each flow rule has k match fields (i.e. $M_i = \{m_1, m_2, \cdots, m_k\}$) and l actions (i.e. $A = \{a_1, a_2, \cdots, a_l\}$). First, we introduce matching relations.

There are two kinds of match fields, fields that can be matched in a range such as IP, and exact match fields such as ethernet type, presenting as either a specific value or a wildcard.

1. Disjoint: F_i and F_j are disjoint when not all match fields overlap (i.e. For F_i and F_j, $\exists x : m_x^i \cap m_x^j = \emptyset, (1 \leq x \leq k))$.
2. Equivalent: F_i equal to F_j when all match fields are the same (i.e. For F_i and F_j, $\forall x : m_x^i = m_x^j, (1 \leq x \leq l))$.
3. Include: F_j include F_i when each match field on F_i is a subset of those on F_j, and at least one match field on F_i is a proper subset (i.e. For F_i and F_j, $\forall x : m_x^i \subseteq m_x^j$, $\exists x : m_x^i \neq m_x^j, (1 \leq x \leq k))$.
4. Correlated: F_i and F_j are correlated when all match fields on F_i are subset, superset, or equal of F_j, and at least one match field on F_i is a proper subset of F_j, one match field on F_j is a proper subset of F_i (i.e. F_i and F_j, $\forall x : m_x^i \cap m_x^j \neq \emptyset$, $\exists x, y : m_x^i \subset m_x^j, m_y^i \supset m_y^j, (1 \leq x \leq k, 1 \leq y \leq k))$.

When two flow rules have a relation on match fields, according to their actions and priority, there are five kinds of conflicts:

1. No conflict: when F_i and F_j are disjoint, no matter what their actions are, they have no impact on each other, in other words, they have no conflict.
2. Redundancy: when F_i and F_j overlap, and they have the same actions, they are redundant. Redundancy has no impact on packet processing, but it takes memories of switches. Reducing the redundancy can optimize switch space consumption and resource allocation.

3. shadow: F_i shadows F_j when F_i includes F_j and $P_i > P_j$, in that case, F_j will never be matched.
4. generalization: F_j is a generalization of F_i when F_i includes F_j and $P_i < P_j$. It's a common conflict, such as table-miss flow rules.
5. correlation conflict: F_i and F_j have correlation conflict when F_i and F_j are correlated and their actions are conflict. Their common match ranges will be impacted [5, 6].

2.2 Conflicts among Multiple Tables

The *goto-table* action directs the flow rules to another flow table, so the final execute action set contains actions of all matched flow rules. The actions of different flow rules may have conflicts. There are mainly four types of actions: output, modify (e.g. modify the source IP and destination IP), goto-table, and drop (See Table 1). The *drop* action conflicts with all other actions. If the same action directs to different values, for example, output on different ports, conflict still happens.

Table 1. Relations of actions

Action	Output	Modify	Goto-table	Drop
Output	Maybe conflict	No conflict	No conflict	Conflict
Modify		Maybe conflict	No conflict	Conflict
Goto-table			Maybe conflict	Conflict
Drop				Conflict

3 Method

Knowledge graph consists of schema level and data level. The schema level presents the abstract of SDN and the relations of network entities with ontology. The data level contains instances of network entities [14]. We first construct the schema level and fill the data level with instances, then do the detection with production rules, and search for results by SPARQL [15].

3.1 Design of Ontology

First, we design the classes of SDN ontology. Classes are the abstract of SDN entities. Two special concepts are superclass and subclass. The subclasses have the characteristics of the superclasses but also have unique characteristics. After classifying the SDN entities, the structure of classes is designed as Fig. 4, containing *Controller, Host, Device, Link, DeviceComponent* (i.e. *Port, FlowTable, Flow*), *FlowComponent* (i.e. *Action*).

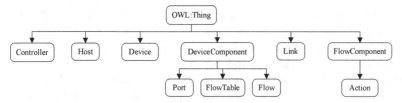

Fig. 4. The classes of SDN ontology

Then design the properties. Properties can be relations with other classes, that is, object properties; or can be their numerical properties, that is, data properties. The basic properties are depicted in Fig. 5, including:

1. Object properties: The connecting relations between components of the SDN, which describe the topology information of SDN.
2. Data properties: Contain some common data values such as names or addresses.

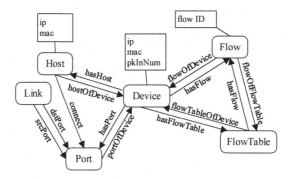

Fig. 5. Basic object properties and data properties

Additionally, flow rules contain lots of network operation information, so it is important to define properties for flow rules. As shown in Fig. 6, includes:

1. Object properties: The relations between flow rules and components during the matching and execution process, including the ports that input or output on, and the next flow rule to be matched (e.g. property *ftMatch*) after the flow rules executing the *goto-table* action, and match relations or conflict types between flow rules.
2. Data properties: The data description required in the flow matching process, including the match fields and the actions.

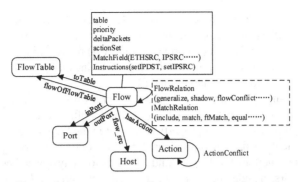

Fig. 6. Object properties and data properties of flow rules

Then define the constrain of properties, including ranges and types of values (See Table 2). For example, the domains of IP are host and device, because hosts and devices have IP addresses, and the range is string; there are also characteristics of properties, such as property *Match* is symmetric.

Table 2. Examples of the constrain of properties

Properties	Domains	Ranges	Characteristics
Ip	Device、host	String	
Match	Flow	Flow	Symmetric
ftMatch	Flow	Flow	Transitive

3.2 Definition of Production Rules

This paper uses production rules to define the path of reasoning. The form of a production rule is as follows (See Fig. 7). Conditions are the premises that return true or false and actions are the conclusions or actions to be performed [16]. Also, the SPARQL, which looks like SQL in form, is used to do the search or filter the result.

$$\textbf{IF } condition_1 \ \& \ condition_2 \ \& \ ...... condition_n$$
$$\textbf{THEN } actions$$

Fig. 7. The form of production rules

Production Rules of Conflicts Detection When Matching in One Table. Usually, to find out the matching relations should first analyze the relations of all the corresponding match fields between two flow rules and then do the classification. But with production rules which only do the binary decision, it should be separated into two parts. First, analyze whether the whole match fields of flow rules overlap. Each condition is replaced with the corresponding field. To analyze whether their intersection is an empty set, we define two builtin functions (supported by jena API) for two kinds of match fields. Specially, to reduce the match of production rules, we define the builtin function *strcmp()* to ensure that the flow-id of f1 is larger than f2.

Then analyze whether the action set of the overlapping flow rule pairs conflict. When matching in one table, if the actions are different, then conflict occurs. So, we only need to compare the set of actions (e.g. property *actionSet* in the knowledge graph).

Second, do the classification, only consider those conflict flow rule pairs. We also define two builtin functions for the two kinds of fields to analyze whether one flow rule of the conflict pairs includes the other, then add the property *include* between them. The production rule for checking the relation *include* refers to Fig. 8. Finally, run the SPARQL to get the result. For example, the relation *include* should be filtered to get the correlation conflict (See Fig. 9).

```
# production rule
For $F_i, F_j$
IF $m_1^i \cap m_1^j \neq \varnothing$ & $m_2^i \cap m_2^j \neq \varnothing$ & $\cdots$ & $m_k^i \cap m_k^j \neq \varnothing$
    THEN $F_i$ and $F_j$ overlap
```

```
# Jena Rule
# IPCross and FieldCross are user-defined builtin functions
[Rule_match_table: (?f1 sdn:flowOfFlowTable ?ft) (?f2 sdn:flowOfFlowTable ?ft) StrCmp(?f1,?f2)
(?f1 sdn:IPSRC ?ipS1) (?f2 sdn:IPSRC ?ipS2) IPCross(?ipS1,?ipS2)
(?f1 sdn:IPDST ?ipD1) (?f2 sdn:IPDST ?ipD2) IPCross(?ipD1,?ipD2)
(?f1 sdn:ETHSRC ?ethS1) (?f2 sdn:ETHSRC ?ethS2) FieldCross(?ethS1,?ethS2)
(?f1 sdn:ETHDST ?ethD1) (?f2 sdn:ETHDST ?ethD2) FieldCross(?ethD1,?ethD2)
-> (?f1 sdn:Match ?f2)]
```

Fig. 8. Example to find the matched flow rules

```
Query for correlation conflict:
SELECT ?f1 ?f2
WHERE{ ?f1 sdn:FlowConflict ?f2.
FILTER NOT EXISTS {?f1 sdn:include ?f2.}
FILTER NOT EXISTS {?f2 sdn:include ?f1.}}
```

Fig. 9. Example to check the correlation conflict

Production Rules of Conflicts Detection When Matching Against Multiple Tables. The *goto-table* action directs the flow rules to another flow table. If the modification actions are executed before, the match fields will change after the modification. The production rules are as follows (See Fig. 10). The flow rules have relation *ftmatch* with the flow rules directed to. Since property *ftmatch* is transitive, we only need to connect the flow rules with the next one, then all the flow rules of the direct path will be connected. The builtin functions constructed before can be reused to find the next flow rule. After that, the rule *action_ftconflict* finds out if the actions are conflict, and those with the same action should also be checked like rule *output_ftconflict* in Fig. 11.

```
# unchanged match fields
[Rule_nextFlow:(?f1 sdn:toTable ?ft) (?f2 sdn:flowOfFlowTable ?ft)
(?f1 sdn:hasAction sdn:unchangedField)
(?f1 sdn:IPSRC ?ipS1) (?f2 sdn:IPSRC ?ipS2) IPCross(?ipS1,?ipS2)
(?f1 sdn:IPDST ?ipD1) (?f2 sdn:IPDST ?ipD2) IPCross(?ipD1,?ipD2)
(?f1 sdn:ETHSRC ?ethS1) (?f2 sdn:ETHSRC ?ethS2) FieldCross(?ethS1,?ethS2)
(?f1 sdn:ETHDST ?ethD1) (?f2 sdn:ETHDST ?ethD2) FieldCross(?ethD1,?ethD2)
-> (?f1 sdn:ftMatch ?f2)]

# change source IP
[Rule_setSRC_nextFlow:(?f1 sdn:toTable ?ft) (?f2 sdn:flowOfFlowTable ?ft)
(?f1 sdn:hasAction sdn:MODIFICATION_ipSRC)
(?f1 sdn:setIPSRC ?ipS1) (?f2 sdn:IPSRC ?ipS2) IPCross(?ipS1,?ipS2)
(?f1 sdn:IPDST ?ipD1) (?f2 sdn:IPDST ?ipD2) IPCross(?ipD1,?ipD2)
(?f1 sdn:ETHSRC ?ethS1) (?f2 sdn:ETHSRC ?ethS2) FieldCross(?ethS1,?ethS2)
(?f1 sdn:ETHDST ?ethD1) (?f2 sdn:ETHDST ?ethD2) FieldCross(?ethD1,?ethD2)
-> (?f1 sdn:ftMatch ?f2)]
```

Fig. 10. Example to find next flow rules

```
[Rule_ftconflict:(?f1 sdn:ftMatch ?f2)
(?f1 sdn:hasAction ?a1) (?f2 sdn:hasAction ?a2) (?a1 sdn:ActionConflict ?a2)
-> (?f1 sdn:ftFlowConflict ?f2)]

[Rule_output_ftconflict:(?f1 sdn:ftMatch ?f2)
(?f1 sdn:outPort ?p1) (?f2 sdn:outPort ?p2) StrNotEqual(?p1,?p2)
-> (?f1 sdn:ftFlowConflict ?f2)]
```

Fig. 11. Example to check conflict

4 Experiment

To evaluate our proposal, we set up our experiment on the topology emulated by Mininet (See Fig. 12). The topology connects with the SDN controller called Open Network Operate System ONOS [17]. Mininet is a virtual network simulation tool that can create a virtual SDN network with switches, hosts, controllers, and links, and supports the OpenFlow protocol. It also provides a Python API to facilitate user-defined development.

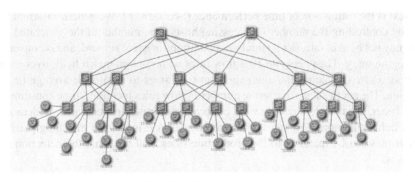

Fig. 12. The test topology

ONOS is an open-source project established by ONF. It adopts a distributed architecture, provides a global view, and supports expansion and fault tolerance.

We build a detection framework written in Java to update the knowledge graph and do the detection, then write a program with python to send the flow rules to the topology through ONOS API. The production rules are verified by constructing flow rules in one of the switches with two kinds of conflicts (See Table 3): 3960 and 8422 are correlation conflict. 8257 is directed to 3967, then directed to 1934, but only 8527 and 1934 conflict. The result in Table 4 shows that the production rules can make the correct detection.

Table 3. The test flow rules

Id(table)	Priority	Match fields	Actions
3960(0)	10	ipv4_dst:10.0.0.10/32	Output:2
8422(0)	10	ipv4_dst:10.0.0.8/29	Output:1
		ipv4_src:10.0.0.0/28	
8257(0)	10	ipv4_dst:10.0.0.27/32	Go to table:1
			output:4
3967(1)	10	ipv4_dst 10.0.0.27/32	Set dstIP:10.0.2.1
			go to table:2
1934(2)	10	ipv4_dst:10.0.2.1/32	Output:5

Table 4. Results of detection

Match	Flow-Conflict	Include	ftMatch	ftFlow-Conflict	Correlation conflict
(3960,8422)	(3960,8422)	-	(8257,3967) (3967,1934) (8257,1934)	(8257,1934)	(3960,8422)

Next is the estimation of time performance (See Table 5). We generate normal flow rules by controlling the number of accessing hosts. The number of the generated flow rules may not be accurate, but it simulates conditions in a real network and is convenient for programming. Then generate 10% flow rules with random match fields to construct conflicts. Each sample repeats the experiment 20 times to obtain the average time of detection. The result shows that as the number of flow rules increases, time consumption grows faster. It may be related to how the abnormal flow rules are generated. With random match fields, the more flow rules there are, the easier it is to form matching pairs, the more triples can be matched to the production rules, and the more the detection time increases.

Table 5. Average time of detection

Num of flow rules	200	400	600	1000	2000	3000
Avg.time(ms)	252	395	543	906	2271	4240

5 Conclusion

This paper presents a method of flow rule conflict detection by knowledge graph. We combine the centralized character of SDN with knowledge graph, which has the ability of knowledge representation and reasoning. The conflicts can be detected correctly by production rules, and administrators can easily modify the production rules or analyze the knowledge reasoning path. The results are certain according to the rules for reasoning, but it also brings a sacrifice on time performance. In the future, we hope to simplify the design of the knowledge graph and the production rules, which may reduce time consumption. Moreover, because of the shareability and reusability of knowledge graph, maybe it can be used for more detections such as loops.

Acknowledgments. This work has been supported by National Key Research and Development Program of China (2020YFB1807700).

References

1. Yu, Y., Li, X., Leng, X., et al.: Fault management in software-defined networking: a survey. IEEE Commun. Surv.Tutorials **21**(1), 349–392 (2019)
2. McKeown, N., Anderson, T., Balakrishnan, H., et al.: OpenFlow: enabling innovation in campus networks. ACM SIGCOMM Comput. Commun. Rev. **38**(2), 69–74 (2008)
3. Pisharody, S., Natarajan, J., Chowdhary, A., et al.: Brew: a security policy analysis framework for distributed SDN-based cloud environments. IEEE Trans. Depend. Secure Comput. **16**(6), 1011–1025 (2019)
4. Khurshid, A., Zhou, W., Caesar, M., et al.: Veriflow: verifying network-wide invariants in real time. ACM SIGCOMM Comput. Commun. Rev. **42**(4), 467–472 (2012)
5. Maldonado-Lopez, F.A., Calle, E., Donosom, Y.: Detection and prevention of firewall-rule conflicts on software-defined networking. In: 2015 7th International Workshop on Reliable Networks Design and Modeling (RNDM), pp. 259–265. IEEE (2015)
6. Khairi, M.H.H., Afiffin, S.H.S., Latiff, N.M.A., et al.: Detection and classification of conflict flows in SDN using machine learning algorithms. IEEE Access **9**, 76024–76037 (2021)
7. Amit, S.: Introducing the knowledge graph: things, not strings. America: official blog of google. http://googleblog.blogspot.com/2012/05/introducing-knowledge-graph-things-not.html 16 May 2012
8. Bodenreider, O.: The unified medical language system (UMLS): integrating biomedical terminology. Nucleic acids research 32(suppl_1), 267–270 (2004)
9. Zhang, W., Wong, C.M., Ye, G.: Billion-scale pre-trained e-commerce product knowledge graph model. In: 2021 IEEE 37th International Conference on Data Engineering (ICDE), pp. 2476–2487. IEEE (2021)
10. Shaoxiong, J., Shirui, P., Eric, C., et al.: A Survey on knowledge graphs: representation, acquisition, and applications. IEEETrans. Neural Netw. Learn. Syst. **33**(2), 494–514 (2022)

11. Xu, G., Cao, Y., Ren, Y., et al.: Network security situation awareness based on semantic ontology and user-defined rules for internet of things. IEEE Access **5**, 21046–21056 (2017)
12. Guang, C., Tonghai, J., Meng, W., et al.: Modeling and reasoning of IoT architecture in semantic ontology dimension. Comput. Commun. **153**, 580–594 (2020)
13. De Souza, T. D. P. C., Rothenberg, C. E., Santos, M. A. S., et al: Towards semantic network models via graph databases for sdn applications. In: Fourth European Workshop on Software Defined Networks, pp. 49–54. IEEE (2015)
14. Li, Z., Zhao, Y., Li, Y., et al: Demonstration of Alarm Knowledge Graph Construction for Fault Localization on ONOS-based SDON Platform. In: 2020 Optical Fiber Communications Conference and Exhibition (OFC), pp. 1–3. IEEE (2020)
15. SPARQL Query Language for RDF. https://www.w3.org/TR/rdf-sparql-query/. Document Status Update 2013/03/26
16. Apache Jena Homepage. https://jena.apache.org/
17. ONOS WiKi. https://wiki.onosproject.org/. Accessed 16 Nov 2020

Risk-Aware SFC Placement Method in Edge Cloud Environment

Ping Zou$^{(\boxtimes)}$ (ID), Shujie Yang (ID), Tao Zhang (ID), and Shitong Wei (ID)

Beijing University of Posts and Telecommunication, Beijing, China
{2021110917,sjyang,zhangtao17,stwei}@bupt.edu.cn

Abstract. Network Function Virtualization (NFV) is a technology that separates software from hardware, NFV increases the manageability, scalability, and flexibility of network function configuration. However, with these conveniences, it is the scheduling and management of complex virtual network resources created by NFV. The key to these problems is the deployment of the Service Function Chain (SFC). There are two major problems in SFC deployment: 1) Complexity of resource scheduling. 2) Vulnerability of SFC. To solve the above problems, we propose a risk-aware SFC deployment method. LSTM (Long Short-Term Memory) is used to predict possible attacks, and DQN (Deep Q Network) uses its results to complete SFC deployments. Our model is validated in a simulation network. The results show that proposed risk-aware SFC deployment is significantly better than traditional resource-oriented deployment in terms of network elasticity, and is not inferior to it in terms of latency.

Keywords: SFC · Attack prediction · Deep reinforcement learning

1 Introduction

Network Function Virtualization (NFV) realizes network functions through software virtualization technology and runs on commercial hardware (i.e. industry-standard servers, storage and switches) [16,17,19]. It can reduce capital investment and energy consumption by integrating network equipment,and quickly customized services according to customer needs. Service Function Chain (SFC) is an important part of NFV, it consists of a series of connected Virtual Network Functions (VNFs) [1,20] that complete a service, as shown in Fig. 1. This technology enables a network request to receive a series of network function services, increases the service customization ability of the network content provider, and provides a wide range of preprocessing, such as firewall, intrusion detection system (IDS), proxy, load balancer, etc.

However, it is a complex project to deploy a series of VNFs in the network [4]. The emergence of NFV has greatly increased resources that need to be planned and managed. In addition, business requirements are usually dynamic, which makes it even harder to deploy SFC. Previous studies have used use graphs and integer linear programming (ILP) [9] to reach the optimal deployment for SFC,

© The Author(s), under exclusive license to Springer Nature Singapore Pte Ltd. 2023
W. Quan (Ed.): ICENAT 2022, CCIS 1696, pp. 105–116, 2023.
https://doi.org/10.1007/978-981-19-9697-9_9

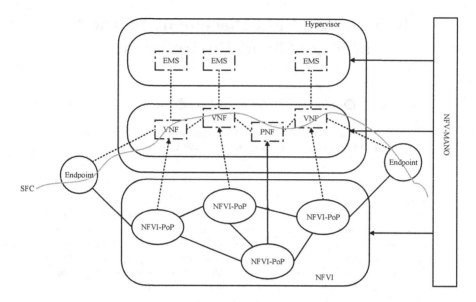

Fig. 1. The model of SFC

one of the methods is to embed SFC into the substrate network according to the resources required by SFC, such as computing power, storage requirements, and network bandwidth. Other solutions using reinforcement learning for solving deployments are also available, such as [8,11].

Above method seems to work well for the problem, but these works have one thing in common: they all solve the optimal placement scheme for SFC by considering relevant resource constraints in the normal network. However,the network may suffer from various attacks during operation, and SFC is in particularly sensitive to attacks [3,18]: Once a node with VNF deployed is attacked, all SFC chains on which VNF is located will fail because they cannot complete their functions. To this end, we propose a risk-aware VNF deployment method. This method first uses the LSTM network to predict the network nodes that may be attacked according to the current network status before deploying the SFC. Then, whole prediction results, together with resources and requests, are sent to the DQN network as a part of the reward. Finally, fetch actions from DQN to update the environment state.

The main contributions of this paper are as follows: (1) Based on the edge cloud scenario and the resource-oriented SFC deployment model, a risk-aware SFC deployment method is proposed. (2) The proposed model is simulated in mininet, and the results show that the proposed method is superior to resource-oriented deployment in network elasticity, and will not bring additional latency.

2   Related Work

In this part, we list the main work in the field of SFC deployment and network attack prediction, focus on the role of reinforcement learning in these fields.

2.1   SFC

Lots of research has been done on how to optimize the deployment of SFC. These studies are mainly divided into two categories. One is to divide the deployment problem into two steps: 1) placement of VNFs. 2) Link to VNFs. This kind of method turns the deployment of SFC into a routing and scheduling problem. When placing VNFs, it is necessary to deal with the resource requirements of possible SFC in the network. Main work in this area includes: Lee et al. [8] uses Q-learning algorithm and pre-deployed VNF resource table to know the connection of SFC. Luizelli [9] uses Dijkstra algorithm to plan SFC routes that meet needs and can dynamically create and destroy VNFs to adapt to different network loads.

Recently, some researchers have applied RL algorithm to guide VNF placement [6]. Pandey et al. [8,11] are committed to using Q-learning algorithm to solve the problem of deploying a single SFC in the edge cloud environment. [12] use DQN to find the optimal deployment scheme for multiple SFCs by minimizing the underlying resource utilization and end-to-end latency. By considering the consumption of cpu, memory, and other resources, as well as the network usage of service functions, Kim et al. used q-learning to dynamically create service chains to achieve load balancing deployment. [7] is a throughput prediction method using random forest regression (RFR) and feedforward neural network (FNN) is proposed. Use the predicted throughput to find a valid SFC path.

2.2   Prediction

Network attack prediction [5] is to use a large amount of network security data to find the behavior and law of hacker intrusion, predict attack behavior that the network system may suffer in the future, then take effective targeted measures to prevent.

At present, the main network attack prediction methods use Markov model, Bayesian network, deep learning model, and so on. Tiresias [13] uses a recurrent neural network (RNN) to predict future events on the machine based on previous observations and provides a mechanism that can identify sudden decline in accuracy and trigger system retraining to ensure system stability. Wang [15] Combine context prediction and mixed strategy Nash equilibrium to predict advanced persistent threat (APT). Fang [2] et al. Proposed a bidirectional recurrent neural network deep learning framework with long-term and short-term memory, which has higher accuracy than statistical methods. Ourstonde [10] and others use the hidden Markov model (HMM) to detect complex Internet attacks, that is, attacks consisting of several steps that may occur over a long period. Sun [14] et al. Analyzed the system call, constructed the dependency graph as a hypergraph, and revealed the attacker's attack path based on Bayesian network and intrusion evidence.

3   Method

3.1   System Overview

This paper will describe its methods based on simplified AT&T CORD (central office re-architected as a data center) architecture. The core technologies of AT&T CORD include disaggregation, software-defined network (SDN), and NFV. AT&T CORD hopes to avoid vendor lock-in.

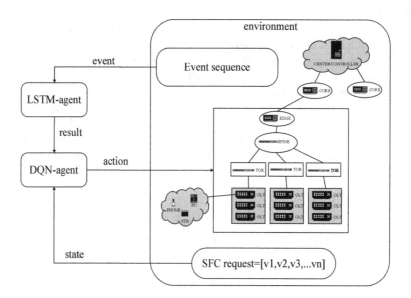

Fig. 2. Simplified model

Based on AT&T CORD, we build model as shown in Fig. 2. The model mainly includes three parts: environment, DQN agent, and LSTM agent. The environment is a simplified version of the AT&T CORD architecture, it completes the simulation of network status and provides the required data and parameters to other two parts. The nodes of environment are divided into five categories:

Data Center (DC), Core Router (CR), Edge Router (ER), and Top of Rank Switch (TOR), Server. LSTM agent completes the prediction of network attack for next time slot and returns its result to DQN agent. Our model defines newly arrived SFC requests as vectors $[v_1, v_2, v_3 ... v_n]$, where v_1 denotes the i-th VNF in the SFC. DQN agent combines current incoming SFC requests and prediction results returned by LSTM agrnt to find an appropriate deployment method for each VNF. Next, the functions and relevant details of each part will be introduced in detail.

3.2   Edge Cloud Attack Prediction

The overview of attack prediction is shown in Fig. 3. LSTM is a neural network with the ability to memorize long-term and short-term information, since it introduced input gate, output gate, and forget gate to avoid the shortcomings of RNN.

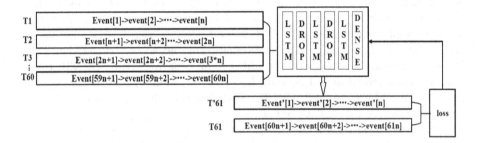

Fig. 3. LSTM architecture

Process of LSTM agent is shown in Algorithm 1. The dataset is some log information collected on several windows hosts. To convert data into sequence event information, LSTM agent sort data in a dataset by time, and extract events that occur on all hosts in the same time interval. Two issues need to be addressed: 1) At one certain time, some hosts may not log events. 2) What is extracted from the database is a time series that must be transformed into attack information before it can be used. For 1), Agent treats no event as a new event. For 2), agent extract all possible event types, analyze the impact of each event on network security, and finally convert the event information into security information.

Algorithm 1. attack_prediction

Input: dataset
Output: $event_t[svr]$, Attack_condition[svr][1]
1: event_seq ← null
2: **for** each event in dataset **do** Pretreatment(event)
3:      $event\_seq$.append()
4: model.add(lstm_cell)

5: model.add(dropout_cell)
6: model.add(dense_layer) model.compile()
7: **for** t in event_seq_size **do**
8:     X.append($event_{t-60}$[svr],$event_{t-59}$[svr]...$event_t - 1$[svr])
9:     Y.append($event_t$[svr])
10: **for** each Xbatch,Ybatch in X,Y **do**
11:     $event_t$[svr],state = model.fit(Xbatch,Ybatch)
12:     $event_t$[svr]=model.predict()
13:     cross_entropy=tf.reduce_mean(tf.nn.softmax_cross_entropy_with_logits(
14: logits=$event_t$[svr], labels=Y))
15:     trian_step=tf.train.AdamOptimizer(1e-4).minimize(cross_entropy)
16: Attack_condition = identify($event_t$[svr])
17: **return** $event_t$[svr], Attack_condition

The constructed LSTM uses a set of events sequences [event[1], event[2], event[3]... Event[n]] as input, where event[i] indicates that event labeled event[i] occurred on node i. To ensure accuracy of prediction, agent combines 60 consecutive events as the input of LSTM. Neural network used for training has six layers, among which LSTM represents long-term and short-term hidden layer, DROP represents the dropout layer added to prevent overfitting, DENSE represents fully connected neural network layer. During training, the results of each prediction will be compared with the real situation to calculate the loss and guide the training process of the network.

After prediction results are obtained, the event vector needs to be identified according to predefined rules. The rules for identification are: events that may cause network failure are marked as attacks.

3.3   Risk-Aware Deployment

DQN combines a neural network with Q-learning algorithm. By the strong representation ability of the neural network, high-dimensional input data is used as state in DQN and input of neural network model. Then neural network model outputs corresponding value (Q value) of each action and select the maximum one to get the most out of it. The key to DQN is the modeling of states, rewards and actions. Next, we will be more specific about these aspects.

Environment. We represent resources of network nodes as a two-dimensional array of sources shaped as [total_server_number, 2], with total_server_number representing number of servers of the entire network architecture. Each row indicates the remaining cpu and memory resources of a node respectively, i.e., source [i] = [n, m], meaning that the server numbered i has n number of CPU resources and m number of memory resources available for use.

The resource quantity level is: DC > CR > ER > TOR > server, in order to fully utilize the resources at each level, the principle of tiered allocation is satisfied in the actual allocation of resources, i.e., the resources at the lower layer are used first, and when the resources of this network are not enough, the network nodes at the upper layer are requested.

Action. After each dqn operation, the model will select an action with greatest benefit. In our model. Action is defined as selecting the next VNF server to deploy. The selected server can be a central data server or an edge server.

State. We define the state of the DQN as the current resource situation occupied by the VNF. For example, for an SFC request $[v_1, v_2, v_3...v_n]$, the state s is defined as the resource requirement of the current vnf. That is, assuming that the currently processed deployment request is v_1, then the current state will be represented using the resource demand vector [CPU1, MEM1] of v_1.

Reward. The definition of reward is key to whether DQN can converge and how well it can be trained. In our model, the reward value is calculated after each VNF is placed, and it is used to minimize the overall latency and increase the resource usage. In addition, the predictions given by the LSTM are combined in order to make the VNF placement avoid the nodes that will be attacked. Thus, our final reward is.

$$
\begin{cases}
reward = (\alpha \times CPU + \beta \times MEM + \delta \times LANT) \times \gamma \\
\gamma = \begin{cases} -1 & if\ node\ is\ attacked\ and\ random\ i\ less\ than\ p \\ 1 & otherwise \end{cases}
\end{cases}
$$

The MEM and CPU parameters in above equation are shown below respectively:

$$CPU = \frac{vnf\_cpu\_require}{total\_cpu}$$
$$MEM = \frac{vnf\_mem\_require}{total\_mem}$$

vnf_cpu_require and vnf_mem_require is the number of cpu/memory resources occupied by currently deployed VNF, total_cpu and total_mem is the total number of cpu/memory resources of the deployed nodes.

In addition to minimizing resource occupancy, another goal of SFC deployment is low latency. We introduce LANT parameter, which is defined as average latency of the SFCs deployed in the whole network. To simplify operation, End-to-End (E2E) network latency is mainly classified into the following categories according to the topological relationship between the source and destination nodes.

– Both VNFs are deployed on the same node. In this case, E2E latency is 1;
– VNFs are deployed on different nodes,the latency is determined according to
  their minimum common ancestor type.

Table 1. Node latency

Ancestor type	Latency
DC	10
CR	8
ER	4
TOR	2

Finally, reward shall be multiplied by attack coefficient. If attacked, the punishment shall be given with a certain probability p.

3.4   Overall-Algorithm

The overall algorithm is as follows:

Algorithm 2. sfc_deploy_lstm_DQN

Input: Q , SFC request$[v_1, v_2, v_3, v_4...v_n]$, $N_s, N_t, N_e, N_d, epsilon$
Output: action,history[VNF,action]
1: env.init()
2: **for** all episodes **do**
3:      **for** all states v_n **do**
4:          **if** $env.N_s \neq \emptyset$ **then**
5:              **if** np.random.rand()<epsilon **then**
6:                  action = random.choice($env.S_s$,env.P_i)
7:              **else**
8:                  action = model.predict(v_n).argmax(Q)
9:          **else if** $env.N_t \neq \emptyset$ **then**
10:             **if** np.random.rand()<epsilon **then**
11:                 action = random.choice(env.S_t,env.P_i)
12:             **else**
13:                 action = model.predict(v_n).argmax(Q)
14:         **else if** $env.N_e \neq \emptyset$ **then**
15:             **if** np.random.rand()<epsilon **then**
16:                 action = random.choice(env.S_e,env.P_i)
17:             **else**
18:                 action = model.predict(v_n).argmax(Q)
19:         **else if** $env.N_d \neq \emptyset$ **then**
20:             **if** np.random.rand()<epsilon **then**

```
21:              action = random.choice(env.Sd,env.P_i)
22:          else
23:              action = model.predict(v_n).argmax(Q)
24:          history.append(v_n,action,v_{n+1})
25:          Attack_condition = attack_prediction(dataset , event_{t-1}[svr])
26:          reward = caculate_reward (history,Attack_condition)
27:          env.update(v_n, a_n,reward)
28:      for all state v_n do
29:          remember(Transition(v_n,action,r,v_{n+1}))
             replay(batch_size)
30: return action,history
```

The algorithm first initializes environment, such as number of network nodes at all levels, capacity information of each node and network topology. For each episode, VNFs of incoming SFC request is traversed. Each VNF will be deployed to substrate network in a hierarchical manner. Only when server does not have a node that can meet the requirements, will considering deploying VNF on TOR, and so on.

For each level, a deployment scheme is chosen randomly with probability epsilon, while optimal action is selected by DQN neural network with probability 1- epsilon. After action is selected, state, action, next_state and reward are stored in history. Based on history, the scoring function will give a stage score, and its result will be used to update the neural network. After each epoch, a part of the history will be randomly selected to update neural network.

4   Evaluation

We have simulated the proposed model and compared it with some similar work, such as [11], and use randomly selection of VNF deployments as a baseline approach. In our experiments, the number of network nodes are shown in Table 1 (Table 2):

Table 2. Node number

Type	Number
DC	1
CR	2
ER	4
TOR	8
server	16

Figure 4 shows the average latency of SFCs with different lengths using different models. For each length, we test 100 testcases and take the average number of hops. As shown in the figure, SFC deployed by random method has the highest average latency among three methods (since it does not take any measures to reduce the latency). Given that similar latency reduction measures, there is no significant difference between the latency of DQN and our approach.

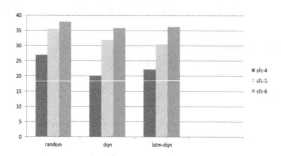

Fig. 4. Latency-model result

Figure 5 shows the failure rate measured for four different SFC lengths. As can be seen in the figure, the probability of deploying the VNF on an attacked node can be significantly reduced due to the prediction of the next moment of each node before each deployment and applying the prediction results to the deployment of the SFCs.

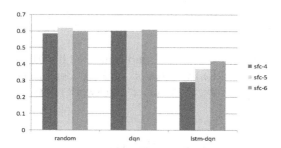

Fig. 5. Failure-model result

Figure 6 shows the reward diagram of DQN when SFC has different lengths. The number of epoches required for DQN from learning to convergence becomes longer as the length grows. That is because longer the SFC is, the harder to learn and find optimal deployment Solutions.

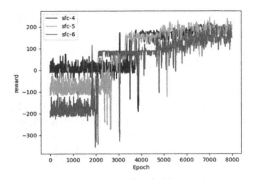

Fig. 6. Reward-length result

5   Conclusion

How to deploy SFC is a critical issue. In this paper, we propose a risk-aware SFC deployment solution to avoid deploying the VNF deployed on network nodes that may be attacked in the near future.

It is worth noting that our approach is not simply to disable a node that may be attacked, but only to reduce its reward with some probability. Such an approach improves the misclassification of nodes while alleviating load imbalance to some extent. The evaluation results show that our approach is more resilient compared to other methods that only target resource constraints and is not inferior to those methods in terms of latency and resource utilization. In the future, we will experiment with different prediction and scheduling methods and analyze what models to use for different network sizes and network characteristics.

References

1. Bari, M.F., Chowdhury, S.R., Ahmed, R., Boutaba, R.: On orchestrating virtual network functions. In: 2015 11th International Conference on Network and Service Management (CNSM), pp. 50–56. IEEE (2015)
2. Fang, X., Xu, M., Xu, S., Zhao, P.: A deep learning framework for predicting cyber attacks rates. EURASIP J. Inf. Secur. **2019**(1), 1–11 (2019)
3. Farris, I., Taleb, T., Khettab, Y., Song, J.: A survey on emerging SDN and NFV security mechanisms for IoT systems. IEEE Commun. Surv. Tutor. **21**(1), 812–837 (2018)
4. Fischer, A., Botero, J.F., Beck, M.T., De Meer, H., Hesselbach, X.: Virtual network embedding: a survey. IEEE Commun. Surv. Tutor. **15**(4), 1888–1906 (2013)
5. Husák, M., Komárková, J., Bou-Harb, E., Čeleda, P.: Survey of attack projection, prediction, and forecasting in cyber security. IEEE Commun. Surv. Tutor. **21**(1), 640–660 (2018)
6. Jeong, S., Kim, H., Yoo, J.H., Hong, J.W.K.: Machine learning based link state aware service function chaining. In: 2019 20th Asia-Pacific Network Operations and Management Symposium (APNOMS), pp. 1–4. IEEE (2019)

7. Kim, S.I., Kim, H.S.: A research on dynamic service function chaining based on reinforcement learning using resource usage. In: 2017 Ninth International Conference on Ubiquitous and Future Networks (ICUFN), pp. 582–586. IEEE (2017)

8. Lee, D., Yoo, J.H., Hong, J.W.K.: Q-learning based service function chaining using VNF resource-aware reward model. In: 2020 21st Asia-Pacific Network Operations and Management Symposium (APNOMS), pp. 279–282. IEEE (2020)

9. Luizelli, M.C., Bays, L.R., Buriol, L.S., Barcellos, M.P., Gaspary, L.P.: Piecing together the NFV provisioning puzzle: efficient placement and chaining of virtual network functions. In: 2015 IFIP/IEEE International Symposium on Integrated Network Management (IM), pp. 98–106. IEEE (2015)

10. Ourston, D., Matzner, S., Stump, W., Hopkins, B.: Applications of hidden Markov models to detecting multi-stage network attacks. In: Proceedings of the 36th Annual Hawaii International Conference on System Sciences, pp. 10–pp. IEEE (2003)

11. Pandey, S., Hong, J.W.K., Yoo, J.H.: Q-learning based SFC deployment on edge computing environment. In: 2020 21st Asia-Pacific Network Operations and Management Symposium (APNOMS), pp. 220–226. IEEE (2020)

12. Pandey, S., Van Nguyen, T., Yoo, J.H., Hong, J.W.K.: EdgeDQN: multiple SFC placement in edge computing environment. In: 2021 17th International Conference on Network and Service Management (CNSM), pp. 301–309. IEEE (2021)

13. Shen, Y., Mariconti, E., Vervier, P.A., Stringhini, G.: Tiresias: predicting security events through deep learning. In: Proceedings of the 2018 ACM SIGSAC Conference on Computer and Communications Security, pp. 592–605 (2018)

14. Sun, X., Dai, J., Liu, P., Singhal, A., Yen, J.: Using Bayesian networks for probabilistic identification of zero-day attack paths. IEEE Trans. Inf. Forensics Secur. 13(10), 2506–2521 (2018)

15. Wang, J., Yi, Y., Zhang, H., Cao, N.: Network attack prediction method based on threat intelligence. In: Sun, X., Pan, Z., Bertino, E. (eds.) ICCCS 2018. LNCS, vol. 11065, pp. 151–160. Springer, Cham (2018). https://doi.org/10.1007/978-3-030-00012-7_14

16. Xu, C., Zhang, T., Kuang, X., Zhou, Z., Yu, S.: Context-aware adaptive route mutation scheme: a reinforcement learning approach. IEEE Internet Things J. 8(17), 13528–13541 (2021)

17. Yue, Y., Cheng, B., Li, B., Wang, M., Liu, X.: Throughput optimization VNF placement for mapping SFC requests in MEC-NFV enabled networks. In: Proceedings of the 26th Annual International Conference on Mobile Computing and Networking, pp. 1–3 (2020)

18. Zhang, T., Kuang, X., Zhou, Z., Gao, H., Xu, C.: An intelligent route mutation mechanism against mixed attack based on security awareness. In: 2019 IEEE Global Communications Conference (GLOBECOM), pp. 1–6. IEEE (2019)

19. Zhang, T., Xu, C., Zhang, B., Shen, J., Kuang, X., Grieco, L.A.: Toward attack-resistant route mutation for VANETs: an online and adaptive multiagent reinforcement learning approach. IEEE Trans. Intell. Transp. Syst. 23, 23254–23267 (2022)

20. Zhang, T., et al.: How to mitigate DDOS intelligently in SD-IOV: a moving target defense approach. IEEE Trans. Ind. Inform. 19, 1097–1106 (2022)

Network Traffic Identification Method Based on Temporal and Multi-scale Spatial Fusion

Mingshi Wen[1], Jiakai Hao[1], Wuwei Zhang[1], Yuting Li[1], Yang Yang[2(✉)], and Shaoyin Chen[2]

[1] State Grid Beijing Power Company, Beijing, People's Republic of China
[2] State Key Laboratory of Networking and Switching Technology, Beijing University of Posts and Telecommunications, Beijing, People's Republic of China
yyang@bupt.edu.cn

Abstract. Network traffic identification is the basic module required to realize any traffic management operation. From network traffic partition and traffic processing (such as alarm, traffic shaping, etc.) to general security operations (such as firewall, traffic filtering, anomaly detection, etc.), network traffic identification is an indispensable part. Traditional port-based and payload-based network traffic identification approaches become less accurate as network traffic encryption technology advances and user privacy concerns are raised. However, the method based on flow statistical features requires a lot of additional calculation in feature extraction, and also requires domain experts to carry out feature engineering, which results in large algorithm cost and poor generalization. Recent studies have introduced DL-based methods, but most current DL-based methods use neural network models to extract network traffic features with problems such as a single feature scale and insufficient information extraction. This paper presents a method based on spatiotemporal fusion about network traffic identification. The model uses ResNet to obtain the spatial features of original traffic at first, then a module for multi-scale feature extraction is added to allow for the multi-scale pooling operation to obtain spatial feature information at various scales, overcoming the single performance limitation of existing DL-based network traffic identification methods. Then, the LSTM is used to further learn network traffic's temporal features, and finally the identification results of the network traffic are obtained based on the extracted spatiotemporal features. Public datasets used in the experiments demonstrate the proposed method's good performance and certain degree of effectiveness.

Keywords: Spatial-temporal fusion · Multi-scale spatial feature extraction · Network traffic identification

1 Introduction

The process of automatically identifying the application or category to which a single data packet or data packet flow carried over a network belongs is referred to as "network traffic identification", and mapping network traffic data to different network applications

© The Author(s), under exclusive license to Springer Nature Singapore Pte Ltd. 2023
W. Quan (Ed.): ICENAT 2022, CCIS 1696, pp. 117–130, 2023.
https://doi.org/10.1007/978-981-19-9697-9_10

or network protocols. As an important research content, network traffic identification is the basic module required to realize any traffic management operation. As a key link in network management, network traffic identification technology provides operators, Internet service providers and network administrators with the ability to automatically identify applications and traffic categories, and plays a key role in understanding network operation status, providing reference basis for network management and control, improving user experience and ensuring the network's steady operation. The accuracy and performance of network traffic identification technology greatly affect the quality of network resource management. Therefore, In order to optimise network management and ensure the long-term development of the Internet, network traffic identification technology's research and development are of utmost importance.

There are numerous ways to identify network traffic, which are categorised as traffic identification methods based on port, payload, flow statistical feature and deep learning. Owing to the continuing expansion of network scale, the network application's types and data volume are proliferating, and the emergence and wide application of technologies such as dynamic ports and traffic encryption, the reliability of conventional payload- and port-based network traffic identification techniques has decreased, and it is no longer applicable to the current network environment. The flow statistical features-based approach of network traffic identification requires a lot of extra computation in feature extraction, and mostly relies on features designed by experts, which is time-consuming and difficult to operate. It has certain limitations in the face of the rapid increase of network traffic types and the rapidly changing network environment. Meanwhile, due to the statistical features can be simulated or tampered with, the identification method using flow statistical features has certain security risks.

Different from the above methods, DL can automatically find and extract the original data's features without feature engineering or relying on expert experience, which has a good application prospect. The techniques DL-based have been successfully applied to the identification of traffic and are extensively employed. However, most methods DL-based have problems such as single feature scale and insufficient information extraction when extracting traffic features using neural network model.

This paper suggests a spatiotemporal fusion-based network traffic identification algorithm, and builds an improved network model MRN-LSTM (Multi-scale ResNet-LSTM) based on the neural network structures of ResNet [1] and LSTM [2]. The model first uses ResNet to preliminarily learn the original traffic's spatial features, and then adds a module for multiscale feature extraction to acquire the spatial features' information of different scales through multi-scale pooling operation. Then, the network traffic's temporal features are further extracted through LSTM. Finally, the network traffic's identification results are obtained using the extracted temporal and spatial features. Compared with RNN model, in the course of long sequence training, LSTM model resolves the issues of gradient disappearance and gradient explosion, and performs better than ordinary RNN in longer sequences; The multi-scale feature extraction module can make relatively good use of the method of global information, extract the spatial feature information of different scales through multi-scale pooling, overcome the performance limitation of the single feature scale of the existing network traffic identification method DL-based, and efficiently address the issue of inadequate information extraction. The model put forward in this paper is adequately capable of extracting information from multi-scale spatial and temporal features, and effectively enhance the ability of network traffic identification.

2 Related Work

Identification of network traffic has gradually grown in importance as a study area in recent years. Many researchers have worked hard to further this field of study, so the network traffic identification technology has developed rapidly. we will introduce three approaches in this part, namely the methods payload- and flow statistical features-based and DL-based.

2.1 Payload Based Network Traffic Identification Method

Payload-based network traffic identification method, which also is known as deep packet detection (DPI), refers to analyzing the data content of the application layer, finding out the matching feature identification rules according to the established network traffic identification rule base, for purpose of identifying the type of network traffic's application(e.g., '\GET' signatures in HTTP traffic). To realize this method, we need to establish a feature identification rule base in advance. When the traffic data is obtained, we first carry out deep packet detection on the data packets to extract the load characteristics, and then use the pattern matching algorithm to determine network traffic's category by analyzing whether the information of payload species matches the feature recognition library. Common DPI rule libraries include libprotected, opendpi, and NDPI, where NDPI contains dedicated protocol decoders for many common protocols (such as HTTP and FTP) [3].

DPI is a computationally intensive traffic identification technique, which involves string matching between payload and application protocol features. When the number of features in the feature rule base reaches a certain scale, the resource overhead is huge, and the network traffic identification's real-time performance is reduced. To solve this problem, a DPI-based mechanism for classifying network traffic was put forth by Khandait et al. [4] and can employ heuristic techniques to classify network flows by scanning network data flows'payload in a single time.

Although DPI is significantly better than port-based network traffic identification method, there are still some problems that cannot be solved: 1) unable to effectively identify encrypted traffic. 2) Unknown traffic cannot be effectively identified. 3) May cause privacy and security problems.

2.2 Flow Statistical Features Based Network Traffic Identification Method

The method for network traffic identification based on flow statistical features is also called the ML-based method for network traffic identification. This method extracts a series of statistical features such as the size, number, average arrival time interval and network flow duration of data packets, and constructs a classification model combined with the method for machine learning (hereinafter referred to as ML) such as SVM, decision tree, KNN[5] and so on, such that network traffic's classification can be achieved. This method can avoid the problem of violating personal privacy.

Although this method can achieve good results in general, it also has some disadvantages, such as requiring domain experts to complete feature engineering and large additional computational overhead.

2.3 Deep Learning Based Network Traffic Identification Method

Driven by the great performance in computer vision and natural language processing, many academics began to apply deep learning to network traffic identification. DL-based methods differ from flow statistical features-based methods or DPI because they extract features without the dependence of professionals. In addition, in comparison to flow statistical features methods, DL-based methods have a greater learning capacity and can therefore achieve a superior performance.

Numerous classic research outcomes based on deep learning's traffic identification techniques have recently been published. A framework called "DeepPacket" was proposed by Lotfolashi et al. [6], which fills the TCP/UDP layer of traffic data in the data preprocessing stage, and produced excellent results by using the pre-sampling technique to address the issue of data sample imbalance. Wei Wang et al. [7] applied one-dimensional and two-dimensional convolutional neural networks (CNNs) respectively so as to extract features from the preprocessed raw traffic data. They then confirmed the superiority of these two methods by looking at the experimental evaluation index results, which led to a significant advancement over the previous network traffic classification technology. Wang et al. [8] also connected the RNN to the CNN model to further extract network traffic's temporal features, realize the detection of network intrusion traffic, and further improved the model's performance. Aceto G et al. [9] presented a fresh DL-based technique called Distiller classifier for classifying network traffic from the perspective of multimodal and multimask, and produced effective results. Shapira T et al. [10] presented a DL-based model called Flowpic for identifying application and classifying encrypted traffic, and the outcomes demonstrate that this technique can produce excellent outcomes.

In summary, we adopted the method DL-based for network traffic identification after analysing the classification's method of various forms of network traffic.

3   Proposed Method

3.1   Overall Architecture

On the basis of CNN and RNN, we develop a network traffic feature identification model, called MRN-LSTM, whose overall architecture is depicted in Fig. 1. The network structure respectively uses ResNet to learn the network traffic's spatial features, and uses LSTM to further learn the network traffic's temporal features. Adding a multi-scale feature extraction module between the ResNet and LSTM network structures can refine the feature granularity and extract multi-granularity spatial features.

In the inference phase, after preprocessing the input original network traffic, ResNet uses a block (including two basicblocks) to learn the network traffic's local spatial

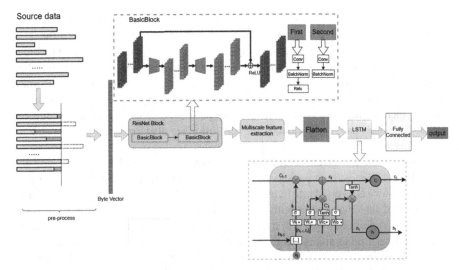

Fig.1. Overall architecture of MRN-LSTM.

features. And then extracts the network traffic's spatial features of multi-scale through the pooling operation of different sizes through the module of extracting features of multi-scale. Then we flatten the tensor obtained from above structure. After that, to further obtain the network traffic's temporal features, an network named LSTM is utilised. Finally, the full connection layer and output layer are applied to complete the operation of classification.

In the proposed model of traffic identification based on integration of time and space, the original traffic data's features are extracted by two aspects of time and space from the original network traffic as input of classifier, and the spatial feature information of different scales is obtained by adding the module of extracting multi-scale features, which overcomes the deep learning traffic classifier existing performance restriction with a single feature scale, and enhances the ability to identify different network traffic.

3.2 Data Preprocessing

As the basic unit of network traffic identification, the hierarchical relationship of network data flow is as follows: data packets consist of multiple traffic bytes, and a series of data packets transmitted during information exchange on the network constitute a network flow. From this, it can be seen that there are obvious temporal features between the data packets of network traffic, while there are spatial fetaures of bytes within the data packets.

Generally speaking, the original network traffic data cannot be utilised directly as the neural network's input, therefore, the dataset must first undergo preprocessing in order to make the traffic data compatible with the neural network's input specifications.

Because the physical link's information is contained in the datalink layer header that is unfavorable of network traffic identification, it is first necessary to remove the Ethernet header. Then Padding the UDP header to 20 bytes with zeros, and masking the

IP in the IP header. At the transport layer, TCP typically has a 20-bytes header, while UDP has only 8 bytes. Zeros need be used to pad the UDP header to match the TCP header's length for the sake of homogenising the data. The original traffic dataset includes some pointless packets because it was obtained from a real network. For example, when establishing a connection, the communication parties need to shake hands three times. During this period, the data packets transmitted do not carry any useful informations for traffic identification, so such irrelevant data packets should be deleted. In addition, some DNS packets used for domain name resolution are also irrelevant packets and are removed from the dataset.

On account of the given neural network's input must be a fixed length, and the payload length of most data packets in the dataset is less than 1480 bytes, the original packet needs to be converted into byte vector, the vector with size over 1500 is truncated, zeros are filled into byte vector with size less than 1500, and finally the byte vector is normalized. In addition, to prevent overfitting caused by the neural network learning to use IP addresses for classification, the IP addresses in the IP header are masked.

After analyzing the composition of the original traffic data, it is found that the data samples are unbalanced, and the number of samples of different categories varies greatly. If such data is used for training, the model's performance will be drastically decreased. To resolve this issue, an undersampling method is used, which, there until classes are roughly balanced, removes the majority of the samples at random.

3.3 Spatial Feature Extraction of Network Traffic

As can be seen from the description in Sect. 3.2, there are spatial features between bytes in the packet. The residual network (ResNet) is applied for extracting the preprocessed network traffic data's spatial features in paper. In order to improve network convergence, ResNet proposes the idea of fitting the residual mappings rather than fitting the expected underlying mappings directly.

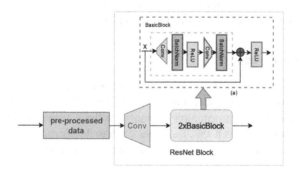

Fig.2. Spatial feature extraction of network traffic based on ResNet

In this paper, the CNN structure (ResNet) is applied for extracting the network traffic's spatial features. Figure 2 depicts the structure of ResNet-based network traffic spatial features extraction. After the preprocessed traffic data is received by the network, the initial convolution operation only increases the number of channels, then through the BasicBlock, which can be connected in series to deepen the network, there is only convolution operation, and no sampling and pooling operation is carried out. The dimensions of input and output are the same without changing the number of channels. The structure diagram of BasicBlock is shown in Fig. 2.(a), which has two layers, each of which contains convolution layer (Conv), batch normalization layer (BatchNorm) and activation function (Relu). The batch normalization layer has an great strength on quickening the pace of the training of the model, improving the model's generalization capability and alleviating the vanishing gradient problem, and in the meantime, it can effectively restrain the issue of model overfitting. The following is the BatchNorm calculating formula:

$$y_i = \gamma \frac{x_i - \mu}{\sqrt{\sigma^2 + \epsilon}} + \beta \tag{1}$$

where γ and β represent the parameters learned by the model, x_i represents a data in the training batch, μ and σ^2 represent the mean and variance of the training data in a training batch, and the denominator is kept from falling to zero by the factor ϵ.

The traditional convolution layer has the problems of information loss and so on when transmitting information. This issue is somewhat resolved by ResNet. The information's integrity is safeguarded by going straight from the input to the output. The learning objective and difficulty are made simpler because the entire network just needs to learn the portion where input and output differ.

Single feature scale and insufficient information extraction are issues with the majority of DL-based traffic identification methods now in use. To address the issue that the conventional convolutional neural network is unable to extract large-scale features, convolutional neural network has insufficient ability to extract global features, Zhao H et al. [11] proposed a pyramid pooling module to obtain different receptive fields' global information and enhance neural networks' ability on obtaining global feature information. In this article, a pyramid pooling-based module for multi-scale feature extraction is presented, after extracting network traffic's coarse-grained spatial features from the previous backbone network, it further obtains spatial feature information of different scales.

Figure 3 depicts the multi-scale feature extraction module. In the multi-scale feature extraction module, "feature pyramid" is obtained by global average pooling operation of different scales for feature maps extracted from backbone network ResNet, and feature maps with sizes of $1 \times 1, 2 \times 2, 3 \times 3$ and 6×6 are generated. Then, the convolution kernel of size 1*1 is used to change the number of channels in feature maps of different sizes to 1/4 of the original. Then, perform bilinear interpolation and upsampling on all feature maps to restore them to the size of the original feature maps, and then use CONCAT to fuse them and connect them with the original features. Finally, the above feature map is subjected to depthwise convolution so that the final feature map has the same quantity of channels as the original feature map of input. The module obtains richer global information by extracting traffic features of different receptive fields, enhances the ability of the model to obtain global information of original traffic, meanwhile, improves the effect about network traffic identification.

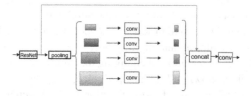

Fig. 3. Multi-scale spatial feature extraction module.

3.4 Temporal Feature Extraction of Network Traffic

The network structure called LSTM is applied for extracting the network traffic data's temporal features in paper.

The LSTM network structure diagram for a single time step is shown in Fig. 4. The input gate decides how much the current network status's information should be preserved into network's internal status, whereas the forget gate specifies how much information about the network's previous state should be erased. At last, the output gate decides how much information ought to be exported from the internal state to the external status at the present moment.

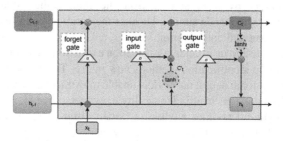

Fig. 4. The LSTM network structure of a single time step.

The input at the present moment, the internal state c_{t-1} from the previous moment, and the external state h_{t-1} from the previous moment are the three inputs that an LSTM unit gets at each time step, as shown in Fig. 4. Wherein three "gates" simultaneously use x_t and h_{t-1} as their inputs. The logistic function is σ. The value output from the "tanh" node is:

$$\tilde{c}_t = \tanh(W_c \cdot [h_{t-1}, x_t] + b_c) \tag{2}$$

In the above formula, the parameter's subscript " t" indicates that it is a "tanh" node parameter. In the same way, the output gate parameter's subscript is "o", the input gate parameter's subscript is "i" and the forget gate parameter's subscript is "f".The above formula is the same as the calculation formula of hidden layer in simple structure recurrent neural network. In LSTM, we call the output of "tanh" node as candidate state $\tilde{c}_t$.

The following equation can be used to determine the input gate:

$$i_t = \sigma(W_i \cdot [h_{t-1}, x_t] + b_i) \tag{3}$$

In the above equation, the domain of σ is (0,1), hence the input gate's value belongs to (0,1). After multiplying the "tanh" node's output value (i.e. candidate state $\widetilde{c_t}$) by the input gate's value, the LSTM updates the internal state with this new value. If the value of i_t goes to zero, then the internal state will only store a very little amount of data about the candidate state $\widetilde{c_t}$, and conversely, if the size of i_t value goes to be close to one, then more information about the candidate state $\widetilde{c_t}$ is saved. The input gate determines how much information is saved in this way, the size of the i_t value indicates how essential the new information is, and the internal state will not hold the unimportant information. The following equation can be used to determine the forget gate:

$$f_t = \sigma(W_f \cdot [h_{t-1}, x_t] + b_f) \tag{4}$$

Similar to the input gate, using the value of f_t to establish the extent to which the previous moment's internal state's imformation must be "forgotten". When the value of f_t approaches 0, the more information is forgotten. The following equation can be used to determine the current cell state c_t:

$$c_t = f_t \circ c_{t-1} + i_t \circ \widetilde{c_t} \tag{5}$$

where "∘" denotes the Hadamard product. Thanks to the forget gate, it can preserve content dated back a long time, and thanks to the input gate, it can deter the present unrelated information from being memorizing.

In the same principle, the following equation can be used to determine the output gate:

$$o_t = \sigma(W_o \cdot [h_{t-1}, x_t] + b_o) \tag{6}$$

The following equation can be used to determine the current output value of LSTM:

$$h_t = o_t \circ tanh(c_t) \tag{7}$$

The internal state c_t at the present moment will output more information to the external state h_t at the present moment when the value of o_t is closer to 1.

In the subsequent model training, the loss function we used is the most common multi-classification loss function called the cross-entropy loss function. The formula is as follows:

$$\text{loss} = -\sum_{i=1}^{n}\sum_{j=1}^{m} \hat{y}_{ij} \log y_{ij} \tag{8}$$

where, correspondingly, n and m stahd for the quantity of samples and the quantity of categories of classification, $\hat{y}_{ij}$ and y_{ij} represent the true probability and classification, $\hat{y}_{ij}$ and y_{ij} represent the true probability and prediction probability of the i_{th} sample data belonging to the j_{th} category respectively.

4 Evaluation

4.1 Dataset

In order to complete the simulation work, our experiments use the "ISCX VPN-nonVPN 2016" network traffic dataset, which is composed of traffic of different applications captured by Wireshark and other tools. In this dataset, data packets generated by different applications could be broken down into multiple categories, including Skype, Facebook, hangouts, and email, chat, file transfer, etc. according to the specific activities that applications participate in during the capture session. Gil et al.[12] have more nitty-gritties regarding the traffic that was gathered and the traffic production procedure. According to the requirements of simulation experiments, an appropriate training set and test set are created from the preprocessed dataset.

4.2 Metrics

We assess each method according to the accuracy (A.), recall (R.) and F1-score (F1.). The following are the definitions:

$$\text{Accuracy} = \frac{TP + TN}{TP + FP + FN + TN} \tag{9}$$

$$\text{Recall} = \frac{TP}{TP + FN} \tag{10}$$

$$\text{F1} = 2 \times \frac{Precision \times Recall}{Precision + Recall} \tag{11}$$

where true positive, true negative, false positive, and false negative are denoted, respectively, by the letters TP, TN, FP, and FN.

4.3 Comparison Algorithm

A total of four different network models were trained in this experiment, and their performances were tested respectively. Finally, the effects of the models were compared.

(1) Lotfollahi M et al. Proposed DeepPacket[6] network model structure, which directly identifies the network traffic's features and is used as this paper's baseline model for reference.
(2) CNN-GRU[13] model combins with gated recurrent unit (GRU) on the basis of the CNN to extract the network traffic's spatiotemporal features.
(3) MRN-LSTM(multi-scale ResNet-LSTM) model is a suggested spatiotemporal fusion-based model for identifying network traffic in this paper, that is, a fine-grained multi-scale feature extraction module is added on the basis of coarse-grained feature extraction ResNet model, and then LSTM network structure is connected.

The above models are gradually improved from DeepPacket to CNN-GRU and MRN-LSTM. Among them, the focus is on the comparison of traffic identification experimental results between the DeepPacket and the model of MRN-LSTM presented in paper.

4.4 Experiments

So as to compare and analyze different activation functions' influence on the model for network traffic identification and select the appropriate activation function to apply to the network model, the experiment selects Relu, Sigmoid and Tanh as the activation functions for model training. Table 1 below displays the experimental outcomes. Relu is employed in this experiment as the network model's activation function because, as seen in the findings in table1, it provides the best level of model accuracy.

Table 1. Acuuracy under different activation functions.

Activation function	Average accuracy
Relu	98.67%
Tanh	98.34%
Sigmoid	97.91%

Similarly, for the purpose of selecting the appropriate optimizer and apply it to the network model, it's needed to analyze different optimizers' influence on the model identification effect. In this experiment, Adam, SGD, Adagrad and RMSprop are chosen as the model's optimizers for training. Table 2 below depicts the experiment's outcomes. Based on the outcomes of experiment in table2, when using Adam as the activation function, the accuracy is higher and the effect is better. Therefore, Adam is used as the optimizer of the network model in this experiment.

Table 2. Acuuracy under different optimizers.

Optimizer	Average accuracy
Adam	98.70%
SGD	94.06%
Adagrad	97.81%
RMSprop	98.42%

The trained models are tested on the test set so as to compare three distinct models' performance for identifying network traffic. The comparison diagrams of accuracy and recall for every model on the test set are created in accordance with the simulation results, as illustrated in Figs. 5 and 6 below.

In Fig. 5 and Fig. 6, the abscissa represents 13 different application categories in the traffic data, and the ordinate shows the accuracy and recall rates of each application category where the network traffic identification model identify test set. The identification effects of the three network traffic identification models for different application traffic are clearly demonstrated from the perspective of accuracy and recall rate respectively.

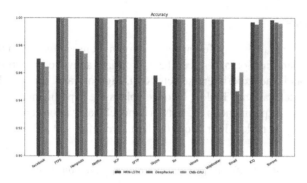

Fig.5. The Accuracy of different methods

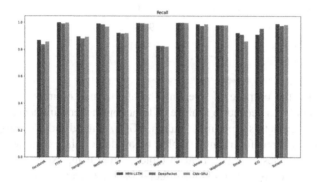

Fig.6. The recall of different methods

The algorithm spatiotemporal fusion-based of network traffic identification presented this paper obtains great results in both accuracy and recall, as shown in the figure.

In order to more intuitively show the comparison of the identification performance of each algorithm model, the average score of the evaluation index of each network traffic identifiction algorithm is calculated based on the outcomes of the simulation experiment. Table 3 below provides a detailed comparison of each model's performance.

Table 3. Performance comparison of various network traffic identification models.

Model	Metrics		
	Accuracy	Recall	F1
DeepPacket	0.9841	0.9358	0.9227
CNN-GRU	0.9853	0.9349	0.9231
MRN-LSTM	0.9879	0.9425	0.9374

According to the model performance effect table and performance comparison diagram of the above models, we discover that the MRN-LSTM model put forward in this paper is more accurate compared with DeepPacket network model and CNN-GRU model in the three indicators of accuracy, recall and F1. Compared with DeepPacket model, CNN-GRU model achieves 98.53%, 93.49% and 92.31% in three indicators respectively, which is better than DeepPacket model. Comparing CNN-GRU and MRN-LSTM models, it can be found that the latter has significantly improved in various indicators, and the classification effect for network traffic is significantly better. Compared with DeepPacket and MRN-LSTM models, the latter is significantly better than the former in accuracy, recall and F1. This shows that adding a module for extracting features of multi-scale into the neural network structure can significantly boost the model's performance and the algorithm's capacity to identify the network.

According to the appeal analysis, the conclusion is that the spatiotemporal fusion-based method for identfying network traffic presented in our paper works well. Additionally, it is proved that extracting features of multi-scale can obviously enhance the model's performance of neural network, which is worth studying.

5 Conclusion

Most DL-based traffic identification methods have the problems of single feature scale and insufficient information extraction when using those models about neural networks to extract network traffic's features. We present a spatiotemporal fusion neural network structure called MRN-LSTM based on deep learning in this paper, which combines ResNet and LSTM for network traffic identification. Then a module is added to the model for extracting spatial features of multi-scale, which overcomes the limitation of the single feature scale of the existing DL-based traffic identification methods, and effectively improves the problem of insufficient information extraction. We verify the effectiveness of MRN-LSTM on public network traffic dataset. The outcomes of the experiment demonstrate that MRN-LSTM performs well in terms of traffic identification.

Acknowledgment. This project is supported by the science and technology project of State Grid Beijing Power Company "AI-based Health Degree Analysis Technology of Power Communication Networks (SGBJXT00XTJS2200587)".

References

1. He, K., Zhang, X., Ren, S., et al.: Deep residual learning for image recognition. In: Proceedings of the IEEE conference on computer vision and pattern recognition, pp: 770–778 (2016)
2. Shi, X., Chen, Z., Wang, H., et al.: Convolutional LSTM network: a machine learning approach for precipitation nowcasting. Advances in neural information processing systems 28 (2015)
3. Xie, G., Li, Q., Jiang, Y., et al.: SAM: self-attention based deep learning method for online traffic classification. In: Proceedings of the Workshop on Network Meets AI & ML, pp. 14–20 (2020)
4. Khandait, P., Hubballi, N., Mazumdar, B.: Efficient keyword matching for deep packet inspection based network traffic classification. In: 2020 International Conference on Communication Systems & Networks (COMSNETS). IEEE, pp. 567–570 (2020)

5. Abeywickrama, T., Cheema, M.A., Taniar, D.: K-nearest neighbors on road networks: a journey in experimentation and in-memory implementation. arXiv preprint arXiv:1601.01549 (2016)

6. Lotfollahi, M., Jafari Siavoshani, M., Shirali Hossein Zade, R., et al.: Deep packet: a novel approach for encrypted traffic classification using deep learning. Soft Comput. 24(3), 1999–2012 (2020)

7. Wang, W., Zhu, M., Wang, J., et al.: End-to-end encrypted traffic classification with one-dimensional convolution neural networks. In: 2017 IEEE International Conference on Intelligence and Security Informatics (ISI). IEEE, pp: 43–48(2017)

8. Wang, W., Sheng, Y., Wang, J., et al.: HAST-IDS: Learning hierarchical spatial-temporal features using deep neural networks to improve intrusion detection. IEEE Access 6, 1792–1806 (2017)

9. Aceto, G., Giuonzo, D., Montieri, A., et al.: DISTILLER: encrypted traffic classification via multimodal multitask deep learning. J. Netw. Comput. Appl. 183, 102985 (2021)

10. Shapira, T., Shavitt, Y.: Flowpic: a generic representation for encrypted traffic classification and applications identification. IEEE Trans. Netw. Serv. Manage. 18(2), 1218–1232 (2021)

11. Zhao, H., Shi, J., Qi, X., et al.: Pyramid scene parsing network. In: Proceedings of the IEEE conference on computer vision and pattern recognition, pp: 2881–2890 (2017)

12. Draper-Gil, G., Lashkari, A.H., Mamun, M.S.I., et al.: Characterization of encrypted and VPN traffic using time-related. In: Proceedings of the 2nd International Conference on Information Systems Security and Privacy (ICISSP), pp: 407–414 (2016)

13. Yao, C.W., Yang, P., Lin, Z.J.: Load forecasting method based on CNN-GRU hybrid neural network. Power Syst. Technol. 44(09), 3416–4342 (2020)

A Trustworthy Content Moderation Scheme Based on Permissioned Blockchain

Yanhua Niu[1,2]([✉]), Shuai Gao[1], and Hongke Zhang[1]

[1] Beijing Jiaotong University, Beijing, China
18111072@bjtu.edu.cn
[2] Academy of Broadcasting Science, Beijing, China

Abstract. Content moderation is one of the most important issues in media industry. With the increasing of media content, most service providers (SPs) have been challenged with huge content moderation workload and tight deadline. We are concerned about the repeated moderation of popular content caused by 'head' effect, and find the lack of trust among SPs is the basic reason. To deal with this, we propose a novel content moderation scheme based on permissioned blockchain, which provides trustworthy moderation data sharing operation. We also design the content moderation mechanism based on video feature, which is used to identify the same video with different formats. Compared with the traditional approach, the proposed scheme can both ensure the integrity of the moderation data and reduce the total computation overhead.

Keywords: Content moderation · Permissioned blockchain · Data sharing

1 Introduction

As media content grows fast and connects more and more people through different terminal devices, media service providers (SPs) have been challenged with the huge content moderation workload and the tight deadline. Great efforts have been made, such as optimizing the artificial intelligence (AI) algorithms, deploying more machine moderation devices, expanding moderator team or entrusting the task to third-party agencies. These approaches speed up the moderation time to some extent, however, the fundamental problem is not solved. As we all know, a best-selling TV series or a popular short video usually attracts tens of thousands of viewers, which is called 'head' effect. To keep users engaged, many SPs prefer to launch the small amount of popular content. Because of the lack of trust among these SPs, the same contents will be moderated separately by each platform, which leads to repeated workloads and computational overhead. Therefore, the trust mechanism among different SPs is one of the important issues of content moderation.

Blockchain is a distributed ledger technology with decentralized, transparent, anti-tampering characteristics. It can effectively reduce the security risk of centralized architecture and has been applied in several domains as a trusted infrastructure such as decentralized DNS [1], energy [2], vehicular social networks [3], etc. In the area of content

© The Author(s), under exclusive license to Springer Nature Singapore Pte Ltd. 2023
W. Quan (Ed.): ICENAT 2022, CCIS 1696, pp. 131–145, 2023.
https://doi.org/10.1007/978-981-19-9697-9_11

moderation, blockchain can provide the trustworthy mechanism for different SPs. With the consensus and anti-tampering mechanism of blockchain, the content moderation records can be transmitted among all the participants securely, which can reduce the repeated moderation task and achieve a traceable, efficient and transparent content moderation mechanism. Until now no research about trustworthy content moderation scheme based on blockchain has been reported.

Motivated by the above challenges and issues, a trustworthy moderation scheme based on permissioned blockchain is proposed. The main contributions of this study can be summarized as follows:

- A permissioned blockchain-based content moderation scheme is proposed. The participants include content moderation demanders (CMDs), content moderation providers (CMPs) and content moderation supervisors (CMSs), and all the participants are under strict admission control and identity management to ensure the authenticity of the identities. CMDs can entrust the moderation task to the specified CMPs according to the points of CMPs.
- A novel content moderation data sharing scheme is proposed to support the trustworthy mechanism. The moderation records are stored in a verifiable and immutable ledger to guarantee the integrity and traceability. The moderated video files are encrypted and stored off chain. The content moderation results can be shared reliably based on blockchain.
- A trial system is implemented and the performance evaluation is conducted. The latency performance evaluation shows that the proposed scheme has little effect on the whole moderation process, and the computational overhead evaluation proves that this solution can reduce the total computational overhead.

The rest of this paper is organized as follows. In Sect. 2, we give an overview of related work. In Sect. 3, we provide the detail scheme based on permissioned blockchain. In Sect. 4, we describe the experimental environment and trail system. In Sect. 5, we conduct the performance evaluation of the proposed scheme. Finally, In Sect. 6, we present the conclusions and future research directions for this work.

2   Related Work

Content moderation is a long-studied problem. Literature [4] analyzed a variety of pre-moderation and post-moderation approaches of location-based user generated content (UGC), including pre-authorization, content filtering, user feedback, etc. Literature [5] proposed a method to detect automatic bots which originated malicious content in fringe social networks. Literation [6] analyzed the performance of three different machine learning models in detecting hate content on Twitter. VideoModerator was proposed to integrate human knowledge with machine insights, with which the risk-aware features can be extracted from multimodal video content [7]. Literature [8] presented a novel on-device solution with unsafe body part annotations and identification of semi-nude images. The above researches mainly focus on improving the accuracy of AI algorithms in a centralized mode, and do not address the repeated content moderation and resource waste caused by the distrust among different institutions.

In the field of video based on blockchain, some research has been carried out on the authenticity and integrity of video content. Literature [9] proposed a deepfake identification method using Ethereum smart contracts to trace and track the provenance and history of video content to its original source. ARCHANGEL was proposed to ensure the integrity of videos for tamper-proofing based on a proof-of-authority blockchain [10]. Literature [11] proposed the use of blockchain to secure and verify the integrity of video files. The video file's hash is permanently secured in the tamper-proof decentralized public ledger after the transaction is confirmed, which can be used as a valid form of evidence in court. Literature [12] proposed a video integrity confirmation scheme in the field of wireless-based IoT devices based on blockchain technologies, by comparing the hash of video frames between IoT devices and a remoted base station. Literature [13] focused on the task of cataloguing CCTV video evidence based on blockchain with a novel digital watermarking application. The above solutions aim to ensure the integrity and anti-tampering capabilities of videos based on blockchain, but do not involve video moderation mechanism.

In the field of content moderation based on blockchain, a few schemes have been put forward. Literature [14] focused on the irreversibly storage of illicit content based on blockchain and proposed a moderation frame for swift and transparent removal of illicit content. WhistleBlower was proposed to detect fake news and allow community members to participate in the identification process based on a public blockchain [15]. However, the above-mentioned researches do not focus on the mutual distrust among different institutions. In fact, we have not found any literature about the specific implementation to provide a trustworthy mechanism for different institutions. In this paper, we describe the design and implementation of the proposed scheme in detail.

3   Proposed Scheme

The proposed scheme focuses on the trust mechanism among different institutions based on blockchain and the main ideas are as follows:

- To ensure the authenticity of the participants, the proposed scheme adopts permissioned blockchain as the underlying technology, which can provide strict access control and identify management to all the participants. Furthermore, the content moderation capability registration transaction is designed to ensure the qualifications and abilities of CMPs.
- To ensure the trustworthy sharing of the moderation records along with the motivation of sharing willingness, the proposed scheme designs content moderation data sharing mechanism and a fundamental credit scoring mechanism.
- To improve the moderation efficiency further, this paper designs the video preprocessing module to extract the video feature and content tag to support the repeated moderation.

The architecture of the trustworthy content moderation scheme based on permissioned blockchain is shown in Fig. 1. Each node belongs to one of the participants.

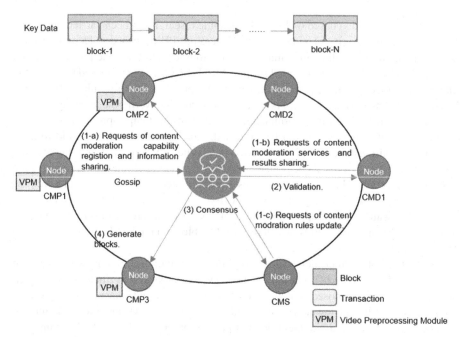

Fig. 1. Content moderation architecture based on blockchain

3.1 Participants of the Blockchain

As the entities corresponding to the blockchain member nodes, there are three types of participants in this scheme, including content moderation service demanders, providers and supervisors.

- Content moderation demanders (CMDs) include new media platforms (such as IPTV SPs, OTT SPs, etc.), online video platforms (such as iQiyi, Youku, Tencent, etc.) and those platforms without sufficient moderation capabilities. CMDs can relieve their work pressure by submitting content moderation requests on demand, and share content moderation results or illicit content features to reduce the repeated workload.
- Content moderation providers (CMPs) include third-party content moderation companies (such as NetEase YIDUN, Tencent Cloud, etc.) and content moderation departments of SPs with spare moderation capabilities. The CMPs that have registered content moderation capabilities in advance can provide third-party content moderation services and share illicit content features to other participants.
- Content moderation supervisors (CMSs) can update content moderation standards and rules to CMPs and solve the problem of inconsistent moderation quality caused by different moderation rules in different areas. With this proposed scheme, CMSs can clearly trace back to the responsible entities and find out where the problem lies.

3.2   Transaction Formats

To support the content moderation service, moderation data sharing and rules update, this paper designs the following transaction formats.

3.2.1   Content Moderation Capability Registration (CMCR)

To ensure the reliable operation of participants and the traceability of nodes' behavior, all participants must register first, and then be allowed to join in the system after strict qualification check. Each participant will be assigned a unique ID called *parti_id*.

The *CMCR* transaction is defined as follows: [*parti_id, parti_name, auth_status, auth_time, exp_time, timestamp, sig*]. The first five fields represent the CMP's ID, name, authentication status, authentication time and expire time, respectively. Once the participants are authenticated, the *auth_status* is set to 1. When the valid time expires, the *auth_status* will be set to 0. *Timestamp* identifies the exact time of the record creation, and *sig* is used to ensure the integrity of the record. The *CMCR* transaction is initiated by CMPs.

3.2.2   Content Moderation Service Request (CMSR)

The *CMSR* transaction is defined as follows: [*cont_id, cont_hash, cont_loc, spec_cmp, parti_id, parti_name, fin_time, timestamp, sig*]. *Cont_id* is composed of the CMD's *parti_id* and the content ID within the CMD, which guarantees *cont_id* is unique. *Cont_hash* is used to verify the integrity of the content. *Cont_loc* refers to the location of the content which is an off-chain storage as described in 3.4. *Spec_cmp* refers to the specified CMP ID of the moderation task. *Parti_id* and *parti_name* are used to identify the CMD. *Fin_time* represents the completion time of the task. The *CMSR* transaction is initiated by CMDs.

3.2.3   Content Moderation Service Response (CMSP)

The *CMSP* transaction is defined as follows: [*cont_id, cont_tag, cont_vf, ncont_hash, ncont_loc, inap_id, inap_loc, rev_id, timestamp, sig*]. *Cont_id* is the unique content ID. *Cont_tag* consists of the characters, events, time of the moderated content. *Cont_vf* is the video feature of the moderated content. *Ncont_hash* is the new hash of the approved video which is used to verify the integrity of video. *Ncont_loc* is the location of the approved content. *Inap_id* and *inap_loc* represent the inappropriate content ID and location. *Rev_id* and *signature* identify the moderator and the CMP. The *CMSP* transaction is initiated by CMPs.

3.2.4   Content Moderation Sharing Declaration (CMSD)

The *CMSD* transaction is defined as follows: [*cont_id, cont_tag, parti_id, parti_name, vali_time, timestamp, sig*]. *Cont_id* refers to the sharing moderation result. *Parti_id* and *parti_name* indicate the sharing entity. *Valid_time* represents the valid sharing time. The *CMSD* transaction is usually initiated by CMDs, since they own the content copyright. Here we call the sharing data providers as SDPs.

3.2.5 Content Moderation Sharing Request (CMShR)

The *CMShR* transaction is defined as follows: [*cont_id, dest_parti_id, from_parti_id, timestamp, sig*]. *Cont_id* refers to the data requested. *Dest_parti_id* refers to the institution who shares the data. *From_parti_id* refers to the sharing data demander. The *CMShR* transaction can be initiated by CMDs or CMPs depending on their content moderation requirement. Here we call the sharing data demanders as SDDs.

3.2.6 Content Moderation Rule Update (CMRU)

The *CMRU* transaction is defined as follows: [*rule_id, rule_hash, rule_object, rule_approch, timestamp, sig*]. *Rule_id* represents the unique rule. *Rule_hash* is used to ensure the integrity of the updated rule. *Rule_object* indicates the illicit object. *Rule_approch* refers to the execution method, such as pruning or mark. The *CMRU* transaction is initiated by CMSs.

3.3 Transaction Procedure Based on Blockchain

Since the procedure based on blockchain of above transactions are similar, here we take the CMCR transaction as an example. Figure 1 illustrates the procedure.

First, the CMP initiates a content moderation capability registration transaction, and then several neighbor nodes are randomly selected to broadcast to the network through the Gossip protocol. To avoid repeated forwarding and reduce network overhead, each node will verify the message before forwarding, and the same message is only forwarded once. Finally, all the nodes run consensus protocol and reach a consensus on the CMCR transaction, and store the qualification information on the blockchain after the transaction is verified by most of the nodes. After the registration is completed, only the registered CMP is allowed to update and revoke the information. Each node maintains a history of the operations based on the blockchain and provides content moderation services based on the latest data files.

3.4 Content Moderation Service Mechanism

Content moderation service mechanism is shown in Fig. 2. CMPs perform the content moderation based on machine moderation system, video preprocessing module (VPM) and manual review system. The storage architecture adopts an on-chain and off-chain model, with which the key data of transactions is stored on-chain and the videos are encrypted and stored off-chain.

On-chain data includes the transactions of content moderation requests, content moderation results, content access control information, etc. Off-chain data includes original videos, moderated videos, evidences, secondary editing files, malicious content archives, etc. For the same video file, all version files and corresponding illicit content files (snapshots) should be saved to facilitate the traceability of records.

To achieve an integrated content moderation service, we design four fundamental procedures, including video preprocessing procedure, content moderation procedure, content moderation data sharing procedure and content moderation responsibility tracing

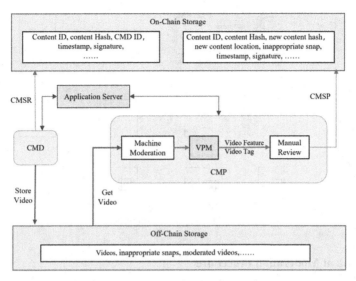

Fig. 2. Content moderation service mechanism

procedure. The first procedure is the basic one to improve the moderation efficiency. The second and the third procedures are both initiated by CMDs with the query of whether the sharing data is the same as the given content exists. If not, the content moderation procedure will be performed. Otherwise, the content moderation data sharing procedure will be performed. The content moderation responsibility tracing procedure is initiated by CMSs, which can clearly trace back to the responsible entities and enforce punishments.

3.4.1 Video Preprocessing Procedure

Currently, the moderation platform in CMP is generally composed of machine moderation system and manual review system. The machine moderation system analyzes the content and identify illicit or inappropriate imagery with AI-powered algorithms. As a result, the content doesn't satisfy the guidelines will be flagged and removed, and the ambiguous content will be submitted to manual review system and determined by moderators.

This paper designs the VPM based on the current content moderation platform in CMP to identify the same video in different format. The VPM extract the video feature based on content hash to ignore transcoding and the content tag which contains the video's main characters, events and occurrence time. The hash is computed over both the audio and the visual components of the video stream.

The video preprocessing process is illustrated in Fig. 3. The VPM extracts the video feature of video A and compares it with the video feature library. If the match is unsuccessful, the video feature is stored in the feature library, and a unique video identifier *AID* is assigned to the video. Video B is the same content as video A and in a different format. When video B enters the system, the match will be successful after video feature extraction and comparison. Then video B will be attached to Video A.

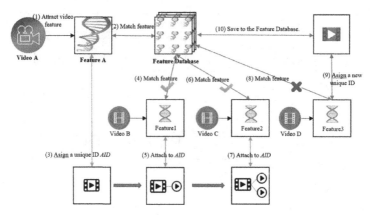

Fig. 3. Video preprocessing process

3.4.2 Content Moderation Procedure

The CMD queries whether the moderation data of the given content exists. If not, the content moderation procedure will be performed as shown in Fig. 4. Otherwise, the *Content Moderation Data Sharing* procedure will be conducted.

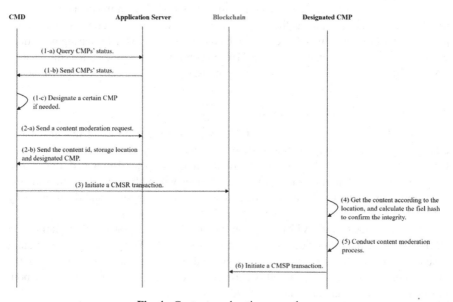

Fig. 4. Content moderation procedure

Step 1: the CMD queries CMPs' status, mainly including the credit score, workload and estimated completion time. Then the CMD designates a CMP if the requirements are met.

Step 2: The CMD sends its content moderation request along with the content size and the designated CMP to the application server. If the designated CMP is *NULL*, the application server will randomly allocate a CMP with less workload, which can ensure load balancing. Then a unique contend ID, storage location and a designated CMP will be sent to the CMD.

Step 3: The CMD initiates a *CMSR* transaction, which contains *cont_id, cont_hash, cont_loc, spec_cmp, parti_id, parti_name, fin_time, timestamp* and *sig. Cont_hash* is the hash of the content being moderated. After the process of consensus, the *CMSR* will be stored on blockchain.

Step 4: The designated CMP obtains the content at the designated location, and calculates the file hash to determine the integrity.

Step 5: The CMP performs moderation and extracts the video feature and the content tag as described in *Video Preprocessing Procedure*. The new moderated content will be stored to off-chain.

Step 6: The CMP initiates a *CMSP* transaction, which cantains *cont_id, cont_tag, cont_vf, ncont_hash, ncont_loc, inap_id, inap_loc, rev_id, timestamp*, and *sig*. The video feature and the content tag will be filled *cont_vf* and *cont_tag* individually. After the process of consensus, the *CMSP* will be stored on blockchain.

3.4.3 Content Moderation Data Sharing Procedure

Traditionally, content moderation data are stored in different separate institutions without data sharing, so the problem of repeated moderation task is severe. This paper designs a trusted data sharing scheme so that institutions could share content moderation results and inappropriate video features. This can greatly reduce the workload of repeated moderation among CMDs and improve the moderation accuracy of the CMPs. To stimulate the data sharing, we design a fundamental credit scoring mechanism. The points of institutions that contribute data will increase, and the points of institutions that use the data will decrease. As far as the SDDs are concerned, the points they need to pay are much lower than the content moderation cost, so this mechanism will not reduce the usage of SDDs.

Figure 5 shows the steps involved in the sharing process.

Step 1: The SDP sends a *CMSD* message, which contains the *cont_id, cont_tag, parti_id, parti_name, vali_time, timestamp*, and *sig*. After the process of consensus, the CMDR transaction will be stored on chain.

Step 2: The SDD queries the sharing data of a given content.

Step 3: If it exists, the SDD initiates a CMShR transaction, which contains *cont_id, dest_parti_id, from_parti_id, timestamp, sig*. The CMShR transaction will be stored on chain after consensus.

Step 4: The blockchain will call the smart contract to increase the points of the SDP and decrease the points of SDD automatically.

Step 5: The application server configures the access rights of sharing data according to the transaction and inform the SDD.

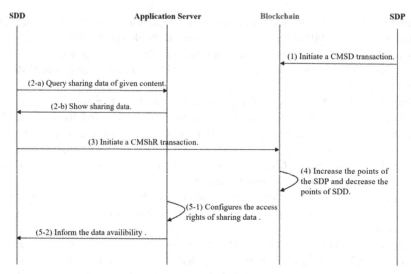

Fig. 5. Content moderation data sharing procedure

3.4.4 Content Moderation Responsibility Tracing Procedure

Content moderation responsibility tracing procedure is initiated by CMSs. Figure 6 shows the steps involved in the responsibility tracing process.

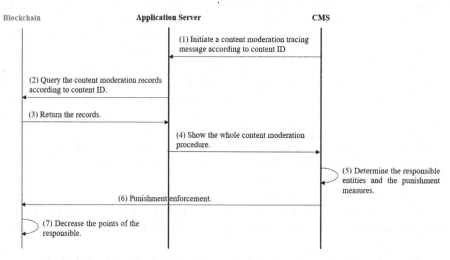

Fig. 6. Content moderation responsibility tracing procedure

Step 1: The CMS Initiates a content moderation tracing message according to content ID.

Step 2: the application server queries the content moderation records from the blockchain according to content ID.

Step 3: the blockchain returns all the records.

Step 4: the application servers shows the whole content moderation records with the detailed CMPs and the relevant moderators.

Step 5: the CMS determines the responsible entities and the punishment measures.

Step 6: the CMS enforce the punishment and all the data will be stored on the blockchain.

Step 7: the blockchain decrease the points of the responsible entities according to the punishment measures.

4 Experimental Environment and Trail System

We developed a trial system with five nodes on the private cloud in our laboratory as shown in Fig. 7, running Ubuntu 18.04.5 LTS operating system with Intel(R) Xeon(R) CPU E5–2650 v2 @ 2.60 GHz, 16 Cores, and 32 Gigabytes of memory. The trail system is based on the ACME consortium blockchain. Figure 8 shows the information of the submitted transaction.

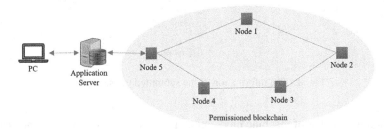

Fig. 7. The trail system topology

5 Performance Evaluation

5.1 Latency Performance Evaluation

Compared with the traditional content moderation approach, the proposed scheme introduces three new latencies: the CMSR transaction latency, video preprocessing latency and the CMSP transaction latency.

The CMSR transaction latency and the CMSP transaction latency are mainly determined by the block generation time of the underlying blockchain system. We test the transaction latency for 50 times, and the average latency is 6.012 s.

The video preprocessing latency depends on the performance of the hardware. Here we refer to the performance parameters of a certain brand of device on the market. A video with 45 min length and 8 Mbps bit rate needs 0.75 h, and a short video with 3 min length and 4 Mbps bit rate needs 0.025 h. Since the video preprocessing and the machine moderation can perform in parallel and the duration of video preprocessing is

概览		输入/输出	
交易大小	966 (bytes)	交易费用	0
交易时间	2022-07-21T03:31:15	交易金额	0
区块高度	480	输出个数	0
交易类型	Coinbase Transaction	输入个数	0

签名信息	pubkey:03b21688e7e133f3032b2927b4aef8af39997cb6e49afb55d2c6db15de4 020ed60;signature:304502203101cfd99c9e334b86dece4da28b626cd20637247 926539822d882820a1c256f022100b0c75416dec13af967d684c0e7ba00a79afd 8a63bab100ab0aad0b34819fef10,address:P14U4gFCF4is3ECgoPi8NP74mPhq5 hEUJBX
备注	{"examineResult":{"createTime":"2022-07-21 11:30:32","id":42,"pathName":"/m nt/data/remote/hawk/分类素材/片段预告/建军大业17.mp4","realUserNam e":"zcqsh1","result":-1,"resultContent":"99采纳88","roleType":"Auditor1","use r":"zcqsh1"},"faceList":[{"description":"test","endTime":28240,"id":10,"label":"落 马官员","scene":"face","startTime":0,"subLabel":"test","suggestion":"block"}]} {"extra_data":{"author":"zcqsh1","hash":"adc628e8a44027fb4b563956cce7d5c4 a7688630f085726c2a75668778ee9a99","strorage":"/mnt/data/remote/hawk/ 分类素材/片段预告/建军大业17.mp4"},"guid":"2d1348b6c80d5e8cefc4d8e9b5 08f891","organization":"012345678901234569") adc628e8a44027fb4b563956c ce7d5c4a7688630f085726c2a75668778ee9a99-2d1348b6c80d5e8cefc4d8e9b 508f891
附加信息	null
请求哈希	0x29d62e1fd836bb32872b749b758f1c9251a08a36e4f9873ca1f8d90017e59cdf

Fig. 8. The information of the submitted transactions

much shorter than that of machine moderation, the video preprocessing latency can be ignored.

Figure 9 illustrates the comparison in duration of the proposed scheme and the traditional one without trusted blockchain. Type 1, type 2 and type 3 refer to the video with 45 min length and 8 Mbps bit rate, the video with 15 min length and 4 Mbps and the video with 3 min length and 4 Mbps bitrate respectively, which are common video format. Compared with the practical business model, the proposed scheme spends about 6 s more. Therefore, the latency of this solutions is much shorter than the current moderation duration, which has little effect on the latency performance.

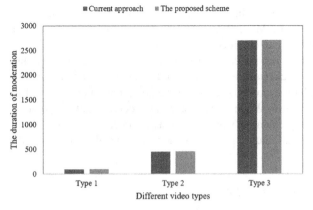

Fig. 9. Comparison in duration

5.2 Computational Overhead Evaluation

To simulate the computational overhead of the proposed scheme, Let $V = \{V_1, V_2, \ldots\ldots, V_N\}$ be the set of content within a given time T, C_T is the current content moderation computational overhead, so we have:

$$C_T = \sum_{i=1}^{N} S_i \alpha$$

Here, S_i is the file size of V_i, and α represents the computational overhead per unit size.

Let V_R be the set of repeated content, and V_S be the set of non-repeated content, then $V_R \subseteq V$, $V_S = V\text{-}V_R$. C_T is the computational overhead of the proposed scheme, including the computation of both regular moderation and the video feature extraction.

$$C_N = \sum_{i=1}^{N} S_i \tau + \sum_{j=1}^{Nr} S_j \alpha \eta + \sum_{k=1}^{N(1-r)} S_k \alpha$$

$$\gamma = |V_R|/N$$

$$0 < \eta \leq 0.5$$

$$0 \leq \gamma \leq 1$$

$$S_i \in V, \ S_j \in V_R, \ S_k \in V_s$$

Here, τ is the computational overhead of video feature extraction and comparison per unit size. γ represents the proportion of the number of repeated videos in set V. η is the video repetition factor, which represents the request number of the same content.

We take 1000 high-definition videos as an example, with an average length of 45 min and a bit rate of 8 Mbps. We refer to the processing time of a certain brand device: 1 MB of video files can be processed in about 1 s.

Figure 10 illustrates the comparison of the proposed scheme and the traditional one without trusted blockchain. $\gamma = 0$ refers to the moderation computational overhead C_T without blockchain and others represent the computation of proposed scheme C_N with different proportion γ. When γ is constant, as η decreases, the computational overhead also decreases. For example, when $\gamma = 20\%$, C_N decreases 10%, 12%, 14%, 16%, 18% respectively. Overall, the proposed scheme can reduce the total computation overhead.

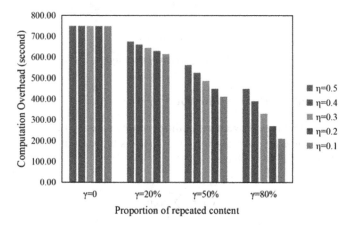

Fig. 10. Comparison in computational overhead

6 Conclusion and Future Work

In this paper, we propose a trustworthy content moderation scheme that enables the institutions to share content moderation data securely and improve the content moderation efficiency. The integrity and security of the moderation data can be ensured by the consortium blockchain among different institutions. Firstly, we design the transaction formats and procedure of capability registration, service request and response, sharing declaration and request. Secondly, we propose the video preprocessing scheme to improve the efficiency of content moderation. Thirdly, we propose the content moderation and data sharing scheme based on consortium blockchain, which can ensure the integrity and security of the moderation data. In theory, the proposed scheme with higher security, efficiency, and credibility, but further research works are still needed.

- We still need to implement the coordinated management between on-chain and off-chain storage based on the trial system. In the future, we will deploy the InterPlanetary File System (IPFS) as our decentralized storage.
- We still need to improve the credit stimulating mechanism for SDPs to motivate them to share data based on the real business data. We will propose an optimized mechanism in the future.

- More functions need to be introduced to this framework, such as content moderation data analysis and quality assessment.

Acknowledgement. This work was supported by the Fundamental Research Fund for Academy of Broadcasting Science, China under project JBKY20220180.

References

1. Ali, M., Nelson, J., Shea, R., Freedman, M.J.: Blockstack: a global naming and storage system secured by blockchains. In: 2016 Annual Technical Conference, pp. 181–194 (2016)
2. Li, Z., Kang, J., Yu, R., et al.: Consortium blockchain for secure energy trading in industrial internet of things. IEEE Trans. Industr. Inf. **169**(1), 3690–3700 (2017)
3. Fan, K., Pan, Q., Zhang, K., et al.: A secure and verifiable data sharing scheme based on blockchain. IEEE Trans. Veh. Technol. **69**(6), 5826–5835 (2020)
4. Coutinho, P., Rui, J.: Moderation techniques for user-generated content in place-based communication. In: 2017 12th Iberian Conference on Information Systems and Technologies (CISTI). IEEE (2017)
5. Ravazzi, C., Malandrino, F., Dabbene, F.: Towards proactive moderation of malicious content via bot detection in fringe social networks. IEEE Control Syst. Lett. **6**, 2960–2965 (2022)
6. Khandelwal, S., Aruna, M.: Comparative analysis of the performance of Machine Learning and Transfer Learning models in detecting hate on Twitter. In: 2022 2nd International Conference on Advance Computing and Innovative Technologies in Engineering (ICACITE), pp. 1097–1100 (2022)
7. Tang, T., Wu, Y., Wu, Y., Yu, L., Li, Y.: VideoModerator: a risk-aware framework for multimodal video moderation in e-commerce. IEEE Trans. Visual Comput. Graph. **28**(1), 846–856 (2022)
8. Pandey, A., Moharana, S., D. Mohanty, P.A., et al.: On-device content moderation. In: 2021 International Joint Conference on Neural Networks (IJCNN), pp. 1–7 (2021)
9. Hasan, H.R., Salah, K.: Combating deepfake videos using blockchain and smart contracts. IEEE Access **7**, 41596–41606 (2019)
10. Bui, T., Cooper, D., Collomosse, J., et al.: ARCHANGEL: tamper-proofing video archives using temporal content hashes on the blockchain. In: 2019 IEEE/CVF Conference on Computer Vision and Pattern Recognition Workshops (CVPRW), pp. 2793–2801 (2019)
11. Gipp, B., Kosti, J., and Breitinger, C.: Securing video integrity using decentralized trusted timestamping on the bitcoin blockchain. In: MCIS 2016 Proceedings, p. 51 (2016)
12. Danko, D., Mercan, S., Cebe, M., and Akkaya, K.: Assuring the integrity of videos from wireless-based IoT devices using blockchain. In: 2019 IEEE 16th International Conference on Mobile Ad Hoc and Sensor Systems Workshops (MASSW), pp. 48–52 (2019)
13. Kerr, M., Han, F., Schyndel, R.: A Blockchain implementation for the cataloguing of CCTV video evidence. In: 2018 15th IEEE International Conference on Advanced Video and Signal Based Surveillance (AVSS), pp. 1–6 (2018)
14. Matzutt, R., Ahlrichs, V., Pennekamp, J., Karwacik, R. and Wehrle, K.: A moderation framework for the swift and transparent removal of illicit blockchain content. In: 2022 IEEE International Conference on Blockchain and Cryptocurrency (ICBC), pp. 1–9 (2022)
15. Ramachandran, G., Nemeth, D., Neville, D., et al.: WhistleBlower: towards a decentralized and open platform for spotting fake news. In: 2020 IEEE International Conference on Blockchain (Blockchain), pp. 154–161 (2020)

Multi-agent Deep Reinforcement Learning-Based Content Caching in Cache-Enabled Networks

Sai Liu[1], Jia Chen[1], Deyun Gao[1(✉)], Meiyi Yang[1], and Junfeng Ma[2]

[1] National Engineering Research Center of Advanced Network Technologies, School of Electronic and Information Engineering, Beijing Jiaotong University, Beijing 100044, China
{21120089,chenjia,gaody,19111045}@bjtu.edu.cn
[2] China Academy of Information and Communication Technology, Beijing 100191, China
majunfeng@caict.ac.cn

Abstract. Deploying popular contents during the off-peak time via node cooperative caching has been proved to be an important measure to alleviate the link burden of wired multi-hop network. However, due to the unknown and time-varying content popularity in practice, it is imminent to optimize the content placement to effectively utilize the limited caching storage. In this paper, to address these issues, we investigate a multi-agent reinforcement learning (DRL) mechanism to intelligently deploy contents in dynamic environments. The optimization of content caching is modeled as a cooperative Markov decision process (MDP) to minimize the content transmission cost in the network. Then, a multi-agent deep deterministic policy gradient-based collaborative caching algorithm (MADDPG-CC) is proposed to solve this optimization problem with the goal of maximizing long-term caching reward. Extensive simulations have demonstrated the superior performance of the proposed algorithm in reducing the content transmission cost compared to existing caching algorithms, as well as its compatibility with variable and dynamic network environments.

Keywords: Collaborative caching · Content transmission cost · Markov decision process · Multi-agent deep deterministic policy gradient

1 Introduction

In recent years, with the boom in new multimedia applications such as short-form video applications, a huge volume of content that requires additional resources has been generated on the network, and this leads to the exceptional growth of network traffic. In order to reduce the burden of content transmit in the

Supported by School of Electronic and Information Engineering, Beijing Jiaotong University.

ⓒ The Author(s), under exclusive license to Springer Nature Singapore Pte Ltd. 2023
W. Quan (Ed.): ICENAT 2022, CCIS 1696, pp. 146–157, 2023.
https://doi.org/10.1007/978-981-19-9697-9_12

network and improve the users' service experience, mobile edge caching (MEC) has been proposed in many studies, such as [1–3]. That is, a limited local cache space is allocated in the edge node to store some popular requested content, and when the user requests for this popular content, the edge node can respond directly to the user's content request. However, as the number of users of these applications proliferates, it is difficult to fully satisfy user demand for popular content by considering caching deployments solely in the edge nodes. And now resource storage and caching technologies are also pervading various network architectures such as content delivery networks (CDNs) and information centre networks (ICNs). So, inspired by this, we consider a wired multi-hop network that can support caching, and the central issue in this type of network scenario is how to make full use of the limited local cache space of the cache nodes to minimize the content transmission cost in the network.

Efficient utilization of limited node cache resources is highly dependent on the content popularity. However, it is dynamic in both time and space, which is a priori unknown. To this end, machine learning is employed to predict content popularity based on historical observations and then optimize content placement, such as [4–6]. In [4], the authors propose a transfer learning-based caching scheme to predict trends in the popularity of user-requested content by extracting rich contextual information from the target and source domains, while the authors in [5] and [6] used multi-armed bandit (MAB) to predict the content popularity. However, the effectiveness of these efforts depends heavily on the accuracy of the predictions, so there is a great deal of uncertainty and ultimately it is difficult to obtain an optimal caching strategy.

The rise and widespread use of reinforcement learning has shown promise in solving the caching decision problem for mobile edge nodes in wireless networks. It adapts to the dynamics of the network environment without the need for prior knowledge of the dynamics of the network environment. To deal with higher dimensional state spaces, deep reinforcement learning (DRL) has started to be used in recent years of research to develop caching strategies. Many of the current studies related to MEC use centralized deep reinforcement learning, where edge nodes in a static network environment are trained centrally to obtain the full caching policy directly, as in [7,8]. However, for the complex network environment and the dynamic content popularity, applying centralized deep reinforcement learning algorithms to this is hardly successful. Then some of the latest research for MEC is starting to use multi-agent deep reinforcement learning algorithms, such as [9–11], in which all agents can not only fully perceive and acquire the state of the complex and changing network environment through distributed learning, but also better collaborative caching between agents through centralized training. However, in all of these studies, the authors only considered the collaborative nature of adjacent edge nodes, which is very different from caching in wired multi-hop networks.

In a wired multi-hop network, the source node generating the content request is directly connected to the network, so there is an interaction between the cache update policy of the source node and the cache policies of the intermediate nodes on the routing path. That is, these cache nodes are all in a cooperative relationship with each other and are not limited to neighboring nodes. So when considering caching in a wired multi-hop network, we need to take full account of the collaboration between all the cache nodes in the network, which also dictates that the edge node caching strategy for wireless networks cannot be directly applied to wired multi-hop networks.

In this paper, we aim to optimize content caching among cooperative nodes by minimizing the expected total transmission cost over a finite time horizon in cache-enabled wired networks without knowing content popularity in advance. In our experiments, we use the reduction in transmission cost as the caching reward compared to caching without requesting content at the cache node, and then we reformulate this content caching as a Markov decision process (MDP) to maximize the total caching reward. In addition, we take into account the complexity network environment and the collaboration between nodes, and choose to use a multi-agent deep reinforcement learning algorithm to train and learn the caching policy. The main contributions of this paper are as follows.

1) Analyzes the problem to optimizing content caching policies in cache-enabled wired multi-hop networks and transmits it as a cooperative MDP by defining the caching reward.
2) Considering the complex and variable nature of the actual network environment and the cooperative relationship between caching nodes, we propose a multi-agent-based intelligent caching algorithm MADDPG-CC.
3) Through extensive simulations, we demonstrate that our algorithm converges up to nearly 10% better and significantly faster in the same network environment compared to various other algorithms. In addition, our algorithms are highly compatible with complex and changing network environments.

2   System Model

2.1   Model Building

When considering a practical network model, we choose to use directed graphs to represent general multi-hop networks, whose general expression is $G = (N, L)$, where N denotes the set of all nodes in this multi-hop network, and L denotes the set of all links between any two adjacent nodes, i.e., $\forall l = (n_1, n_2) \in L, N_s \ll N_c$. In addition, we assume that a total of M different content (e.g., video, audio, image, text, etc.) is stored in the content library of this multi-hop network. The content base of the entire network is denoted by E, i.e., $E = \{e_1, e_2, ..., e_m, ..., e_M\}$, and in the model, we set the size of a content to 1 and represent the different contents with different natural numbers. The nodes in this network are divided into two types, server nodes and cache nodes, whose sets are denoted as N_s and N_c respectively, and $N = N_s \cup N_c, N_s \ll N_c$. Each cache node i has a local cache space D_i of size V, i.e., $D_i = \{d_1^i, d_2^i, ..., d_v^i, ..., d_V^i\}, V \ll M$. And each server node s has a local cache space that is larger than the cache node. For each content e_m in the network content library E, there exists a server node s that stores it uniquely and fixedly, i.e., the content in the entire network content library is stored non-repeatedly in each server node in the network.

In addition, we divide a longer period of time T into different time slot t, i.e., $T = \{1, 2, ..., t\}$. We assume that all cache nodes i, except server node s, receive a certain number of content requests at each time slot t. We denote the set of content requests from cache node i at time slot t as $b_i(t)$, i.e., $b_i(t) = \{b_{i,1}^t, b_{i,2}^t, ..., b_{i,w}^t, ..., b_{i,W}^t\}$, where $b_{i,w}^t$ indicates the specific content of the request, while W is the total number of all content requests received by cache node i at time slot t. To ensure that the number of content requests received by each cache node i within each time slot better matches a realistic scenario, we set the number of content requests W received by each cache node i within each time slot to follow an independent Poisson distribution process with arrival rate λ_i. In addition, for the request contents received by each cache node i at each time slot t, we set it to follow $Zipf$ distributions with parameter α.

As mentioned earlier, for each cache node i there is a finite size of local cache space D_i. In this paper, we define the set of local cache contents maintained by all cache nodes in time slot t as the cache matrix $x(t)$, and $x(t) = \{x_i(t), \forall i \in N_c\}$, where $x_i(t)$ represents the vector consisting of the local cache contents maintained by cache node i in time slot t. It is important to note here that the total amount of content stored in the local cache space per time slot t for each cache node i must not exceed the maximal cache space V for that node, and that both the content stored in the local cache space for each cache node i and the requested content from each cache node i should be available for matching within the server nodes in the network.

In network G, each link is assigned a fixed weight as the data transmission cost of that link, after taking into account the various types of transmission costs of the link (e.g., transmission delay, energy consumption, traffic, etc.). In this paper, we set cache nodes to communicate with server nodes according to the least weighted path. So the request $b_{i,m}$ for content m from cache node i complete the transmission of the content request and response with the target server node s, where content m is stored, via the least weighted path $p_{i,s}^m$. In addition, it is also important to note that the cost of transmitting the content request itself across the network is minimal compared to the content response. Therefore, in this paper, we ignore the request transmission cost. Moreover, during the transmission of request $b_{i,m}$ along the path $p_{i,s}^m$, if the intermediate cache node j passes through a successful match for content m, the transmission is terminated and cache node j follows the reverse symmetric path, not necessarily the path of least weight of cache nodes i and j, and responds directly to the request $b_{i,m}$ from the cache node i.

2.2   Problem Transformation

Based on the main idea of deep reinforcement learning, we transmit the problem to optimizing content caching policies in cache-enabled wired multi-hop networks into a MDP, in which each cache node acts as an agent and the cache-enabled network acts as environment. Define the each critical elements of MDP as follows:

State: The state of each agent reflects the local network environment. So, when we define the state of each agent, it should include the storage state of the agent's local cache space and the state of content requests received by the agent. In turn, the global state can be defined as $s(t) = \{x(t), b(t)\}$, $x(t) = \{x_{i,m}(t), \forall i \in N_c, \forall m \in E\}$ denotes the vector consisting of the contents stored in the local cache space of agent i at time slot t, and $b(t) = \{b_{i,m}(t), \forall i \in N_c, \forall m \in E\}$ denotes the vector of all request contents received by agent i at time slot t. So the state of agent i at time slot t can then be expressed as $s_i(t) = \{x_i(t), b_i(t), \forall i \in N_c\}$, where $b_i(t)$ is a vector of dimension M (M denotes the size of the content library in this network), and the index corresponding to each position in the vector indicates the specific content requested. The value corresponding to the index at each position indicates the number of times agent i requests that content at time slot t. Our goal is to continuously train the neural network at time slot $t+1$ using the global state $s(u)$ of some historical time slots, $u \in \{1, 2, 3, ..., t\}$, with the rewards obtained from these time slots, and then learn to obtain the optimal caching policy for each agent within time slot $t+1$.

Action: At the end of time slot t, agent i gets its state vector $x_i(t)$ as input to its actor network, and the output from the actor network is the caching policy $p_i(t)$ of agent i, where $p_i(t)$ is a vector of dimension M, and the specific value in the vector represents the value of the indexed content of the corresponding location of the cache selected by agent i, i.e., the larger the value, the bigger reward will be given for caching its corresponding indexed content. We then note the value of the first V index positions of the value according to the cache policy $p_i(t)$ as 1, and the rest of the index positions as 0. Thus we can obtain the cache action vector $a_i(t)$ consisting of 0, 1 binary numbers, and the index corresponding to the vector position where the number 1 is located indicates the request content that agent i should cache updates. So the global action matrix at time slot t can be defined as $a(t) = \{a_i(t), \forall i \in N_c\}$.

Reward Function: At time slot t, we define the transmission cost spent by target server node s to respond to the agent i that sends the request $b_{i,m}(t)$ with content m via the path $p_{i,s}^m$ as $C_{i,s}^m$, and we define the transmission cost spent by cache node j on the path $p_{i,s}^m$ storing content m to respond directly to agent i via the reverse symmetric path as $C_{i,j}^m$. And the difference between the above two costs we define as the reward given to cache node j by caching content m. We define that the set of intermediate nodes contained in the path $p_{i,s}^m$ is $N_{i,p_{i,s}^m,s}$, $i, s \in N_{i,p_{i,s}^m,s}$, then $C_{i,s}^m$ can be expressed as:

$$C_{i,s}^m = \sum_{f,k \in N_{i,p_{i,s}^m,s}} W_{l_{f,k}} \tag{1}$$

where $W_{l_{f,k}}$ is the link weight corresponding to the link $l_{f,k}$ between node f and node k.

Likewise, let the set of intermediate nodes contained in the path $p_{i,j}^m$ between agent i and agent j be $N_{i,p_{i,s}^m,j}$, $i,j \in N_{i,p_{i,s}^m,j}$, then $C_{i,j}^m$ can be expressed as:

$$C_{i,j}^m = \sum_{f,k \in N_{i,p_{i,s}^m,j}} W_{l_{f,k}} \tag{2}$$

We set $y_{i,j}^m(t)$ to be a binary judgment marker. If the request $b_{i,m}(t)$ from agent i to content m is the first to match successfully in the local cache space of agent j at time slot t, then $y_{i,j}^m(t)$ set to 1, otherwise, set to 0. Then the total reward $r_j(t)$ obtained by agent j at time slot t can be expressed as:

$$r_j(t) = y_{i,j}^m(t) \sum_{i \in N_c} \sum_{m \in b_i(t)} \left(C_{i,s}^m - C_{i,j}^m \right) \tag{3}$$

To reduce the order of magnitude of the reward value obtained by each agent in each time slot, we use the reduction $\bar{r}_i(t)$ in the average transmission cost of the response to each content request in agent$i$ at time slot t, as the reward obtained by agent i in that time slot as a result of caching content $x_i(t)$, i.e., $\bar{r}_i(t) = r_i(t)/W$. Thus, we can obtain the vector set of rewards for all agents at time slot t as $r(t) = \{\bar{r}_i(t), i \in N_c\}$.

2.3   MADDPG-Based Cooperative Caching Algorithm

The MADDPG [12] algorithm is an Actor-Critic based algorithm that uses a centralized training and decentralized execution architecture. As can be seen in Fig. 1, it is an architecture consisting of multiple actor-critic. During training, each agent's actor network obtains local observation, while the agent's critic network obtains global observation (i.e., the local observation and actions of other agents) for centralized global training. Once the model is trained, it only needs the agent to interact with the environment to obtain the optimal action decision. The MADDPG algorithm has three main features: (i) the agents are centralized training, decentralized execution; (ii) the dynamical model of the environment does not need to be known; and (iii) the cooperative or competitive environment is applicable.

In this subsection we propose a cooperative caching algorithm based on MADDPG, called MADDPG-CC. The algorithm treats each cache node in the network as a separate agent, and the content deployment policy of each cache node is trained collaboratively via the continuous interaction between all agents and the network environment, to minimize the transmission cost. By defining the input states, output actions and reward functions for each agent in the previous sub-section, we give the specific training learning process of the MADDPG-CC algorithm in interaction with the network environment in the form of pseudo-code, see Algorithm 1.

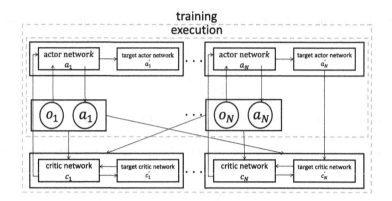

Fig. 1. MADDPG algorithm framework.

Algorithm 1. MADDPG-CC

Input: Initialize online parameters of actor network and online parameters of critic network for each agent; Initialize the local cache contents of all server nodes in the network.

Output: Average Reward

    for episode=1 to max-episode-number **do**

        Initialize the global local cache matrix $x(0)$;

        Initialize the global content request matrix $b(0)$;

        Observe the global state matrix $s(0)$

        for t=1 to max-episode-length **do**

            For each agent i, observe a policy $p_i(t)$ by current state $s_i(t)$;

            For each agent i, execute action $a_i(t)$ with respect to policy $p_i(t)$;

            Observe new the global local cache matrix $x(i+1)$;

            For each agent i obtains request vector $b_i(t+1)$;

            Observe the global reward $r(t)$;

            Obtain the global state matrix $s(t+1)$;

            $s' \leftarrow s(t+1)$;

            Store $\{s(t), a(t), r(t), s'\}$ in replay buffer D;

            $s(t) \leftarrow s(t+1)$;

        end for

        for agent i=1 to N_c **do**

            Sample a random mini batch of S samples $\{s^k, a^k, r^k, s'^k\}$ from D;

            Set target network;

            Minimizing the loss and update the critic network;

            Update the actor network;

        end for

        Update target network parameters for each agent i;

    end for

---

3   Simulation Experiments

In this section, we conduct extensive simulation experiments to verify the performance of the MADDPG-CC algorithm in various complex and dynamic network environments.

3.1   Experimental Simulation Environment

Building the network environment required for our simulation experiments, we choose to use the US Abilene Network. In this network topology, 11 nodes and 14 links are included. In the simulation experiments, we choose three of the nodes as server nodes, each of which stores one-third of the content of the network content library, and the remaining eight nodes as cache nodes, each of which acts as an independent agent. Each cache node follows an independent Poisson distribution process to generate the number of content requests for that cache node. Unless otherwise specified, we set the simulation parameters as follows: the arrival rate of the Poisson distribution $\lambda = 100$, the network content library size $M = 120$, the local cache space size of each cache node $V = 15$ and $Zipf$ distribution with the parameter $\alpha = 0.8$. In addition, each link is assigned a weight derived from TOTEM project [13]. Finally, some key parameters in the implementation of our algorithm are given in Table 1.

Table 1. Parameters for algorithm.

Parameters	Values
Agent number	8
Size of replay buffer	1000000
Size of mini-batch	1024
Learning rate	0.001
Discount	0.95
Maximum number of episodes	2500
Number of slots in each episode	50

3.2   Experimental Results

In this section, we analyze our proposed algorithm from two main aspects, the training process of MADDPG-CC in different network environments and the performance comparison between different algorithms, to demonstrate its superiority in performance.

Training Process in Different Network Environments. First, we verify the compatibility of our algorithm in various complex and dynamic network environments by varying the following variables in the network environment to obtain different convergence results.

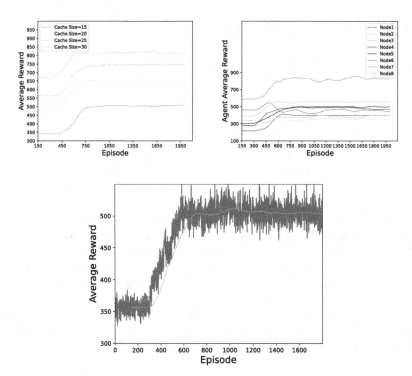

Fig. 2. Convergence curves of MADDPG-CC in different network environments: (a) Different local cache space sizes ($V = 15, 20, 25, 30$). (b) Different *Zipf* distribution parameters for different cache nodes ($\alpha = 0.2, 0.4, 0, 6, 0.8, 1.0, 1.2, 1.4, 1.6$). (c) Alternating *Zipf* distribution parameters ($\alpha = 0.8$ or 1.6).

The Size of Local Cache Space for Cache Nodes. Figure 2a shows the training curves of our algorithm for cache nodes with local cache space sizes of 15, 20, 25 and 30, and the results show that our algorithm still has good convergence results in these network environments. Moreover, as the local cache space of the cache node increases, the hit rate of the requested content at the intermediate cache nodes also increases, so the final convergence result obtained also increases.

Zipf Distributions of Cache Nodes. Figure 2b shows the convergence of the average reward value obtained by each cache node when the parameters of *Zipf* distributions followed by our algorithm in generating the requested content of different cache nodes are set to different values (cache node 1 to cache node 8 are set to 0.2, 0.4, 0.6, 0.8, 1.0, 1.2, 1.4, 1.6 in that order), from which we can see that all the cache nodes also converge separately. The difference in the final convergence results of different cache nodes is due to their specific positions in the network topology and the different link weights.

In addition, when conducting simulation experiments, we also simulated a network environment with dynamic and complex changes in the request content popularity of cache nodes by setting the parameter α of $Zipf$ distributions followed by the request content of cache nodes to 0.8 at odd episodes and 1.6 at even episodes, and the obtained training curves are shown in Fig. 2c, and the final convergence results demonstrate that the MADDPG-CC algorithm also shows good performance when training cache nodes with dynamically changing request content popularity, thus indicating that our algorithm is predictive of the changing trend of request content popularity.

Performance Comparison of Different Algorithms. To verify the performance difference between our proposed algorithm and other traditional caching algorithms as well as centralized reinforcement learning algorithms, we consider the following three algorithms chosen to compare with our proposed algorithm: least recently used (LRU), least frequently used (LFU) and deep deterministic policy gradient (DDPG).

The convergence of the average reward value curve obtained by the four algorithms is shown in Fig. 3. Since the training result data-set obtained from each training was too large, we considered taking an average every 150 episodes when plotting, and then plotted the convergence curve based on the obtained average value, so the starting value of the number of episodes in the horizontal coordinate is 150 instead of 0. In addition, for the initial 400 episodes, the agent only interacts with the network environment, completes online learning and generates experience bars, but does not update the actor and critic networks, so we can see from the figure that the average reward obtained by the two algorithms, MADDPG-CC and DDPG, do not change during this phase. After 400 episodes, the agent starts to update the parameters of the neural network by extracting experience entries from the replay buffer, so in the interval from 400 to 750, the result curves of the two algorithms start to rise significantly, and it can be seen that the MADDPG-CC algorithm converges significantly faster than DDPG. After 750 episodes, the results of both algorithms slowly converge, and from the final convergence results we can also see that the convergence results obtained by the two deep reinforcement learning algorithms are much greater than those obtained by the two traditional algorithms, LRU and LFU. And the final convergence value obtained by the MADDPG-CC algorithm is also slightly greater than that obtained by DDPG. We believe that the reason why the final convergence results of the two deep reinforcement learning algorithms are relatively close is that the size of the network content library set in the simulated experimental environment is small, so the advantages of our algorithm are not reflected.

In order to verify our above idea, we adjusted the size of the network content library in the simulation environment from 120 to 240 and 600 respectively, with other parameters unchanged, and re-trained the two algorithms with MADDPG-CC and DDPG, and the results are shown in Fig. 4. When the size of the content library is adjusted to 240 and 600, the difference between the convergence results

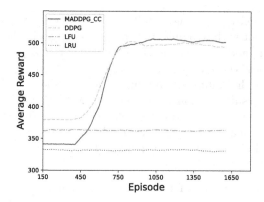

Fig. 3. Convergence curves for the four algorithms.

of the two algorithms is more obvious. Moreover, we can clearly see from all three figures that the convergence speed of the MADDPG-CC algorithm is also significantly faster than that of DDPG.

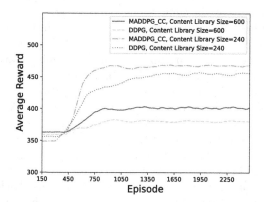

Fig. 4. Convergence curves of MADDPG-CC and DDPG at content library sizes of 240 and 600.

4   Conclusion

In this paper, we address the problem of content caching in wired multi-hop networks with the aim of minimizing long-term content transmission cost. Due to the dynamic and random nature of the network environment, we remodel this caching decisions making problem as a MDP and address it by learning caching policy directly online based on the proposed MADDPG-CC framework. Based on extensive simulation results, we demonstrate that our proposed algorithm is well compatible with various dynamically changing network environments.

Furthermore, our experimental results demonstrate the superior performance compared to current existing algorithms in different network environments.

Acknowledgements. This work is supported by the National Key Research and Development Program of China (grant no. 2018YFE0206800), the fundamental research funds for the central universities (no. 2021YJS013), and the National Natural Science Foundation of China (grant no. 61971028).

References

1. Yao, J., Han, T., Ansari, N.: On mobile edge caching. IEEE Commun. Surv. Tutor. **21**(3), 2525–2553 (2019)
2. Qiu, L., Cao, G.: Popularity-aware caching increases the capacity of wireless networks. IEEE Trans. Mob. Comput. **19**(1), 173–187 (2019)
3. Wang, R., Zhang, J., Song, S., Letaief, K.B.: Mobility-aware caching in D2D networks. IEEE Trans. Wirel. Commun. **16**(8), 5001–5015 (2017)
4. Hou, T., Feng, G., Qin, S., Jiang, W., Letaief: Proactive content caching by exploiting transfer learning for mobile edge computing. IEEE Trans. Wirel. Commun., 1–6 (2017). Proc. GLOBECOM
5. Song, J., Sheng, M., Quek, T.Q.S.: Learning-based content caching and sharing for wireless networks. IEEE Trans. Commun. **65**(10), 4309–4324 (2017)
6. Blasco, P., Gndz, D.: Learning-based optimization of cache content in a small cell base station. In: Proceedings of the ICC, pp. 1897–1903, June 2014
7. Zhong, C., Gursoy, M.C., Velipasalar, S.: A deep reinforcement learning-based framework for content caching. In: Proceedings of the CISS, pp. 1–6, March 2018
8. Zhu, H., Cao, Y., Wang, W., Jiang, T., Jin, S.: Deep reinforcement learning for mobile edge caching: review, new features, and open issues. IEEE Netw. **32**(6), 50–57 (2018)
9. Jiang, W., Feng, G., Qin, S., et al.: Multi-agent reinforcement learning for efficient content caching in mobile D2D networks. IEEE Trans. Wirel. Commun. **18**(3), 1610–1622 (2019)
10. Feriani, A., Hossain, E.: Single and multi-agent deep reinforcement learning for AI-enabled wireless networks: a tutorial. IEEE Commun. Surv. Tutor. **23**, 1226–1252 (2021)
11. Wang, F., Wang, F., Liu, J., Shea, R., Sun, L.: Intelligent video caching at network edge: a multi-agent deep reinforcement learning approach. In: IEEE INFOCOM 2020-IEEE Conference on Computer Communications, pp. 2499–2508. IEEE (2020)
12. Lowe, R., Wu, Y., Tamar, A., Harb, J., Abbeel, P., Mordatch, I.: Multi-agent actor-critic for mixed cooperative-competitive environments (2017). arXiv preprint arXiv:1706.02275
13. TOTEM progect. https://www.cs.utexas.edu/yzhang/research/AbileneTM/. Accessed 4 Oct 2003

Heterogeneous Networks and Network Integration

Mutual Authentication Protocol in a Distributed Heterogeneous Environment: A Blockchain-Based Approach

Ningyu An[1], Xiao Liang[1], Xuan Wang[1], Ruimiao Wang[2(✉)], Shuai Yuan[3], and Zhitao Guan[2]

[1] Artificial Intelligence on Electric Power System State Grid Corporation Joint Laboratory, State Grid Smart Grid Research Institute Co., Ltd., Beijing 102209, China
[2] School of Control and Computer Engineering, North China Electric Power University, Beijing 102206, China
wangruimiaowrm@163.com
[3] Department of Finance, Operations, and Information Systems (FOIS), Brock University, St. Catharines, ON, Canada

Abstract. Most of the existing identity-based authentication solutions rely on a centralized key generation center, resulting in the potential risk of single point of failure. Furthermore, there is a lack of heterogeneous authentication schemes that can realize authentication between users in different cryptosystems. In this study, we first present an identity-based authentication protocol with distributed authorization centers based upon blockchain. Next, we extend our fundamental protocol to a heterogeneous environment by considering the mutual authentication between the Public Key Infrastructure (PKI)-based and the identity-based systems. Finally, the proposed work is validated through the comparisons with the benchmarks.

Keywords: Identity-based authentication · Heterogeneous authentication · Blockchain

1 Introduction

The Internet changes the way people live and work in a variety of domains and perspectives [1]. It also plays an increasingly important role in shaping social behavior. Meanwhile, the issues pertaining to security and privacy have become the key consideration given the current heterogeneity in Internet services and user expectations. Therefore, ensuring the security over long periods of time becomes a major challenge for stakeholders.

Typically, authentication techniques are required to confirm the user identity in the network, and also to determine whether it is consistent with its real-world counterpart. Therefore, it serves as an important tool for safety and security in the cyberspace by preventing forged identities and/or repudiation.

© The Author(s), under exclusive license to Springer Nature Singapore Pte Ltd. 2023
W. Quan (Ed.): ICENAT 2022, CCIS 1696, pp. 161–171, 2023.
https://doi.org/10.1007/978-981-19-9697-9_13

The common protocols for user authentication include password-based authentication [2], biometric-based authentication [3, 4], symmetric cryptography-based authentication [5], and asymmetric (i.e., public-key) cryptography-based authentication [6, 7]. However, password-based systems are known to be susceptible to the risks of password loss, while there are also privacy risks such as genetic information leakage in biometric-based systems. In addition, symmetric cryptography requires both parties to share a common key through a channel where security issues may occur during its exchange. Therefore, the public-key cryptography-based systems are adopted by the majority of Internet service providers who run more mission-critical tasks or have a low tolerance for risk.

The traditional asymmetric cryptography [8] is based on public key infrastructure (PKI) which facilitates the distribution and use of public keys and establishes a trust hierarchy. Many steps, such as the generating, distributing, storing and revoking of the public-key certificate are involved in PKI-based system. Shamir et al. [9] propose the concept of identity-based cryptography where the user's identity serves as its public key. This approach simplifies the certificate management process in PKI-based systems, however, a specific key generation center (KGC) for private keys is also necessary. In cases where the KGC crashes or is compromised, the failures inevitably render the service unavailable. Furthermore, most of the existing authentication protocols are homogeneous, i.e., the same cryptosystem is used on both parties, thus making it an obstacle to wider adoption in a heterogeneous context.

Motivated by the prior limitations, we first propose an identity-based authentication protocol with distributed authorization centers based on blockchain [10, 11]. The (t, n) -threshold secret sharing [12] is used where key shares are distributed to n nodes on the blockchain, such that more than t nodes can cooperate for the purpose of key generating. Therefore, the risk of single point of failure from centralized management can be mitigated. In addition, considering the possible authentication between the PKI-based and the identity-based systems, we also present a solution in the heterogeneous environment by extending our fundamental protocol.

2 Related Work

Park et al. [13] introduce a lightweight PKI-based authentication scheme to enhance the data security in the cloud environment by detecting fake network functions. Xu et al. [14] develop a blockchain-based identity management and authentication scheme for mobile network. The user's identity and the public key can be stored on the blockchain, while the identity information can also be independently managed by the individual. Jiang et al. [15] propose a heterogeneous cross-domain authentication scheme between the PKI-based and certificateless public-key systems. It applies proxy blind signature technology to achieve identity blindness on both parties during authentication, while it requires a trusted certification center to authorize the third-party agents. Tan et al. [16] model a blockchain-based distributed identity authentication scheme for IoT devices where it addresses the problems of low compatibility and weak anti-attack capability due to centralized platform for authentication. However, it does not support cross-domain authentication. Li et al. [17] suggest an end-to-end authentication and key exchange protocol for the Internet of Things based on physical unclonable function. This method provides forward secrecy and does not require certificate management. Irshad et al. [18] develop a multi-server authentication protocol for mobile cloud environment, however, the trusted authority must disclose the shared secret to all servers thus may incur privacy leakage. Zhang et al. [19] study an anonymous authentication and key agreement protocol for the Internet of Vehicles based on certificateless aggregated signatures. This approach uses temporary identities and pre-signatures to protect the privacy of vehicle information. Tang et al. [20] develop a multi-authority identity-based identification scheme through bilinear pairing while removing a trusted party. But mutual authentication cannot be accomplished by both works.

3   Background

3.1   Bilinear Pairings

Let $\mathbb{G}_0$ and $\mathbb{G}_T$ be two multiplicative cyclic groups with order q, which is a large prime. A bilinear pairing $e : \mathbb{G}_0 \times \mathbb{G}_0 \rightarrow \mathbb{G}_T$ from $\mathbb{G}_0$ to $\mathbb{G}_T$ satisfies the following conditions:

1) *Bilinearity*: For any $P, Q, R \in \mathbb{G}_0$ and all $a, b \in \mathbb{Z}_q$, $e(P^a, Q^b) = e(P, Q)^{ab}$ or $e(PQ, R) = e(P, R) \cdot e(Q, R)$.
2) *Non-degeneracy*: There exists $P, Q \in \mathbb{G}_0$ such that $e(P, Q) \neq 1_{\mathbb{G}_T}$, which means it won't map all pairs of elements in $\mathbb{G}_0 \times \mathbb{G}_0$ to the identity element of group $\mathbb{G}_T$.
3) *Computability*: For any $P, Q \in \mathbb{G}_0$, there's an efficient algorithm to compute $e(P, Q)$.

3.2   Lagrange Interpolation Polynomial

For a given function $y = f(x)$ where $n + 1$ points are known as: $(x_0, y_0), (x_1, y_1), ..., (x_n, y_n)$, we can derive a polynomial $L(x) = \sum_{i=0}^{n} y_i \ell_i(x)$ of degree no more than n such that:
$$L(x_i) = y_i, i = 0, 1, ..., n,$$
where $\ell_i(x) = \prod_{j=0, j\neq i}^{n} \frac{x-x_j}{x_i-x_j}$ is Lagrange fundamental polynomial, denoted by $\Delta_{i,n}(x)$.

4   Identity-Based Authentication Protocol

We first introduce the fundamental identity-based authentication protocol, which contains the following three entities:

Key Generation Center (KGC): KGC creates the public parameters, master public key and master private key of the system, then distributes the share of the master private key to each authorized node.

Authorized Nodes: Authorized nodes are on the blockchain where they receive their own private keys from the KGC and generate partial private keys for users pertaining to the identity. We assume that there are n authorized nodes in the system, and more than t authorized nodes can create partial private keys for users.

Users: Each user obtains her partial private keys from authorized nodes and calculates her own private key based on these keys. Users are also capable of authenticating each other.

The proposed protocol is presented as follows:

4.1 Initialization

The KGC creates two multiplicative cyclic groups $\mathbb{G}$ and $\mathbb{G}_T$ of order q, where $\mathbb{G}$ is generated by g, and performs a bilinear pairing $e : \mathbb{G} \times \mathbb{G} \to \mathbb{G}_T$.

Then the KGC decides two hash functions $H : \{0, 1\}* \to \mathbb{Z}_q$ and $H_1 : \{0, 1\}* \to \mathbb{G}$. The public parameter of the system is $par = \{\mathbb{G}, \mathbb{G}_T, e, q, g, H, H_1\}$.

4.2 Key Generation for Authorized Nodes

The KGC selects t random numbers $s, a_1, ..., a_{t-1} \in \mathbb{Z}_q^*$ to derive a polynomial $f(x) = s + a_1 x + a_2 x^2 + ... + a_{t-1} x^{t-1}$ of degree $t - 1$, and sets $P = g^s$ as the system public key.

Then the KGC assigns an ID $Node_i$ to each authorized node i, $(i = 1, 2, ..., n)$, and also sends $nsk_i = f(Node_i)$ as the private key.

4.3 Key Generation for Users

When an individual user decides to join the system, she first needs to send a request to the authorized nodes to generate her own private key. The request includes her ID $User_i$ and a random number $k_i \in \mathbb{Z}_q$.

Upon receiving the request, the authorized node $Node_j$ computes $c_i = H(g^{k_i}, User_i)$ and sends $sk_{j,i} = H_1(User_i)^{c_i \cdot nsk_j}$ back to $User_i$ through a secure channel.

Once the $sk_{j,i}$ from more than t authorized nodes are received, $User_i$ is able to calculate her own private key in the following way:

$$
\begin{aligned}
usk_i &= H_1(User_i)^{k_i} \cdot \prod_{j=1}^t sk_{j,i}^{\prod_{k=1,k\neq j}^t \frac{Node_k}{Node_k - Node_j}} \\
&= H_1(User_i)^{k_i} \cdot \prod_{j=1}^t H_1(User_i)^{c_i \cdot nsk_j \cdot \Delta_{j,t}(0)} \\
&= H_1(User_i)^{k_i} \cdot H_1(User_i)^{c_i \cdot \sum_{j=1}^t f(Node_j) \cdot \Delta_{j,t}(0)} \\
&= H_1(User_i)^{k_i + c_i \cdot f(0)} \\
&= H_1(User_i)^{k_i + c_i \cdot s}.
\end{aligned}
$$

4.4 Authentication

When it is required for a given user to prove her identity, she interacts with the verifier through the protocol shown in Fig. 1. Details of the steps are as follows:

1) $User_i$ selects a random number $t_1 \in \mathbb{Z}_q^*$, and then sends $T_1 = H_1(User_i)^{t_1}$ to the verifier;

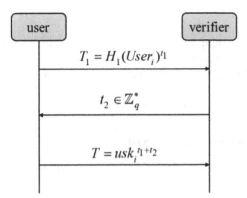

Fig. 1. Identity-based authentication.

2) The verifier selects a random number $t_2 \in \mathbb{Z}_q^*$ and sends it to $User_i$;

3) Upon receiving t_2, $User_i$ computes and sends $T = usk_i^{t_1+t_2}$ to the verifier;

4) Once T from $User_i$ is received, the verifier computes $c_i = H(g^{k_i}, User_i)$. Only if $e(T, g) = e(T_1 \cdot H_1(User_i)^{t_2}, g^{k_i} \cdot P^{c_i})$, the authentication is completed successfully.

We also prove the correctness of such verification as follows:

$$
\begin{aligned}
&e(T, g) \\
&= e(usk_i^{t_1+t_2}, g) \\
&= e(H_1(User_i)^{(k_i+c_i \cdot s) \cdot (t_1+t_2)}, g) \\
&= e(H_1(User_i)^{t_1+t_2}, g^{k_i+c_i \cdot s}) \\
&= e(T_1 \cdot H_1(User_i)^{t_2}, g^{k_i} \cdot P^{c_i}).
\end{aligned}
$$

5 Mutual Authentication Protocol in Heterogeneous Environment

In order to accomplish the mutual authentication between users in a variety of cryptosystems, we now extend our fundamental identity-based authentication protocol to a more complex and heterogeneous environment, where the authentications between the PKI-based and the identity-based systems can be supported.

The extended protocol consists of four entities: KGC, Authorized Nodes, Users and Certification Authority (CA).

The KGC and Authorized Nodes maintains status quo as the fundamental protocol in Sect. 4.

Users: Users include those in both PKI-based and identity-based systems.

Certification Authority: The CA generates public and private key pairs for users in the PKI-based system.

The extended protocol is presented as follows:

5.1 Initialization

The KGC creates two multiplicative cyclic groups $\mathbb{G}$ and $\mathbb{G}_T$ of order q, where $\mathbb{G}$ is generated by g, and performs a bilinear pairing $e : \mathbb{G} \times \mathbb{G} \to \mathbb{G}_T$.

Then the KGC decides three hash functions $H : \{0, 1\}* \to \mathbb{Z}_q$, $H_1 : \{0, 1\}* \to \mathbb{G}$ and $H_2 : \mathbb{G}_T \to \mathbb{Z}_q$.

The public parameter of the system is $par = \{\mathbb{G}, \mathbb{G}_T, e, q, g, H, H_1, H_2\}$.

5.2 Key Generation for Authorized Nodes

This step maintains status quo as the fundamental protocol in Sect. 4.2.

5.3 Key Generation for Users

1) *For users in the identity-based system:*
   This step maintains status quo as the fundamental protocol in Sect. 4.3.
2) *For users in the PKI-based system:*
   When a given user i decides to join the PKI-based system, the CA selects a random number $x_i \in \mathbb{Z}_q^*$ as the private key for the user. Thus, the associated public key is $pk_i = g^{x_i}$.

5.4 Authentication

When user j in the PKI-based system requests to interact with user i in the identity-based system, the authentication is performed as shown in Fig. 2.

1) User i selects a random number $t_1 \in \mathbb{Z}_q^*$, and then sends $T_1 = H_1(User_i)^{t_1}$ to user j;
2) User j selects a random number $t_2 \in \mathbb{Z}_q^*$ and sends it to user i;
3) Upon receiving t_2, user i selects $R \in \mathbb{G}_T$ and computes $T = e(usk_i^{t_1+t_2}, pk_j) \cdot R$, $h = H_2(R)$. Then user i sends T and h to user j;
4) Once T and h are received, user j computes $c_i = H(g^{k_i}, User_i)$, $R' = T/e(T_1 \cdot H_1(User_i)^{t_2}, pk_j^{k_i} \cdot P^{sk_j \cdot c_i})$ and $h' = H_2(R')$.

   If $h = h'$, user j sends R' to user i. Otherwise, the authentication fails and j returns $\perp$.

5) Upon receiving R' from user j, the authentication is completed successfully only if $R = R'$.

We also prove the correctness of such verification as follows:

$$T = e(usk_i^{t_1+t_2}, pk_j) \cdot R$$
$$= e(H_1(User_i)^{(k_i+c_i \cdot s) \cdot (t_1+t_2)}, g^{sk_j}) \cdot R$$
$$= e(H_1(User_i)^{t_1+t_2}, g^{sk_j \cdot (k_i+c_i \cdot s)}) \cdot R$$
$$= e(T_1 \cdot H_1(User_i)^{t_2}, pk_j^{k_i} \cdot P^{sk_j \cdot c_i}) \cdot R.$$

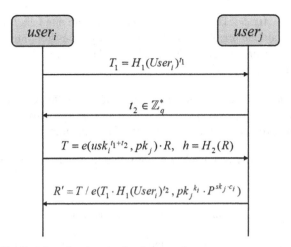

Fig. 2. Mutual authentication between heterogeneous systems.

6   Security and Performance Analysis

In this section, we evaluate the security and performance of the proposed protocol through the comparisons with existing benchmarks.

6.1   Security Analysis

We first analyze the security of the protocol from the following perspectives.

Mutual Authentication: Only the user with private key usk_i can calculate $e(usk_i^{t_1+t_2}, pk_j)$, which is equivalent to $e(T_1 \cdot H_1(User_i)^{t_2}, pk_j^{k_i} \cdot P^{sk_j \cdot c_i})$, in the meantime, only the user with private key sk_j can calculate $R' = T/e(T_1 \cdot H_1(User_i)^{t_2}, pk_j^{k_i} \cdot P^{sk_j \cdot c_i})$, which is equivalent to R. Therefore, the mutual authentication is achieved.

Denial of Service (DoS) Attack: Since keys are generated by distributed nodes on the blockchain in our protocol, the remaining nodes can still cooperate even if some nodes are compromised. Therefore, it is resistant to the DoS attack.

Replay Attack: Since random numbers t_1 and t_2 are introduced in our protocol, in cases where the user receives repeated T_1 or t_2, the authentication will be considered illegal. Therefore, it is resistant to the replay attack.

Internal Attack: The internal attacker may obtain the identity of the users, while the secret value s selected by the KGC and the private key share of the authorized nodes cannot be observed, thus they cannot obtain the user's private key. Therefore, it is resistant to the internal attack.

External Attack: Even though an external attacker may obtain the public parameters of the system, the secret value s cannot be calculated unless the discrete logarithm problem is solved. In other words, the external attacker cannot get the user's private key. Therefore, it is resistant to the external attack.

Man-in-the-Middle Attack: Due to the existence of random numbers t_1 and t_2, the middleman cannot obtain the private keys of the parties by eavesdropping. In other words, message tampering cannot be performed by the attacker. Therefore, it is resistant to the man-in-the-middle attack.

Impersonation Attack: IN cases where an attacker decides to impersonate a user during authentication, to get the private key of at least one party is equivalent to solving the discrete logarithm problem. Therefore, it is resistant to the impersonation attack.

Next, we compare our extended protocol in Sect. 5 with existing benchmarks, as shown in Table 1.

Table 1. Comparisons on security.

	[15]	[20]	[21]	[22]	[23]	Our work
Mutual authentication	√	×	√	×	√	√
Heterogeneous authentication	√	×	×	×	×	√
Resist DoS attack	×	√	×	√	√	√
Resist replay attack	√	√	√	√	×	√

6.2 Performance Analysis

Let T_{ecpm} be the elliptic curve point multiplication operation, T_{par} be the bilinear pairing, T_{mtp} be the map-to-point operation, T_{exp} be the exponential operation, and T_{mul} be the multiplication operation carried out by the elements in the group respectively. Also, (I) denotes our fundamental authentication protocol in Sect. 4 and (II) denotes the extended protocol in Sect. 5. As a result, we compare our protocols with existing benchmarks in terms of computational costs, as shown in Table 2. We also provide the computation time based on Charm 0.43 [24] in Python in Table 3. Note that each instance is the mean derived from 100 tests and the configuration of the experimental equipment is: Intel(R) Core (TM) I5-6300HQ CPU @ 2.30 ghz, 4 GB RAM.

Next, we compare our work with existing schemes over the communication costs as shown in Table 4, where $|\mathbb{G}|$ represents the size of the elements in group $\mathbb{G}(512\text{bit})$, $|\mathbb{G}_T|$ represents the size of the elements in group $\mathbb{G}_T(512\text{bit})$, $|\mathbb{Z}_q|$ represents the size of elements in $\mathbb{Z}_q(160 \text{ bit})$.

Table 2. Comparisons on computational cost (ms).

		Computational cost	Total cost
[15]	User	$4\,T_{mtp} + 9\,T_{ecpm} + 2\,T_{\exp} + 6\,T_{mul} = 83.526$	171.056
	ISP	$4\,T_{mtp} + 10\,T_{ecpm} + 2\,T_{\exp} + 6\,T_{mul} = 87.530$	
[20]	Prover	$T_{par} + T_{mtp} + 2\,T_{\exp} = 22.874$	49.279
	Verifier	$2\,T_{par} + T_{mtp} + 2\,T_{\exp} + T_{mul} = 26.405$	
[21]	User	$T_{mtp} + 3\,T_{ecpm} + 3\,T_{\exp} = 36.418$	62.549
	CSP	$2\,T_{par} + T_{ecpm} + 3\,T_{\exp} + T_{mul} = 26.131$	
[23]	User	$3\,T_{ecpm} + T_{\exp} = 17.044$	41.643
	Service provider	$3\,T_{par} + T_{ecpm} + 2\,T_{\exp} + T_{mul} = 24.599$	
(I)	Prover	$2\,T_{\exp} + T_{mtp} = 19.374$	50.842
	Verifier	$2\,T_{par} + T_{mtp} + 3\,T_{\exp} + 2\,T_{mul} = 31.468$	
(II)	User in the identity-based system	$T_{par} + T_{mtp} + 2\,T_{\exp} + T_{mul} = 22.905$	50.873
	User in the PKI-based system	$T_{par} + T_{mtp} + 3\,T_{\exp} + 2\,T_{mul} = 27.968$	

Table 3. Computation time (ms).

Operation	Time
T_{ecpm}	4.004
$T_{\exp}$	5.032
T_{mtp}	9.310
T_{par}	3.500
T_{mul}	0.031

Table 4. Comparisons on communication costs (bit).

	Communication cost
[15]	$12\,|\mathbb{G}| + 2\,|\mathbb{Z}_q| = 6464$
[20]	$|\mathbb{G}_T| + |\mathbb{G}| + 2\,|\mathbb{Z}_q| = 1344$
[21]	$2\,|\mathbb{G}| + 2\,|\mathbb{Z}_q| = 1344$
[23]	$|\mathbb{G}_T| + 2\,|\mathbb{G}| + 2\,|\mathbb{Z}_q| = 1856$

(*continued*)

Table 4. (*continued*)

	Communication cost
(I)	$2 |\mathbb{G}| + |\mathbb{Z}_q| = 1184$
(II)	$2 |\mathbb{G}_T| + |\mathbb{G}| + 2 |\mathbb{Z}_q| = 1856$

7 Conclusion

In this paper, we first propose an identity-based authentication protocol with distributed authorization centers based on blockchain. To mitigate the risk of single point of failure, the (t, n)-threshold secret sharing technology is applied such that at least t out of n nodes on the blockchain can cooperate to generate private keys for users. Meanwhile, the protocol uses the identity of users as the public key to facilitate certification management. Furthermore, we also extend our fundamental protocol to a more complex heterogeneous environment where authentication can be performed mutually between the PKI-based and the identity-based systems. Finally, we evaluate our work through the analysis and comparisons with the benchmarks.

Acknowledgment. This work is supported by the science and technology project in State Grid Corporation of China entitled "Research on Information Security Supporting and Identity Management Key Technologies for Energy and Power Blockchains" (Grant No. 5700-202158411A-0-0-00).

References

1. Liao, S., Wu, J., Mumtaz, S., et al.: Cognitive balance for fog computing resource in internet of things: an edge learning approach. IEEE Trans. Mob. Comput. **21**(5), 1596–1608 (2022)
2. Xu, J.: Analysis and improvement on security of authentication scheme based on password. J. Shandong Univ. Technol. (Nat. Sci. Ed.) **33**(03), 19–22 (2019)
3. Hemalatha, S.: A systematic review on Fingerprint based Biometric Authentication System. In: 2020 International Conference on Emerging Trends in Information Technology and Engineering. IEEE, New York (2020)
4. Ma, Z., Yang, Y., Liu, X., et al.: EmIr-Auth: eye movement and iris-based portable remote authentication for smart grid. IEEE Trans. Industr. Inf. **16**(10), 6597–6606 (2020)
5. Chen, X.L., Su, H., Yang, D.Y.: Application of Kerberos in authentication of existing system. Cyberspace Secur. **13**(01), 23–28 (2022)
6. Wang, J., Wu, L., Choo, K.-K.R., He, D.: Blockchain-based anonymous authentication with key management for smart grid edge computing infrastructure. IEEE Trans. Ind. Inf. **16**(3), 1984–1992 (2020)
7. Vijayakumar, P., Obaidat, M.S., Azees, M., et al.: Efficient and secure anonymous authentication with location privacy for IoT-based WBANs. IEEE Trans. Ind. Inf. **16**(4), 2603–2611 (2020)
8. Yang, W., Wang, N., Guan, Z., et al.: A practical cross device federated learning framework over 5G networks. IEEE Wirel. Commun. **99**, 1 (2022)

9. Shamir, A.: Identity-based cryptosystems and signature schemes. In: Blakley, G.R., Chaum, D. (eds.) CRYPTO 1984. LNCS, vol. 196, pp. 47–53. Springer, Heidelberg (1985). https://doi.org/10.1007/3-540-39568-7_5

10. Zeng, S.Q., Huo, R., Huang, T., et al.: Survey of blockchain: principle, progress and application. J. Commun. **41**(01), 134–151 (2020)

11. Lin, X., Wu, J., Bashir, A.K., et al.: Blockchain-based incentive energy-knowledge trading in IoT: Joint power transfer and AI design. IEEE Internet Things J. **9**(16), 14685–14698 (2022)

12. Shamir, A.: How to share a secret. Commun. ACM **22**(11), 612–613 (2011)

13. Park, S., Kim, H., Ryou, J.: Utilizing a lightweight PKI mechanism to guarantee a secure service in a cloud environment. J. Supercomput. **74**(12), 6988–7002 (2018). https://doi.org/10.1007/s11227-018-2506-3

14. Xu, J., Xue, K., Tian, H., et al.: An identity management and authentication scheme based on redactable blockchain for mobile networks. IEEE Trans. Veh. Technol. **69**(6), 6688–6698 (2020)

15. Jiang, Z.T., Xu, J.J.: Efficient heterogeneous cross-domain authentication scheme based on proxy blind signature in cloud environment. Comput. Sci. **47**(11), 60–67 (2020)

16. Tan, C., Chen, M.J.: Research on distributed identity authentication mechanism of IoT device based on blockchain. Chin. J. Internet Things **4**(02), 70–77 (2020)

17. Li, S., Zhang, T., Yu, B., et al.: A provably secure and practical PUF-based end-to-end mutual authentication and key exchange protocol for IoT. IEEE Sens. J. **21**(4), 5487–5501 (2021)

18. Irshad, A., Chaudhry, S.A., Alomari, O.A., et al.: A novel pairing-free lightweight authentication protocol for mobile cloud computing framework. IEEE Syst. J. **15**(3), 3664–3672 (2021)

19. Zhang, W.F., Lei, L.T., Wang, X.M., et al.: Secure and efficient authentication and key agreement protocol using certificateless aggregate signature for cloud service oriented VANET. Acta Electron. Sin. **48**(09), 1814–1823 (2020)

20. Tang, F., Bao, J., Huang, Y., et al.: Identity-based identification scheme without trusted party against concurrent attacks. Secur. Commun. Netw. **2020**, 1–9 (2020)

21. He, D., Kumar, N., Khan, M.K., et al.: Efficient privacy-aware authentication scheme for mobile cloud computing services. IEEE Syst. J. **12**(2), 1621–1631 (2018)

22. Karati, A., Amin, R., Islam, S.H., et al.: Provably secure and lightweight identity-based authenticated data sharing protocol for cyber-physical cloud environment. IEEE Trans. Cloud Comput **9**(1), 318–330 (2021)

23. Chaudhry, S.A., Kim, I.L., Rho, S., et al.: An improved anonymous authentication scheme for distributed mobile cloud computing services. Clust. Comput. **22**(1), 1595–1609 (2019)

24. Akinyele, J.A., Garman, C., Miers, I., et al.: Charm: a framework for rapidly prototyping cryptosystems. J. Cryptogr. Eng. **3**(2), 111–128 (2013)

Performance Evaluation of Transmission Protocols Based on Satellite Networks

Wentai Xiao and Kuayue Chen[✉]

School of Electronic and Information Engineering, Beijing Jiaotong University,
Beijing 100044, China
21120033@bjtu.edu.cn

Abstract. In face of the continuous expansion of user scale under
the rapid development of the Internet, communication devices in many
remote areas and complex natural scenarios cannot use terrestrial networks for communication. Satellite networks have become the first choice
for communication in complex environments. However, the characteristics of long delay, high bit error rate and intermittent link interruption
of satellite networks leads to existing terrestrial transmission protocols
such as TCP have always been poor performance in satellite networks
environment. TCP protocol interprets the high frequency of packet loss
in satellite networks as network congestion and implements certain congestion control measures to prevent further congestion. However, most of
the packet loss in satellite networks is caused by transmission errors and
congestion control measures will have no help at this time. Therefore,
the transmission protocol needs to be improved and optimized for the
satellite network environment to make full use of the link. This paper
first introduces the different variants of the TCP protocol, and then introduces the current new network protocol QUIC, finally uses NS-3 network
emulators to compare their performance and points out the improvement
direction of satellite network transmission protocol.

Keywords: Satellite networks · Transmission protocol · Network
simulator 3

1 Introduction

The Transmission Control Protocol (TCP) complements the Internet Protocol
(IP) and is therefore also known as the TCP/IP protocol. The TCP protocol can
provide reliable, ordered, and error-checked stream-based transmission services
for hosts in the network. TCP is a connection-oriented transmission protocol,
before data transmission both hosts need to perform three-way handshake to
establish a connection. After the data transmission is completed, two hosts terminate the connection by four times interactions. During the data transmission
process, TCP adopts the retransmission mechanism, congestion control and flow
control to ensure transmission quality. It has been widely used since it was
proposed in the 1970s, even nowadays it also plays an important role in data
transmission. The current mainstream application, such as HyperText Transfer

© The Author(s), under exclusive license to Springer Nature Singapore Pte Ltd. 2023
W. Quan (Ed.): ICENAT 2022, CCIS 1696, pp. 172–183, 2023.
https://doi.org/10.1007/978-981-19-9697-9_14

Protocol (HTTP), Simple Mail Transfer Protocol (SMTP), File Transfer Protocol (FTP), etc., all based on TCP protocol.

However, in the satellite networks environment, the characteristics of high delay and high bit error rate completely deviate from the runtime environment of the TCP. In the terrestrial network environment, the transmission media is mostly based on optical fiber or network cable, so the bit error rate is low enough. And if there is a loss of packets, it is very likely that the network intermediate equipment randomly discards the packets due to network congestion. Therefore, TCP treats packet loss events as the basis for judging network congestion. When the network is congested, it will implement a backoff algorithm to reduce the amount of data prepare to send to prevent network congestion from aggravating. With the upgrading of network equipment, ability of various network equipment to process packets has been greatly enhanced, the probability of congestion is also reduced, and the congestion window will be maintained at a high level. Therefore, TCP protocol has good performance in terrestrial networks environments. In satellite networks, the scenes of high delay and high bit error rate is ubiquitous. High delay will cause the congestion window expands slowly, and high bit error rate will lead to frequently start the backoff mechanism, reducing the congestion window. Both of the above situations will result poor performance in throughput. Therefore, how to adapt the transmission protocol to the high delay and high bit error rate environment is one of the main problems in the development of satellite networks.

This paper shows the performance of different transmission protocols in the satellite network environment. In the Sect. 2, we mainly discuss the working mechanism and characteristics of different transmission protocols. Section 3 introduces the experimental topology based on NS-3 and analyzes the results. In Sect. 4, we conclude this paper and provides the improvement direction of the satellite network transmission protocol.

2 Transmission Protocols

In this section the main characteristics of some TCP variants and new protocol are introduced, we mainly focus on their working mechanism, advantages and disadvantages.

2.1 TCP Reno

TCP Reno is an early version of TCP protocol, which is mainly divided into four states:

Slow Start. It is the initial state when connection is established, and congestion window increases exponentially in this state.

Congestion Avoidance. This state is entered when the congestion window exceeds the slow start threshold, during this state congestion window increases linearly.

Fast Retransmission. When the sender receives three consecutive repeated acknowledgments, it immediately retransmits the lost message without waiting for the retransmission timer to expire.

Fast Recovery. After fast retransmission state, fast recovery state entered. In this state, slow start threshold is set to half of the current congestion window, and the size of the congestion window is set to the slow start threshold [1]. Each time another duplicate packet is received, congestion window will increase by one. When the new acknowledgment (ACK) is received, congestion window is set to slow start threshold, and then the sender exits this state and enters congestion avoidance state again.

Due to the existence of slow-start state, TCP Reno can gradually detect the current network status and execute a backoff algorithm when the network is congested, which largely ensures the smoothness of terrestrial network environment [2]. However, when packet loss events occur continuously, TCP Reno will repeatedly enter fast retransmission state and fast recovery state, and congestion window will be halved each time it enters the fast recovery state. As the congestion window continues to shrink, throughput of Reno will significantly reduce.

2.2   TCP NewReno

TCP NewReno makes some modifications to the algorithm of the data sender on the basis of TCP Reno: two new concepts are added in the fast recovery state: partial response ACK and recovery response ACK. These two kinds of ACK messages are used to distinguish the situation of losing multiple messages in one congestion from multiple congestion. The ACK received in the fast retransmission state is recorded as ACK_x. And when first ACK_x has been received, the packet with the largest sequence that has been sent is recorded as PKT_{max}. When the ACK_x received is not a PKT_{max}'s acknowledgement message, $ACKx$ is a partial response ACK_x, and when ACK_x happens to be a PKT_{max} response message, ACK_x is a recovery response ACK.

When receiving a partial response during fast recovery state, sender will retransmit the next packet of the packet confirmed by the partial response, and continue to send new data packets if the congestion window allows. When receiving the recovery response, the sender considers that all discarded packets have been retransmitted, so it sets congestion window equals to slow start threshold and exits fast recovery state. Therefore, when multiple packets are lost at one time, NewReno will exit the fast recovery state until retransmitting all lost packets and receiving a recovery response, avoiding the continuous decrease of congestion window caused by entering the fast recovery state multiple times. In this case, the robustness and throughput of TCP got improved [3].

However, without selective retransmission, TCP NewReno retransmits at most one packet per round-trip time (RTT), which is still inefficient. In addition, the generation of duplicate ACKs can be caused by replication of ACK or data segments by the network, in which case the sender will still retransmit.

2.3   TCP Bic

TCP Bic proposes a binary search algorithm for searching the optimal congestion window. The algorithm sets a multiplicative reduction factor β, and also uses a multiplicative reduction method to reduce the congestion window. When congestion occurs, the size of congestion window is W_{max}, and after multiplication reduction the congestion window is W_{min}, which equals to $\beta \cdot W_{max}$. The Bic algorithm considers that the optimal congestion window W is larger than the multiplicatively reduced congestion window W_{min}, and smaller than the congestion window W_{max} which makes the link just saturated [4].

After the fast recovery state, the Bic algorithm uses binary search between W_{min} and W_{max} to find the optimal congestion window, that is, every time an ACK packet is received, the congestion window is set to the midpoint of W_{min} and W_{max}, and the value of W_{min} is updated at the same time. When congestion window is close to W_{max}, the congestion window will grow slowly. If there is no packet loss at this time, it will continue to grow at a slow rate until reaches the W_{max}, so the congestion window can maintain a good stability around the W_{max}. When the congestion window exceeds W_{max}, algorithm considers that the current congestion window is not a saturation point, more data can be accommodated in the network, so a larger congestion window value is waiting to be explored. Therefore, Bic algorithm uses a window growth function that is symmetric to the binary search to detect the maximum value of the congestion window.

Although the Bic algorithm has good stability, it also has shortcomings. Since the growth of congestion window in the Bic algorithm are driven by ACK packets, the window growth function of the Bic algorithm is more aggressive than the standard TCP protocol when the RTT is short. So there is a problem of unfair bandwidth competition.

2.4   TCP Cubic

TCP Bic achieves good scalability and stability in high-speed networks. But TCP Bic's window growth function is still too aggressive for standard TCP, especially in short RTT or low-speed environment. So with TCP Cubic, Cubic retains the stability of TCP Bic, while simplifying window control and enhancing fairness. Cubic replaces the congestion window growth function of TCP Bic with a cubic function (including concave function and convex function part), which greatly simplifies the window adjustment algorithm of TCP Bic. A key feature of Cubic is that its window growth depends only on the time between two congestion events. Therefore, window growth has nothing to do with RTT. This feature allows Cubic streams to compete with other TCP variants in the same network without relying on the connection's RTT, solving the problem of poor BIC fairness [5]. This feature enhances the TCP friendliness of the protocol when the RTT is short, since the window growth rate is fixed.

The window growth function of Cubic is a cubic function, which is very similar to the window growth function of TCP Bic. When a packet loss event occurs,

Cubic will record the size of the congestion window at this time as W_{max}, and a small coefficient β performs a multiplicative reduction of the congestion window, where β is a window reduction constant, followed by normal fast retransmission and fast recovery. After entering congestion avoidance from the fast recovery state, the concave contour of the cubic function is used to increase the window, and then the convex contour of the cubic function is used to start exploring a new maximum window [6].

The window growth function of Cubic is described as follows:

$$W(t) = C(t - K)^3 + W_{max} \tag{1}$$

where $W(t)$ is the size of congestion window at time t, C is a constant parameter used to control the convergence of algorithm, t is the time when the last packet loss event happend, K is the time taken for congestion window to increase from W to W_{max}. The value of K can be inferred from $W(0) = \beta \cdot W_{max}$. Every time an ACK packet is received during the congestion avoidance state, Cubic uses Equation (1) to calculate the congestion window growth rate at the next RTT.

Although the Cubic algorithm is RTT independent in terms of the growth of the congestion window, there is also some drawback within: when the bandwidth of link changes, it will take a long time for Cubic to enter the stage of detecting the next W_{max} from the stable point. And it is more likely to cause bufferbloat, in the Reno algorithm, if the link is congested due to the large buffer, its RTT will also become larger, so the growth of congestion window will also become slower, but in the Cubic algorithm, the growth of congestion window has nothing to do with RTT, and it will be easier to aggravate the link burden.

2.5   TCP Westwood

Different from the congestion control based on packet loss, TCP Westwood monitors the reception rate of ACK packets and estimates the data transmission rate. When the sender detects packet loss, timeout or 3 repeated ACK packets, the sender sets the congestion window and slow start threshold according to the estimated sending rate.

TCP Westwood evaluates the bandwidth of the current sampling point as follows:

$$b_k = \frac{d_k}{t_k - t_{k-1}} \tag{2}$$

where d_k represents the amount of data sent between t_k and t_{k-1}. t_k, t_{k-1} represent the current time when the ACK packet is received and the time when the last ACK was received. In order to remove the rate sampling noise caused by the ACK packet, Westwood applies a low-pass filter to the sampling rate to obtain the low-frequency part of available bandwidth. The discrete-time filter is generated by Eq. (3) as follows:

$$\hat{b}_k = a\hat{b}_{k-1} + \frac{(1-a)}{2}[b_k + b_{k-1}] \tag{3}$$

It can be considered that the current estimation of bandwidth is a smooth sampling of the last estimation of bandwidth and the last two bandwidths. Westwood avoids too conservative window reduction operation and adopts additive increase and adaptive decrease congestion control mechanism. Compared with the congestion control algorithm based on packet loss, Westwood is more suitable for TCP connections of wireless links. It not only improves the throughput of wireless networks, but also has good fairness and interoperability with existing networks [7]. TCP Westwood proposed a similar idea to google BBR as early as the late 1990s, estimating network capacity by continuously measuring bandwidth and minimum RTT.

2.6   TCP Vegas

TCP Vegas controls the congestion window by measuring the round-trip time of packets. The slow-start algorithm is improved in Vegas and a more cautious way is used to increase the congestion window to reduce unnecessary packet loss. Compared with TCP Reno, congestion window of Vegas is doubled every two RTTs. Therefore, the congestion window will not change during one of the RTTs, and the sender will compare the difference between the actual sending rate and the expected sending rate in real time. When the difference reaches the threshold γ, Vegas enters the congestion avoidance phase.

Vegas calculates the expected sending rate and the actual sending rate during the process of data transmission and estimates the congestion in the network through the difference between the expected and the actual [8]. The calculation method of the expected sending rate is:

$$Excepted = cwnd/baseRTT \tag{4}$$

and the calculation method of the actual rate is:

$$Actual = cwnd/RTT \tag{5}$$

where $cwnd$ represents the current congestion window size, RTT is the round-trip time, and $baseRTT$ refers to the round-trip time of a data packet when the network is not congested. In general, $baseRTT$ is the minimum value of the round-trip time. Vegas satisfies the following inequality relationship by adjusting the size of congestion window.

$$\alpha \le D = (Expected - Actual) \cdot baseRTT \le \beta \tag{6}$$

where α and β are congestion thresholds, which are used to judge whether there is congestion in the network. When $D < \alpha$, it means that the network is in good condition. When the next ACK packet arrives, the size of the congestion window is linearly increased to make full use of the bandwidth. When $D > \beta$, it indicates that there is congestion in the network or is about to occur. When the next ACK packet arrives, the size of congestion window needs to be reduced to decrease the sending rate. Vegas reduces the congestion window by 75% instead of 50%.

In terms of the retransmission mechanism, Vegas checks whether it times out every time it receives a duplicate ACK response. If it times out, Vegas will directly retransmit the packet without extra waiting. This makes packet loss detection more timely.

2.7   TCP BBR

TCP BBR is a new TCP congestion control algorithm published by Google. It has been widely used within Google and with the official release of Linux kernel version 4.9. The name of BBR is an acronym for Bottleneck Bandwith and Round-trip propagation time, indicating that the main operating mechanism of BBR: congestion control is performed by detecting two indicators of bandwidth and RTT.

BBR believes that the maximum throughput that a network link can transmit depends on the physical delay round-trip propagation time, abbreviated as RTprop in BBR, on the network link and the bandwidth of the segment with the lowest speed on the link, bottle-neck bandwidth, abbreviated as BtlBw. Their product is called BDP (Bottle-neck Bandwidth Delay Production),that is the maximum amount of data buffered by the link is filled with data without filling the intermediate link device [9]. What BBR pursues is the optimal point of data transmission rate reaching BDP.

In order to estimate the optimal value of BDP, BBR has designed four operating states, namely STARTUP, DRAIN, PROBE_BW, PROBE_RTT.

STARTUP. When the connection is established, the BBR gradually increases the sending rate in slow start state as stander TCP does, and then calculates the BDP according to the ACK packets received. When BDP no longer increases, BBR enters the congestion avoidance state, this process is completely regardless of whether there is packet loss. During the slow start state, since the buffer of the intermediate device will hardly be filled, the minimum delay in this process is the initial estimated minimum delay and the maximum bandwidth at the end of slow start is the initial estimated maximum delay.

DRAIN. In order to empty the data that may be filled into the buffer during the STARTUP state, BBR will enter the DRAIN state, during which the transmission rate will be reduced. If there is data in the buffer, reducing the transmission rate will decrease transmission delays, until the delay stops falling.

PROBE_BW. After the DRAIN state, a steady state is entered, which alternates the probe bandwidth and delay. The PROBE_BW state is a positive feedback system: periodically try to increase the packet sending rate, and if the rate of received acknowledgments also increases, increase the packet sending rate further. Specifically, set every 8 RTTs as a period, in the first RTT, try to send data at a speed of 5/4 of the estimated bandwidth, and in the second RTT, in order to drain the extra packets sent by the previous RTT, send data at 3/4 of the estimated bandwidth. In the remaining 6 RTTs, use the estimated bandwidth to send packets (the estimated bandwidth may be updated in the previous process). This mechanism enables BBR to rapidly increase the sending rate when the bandwidth increases, but it takes a certain time for the BBR to decrease to a stable level when the bandwidth decreases [10].

PROBE_RTT. In addition to bandwidth detection, BBR also performs minimum delay detection. Every 10s, if the minimum RTT does not change, that is a lower delay is not found, the PROBE_RTT state is entered. This state lasts only 200ms and the congestion window is fixed at 4 packets during this time, that is, almost no packets are sent. The minimum delay measured during this time period serves as the new delay estimate.

Through the periodic operation of the above four states, the BBR algorithm can more accurately estimate the amount of data that can be carried in the current link, and dynamically adjust the size of the congestion window and the data transmission rate according to BDP and RTT, because the BBR algorithm does not consider the loss of packet. Therefore, the packet loss is no longer a signal of congestion. In the environment of high bit error rate, the BBR algorithm has better performance.

2.8   QUIC

The full name of the QUIC protocol is Quick UDP Internet Connections, which is a new application layer protocol based on the UDP protocol. The main feature of the QUIC protocol is the 0-RTT handshake and forward security, which improves efficiency and security during the connection establishment and data transmission [11]. At the same time, the QUIC protocol implements the reliable transmission characteristics of the TCP protocol. Especially in the data packet retransmission stage. Further more, it can distinguish the original data packet from the retransmitted data packet, which solves the problem of retransmission ambiguity in the standard TCP protocol. In terms of congestion control, QUIC implements a variety of TCP congestion control methods at the application layer, such as NewReno, Cubic, BBR, etc., which can be set very flexibly, even customize private algorithms according to specific scenarios and set a unique setting for each QUIC connection.

3   Testbed and Experiment

In order to test the throughput performance of different transmission protocols in the satellite network environment, we build the following topology in NS-3:

As shown in the Fig. 1, the topology consists of two terminal nodes and two routers, one terminal node acts as an FTP-like server, and the other terminal node acts as a client. The two end nodes communicate through two routers.

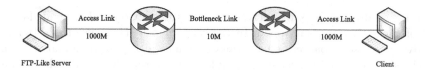

Fig. 1. Testbed topology in NS-3.

Select the communication environment between LEO satellites for simulation, the bandwidth of the two access links connecting the terminal node to the router is set to 1000M, and the propagation delay of access link is fixed at 10 ms; the bandwidth of the bottleneck link between the routers is set to 10M, 50 ms. In addition, set up a FIFO queue on the bottleneck link between routers, the queue can hold a maximum of 100 packets, when the queue is full, it will drop one packet from the tail, at the same time, set packet drop rate in the bottleneck link to simulate the high bit error rate characteristics of satellite networks. We will conduct experiments under different round-trip times and pack drop rates using TCP Reno, TCP NewReno, TCP Bic, TCP Cubic, TCP Vegas, TCP Westwood, TCP BBR and QUIC.

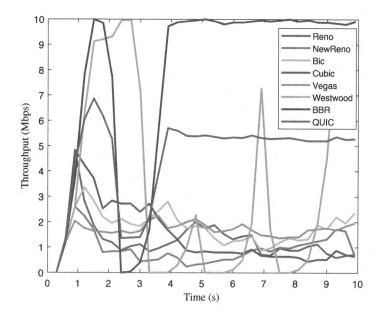

Fig. 2. 140 ms RTT and 1% drop rate.

Figure 2 shows the throughput performance of different transport protocols under the environment with RTT of 140 ms and packet loss rate of 1%. At the beginning of the experiment the BBR first goes through the STARTUP state, and sends fully to fill up the buffer in the network. During 2 s to 3 s, the BBR enters the DRAIN state, which reduces the congestion window to the minimum to detect the shortest RTT, and then the BBR periodically enters the PROBE_BW and PROBE_RTT states, and maintains the throughput at around 10 Mbps, which achieving better link utilization. During s to 10 s the performance of Westwood fluctuates greatly. The reason is that Westwood is extremely sensitive to bandwidth. After the buffer is filled, Westwood detects a drop in available bandwidth through RTT and immediately reduces the congestion window. After the buffer gradually released, the RTT is shortened accordingly, and the available bandwidth is increased. Therefore, Westwood will increase the congestion window again, and the final throughput will fluctuate in a jagged manner. In this experiment, the QUIC protocol adopts the BBR algorithm, so the performance of the QUIC protocol is roughly the same as that of the BBR, but since QUIC is based on the UDP protocol for datagram transmission, it is less efficient than streaming transmission in terms of splitting and assembling a large amount of data. Vegas is more sensitive to changes in RTT. During 0 s to 2 s, as the buffer is filled, the RTT continues to increase. Vegas constantly adjusts the congestion window to adapt to the RTT, and the final throughput is maintained at about 2 Mbps. Bic algorithm adopts the binary search method, which has a faster window growth rate than Reno and NewReno after the fast recovery state. In the presence of a bottleneck link, Cubic is more likely to cause bufferfloat to aggravate the congestion, resulting in its own throughput is also at a low level. Reno and NewReno are congestion control algorithms based on packet loss. In the high bit error rate and long RTT environment, the congestion window increases slowly, and due to frequent packet loss, the algorithm frequently starts the congestion control mechanism to continuously reduce the size of the congestion window, which eventually leads to poor performance in throughput.

Figure 3 shows the environment where the RTT is at 140 ms and the packet loss rate is at 2%. It can be seen that the performance of the congestion control algorithm based on bandwidth and RTT estimate is still better than the congestion control algorithm based on packet loss. Among them, the performance of BBR and Westwood algorithms is more outstanding, but due to the further increase of the packet loss rate, the frequent loss of ACK data packets leads to fluctuations in bandwidth calculation. With the passage of time, the packet loss-based congestion control algorithm's growth rate of the window has been much lower than the speed of the window shrinking, and the final throughput is only maintained at the level of about 0.5 Mbps.

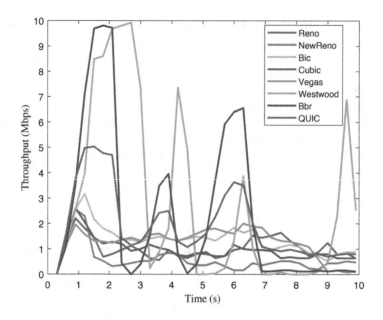

Fig. 3. 140 ms RTT and 2% drop rate.

4   Conclusion

This paper first introduces various transmission protocols currently used and tests the transmission performance of different transmission protocols in the satellite network environment. Finally, the following conclusions are drawn: the traditional transmission protocol based on packet loss does not perform well in the satellite network environment. The reason is that in the environment of unstable satellite network link quality, frequent packet loss will inevitably lead to frequent activation of the congestion control mechanism, which greatly affects transmission performance such as throughput. Congestion control algorithms based on bandwidth and RTT estimation have better performance in the satellite network environment. They do not consider the impact of packet loss on transmission, but directly adjust the amount of data that can be accommodated in the link. This design idea is not only suitable for the satellite network environment, but also for the long fat link in the terrestrial network environment.

In view of the fact that the current congestion control algorithm based on bandwidth and RTT estimation has problem that the bandwidth estimation fluctuates greatly when the bit error rate is high. In the future, the development of the transmission protocol in the satellite network environment can add an end-to-end data recovery mechanism, so as to further eliminate the influence of high bit error rate on link state estimation.

Acknowledgements. This paper is supported by the Fundamental Research Funds for the Central Universities under Grant No. 2020JBM013.

References

1. Ratna Pavani, K., Sreenath, N.: Performance evaluation of TCP-Reno, TCP-Newreno and TCp-westwood on burstification in an OBS network. In: 2012 18th International Conference on Advanced Computing and Communications (ADCOM), pp. 19–24 (2012). https://doi.org/10.1109/ADCOM.2012.6563579

2. Sisalem, D., Schulzrinne, H.: Congestion control in TCP: performance of binary congestion notification enhanced TCP compared to Reno and Tahoe TCP. In: Proceedings of 1996 International Conference on Network Protocols (ICNP-96), pp. 268–275 (1996). https://doi.org/10.1109/ICNP.1996.564953

3. Chaudhary, P., Kumar, S.: Comparative study of TCP variants for congestion control in wireless network. In: 2017 International Conference on Computing, Communication and Automation (ICCCA), pp. 641–646 (2017). https://doi.org/10.1109/CCAA.2017.8229880

4. Nirmala, M., Pujeri, R.V., Valarmathi, M.L.: An adaptive window increment based BIC TCP algorithm for improved data transfer in satellite network. In: 2015 International Conference on Advanced Computing and Communication Systems, pp. 1–8 (2015). https://doi.org/10.1109/ICACCS.2015.7324093

5. Miyazawa, K., Yamaguchi, S., Kobayashi, A.: Drain asynchronization for cyclic throughput fluctuation of cubic TCP and TCP BBR. In: 2020 IEEE 9th Global Conference on Consumer Electronics (GCCE), pp. 588–589 (2020). https://doi.org/10.1109/GCCE50665.2020.9291713

6. Abdeljaouad, I., Rachidi, H., Fernandes, S., Karmouch, A.: Performance analysis of modern TCP variants: a comparison of cubic, compound and new reno. In: 2010 25th Biennial Symposium on Communications, pp. 80–83 (2010). https://doi.org/10.1109/BSC.2010.5472999

7. Tekala, M.: TCP Westwood with limited congestion window. In: 2009 International Conference on Advanced Computer Control, pp. 687–692 (2009). https://doi.org/10.1109/ICACC.2009.142

8. Servati, S., Taheri, H., Nesary Moghaddam, M.: Performance enhancement for TCP Vegas in slow start phase over a satellite link. In: 2008 International Symposium on Telecommunications, pp. 510–514 (2008). https://doi.org/10.1109/ISTEL.2008.4651355

9. Miyazawa, K., Yamaguchi, S., Kobayashi, A.: Performance evaluation of TCP BBR and cubic TCP in smart devices downloading on Wi-Fi. In: 2020 IEEE International Conference on Consumer Electronics - Taiwan (ICCE-Taiwan), pp. 1–2 (2020). https://doi.org/10.1109/ICCE-Taiwan49838.2020.9258327

10. Sasaki, K., Yamaguchi, S.: A study on bottleneck bandwidth estimation based on acknowledge reception on TCP BBR. In: 2020 IEEE 44th Annual Computers, Software, and Applications Conference (COMPSAC), pp. 1107–1108 (2020). https://doi.org/10.1109/COMPSAC48688.2020.0-117

11. Quadrini, M.: Performance evaluation of a QUIC-based proxy architecture over a hybrid satellite-terrestrial backhaul network. In: 2019 International Symposium on Advanced Electrical and Communication Technologies (ISAECT), pp. 1–5 (2019). https://doi.org/10.1109/ISAECT47714.2019.9069738

Optimizing Communication Topology for Collaborative Learning Across Datacenters

Long Luo[1](✉)(iD), Shulin Yang[1], Wenjiao Feng[1], Hongfang Yu[1](✉)(iD), Gang Sun[1], and Bo Lei[2]

[1] University of Electronic Science and Technology of China,
Chengdu, People's Republic of China
llong@uestc.edu.cn

[2] China Telecom Corporation Limited Research Institute, Beijing, China
leibo@chinatelecom.cn

Abstract. Federated learning (FL) is emerging as an increasingly important and popular paradigm for collaboratively training high-quality machine learning (ML) models over massive amounts of data stored by geo-distributed datacenters. However, the communication efficiency of gradient aggregation during the training process comes as a primary bottleneck that impedes the adoption of FL, especially in cross-silo settings, as the available bandwidth of inter-datacenter links connecting data silos is often very limited. To improve the training efficiency of cross-silo FL between datacenters, we propose TOPOADOPT, an efficient communication topology design for gradient aggregation to overcome the communication bottleneck of cross-silo model training. TOPOADOPT uses multiple aggregators to share aggregation load and tree-based hierarchical aggregation to reduce bandwidth consumption from clients to aggregators. For better performance, it jointly optimizes the parameter assignment among aggregators and the construction of aggregation trees. We formulate this optimization problem as a mixed-integer nonlinear programming model and develop efficient algorithms to find satisfactory communication topologies in reasonable computational time. The experimental results show that TOPOADOPT achieves significant speedup, up to $5.2\times$, in gradient aggregation completion time compared to existing solutions.

Keywords: Collaborative learning · Communication · Topology

1 Introduction

The demand for model training is growing at an unprecedented rate with the great success and widespread application of ML techniques in many fields [1]. Traditionally, to improve the prediction performance of applications, model training is performed in the cloud, which requires collecting massive amounts of data into a single large-scale datacenter to learn high-quality ML models. In many industries, however, vast amounts of data are often owned by disparate organizations such as banks and hospitals that are unwilling or legally prohibited from sharing their privacy-sensitive data.

This work was funded by the National Natural Science Foundation of China (62102066), the Open Research Projects of Zhejiang Lab (No. 2022QA0AB02), and CNKLSTISS.

W. Quan (Ed.): ICENAT 2022, CCIS 1696, pp. 184–197, 2023.
https://doi.org/10.1007/978-981-19-9697-9_15

Cross-silo federated learning offers an attractive solution to build models without sharing the raw training data. It enables participating clients (*e.g.*, data silos or data center) to collaboratively train a global ML model by computing gradients locally and just exchanging gradients periodically over the network for global aggregation. Although the data centers have abundant computing power for local gradient computation, they are typically connected by reliable WAN links with very limited available bandwidth for gradient aggregation [2]. Compared to the computation time of local training within each data center, the communication time of gradient aggregation among multiple data centers contributes significantly to the overall training time and has become a performance bottleneck of cross-silo FL systems [3].

An effective way to improve training efficiency is to optimize the communication logic topology of gradient aggregation in each model training iteration [1,2,4–7]. The gradient aggregation conventionally relies on a star-like communication topology [8], in which a central aggregator combines gradients from all clients and pushes the aggregated results back to clients for model update. Obviously, the central single aggregator can easily become a candidate for congestion and slow down the aggregation speed. To prevent the aggregator from becoming a bottleneck, many recent works (*e.g.*, [2,5,7,9]) suggest using tree-like communication topology, which reduces the communication overhead from clients to the aggregator through hierarchical aggregation. Other recent work suggest employing multiple aggregators and carefully distributing model parameters and aggregation load among aggregators to alleviate aggregation load on a single node [4]. However, these proposals can be inefficient (as detailed in Sect. 2.2) in the cross-silo scenario because they are dedicated to data centers or cross-device scenarios, relying on specific topological properties of these scenarios that are not available in the cross-datacenter scenario.

Besides, a lot of current research works on cross-silo FL emphasize the privacy and security issues and often use techniques like additively homomorphic encryption to ensure no gradient is disclosed during aggregation [3]. The homomorphic encryption operation is well known to result in hundreds of times size inflation of gradients after encryption, which in turn greatly increases communication overhead and time. Therefore, optimizing the communication topology for FL is urgently needed to help FL silos take less time to complete the gradient aggregation across datacenters.

In this paper, we present TOPOADOPT, an efficient communication topology design for aggregating gradients across datacenters during collaborative training among FL silos. The key goal of TOPOADOPT is to increase model training efficiency by minimizing the communication time of gradient aggregation for FL silos. At the core, to avoid the communication bottleneck, TOPOADOPT leverages aggregator-centric and tree-like communication topology to perform hierarchical aggregation and employs multiple aggregators to balance aggregation load. For greater communication efficiency, it jointly optimizes the aggregator parameter assignment and aggregation tree construction when designing communication topologies. To find the near-optimal topologies in real time, we formulate this optimization problem and propose efficient searching algorithms based on problem decomposition and simple linear programming.

In summary, the contributions of this work are as follows.

1. To the best of our knowledge, this paper is the first work to explicitly optimize all components in an aggregator-centric communication topology that may affect the

time for FL silos to complete gradient aggregation across data centers, including aggregator parameter assignment and hierarchical aggregation tree construction.

2. A thorough analysis of the drawbacks of existing aggregator-centric topology designs (Sect. 2).
3. A mixed-integer nonlinear programming that describes the optimal communication topology design problem (Sect. 3.2), and efficient algorithms that solve this optimization problem efficiently (Sect. 3.3).
4. Numerical results show significant speedups in the completion of gradient aggregation under various workloads and FL scales (Sect. 4).

We introduce the background and motivation in Sect. 2, and propose our solution together with problem formulation, analysis and algorithm design in Sect. 3. Performance evaluation follows in Sect. 4 and Sect. 5 concludes the paper.

2 Background and Motivation

Cross-silo FL is becoming increasingly popular for collaborative training among different organizations such as banks [10], hospitals [11], and *etc*. In this paper, we focus on the communication optimization, especially optimizing the communication topology of gradient aggregation, in cross-silo FL systems. In what follows, we briefly introduce the background about communication in cross-silo FL and then examine related solutions by using an example to show their limitations and the motivation of this work.

2.1 Communication in Cross-Silo Federated Learning

Cross-silo FL generally has a small number of reliable data silos (*e.g.*, data centers or edge clusters) with abundant computing resources and datasets [12]. These geo-distributed data silos (a.k.a, clients) collaboratively learn an ML model, by sharing only model gradients rather than private datasets. Many of today's production distributed machine learning frameworks (*i.e.*, TensorFlow and MXNet) adopt the synchronous data parallelism paradigm, and the training of cross-silo FL is an iterative procedure. As Fig. 1 illustrates, in each training round, clients first train their local models to derive gradients in parallel and then upload calculated gradients for aggregation.

Among the gradient synchronization paradigms, the PS architecture [8] is popular and widely adopted in today's cross-silo FL systems. In this architecture, the orchestrator computes an overlay communication topology to control gradient aggregation based on the available bandwidth between data silos. Currently, these topologies are typically aggregator-centric where a logical central aggregator globally aggregates the gradients learning by participating clients over WAN connections. Thus, in this paper, we focus on optimizing the aggregator-centered communication topology for gradient aggregation in cross-silo FL.

2.2 Related Work and Their Limitations

Figure 2 demonstrates the space of existing solutions, using a FL instance with five participating data silos. In production cross-silo FL environment, star-like communication

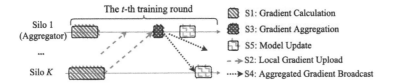

Fig. 1. The typical workflow (S1–S5) of the model training in cross-silo FL, in which communication (S2, S4) happens for gradient aggregation.

topology (STAR) is the most prevailing employed topology, where a single aggregator gathers gradients from all other silos using one-hop direct communication. Obviously, STAR can be suboptimal in terms of completion time (the time between the start of gradient transfer and the completion of aggregation) because it makes the aggregator a candidate for congestion. In fact, the performance of STAR directly depends on the bottleneck link. Taking the network in Fig. 2(a) as an example, the minimum bandwidth, 0.25 as link $d \rightarrow a$, of inter-silo communication links makes the STAR-based solution in Fig. 2(b) have a completion time of 4 if the size of gradients is 1.

To alleviate the performance bottleneck of STAR, recent works propose tree-like topologies (TREE) to perform hierarchical aggregation with the help of programmable switches [5,7] or NFV technologies [13]. In a TREE topology, each node adds up gradients from its children and itself and passes this sum to parent node for further aggregation, which reduces traffic going to aggregators and through the network. This design leverages the associativity property of gradient aggregation, namely $g_1 \oplus g_2 \oplus g_3 \oplus g_4 \equiv (g_1 \oplus g_2) \oplus (g_3 \oplus g_4)$ if $\oplus$ denotes the aggregation operation of gradients.

Existing TREE-based solutions (*e.g.*, [5,9]) typically are dedicated to high-performance data center networks. For example, the state-of-the-art TREE-based solution [9] may compute a symmetrical tree as in Fig. 2(c) and take a time of 2, 50% less than STAR, to complete the gradient aggregation for the FL instance in Fig. 2.

Another idea to improve communication efficiency is adopting multiple aggregators that each of which maintains different parts of parameters and undertakes the corresponding gradient aggregation task. The-state-of-the-art solution following this design is PSLD [4], which selects several nodes with the highest capabilities as aggregators and distributes parameters among these aggregators in proportion to their capabilities. For the FL example in Fig. 2, it chooses silo a and b as aggregators and builds a star-like topology for each aggregator as in Fig. 2(d), reducing completion time from 4 to 1.73.

To further improve performance, an idea is to use multiple aggregators in TREE as it is generally expected to achieve a shorter completion time than STAR. Unexpectedly, for this example, we observe that this TREE-based solution achieves a completion time of 1.73, same as STAR-based solution, when it is extended to use multiple aggregators as Fig. 2(e) shows. One reason is that existing solutions build aggregation trees for multiple aggregators independently, ignoring the bandwidth contention among multiple trees. Besides, existing parameter assignment solutions are designed for STAR and do not take into account the impact of TREE hierarchical aggregation on traffic load.

Moreover, we observe that the optimal topology, as in Fig. 2(f), can reduce aggregation time from 1.73 to 1.2 compared to the solutions in Fig. 2(d) and Fig. 2(e).

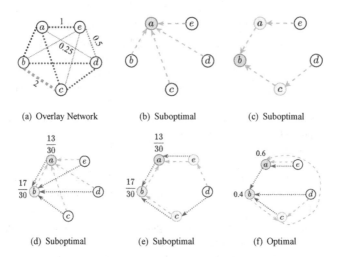

Fig. 2. Example of optimizing the communication topology for gradient aggregation of cross-silo FL. (a) An instance of FL with five geographically distributed data silos (a-e), and their possible direct communications can be abstracted as an overlay network, where the numbers next to links denote available bandwidth. Existing solutions based on STAR-like topology and TREE-like topology with a single aggregator in (b) and (c) and with multiple aggregators (each aggregator maintains a fraction of parameters proportional to the node bandwidth capacity) in (d) and (e) can be suboptimal. They take a time of 4, 2, 1.73, and 1.73, respectively, to complete if gradient data has a size of 1 (detailed discussion in Sect. 2.2), while the optimal topology in (f) reduces the completion time to 1.2.

Inspired by the limitations of existing solutions, we focus on the effect of communication topology on the duration of gradient aggregation and study how to design communication topologies that minimize the aggregation time of gradients in each round.

3   TOPOADOPT: Communication Topology and Parameter Distribution Optimization

In this section, we propose TOPOADOPT, an algorithm that runs at a centralized orchestrator to determine the communication topologies for periodical gradient aggregation during the training process.

3.1   Design Overview

At a high level, TOPOADOPT computes the communication topologies by taking into account end-to-end latency and available bandwidth between silos to control gradient aggregation, as shown in Fig. 3. Each pair of silos uses probing packets to measure end-to-end delays and available bandwidths and reports them to the orchestrator. TOPOADOPT then constructs a connectivity graph among silos and based on which designs communication topologies. Basically, TOPOADOPT follows the design of hierarchical tree topology and adopts multiple aggregator instances for parameter maintenance and gradient aggregation. The core idea of TOPOADOPT is to jointly optimize the selection of

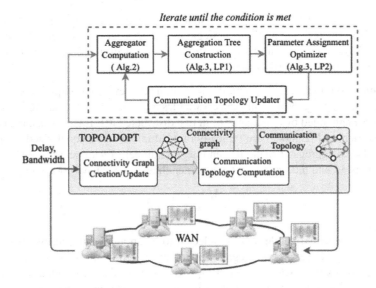

Fig. 3. Overview of TOPOADOPT

aggregators, the parameter assignment among aggregators, and the tree-like aggregation topology with each aggregator as the root, so that the gradient aggregation in each communication round takes less time to complete.

3.2 Problem Formulation

Networks: We consider a set of data silos $\mathcal{N}$ that participate in collaborative learning. We use a complete connectivity directed graph $G = (\mathcal{N}, E)$ to capture the possible direct communications among these data silos. Each pair of silos is generally connected in G by a link except for those blocked from communicating by specific configurations of NAT or firewall. By using communication link $\ell(i, j) \in E$, silo i can directly transmit its gradients to silo j. The data transfer over link $\ell(i, j)$ experiences a propagation delay $d^{\text{pr}}_{\ell(i,j)}$ depending on distance and queuing delays and a transmission delay $d^{\text{tr}}_{\ell(i,j)}$ depending on available bandwidth $b_{\ell(i,j)}$ and gradient size. The time interval $d_{\ell(i,j)}$ between the beginning of transferring gradients from silo i and the receiving of i's gradients by j can be calculated through

$$d_{\ell(i,j)} = d^{\text{tr}}_{\ell(i,j)} + d^{\text{pr}}_{\ell(i,j)} \tag{1}$$

Decisions: Obviously, gradient aggregation does not need to use all potential connections in G. The communication topology design problem is actually to find a connected subgraph G^c of G that contains a subset of links $E^c \subset E$ connecting all nodes in $\mathcal{N}$. Silos follow G^c to transfer gradients. To mitigate congestion caused by using a single aggregator, we consider multiple aggregators and let each aggregator maintain a subset of parameters and take the aggregation task of corresponding gradients. Then, we compute a group of subgraphs of G, denoted by $\boldsymbol{G}^c$. The following decisions need to be made to compute G^c: ① parameter assignment, selecting aggregators and assigning fraction of parameters among these aggregators and ② aggregation trees construction, a tree is built for an aggregator to aggregate the gradients of the parameters maintained by this aggregator from participating silos.

Constraints: Without loss of generality, we assume that every participating silo can be selected as an aggregator and introduce variables $x_u \in [0, 1]$ to denote the fraction of parameters maintained by aggregator u. In real distributed ML frameworks, the parameters of a training ML model are typically divided into a set of equal-sized parameter slices, and each aggregator maintains an integral number of parameter slices [4]. If the model size is M and the size of each parameter slice is β, we have constraint (2).

$$\sum_u \lceil \frac{M \times x_u}{\beta} \rceil \geq M \tag{2}$$

Given that each silo node may be selected to be an aggregator, let binary $y_{u,\ell(i,j)}$ denote whether the tree-like aggregation topology rooted at silo u uses link $\ell(i, j)$ to transfer gradients from silo i to j. Let $\mathcal{A}_u \subset \mathcal{N}$ denote the set of adjacent nodes of u in G. Since each aggregator u is the root of a tree aggregation topology, it should have at least one incoming link for gradients gathering as (3) shows and no outgoing communication link as constrained in (4).

$$\sum_{j \in \mathcal{A}_u} y_{u,\ell(j,u)} \geq x_u, \quad \forall u \in \mathcal{N} \tag{3}$$

$$\sum_{j \in \mathcal{A}_u} y_{u,\ell(u,j)} = 0, \quad \forall u \in \mathcal{N} \tag{4}$$

To build an aggregation tree towards each aggregator, each data silo uses an outgoing link for transferring the corresponding gradients, as indicated by (5).

$$\sum_{j \in \mathcal{A}_i} y_{u,\ell(i,j)} = \lceil x_u \rceil, \quad \forall u, i : i \neq u \tag{5}$$

As mentioned before, each pair of silos (i, j) reports the measured propagation delay $d^{pr}_{\ell(i,j)}$ and available bandwidth $b_{\ell(i,j)}$ to the orchestrator. The orchestrator can compute the transmission delay $d^{tr}_{\ell(i,j)}$ through

$$d^{tr}_{\ell(i,j)} = \frac{\sum_u \beta \times \lceil \frac{M \times x_u}{\beta} \rceil \times y_{u,\ell(i,j)}}{b_{\ell(i,j)}} \tag{6}$$

Accordingly, we compute $d_{\ell(i,j)}$ as in (1) and the time $t_{u,i}$ for node i to aggregate the gradients maintained by aggregator u. $t_{u,i}$ depends on $d_{\ell(i,j)}$ and the delay to receive gradients from downstream nodes in aggregation tree, as (7) denotes.

$$t_{u,i} \geq t_{u,j} \times y_{u,\ell(i,j)} + d_{\ell(i,j)}, \quad \forall u, i \in \mathcal{N}, j \in \mathcal{A}_i \tag{7}$$

Aggregation Minimization Problem: Given that multiple aggregators may be used, minimizing the maximum completion time of gradient aggregation among aggregators

Algorithm 1. Simulated Annealing Main Routine

Input: $\{b_{i,j}, \forall i,j \in \mathcal{N}\}$ ▷ Communication Bandwidth
Output: $\mathcal{S}^*, \mathcal{E}^*, \mathcal{T}^*$ ▷ Aggregators, throughput, completion time
1: $\mathcal{S}^{current} \leftarrow u* = \arg\max_{u \in \mathcal{N}} \sum_{v \in \mathcal{A}_u} b_{u,v}$;
2: $\mathcal{E}^{current}, \mathcal{T}^{current} \leftarrow EnergyCompute(\mathcal{S}^{current})$;
3: $\Phi \leftarrow \mathcal{E}^{current}, \mathcal{S}^* \leftarrow \mathcal{S}^{current}, \mathcal{T}^* \leftarrow \mathcal{T}^{current}$;
4: **while** $\Phi > \epsilon$ **do:**   ▷ Iteration
5:     $\mathcal{S}^{neighbor} \leftarrow NeighborCompute(\mathcal{S}^{current})$;
6:     $\mathcal{E}^{neighbor}, \mathcal{T}^{neighbor} \leftarrow EnergyCompute(\mathcal{S}^{neighbor})$;
7:     **if** $\mathcal{E}^{neighbor} > \mathcal{E}^{current}$ **then**
8:         $\mathcal{S}^* \leftarrow \mathcal{S}^{neighbor}, \mathcal{T}^* \leftarrow \mathcal{T}^{neighbor}, \mathcal{E}^* \leftarrow \mathcal{E}^{neighbor}$;
9:     **end if**
10:     **if** $\mathcal{Q}(\mathcal{E}^{current}, \mathcal{E}^{neighbor}, \Phi) > Rand(0,1)$ **then**
11:         $\mathcal{S}^{current} \leftarrow \mathcal{S}^{neighbor}, \mathcal{T}^{current} \leftarrow \mathcal{T}^{neighbor}, \mathcal{E}^{current} \leftarrow \mathcal{E}^{neighbor}$;
12:     **end if**
13:     $\Phi \leftarrow \Phi \times \zeta$;
14: **end while**

can result in a minimum completion time of gradient aggregation per communication round. We can formulate the aggregation minimization problem as follows.

$$\min \max_u (t_{u,u} \times \lceil x_u \rceil) \tag{8}$$

$$\text{s.t.} \quad (2) - (7)$$

$$x_u \in [0,1], \forall u \tag{9}$$

$$y_{u,\ell(i,j)} \in \{0,1\}, \forall u, \ell(i,j) \tag{10}$$

$$t_{u,u} \geq 0, \forall(u,u) \tag{11}$$

NP-Hardness. The above problem is generally NP-hard in theory because of the non-linear objective (8), non-linear constraint such as (7) and integer variables y.

3.3 Algorithm Design

For the above problem, if aggregation trees (the values of variables y) are known, it only needs to optimize the parameter assignment (variables x) that is easy to solve. A naive approach is to separately optimize aggregation trees and parameter assignment. However, as this two decisions are highly coupled with each other, the one-shot greedy approach does not yield good performance results. Besides, finding the global optimal communication topology is computationally expensive. Therefore, we use simulated annealing [14] to search for an approximate solution in reasonable computational time.

Simulated Annealing Main Routine (Algorithm 1). We use aggregators as the state and aggregation throughput as energy in simulated annealing. Algorithm 1 chooses the silo with the maximum bandwidth capacities as the initial state (line 1) and the corresponding approximate optimal aggregation throughput (the minimum aggregation completion time) as initial temperature (line 3). It uses iterative search to find

---

Algorithm 2. Compute Neighbor State (NeighborCompute)

1: **function** $NeighborCompute(\mathcal{N}^s)$;
2: $m \leftarrow \lceil |\mathcal{N}^s| \times \alpha \rceil$;   ▷ $\alpha \in (0,1]$
3: Select m nodes $\mathcal{N}^a$ from $\mathcal{N} - \mathcal{N}^s$;
4: Select m nodes $\mathcal{N}^r$ from $\mathcal{N}^s$;
5: $\mathcal{N}^{neighbor} \leftarrow \mathcal{N}^s - \mathcal{N}^r + \mathcal{N}^a$;
6: Select q_1 nodes $\mathcal{N}^1$ from $\mathcal{N} - \mathcal{N}^{neighbor}$ and select q_2 nodes $\mathcal{N}^2$ from $\mathcal{N}^{neighbor}$,   ▷
   $1 \le q_1 \le |\mathcal{N} - \mathcal{N}^{neighbor}|, 1 \le q_2 \le |\mathcal{N}^{neighbor}|$;
7: Let $\mathcal{N}^{neighbor} \leftarrow \mathcal{N}^{neighbor} + \mathcal{N}^1$ with probability p_1;
8: Let $\mathcal{N}^{neighbor} \leftarrow \mathcal{N}^{neighbor} - \mathcal{N}^2$ with probability p_2;
9: **return** $\mathcal{N}^{neighbor}$

---

the topologies with the maximum aggregation throughput (line 4–15). In each iteration, it uses $NeighborCompute$ function to compute a neighbor state and uses $EnergyCompute$ function to compute the energy of neighbor state. It records the optimal state $\mathcal{S}^*$, topologies $\mathcal{T}^*$, and energy $\mathcal{E}^*$, jumps to a neighbor state with a probability of $e^{\frac{\mathcal{E}^{current} - \mathcal{E}^{neighbor}}{\Phi}}$, and decreases the value of Φ by a factor of ζ at the end of each iteration.

NeighborCompute Subroutine (Algorithm 2). Basically, this algorithm randomly generates a neighbor state of current state. To create a neighbor state, it first replaces some aggregators in current state with other silos (line 3–5) and then probabilistically removes a certain number of aggregators and adds some as a complement (line 6–9).

EnergyCompute Subroutine (Algorithm 3). Given a set of aggregators, we still need to solve the aggregation tree construction subproblem and the parameter assignment subproblem. To solve this two subproblems, we use an EnergyCompute algorithm which finds the possible highest energy (the minimum aggregation completion time) under current state.

Firstly, it generates candidate aggregation trees via solving a feasibility problem LP1. Each feasible solution of LP1 is a collection of aggregation tree candidates where each is built with an aggregator as the root. Notice that some aggregate "trees" resulting from solving LP1 may include loops, and we consider the corresponding solution as infeasible. To compute k feasible solutions of LP1, we can use optimization solver Gurobi and set the solver parameter *poolsolutions* to k.

$$\textbf{LP1} \qquad \sum_{j \in \mathcal{A}_u} y_{u,\ell(j,u)} \ge 1, \qquad\qquad \forall u \in \mathcal{N}^s \qquad (12)$$

$$\sum_{j \in \mathcal{A}_u} y_{u,\ell(u,j)} = 0, \qquad\qquad \forall u \in \mathcal{N}^s \qquad (13)$$

$$\sum_{j \in \mathcal{A}_i} y_{u,\ell(j,i)} \ge \sum_{j \in \mathcal{A}_i} y_{u,\ell(i,j)}, \qquad \forall u, i : i \ne u \qquad (14)$$

$$\sum_{i,j \in \mathcal{A}_i} y_{u,\ell(j,i)} \le \Gamma, \qquad\qquad \forall u \in \mathcal{N}^s \qquad (15)$$

Then, we compute the optimal parameter assignment for every collection of candidate aggregation trees and find the collection that yields the highest energy (the minimal

---

Algorithm 3. Compute State Energy (EnergyCompute)

1: **function** $EnergyCompute(\mathcal{N}^s)$
2: Compute a groups $\mathcal{P}$ of candidates for the aggregate topology by solving the feasibility problem LP1;   ▷ The topologies with cycles (loops) are excluded in $\mathcal{P}$
3: **for each** $P \in \mathcal{P}$ **do**   ▷ Iteration
4:     Solve LP2 to obtain fractional values of $\tilde{\boldsymbol{x}}$;
5:     Compute $w_i \leftarrow \frac{M \times \tilde{x}_i}{\beta}, \forall i \in \mathcal{N}^s$;
6:     Let $\mathcal{N}^{re} \leftarrow \{i | w_i \notin \mathbb{N}^+, \forall i \in \mathcal{N}^s\}$;
7:     Let $\mathcal{N}^{in} \leftarrow \{i | w_i \in \mathbb{N}^+, \forall i \in \mathcal{N}^s\}$;
8:     **while** $|\mathcal{N}^{re}| > 1$ **do**   ▷ Compute integer solutions
9:         Select $(i,j) \in \mathcal{N}^{re}$ and let $\bar{w}_i = \lceil \tilde{w}_i \rceil$ and $\bar{w}_j = \lfloor \tilde{w}_j \rfloor$;
10:         $\mathcal{N}^{re} \leftarrow \mathcal{N}^{re} \setminus \{(i,j)\}, \mathcal{N}^{in} \leftarrow \mathcal{N}^{in} \cup \{(i,j)\}$;
11:     **end while**
12:     **if** $|\mathcal{N}^{re}| == 1$ **then**
13:         Let $\bar{w}_i = \frac{M}{\beta} - \sum_{j \in \mathcal{N}^{in}} \bar{w}_j, \forall i \in \mathcal{N}^{re}, \mathcal{N}^{in} \leftarrow \mathcal{N}^{in} \cup \{i\}$;
14:     **end if**
15:     Compute aggregation time t_P according to $\bar{\boldsymbol{w}}$;
16: **end for**
17: **return** $th^* = \max_P \frac{1}{t_P}$.

---

aggregation time). Given a specific collection of aggregation trees $(\boldsymbol{y})$, we solve a linear programming (LP2) to compute the optimal parameter assignment $(\boldsymbol{x})$ and aggregation time. In LP2, we relax the constraint that the number of parameter slices assigned to aggregators should be integer and rewrite the parameter assignment optimization problem to minimize aggregation time. After optimally solving this relaxed problem, we calculate a satisfactory integer number of parameter slices to be assigned to each aggregator (lines 6–18). After iteration, Algorithm 3 returns the highest energy and the corresponding topologies.

$$\textbf{LP2} \quad \min t \tag{16}$$

$$\sum_{u \in \mathcal{N}^s} x_u = 1 \tag{17}$$

$$t_{u,i} \geq t_{u,j} + \frac{\sum_u M x_u}{b_{\ell(i,j)}} + d^{pr}_{\ell(i,j)}, \qquad \forall u, i \in \mathcal{N}, j \in \mathcal{A}_i \tag{18}$$

$$t_{u,u} \geq t, \qquad \forall u \in \mathcal{N}^s \tag{19}$$

4   Performance Evaluation

In this section, we evaluate the effectiveness of TOPOADOPT in reducing gradient aggregation time in each communication round for cross-silo FL through simulations. Extensive results show that TOPOADOPT outperforms the state-of-the-art and reduces the completion time of gradient aggregation significantly.

4.1   Methodology

Network and Workloads. We consider n data silos collaboratively train an ML model in each experiment and vary it to simulate cross-silo FL with different scales. To simulate the heterogeneous available WAN bandwidth between these silos, the communication bandwidth of each pair of silos is randomly set to [20 Mbps, 500 Mbps] according to real environment. We omit the end-to-end delay in milliseconds for the WAN because it is insignificant compared to the transmission delays in the tens or even hundreds of seconds shown by the experimental results. To simulate different workloads, we use two popular ML models, ResNet50 and VGG16, with different model sizes for FL.

Baselines. We compare TOPOADOPT to *PLink* [9] and *PSLD* [4]. *PLink* is state-of-the-art tree-based topology design, which divides nodes into groups based on node affinity and builds a 2-level hierarchical aggregation topology adapting to network conditions. Note that the design of *PLink* also captures the hierarchical communication topologies used in cloud-edge-device FL applications. *PSLD* is the state-of-the-art parameter assignment solution which assigns model parameters among multiple aggregator instances adapting to node capacities.

Simulator and Metrics. We develop a flow-level simulator with Python 3 to simulate the gradient aggregation process that uses the communication topologies designed by baseline solutions and TOPOADOPT. It employs the off-the-shelf Gurobi optimization solver to solve LP1 and LP2 in TOPOADOPT. For time efficiency, we set the Gurobi solver parameter *poolsolutions* = *10* to compute ten groups of candidate aggregation trees when solving LP1. Our primary metric to quantify performance is the completion time of gradient aggregation in each communication round during the training. We compare baselines and TOPOADOPT in every experiment run and report the average completion time of 10 trials for every parameter setting. Besides, we also compute the speedup of TOPOADOPT over baselines. Taking comparing scheme X with TOPOADOPT as an example, we compute speedup $= \frac{\text{completion time (X)}}{\text{completion time (TOPOADOPT)}}$.

4.2   Experimental Results

Effectiveness of TOPOADOPT. Figure 4 shows that the completion times of all solutions grow as the number of participating silos increases from 10 to 50, and TOPOADOPT always outperforms *PSLD* and *PLink* in all experiments.

Figure 4(a) shows that TOPOADOPT reduces completion times to no more than 18 s, achieving up to 5.2× and 3.9× speedups on ResNet50 compared to *PSLD* and *PLink*, respectively. Among compared baselines, *PLink* achieves shorter completion times than *PSLD*. These results indicate that, compared to optimizing aggregator parameter assignment, optimizing aggregation tree can be more beneficial to alleviate the communication bottleneck during gradient aggregation and effectively reduce the corresponding completion time of gradient aggregation.

Figure 4(b) shows that the completion time of training VGG16 is much longer than that of training ResNet50 due to the larger model size. The results also show that, compared to *PSLD* and *PLink* that take hundreds of seconds to complete, TOPOADOPT can always complete gradient aggregation in dozens of seconds. Interestingly, *PSLD* and *PLink* achieve comparable performances and neither can always beat the other when n increases from 10 to 50. These results indicate that, optimizing parameter assignment among aggregators and optimizing aggregation tree have similar effects on improving communication efficiency of gradient aggregation for training large ML models like

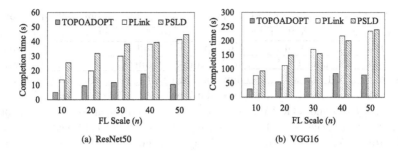

Fig. 4. TOPOADOPT significantly reduces the completion time of gradient aggregation in training different ML models at different FL scales.

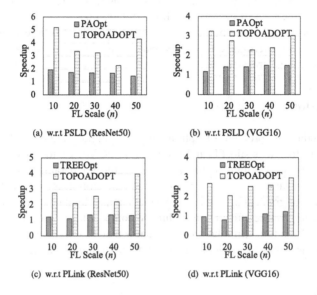

Fig. 5. Performance breakdown: the benefits of optimizing parameter assignment (PAOpt) and optimizing aggregation tree (TREEOpt) of TOPOADOPT in speeding up gradient aggregation.

VGG16. However, they are not as efficient as TOPOADOPT because TOPOADOPT optimizes not only the parameter assignment but also the aggregate tree construction.

Performance Breakdown. At the design of TOPOADOPT, it jointly optimizes the aggregation tree construction and aggregator parameter assignment for communication topologies. We here examine the performance of TOPOADOPT when it is artificially limited to use a single aggregator and only optimize the aggregation tree (denoted by *TREEOpt*) and when it is limited to use star-like topologies and only optimize the aggregator parameter assignment (denoted by *PAOpt*), respectively.

Figure 5(a), 5(b) show the speedups of *PAOpt* and TOPOADOPT over *PSLD*. *PAOpt* achieves relatively stable speedups over *PSLD*, up to 1.9× and 1.5× for training ResNet50 and VGG16, respectively. These results indicate the superiority of TOPOAD-

OPT that it can still outperform prior related work even though only optimizing aggregator parameter assignment. Moreover, compared to only optimizing parameter assignment in *PAOpt*, TOPOADOPT can bring up to 3.2× and 2.1× additional performance gain for ResNet50 and VGG16 by simultaneously optimizing the aggregation tree.

Figure 5(c), 5(d) show the speedups of *TREEOpt* and TOPOADOPT over *PLink*. *TREEOpt* achieves relatively stable speedups over *PLink*, up to 1.3× and 1.2× for training ResNet50 and VGG16, respectively. This improvement is not significant as *PAOpt*. However, TOPOADOPT brings up to 2.6× and 1.7× additional performance gain for ResNet50 and VGG16 by optimizing parameter assignment and aggregation tree together.

The above results confirm that TOPOADOPT outperforms existing works even when it is limited to optimize only the aggregation tree construction or parameter assignment alone. However, the gain of each is also limited. Optimizing this two jointly is more effective in improving the communication efficiency. Besides, in our tests, the proposed algorithms can always terminate within seconds, indicating that TOPOADOPT is ready for deployment in real cross-silo FL systems.

5 Conclusion

This paper studies the problem of optimizing the communication topology of gradient aggregation for cross-silo FL and proposes TOPOADOPT to solve this problem. TOPOADOPT relies on a joint optimization of aggregator parameter assignment and hierarchical aggregation trees to improve communication efficiency and reduce the completion time of gradient aggregation. We mathematically model this joint optimization problem and propose efficient algorithms to compute topologies that minimize the gradient aggregation time. Simulation results show that TOPOADOPT significantly outperforms existing works in accelerating the completion of gradient aggregation.

References

1. Verbraeken, J., et al.: A survey on distributed machine learning. ACM Comput. Surv. (CSUR) **53**(2), 1–33 (2020)
2. Hsieh, K., et al.: Gaia: geo-distributed machine learning approaching LAN speeds. In: NSDI, pp. 629–647 (2017)
3. Zhang, C., et al.: BatchCrypt: efficient homomorphic encryption for cross-silo federated learning. In: USENIX ATC, pp. 493–506 (2020)
4. Chen, Y., et al.: Elastic parameter server load distribution in deep learning clusters. In: SoCC, pp. 507–521 (2020)
5. Sapio, A., et al.: Scaling distributed machine learning with in-network aggregation. In: NSDI, pp. 785–808 (2021)
6. Marfoq, O., et al.: Throughput-optimal topology design for cross-silo federated learning. In: NeurIPS, vol. 33, pp. 19 478–19 487 (2020)
7. Lao, C., et al.: ATP: in-network aggregation for multi-tenant learning. In: NSDI, pp. 741–761 (2021)
8. Li, M., et al.: Scaling distributed machine learning with the parameter server. In: OSDI, pp. 583–598 (2014)

9. Luo, L., et al.: Plink: efficient cloud-based training with topology-aware dynamic hierarchical aggregation. In: MLSys, pp. 1–13 (2020)
10. Fate (federated AI technology enabler) (2019). https://github.com/FederatedAI/FATE
11. Courtiol, P., et al.: Deep learning-based classification of mesothelioma improves prediction of patient outcome. Nat. Med. **25**(10), 1519–1525 (2019)
12. Kairouz, P., et al.: Advances and open problems in federated learning. Found. Trends® Mach. Learn. **14**(1–2), 1–210 (2021)
13. Shouxi, L., et al.: Eliminating communication bottlenecks in cross-device federated learning with in-network processing at the edge. In: IEEE ICC, pp. 1–6 (2022)
14. Kirkpatrick, S., Gelatt Jr., C.D., Vecchi, M.P.: Optimization by simulated annealing. Science **220**(4598), 671–680 (1983)

Design of Reliable Parallel Transmission System in Complex Heterogeneous Network

Xuan Zhang, Xiaoya Zhang[✉], Yuyang Zhang, Wenxuan Qiao, and Ping Dong

School of Electronic and Information Engineering, Beijing Jiaotong University, Beijing, China
{20120166,pdong,zhyy,19111033,18111040}@bjtu.edu.cn

Abstract. Today's terminal equipment is often equipped with multiple network interfaces, and the traditional TCP/IP protocol can only transmit data using a single network interface and cannot take advantage of the network environment where multiple heterogeneous networks coexist today [1]. The multi-channel parallel transmission technology emerging in recent years can use multiple wireless network interfaces to transmit data in parallel, to make full use of heterogeneous network resources for reliable transmission, which is an important means to improve network quality. At present, there are two mainstream protocols for multi-path parallel transmission technology, MPTCP and SCTP [2, 3]. Although both protocols can use multiple wireless links to transmit data, they do not perform well in the actual use scenarios of complex heterogeneous networks. Reliable transmission cannot be completed in mobile and high packet loss rate scenarios, and because the two are not widely integrated into the TCP/IP protocol stack, there are problems such as deployment difficulties. In order to achieve reliable transmission in scenarios with severe network fluctuations, we have designed a multi-channel parallel transmission system to achieve reliable transmission in different scenarios. In terms of scheduling algorithm, we design a mechanism that can adaptively switch scheduling schemes according to transmission scenarios. In terms of cache sorting, we have designed a reasonable cache mechanism, which can well alleviate the drop in the sending rate caused by the disorder of the receiving end. According to the test results, the system can achieve reliable transmission in different transmission environments.

Keywords: Parallel transmission · Bandwidth fluctuation · Transmission scheduling

1 Introduction

The cellular network has basically covered the whole world since its construction, allowing people to enjoy fast network services. The 5G mobile communication system will provide new high-quality wireless services, and users will enjoy faster network services. However, on high-speed trains, there is currently no reliable and stable in-vehicle network to provide access. Users in high-speed trains are in high-speed closed spaces, and the received wireless signals will have Doppler effects. In addition, trains operate in sparsely

W. Quan (Ed.): ICENAT 2022, CCIS 1696, pp. 198–208, 2023.
https://doi.org/10.1007/978-981-19-9697-9_16

populated areas, and the density of base stations Therefore, the network experience on high-speed trains is unsatisfactory, and a single wireless network cannot meet the needs of users, so wireless multipath transmission has become a research hotspot for scholars [4]. However, traditional multi-path transmission scheduling algorithms do not perform well in heterogeneous network environments, and even perform worse than single-path in scenarios with high delay and packet loss rate. Therefore, the future development trend is to have a set of stable and reliable multi-path operation. transport mechanism [5].

First of all, the difference between each link in a heterogeneous network often leads to serious disorder at the receiving end. In order to keep the data packets delivered by different sub-flows in a basic order, it is necessary to allocate data packets in advance according to the characteristics of each sub-flow. According to the delay of the substream, the time when the data packet arrives at the opposite end is estimated, and the transmission link of the data packet is adjusted on this basis [6, 7]. In addition, in a dynamically changing heterogeneous network scenario, how to quickly determine whether a link has lost packets, and how to adjust the retransmission policy after packet loss so that the receiving end can quickly obtain the retransmitted data packets, so that the sorted data can be delivered to the The upper-layer applications also need further research [8].

The contributions of this paper can be summarized as follows: First, a multi-link reliable parallel transmission system is proposed, and the system modules are described. Secondly, a scheduling scheme that adjusts the transmission scheme according to the network transmission environment is proposed. Thirdly, the reliability of the system is verified through the actual system test.

The structure of the paper is arranged as follows. We discuss related work on existing multi-link parallel transmission schemes in Sect. 2. Section 3 presents the architecture of the multi-link parallel system. In Sect. 4, we detail the scheduling scheme. In Sect. 5, we demonstrate that our system can achieve reliable transmission through actual system tests.

2 Related Work

Given that most applications in the current Internet are based on TCP, Huitema proposed the idea of TCP-based multi-path transmission control as early as 1995. After years of research and exploration, IETF standardized it in 2009. In multi-path TCP By adding a layer of management layer to manage multiple TCP substream data at the same time, to improve the transmission effect, and because the same socket as TCP is used in the application layer, it achieves good compatibility. Compared with single-path transmission, the advantages of multi-path transmission are mainly reflected in two aspects: (1) The role of multi-path transmission is particularly prominent in static or low-speed mobile wireless network environments, the reason is that in addition to The gain in data transmission rate brought about by inverse multiplexing of channels, when users enter or exit coverage, links can be added or dropped without interrupting end-to-end connections [9, 10]; (2) In data centers such as It also has outstanding performance in application scenarios, the reason being that multi-channel parallel transmission can balance a single connection across multiple interfaces, thus achieving very high transmission efficiency [11, 12]. At present, the research on multi-channel parallel transmission mainly focuses on the research of packet scheduling strategy and congestion control.

In terms of multi-link scheduling, Chebrolu et al. proposed a scheduling algorithm in the multi-path transmission mechanism of IP in IP encapsulation, the earliest delivery path first (EDPF) algorithm, through the estimated packet transmission time based on to schedule packets to ensure that they meet their playback deadlines. Scholars such as Rodriguez proposed two scheduling mechanisms, the packet-oriented scheduling mode and the flow-oriented scheduling mode: when a proxy server exists, the packet-oriented scheduling mode is used to transmit packets on the same TCP stream. Multipathing; when a proxy server does not exist, a flow-oriented scheduling mode is used to arrange all packets belonging to the same flow onto the same path. Scholars such as Evanson et al. proposed a multi-link proxy (MLP) to distribute packets using a WRR-based scheduling mechanism according to the estimated throughput ratio of the available paths [13].

In terms of receiving buffers, since the receiving buffers are not infinite, and because the data packets may be out of order during the transmission process, these data packets cannot be directly delivered to the application layer after arriving at the receiving end, but are received at the receiving end. Because the sending window is limited by the congestion window and the remaining buffer space, the out-of-order data packets occupying the buffer may affect the sending speed of the sender. Dreibholz T et al. proposed a cache segmentation scheme. When the multiple sub-stream paths of multi-path transmission are quite different, if a certain sub-path occupies too much receiver cache, it will lead to other sub-paths. Even if the path is in good condition, it cannot continue to send data. The author divides the buffer of the receiving end according to the number of paths, and feeds it back to the sending end through the receiving window. The sending terminal path performs flow control according to this value [14, 15].

Through the above analysis, we can conclude that most of the existing research is based on the static environment, focusing on improving the effect of multi-link bandwidth aggregation, or using methods such as network coding to improve the reliability of transmission, but in high-speed mobile environment or When other high-loss network environments provide emergency network supply services, due to the large differences in the performance of each network link, there will be a problem of mutual restriction of link performance. For example, in a static environment, it is necessary to provide services that are too high and too wide, and provide additional reliability guarantees in the case of poor link quality. Therefore, we propose a reliable transmission mechanism in the scenario of network fluctuation, which can solve the problem of large performance fluctuation during the transmission process and adaptive scheduling for different scenarios, so as to meet the transmission requirements in different scenarios.

3   Introduction to Parallel Transmission System

In this section, the architecture of the heterogeneous link parallel transmission system will be introduced. This paper proposes a system capable of adaptive and reliable transmission in different scenarios. The system consists of Smart Collaborative Router (SMR) and Smart Aggregation Router (SAR). As shown in Fig. 1, the system can be divided into connection management module, data transceiver Management module, link state detection module and link hierarchical scheduling module, the following will introduce the role of each module in the system in detail.

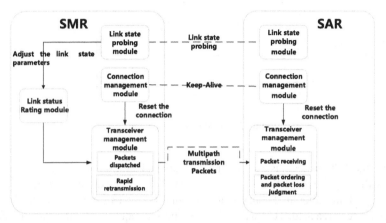

Fig. 1. System structure of heterogeneous network parallel transmission

3.1 Connection Management Module

The connection management module is responsible for the socket connection of multiple links between SAR-SMR and the maintenance of the link status, and keeps the link alive through heartbeat packets and detects the connectivity of the link. For links with abnormal connection status To reset the connection and reconnect the link with abnormal link status in time, the basic work flow of the link management module is: firstly establish a socket connection between multiple links, and when receiving the Update the time when the link receives the data packet, send heartbeat packets at regular intervals to keep the link alive, obtain the current time and calculate the arrival time of the last data packet on this link, if the time difference is greater than the set threshold, disconnect and reconnect.

3.2 Transceiver Management Module

The multi-link reliable transmission mechanism uses TCP to transmit data, and its packet header format is designed as shown in Fig. 2:

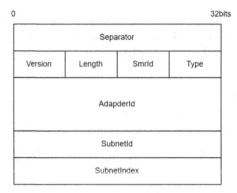

Fig. 2. Header format design

Since the TCP protocol is a streaming protocol and has no boundaries, the operating system will optimize the buffer when sending TCP data. For example, the buffer is 1024 bytes in size. If the amount of data sent in one request is relatively small, there is no When the buffer size is reached, TCP will combine multiple requests into the same request to send, thus forming a sticky packet problem. If the amount of data sent in one request is relatively large and exceeds the buffer size, TCP will split it into multiple transmissions, thus causing the problem of unpacking. Therefore, a 32-bit separator is added to the header of the message to solve the problem of sticking and unpacking. Version is used to distinguish the version number that identifies the header format to distinguish different header versions; the Length field is used to identify the length of the data it carries, and the SmrId field is used to identify the number of the SMR/SAR to inform the other party of the SAR/SMR being communicated. Number; since there are multiple network ports on the SMR, the AdapterId field is added to the header to identify the name of the network port that sends the data packet; the SubnetId field is used to mark the subnet to which the data is sent, which is then forwarded by the router; SubnetIndex The field is used to identify the number of the sent data packet, which is used for subsequent data packet sorting; the Type field is used to identify the type of the data packet. Currently, the types of data packets are divided into ordinary data packets, heartbeat packets, retransmission request packets and retransmission response packets. The normal data packet is responsible for transmitting data, and the heartbeat packet is responsible for maintaining the connection of multiple links in the connection management module, and the retransmission request packet and the retransmission response packet are responsible for the retransmission of lost data packets.

3.3 Link State Detection Module

The link status update module is responsible for updating the link status. Here, a thread independent of data transmission is started to update the link status. The number of unpacked and unsend packets on each link is maintained through the getsockopt system call. For the link that exceeds the threshold value is marked as unavailable, otherwise the RTT of the link is calculated. The delay here includes two parts, one part is the propagation delay, and the other part is the queuing delay of the link, which is used by the scheduling module.

The basic flow of link status update is as follows:

(i). Start a separate thread for the link state update module.

(ii). Use the system call to obtain the parameters of the socket connection. If the return value is 0, it means that the link status is abnormal, and the connection needs to be re-established. Otherwise, it will enter the parameter update state.

(iii). Record the number of unacknowledged packets on the link. If the number of unacknowledged packets exceeds the threshold, the link will be marked as temporarily unavailable.

(iv). Record the number of unsent packets on the link and mark the link status as temporarily unavailable if the number of unacknowledged packets exceeds the threshold.

(v). Calculate the link delay. The delay here includes two parts, one is the propagation delay, and the other is the queuing delay of the link. The calculation of the delay is estimated by using Eq. (1).

$$PRtt_i = Rtt_i + \left(\frac{unsend_i}{cwnd_i * mss_i} \right) * Rtt_i \qquad (1)$$

where $PRtt_i$ is the estimated delay, Rtt_i is the propagation delay, and $(\frac{unsend_i}{cwnd_i*mss_i}) * Rtt_i$ is the estimated time that the data packet needs to be queued in the link.

(vi). Add the link whose status has been updated to the available set for the subsequent scheduling and sending module to select the optimal scheduling scheme to send data packets.

3.4 Link State Classification Module

The link state classification module divides the quality of the link into different levels and adopts different transmission methods. In order to manage the state, the link state machine as shown in the figure is designed (Fig. 3):

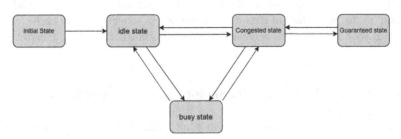

Fig. 3. Link state transition

The link status grading module divides the link status into five priorities respectively, for the scheduling module to make sending judgments according to the link priorities. For the initial state, there are no data packets to be sent or unacknowledged on the link, and data packets are sent to this state first. As the number of data packets in different states on the link changes, the link state also follows. transfer. When there is a small amount of unsent or unacknowledged data on the link, the link transitions from the initial state to the idle state, and when the number of unsent packets maintained on the link reaches the threshold, it means that a lot of data is accumulated on the link Packet, thus transitioning to the busy state. On the basis that the link is in a congested state, the unreplied data packets reach the threshold, indicating that there are many data packets on the link that have been sent but there is no ACK, and the link state is poor, so it transitions to a congested state. If the RTT reaches the threshold, the link is transferred to guaranteed state operation.

4   Design of Cache Sorting Mechanism

Receive buffering is an important module to ensure reliable transmission. It can shield the quality difference between links, try to make the data packets can be delivered to the upper-layer application in an orderly manner, and avoid the decrease of bandwidth due to disorder. For each data packet, there is a unique The ID to identify the duplicate data packets will be removed in the cache, otherwise it will be put into the set of arriving data packets and enter the data packet sorting process. For the ordered data packets in the cache, route forwarding is performed directly. To avoid cache breakdown, a cache threshold is designed in the system, that is, the cache can accommodate the maximum number of data packets, in addition to the expected packets arriving in an orderly manner. After reaching the threshold, the expected packet is a possible potential packet loss and enters the process of fast retransmission. Finally, it is judged whether the data packets in the cache have reached the cache threshold. The maximum cache threshold here is the RTO of TCP, that is, the timeout retransmission time, to avoid triggering the timeout retransmission of TCP. The calculation of the minimum threshold is Eq. (2), that is the difference between the maximum delay and the minimum delay of the link

$$Diff(t) = \max\left(\left|Link_i - Link_j\right|\right), \ i, j = 1, 2 \ldots \ldots n, \tag{2}$$

In addition, the upper limit of the timeout time set here is dynamically adjusted according to the proportion of data packets arriving in sequence in the cache, and the delivery as soon as possible is achieved by allowing some data packets to arrive out of sequence.

5   A Reliable Scheduling Scheme for Parallel Transmission

According to different transmission scenarios, a scheduling transmission mechanism is designed. The status of all links is updated before data packets are sent. If the status of all links exceeds the delay or packet loss threshold, it will enter the state of guaranteed transmission. If the redundant data packets do not reach the guaranteed state threshold, the best link state is selected and sent according to the delay detected by the link state detection module.

The specific process of scheduling sending is as follows:

(i)   Update the status of all links and remove the link with abnormal status from the set of available links.
(ii)   If all the links are higher than the packet loss/delay threshold, it is considered that the status of the links is very poor, and the steps are entered.
(iii)   Otherwise go to step 3.
(iv)   Select the link with the highest wired level in the set of available link states. If there are multiple links with the same priority level, select the link to be finally sent according to the predicted delay of the link.
(v)   The sending state is in the overall guaranteed sending state. Multiple links send redundant packets to ensure that the data packets can finally reach the receiving end, reducing the probability of retransmission.

6   Comparative Testing

In this section, the proposed parallel transmission scheme will be tested. The test environment built based on the actual application environment is shown in the figure. In this test scenario, the in-vehicle equipment SMR is placed in the laboratory, and the cloud server is used as the SAR. The SMR communicates with the Link Aggregation Server SAR via 4G links of 3 different operators. The test equipment is used as the hanging equipment of the in-vehicle equipment for performance testing (Fig. 4).

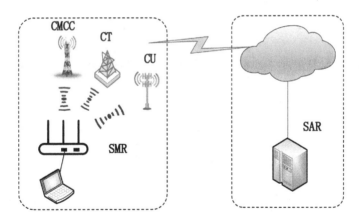

Fig. 4. Testing scenarios

The EDPF multi-link transmission method is a kind of classical multi-link transmission method. The method works on the sender side to ensure that the data transmitted by the heterogeneous network arrives at the receiver side in an orderly manner. The core idea is to calculate the time it takes for a data packet to be sent from each available link to the opposite end before each packet is sent, and then send the data packet from the link with the shortest time. The entire communication process ensures that the continuously sent data packets are still in order after reaching the receiving end through the heterogeneous link through accurate link estimation and strict mathematical calculation. In this test, the parallel transmission mechanism of EDPF and heterogeneous network will be used.

6.1 The Out-of-Order Degree Test of the Data Packets at the Receiving End

Record the sending of data packets at the sending end and the receiving sequence of the receiving buffer. The received result is shown in Fig. 5. It can be seen that compared with the EDPF transmission mechanism, the receiving buffer of the multi-link parallel transmission mechanism can smooth the chain well. The difference between the paths, so that the packets are delivered in order (Fig. 6).

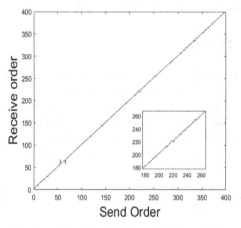

Fig. 5. Disorder degree based on EDPF parallel transmission mechanism

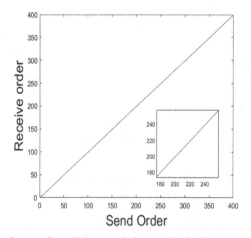

Fig. 6. Disorder degree of parallel transmission mechanism in heterogeneous network

6.2 Bandwidth Comparison Test

The bandwidth comparison test results are shown in Fig. 7.

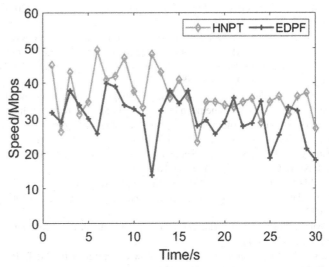

Fig. 7. Comparison of heterogeneous network parallel transmission and bandwidth fluctuation of EDPF mechanism

It can be seen that the parallel transmission mechanism of heterogeneous networks is better than the parallel transmission mechanism based on EDPF in terms of stability and average bandwidth and can complete the transmission in the case of network fluctuations.

7 Conclusion

As people's requirements for network quality are getting higher and higher, multi-link parallel transmission can complete a variety of network resources and take advantage of today's heterogeneous network environment, whether in static or high-speed mobile scenarios. It is of great practical significance to provide reliable and stable transmission services. The parallel transmission mechanism in the heterogeneous network proposed in this paper can give full play to the advantages of multiple links and solve the problem of unstable transmission rate caused by differences between multiple links. The reliability of transmission in different scenarios has been tested, and the comparison test shows that the multi-link parallel transmission mechanism has a good performance in terms of bandwidth and transmission stability.

Acknowledgment. This work was supported in part by the China Postdoctoral Science Foundation under grant 2021M690343, and in part by the Fundamental Research Funds for the Central Universities under grant 2021RC247, and in part by the National Natural Science Foundation of China (NSFC) under grant No. 61872029.

References

1. http://www.gov.cn/xinwen/2020-12/23/content_5572460.htm,2020-12-23
2. Qiao, W., et al.: A bottleneck-aware multipath scheduling mechanism for social networks. In: ICC 2021–IEEE International Conference on Communications, pp. 1–6 (2021). https://doi.org/10.1109/ICC42927.2021.9500794
3. Lin, M., Zhang, Y., Qiao, W., Dong, P.: Design of mobile device cooperative transmission system under wireless network fluctuation. In: 2022 IEEE 10th Joint International Information Technology and Artificial Intelligence Conference (ITAIC), pp. 635–639 (2022). https://doi.org/10.1109/ITAIC54216.2022.9836595
4. Chen, X., Dong, P., Zhang, Y., Qiao, W., Yin, C.: Design of adaptive redundant coding concurrent multipath transmission scheme in high-speed mobile environment. In: 2021 IEEE 5th Advanced Information Technology, Electronic and Automation Control Conference (IAEAC), pp. 2176–2179 (2021). https://doi.org/10.1109/IAEAC50856.2021.9391038
5. Liu, S., Huang, J., Jiang, W., et al.: Reducing traffic burstiness for MPTCP in data center networks. J. Netw. Comput. Appl. **192**, 103169 (2021)
6. Silva, A.C., Martins, R., Verdi, F.L.: Empowering applications with RFC 6897 to manage elephant flows in datacenter networks. In: IEEE International Conference on Cloud Networking, pp. 1–6 (2017)
7. Chao, L., Wu, C., Yoshinaga, T., et al.: A brief review of multipath TCP for vehicular networks. Sensors **21**(8), 2793 (2021)
8. Huang, J., Li, W., Li, Q., et al.: Tuning high flow concurrency for MPTCP in data center networks. J. Cloud Comput. **9**(1), 1–15 (2020)
9. Zhang, J., Ma, L., Cai, Z., Wang, X.: Network coding-based multipath content transmission mechanism in content centric networking. In: 2017 IEEE 9th International Conference on Communication Software and Networks (ICCSN), Guangzhou, pp. 1012–1015 (2017)
10. Tang, F., Zhang, H., Yang, L.T.: Multipath cooperative routing with efficient acknowledgement for LEO satellite networks. IEEE Trans. Mob. Comput. **18**(1), 179–192 (2018)
11. Zeng, J., Ke, F., Zuo, Y., et al.: Multi-attribute aware path selection approach for efficient MPTCP-based data delivery. J. Internet Serv. Inf. Secur. **7**(1), 28–39 (2017)
12. Hou, J., Hou, D., Tao, B., et al.: Performance analysis of MPTCP under high load based on SDN environment. In: Li, W., Tang, D. (eds.) Mobile Wireless Middleware, Operating Systems and Applications. MOBILWARE 2020. LNICS, Social Informatics and Telecommunications Engineering, vol. 331, pp. 57–68. Springer, Cham (2020). https://doi.org/10.1007/978-3-030-62205-3_5
13. Qiao, W., Dong, P., Du, X., Zhang, Y., Zhang, H., Guizani, M., et al.: QoS provision for vehicle big data by parallel transmission based on heterogeneous network characteristics prediction (2022)
14. Huang, Y., Dong, P., Zhang, Y., Zhang, X. Distributed management system architecture of multi-link mobile tunnel network. In: 2022 IEEE 10th Joint International Information Technology and Artificial Intelligence Conference (ITAIC), pp. 662–666 (2022). https://doi.org/10.1109/ITAIC54216.2022.9836798
15. Zhang, X., Dong, P., Du, X., Zhang, Y., Zhang, H., Guizan, M.: Study on characteristics of metric-aware multipath algorithms in real heterogeneous networks. In: 2021 IEEE Global Communications Conference (GLOBECOM), pp. 1–6 (2021). https://doi.org/10.1109/GLOBECOM46510.2021.9685343

Design of Privacy-Preserving in Multi-link Vehicle-Ground Communication

Rui Sun, Yuyang Zhang[✉], Zongzheng Wang, Xiaoya Zhang,
and Ping Dong

School of Electronic and Information Engineering, Beijing Jiaotong University,
Beijing 10004, China
{20120105,zhyy,18111035,18111040,pdong}@bjtu.edu.cn

Abstract. Multi-link vehicle-ground communication uses the integration of WiFi, cellular and other wireless communication technologies to solve the problem of network service quality in high-speed mobile networks, and it is also accompanied by more security issues. For example, the identity authentication problem caused by the frequent switching of IP addresses of the in-vehicle equipment, and the application data information is vulnerable to eavesdropping attacks. On the one hand, the mobility characteristics of in-vehicle devices make it more difficult to achieve device privacy-preserving, and on the other hand, the multi-homed characteristics of in-vehicle devices also provide us with new ideas for privacy-preserving. So we propose a privacy-preserving scheme based on shard scheduling and reorganization in multi-links. This scheme takes into account the data source authentication problem when the link IP is switched frequently, and adopts an identity-based non-interactive authentication scheme. At the same time, the shared key generated by the authentication part can also provide the possibility for data encryption. Using the multi-homing feature, we realize that the original data packet is fragmented and sent from different links, and the ring buffer is used at the receiving end to receive and reassemble, and the fixed-length padding scheme is used to blur the length characteristics of the data packet. Finally, the data aggregation bandwidth is used to evaluate the scheme, which proves the feasibility of the scheme in the heterogeneous multi-link vehicle-ground communication scenario.

Keywords: Multi-link vehicle-ground communication ·
Privacy-preserving · Data aggregation · Fixed-length padding

1 Introduction

With the rapid development of our country's transportation industry, the number of passengers carried by high-speed rail and automobiles has increased year by year. However, the network quality on fast-moving in-vehicle devices is not satisfactory. In order to improve the quality of network services in fast moving scenarios, heterogeneous converged networks use existing network resources such as 4G, 5G, and WiFi to increase network bandwidth, but there are more complex security issues than single networks. In addition, the user's real-name information, transaction information and other private data, the location, movement trajectory, and application data of in-vehicle devices need to be protected [1].

The in-vehicle device of the smart car networking is a multi-interface router that supports access to 4G, 5G, WiFi and other network resources [2]. Using the multi-homing feature can reduce the connection interruption problem of the link during the mobile handover process, and also allow us to make full use of the existing heterogeneous network resources.However,it also brings more security challenges. The vehicle communication topology is shown in Fig. 1.

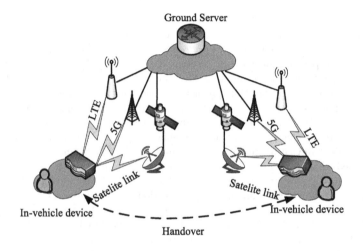

Fig. 1. Vehicle-ground communication topology.

In a wireless heterogeneous network, passive attacks the channels may suffer include traffic analysis, eavesdropping and intercepted information [3]; active attacks such as replay, denial of service, and data tampering. Packet source authentication can solve denial of service attacks and IP spoofing to some extent. However, the highly dynamic and multi-homed characteristics of in-vehicle devices make end-to-end data source authentication from in-vehicle devices to infrastructure have higher requirements, such as lower authentication delay and overhead.

Privacy-preserving is divided into data privacy-preserving, as well as the identity and location protection of both communication parties [4]. Traffic analysis mainly threatens data privacy. It is based on Shannon's perfect secrecy principle [5], which is if the original communication traffic can be changed to conform to a predetermined statistical characteristic pattern, the traffic in the channel will lose its analytical significance. In order to prevent traffic analysis, traffic obfuscation technology confuses traffic characteristics, such as packet length distribution, time distribution, etc. Therefore, methods such as encryption, random padding, and random delay adjustment are often used to obfuscate traffic.

In order not to increase the transmission delay of some application data at the vehicle end, the random delay method is not considered. At the same time, traffic filling will cause a lot of bandwidth waste. Therefore, the use of traffic slicing method in combination with the multi-path advantage brings a new direction to the research on the security of smart car networking.

2   Related Work

2.1   Privacy-Preserving in Vehicle-Ground Communication

The privacy-preserving of the vehicle-ground communication network can be divided into three layers, the perception layer, the network layer and the application layer. Here we mainly discuss the privacy-preserving based on the network layer. The privacy-preserving schemes in this layer are mainly divided into three categories, privacy-preserving based on anonymity [6], privacy-preserving based on ambiguity [7] and privacy-preserving based on cryptography [8]. Anonymity is to hide the identities of the real communication parties. The privacy-preserving based on ambiguity mainly adds noise to obfuscate the real data. The privacy-preserving based on cryptography can use traditional encryption methods to encrypt data, and at the same time, it needs to consider the problem of encryption overhead.

2.2   Link Padding

There are fixed rate filling techniques such as BuFLO [9] scheme for the study of flow filling scheme. That is, the size of the fixed-length data packet is determined, the speed at which the data packet is sent is determined, and the minimum length of the continuous data packet transmission is determined. Adaptive filling technology [10], if an abnormally large time gap is found in the current data stream, it fills the time gap to prevent the time gap from becoming a significant feature. Correlation link padding [11] focuses on ingress traffic rates. Whether and how much masquerading traffic needs to be generated is based on the rate of traffic entering the system.

2.3   Multi-path Anonymity Technology

Onion routing [12] is a typical example in the field of anonymous network research. This technology mainly performs multi-level transmission and data encryption, so that the transmitted data has extremely high security, and hides the source address and destination address at the same time. An anonymous network technology that echoes the onion routing technology is Garlic routing [13]. Compared with onion routing, which establishes a multi-relay communication link between two communication nodes, garlic routing technology establishes multiple communication links for two communication nodes to realize parallel data transmission, so as to prevent data tracking and capture.

Duan Guihua et al. [14] developed an anonymous communication mechanism that does not require key infrastructure. The mechanism divides the information and then encodes it for transmission.The intermediate node randomly selects the coding coefficients to encode the fragmentation information and then forwards it, and the encoding coefficients and encoded information are separated and transmitted along different paths,so that information can be transmitted anonymously without the need for a key mechanism.

He W [15] et al. proposed the Slice Mixed Aggregation Scheme (SMART). After the original data is fragmented, it is encrypted and routed to the next node. When the node receives the encrypted fragmented data, it decrypts it with the shared key, and finally aggregates the data.

Through the above analysis, we can conclude that most of the existing research is based on a specific network or single-channel anonymity scheme. In a heterogeneous network environment, it is necessary to consider the problem of switching the IP address of a single network card and the packet loss under network instability. Therefore, we propose the following privacy protection scheme in multi-link vehicle-ground communication to meet the requirements of privacy protection and bandwidth in multi-link vehicle-ground communication system.

3   The Introduction of Privacy-Preserving in Multi-link Vehicle-Ground Communication System

In this section, the multi-link vehicle-ground communication privacy protection system will be introduced. The system consists of two communication entities: a mobile in-vehicle device and a ground server, as shown in Fig. 2. The whole system can be divided into four parts, which are data encryption and authentication part, fragmentation and reorganization part, link perception part, and virtual packet construction and sending part.

3.1   Data Encryption and Authentication

Realize packet source authentication and integrity detection by using identity-based authentication method, and the shared key is realized by using the bilinear pairing principle of the elliptic curve.

3.2   Link Perception

Implementation of the re-authentication mechanism. The in-vehicle device uses the NetLink mechanism to monitor the changes of the network card at all times. When the IP address of the network card changes, first report that the network card is offline and then bind a new network card, and recalculate the public key and shared key. The ground server returns the network card information of the peer end by the detection packet, and recalculates the public key and shared key.

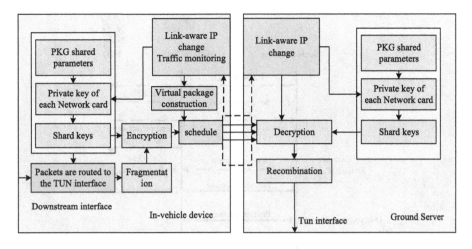

Fig. 2. Multi-link vehicle-ground communication privacy protection system

3.3   Fragmentation and Reorganization

After the data packet is fragmented, the fragment header is encapsulated, and the ring buffer is used to receive it. The network card of the receiving end always monitors the arrival of the fragment. The receiving end has three states: form a frame of data and forward it to the virtual network interface, continue to monitor when reorganizing, and receive the next data packet fragment if the fragment is lost.

3.4   Virtual Packet Construction and Sending

Construction and transmission of redundant packets. After monitoring the speed of the virtual network interface, the data packets are fragmented and forwarded from different links,the speed and data packet lengths on these links are the same. Virtual packets need to be constructed to send within the allowable range of bandwidth.

4   Authentication Mechanism

The overall authentication process is shown in Fig. 3.

4.1   System Initialization

In-vehicle device and ground server register with PKG to obtain the private key,PKG needs to broadcast its own public parameters after initializing itself. These public parameters are $<G, G_T, e, P, P_{pub}, H>$, we can see P as a point on the elliptic curve, G is a cyclic addition group produced in P. G_T is a multiplicative group with the same level q produced in P at the same time, and

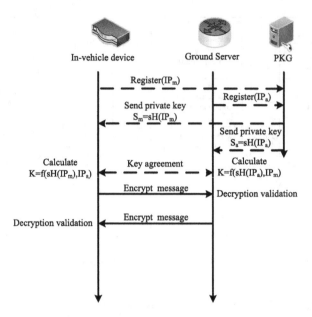

Fig. 3. Authentication encryption process

$\hat{e} : G \times G \to G_T$. PKG randomly generated $s \in \mathbb{Z}_q$, then calculated the public key $P_{pub} = sP$. And $H : \{0,1\}^* \to G$ represents the mapping of bit strings of arbitrary length to the group G, and having the flowing properties.

$$\forall P, P', Q, Q' \in G \to \hat{e}(aP, bQ) = \hat{e}(P, Q)^{ab} = \hat{e}(P, aQ)^b = \hat{e}(bP, Q)^a \quad (1)$$

4.2   Register to Get Private Key

Map the public key of each network card of the communication entity to G according to $Q_m = H\,(IP_m)$, $Q_a = H\,(IP_a)$, $Q_m\,Q_a$ is respectively their public key. PKG will generate their corresponding private keys $S_a = sH\,(IP_a)$, $S_m = sH\,(IP_m)$, then send them in a secure way.

4.3   Authentication Communication

In this way, the shared key is obtained by its own private key and the IP address of the other party according to the flowing equation, and the shared key is used for encryption and authentication.

$$\begin{aligned}
K_{ma} &= e\,(S_m, H\,(IP_a)) = e\,(sH\,(IP_m)\,, H\,(IP_a)) \\
&= e\,(H\,(IP_m)\,, H\,(IP_a))^s \\
&= e\,(H\,(IP_m)\,, sH\,(IP_a)) = e\,(H\,(IP_m)\,, S_a) = K_{am}
\end{aligned} \quad (2)$$

5   Fragmentation Reorganization Mechanism

The fragment header design is shown in Fig. 4, and the design synchronization word is AFAE. The total length of the data refers to the data length of the UDP data packet before fragmentation. The total number of fragments is related to the length of our fixed fragment, and the fragment number is used to prepare the receiver to reassemble the data packet. The size of the current fragment data is mainly because the value of the last shard will be different from other shards. A sequence number is added to each UDP data packet in preparation to reduce the packet loss rate.

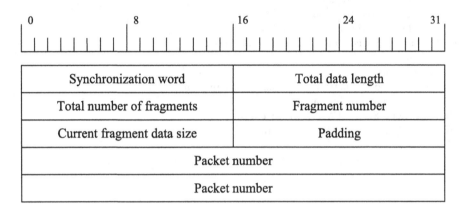

Fig. 4. The design of fragment header.

5.1   Fragment

Monitor the tun netcard through the select function. When a data packet arrives on the tun netcard, the length of the fragmented data packet is calculated and stored according to the actual data packet length returned by the read function. The size of the last slice is the length of the data packet minus the fixed size of the slice, and the length of the other slices is the fixed size of the slice. If the size of the last fragment is 0, the total number of fragments returned is the packet length divided by the fragment fixed size, otherwise the packet length divided by the fragment fixed size plus one. Encapsulate the fragmented data packet according to the total number of fragments returned, to determine whether it is the last fragment, and if so, copy the data circularly until the length is a fixed size. This also belongs to the small amount of padding mentioned in the design scheme.

5.2   Reorganization

Algorithm 1. Fragmentation Reorganization.

Input: The packet piece,p_n;

   The total length of the received packet,R_L;

   The number of fragments received,R_c;

   The sequence number of fragment the currently received packet,a_n;

   The total number of fragment of the currently received packet,a_c;

   The total length of fragment of the currently received packet,a_L;

   The piece length of fragment of the currently received packet,a_l;

   The stored sequence number of fragment,s_n;

   The stored total number of fragment,s_c;

   The stored total length of fragment,s_L;

Output: The Successfully reorganized packets,P;

1: *listen*:
2: **while** 1 **do**
3:      Detected the network port has packet piece,p_n
4:      Copy data to ring buffer
5:      **if** sync word AFAE detected **then**
6:          **if** $R_L=0$ **and** $R_c=0$ **then**
7:              $s_n \leftarrow a_n$
8:              $s_L \leftarrow a_L$
9:              $s_c \leftarrow a_c$
10:             $R_L \leftarrow R_L+a_l$
11:             $R_c \leftarrow R_c+1$
12:             **goto** *listen*
13:         **else if** $s_n \neq a_n$ **or** $s_L \neq a_L$ **or** $s_c \neq a_c$ **then**
14:             $R_L \leftarrow 0$
15:             $R_c \leftarrow 0$
16:             **goto** *listen*
17:         **else**
18:             $R_L \leftarrow R_L+a_l$
19:             $R_c \leftarrow R_c+1$
20:             **if** $R_c=a_c$ **then**
21:                 Discard the fill of the last piece
22:             **end if**
23:             **if** $R_c=s_c$ **and** $R_L=s_L$ **then**
24:                 Successfully reorganized packets,P
25:                 **goto** *listen*
26:             **else**
27:                 **goto** *listen*
28:             **end if**
29:         **end if**
30:     **end if**
31: **end while**

According to the fragment header field, determine the three states of the receiver: form a frame of data and forward it to the virtual network interface, continue to monitor when reorganizing, and receive the next data packet fragment if the fragment is lost. Judging whether it is the last piece, and if it is, the padding data is discarded. Algorithm 1 explained the process in detail.

6   Experiment

6.1   Authentication Mechanism Comparison Test

Comparing the performance of the proposed scheme with IPSec, Table 1 illustrates link parameter settings such as packet loss, bandwidth, and delay of virtual machine. And the algorithm for calculating HMAC are both SHA256. The distinct varieties of the our scheme and IPSec in the field of bandwidth, and out-of-order number, packet loss rate are show in Fig. 5. Overall, the bandwidth consumption of the proposed scheme is slightly less than IPSec. And the bandwidth consumption is related to the length of the added authentication header. The proposed scheme adds a 32-byte header to each data packet. However, in addition to the AH header of 28 bytes, the tunnel mode of the AH packet also adds a new IP header of 20 bytes. Although the difference in measured bandwidth is not large, the proposed scheme out-of-order number is about 24 packets, and the IPSec out-of-order number is about 70 packets. The packet loss rate of the proposed scheme is about 15%, and the IPSec packet loss rate is about 17%. This is because the proposed scheme is coupled to the multi-link program, so it has a smaller processing delay than IPSec. And compared with IPSec, this scheme does not require certificate transmission and DH parameter exchange to establish a connection, which greatly reduces the risk of more delay in establishing a connection when the packet loss rate is high.

Table 1. Links configuration.

Parameters	LinkA	LinkB	LinkC
Loss rate (%)	1.0%	1.5%	2.0%
Bandwidth	4 Mbps	4 Mbps	4 Mbps
Delay	50 ms	40 ms	60 ms

6.2   Fragmentation Reorganization Mechanism Comparison Test

We measured the tunnel bandwidth in the wired environment as shown in Fig. 6, and measured the bandwidth without fragmentation to be about 450 Mbit/s in the single-path case, and the bandwidth of the fragmentation to be about 350 Mbit/s. Fragmentation headers have bandwidth consumption, as well as added

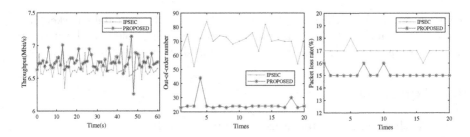

Fig. 5. Comparison with IPSec.

padding for fixed length. Fragmentation is sensitive to the packet loss rate. If the packet loss rate of the link is b% and it is divided into three fragments,the packet loss rate will be between b% and 3b%.

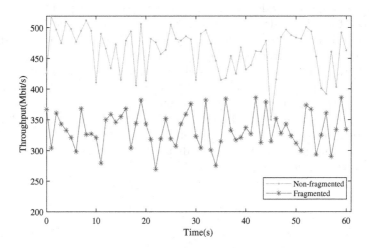

Fig. 6. Bandwidth aggregation efficiency.

7   Conclusion

Aiming at the multi-homing characteristics of in-vehicle devices in multi-link vehicle-ground communication and the problem that the IP address will change, we propose a privacy protection scheme based on fragmentation scheduling and reorganization in multi-link. This scheme takes into account the data source authentication problem when the link IP is switched frequently, and adopts an identity-based authentication scheme that does not require interaction. At the same time, the shared key generated by the authentication part can also provide the possibility for data encryption,and comparing with IPSec's host-to-host tunneling mode, we can see that it is better than IPSec in the performance of out-of-order and packet loss rate. Using the multi-homing feature, the original packets are partitioned and sent from different links. The ring buffer is used to receive and regroup the packets. Finally, the scheme is evaluated by data aggregation bandwidth, and the loss of tunnel bandwidth after fragmentation is in a controllable range.

Acknowledgements. This work was supported in part by the National Natural Science Foundation of China under Grant 92167204, 62072030, and in part by the China Postdoctoral Science Foundation under grant 2021M690343, and in part by the Fundamental Research Funds for the Central Universities under grant 2021RC247.

References

1. Srinivas, J., Das, A.K., Wazid, M., Vasilakos, A.V.: Designing secure user authentication protocol for big data collection in IoT-based intelligent transportation system. IEEE Internet Things J. **8**(9), 7727–7744 (2020)
2. Zhang, X., Dong, P., Du, X., Zhang, H., Guizani, M.: Space-ground integrated information network enabled internet of vehicles: architecture and key mechanisms. IEEE Commun. Stand. Mag. **4**(4), 11–17 (2020)
3. Cheema, A., et al.: Prevention techniques against distributed denial of service attacks in heterogeneous networks: a systematic review. Secur. Commun. Netw. **2022** (2022)
4. Song, J., Wang, W., Gadekallu, T.R., Cao, J., Liu, Y.: EPPDA: an efficient privacy-preserving data aggregation federated learning scheme. IEEE Trans. Netw. Sci. Eng. (2022)
5. Shannon, C.E.: Communication theory of secrecy systems. Bell Syst. Tech. J. **28**(4), 656–715 (1949)
6. Xu, X., Chen, H., Xie, L.: A location privacy preservation method based on dummy locations in internet of vehicles. Appl. Sci. **11**(10), 4594 (2021)
7. Xiong, P., Li, G., Ren, W., Zhu, T.: LOPO: a location privacy preserving path optimization scheme for spatial crowdsourcing. J. Ambient Intell. Humanized Comput., 1–16 (2021)
8. Gai, K., Qiu, M., Zhao, H.: Privacy-preserving data encryption strategy for big data in mobile cloud computing. IEEE Trans. Big Data **7**(4), 678–688 (2017)
9. Dyer, K.P., Coull, S.E., Ristenpart, T., Shrimpton, T.: Peek-a-boo, i still see you: why efficient traffic analysis countermeasures fail. In: 2012 IEEE Symposium on Security and Privacy, pp. 332–346. IEEE (2012)
10. Shmatikov, V., Wang, M.-H.: Timing analysis in low-latency mix networks: attacks and defenses. In: Gollmann, D., Meier, J., Sabelfeld, A. (eds.) ESORICS 2006. LNCS, vol. 4189, pp. 18–33. Springer, Heidelberg (2006). https://doi.org/10.1007/11863908_2
11. Wang, W., Motani, M., Srinivasan, V.: Dependent link padding algorithms for low latency anonymity systems. In: Proceedings of the 15th ACM Conference on Computer and Communications Security, pp. 323–332 (2008)
12. Roy, P., Kumar, R.: Onion encrypted multilevel security framework for public cloud. In: 2022 2nd International Conference on Power Electronics & IoT Applications in Renewable Energy and its Control (PARC), pp. 1–5. IEEE (2022)
13. Ali, A., et al.: TOR vs I2P: a comparative study. In: 2016 IEEE International Conference on Industrial Technology (ICIT), pp. 1748–1751. IEEE (2016)

14. Duan, G.H., Wang, W.P., Wang, J.X., Yang, L.: Anonymous communication mechanism with multi-paths network coding. J. Softw. **21**(9), 2338–2351 (2010)
15. He, W., Liu, X., Nguyen, H., Nahrstedt, K., Abdelzaher, T.: PDA: privacy-preserving data aggregation in wireless sensor networks. In: IEEE INFOCOM 2007–26th IEEE International Conference on Computer Communications, pp. 2045–2053. IEEE (2007)

Smart Mobile Router Wireless Heterogeneous Network Access Mechanism

Dezhen Li[1] , Wenxuan Qiao[1]([⊠]) , Xiangyu Ren[2] , Yuyang Zhang[1] ,
Xiaoya Zhang[1] , and Ping Dong[1]

[1] Beijing Jiaotong University, Beijing, China
{20120063,19111033,zhyy,18111040,pdong}@bjtu.edu.cn
[2] The University of Queensland, Brisbane, Australia
xiangyu.ren@uqconnect.edu.au

Abstract. Under the current international security situation, national communication information security is facing a severe test. At the same time, our traffic network is developing rapidly, and it is also an urgent problem to achieve high quality communication services under the high-speed mobile scene. Traditional solutions include building a dedicated mobile communication system such as GSM-R and increasing the coverage area of mobile network base stations, but these solutions are either limited in scope of application or too high in construction cost, which cannot meet the development needs. In order to provide secure and reliable communication services in high-speed mobile scenarios, we design a device that can integrate multiple wireless heterogeneous networks based on the intelligent fusion network theory. This paper will introduce the design and implementation process of the wireless heterogeneous network access mechanism of the device. The device can access multiple wireless heterogeneous networks at the same time and use multiple links to provide high-quality network services for users. The device can also select the network with the best performance to provide services for users. After a lot of tests and long-term practical operation, the mechanism can better realize the network access and network selection of devices, and then realize to provide users with reliable and high-quality network services.

Keywords: Smart mobile router · Network access · Multi-attribute decision making

1 Introduction

With the breakthrough construction of high-speed railway mileage in China, high-speed railway has become an important infrastructure for promoting our national economy and an important travel mode for People's Daily life. As a result, the communication quality problems in ensuring high-speed mobile scenarios become more and more important and urgent. At the same time, with the frequent occurrence of extreme climate and natural disasters around the world, people are often faced with the need to obtain high-quality emergency support communications in various difficult situations. In addition, the current international security situation is facing a severe test, national information security is in urgent need of credible, secure, stable party and government special communication system. From the technical point of view, the current TCP/IP Internet system has serious problems. Its security problems and unfriendly support for mobility make it unable to provide high-quality services in the above important application scenarios. Based on the intelligent fusion network system proposed by Hongke Zhang, an academician of Beijing Jiaotong University, the intelligent fusion network system can integrate different heterogeneous networks such as 4G/5G cellular mobile network, Ethernet, satellite network and proprietary identification network, so as to provide users with high-quality, secure and stable communication services.

Under the current development form, realizing the fusion of various heterogeneous networks and providing the cooperative transmission capability of various heterogeneous networks is the development goal of intelligent fusion network system. At the present stage, the intelligent fusion network system mainly integrates cellular mobile networks of different manufacturers and different formats, which can initially provide multi-link communication for users. The network fusion capability of the smart converged network system is realized based on the cooperation between the smart mobile router and the smart aggregation router. The heterogeneous network fusion access of the smart mobile router is the basis of the smart converged network (Fig. 1).

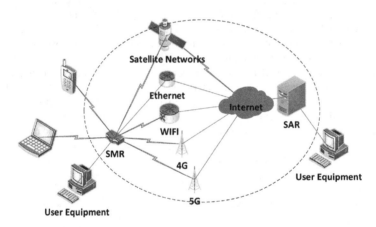

Fig. 1. Heterogeneous network cooperative transmission.

To adapt to the expanding application scenarios, the design of smart mobile router should solve the following problems:

1. System compatibility problems. Due to the complex and diverse application environment in China, different users have different requirements on device performance. To comprehensively improve the application scope of service products, we designed intelligent mobile router devices based on x86 architecture and ARM architecture. At the same time, to reduce the difficulty of development and maintenance, it is necessary to adapt the two types of devices.

2. The scalability of the equipment to the accessible network. The existing smart finance network equipment has good access ability to 4G network, but there are still

problems in support of 5G network and proprietary VPDN card. It needs to invest special manpower for adaptation during expansion, so it cannot be used as needed.

3. It does not have the ability to independently check and monitor the availability of the network it accesses. The current intelligence combines passive access network equipment is corresponding cellular mobile networks, cannot take the initiative to check and monitor the availability of the access network, resulting in the access network has appeared in the process of actual use is not available, but there is no timely detected and equipment for network switch, unable to provide users with stable network services.

Aiming at the above problems, this paper designs a new wireless heterogeneous network access mechanism of smart mobile router and describes the system structure of the mechanism. Then a network selection algorithm based on multi-attribute decision making is designed to enable SMR to provide users with better network services according to the connected network performance. Finally, the function of the mechanism is verified by a large number of system measurements.

The structure of this paper is as follows. In Sect. 2, the paper will discuss the existing wireless heterogeneous network related technologies. Section 3 introduces the system structure of wireless heterogeneous network access mechanism of smart mobile router. In Sect. 4, the network selection strategy of access mechanism is introduced in detail. In the Sect. 5, the system is proved to be effective and reliable through the actual system test.

2 Related Work

Because the wireless heterogeneous networks to which this system is currently connected are different cellular mobile networks, this chapter only introduces the technological development related to cellular mobile networks. Cellular mobile communication is a cellular wireless network, in which terminals and network devices are connected through wireless channels, so that users can communicate with each other in activities. Its main feature is the mobility of the terminal and has the function of switching and automatic roaming across the local network.

With the continuous development of information technology, the commercial deployment of the fifth-generation mobile communication system has been realized. Among them, the first generation of cellular mobile communication system (1G) uses analog voice modulation technology and frequency division multiple access technology (FDMA) to provide users with analog voice services, but its bandwidth is limited, unable to carry out long-distance roaming. The second generation of cellular mobile communication system (2G) has realized the transformation from analog system to digital system and can provide users with digital voice services. 2G system has many standards, among which the most important is the adoption of Time Division Multiple Access (TDMA). The Global System for Mobile Communications (GSM) with TDMA Access technology and IS-95 with Code Division Multiple Access (CDMA) Access technology, its bandwidth is greatly improved compared with 1G, which can provide users with low-speed data services. The third-generation cellular mobile communication system (3G) is a mobile communication system which can provide voice and data services at the same time. Its mainstream standard is Wideband CDMA. WCDMA, CDMA2000 and

Time Division-Synchronous Code Division Multiple Access (TD-SCDMA), the third generation of mobile communication systems to solve the main drawbacks of 1G, 2G, it provides mobile multimedia services including voice, data, video, and other rich content. The fourth-generation mobile communication technology (4G) is improved based on 3G. It combines WLAN technology and 3G communication technology, through Orthogonal Frequency Division Multiplexing, A series of key technologies, such as OFDM [1] technology, MIMO technology, smart antenna technology and Software Defined Radio (SDR) technology, have greatly improved the signal and stability of wireless communication, and can achieve transmission rates as high as 100 Mbps [2].

On June 6, 2020, the fifth-generation mobile communication technology (5G) officially entered the commercial phase in China. 5g using LDPC, Polar new coding scheme [3] and more robust performance of large-scale antenna technology, makes the 5g can support higher transfer rate and better coverage, its overall characteristic is to have a high rate, low time delay and large connection, can realize people, machine, objects connected, for the advent of the era of human all interconnected possibility [4] provides the basis.

However, due to the limitation of the network construction ability of operators, a single network cannot ensure that users' devices have reliable and high-quality network services anytime and anywhere. National Engineering Research Center for Mobile Private Network of Beijing Jiaotong University proposed the theoretical system of "intelligent fusion network" and its key mechanism based on the previous theoretical research of "identification network" [5, 6] and "intelligent identification network" [7] and designed the key network equipment with "intelligent integration identification network" as the core. This system provides users with efficient and reliable network resources and services by intelligently integrating various heterogeneous networks in the domestic cyberspace and combining bandwidth resources of various dimensions [8, 9].

Based on the theory of smart fusion network, this paper designs and implements the network access mechanism of its key device: smart mobile router. By simultaneously integrating the cellular mobile networks of the three major operators in China, it can provide users with stable and reliable basic network services.

3   System Introduction

This chapter will introduce the system structure of wireless heterogeneous network access mechanism of smart mobile router. The system structure is shown in Fig. 2. According to the function, the system structure of the whole access mechanism is divided into hardware adaptation module, data storage module, resource sensing and management module, and network access and processing module. This chapter describes each module of the system in detail.

3.1   Hardware Adaptation Module

In order to realize the device access to different heterogeneous cellular networks, the first need in the device hardware support. In this paper, multiple wireless communication modules are integrated in the device of SMR, and then the GobiNet driver protocol

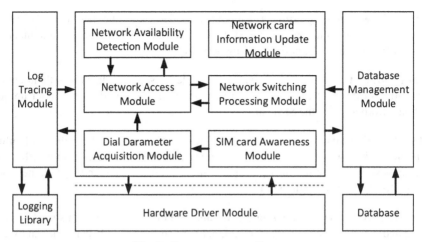

Fig. 2. System structure diagram.

designed by Qualcomm is used to realize the hardware driver of the communication module. However, this driver only realizes the driver of the communication module, which cannot ensure the logical correspondence between the module naming sequence and the module location sequence. Moreover, the driver will make the communication module generate USB devices in the device system, which does not match the naming rules of network devices required by the intelligent fusion network system. The function of the hardware adaptation module is to achieve one-to-one correspondence between the logical sequence and the physical location sequence of the communication module in the system and map the virtual network adapter device name of the communication module into the device name required for intelligent converged network services.

3.2 Data Storage Module

This module is used to manage and store system running data and related parameter data, including log information management module and database management module.

Log Information Management Module. This module is used to record the log information of the system running status and manage the log files generated by the system.

Database Management Module. This module firstly manages and maintains the operating parameters of the system, and then records the data and information to be used in the following maintenance.

3.3 Resource Awareness and Management Module

The module senses the status of the network adapter in the device, authentication parameters required for network access, and network parameters, and manages the display information of the network connected to the device.

SIM Card Awareness Module. The module is used to update the status of the SIM card in the communication module for the system to determine whether the communication module can connect to the corresponding network.

Dialing Parameter Update Module. The module is used to update the authentication information of the SIM card inserted in the communication module and other unique marking information of the SIM card.

Network Availability Detection Module. The module is used to check the availability of the network to which the communication module connects, determine whether the user can access the Internet through the communication module, and provide network services for the user through the link.

Network Card Information Update Module. The main function of this module is to update and maintain the network standard, network signal strength, network bandwidth and other information of the communication module network card equipment, so as to display the front-end call to the user for viewing.

3.4 Network Access and Processing Module

Functionally, this module is the core module of the system, which is used to realize the network access function of SMR and the network switching decision when the network environment of the device changes.

Network Access Module. The function of the module is to determine whether the communication module needs to perform network access operations according to the parameter status of the communication module. If so, run the dialing program to realize the network access of the communication module.

Network Switching Processing Module. This module will collect the network status parameter information of the communication module in the current device, such as signal strength, bandwidth, delay, delay jitter, packet loss rate, etc., and then determine the network connected by the current network adapter according to the multi-attribute decision algorithm, so as to select the optimal network.

4   Network Selection Strategy

Heterogeneous wireless network selection, that is, according to the performance of the network to select the best network among alternative networks. Algorithms have network selection algorithm based on received signal strength, the network selection algorithm based on multiple attribute decision making, based on fuzzy logic and neural network [10, 11] network selection algorithm, the network selection algorithm based on game theory [12, 13] of network selection algorithm based on context awareness, [14] network selection algorithm based on decision function, etc.

In order to consider the network attributes more comprehensively, realize the selection of the optimal network, and relatively balance the algorithm complexity of the whole system, this paper adopts the network selection algorithm based on multi-attribute decision making, and implements it according to the entropy weight method [15]. In information theory, information entropy is expressed as the amount of information, which is inversely proportional to the amount of information contained. In network selection, this feature can be used to express the relative importance degree of a certain network decision attribute in each candidate network. The quantitative representation of the difference of network attribute parameters in candidate networks can be expressed by the information entropy and entropy weight corresponding to the attribute parameters.

Assuming that the SMR device has M candidate networks, and each network selects N decision attributes, the M × N dimensional decision matrix is as follows:

$$A = \left(a_{ij}\right)_{m \times n} \tag{1}$$

where a_{ij} is the jth attribute of the ith network.

The attributes of the decision matrix are standardized [16] to obtain the standardized matrix:

$$R = \left(r_{ij}\right)_{m \times n} \tag{2}$$

Then the normalized matrix is normalized to obtain the normalized matrix:

$$r'_{ij} = \frac{r_{ij}}{\sum_{i=1}^{m} r_{ij}}, 1 \leq i \leq m, 1 \leq j \leq n. \tag{3}$$

According to the definition of normalized matrix and information entropy, the information entropy of attribute J can be obtained as follows:

$$H_j = -\frac{\sum_{i=1}^{m} r'_{ij} \ln r'_{ij}}{\ln m}, 1 \leq j \leq n. \tag{4}$$

Finally, according to the information entropy of attribute j, the entropy weight of attribute j can be obtained:

$$w_j^{EW} = \frac{1 - H_j}{n - \sum_{j=1}^{n} H_j}, 1 \leq j \leq n. \tag{5}$$

After the entropy weights of each attribute are obtained, the normalized network attribute parameters are weighted and summed to get the evaluation score of the network, and the network with the highest score is the optimal network.

5 Functional Test

This chapter shows the results of the network selection algorithm of the access mechanism. The SMR device based on this paper provides six candidate networks, and each network selects network attributes such as signal strength, bandwidth, delay, delay jitter and packet loss rate as the decision basis. The Signal strength is expressed as Reference Signal Receiving Power (RSRP), and its unit is dBm.

When the attribute parameters of the network connected to the current device are obtained in a certain scenario, the normalized matrix of the current decision matrix can be obtained according to Eqs. (2) and (3) in Sect. 4, and then the entropy weight matrix of each attribute can be obtained. The performance evaluation score of each network can be obtained by multiplication of the two. At the same time, the graph can be drawn according to the normalized matrix of attribute parameters, and the advantages and disadvantages of network performance can be judged intuitively from the graph.

As shown in Fig. 3, this figure is the normalized result of the attribute parameters of the network connected to the 6 communication modules in the device when the device moves slowly indoors.

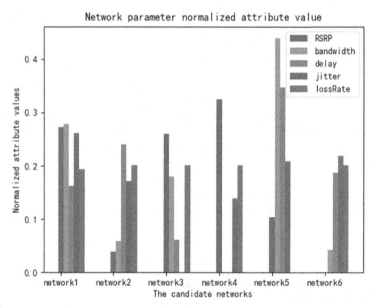

Fig. 3. Indoor, network parameters normalized attribute values.

According to formula (5), the entropy weight of each network attribute parameter in this scenario can be obtained as [0.238, 0.307, 0.199, 0.135, 0.121], The evaluation score of the candidate network can be obtained by multiplying it with each attribute value in the normalized matrix: [0.242, 0.123,0.153,0.120,0.257,0.104], therefore, the fifth network has the best comprehensive performance.

As shown in Fig. 4, the figure shows the result of normalization of the attribute parameters of the network connected by the six communication modules of the equipment when the equipment moves slowly outside.

According to the formula (5) the scenario can be obtained under various network properties parameters of entropy value is [0.250, 0.313,0.162,0.142,0.133], the evaluation score of the candidate network can be obtained by multiplying it with each attribute

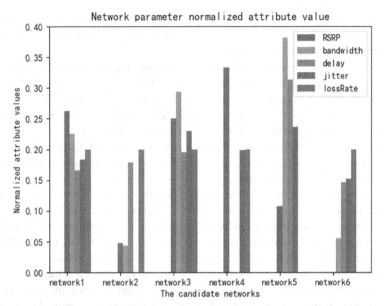

Fig. 4. Outdoor, network parameters normalized attribute values.

value in the normalized matrix: [0.216, 0.081,0.245,0.138,0.230,0.089]. Therefore, the third network has the best comprehensive performance.

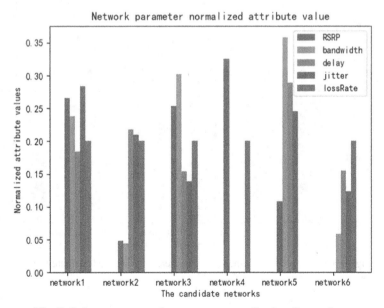

Fig. 5. Laboratory, network parameters normalized attribute values.

As shown in Fig. 5, the figure shows the result of normalization of the attribute parameters of the network connected by the six communication modules of the equipment when the equipment is obscured in the laboratory.

According to the formula (5) the scenario can be obtained under various network properties parameters of entropy value is [0.246, 0.303, 0.154, 0.167, 0.132], and the evaluation score of the candidate network can be obtained by multiplying it with each attribute value in the normalized matrix: [0.239, 0.120, 0.227, 0.106, 0.220, 0.088], so the comprehensive performance of one of the first network optimal.

As shown in Fig. 6, the figure shows the result of normalization of the attribute parameters of the network connected by six communication modules when the device is on a mobile car in the urban area.

According to the formula (5) the scenario can be obtained under various network properties parameters of entropy value is [0.117, 0.114, 0.086, 0.068, 0.615], and the evaluation score of the candidate network can be obtained by multiplying it with each attribute value in the normalized matrix: [0.090, 0.048, 0.104, 0.038, 0.074, 0.032], so the second the comprehensive performance of the optimal of the network.

Based on the above test results, it can be concluded that this mechanism can better select a suitable network for users in various scenarios and can meet the needs of smart mobile routers to integrate a variety of wireless heterogeneous networks to provide high-quality network services for users.

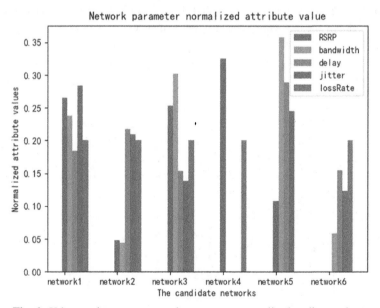

Fig. 6. Urban environment, network parameters normalized attribute values.

6 Conclusion

In the face of increasingly complex application scenarios and severe security requirements, the traditional single network service model is no longer suitable, and heterogeneous network fusion has become a new trend. The smart mobile router and its subsequent smart fusion network constructed in this paper can fully integrate into a variety of wireless heterogeneous networks and provide users with high-quality network services in most scenarios. In some special, signal coverage is weak environment can also provide users with basic network services, increase the application range of its products and service quality.

Acknowledgment. This work was supported in part by the China Postdoctoral Science Foundation under grant 2021M690343, and in part by the Fundamental Research Funds for the Central Universities under grant 2021RC247, and in part by the National Natural Science Foundation of China (NSFC) under grant No. 61872029.

References

1. Sharma, V., Singh, G.: On BER assessment of conventional- and wavelet-OFDM over AWGN channel. Optik **125**(20), 6071–6073 (2014)
2. He, J., Ma, Y., Yang, J.: Discussion on 4G communication technology. China New Commun. **21**(13), 4 (2019)
3. Arikan, E.: Channel polarization: a method for constructing capacity-achieving codes for symmetric binary-input memoryless channels. IEEE Trans. Inf. Theory **55**(7), 3051–3073 (2009)
4. Tian, Y.: Research status and development trend of 5G network technology. Comput. Netw. **47**(04), 39 (2021)
5. Zhang, H., Su, W.: Fundamental research on the architecture of new network——universal network and pervasive services. Electron. J. **04**, 593–598 (2007)
6. Feng, B., Zhou, H., Zhang, H., et al.: HetNet: a flexible architecture for heterogeneous satellite-terrestrial networks. IEEE Network **31**(6), 86–92 (2017)
7. Zhang, H., Quan, W., Chao, H., et al.: Smart identifier network: a collaborative architecture for the future internet. IEEE Network **30**(3), 46–51 (2016)
8. Quan, W., Liu, Y., Zhang, H., et al.: Enhancing crowd collaborations for software defined vehicular networks. IEEE Commun. Mag. **55**(8), 80–86 (2017)
9. Zhang, H., Feng, B., Quan, W.: Fundamental research on smart integration identifier networking. Electron. J. **47**(05), 977–982 (2019)
10. Hasan, M., Shahjalal, M., Chowdhury, M.Z., et al.: Fuzzy logic based network selection in hybrid OCC/Li-Fi communication system. In: 2018 Tenth International Conference on Ubiquitous and Future Networks (ICUFN), Prague, Czech Republic, pp. 95–99. IEEE (2018)
11. Chen, J., Wang, Y., Li, Y., et al.: QoE-aware intelligent vertical handoff scheme over heterogeneous wireless access networks. IEEE Access **6**, 38285–38293 (2018)
12. Wang, X., Liu, B., Su, X., et al.: Evolutionary game based heterogeneous wireless network selection with multiple traffics in 5G. In: 2019 26th International Conference on Telecommunications (ICT), Hanoi, Vietnam, pp. 80–84. IEEE (2019)
13. Monteiro, A., Souto, E., Pazzi, R., et al.: Context-aware network selection in heterogeneous wireless networks. Comput. Commun. **135**, 1–15 (2019)

14. Ahuja, K., Singh, B., Khanna, R.: Network selection in wireless heterogeneous environment by CPF hybrid algorithm. Wireless Pers. Commun. **98**(3), 2733–2751 (2018)
15. Yu, H., Zhang, B.: A heterogeneous network selection algorithm based on network attribute and user preference. Ad Hoc Netw. **72**, 68–80 (2018)
16. Liao, Y., Liu, L., Xing, C.: Investigation of different normalization methods for TOPSIS. Trans. Beijing Inst. Technol. **32**(5), 871–875 (2012)

A Comparative Study on Routing Convergence of IP-Based and ICN-Based Routing Protocols in Satellite Networks

Fei Yan[1]([✉]), Hongbin Luo[1,2], Shan Zhang[1,2], Zhiyuan Wang[1], and Peng Lian[1]

[1] School of Computer Science and Engineering, Beihang University, Beijing, China
{yanfeienter,luohb,zhangshan18,zhiyuanwang,penglian}@buaa.edu.cn
[2] National Laboratory for Software Development Environment, Beihang University, Beijing, China

Abstract. The mobility of satellites makes it highly challenging to design routing protocols for satellite networks. In this paper, we investigate the adaptability of IP-based and ICN-based routing protocols in satellite networks. Specifically, we conduct a comparative study on the classic IP-based and ICN-based routing mechanisms (i.e., OSPF and NLSR). Moreover, we implement the above routing protocols on OMNeT++ and present extensive comparative simulation results to explore the impact of satellite mobility on the convergence time and messaging overhead. We unveil several critical and counter-intuitive insights in terms of the snapshot length (i.e., period of a stable topology) as well as the convergence time and messaging overhead incurred by OSPF and NLSR in satellite networks. First, the evaluation results show that the snapshot length in a small-scale constellation may not be larger than that of a large-scale constellation. Second, OSPF converges at least 43.49% faster and incurs less messaging overhead than NLSR.

Keywords: Satellite networks · Information-Centric Networking (ICN) · Internet Protocol (IP) · Routing protocol

1 Introduction

Low earth orbit (LEO) satellite networks have been increasingly popular in industry and academia for their wide coverage and potential low-latency transmission [1]. The advantages above have attracted many cutting-edge companies to deploy the satellite Internet, which includes Starlink,[1] OneWeb,[2] etc. These companies aim to provide global Internet coverage for devices around the world. This goal requires that the satellites should process information and communicate with each other directly through the *inter-satellite links* (or simply *links*), which include *inter-plane* and *intra-plane* links. Due to the mobility of LEO satellites, the links may be intermittent, thus causing frequent topology changes.

---

[1] https://www.starlink.com.
[2] https://oneweb.net.

© The Author(s), under exclusive license to Springer Nature Singapore Pte Ltd. 2023
W. Quan (Ed.): ICENAT 2022, CCIS 1696, pp. 233–245, 2023.
https://doi.org/10.1007/978-981-19-9697-9_19

Hence it is crucial to develop a proper routing protocol that can accommodate the topology characteristics. This paper will investigate the adaptability of IP-based and ICN-based routing in satellite networks. We will focus on the routing convergence and the overhead (caused by the control messages).

The IP-based routing protocols have been mature in terrestrial networks with stable connections. Most previous studies on the routing issue in satellite networks (e.g., [2,3]) focus on IP-based routing. Nevertheless, the previous studies failed to capture topology dynamics' impact on the convergence time and overhead under IP-based routing in satellite networks. This is the key question we tend to explore in this paper: *what is the impact of the topology dynamics on the convergence time of routing protocols in satellite networks?*

Information-Centric Networking (ICN) [4,5] is usually believed to be capable of mitigating the topology dynamics. Moreover, the in-network caching of ICN makes it possible to reduce the content transmission cost and retrieval delay [6]. The advantages of ICN are crucial for satellite networks. However, there are few studies on the ICN-based routing protocol in satellite networks, let alone the performance comparison between IP-based and ICN-based routing in satellite networks. To fill this void, we will conduct an extensive performance evaluation on the IP-based and ICN-based routing protocols in satellite networks.

To explore the adaptability of IP-based and ICN-based routing in satellite networks, we conduct a comparative study on IP-based and ICN-based routing mechanisms. Specifically, we focus on classic IP-based and ICN-based routing protocols, i.e., Open Shortest Path First Routing Protocol (OSPF) [7], and Named-data Link-State Routing Protocol (NLSR) [8]. Moreover, we implement the above routing protocols on OMNeT++ and evaluate the impact of satellite mobility on the convergence time and control messages. Our results unveil several counter-intuitive and critical insights regarding the period of a stable topology (i.e., snapshot) and convergence time. The details are as follows:

- *Impact of Constellation on the Snapshot Length:* The satellite mobility will lead to a topology change. We show that the number of satellites in orbit (instead of the number of orbits) affects the snapshot in the polar satellite constellation. That is, more satellites in orbit will not necessarily lead to a longer snapshot length. It depends on the angular distance of the satellites to the link handover latitude in the constellation. To this end, the convergence time of a routing protocol is not strictly increasing in the constellation scale.
- *Routing Convergence Time:* Our simulation results show that OSPF converges at least 43.49% faster than NLSR. The reason is that the IP-based routing protocol should rapidly propagate all the network topology changes to the entire network to guarantee network reachability. In contrast to the OSPF, the NLSR does not need to converge fast due to the alternative paths found by the forwarding plane. Thus the network topology change messages are exchanged among the satellites hop-by-hop in NLSR.
- *Messaging Overhead:* Our evaluation results indicate that the ICN-based routing protocol could incur much more messaging overhead than the IP-based routing protocol for satellite networks. The reason is that NLSR uses Inter-

est/Data packets to maintain the adjacency relationship and exchange routing update messages in a hop-by-hop manner, which increases the exchanging of messages among the adjacent satellites.

The rest of this paper is organized as follows. Section 2 reviews the related studies on the satellite network routing. Section 3 introduces the preliminaries for satellite networks. Section 4 compares IP-based and ICN-based routing mechanisms. Section 5 presents the packet-level experimental results. Finally, we conclude this paper in Sect. 6.

2 Literature Review

This section introduces the previous studies on the IP-based routing protocols in satellite networks and ICN-based satellite networking.

IP-Based Routing for Satellite Networking: Most studies adopt the Virtual Node (VN) (e.g., [9,10]) and the Virtual Topology (VT) (e.g., [11,12]) topology control strategies to tackle the mobility issue in satellite networks. For example, Ekici *et al.* in [9] proposes the VN mechanism, which aims to create a virtual network with global coverage relying on the logical locations of the satellites. The VT mechanism divides the satellite network into a series of snapshots, so the topology within each snapshot is fixed. The satellite routing converts to a static routing problem within each snapshot. However, the above routing algorithms cannot deal with irregular link failures in certain snapshots.

Several studies integrated the above topology control strategies with the link-state routing to deal with the occasional link failures in satellite networks (e.g., [2, 13,14]). For example, Xu *et al.* in [13] propose OSPF+ (i.e., an extended version of OSPF), which modifies the neighbor state machine to achieve efficient Link-state database synchronization. Pan *et al.* in [2] follows OSPF and integrates the dynamic link detection with the regular routing table updates to reduce the onboard satellite memory. Zhang *et al.* in [14] focus on the efficiency and scalability of routing protocols and develop an Area-based SatellitE Routing (ASER) protocol, which inherits the basic functionality of OSPF.

ICN-Based Satellite Networking: Different from the IP's push-based communication paradigm, ICN adopts a pull-based (i.e., receiver-driven) communication paradigm. In ICN, the information retrieval is connectionless; thus, it has the potential to address the mobility issue of satellites (i.e., [6,15]). In recent years, there are many studies on designing the satellite network based on the ICN paradigm, which includes the ICN-based satellite architecture (e.g., [16,17]), the in-network caching strategy (e.g., [18,19]), the efficient data retrieving (e.g., [20,21]), and the information-centric integrated satellite-terrestrial networks (e.g., [22,23]). However, there are few studies on the ICN-based routing design for satellite networks, let alone the performance comparison between IP-based and ICN-based routing in satellite networks.

In this paper, we will apply the ICN-based routing protocol (i.e., NLSR) in the satellite network. Moreover, we will compare the IP-based and ICN-based routing performance to explore their adaptability in the satellite network.

3   Preliminaries for Satellite Networks

3.1   Polar Satellite Constellation

Satellites and Orbit Planes: We consider a polar satellite constellation with a total of N_S orbital planes and a total of M_S satellites on each plane. All the satellites orbit at the altitude of h km. We let $\{S_{i,1}, S_{i,2}, ..., S_{i,M_S}\}$ denote the satellites on the i-th orbital plane. The satellites in the same plane are distributed uniformly, thus the angular distance between two adjacent satellites in the same plane is $\omega_S = 2\pi/M_S$.

Satellite Links: Each satellite has at most four links, which include *inter-plane* and *intra-plane* links. For example, the link between satellite $S_{i,j}$ and satellite $S_{i,j-1}$ is an *intra-plane* link, while the link between $S_{i,j}$ and $S_{i-1,j}$ is an *inter-plane* link. In particular, as illustrated in Fig. 1, there is a *seam* between the first and last plane due to the satellites moving in opposite directions. So the *inter-plane* links between the first and last plane will be switched off. As shown in Fig. 1, the $S_{i,j}$ has four links with adjacent satellites $\{S_{i,j-1}, S_{i,j+1}, S_{i-1,j}, S_{i+1,j}\}$, and $S_{i-1,j}$ has three links with adjacent satellites $\{S_{i,j}, S_{i-1,j+1}, S_{i-1,j-1}\}$.

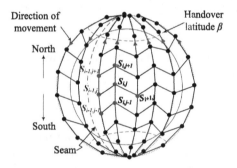

Fig. 1. Polar satellite constellation model

3.2   Duration of a Stable Topology

The satellite mobility will affect the link connection. Specifically, the *inter-plane* link will switch off due to the physical limitations of satellite antennas. By contrast, the *inter-plane* link will be re-established when all the corresponding satellites leave the polar zone. We let β denote the corresponding link handover latitude. We follow the previous studies (e.g., [12,24]) and define the time period between two consecutive regular topology changes as a *snapshot* of the satellite network. That is, given a total of K regular topology changes, we divide the time horizon in the satellite network system into K snapshots, i.e., $[t_0, t_1], \cdots,$ $[t_k, t_{k+1}], \cdots, [t_{K-1}, t_K]$. The regular topology changes occur at the time slots

$\{t_1, t_2, ..., t_K\}$ when the satellites run into or away from the polar zone. Mathematically, we let δ_k denote the snapshot period length of the k-th snapshot period $[t_{k-1}, t_k]$. That is, we have

$$\delta_k \triangleq t_k - t_{k-1}. \tag{1}$$

Note that the snapshot period length could be different due to satellite mobility. We let $\delta_{min} \triangleq \min_k \delta_k$ denote the *minimal snapshot length*, which represents the shortest duration of a stable satellite network topology. Moreover, we let $\delta_{max} \triangleq \max \delta_k$ denote the *maximal snapshot length*, which represents the longest duration of a stable satellite network topology.

4   Comparison Between IP-Based and ICN-Based Routing Mechanisms

In this section, we consider the two typical routing protocols, which rooted in the two classic networking (i.e., IP and ICN).

- OSPF is a classic IP-based routing protocol [7]. It has been widely used to distribute IP routing information on the Internet.
- NLSR is a classic ICN-based routing protocol [8], which is the counterpart to OSPF in this work.

Note that both OSPF and NLSR can achieve topology change detection, link-state synchronization, and routing re-calculation. Therefore, we perform a comparative study of OSPF and NLSR in terms of *link-state detetcion*, and *link-state synchronization* in the following.

4.1   Link-State Detection

Both OSPF and NLSR adopt the *hello mechanism* to detect the link-state changes (i.e., link establishment and failure detection). Specifically, when a satellite starts, it sends hello packets to its adjacent satellites and receives their returned hello packets. For example, as shown in Fig. 2(a), satellite $S_{1,1}$ and satellite $S_{2,1}$ send hello packets to their neighbors once OSPF is enabled on $S_{1,1}$ and $S_{2,1}$. A neighboring relationship is established in $S_{1,1}$ when $S_{1,1}$ sees its Router ID listed in the neighbor's Hello packet. A similar process is carried out in the NLSR satellites, which used NDN's Interest/Data pakcets. Specifically, NLSR sends *hello interest* to its neighboring satellites and receives their *hello data* packets. As shown in Fig. 2(b), the satellite $S_{1,1}$ periodic sends the *hello interest* to satellite $S_{2,1}$, and will receive a response (i.e., *hello data*) to its *hello interest*. Then, the satellite $S_{1,1}$ changes the adjacency status to active.

In link failure detection, OSPF and NLSR satellites send a periodic hello packet to each neighboring satellite, as illustrated in Fig. 2. Specifically, as shown in Fig. 2(a) and Fig. 2(b), the satellite (i.e., $S_{2,1}$) sends periodic hello packet to the neighboring satellite (i.e., $S_{3,1}$). If the hello message is timed out, the

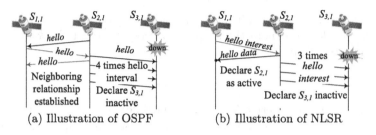

Fig. 2. Link-state detection in OSPF and NLSR

satellite $S_{2,1}$ will try sending it a few times (i.e., four times and three times in OSPF and NLSR, respectively) at intervals. If there is no response from the satellite $S_{3,1}$ during this period, the satellite $S_{2,1}$ will declare the satellite $S_{3,1}$ is changed to inactive. As a consequence, the satellite $S_{2,1}$ creates a new link-state advertisement (LSA) once the link-state change is detected and triggers synchronization of the latest link-state within the satellite network.

4.2   Synchronization of Link-State

The IP-based and ICN-based routing employ a distinct mechanism to propagate the link-state changes in the network. We take Fig. 3 as the example, explore the differences in network changes dissemination manner between IP-based and ICN-based routing, and discuss the underlying reasons.

IP-Based Routing Mechanism: The IP paradigm was designed to be centric on communication between hosts in the network. It assigns identifiers (i.e., IP addresses) to all the hosts (or nodes). Thus, the IP-based routing tables record the reachability information to the hosts in order to retrieve information and generate the forwarding information base (FIB) table for packet forwarding. This means that the FIB table strictly follows the routing table. Therefore, the IP-based routing needs to rapidly propagate the link-state changes to the entire network in order to guarantee network reachability. As a consequence, in IP-based routing protocol, the node propagates the network topology changes to the entire network by flooding (i.e., OSPF).

As illustrated in Fig. 3(a), if the link between $S_{2,2}$ and $S_{3,2}$ is interrupted or restored, the affected satellites create a new LSA (i.e., $S_{2,2}$ and $S_{3,2}$) describing the change and flood the latest LSAs within the networks, respectively. For instance, as shown in Fig. 3(a), the $S_{2,2}$ will flood the generated LSA to all other OSPF neighbors (i.e., $S_{1,2}$, $S_{2,1}$, and $S_{2,3}$). Similarly, the intermediate satellite (i.e., $S_{1,2}$) will flood the received LSA out of all its interfaces but the coming interface. As a result, there are much more duplicate link-state update messages in the satellite network (i.e., $S_{2,2} \rightarrow S_{1,2} \rightarrow S_{1,3} \rightarrow S_{2,3} \rightarrow S_{2,2}$).

ICN-Based Routing Mechanism: Different from IP networking, ICN focuses on content [4]. Particularly, every piece of content has a content name, regardless of where the content is stored. In addition, to obtain a piece of content,

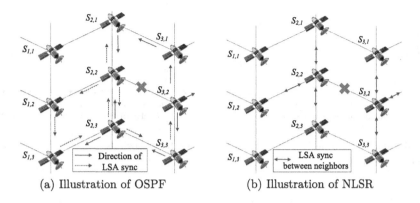

(a) Illustration of OSPF   (b) Illustration of NLSR

Fig. 3. Synchronization of link-state in OSPF and NLSR

a user sends out an Interest packet with the name of the desired content. In such cases, the role of routing is to advertise content names of content routers, disseminate network topology, and compute the routing table to guide the Interest packet forwarding, as the classic routing in NDN (i.e., NLSR). Moreover, ICN's forwarding plane can detect the network faults on its own since the forwarding plane is the actual control plane. This fundamental change results in an ICN device that can handle network failure locally and quickly without the fast routing convergence requirement. Therefore, routing in ICN no longer needs to handle link-state changes immediately in the network, which leads to the routing update in a hop-by-hop manner (i.e., Psync [25] mechanism in NLSR).

We now illustrate the basic process of LSA sync in Psync, with the help of Fig. 3(b), $S_{2,2}$ and $S_{3,2}$ will create a new version of *LSA* whenever its adjacency changes (i.e., the link between $S_{2,2}$ and $S_{3,2}$ is interrupted). If there is no *pending sync interest* in Pending Sync Interest (PSI) table in $S_{2,2}$ and $S_{3,2}$, they have to wait for the *sync timer* expiration before sending a *Sync Interest* packet. Thereby, the satellite $S_{2,2}$ may take one *sync interval* to synchronize the *LSA* with the adjacent satellites $S_{1,2}$ in the worst case. A similar process is performed on each satellite in a hop-by-hop manner. In the worst case, the time required for the latest LSA to travel from one satellite to the furthest one is equal to the number of *hops* multiplied by the *syncInterval*. Thus NLSR may take more time to converge than OSPF, which will be introduced later in Sect. 5.3.

5 Performance Evaluation

5.1 Simulation Setup

We conduct extensive packet-level experiments based on OMNeT++ to evaluate the performance of IP-based and ICN-based routing (i.e., OSPF and NLSR) in Iridium-like satellite networks. Specifically, we consider two sets of constellations to explore the impact of constellations on the snapshot. The first one is the

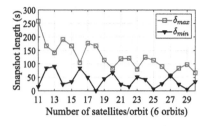
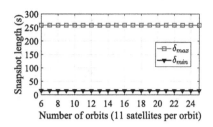

Fig. 4. Snapshots length with different satellites per plane

Fig. 5. Snapshots length with different orbit planes

constellations with six orbital planes and set the number of satellites on each plane as $\{11, 12, ..., 30\}$. Another one is the constellations with 11 satellites per plane and set the number of orbits as $\{6, 7, ..., 25\}$. What's more, we then evaluate the convergence time and the messaging overhead. More specifically, we focus on the three constellations (i.e., 6×11, 6×16, and 8×12), which differ in the number of orbital planes and the number of satellites per plane.

In the above experiments, the satellites are located at an altitude of 780km, in which the link handover latitude is 65°C. The simulation lasts for one satellite orbit period (i.e., 6018 s).

5.2 Duration of a Stable Topology

Impact of Number of Satellites Per Orbit on Snapshot: Figure 4 shows the snapshot period length under the different number of satellites per orbit, which has six orbits. Specifically, the horizontal axis represents the number of satellites per orbit. The δ_{max} and the δ_{min} represent the longest and shortest duration of a stable topology, respectively. We have the following observations:

- As shown in Fig. 4, we can see that the δ_{max} and δ_{min} are decreasing with the number of satellites of the orbital plane increase. However, there are fluctuations in the δ_{max} curve and δ_{min} curve. The reasons for the above observations are two-fold. First, the angular distance between the satellites (i.e., ω_S) in the same plane becomes smaller when the number of satellites M_S increases, causing the smaller snapshot length for the whole constellation. Second, the angular distance of the satellites to the link handover latitude β will vary with constellations, resulting in distinct snapshot lengths.
- From Fig. 4, we find that more satellites in the plane will not necessarily lead to a longer snapshot length. For example, the constellation with 14 satellites in each orbit has a smaller δ_{min} than the constellation with 13 satellites in each orbit. The reason is that the snapshot length is affected by the angular distance of the satellite to the link handover latitude in the constellation.

Impact of Number Orbits on Snapshot: Figure 5 plots the snapshot period length under a different number of orbital planes, having 11 satellites per plane.

From Fig. 5, we can see that the value of δ_{max} or δ_{min} is a constant value in the constellations with the same number of satellites per plane. This means that the number of satellites of the orbital plane (instead of the number of orbital planes) affects the snapshot in the polar satellite constellation. The reason is that the angular distances of the satellites to the handover latitudes are the same when having constellations with different orbital planes.

5.3   Routing Convergence and Messaging Overhead

IP-Based Protocol: Figure 6 investigates the average convergence time for the regular topology changes under OSPF. Specifically, the horizontal axis represents the LSA retransmission interval of the protocol. The vertical axis represents the average convergence time. The curve 6×11 represents the constellations with six orbital planes and 11 satellites per plane. It similarly means for the other curves in Fig. 6. We have the following observations:

- From Fig. 6, we can see that the average convergence time of OSPF increases with the LSA *retransmission interval*. This is because each recipient validates the LSA update and sends an acknowledgment back to the sending satellite that confirms that it received the flooded LSA. This means that the advertising satellite will re-send the LSA when its *retransmission timer* is out, causing the convergence time to increase.
- Comparing Constellation 6×11 (i.e., 66 satellites) with Constellation 6×12 (i.e., 72 satellites) in Fig. 6, we find that the convergence time of OSPF in a larger constellation may not be larger than that of a smaller constellation. The reason is that the routing protocol cannot converge within the snapshot. In other words, a link state change occurred before the last routing change was completed, which caused a convergence time accumulation. This is the reason why the convergence time of OSPF increases sharply when the *retransmission interval* is greater than ten seconds in Constellation 6×11.

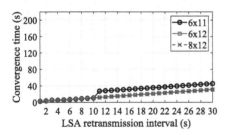

Fig. 6. Convergence time of OSPF

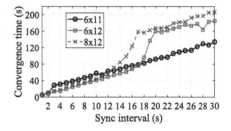

Fig. 7. Convergence time of NLSR

ICN-Based Protocol: Figure 7 shows the average convergence time for the regular topology changes under NLSR. Specifically, the horizontal axis represents the sync interval of the protocol. We have the following observations:

- As shown in Fig. 7, we can see that the convergence time of NLSR increases with the sync interval. The reason is that the synchronization time plays a vital role in the convergence time of NLSR since the latest LSAs are exchanged among satellites hop-by-hop in NLSR.
- From Fig. 7, we find that the convergence time of NLSR increases sharply when the *sync interval* is greater than 16 s in Constellation 8×12. The reason is that the routing cannot converge within the snapshot when the *sync interval* increases. Hence there is the convergence time accumulation in the next round of routing convergence.
- By comparing IP-based with ICN-based routing protocols in Fig. 6 and Fig. 7, we find that OSPF converges at least 43.49% faster than NLSR on the constellation 6×12 with 72 satellites. This is because OSPF and NLSR adopt distinct mechanisms to propagate the link-state to the entire network. Specifically, the LSA update messages can rapidly propagate the entire network by flooding in OSPF. In contrast to the OSPF, NLSR periodically exchanges the LSA update messages among the satellites hop-by-hop.

Control Message: To measure the messaging overhead, we collect the total amount of control messages yielded by OSPF and NLSR during their orbital period (i.e., 6018 s), respectively. Specifically, the size of the message is determined by its LSA header fields, and IP packet header in OSPF [7]. For NLSR, a message contains the essential fields (i.e., the name, the sequence number, and expiration time in LSA[3]). The size of the messages in NLSR may have little difference in the real world but has little impact on our evaluation.

Figure 8 shows the total message amount under OSPF and NLSR in the constellation with 66 and 96 satellites, respectively. Specifically, the horizontal axis represents the average convergence time, and the vertical axis represents the total message amount with the Million bytes (M bytes). What's more, the subfigure is the control messages amount under OSPF. By comparing OSPF and NLSR in Fig. 8(a) and (b), we can see that OSPF has less control messages than NLSR. This is because the NLSR uses NDN's Interest/Data packets to maintain the adjacency relationship and exchange routing update messages, which bring much more messages exchanged among the adjacent satellites.

---

[3] https://github.com/named-data/NLSR/blob/master/src/lsa/lsa.hpp.

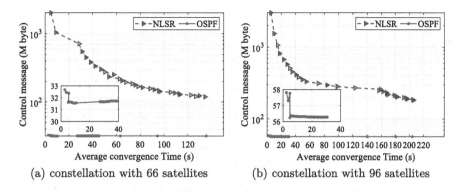

(a) constellation with 66 satellites   (b) constellation with 96 satellites

Fig. 8. Message amount with different network scales

6   Conclusion

This paper investigates the adaptability of IP-based and ICN-based routing protocols (i.e., OSPF and NLSR) for satellite networks. Specifically, we perform a comparative study of OSPF and NLSR in terms of link-state detection and synchronization of link-state. We implemented the above routing protocols on the OMNeT++ platform. Moreover, we conducted extensive packet-level evaluations to explore the duration of a stable topology and the performance of IP-based and ICN-based routing in terms of convergence time and messaging overhead. Our results reveal several critical insights. For example, a larger satellite constellation may not increase the convergence time, which is impacted by snapshot length. Moreover, the ICN-based protocol takes longer to converge than the IP-based protocol and incurs more messaging overhead.

In the future, we will further compare IP-based and ICN-based routing in terms of packet delivery performance (i.e., packet delivery ratio, packet delay).

Acknowledgements. This work was supported in part by the National Key R&D Program of China under Grant 2019YFB1802803, in part by the Nature Science Foundation of China under Grant 62202021, 62271019, in part by Beijing Municipal Natural Science Foundation under Grant L192028, in part by State Key Laboratory of Software Development Environment under Grant SKLSDE-2022ZX-18, in part by the Fundamental Research Funds for the Central Universities, and in part by Grant DXZT-JC-ZZ-2016-008.

References

1. Handley, M.: Delay is not an option: low latency routing in space. In: Proceedings of the 17th ACM Workshop on Hot Topics in Networks, Redmond, WA, USA, pp. 85–91 (2018)
2. Pan, T., Huang, T., Li, X., Chen, Y., Xue, W., Liu, Y.: OPSPF: orbit prediction shortest path first routing for resilient LEO satellite networks. In: Proceedings

of IEEE International Conference on Communications, Shanghai, China, pp. 1–6 (2019)

3. Kumar, P., Bhushan, S., Halder, D., Baswade, A.M.: fybrrLink: efficient QoS-aware routing in SDN enabled future satellite networks. IEEE Trans. Netw. Service Manag **19**(3), 2107–2118 (2022)

4. Jacobson, V., Smetters, D.K., Thornton, J.D., Plass, M.F., Briggs, N.H., Braynard, R.: Networking named content. In: Proceedings of the 5th International Conference on Emerging Networking Experiments and Technologies, Rome, Italy, pp. 1–12 (2009)

5. Seskar, I., Nagaraja, K., Nelson, S.C., Raychaudhuri, D.: MobilityFirst future internet architecture project. In: Proceedings of the 7th Asian Internet Engineering Conference, Bangkok, Thailand, pp. 1–3 (2011)

6. Siris, V.A., Ververidis, C.N., Polyzos, G.C., Liolis, K.P.: Information-centric networking (ICN) architectures for integration of satellites into the future internet. In: Proceedings of the 2012 IEEE First AESS European Conference on Satellite Telecommunications (ESTEL), Rome, Italy, pp. 1–6 (2009)

7. Moy, J.: OSPF version 2. RFC 2328, pp. 1–244 (1998)

8. Wang, L., Lehman, V., Hoque, A.K.M.M., Zhang, B., Yu, Y., Zhang, L.: A secure link state routing protocol for NDN. IEEE Access **6**, 10470–10482 (2018)

9. Ekici, E., Akyildiz, I.F., Bender, M.D.: A distributed routing algorithm for datagram traffic in LEO satellite networks. IEEE/ACM Trans. Netw. **9**(2), 137–147 (2001)

10. Chen, Q., Guo, J., Yang, L., Liu, X., Chen, X.: Topology virtualization and dynamics shielding method for LEO satellite networks. IEEE Commun. Lett. **24**(2), 433–437 (2020)

11. Werner, M.: A dynamic routing concept for ATM-based satellite personal communication networks. IEEE J. Sel. Areas Commun. **15**(8), 1636–1648 (1997)

12. Fischer, D., Basin, D.A., Eckstein, K., Engel, T.: Predictable mobile routing for spacecraft networks. IEEE Trans. Mob. Comput. **12**(6), 1174–1187 (2013)

13. Xu, M., Xia, A., Yang, Y., Wang, Y., Sang, M.: Intra-domain routing protocol OSPF+ for integrated terrestrial and space networks. J. Tsinghua Univ. (Sci. Technol.) **57**(1), 12–17 (2017)

14. Zhang, X., Yang, Y., Xu, M., Luo, J.: ASER: scalable distributed routing protocol for LEO satellite networks. In: 46th IEEE Conference on Local Computer Networks, Edmonton, AB, Canada, pp. 65–72 (2021)

15. Liang, T., Xia, Z., Tang, G., Zhang, Y., Zhang, B.: NDN in large LEO satellite constellations: a case of consumer mobility support. In: Proceedings of the 8th ACM Conference on Information-Centric Networking, Paris, France, pp. 1–12 (2021)

16. Detti, A., Caponi, A., Blefari-Melazzi, N.: Exploitation of information centric networking principles in satellite networks. In: Proceedings of the 2012 IEEE First AESS European Conference on Satellite Telecommunications (ESTEL), Rome, Italy, pp. 1–6 (2012)

17. Li, J., Xue, K., Liu, J., Zhang, Y., Fang, Y.: An ICN/SDN-based network architecture and efficient content retrieval for future satellite-terrestrial integrated networks. IEEE Netw. **34**(1), 188–195 (2020)

18. Wu, H., Li, J., Lu, H., Hong, P.: A two-layer caching model for content delivery services in satellite-terrestrial networks. In: Proceedings of the 2016 IEEE Global Communications Conference, Washington, DC, USA, pp. 1–6 (2016)

19. Liu, S., Hu, X., Wang, Y., Cui, G., Wang, W.: Distributed caching based on matching game in LEO satellite constellation networks. IEEE Commun. Lett. **22**(2), 300–303 (2018)

20. Liu, Z., Zhu, J., Zhang, J., Liu, Q.: Routing algorithm design of satellite network architecture based on SDN and ICN. Int. J. Satell. Commun. Netw. **38**(1), 1–15 (2020)
21. Yang, Y., Song, T., Yuan, W., An, J.: Towards reliable and efficient data retrieving in ICN-based satellite networks. J. Netw. Comput. Appl. **179**, 102982 (2021)
22. de Cola, T., Gonzalez, G., V, V.E.M.: Applicability of ICN-based network architectures to satellite-assisted emergency communications. In: Proceedings of the 2016 IEEE Global Communications Conference, Washington, DC, USA, pp. 1–6 (2016)
23. de Cola, T., Blanco, A.: ICN-based protocol architectures for next-generation backhauling over satellite. In: Proceedings of 2017 IEEE International Conference on Communications, Paris, France, pp. 1–6 (2017)
24. Wang, J., Li, L., Zhou, M.: Topological dynamics characterization for LEO satellite networks. Comput. Netw. **51**(1), 43–53 (2007)
25. Zhang, M., Lehman, V., Wang, L.: Scalable name-based data synchronization for named data networking. In: Proceedings of the IEEE Conference on Computer Communications, Atlanta, GA, USA, pp. 1–9 (2017)

Subarea Route Fusion Mechanism Based on Virtual Links

Jinwen Qin[1], Wenlong Chen[1] , and Chengan Zhao[2](✉)

[1] Information Engineering College, Capital Normal University, Beijing 100048, China
[2] School of Management, Capital Normal University, Beijing 100048, China
zhaochengan@cnu.edu.cn

Abstract. With the rapid expansion of cyberspace, the performance-oriented traditional Internet architecture faces serious security threats. Based on this, this paper proposes a Virtual Link-Based Sub-Area Route Fusion Model. Divareas within Autonomous Systems (ASes) into isolated areas according to security requirements, on the basis of ensuring that the topology of each isolated area is transparent and invisible, the virtual link is used to route between the adjacent areas. The virtual link optimal construction algorithm is designed for the global traffic cost and the link backup path. Then, as shown by the experimental results, through real experiments, we show that establishing fewer virtual links can effectively maximize the global traffic cost optimization, and we can also provide a backup for most and even all links. At the same time, the virtual link can be automatically adapted and quickly reconstructed, reducing the routing cost and time, and balancing the security requirements, routing efficiency and cost.

Keywords: Virtual link · Isolated area · Sub-area route fusion

1 Introduction

With the rapid change and development of Internet technologies, network security accidents occur frequently, calling for stronger security demands for networks. In an intra-domain area, the Open Shortest Path First (OSPF) protocol updates the topology by publishing link state advertisements, and each node knows the topology information of the area. Once a node router is hijacked, the topology information of the entire domain will be leaked, and the attacker will flood the wrong routing information through the router, which will bring routing changes in the network, resulting in serious consequences such as data leakage. In the worst case, it will even cause the breakdown of the entire system. At the same time, each routing area divided by the OSPF protocol will hide the internal topologies by stop publishing topology information. Because other areas cannot be used for routing, the final shortest path is not optimal. Moreover, since the security levels of devices in a network are different, some network devices or areas may have higher security requirements.

To solve the above problems, this paper proposes a lightweight subarea route fusion mechanism, which alleviates the problem of reduced efficiency under the premise of

W. Quan (Ed.): ICENAT 2022, CCIS 1696, pp. 246–257, 2023.
https://doi.org/10.1007/978-981-19-9697-9_20

meeting the security requirements of each Isolated Area (IA) in the domain. The IAs are further divided within the OSPF internal routing area to meet the fine-grained security requirements. Virtual links are established between Border Nodes (BNs) in the IA under the premise of ensuring each isolation area is transparent and invisible, so that the IAs can use each other for route fusion to obtain a better shortest path. In this paper, we aim to maximize the benefits brought by establishing virtual links, i.e., to bring the greatest possible benefits with the smallest possible establishing cost.

The main contributions of this paper include: (1) The different routing areas are transparent and invisible to each other, and the topology information is only transmitted within the area. (2) The routing system is integrated through virtual links between areas. When a node in an area is routed, the routing states of other areas are mapped in real time through virtual links to ensure the optimality of the overall routing across areas. (3) Network managers can integrate management strategies by configuring virtual links. (4) It is exactly the same as the forwarding level of ordinary routing transmission.

Section 2 introduces related work; Sect. 3 describes the specific idea of the model and the routing design between IAs; Sect. 4 presents the optimal establishing method of virtual links; Sect. 5 introduces the performance analysis of this mechanism and the experimental results of real deployment; Finally, Sect. 6 concludes the paper.

2 Related Work

At present, the inter-domain routing policy Border Gateway Protocol (BGP) has been widely studied. It is based on an unconditional trust mechanism between autonomous domains. But this is also the main reason why BGP suffers from various path manipulation attacks. The research on inter-domain routing security has been going on for decades, and routing leakage is considered as one of the important security problems. The main challenge in detecting route leaks is that the business relationship between ASes is kept secret [1]. To detect route leaks, [2] proposes a probabilistic algorithm ProbLink, which reveals key AS interconnecting properties derived from random signals, overcoming the challenge of inferring hard links. TopoScope [3] can be used to accurately recover AS relationships from fragmented observations. TopoScope discovers intrinsic similarities between groups of Adjacent Links (ALinks) and infers relationships that cannot be directly observed on hidden links. But their speculative technique [3] still has errors on some key links. [4] proposed a centralized scheme S-BGP based on the Public Key Infrastructure (PKI) architecture to address most of the security vulnerabilities by using a combination of IP Security (IPsec) protocols, a new BGP path attribute that includes "authentication" and PKI. A method of protecting BGP is implemented for secure inter-domain routing, i.e., using RPKI-based BGPSec [5] to defend against prefix hijacking and path tampering. However, the above methods have some common problems, e.g., the single point of failure of damaged nodes, which will make the entire security mechanism invalid. Moreover, the deployment is difficult and the management is complicated. Lukas Mastilak believes that blockchain-based security inter-domain routing solves the problem of security mechanism failure caused by a single point of failure and it improves the security levels [6]. [7] proposed ROAchain, a new blockchain-based BGP security infrastructure. Unlike RPKI, ROAchain is a decentralized architecture where each AS maintains a globally consistent and tamper-proof ROA repository to verify the legitimacy of routing sources and prevent BGP prefix hijacking. To ensure the strong consistency, scalability, and security of ROAchain, a new consensus algorithm is proposed, which introduces the trustworthiness value, the collective signature, and the sharding and penalty mechanisms. However, blockchain-based secure inter-domain routing suffers from low scalability and high convergence delay.

Besides, when an autonomous network is large enough, the OSPF protocol also has security and performance bottlenecks [8]. To reduce bandwidth consumption inside the autonomous domain and meet the security requirement that some networks can shield the internal layout details of their own networks on the basis of interconnection, a hierarchical OSPF routing protocol is proposed [9]. The implementation of this protocol is based on dividing an autonomous domain into a backbone area and a non-backbone area. The non-backbone area can be divided into multiple subareas, and the link information including detailed routing selection and time cost is only exchanged within the area to which it belongs [10]. However, since the non-backbone area must be directly connected to the backbone area, an Area Border Router (ABR) is required to summarize the link information of each area and finally send it to the backbone area, which then forwards various link information to other areas [11]. Topological transparency cannot be guaranteed between areas and each area is used for routing, resulting in longer shortest paths between a large number of nodes and reduced routing efficiency.

In addition, when OSPF performs multi-area division [12, 13], it is extremely possible to fail to follow the existing criteria for area division, and only non-standard heterogeneous division can be used, which eventually leads to network communication failure [14]. In view of the current inter-domain communication problem caused by multi-area OSPF remote heterogeneous routing and split heterogeneous routing, researchers use virtual connections [15] to stretch and extend the scope of the backbone area to adjacent non-backbone areas, so that the non-backbone areas that are supposed not to be connected to the backbone areas are directly connected to the backbone areas logically to achieve interconnection. However, the logical channel established by virtual links only realizes the point-to-point communication between the two ABRs. The inability to perform route fusion between areas and low routing efficiency still exists.

The virtual link technology has also been applied in inter-domain routing. [16] proposed an inter-domain awareness routing protocol based on virtual links as a potential routing solution for the future mobile Internet. The proposed architecture has been proven able to provide better support and flexibility for routing to wireless devices, network-assisted multi-path routing, routing to multiple interfaces (multi-homing), and Anycast services.

3   Virtual Link-Based Sub-area Route Fusion Model

The sub-area route fusion mechanism based on virtual links proposed in this paper is to divide smaller IAs within the OSPF routing area and establish virtual links between the BNs of two AAreas to solve the problem of reduced routing efficiency caused by area division. To maximize the benefits brought by establishing virtual links, different virtual link establishing strategies are proposed for different optimization goals.

3.1   A Subsection Sample

Isolated Area (IA). A locally interconnected structure whose topology is transparent and invisible to the outside world. There are no duplicate nodes between any two IAs, i.e., no node belongs to two IAs at the same time. Figure 1(a) shows two typical IAs. In Fig. 1(b), although the nodes in IA_p are distributed around IA_q (the physical location has a containment relationship), they are still two completely disjoint areas. For the convenience of analysis, all the subsequent topology structures of the paper are as shown in Fig. 1(a).

Boundary Node of IA (BN). A node in an IA that is connected to other IAs are called Boundary Nodes (BNs). In Fig. 1(a), nodes A and B are boundary nodes of IA_q, and nodes C and D are boundary nodes of IA_p.

Area Adjacency. For two IAs, if there is a direct link between their BNs, the two IAs are called Adjacent Areas (AArea) to each other. A link whose nodes at both ends of the link belong to different AAreas is an Adjacent link (ALink). As shown in Fig. 1, the two IAs in the four topologies are adjacent to each other. If two IAs are connected by only one link, they are called one-way AAreas. The routing between the two areas in this topology is relatively simple and cannot support virtual links and route fusion, which is not the research object of this paper. (Cross-area virtual links are not considered here.)

Virtual Link. It is a link virtually established between two BNs in the IA, and its real transmission path is established based on the AArea of the IA.

For two adjacent areas IA_p and IA_q, there are physical links link(a,c) and link(b,d), $a,b \in IA_p, c,d \in IA_q, a \neq b$. A virtual link vlink(a,b,q) can be configured in IA_p, indicating that the two ends of the virtual link are nodes a and b, and the transmission path of the virtual link is established based on IA_q. Among them, c and d can be the same node.

Due to the phenomenon of asymmetry bidirectional path in Internet transmission, $\overrightarrow{vlink}\ (a,b,q)$ is used to explicitly indicate that the data transmission direction is $a\text{->} b$, while $\overrightarrow{vlink}\ (b,a,q)$ indicates that the data transmission direction is $b\text{->}\ a$. In the subsequent description of this paper, if not explicitly stated, the link weights are all bidirectional equivalents.

Let the optimal path from c to d in IA_q be $path(c,d)$, then the physical transmission path of $\overrightarrow{vlink}\ (a,b,q)$ is shown as Formula (1):

$$vpath(a, b, q) = \{a, path(c, d), b\} \tag{1}$$

If the above virtual link can be established, IA_q is considered able to support IA_p, which is expressed as: $q \rightarrowtail p$. This indicates that nodes a and b in IA_p may use different AAreas to establish multiple virtual links.

The cost of a virtual link is the sum of the costs of each link on its real path, expressed as Formula (2):

$$C\left(\overrightarrow{vlink}(a, b, q)\right) = C(link(a, c)) + C(path(c, d)) + C(link(d, b)) \tag{2}$$

When the link and path costs have bidirectional non-equivalents, Formula (1) represents the virtual link cost in the $a\text{-}> b$ direction. If not explicitly stated, the two-way cost is considered to be equivalent.

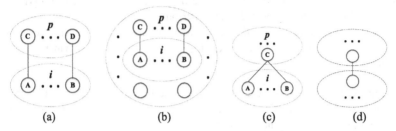

Fig. 1. Analysis of relationships between IAs.

In Figs. 1(a) and 1(b), the two IAs can support each other. In Fig. 1(c), IA_q can support IA_p, whereas IA_p cannot support IA_q. The two IAs in Fig. 1(d) cannot support each other (Table 1).

Table 1. Symbols and descriptions.

Symbols	Descriptions
IA	Isolated areas
BN	Boundary nodes of IAs
$vlink(a,b,q)$	The virtual link established in IAq with end nodes a and b
k	Number of established virtual links constrained by the administrator
μ	Comprehensive optimization capability of a single virtual link
CT	Global traffic cost
CT_{min}	Minimum global traffic cost (establishing all virtual links)
CT_i	Possible minimum global traffic cost establishing i virtual links
$T_{(m,n)}$	Traffic between nodes m and n
S_V_L	The set of all the virtual links can be established in an IA
S_Vcost	Minimum (target) set of virtual links that minimize the global traffic cost
S_L	Set of links that can be optimized
S_Vlink	The smallest (target) set of virtual links that can optimize all links
B	Indicating whether a virtual link has a backup path
N_β	Total number of links with backup paths
TB	Total number of links (establishing all virtual links) with backup paths after optimization

3.2 Inter-area Routing Design Within IAs

After an IA is established, inter-area routing can be regarded as traditional BGP inter-area routing, and each BN can import routes from AAreas. It is obvious that indirectly connected IAs can also import routes to each other through multiple adjacencies to ensure the access of the entire IP network. For the same IA, if multiple BNs import routes of the same IP, the nodes in the IA will select the egress node according to the intra-area routing metrics. In the topology of Fig. 2, for all the packets whose destination IPs belong to IA_1, nodes K, J, and G will select node G, while nodes H and F will select node F.

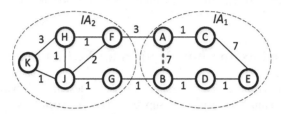

Fig. 2. IAs example topology 1.

Given two AAreas IA_p and IA_q, IA_p has virtual links $vlink(a,b,q)$. Then the nodes in IA_p will perform the Shortest Path Tree (SPT) calculation based on the fusion topology of the virtual links. The shortest paths to some destination nodes in IA_q will contain virtual links. Then, for these destination nodes, the real nodes involved in the virtual links should adjust their next-hops, which is consistent with the Shortest Path First (SPF) calculation result.

For example, in the topology of Fig. 2, before $vlink$ (A,B,2) is established, the next-hop from node J to node A is node G. Because for two reachable BNs F and G, the path from node J to node G is better. After $vlink$ (A,B,2) is established, the SPT algorithm is performed for all the nodes in IA_1. The destination nodes that will be reached through virtual links include: nodes A, B, C, and D. Therefore, the nodes included in the virtual links should adjust their next-hops for these destination nodes. At this point, the next-hop from node J to node A should be adjusted to node F.

In addition, because the virtual link $vlink$ (a,b,q) is configured in IA_p, some nodes in IA_p will also adjust their next-hops according to the calculation result using the new SPF algorithm. For example, in the topology shown in Fig. 2, the next-hops from nodes A and C to B were originally C and E, respectively, while their next-hops after the virtual link was established were F and A, respectively. The changed paths include A to B, C to B, and A to D.

Given AAreas IA_p and IA_q, IA_p has a virtual link $vlink$ (a,b,q), whose corresponding ALinks are $link$ (a,c) and $link(b,d)$, $a,b \in IA_p$, $c,d \in IA_q$, $a \neq b$.

In IA_q, $vpath$ (a,b,q) involves topology fusions of nodes and IA_p, calculating the shortest path to each node in IA_p and obtaining the next-hops. Note that the calculation does not involve the corresponding virtual link $vlink$ (a,b,q). For this task, this paper designs a lightweight incremental computing method. The main idea is as follows, for any node y in IA_p, nodes a and b have already obtained the shortest path cost to y, which are C $(path(a,y))$ and C $(path(b,y))$, respectively. Next, using any node x in $vpath(a,b,q)$ to calculate the path cost to nodes a and b, which are C $(path(x,a))$ and C $(path(x,b))$, respectively. Let $path(c,d) = \{n_1, n_2, ..., n_j\}$ $(n_1 = c, n_j = d)$ and $vpath(a,b,q) = \{a, n_1, n_2, ..., n_j, b\}$. If the sequence of node x on the path is n_l, $l < 1 < j$.

Obviously, the next-hop of $x\text{->}y$ is also obtained in the above calculation process. The next-hops of BNs a and b to some destination nodes may be virtual links $vlink$ (a,b,q), and special handling is required in this case. For nodes a and b, the actual forwarding next-hops of the virtual link should be filled with nodes c and d, respectively. In Fig. 2, the actual next-hops corresponding to the virtual links of nodes A and B are nodes F and G, respectively. (Note, if there are multiple virtual links, they should be calculated together.)

4   The Optimal Establishing Method for Virtual Links

When establishing virtual links, different methods are designed for two different goals, i.e., global cost and link backup path. To support the above two methods, the optimization capability of a single virtual link is analyzed first. CT is the global traffic cost, C $(path$ $(m,n))$ is the shortest path cost between nodes m and n, and $T_{(m,n)}$ is the traffic between nodes m and n.As shown in Formula (3):

$$CT = \sum_{m,\, n \in S\_N,\, m \neq n} C(path(m, n)) \cdot T_{(m,n)} \tag{3}$$

β indicates whether a link has a backup path, and N_β indicates the total number of links with backup paths in the IA. As shown in Formula (4)

$$\beta_{m \to m.neighbor} = \begin{cases} 0,\ link\,(m,\, m.neighbor)\,Without\,backup\,path \\ 1,\ link\,(m,\, m.neighbor)\,With\,backup\,path(s) \end{cases},\ \forall m \in S\_N \tag{4}$$

$$N_\beta = \sum \beta_{m \to m.neighbor},\ \forall m \in S\_N$$

When establishing all the possible virtual links in an IA, the minimum global traffic cost CT_{min} and the Total number of links with Backup paths (TB) in the IA at this time can be obtained. It is clear that when establishing all the possible virtual links in the IA, the maximum number of links can be obtained. Then, based on different goals, the analysis on the optimization capability of a single virtual link has the following three situations: 1) the global traffic cost that can be optimized by this virtual link; 2) the number of links without backups that can be optimized by this virtual link, i.e., the number of optimized Origin-Destination pairs; 3) The comprehensive optimization capability μ (a normalized value) of the virtual link.

4.1   Optimization of Global Traffic Cost

The first optimization goal of this paper is to find the smallest set of virtual links, in which the number of elements in this set should not be greater than k and the set of virtual links can maximize the global traffic cost, i.e., to maximize the reduction of global traffic. Given the isolated area IA_p, the selection method of the virtual link set satisfies Formula (5):

$$min\{x|x = |S_{Vcost}|, CT = min\{CT_k, CT_{k-i}\}, i < k\}; |S\_V_{cost}| \leq k \qquad (5)$$

where S_V_{cost} is the set of target virtual links, CT_i is the minimum global traffic cost that can be obtained when i virtual links are established. Aiming at this optimization goal, the main solution is as follows: Denote the set of all the possible virtual links in IA_p as S_V_L and identify the virtual link that may not optimize the global traffic cost according to the above analysis of the optimization capability of a single virtual link. Then, establish all the virtual links in S_V_L that can optimize the global traffic cost. At this point, the global traffic cost is CT_{min}. After that, analyze and judge the virtual links in the set in turn, i.e., whether the global traffic cost CT changes when a virtual link is deleted. If it remains the same, delete the virtual link from set S_V_L; if the global traffic cost increases, reserve it. Assume the number of elements in set S_V_L is g: if g is less than k, S_V_L is the target set S_V_{cost}; if g is greater than k, delete a certain virtual link in the set. When the number of elements in the set is g-1, the virtual links minimizing the global traffic are gathered. If g-1 is greater than k, repeat the operation until the number of elements in this set is less than or equal to k and the condition $CT_k < CT_{k-i}$ is met. At last, the final set is the target set S_V_{cost}.

4.2 Optimization of Links Without Backups

The second optimization goal of this paper is to provide backup paths for the most links by establishing the smallest set of virtual links. Similarly, the number of elements in the target set should not be greater than k. The main idea of this subsection is as follows: S_V_{link} is a set of target virtual links, which is also a subset of S_V_L. When establishing all the virtual links in set S_V_L, it can be inferred that N_β at this time is TB. It is necessary to identify the smallest subset S_V_{link}, i.e., the number of elements x in this set is the smallest, so that N_β still equals to TB. The description of the above strategy can be expressed as Formula (6):

$$min\{x|x = |S_{Vlink}|, N_\beta = TB\}; |S\_V_{link}| \leq k \qquad (6)$$

Each virtual link corresponds to a set of links that can be optimized currently and the corresponding number of elements v in this set. The algorithm is described as follows:

1) Calculate the links that can be optimized. Let the set be S_L; 2) Given a set for each virtual link, the set contains all the links that can be optimized by the virtual link, and the set element value is the number of links that can be optimized by the virtual link; 3) Select the virtual link with the most corresponding set elements before deleting the links that can be optimized in this set from the set mapped by other virtual links. Update the element value of the set corresponding to the remaining virtual links and reduce the k value by 1; 4) Select the virtual link with the most set elements and delete the elements in this set from other sets until $k = 0$, or when the number of set elements corresponding to the remaining virtual links is 0, the minimum virtual link set is obtained.

5   Experimental Analysis

5.1   Optimization Capability Analysis of a Single Virtual Link

For a given topology, the optimization capability of a single virtual link is first analyzed. Taking Fig. 3 as an example, the ANS topology [17] is arbitrarily divided into two IAs, and Fig. 3(a) is one of the random divisions. In this case, four BNs can be obtained, and a total of six virtual links can be established, as shown in Fig. 3(b).

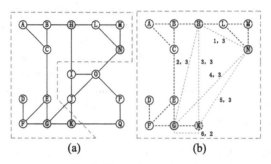

(a)   (b)

Fig. 3. Example topology 2.

In this case, the optimized global cost, the number of links, the number of OD pairs and the corresponding comprehensive optimization capability that can be optimized by each virtual link are as shown in Fig. 4:

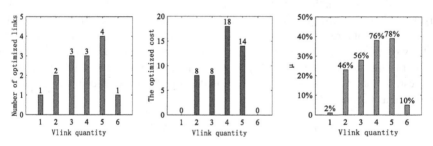

Fig. 4. Optimization capability of a single virtual link.

5.2   Optimization Capability of Multiple Virtual Links

TO illustrate that most of the link cost paths can be optimized only by deploying a few virtual links, the real topologies ANS, ABLIENE, PEER1 and ARPANET are selected [17]. We randomly divide them each into two IAs to calculate the global traffic cost that can be optimized by different number of virtual links under various scenarios and the relationship between them is analyzed. As shown in Fig. 5, for most common topologies, only a few virtual links are needed for ideal optimization.

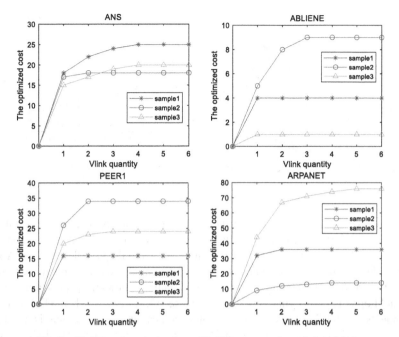

Fig. 5. Global cost optimization with different number of virtual links.

5.3 Experiment with Real Equipment

Path Optimization Cost. According to the OSPF protocol, we build a real experimental network. Its topology is as shown in Fig. 6:

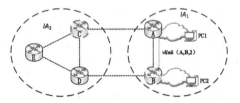

Fig. 6. Real experimental network example.

In the topology of Fig. 6, the path cost is the delay. Under Scenario 1, no virtual link is established, and PC1 and PC2 communicate via path A-B. At the 10th second, the delay of link AB increases and the path weight increases accordingly. The packet sent from PC1 to PC2 still transmits through path A-B, and the number of path hops is always 2. Under Scenario 2, *vlink* (A,B,2) is established and the delay is also increased at the 10th second. The real path of virtual link (*vpath*) is A-C-D-B, so the traffic from PC1 to PC2 in the first 10 s also transmits through path A-B. But as the delay of link AB increases, the path cost of *vlink* (A,B,2) becomes smaller. The path taken by traffic is switched to A-C-D-B, and the number of hops is also changed from 2 to 4. The packet transmission Round Trip Time (RTT) and hop-counts are as shown in Fig. 7:

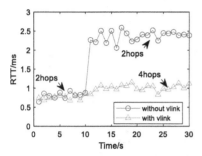
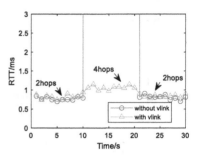

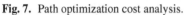

Fig. 7. Path optimization cost analysis.   **Fig. 8.** Optimized link analysis.

Link Optimization. Virtual links can also be used to provide backup paths for links. In the topology of Fig. 6, when no virtual link is established, if link AB fails and disconnects within 10 to 20 s, PC1 and PC2 cannot communicate. After the virtual link vlink (A,B,2) is established, if link AB is disconnected, the traffic can be switched to path A-C-D-B, and the two PCs can still communicate normally. Figure 8 shows the packet transmission RTT and hop-counts of virtual links. As can be seen from Fig. 8, when a link fails and disconnects, the RTT of packet transmission becomes infinite when there is no virtual link, and the RTT of packet transmission when there is a virtual link is only slightly higher than that when no fault occurs. Figure 8 shows that after *vlink (*A,B,2) is established, the number of hops changes from 2 to 4 within 10 to 20 s, indicating that the traffic transmits through virtual links at this time.

6   Conclusion

This paper proposes a intra-domain sub-area route fusion mechanism based on virtual links. On the basis of ensuring inter-domain topology transparency, it can also use AAreas for routing through virtual links to achieve optimal transmission efficiency. To improve the overall network performance, two optimal establishing algorithms of virtual links are designed for two different optimization goals (i.e., global traffic cost and links backup path). Aiming at the problem that topologies may be leaked through the TTL information of a packet, the strategy of randomly modifying the TTL value of adjacent nodes is adopted, which solves the security problem that may be caused by establishing virtual links based on AAreas. According to the analysis result, the virtual links designed in this paper can not only meet the task requirements, but also reduce the routing convergence time, better balancing the security requirements as well as routing efficiency and cost.

It has been well-proved from the real experiments of four topologies ANS, ABLIENE, PEER1 and ARPANET that, in terms of virtual link optimization efficiency, requiring only a few virtual links to achieve the maximization of global traffic cost optimization. In dealing with virtual link failures, the real paths of virtual links can be adaptively and quickly reconfigured without affecting intra-domain routing, reducing routing overhead and convergence time.

Acknowledgment. We gratefully acknowledge the support from the National Key Research and Development Program of China (2018YFB1800403), the National Natural Science Foundation of China (61872252) and the Beijing Natural Science Foundation (4202012).

References

1. Zeng, M., Li, D., Zhang, P., et al.: Federated route leak detection in inter-domain routing with privacy guarantee (2021)
2. Jin, Y., Scott, C., Dhamdhere, A., Giotsas, V., Krishnamurthy, A., Shenker, S.: Stable and practical AS relationship inference with problink. In: 16th USENIX Symposium on Networked Systems Design and Implementation (NSDI 2019), pp. 581–598 (2019)
3. Jin, Z., Shi, X., Yang, Y., Yin, X., Wang, Z., Wu, J.: Toposcope: recover as relationships from fragmentary observations. In: Proceedings of the ACM Internet Measurement Conference, pp. 266–280 (2020)
4. Seo, K., Lynn, C., Kent, S.: Public-key infrastructure for the Secure Border Gateway Protocol (S-BGP). In: Darpa Information Survivability Conference & Exposition II. IEEE (2001)
5. Sriram, K., Lepinski, M.: BGPsec protocol specification (2017)
6. Mastilak, L., Galinski, M., Helebrandt, P., et al.: Enhancing border gateway protocol security using public blockchain. Sensors **20**(16), 4482 (2020)
7. He, G., Su, W., Gao, S., Yue, J., Das, S.K.: ROAchain: securing route origin authorization with blockchain for inter-domain routing. IEEE Trans. Netw. Serv. Manag. **18**(2), 1690–1705 (2020)
8. Kleinrock, L., Kamoun, F.: Hierarchical routing for large networks: performance evaluation and optimization. Comput. Netw. **1**, 155–174 (1977)
9. Piper, B.: Open Shortest Path First (OSPF) (2020)
10. Clausen, T.: Optimized link state routing protocol. RFC 3626 (2003)
11. Spagnolo, P., Henderson, T.: Comparison of proposed OSPF MANETExtensions. In: Proceedings of IEEE MILCOM, October 2006
12. Zinin, L., Yeung, D.: Alternative implementations of OSPF area border routers. Request for Comments: 3509, April 2003
13. Murphy, P.: The OSPF not-so-stubby area (NSSA) option, Request for Comments: 3 101 (Obsoletes: 1587), January 2003
14. Ogier, R., Spagnolo, P.: MANET extension of OSPF using CDS flooding, <draft-ogier-manet-ospf-extension-08.txt>, October 2006
15. IEEE standard for control and management of virtual links in ethernet-based subscriber access networks. In: IEEE Std 1904.2-2021, pp.1–112, 13 July 2021. https://doi.org/10.1109/IEE ESTD.2021.9483874
16. Mukherjee, S., Sriram, S., Raychaudhuri, D.: Edge-aware inter-domain routing for realizing next-generation mobility services. In: 2017 IEEE International Conference on Communications (ICC), pp. 1–6 (2017). https://doi.org/10.1109/ICC.2017.7997140
17. http://www.topology-zoo.org/dataset.html. Accessed 29 Aug 2022

Secure Network Slicing Scheme with Signature Authentication and User Trust

Yiming Luo and Wei Quan[✉]

School of Electronic and Information Engineering, Beijing Jiaotong University, Beijing, China
{20120085,weiquan}@bjtu.edu.cn

Abstract. With the development of the slicing network, slicing service providers need to protect the needs of users for differentiated services and they prefer to provide public APIs to users. However, attacks against public APIs pose challenges to the security of user identity authentication. In this paper, we design a network slicing scheme based on signature authentication and user trust, which provides a standardized and unified security access method through RESTful API. It can make access decisions according to the relevant attributes of users. Besides, we proposed a flexible model for the slicing network, featured by user trust and a decision model. The experiment shows that the scheme can ensure the anti-tampering and anti-counterfeiting of the slicing scheme, prevent replay attacks, enhance the non-repudiation of information and enhance the access judgment ability of the slicing scheme.

Keywords: Slicing network · Signature authentication · User trust

1 Introduction

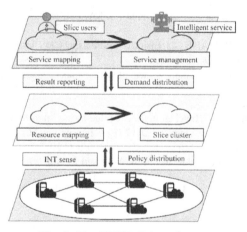

Fig. 1. The SINET slicing scheme

With the development of cloud network technology, the traditional network can no longer meet people's needs, and some flexible network schemes have been proposed. Zhang et.al proposed the Smart Identifier NETwork (SINET), which is a new network architecture [1]. The SINET slicing scheme is shown in Fig. 1. SINET can meet personalized service requirements by integrating multi-dimensional resources, and can provide users with differentiated and customized network services. The overall architecture of SINET has three layers, which are divided into intelligent service layer, resource adaptation layer and network component layer from top to bottom. The intelligent service layer is responsible for managing the service management function that describes the slice service identity and specific behavior, as well as the service query function that manages the mapping relationship between the identity and the behavior description. The resource adaptation layer can dynamically match the corresponding network slice scheduling algorithm according to the service requirements issued by the upper layer, manage the network slice scheduling information and send it to the network component layer to generate the corresponding Network Slice Instance (NSI).

Network slicing [2] refers to abstracting various physical network resources at the bottom layer into virtual resources through network function virtualization (NFV) [3], software defined networking (SDN) [4] and other technologies, transforming network information into digital information convenient for calculation, and providing basis for unified scheduling and unified management of the upper intelligent service layer. Slice users will propose differentiated service requirements when using the SINET, and the requirements will be transferred to the intelligent service layer for analysis and management. The intelligent service layer will abstract the physical network into a logical network, and adapt this demand to the logical network. It will customize the NSI to provide services for slice users, and issue the orchestration command to the resource adaptation center where the slicing cluster is located [5]. The resource adaptation center will map the scheduling commands to the reasonable scheduling of network nodes according to the appropriate slicing scheduling algorithm. In addition, the underlying slice cluster will feed back the network topology information to the upper layer for unified abstraction and management analysis through the In-band Network Telemetry (INT) and other technologies [6].

The SINET realizes the supply and service of new network integration by combining communication and information technology. This process requires to ensure the basic performance requirements of communication services. In addition, it also proposes to implement differentiated services, which requires the SINET to provide a unified slice for unified scheduling and management. Unified scheduling means that the network needs to support the abstraction of existing resources into a logical service, and change the business requirements of slicing users into the call requirements of abstract resources. Unified management means the SINET can describe the state of the whole slicing scheme by collecting the parameter information of the underlying network and the relevant requirements of slicing users, and constructing relevant models. Unified scheduling and unified management can optimize the utilization of cloud resources in network slices. At present, the security assurance technology of the slicing scheme is not yet mature, and there are many security risks. Among them, identity simulation and information leakage caused by resource competition between slices are the main challenges [7].

2 Related Works

RESTful API is the most popular interface design specification, which is widely used. Many application implementations follow this style. Literature [8] considers the requirements met by RESTful API services and analyzes the basic principles of API security. Literature [9] analyzed that RESTful architecture can effectively constrain and help to achieve a simpler, lighter, and more scalable scheme, but there is no unified defense design for possible risks such as identity simulation, replay attack, and identity denial.

In the research on defense against risks such as identity simulation, literature [10] proposed a role-based model for managing heterogeneous access control policies, but the model's processing performance will be degraded when facing user access of SDN network structure. Literature [11] proposed a decision cloud security risk assessment method based on conflict roles, but this method will increase the assessment time and is not suitable for the scenario of massive slicing users of the slicing scheme. The number of users of the slicing scheme will continue to increase, forming a role scheme with complex relationships and difficult to manage, which greatly increases the management workload.

In the scenario of slicing arrangement, literature [12] groups the underlying servers and evaluates the security performance according to the different groups. However, this evaluation method will reduce the performance when facing the arrangement requirements of a large number of slicing users. Literature [13] has designed an identity attribute based storage and access control mechanism to encrypt the image storage index and upload it to the blockchain. When the number of slicing users increases, the cost and time complexity will increase dramatically. Literature [14] proposed a context aware access control framework based on fog. When it is applied to slicing networks, it faces the risk that user data dimensions are too large to process relevant data.

The security threats that may be caused by users in the slicing scheme should be further studied. Literature [15] proposed a combination of k-means and cuckoo search algorithm to resist privacy threats. Literature [16] systematically analyzed the security requirements of the scenarios used by network slicing while sharing resources among multiple tenants, and analyzed the main security challenges of network slicing. Literature [17] designed an elastic slice deployment strategy for operating costs, but ignored user attributes. Literature [18] enhanced the security of the slicing network by dynamically migrating virtual machines, but it could not resist attacks based on the access interface.

3 SINET Access RESTful API Signature Authentication

3.1 RESTful API Introduction

RESTful API is a design specification for Internet software architecture [19], which is based on HTTP protocol. The slicing system side does not store relevant information about slicing users, which perfectly fits the cloud computing mode of the slicing network. Slicing users can interact with the slicing system through this exposed API. In this mode, unified resource identifiers are used to access data. The business operates on resources by using a set of simple and well-defined operations. The client and server exchange resource representations by using standardized interfaces and protocols. Metadata about resources is available and used to control caching and perform authentication or access control. Most importantly, every interaction with the server must be stateless. All these principles help the application become simple, lightweight and fast, and can well adapt to the access scenarios of the slicing system. However, with the development of the slicing network, there are more and more attacks against RESTful APIs, such as tampering, forgery, replay attacks and identity repudiation. In most cases, attackers will push a large number of messages to the server or network to make the service provider collapse, making it impossible to use related APIs.

HTTP basic authentication is one of the common authentication methods, which uses a Base64 encoded user ID/password pair as the user's identity certificate. It is not safe to use it without HTTPS [20], so it needs to be modified and strengthened to be suitable for the SINET slicing system.

3.2 RESTful API Design

When users access the smart financial identification network slicing system, the open API interface will face some security problems, such as the risk of camouflage attack, tampering attack, replay attack and data information disclosure. The SINET Access RESTful API signature authentication module is designed. RESTful API is a set of Internet API design theory based on HTTP protocol. The module is designed to achieve the identity authentication of the slice user, that is, to confirm the operator's identity in the computer and computer network system. The computer can only identify the user's digital identity. The purpose of the signature authentication module is to verify the legitimacy of the identity of the access person, which includes two parts: slice user generated signature and SINET slice system verification signature. Specific process:

(1) Slice users generate data summaries and signatures, and carry signature requests;
(2) SINET receives the request, gets the signature, and parses the summary data from the request according to the summary algorithm;
(3) SINET gets the signature, data digest, and checks the signature according to the signature algorithm.

Fig. 2. Signature generation process

As shown in Fig. 2, metadata is public, and digest information is calculated from metadata through digest algorithm. The algorithm is public to slice users, and then the data digest and key are used to generate a signature through the signature algorithm. The signature algorithm is open to slicing users, which can generally be a hash algorithm or an encryption algorithm. Finally, the request metadata and the final signature are sent to SINET. After SINET obtains the data, it will calculate the digest information according to the public digest algorithm, then calculates the signature according to the public signature algorithm, and finally compares whether the signatures are equal.

The summary algorithm is disclosed by SINET to slicing users. The summary algorithm used here splices the key fields of the request together: *StringToSign* = *SINET_Access_Key* + *ContentMD5* + *ContentType* + *Expires* + *SignatureMethod* + *Timestamp* + *URI*. *SINET_Access_Key* is used to declare the identity of the initiator and complete user identity verification together with the signature algorithm and signature. The purpose of *SignatureMethod* is to let the slicing user specify the signature algorithm, and complete user authentication together with *SINET_KEY* and signature. *ContentMD5*, *ContentType*, and *URI* are used to determine the slicing business request to avoid being tampered or forged after the request is intercepted. *Timestamp* and *Expires* are used to identify the validity period of a request and to avoid replay attacks to some extent.

3.3 Security Functions

The SINET Access RESTful API signature authentication module implement the following security functions. First, it can prevent tampering and forgery. After obtaining the request, the malicious slicing user tampers with the field or forges the business request, which is a violation of the information integrity. To prevent requests from being tampered or forged, the data digest generated contains all the key information of the slicing business. The attacker's tampering with the data field will lead to the final change of the signature. This signature authentication process can enable the SINET slicing system to identify the integrity of the information and identify whether the content has changed. Second, it can prevent replay attacks. A malicious slicing user can obtain a valid network request through network monitoring, and then repeatedly make the request. The timestamp mechanism can defend against replay attacks. The digest algorithm contains the request validity information, limits the window time available for signature, and can prevent replay attacks to a certain extent. Finally, it can prevent repudiation. The non-repudiation of information can be achieved through digital signature technology. The algorithm includes summaries of various data fields of the business, which can ensure that the information is non-repudiation.

4   Design of Trust and Access Decision

Although SINET has changed the shortcomings of low scalability and insufficient efficiency of the traditional network structure, it simplifies the system authorization process and enables users to have greater ability to obtain data, which increases the risk of the network to a certain extent. In many slice deployment schemes, changes in user attributes are not considered, and the protection of resources is insufficient.

As a new network architecture, SDN separates logical control from data forwarding. Various development software based on the application layer realizes the optimal configuration of network resources and functions. In research and applications, unauthorized malicious access and other external threats are also the hot issues in the SDN network security study. Therefore, access control of users' resource access is an effective way to ensure network security while providing users with services such as data access. At the same time, the current research ignores the user side's impact on the mapping security in the slice mapping process, and needs to evaluate its security level by modeling the user side, which is an important part of the slicing system.

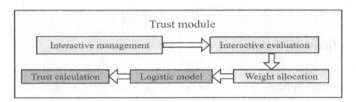

Fig. 3. Trust model

As shown in Fig. 3, a slice user trust module is designed to enhance the security of SINET system authorization process. The interaction management module is responsible for managing the historical interaction between users and slices. The main function of the interaction evaluation module is to improve the user trust when the interaction evaluation is good, otherwise, reduce the user trust. The weight allocation module allocates higher weight for recent interaction evaluation and lower weight for past interaction evaluation to meet the impact of time on user trust; Finally, it is applied to the Logistic curve model to model the growth rate of user trust.

4.1 Calculation of User Trust

The trust degree is calculated according to the historical interaction between the slicing user and the slicing service. When the interaction evaluation is good, the user trust degree is improved, and vice versa. And considering the impact of time on trust, the impact of recent interaction evaluation on user trust should account for a large proportion. The user trust falls within the range (0,1), which is convenient for users to make classified decisions.

The model details the growth rate of user trust based on the Logistic curve model. Logistic curve has a slow growth at the initial stage, and a gradual acceleration at the middle stage. After reaching a certain level, the growth rate gradually decreases, and finally approaches a horizontal line.

In order to consider the impact of time on user trust, aging function is introduced to assign higher weight to recent interaction evaluation and lower weight to past interaction evaluation. The aging function formula is determined as:

$$T_n = \sum_{i=1}^{n} \alpha^{(n-i)} \beta_i, \tag{1}$$

where, n represents the number of times users visit and interact with slice resources. α is the aging factor, $0 < \alpha < 1$, and β_i is the evaluation of each interview interaction. When the interaction is positive, the evaluation is good, at this time, $\beta_i > 0$, and when the interaction is negative, the evaluation is poor, at this time, $\beta_i < 0$. Take the above T_n as the input, and use the Logistic model function to calculate the user trust. Trust calculation formula:

$$D_{i,j}(T_n) = \frac{1}{1 + ae^{-bT_n}}, \tag{2}$$

where, a is the displacement parameter of X axis, b is the growth rate, $D_{i,j}$ indicates the trust degree of resource j to user i, and the result of $D_{i,j}$ is between 0 and 1.

4.2 Access Decision Module

The controller needs to judge the user's access request according to the user's trust degree and access control policies. First, users are divided according to their trust degree. If users have high trust degree and good historical interaction evaluation, they are allowed to access resources and issue long-term effective tables. The drop tables are issued when user's trust is low, and then access is denied. If the access control policies are met, users are allowed to access resources and issue short-term effective tables. If the conditions are not met, access is denied. By introducing the user trust degree and setting the effective duration of the tables, the efficiency of the access decision can be improved, and the dynamic change of the user's access to resources can be achieved. The implementation process is shown in Fig. 4:

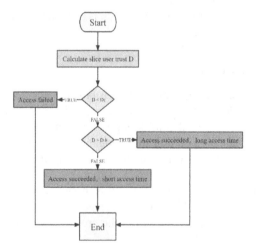

Fig. 4. Access decision process

4.3 Security Functions

As one of the security constraints of the slice deployment method based on the SINET identification network, it can combine the security isolation evaluation value to improve the performance of slice deployment and resist side channel attacks.

The access control method based on trust degree updates the trust degree of users according to the evaluation of their historical behavior, reflecting the trust degree of resources to users as the basis for access authorization. With the change of trust degree, the function of dynamically granting access rights can be realized.

5   Simulation

5.1   Experimental Environment

The testbed has a host with Intel (R) Core (TM) i7-12,700H 2.30 GHz and 16.0 GB RAM. The network is generated using Mininet, and the control tables are distributed using the OpenFlow southbound protocol. The experimental model is shown in Fig. 5.

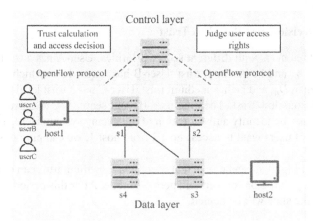

Fig. 5. Experimental topology

5.2   Signature Authentication Security Test

First, we need to ensure that the RESTful API signature authentication model designed can correctly authenticate the identity of the slicing user. First, we assign a slicing user a user ID: sinetSlice and a secret key: 871288641ce7834. Second, the user carries the ID and key to perform the signature operation we designed on the client. Finally, the signature result is encapsulated into the HTTP header and sent to the SIENT slicing system, as shown in Fig. 6.

```
Header:
Authorization : SINET sinetSlice:AnMLEb7Hs8xGZZI6IU/xsks1eKE=
```

Fig. 6. Slice client signature and header

```
16:24:02.083 [main] INFO utils.BasicAuthorizationUtil - SINET slice system signature: AnMLEb7Hs8xGZZI6IU/xsks1eKE=
16:24:02.083 [main] INFO utils.BasicAuthorizationUtil - Authentication succeeded
```

Fig. 7. Successful signature verification of the slicing system

```
16:24:02.083 [main] INFO utils.BasicAuthorizationUtil - SINET slice system signature: qfB/Nhivhy/YGucTwxcGXedI0yA=
16:24:02.083 [main] INFO utils.BasicAuthorizationUtil - Authentication failed
```

Fig. 8. Signature verification of slicing system failed

After receiving the HTTP request, the slicing system will generate another signature. After comparing the two signatures, if they are the same, the user can be classified to be legitimate. As shown in Fig. 7, it is allowed to perform other operations. Tampering, forgery of data fields and replay attacks which change the timestamp will change the signature and cause authentication failure, as shown in Fig. 8.

5.3 Access Decision Test Based on Trust

We consider three users with different secure priorities. User-A has a trust level which is higher than D_h, and he has high trust. User-B has a trust level which is higher than D_l and lower than D_h, and he has medium trust. User-C has a trust level which is lower than D_l and he has low trust. Then the user ID and secret key are given to them, so that they can pass the identity authentication of the slicing system. Here, assuming that the three types of users want to access host 2 from host 1, we can ping to simulate this requirement.

As shown in Fig. 9, it can be seen that user-B with medium trust can only obtain the communication permission for a certain period of time. After this period is used up, his request to use the slice will be denied.

Fig. 9. Limited time window for users with medium trust

As shown in Fig. 10, when user-C attempts to obtain the permission to use the slice, the slice system log will judge that it does not meet the access conditions according to its trust, and give the log "The user trust is lower than the threshold and access is denied", indicating that the user cannot obtain the communication permission of the slice. When users try to use the slicing network from h1 to h2, they will also find that they cannot connect. The specific performance is that all data packets are discarded.

Fig. 10. Low trust users without permission

As shown in Fig. 11, when user-A with high trust attempts to obtain the permission to use a slice, the slice system log judges that he or she has access permission for a long time based on his or her trust, and gives the log "The user trust is more than the threshold and access is allowed for a long time!", The user is prompted that he/she can obtain the communication permission of the slice for a long time. When users try to use the slicing network from h1 to h2, they will also find that they can obtain the permission to use the slicing network for a long time. The specific performance is that all packets are transmitted normally.

Fig. 11. High trust users have long-term access rights

5.4   Scheme Performance Test

As shown in Fig. 12, In order to check the security performance of the above scheme, we constructed 100 normal requests from slicing users and 10000 malicious requests to enable them to access the slicing system at the same time. And observe the safety performance of the scheme from three indexes includes user access success rate, malicious request interception rate and customer demand satisfaction rate. We can see that when

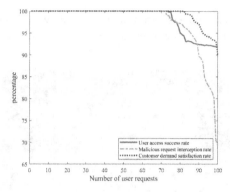

Fig. 12. Relevant parameters of slice security test experiment

the user request reaches 75, all indicators are degraded to varying degrees, but malicious requests can still be intercepted to a certain extent to ensure the access needs of normal users.

6   Conclusion

In this paper, a SINET Access RESTful API signature authentication is designed to ensure that the slicing scheme is tamper proof, forgery proof, and can prevent replay attacks, thus enhancing the non-repudiation of information. SINET simplifies the scheme authorization process, making users have greater ability to obtain data, which increases the network risk to a certain extent. We design a slice user trust attribute and an access decision to improve the ability of slicing scheme to judge user requirements, and enhances the security identification of user attributes. The experiment shows that the slice security is guaranteed. In the future work, we will consider how to properly integrate user attributes with the process of slicing data transmission.

Acknowledgement. This work is supported by the Fundamental Research Funds for the Central Universities under Grant No. KWJBGP22003536.

References

1. Guan, J., Yan, Z., Yao, S., Xu, C., Zhang, H.: GBC-based caching function group selection algorithm for SINET. J. Netw. Comput. Appl. **85**, 56–63 (2016)
2. NGMN Alliance. 5G white paper (2015)
3. Network Functions Virtualisation. Introductory White Paper. SDN and OpenFlow World Congress, 22–24 October 2012
4. Li, E.L., Mao, Z.M., Rexford, J.: Toward software-defined cellular networks. In: European Workshop on Software Defined Networking. IEEE Computer Society (2012)
5. Huang, H., Guo, S., Wu, J., et al.: Service chaining for hybrid network function. IEEE Trans. Cloud Comput. **7**(4), 1082–1094 (2017)

6. Sallent, O., Perez-Romero, J., Ferrus, R., et al.: On radio access network slicing from a radio resource management perspective. IEEE Wirel. Commun. **24**(5), 166–174 (2017)
7. Aljuhani, A., Alharbi, T.: Virtualized network functions security attacks and vulnerabilities. In: Computing & Communication Workshop & Conference, pp. 1–4. IEEE (2017)
8. Kornienko, D.V., Mishina, S.V., Shcherbatykh, S.V., Melnikov, M.O.: Principles of securing RESTful API web services developed with python frameworks. J. Phys. Conf. Ser. **2094**(3), 032016 (2021)
9. Hui, W., Yu, S.G., Yan, Z.Q., Min, L.K., Meng, X., Yuan, Z.Y.: The design and implementation of a service composition system based on a RESTful API. Intell. Autom. Soft Comput. **25**(3), 159–168 (2019)
10. Singh, M.P., Sural, S., Vaidya, J., Atluri, V.: A role-based administrative model for administration of heterogeneous access control policies and its security analysis. Inf. Syst. Front. (2021). (prepublish)
11. Han, J., Zhan, J., Xia, X., Fan, X.: A practical conflicting role-based cloud security risk evaluation method. Recent Adv. Comput. Sci. Commun. **14**(3), 874–886 (2021)
12. Liang, X., Gui, X., et al.: Mitigating cloud co-resident attacks via grouping-based virtual machine placement strategy. In: IEEE International Performance Computing & Communications Conference, pp.1–8. IEEE (2017)
13. Zhou, X., Lin, Z., Huang, J.: An image access control scheme in the blockchain environment. In: Proceedings of 2021 2nd International Conference on Electronics, Communications and Information Technology (CECIT 2021), pp. 248–253 (2021). https://doi.org/10.26914/c.cnk ihy.2021.065421
14. Kayes, A.S.M., Rahayu, W., Watters, P., Alazab, M., Dillon, T., Chang, E.: Achieving security scalability and flexibility using fog-based context-aware access control. Future Gener. Comput. Syst. **107**(C), 307–323 (2020)
15. Murugaboopathi, G., Gowthami, V., Wagner, N., Sundhararajan, Le Hoang, S., Meng, J.: Slicing based efficient privacy preservation technique with multiple sensitive attributes for safe data distribution. J. Intell. Fuzzy Syst. **40**(2), 2661–2668 (2021)
16. Cunha, V.A., et al.: Network slicing security: challenges and directions. Internet Technol. Lett. **2**(5) e125 (2019)
17. Ghaznavi, M., Khan, A., Shahriar, N., et al.: Elastic virtual network function placement. In: IEEE International Conference on Cloud Networking, pp. 255–260. IEEE (2015)
18. Moon, S., Sekar, V., Reiter, M.K.: Nomad: mitigating arbitrary cloud side channels via provider-assisted migration (2015)
19. Lei, G., Zhang, C., Li, S.: RESTful web of things API in sharing sensor data. In: 2011 International Conference on Internet Technology and Applications (2011)
20. Inoue, T., Katayama, Y., Sato, H., et al.: iAuth: HTTP authentication framework integrated into HTML forms, pp. 425–430 (2010)

Network Service Quality Assurance and Security

Online Hybrid Kernel Learning Machine with Dynamic Forgetting Mechanism

Yuhua Wang[1,2] , Deyu Li[1] , Yuezhu Xu[1(✉)] , and Hao Wang[1]

[1] College of Computer Science and Technology, Harbin Engineering University, Harbin, China
{wangyuhua,deyu520,xuyuezhu,wanghao1996}@hrbeu.edu.cn
[2] Modeling and Emulation in E-Government National Engineering Laboratory, Harbin, China

Abstract. This paper, for the purpose of meeting challenges of fewer resources of storage and calculation in the detection of ICS intrusion as well as real-time requirements, has particularly designed an online hybrid kernel learning machine with dynamic forgetting mechanism. First, on the basis of online kernel limit learning machine, a dynamic forgetting mechanism is designed to dynamically adjust the amount of forgetting data according to the current block error, which reduces the system burden and improves the detection accuracy. Then, it replaces the former single kernel function with a hybrid kernel function, which successfully advances the accuracy rate and generalized performance. Finally, a hybrid noise-reducing autoencoder is created to perform dimensional reduction of industrial data with huge dimensions, resulting in the improvement of algorithm and efficiency. The validity and superiority of the proposed online hybrid kernel learning machine with dynamic forgetting mechanism are verified through simulation experiments.

Keywords: Online learning · Forgetting mechanism · Noise-reducing autoencoder · Machine learning · Intrusion detection · Industry-oriented control system

1 Introduction

With the conceptual development and revolutionized evolution of "Industry 4.0", traditional production environment of industrial control systems has been broken, and furthermore the high-speed development of the automation has led to a great increase in the amount of equipment and system functions of industrial control systems [1]. However, the vigorous development of the industrial Internet system has been increasingly troubled and challenged by the hidden security problems, which have seen more serious effects. Industrial control systems were

---

This work was supported by the National Key R&D Program of China under Grant No. 2020YFB1710200 and the High Performance Research Center of Harbin Engineering University.

originally custom-oriented designed for closed internal networks while communication protocols were exclusively designed by device manufacturers, thus the internal networks could not be directly connected to industrial control systems. Therefore, no more efforts have been paid by designers to consider network security issues at the beginning of the design, but more works have been done to ensure reliability and physical security of the system [2]. Nowadays most industrial control protocols are short of measures of basic authentication and behavioral authentication. The operating systems deployed in industrial hosts exacerbate the security risks. Intrusion detection systems for traditional IT systems are not well suited to satisfy ICS systems, especially in terms of computing consumption and real-time performance.

Currently researchers are working to protect industrial control systems from attacks in cyberspace. A new whitelist-based intrusion detection method, proposed by Nakai [3], applies a X-mean clustering method to generate state models from control data collected from power plants. It uses SVM to estimate the current operating state and then generates whitelist detection rules for the normal operating state, and finally monitors the power plant network through the generated whitelist rules. Pan et al. [4] uses the method of data mining to extract a series of temporal characteristics of industrial control systems and construct a corresponding system anomaly model, which could determine whether the system is under attack by matching the current system state with the constructed model. In contrast to the approach proposed by Pan, the literature [5] detects whether there are violations of the corresponding rules in the system by defining system normal rules. Yu et al. [6] proposes a deep packet inspection algorithm for Modbus protocol, which could extract the corresponding data load by modeling the normal state of the system and determine the abnormal behavior once there are abnormal packets.

Most algorithms for ICS intrusion detection fail to consider the real-time requirements of the system [7]. This paper, adopting an online learning approach, designs a dynamic forgetting mechanism on top of the online kernel extreme learning machine to introduce the error of the current model in the data block into the mechanism, which could alleviate the system consumption and avoid dimensional disasters. In order to avoid the drawbacks of single kernel function, a linear mixing method is specially adopted by this paper to linearly mix polynomial kernel function and Gaussian kernel function, which further improves the learning ability and generalization ability of the model. Finally, for the problem of high dimensionality of industrial data, a hybrid encoder is designed to improve the model training efficiency.

2   DAE-DFOS-HKELM

2.1   Hybird Kernel Function

In 2012, Huang et al. introduced the kernel function of kernel learning method into ELM algorithm and constructed KELM with least-square optimal solution, in which simulation experiments were implemented to demonstrate that KELM algorithm could process data more simply and improve its convergence speed and classification performance. The output function of KELM is shown in Eq. (1).

$$f(x) = h(x)H^T \left(C^{-1}I + HH^T\right)^{-1} T = \begin{bmatrix} K(x, x_1) \\ \vdots \\ K(x, x_N) \end{bmatrix} \left(\frac{I}{C} + HH^T\right)^{-1} T \quad (1)$$

The constant C is the penalty term parameter, I is the unit matrix, the choice of the kernel function can greatly affect the performance of the KELM model. Therefore, it is important to find a suitable kernel function for the KELM model. Currently, there is no specification for the selection of the kernel function, which relies more on empirical values. There are three main kernel functions that are most widely used in research: RBF kernel function, Sigmoid kernel function and polynomial kernel function, and the three kernel function forms are shown below.

Polynomial kernel function [8]:

$$K(x, x_i) = ([x \cdot x_i + b]^p) \quad (2)$$

RBF kernel function [9]:

$$K(x, x_i) = \exp\left(-||x - x_i||^2/2\sigma^2\right) \quad (3)$$

Sigmoid kernel function [10]:

$$K(x, x_i) = \tanh\left(v(x \cdot x_i) + c\right) \quad (4)$$

Global kernel functions are more generalized across categories and see most applications in multi-category classification tasks. The polynomial function is a kind of typical global kernel function. The distance of the data points may affect the function values taking from the polynomial kernel function. The core idea of the kernel function is to project data into a higher dimensional space through an implicit mapping. p is used to control the mapping dimension, and the complexity of the overall model. RBF kernel function, a typical local kernel function, has been provided with a good learning ability and thus can approximate the sample with low error. Nevertheless it bears a strong localization.

It is necessary for the traditional ELM algorithm to configure the number of hidden layer neurons and assign the weights and biases randomly, and hence it will produce unpredictable result fluctuations on the model [11]. The introduction of kernel functions may solve the difficulty of manually setting the number of nodes and bias, however, most of the current KELM algorithms only use single kernel functions, which have seen some drawbacks. Therefore, a hybrid kernel function is naturally established in this paper to extend the limitations of the single kernel function in learning sample features. From the basic requirements of the kernel function to be established, it can be seen that the Mercer condition can still be satisfied by mixing the two with a linear method. The hybrid kernel function is shown below:

$$K_{hybird}(x, x_i) = w \cdot \exp\left(-\frac{\|x - x_i\|^2}{a}\right) + (1 - w) \cdot (x \cdot x_i + b)^p, w \in [0, 1] \quad (5)$$

2.2 Dynamic Forgetting Mechanism

Based on the value of the online learning model, Liang et al. [12] proposed an online sequence limit learning machine that could continuously update the output weights in a short period of time. In this paper, a dynamic forgetting mechanism is specially designed and integrated into the process of sequence learning, following the inspiration work of Liang.

Most KELM-based online or incremental learning methods see the data samples incorporated into the model as equally valuable [13]. Obviously, it is unrealistic fort his approach of "weight equalization" among samples to practice in the process of modeling dynamic nonlinear time-varying systems with mapping, particularly in systems like industrial control systems with continuous operation and significant time-varying data, where the newly arrived data should have a greater reference value in modeling [14]. At the same time, whenever the current model performs poor matching to the previous data block, the original data should be discarded appropriately during the updating operation of the weights online. The online kernel limited learning machine with forgetting is defined as follows: Definition 1: Assuming that the data stream $S = (x_1, y_1), (x_2, y_2), \cdots, (x_n, y_n)$, x_j is a d-dimensional input vector and t_j is the corresponding output value, then the ELM with forgetting factor is defined as:

$$\min : L = \frac{1}{2}\gamma^N \|\beta\|^2 + \frac{1}{2}C \sum_{j=1}^{N} \gamma^{N-j} \varepsilon_j^2 \quad (6)$$

$$\text{s.t.} : h(x_j)\beta = t_j^T - \varepsilon_j^T, j = 1, 2, \cdots, N$$

Compared with OS-ELM, Eq. (6) introduces a parameter γ, called the forgetting factor, and $0 \ll \gamma < 1$. Solving Eq. (6), the output weights are obtained as:

$$\beta = \left(c^{-1}\gamma^N I + H^T BH\right)^{-1} H^T BT_N \quad (7)$$

$$E = \text{diag}\,\gamma^{N-1}, \gamma^{N-2}, \cdots, 1$$

Convert Eq. (7):

$$\left(c^{-1}\gamma^N I + H^T BH\right)^{-1} = H^T \left(c^{-1}\gamma^N B^{-1} + HH^T\right)^{-1} \quad (8)$$

Substituting the equations into (6) and (7):

$$\beta = H^T \left(c^{-1}\gamma^N B^{-1} + HH^T\right)^{-1} T_N \quad (9)$$

the kernel weight vector can be updated according to $c^{-1}\gamma^N B^{-1}$.

In this paper, it combines the value of γ with the prediction error of the current data block and designs a dynamic forgetting mechanism, so that the value of γ varies automatically with the prediction error e_f. If the prediction error e_f of the current training data is smaller than the set error θ, it means that the trained model can fit the current data well. Then the value of γ should be infinitely close to 1, meaning complete retention of the original data. In the case that the prediction error is greater than θ, γ should tend to be a smaller value along the special curve, and the following correction function is proposed in this paper to modify the value of γ:

$$\gamma = \frac{1}{1 + e^{(||e_f||-\delta)}} \tag{10}$$

As new data arrives, the forgetting factor can be dynamically adjusted according to the data error, and the function image is shown in Fig. 1.

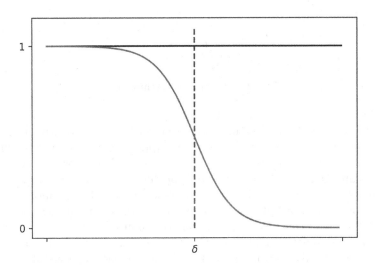

Fig. 1. Forgetting mechanism function graph

2.3 Building DAE-DFOS-HKELM Algorithm

Autoencoder is composed of three parts: encoder, hidden layer, and decoder [15]. The role of the decoder is mainly to extract the potential features of the data samples, which is also called the output layer. It can be represented by the decoding function $z = g_{\theta'}(y)$, the encoding grid consists of two parts of the encoder and the decoder. Since industrial data tends to be high-dimensional the auto encoder always has fewer nodes in the hidden layer, so data compression can be achieved when processing data which similar to the training set. At runtime, the training of the self-encoder on a particular dataset is achieved by increasing or decreasing the number of neurons in the hidden layer, adding penalty terms, and reducing the dimensionality. The relative sizes of the set input and output layers determine whether the data is downscaled or not [16] (Fig. 2).

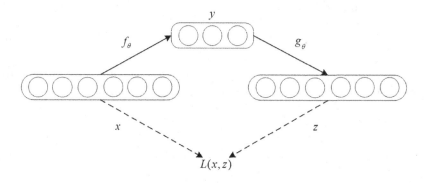

Fig. 2. Auto encoder architecture

In the decoding grid section, a nonlinear coding function is used to represent the mapping relationship between the input layer vectors and the implied layer vectors. The reconstruction error between these two layers is denoted by $L(x, z)$. Through the back propagation algorithm, the AE network cross entropy parameters is fine-tuned so that the minimum value can be obtained.

The noise reduction autoencoder adds noise to the normal autoencoder. After that, Autoencoder can encode and decode contaminated or even corrupted raw data. An autoencoder enabling tothatcan fully recover the original information is not always regarded as the best performer. If the autoencoder can still recover the original data information after the noise is added, such an autoencoder will learn features with stronger robustness [17]. Meanwhile, the DAE method can erase some features randomly without changing the AE network structure. The input data x becomes $\tilde{x}$. Then, $\tilde{x}$ is encoded and decoded. Eventually, the reconstructed vector $Z = g(f(\tilde{x}))$ made to approximate the original data as much as possible, at which point the loss function in the training process changes from the original $L(x, g(f(x)))$ to $L(x, g(f(\tilde{x})))$.

The principle of noise reduction auto-coding is shown in Fig. 3.

Finally, a noise reduction autoencoder is used in this paper to construct a four-layer hybrid encoder for reducing the dimensionality of industrial data, and the overall model is divided into the following four main stages.

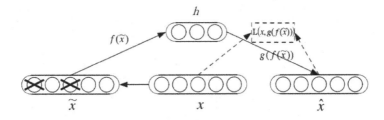

Fig. 3. Noise reduction auto-encoder architecture

1. Data preprocessing: the symbolic attribute features in the NSL-KDD data were numerized, and then converted to between [0, 1] in order to avoid the impact of data metric units on the model.
2. DAE feature extraction and dimensionality reduction: the dataset is trained with the noise-reducing autoencoder, and the dataset is reconstructed with the extracted low-latitude features.
3. DFOS-HKELM Initialization Learning: the noise-reduced encoder-dimensioned data is labeled as reliable data for initial learning.
4. DAE-DFOS-HKELM model validation: A portion of the extracted data is fed into the model, and the effectiveness of the model is determined based on the prediction results given by the model.

3 Experiments

In this paper, experiments are conducted by using the NSL-KDD standard dataset. The main validation of the model depends on accuracy, omission rate and F-score. Such practice aims to verify the effectiveness of the proposed hybrid kernel function and DAE for noise reduction of the data. In order to verify the effectiveness of the hybrid kernel, the Gaussian kernel function and the polynomial kernel function are analyzed in Fig. 4(a). The test point is taken as 0.2, The value of p is 2, and the value of b is between 0.2 and 1.0. In Fig. 4(b), b takes the value 1, p takes the value from 1 to 5. According to Fig. 4, the output of the polynomial kernel function increases with the increase of the input and affects the output of the kernel function regardless of the distance between the sample point and the test point, which fully illustrates the strong universality of the polynomial kernel function and reveals the weak learning ability of the polynomial kernel function.

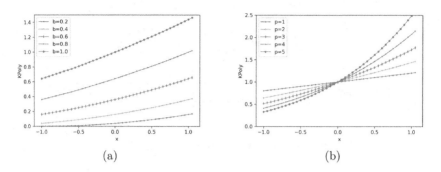

Fig. 4. Polynomial kernel functions with different b and p

In the Gaussian kernel function, the test point is also taken as 0.2, and the Gaussian kernel function a varies from 0.02 to 0.5. Figure 5 shows that unlike the polynomial kernel function, the closer to the test sample point, the better the model works, which indicates the poor generalization ability of the Gaussian kernel function. The closer the sample point is to the test point, the learning ability will be stronger. The hybrid kernel function proposed in this paper combines the advantages of both kernel functions and enhances the kernel function from two different dimensions to avoid the drawbacks of a single kernel function. According to the above analysis, the hybrid functions a, b, p are set to 0.18, 1 and 2 respectively. The weight parameter w is changed from 0 to 1.

In order to determine the value of w, this paper has done several experiments, and the experimental results are shown in Fig. 6. The overall accuracy of the

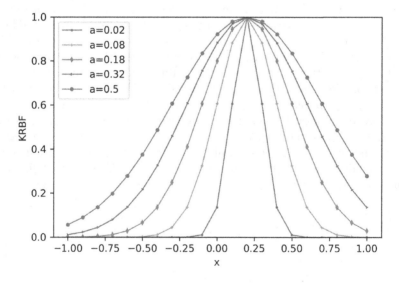

Fig. 5. Gaussian kernel function with different a

model and the recall rate of each sample are higher when the final value of w is 0.938.

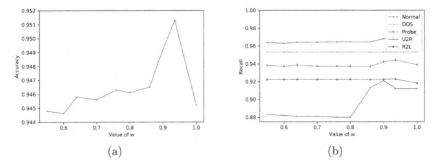

(a)   (b)

Fig. 6. Different kernel function weights under NSL-KDD dataset

To verify the effectiveness of the hybrid kernel function, the algorithm of the hybrid kernel function designed in this paper is compared with the OS-KELM with a single kernel function as shown in Fig. 7. The polynomial kernel function has stronger generalization ability and weaker learning ability, so the false alarm rate of OS-KELM using polynomial kernel function is lower and the leakage rate is higher. In contrast, the RBF kernel function is a typical local kernel function with strong learning ability and weak generalization ability, and it is easy to fall into the local optimum, so its false alarm rate is higher and the leakage rate is lower. The hybrid kernel function proposed in this paper is a good combination of the advantages of RBF kernel function and polynomial kernel function, and it achieves better results than the single kernel function in both leakage rate and false alarm rate detection, and the accuracy of the model is also slightly improved than that of the single kernel function.

In order to verify the feature extraction effect of noise reduction auto-coding, this paper uses the mean square error to measure the difference between the data set after parsimony and the original data set, and verifies whether the data set after DAE dimensionality reduction meets the criteria by MSE.

The data categories in the NSL-KDD dataset are divided into five categories, Normal, Dos, U2R, R2L, and Probe. The dataset is pre-processed to obtain a total of 122-dimensional data features. The 122-dimensional data features are input into the noise reduction autoencoder, and the output method is chosen as 8-dimensional coding. The network structure of the four-layer noise reduction autoencoder is set with the structure of 122-100-50-20-8 neuron numbers, which are named DAE1-122-100, DAE2-100-50, DAE3-50-20, and DAE4-20-8, respectively. The training times of the encoder model are 10 times. The error variation curves of each layer are shown in the following Fig. 8(a).

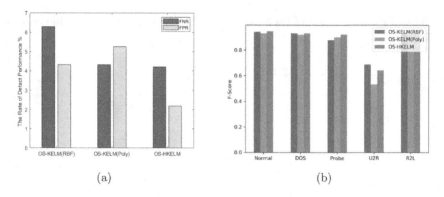

Fig. 7. Comparison of overall effects of models

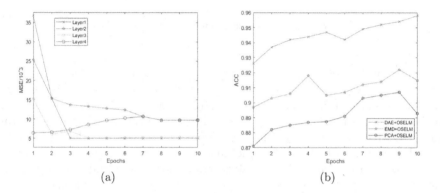

Fig. 8. Different simplification methods

It is very obvious from the curves of DAE reconstruction errors in Fig. 8 that after seven training times, the MSE of most layers has been lower than 0.09. Therefore, it can be considered that when the training times of DAE exceed seven times, each data after noise reduction process has met the criteria and can be used in the subsequent learning tasks.

In addition to verify the effectiveness of the 8-dimensional features extracted by the noise reduction encoder, other feature extraction algorithms of DAE are compared in this paper, and the results are shown in Fig. 8(b). Using the accuracy rate as the judging criterion for the three models, generally speaking, the higher the accuracy rate, the better the model effect. The accuracy of the DAE+OSELM method in ten experiments has a greater advantage over the other two methods, which verifies the effectiveness of the designed DAE.

Figure 9 shows the comparison of training time between DAE-DFOS-HKELM, SVM and DFOS-HKELM. It can be seen from Fig. 9 that the overall training time of the algorithm has decreased significantly after the online learning mode is adopted. Through the comparative experiments of DFOS-HKELM and DAE-DFOS-HKELM, it can be proved that the training speed of the overall model still drops exponentially after the dimension reduction of DAE, and the accuracy rate is almost the same, which fully proves the feasibility of reducing the dimension of industrial data through DAE.

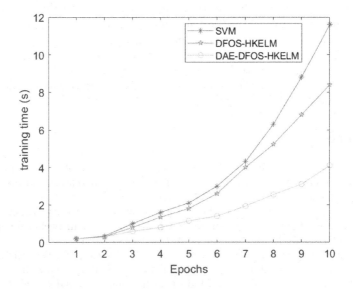

Fig. 9. Comparison of algorithm training time

The final experimental results of the algorithm for the adaptive forgetting mechanism proposed in this paper are shown in Table 1.

Table 1. Experiments

Algorithms	Normal	DOS	Probe	U2R	R2L
SVM	96.14	95.37	83.02	37.25	64.95
OS-KELM	95.23	94.92	82.56	42.1	77.23
FOS-KELM	96.47	93.98	81.72	41.74	77.64
RFOS-KELM	96.51	94.22	80.10	44.34	78.84
DAE-DFOS-HKELM	**96.78**	**94.57**	**82.14**	**55.5**	**81.89**

4 Conclusion

A dynamic forgetting mechanism is specially designed in this paper on the basis of online kernel extreme learning machine for industrial control systems, featuring few computing resources, high real-time requirements and large data dimensionality. The experiments demonstrate the superiority of this method. The drawbacks of single kernel functions are avoided by introducing hybrid kernel functions. Finally, the hybrid encoder is used to reduce the dimension of the data, which further reduces the burden of the system. Although the algorithm is designed based on an online learning approach, the algorithm still does not practice real-time operation in the true sense, and it remains to be proven how well the algorithm performs with streaming data.

Acknowledgements. This work was supported by the National Key R&D Program of China under Grant No. 2020YFB1710200 and the High Performance Research Center of Harbin Engineering University.

References

1. Wollschlaeger, M., Sauter, T., Jasperneite, J.: The future of industrial communication: automation networks in the era of the Internet of Things and Industry 4.0. IEEE Ind. Electron. Mag. **11**(1), 17–27 (2017)
2. Evdokimov, S., Fabian, B., Günther, O., Ivantysynova, L., Ziekow, H., et al.: RFID and the internet of things: Technology, applications, and security challenges. Found. Trends® Technol. Inf. Oper. Manag. **4**(2), 105–185 (2011)
3. Nakai, T., Ichikawa, S., Kobayashi, N., Hata, K., Sawada, K.: Whitelisting cyber attack detection according to estimated operational states for CPS. In: 2019 IEEE 17th International Conference on Industrial Informatics (INDIN), vol. 1, pp. 440–445. IEEE (2019)
4. Pan, S., Morris, T., Adhikari, U.: Classification of disturbances and cyber-attacks in power systems using heterogeneous time-synchronized data. IEEE Trans. Ind. Inform. **11**(3), 650–662 (2015)
5. Mitchell, R., Chen, R.: Behavior-rule based intrusion detection systems for safety critical smart grid applications. IEEE Trans. Smart Grid **4**(3), 1254–1263 (2013)
6. Yusheng, W., Kefeng, F., Yingxu, L., Zenghui, L., Ruikang, Z., Xiangzhen, Y., Lin, L.: Intrusion detection of industrial control system based on Modbus TCP protocol. In: 2017 IEEE 13th International Symposium on Autonomous Decentralized System (ISADS), pp. 156–162. IEEE (2017)
7. Hu, Y., Yang, A., Li, H., Sun, Y., Sun, L.: A survey of intrusion detection on industrial control systems. Int. J. Distrib. Sen. Netw. **14**(8), 1550147718794615 (2018)
8. Padierna, L.C., Carpio, M., Rojas-Domínguez, A., Puga, H., Fraire, H.: A novel formulation of orthogonal polynomial kernel functions for SVM classifiers: the Gegenbauer family. Pattern Recogn. **84**, 211–225 (2018)
9. Han, S., Qubo, C., Meng, H.: Parameter selection in SVM with RBF kernel function. In: World Automation Congress 2012, pp. 1–4. IEEE (2012)
10. An-na, W., Yue, Z., Yun-tao, H., Yun-lu, L.: A novel construction of SVM compound kernel function. In: 2010 International Conference on Logistics Systems and Intelligent Management (ICLSIM), vol. 3, pp. 1462–1465. IEEE (2010)
11. Ding, S., Xu, X., Nie, R.: Extreme learning machine and its applications. Neural Comput. Appl. **25**(3), 549–556 (2014)
12. Liang, N.Y., Huang, G.B., Saratchandran, P., Sundararajan, N.: A fast and accurate online sequential learning algorithm for feedforward networks. IEEE Trans. Neural Netw. **17**(6), 1411–1423 (2006)

13. Zhang, W., Xu, A., Ping, D., Gao, M.: An improved kernel-based incremental extreme learning machine with fixed budget for nonstationary time series prediction. Neural Comput. Appl. **31**(3), 637–652 (2019)

14. Guo, W., Xu, T., Yu, J.J., Tang, K.M.: Online sequential overrun learning machine based on M-estimator and variable forgetting factor. J. Electron. Inf. **40**(6), 1360–1367 (2018)

15. Ashfahani, A., Pratama, M., Lughofer, E., Ong, Y.S.: DEVDAN: deep evolving denoising autoencoder. Neurocomputing **390**, 297–314 (2020)

16. Rifai, S., Vincent, P., Muller, X., Glorot, X., Bengio, Y.: Contractive auto-encoders: explicit invariance during feature extraction. In: ICML, vol. 23, no. 1, pp. 69–101 (1996)

17. Chen, M., Xu, Z., Weinberger, K., Sha, F.: Marginalized denoising autoencoders for domain adaptation. arXiv preprint arXiv:1206.4683 (2012)

TraCGAN: An Efficient Traffic Classification Framework Based on Semi-supervised Learning with Deep Conventional Generative Adversarial Network

Yixin Chen[✉] and Shuai Wang

Guangdong Research Institute, China Telecom Corp Ltd.,
Guangzhou, Guangdong, China
{chenyx34,wangshuai8}@chinatelecom.cn

Abstract. Traffic classification is an engineering technology widely used in network design, service differentiation, accounting, cyber security, etc. Internet technology developed rapidly in recent years. Meanwhile, web applications become varied, and the scale of web service traffic increases dramatically. Hence it remains an open problem to classify different service traffic. To deal with this issue, we propose TraCGAN, an improved deep conventional generative adversarial network (DCGAN) model based on a semi-supervised learning method. We adopted and adjusted the internal network structure of DCGAN so that TraCGAN could work as a semi-supervised model. A softmax layer is added, and the input and output are redesigned to classify characteristic representations of network traffic. TraCGAN can recognize multiclass traffic accurately on traffic classification tasks, including traffic produced by the generator. Our experimental results show it reaches state-of-the-art performance compared with the baseline 2D-CNN.

Keywords: Traffic classification · Generative adversarial network · Convolutional neural network · Semi-supervised learning

1 Introduction

The variety and complexity of Internet traffic increase with the proliferation of mobile devices and heterogeneous communication technologies, including 5G, D2D, SDN, Green Communications, etc. Enormous challenges arise from these technical transitions of network management, like QoS provisioning. Besides, the rapid development of video streams and web applications enlarges the scales of Internet traffic, making traffic classification a more high-dependent task on time efficiency and computational performance. As the modern Internet becomes a critical daily and industrial infrastructure, network traffic classification becomes a significant research task for its extensive applications in network design, traffic

W. Quan (Ed.): ICENAT 2022, CCIS 1696, pp. 286–297, 2023.
https://doi.org/10.1007/978-981-19-9697-9_23

engineering, content-sensitive pricing, and network security. Therefore, many research communities have proposed several traffic classification approaches, along with networking industries and internet service providers [1,4,13,19].

The state of the art relevant to traffic classification experienced great changes last decades. In the early 1980s, Internet technology was not relatively developed as it is now. Upper-level applications were very limited, and many common web applications have their own IANA registered ports (e.g., HTTP has IANA registered port 80), assigned from 0 to 1024, usually called well-known ports [13]. At that time, people used well-known ports to identify most web applications. With the wide use of NAT in IPv4, and many applications using dynamic ports to disguise filters and firewalls, port-based traffic classification approaches have become unreliable. Nevertheless, using transport layer ports to identify common web applications is very fast, simple, and inexpensive. For these reasons, it is now a supplementary method under the condition of low accuracy requirements.

In order to improve the accuracy of traffic identification, deep packet inspection (DPI) was widely used afterward as an efficient and accurate traffic classification tool in web application firewalls (WAF), traffic analyzers, and intrusion detection systems (IDS). Though DPI has excellent performance, it is computationally expensive for inspecting packet content and performing complicated syntactical matching. Besides, the payload-based traffic classification approach is easily prevented by encryption or protocol encapsulation. The future direction of the development of traffic classification techniques is bypassing packet content inspection, for instance, host communication patterns recognition, machine learning (ML) [1,19], or active learning (AL) [18].

In this paper, we proposed a semi-supervised learning generative adversarial network TraCGAN to distinguish traffic protocols. TraCGAN was implemented based on deep conventional generative adversarial networks (DCGAN) [14] and can use a small number of labeled samples and many unlabeled samples to achieve good performances. We improved the training process of GAN [7] and modified the generator and discriminator network structure in a semi-supervised learning way [15]. The major contributions of this paper are as follows:

- We designed a content-free traffic classifier, TraCGAN, based on deep conventional generative adversarial network and semi-supervised learning. Experimental results show it is accurate enough to achieve state-of-the-art performance as the baseline model 2D-CNN.
- We adjusted the internal structure of TraCGAN, designed the input and output, and optimized the training process to increase the accuracy rate and accelerate the convergence of the generator and discriminator.

The rest of the paper is structured as follows. Section 2 briefly introduces the standard techniques, evaluation metrics, and ML and DL-based approaches in traffic classification. Section 3 introduces theoretical knowledge about generative adversarial networks and semi-supervised learning mathematically. Section 4 describes the details of the structure and working process of TraCGAN. Then in Sect. 5, the implementation of TraCGAN and experimental results are presented. Finally, Sect. 6 concludes the paper.

2   State of Art

2.1   Traffic Classification

A) The most used techniques. The most used techniques in traffic classification are port-based approaches, payload-based approaches, and statistics-based approaches [13,19].

- *Port-based approaches:* use transport layer ports (TCP or UDP ports) to infer common web applications, often used as an auxiliary method.
- *Payload-based approaches:* examine packet content and compare with signatures from stored feature library to identify packet patterns associated with every application.
- *Statistics-based approaches:* classify traffic using pre-defined statistic characteristics. Typical examples are machine learning, chi-square test, principal component analysis, etc. Among them, deep learning has been considered a very promising technique in recent years.

B) The granularity of traffic objects. Flows or traffic have a wide range of granularity, and which granularity to use depends on the actual classification requirements [1,4]. The key element that identifies a flow is usually called 5-tuple, including {source IP, source port, destination IP, destination port, transport level protocol}.

- *Flows:* include the 5-tuple of any single direction of traffic.
- *Bidirectional flows:* include the 5-tuple of both directions of traffic.
- *TCP connections:* include 5-tuple and some TCP flags (i.e., SYN, FIN, RST) or TCP state machines.
- *Application categories:* include applications with similar internal characteristics, i.e., chat, video, web, mail, and file sharing.
- *Application:* include a specific web application or protocol, i.e., Skype, Wechat, HTTP, SMTP, FTP.

C) Evaluation metrics. The generally accepted metrics for evaluation are overall accuracy, precision, recall, and F-measure, often summarized in the form of a confusion matrix [13].

- *Precision:* the ratio of the number of correct samples to the total number of retrieved samples.
- *Recall:* the percentage of objects from a given class that are properly attributed to that class.
- *Overall accuracy:* the ratio of the number of correctly classified samples to the total number of samples.

2.2   ML and DL-Based Approach of Traffic Classification

Machine learning and deep learning algorithms have been widely applied in the research of traffic classification. ML-based approaches need to artificial design statistic characteristics they used, while DL-based approaches need to adjust the input format and the DL network structure according to various issues [11]. Despite many deficiencies, deep learning is still considered a promising technique to deal with privacy issues of packet content examination in traffic classification.

In [17], Shafiq et al. captured several online traffic of web applications, including DNS, FTP, P2P, IM, and MAIL, then they applied three ML algorithms to this traffic. Experimental results showed that all the algorithms achieved high accuracy, while the C4.5 decision tree algorithm provided 97.57% highly precise results. Some researchers explored encrypted traffic classification [16,20]. Moustafa N. [12] proposed an AdaBoost ensemble learning method developed by decision tree, Naive Bayes (NB), and artificial neural network (ANN) to detect malicious packets. Network traffic applications included DNS, HTTP, and MQTT protocols utilized in IoT networks. Their ensemble method achieved a 99.54% accuracy rate and a 98.93% detection rate. Aceto G. [2] proposed a DL-based mobile and encrypted traffic classification framework. The granularity of traffic objects, input format, and traffic classification targets will influence the DL network architecture produced by their scheme. They validated this framework with random forest and 2D-CNN algorithms on three mobile traffic datasets, and achieved outstanding high F-measure. Chen [3] used an optimized 2D-CNN model, NTCNET, to classify network traffic automatically. Experimental results showed their approach performs better than simple 2D-CNN and LeNet with 99.66% accuracy on the Moore dataset.

In general, it is convenient to extract statistically significant features from an identified object in traditional ML methods, such as packet length, inter-arrival time, and flow duration. These features are usually payload-independent and thus can circumvent the problems of encrypted content and privacy issues. However, payload-independent features can only classify traffic into different flows at Layer 4. When it comes to application category identification, it is necessary to extract several significant fields from relevant protocol headers. Besides, finding effective features is an intractable problem that adds complexities to ML-based approaches.

3   Generative Adversarial Network

3.1   GAN

Generative Adversarial Networks (GAN), belonging to generative models, is based on game theory and are often combined with other DL networks such as recurrent neural network (RNN) or CNN. GANs compose of two independent neural networks. The generator attempts to capture the actual data distribution to generate new samples, while the discriminator, usually a binary classifier, strives to discern precisely between real and fake samples [5,8]. When both parts are well-trained, GANs can generate new synthetic data that resembles real data and classify fake samples at the same time.

GAN is drawing attention in the field of DL-based traffic classification. It can partially overcome traffic data shortage and imbalanced traffic data of network attack detection issues [9]. Therefore, many GAN models, such as DCGAN [14], Least Squares GAN, and Conditional GAN (CGAN) [10], are considered to work on traffic classification tasks.

The original GAN [7] is implemented by combing multi-layer perceptron (MLP) straightforwardly. To describe The original GAN mathematically, define $p_z(z)$ as the distribution of the output fake data of the generator, where z is the input noise variable of the generator. In order to learn the distribution p_g over real data distribution x, the generator acts like a differentiable function, mapping z from noise space to data space as $G(z, \theta_g)$ with parameters θ_g. On the other hand, the discriminator $D(x, \theta_d)$ with parameters θ_d outputs is a single scalar $D(x)$. $D(x)$ denotes the probability that x was from the data rather than the generator. The original objective function of basic GAN is

$$\min_G \max_D V(D, G) = \mathbb{E}_{x \sim p_{data}}[\log D(x)] + \mathbb{E}_{z \sim p_z(z)}[\log(1 - D(G(z)))]. \quad (1)$$

Early in learning, the discriminator can reject fake samples with high confidence because the generator network is too poor that fake samples are prominently different from real samples. In this situation, $\log(1 - D(G(z)))$ saturates. Therefore we train the generator to maximize $\log D(G(z))$ vicariously, and the objective function becomes

$$\max_{G,D} V(D, G) = \mathbb{E}_{x \sim p_{data}}[\log D(x)] + \mathbb{E}_{z \sim p_z(z)}[\log D(G(z))]. \quad (2)$$

The new objective function provides much stronger gradients early than the old one and converges to the same fixed point of G and D [7]. Theoretically, distribution p_g ends to converge to p_{data} if G and D have enough capacity.

3.2 Semi-surpervised Learning Based on GAN

As the original GAN models can generate fake data that resembles real data, we can also do semi-supervised learning with any standard classifier by simply adding samples from the generator to real dataset [21, 22], labeling them with a new "generated" class $y = K + 1$.

$$L = -\mathbb{E}_{x,y \sim p_{data}}[\log p_{model}(y|x)] + \mathbb{E}_{x \sim G}[\log p_{model}(y = K + 1|x)]$$
$$= L_{supervised} + L_{unsurpervised}, where$$
$$L_{unsurpervised} = -l\mathbb{E}_{x,y \sim p_{data}}[\log 1 - p_{model}(y = K + 1|x)]$$
$$+ \mathbb{E}_{x \sim G}[\log p_{model}(y = K + 1|x)],$$
$$L_{supervised} = -\mathbb{E}_{x,y \sim p_{data}(x,y)}[\log p_{model}(y|x, y < K + 1)]. \quad (3)$$

Because of the generator, half of the training data is fake data. For unlabeled data, we adopt unsupervised learning to maximize the probability $D(x)$ that x was from the data rather than the generator, with no need to specify which category it is. If we substitute $D(x) = 1 - p_{model}(y = K+1|x)$, we have the loss function of unsupervised learning according to the standard GAN:

$$L_{unsupervised} = -\mathbb{E}_{x \sim p_{data}}[\log D(x)] + \mathbb{E}_{z \sim p_z(z)}[\log(1 - D(G(z)))]. \quad (4)$$

The optimal solution for minimizing both $L_{supervised}$ and $L_{unsupervised}$ is to have $exp[l_j(x)] = c(x)p(y = j, x), \forall j < K+1$ and $exp[l_{K+1}(x)] = c(x)p_{G(x)}$ for some undetermined scaling function $c(x)$ [15].

4   The Proposed Method TraCGAN

4.1   The Workflow of TraCGAN

In the TraCGAN process, as shown in Fig. 1, select the noise dimension as same as the input data. For training set $D = \{(x^l, y^l)|l = 1, 2, ..., n\}$, $x^l = (x_1^l, x_2^l, ..., x_k^l, ..., x_m^l)$ is samples with m features extracted from traffic data, y^l is label of x, where n is total numbers of training samples, N is different classes. To do semi-supervised learning with TraCGAN, we added samples from the generator to the original dataset [15], labeling them with a new class $y = N+1$.

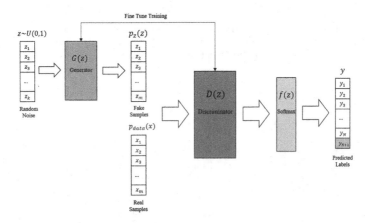

Fig. 1. The workflow of TraCGAN. Input random noise variable z with standard normal distribution to the generator and get fake samples as the distribution of real data. Reshape the real and fake samples into the input form of TraCGAN. The discriminator will learn the characteristic representations so that the softmax layer transforms them into the appropriate output results.

Finally, TraCGAN mainly includes the generator $G(z)$ and the discriminator $D(z)$. Produced k-dimension random noise z are fed into the generator, generating fake samples with distribution $p_z(z)$ after several epochs of fine-tuning training. Then fake samples with label $y = N+1$ are predicted by the discriminator, along with actual samples labeled from 1 to N. We replaced the Sigmoid layer on the top of basic GANs with the Softmax layer to output multiple classification labels.

4.2 Details of TraCGAN Structure

We adopted several pieces of advice in [14] to train a 2D-CNN network gen-
eratively. Details of the structure in TraCGAN are shown in Fig. 2. First, we
replaced any pooling layers in CNN with strided convolutions layers in the discriminator and fractionally strided convolutions layers in the generator. This
structure allows the network to learn its spatial down-sampling. Then, we used
ReLU activation in the generator and LeakyReLU activation in the discriminator. Compared with the ReLU activation, LeakyReLU activation can avoid the
problem of the gradient vanishing during training.

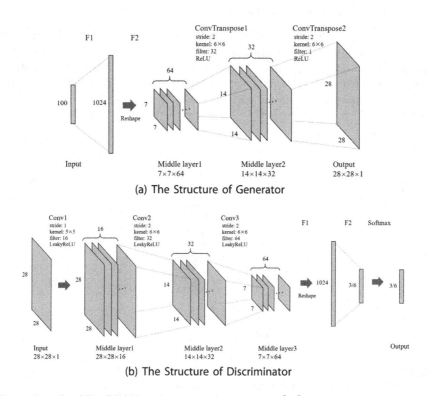

(a) The Structure of Generator

(b) The Structure of Discriminator

Fig. 2. Details of TraCGAN architecture. According to [14], we use three strided convolutions layers in the discriminator and two fractionally strided convolutions layers in
the generator.

In the generator, we inputted 100-dimensional random noises z with the uniform distribution. It is projected to a small spatial extent convolutional repre-
sentation($7 * 7 * 64$) by two full-connected layers. The generator of TraCGAN is
composed of 2 fractional strided convolutions layers. The first fractional-strided
convolutions layer has 32 filters with a kernel size of $6 * 6$, and the second
fractional-strided convolutions layer has a filter size of $6 * 6$. The stride is 2.

The output of the generator is a 28 * 28 * 1 tensor that may contain hidden representations of traffic characteristics.

In the discriminator, we used the format of the current DL baseline, the first 784 bytes of the Layer 4 payload, and reshaped the payload(784 * 1) into a convolutional representation(28 * 28 * 1). The discriminator is composed of 3 strided convolutions layers and two full-connected layers. The first strided convolutions layer has 16 filters with a kernel size of 5 * 5 and a stride of 1; the second one has 32 filters with a size of 6 * 6 and a stride of 2; the third one has 64 filters with a size of 6 * 6 and a stride of 2. Finally, we employed the Softmax layer instead of the Sigmoid layer to output normalized probabilities of multiple traffic categories. Therefore, after flattening into a 1024-dimensional vector, it is input to a Softmax layer to predict traffic labels.

5   Experimental Results

5.1   Description of Open Source Datasets

Most traffic classification studies use their private traffic datasets for individuals or companies, which affects the reliability of the classification results. However, public traffic datasets rarely contain encrypted traffic, which cannot guarantee the robustness and generalization performance of the models trained on these datasets. So we chosen the ISCXVPN2016 traffic dataset [6], as shown in Table 1. The traffic data it provides are original, and it contains the main popular internet applications at present.

Table 1. Description of ISCXVPN2016 dataset

Encrypted	Category	Applications	Total
VPN/nonVPN	Email	SMTP, POP3, IMAP	11746
	Online chat	ICQ, Skype, Facebook, AIM, torTwitter	33900
	Video steaming	Vimeo, Youtube, Netflix, Spotify	97867
	File transfer	SCP, SFTP	20119
	VoIP	Hangouts, voipbuster	43056

The ISCXVPN2016 dataset collects 14 applications, divided into 7 categories: BROWSING, CHAT, STREAMING, MAIL, VOIP, P2P, and FT. However, some traffic, such as Facebook traffic, can be classified as BROWSER or STREAMING simultaneously. We kept only five categories: Email, Online chat, Video steaming, File transfer, and VoIP. BROWSING traffic was divided into Online chat and Video steaming, and P2P traffic was divided into File transfer, as shown in Table 1.

5.2 Discussion About Experiment Results

A) Experiment settings. The experimental environment parameters are shown in Table 2. We conducted experiments with an Intel Core i7-1165G7 CPU @ 2.80 GHz, 16 GB RAM, and an external GPU (Nvidia GeForce MX450) on DL Platform TensorFlow as the back-end support.

Table 2. Experimental environment parameters

Category	Parameters
OS	Windows 10 Professional
RAM	16.0 GB
CPU	Intel Core i7-1165G7 CPU @ 2.80 GHz
GPU	Nvidia GeForce MX450
Program environment	Python 3.6.13
DL environment	CUDA 10.0.130, CuDNN 7.6.5
DL platform	TensorFlow-GPU 2.0.0

B) Model training. The training method is the mini-batch stochastic gradient descent technique. We trained for 500 epochs with a mini-batch size of 64. Other hyper-parameters was set: learning rate $\gamma = 10^{-4}$, momentum $\beta = 0.9$. The decay is initialized to 10^{-3} and will keep changing with epochs (Fig. 3).

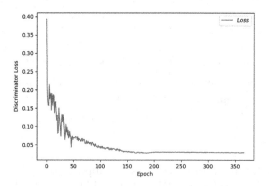

Fig. 3. The loss function curve.

C) Classification experiments on 3 labels. Table 3 and 4 present the confusion matrix and the performance measures for 2D-CNN and TraCGAN models. In the experiment, we added 25000 fake samples to perform classification experiments on three labels in a semi-supervised way. To measure prediction accuracy, we consider precision, recall, and accuracy based on the confusion matrix for our experiments.

As shown in the confusion matrix Table 3, most samples of VPN and non-VPN are predicted accurately. By examining the misclassified samples, we found that both classifiers tend to classify those misclassified samples as fake. This suggests that these misclassified samples may not have typical characteristics of the category they belong to or the others.

Table 4 compares the performance measures precision, recall, and accuracy. Compared with the results of 2D-CNN, the accuracy of TraCGAN is 0.894, slightly lower than the accuracy of 2D-CNN. The precision of VPN is 0.967, and the precision of non-VPN is 0.902. Since the total number of VPN and non-VPN samples is much larger than the fake samples, the precision of the fake sample is much lower than the others, obviously. Even so, the recall of fake samples is 0.936, which shows TraCGAN can still correctly identify fake samples despite this class-imbalance problem. In summary, TraCGAN reaches state-of-the-art performance as the baseline 2D-CNN.

Table 3. The confusion matrix for 2D-CNN and TraCGAN

Classifier	Actual class	Predicted class			Total
		Non-VPN	VPN	Fake	
2D-CNN	Non-VPN	62116	3311	3745	69172
	VPN	6904	122114	8498	137516
	Fake	1432	1665	21903	25000
TraCGAN	Non-VPN	62531	3106	3535	69172
	VPN	6174	121289	10053	137516
	Fake	647	956	23397	25000

Table 4. The performance measures for 2D-CNN and TraCGAN

Classifier	Evaluation metrics	Actual class		
		Non-VPN	VPN	Fake
2D-CNN	Precision (%)	88.2	96	64.14
	Recall (%)	89.8	91.5	87.6
	Accuracy (%)	90.1		
TraCGAN	Precision (%)	90.2	96.7	63.3
	Recall (%)	90.8	90.7	93.6
	Accuracy (%)	89.4		

6 Conclusion

In this paper, a deep conventional generative adversarial network model with semi-supervised learning, TraCGAN, was proposed to overcome the network traffic data shortage and improve the performance of the traffic classifier. Besides, we optimized the internal structure of DCGAN and the training process to increase the accuracy rate and accelerate the convergence of the generator and discriminator. Experimental results show it is accurate enough to achieve state-of-the-art performance as the baseline 2D-CNN. In the next step, we will keep the balance of all kinds of samples to avoid the class-imbalance problem.

References

1. Aceto, G., Ciuonzo, D., Montieri, A., Pescapé, A.: Mobile encrypted traffic classification using deep learning: experimental evaluation, lessons learned, and challenges. IEEE Trans. Netw. Serv. Manag. **16**(2), 445–458 (2019)
2. Aceto, G., Ciuonzo, D., Montieri, A., Pescapé, A.: Toward effective mobile encrypted traffic classification through deep learning. Neurocomputing **409**, 306–315 (2020)
3. Chen, L., Liu, J., and Xian, M. Network traffic classification using deep learning. Int. J. Artif. Intell. Tools **29**(07n08), 2040008 (2020)
4. Dainotti, A., Pescape, A., Claffy, K.C.: Issues and future directions in traffic classification. IEEE Netw. **26**(1), 35–40 (2012)
5. Dash, A., Ye, J., Wang, G. A review of generative adversarial networks (GANs) and its applications in a wide variety of disciplines-from medical to remote sensing. arXiv preprint arXiv:2110.01442 (2021)
6. Draper-Gil, G., Lashkari, A.H., Mamun, M.S.I., Ghorbani, A.A.: Characterization of encrypted and VPN traffic using time-related features. In: ICISSP (2016)
7. Goodfellow, I., et al.: Generative adversarial nets. In: Advances in Neural Information Processing Systems 27 (2014)
8. Gui, J., Sun, Z., Wen, Y., Tao, D., Ye, J.: A review on generative adversarial networks: algorithms, theory, and applications. IEEE Trans. Knowl. Data Eng. (2021)
9. Kim, C.-I., Kim, M., Jung, S., Hwang, E.: Simplified Fréchet distance for generative adversarial nets. Sensors **20**(6), 1548 (2020)
10. Kim, M.: ML/CGAN: network attack analysis using CGAN as meta-learning. IEEE Commun. Lett. **25**(2), 499–502 (2020)
11. Liu, X., You, J., Wu, Y., Li, T., Li, L., Zhang, Z., Ge, J.: Attention-based bidirectional GRU networks for efficient HTTPS traffic classification. Inf. Sci. **541**, 297–315 (2020)
12. Moustafa, N., Turnbull, B., Choo, K.-K.R.: An ensemble intrusion detection technique based on proposed statistical flow features for protecting network traffic of internet of things. IEEE Internet Things J. **6**(3), 4815–4830 (2018)
13. Nguyen, T.T., Armitage, G.: A survey of techniques for internet traffic classification using machine learning. IEEE Commun. Surv. Tutor. **10**(4), 56–76 (2008)
14. Radford, A., Metz, L., Chintala, S. Unsupervised representation learning with deep convolutional generative adversarial networks. arXiv preprint arXiv:1511.06434 (2015)

15. Salimans, T., Goodfellow, I., Zaremba, W., Cheung, V., Radford, A., Chen, X.: Improved techniques for training GANs. In: Proceedings of the 30th International Conference on Neural Information Processing Systems, NIPS 2016, pp. 2234–2242 (2016). https://doi.org/10.5555/3157096.3157346

16. Secchi, R., Cassarà, P., Gotta, A.: Exploring machine learning for classification of QUIC flows over satellite. In: ICC 2022 - IEEE International Conference on Communications, pp. 4709–4714 (2022)

17. Shafiq, M., Yu, X., Wang, D.: Network traffic classification using machine learning algorithms. In: Xhafa, F., Patnaik, S., Zomaya, A.Y. (eds.) IISA 2017. AISC, vol. 686, pp. 621–627. Springer, Cham (2018). https://doi.org/10.1007/978-3-319-69096-4_87

18. Shahraki, A., Abbasi, M., Taherkordi, A., Jurcut, A.D.: Active learning for network traffic classification: a technical study. IEEE Trans. Cogn. Commun. Netw. $8(1)$, 422–439 (2022)

19. Sheikh, M.S., Peng, Y.: Procedures, criteria, and machine learning techniques for network traffic classification: a survey. IEEE Access $\mathbf{10}$, 61135–61158 (2022)

20. Wang, M., Zheng, K., Luo, D., Yang, Y., Wang, X.: An encrypted traffic classification framework based on convolutional neural networks and stacked autoencoders. In: 2020 IEEE 6th International Conference on Computer and Communications (ICCC), pp. 634–641 (2020)

21. Wang, P., Wang, Z., Ye, F., Chen, X.: ByteSGAN: a semi-supervised generative adversarial network for encrypted traffic classification in SDN edge gateway. Comput. Netw. $\mathbf{200}$, 108535 (2021)

22. Wang, S., Wang, Q., Jiang, Z., Wang, X., Jing, R.: A weak coupling of semi-supervised learning with generative adversarial networks for malware classification. In: 2020 25th International Conference on Pattern Recognition (ICPR), pp. 3775–3782. IEEE (2021)

Brief Analysis for Network Security Issues in Computing Power Network

Shizhan Lan[1,2]([✉]) and Jing Huang[3]

[1] School of Software Engineering, South China University of Technology, Guangzhou 510006, China
lanshizhan@gx.chinamobile.com
[2] China Mobile Guangxi Branch Co., Ltd., Nanning 530012, China
[3] EVERSEC (Bei Jing) Technology Co., Ltd., Beijing 100191, China

Abstract. Network security is the cornerstone of computing power network. It is necessary to improve network security awareness, monitoring, early warning, disposal and evaluation capabilities of computing power network in all aspects. It makes a comprehensive analysis on network security issues in computing power network from dimensions of computing facility security, network facility security, combination and scheduling security, operation service security, data security, etc. It is set up gradually evolving atomic power security capabilities for building a ubiquitous security network computing brain. It identifies data assets through active and passive methods, sorts out data assets through in-depth scanning and information completion, supports preset templates formation according to AI (artificial intelligence) models, regular expression matching, keywords, combination rules, etc. It classifies data according to information sensitivity, and visually displays data in charts. In view of serious security risks faced by computing networking services such as network attacks and data privacy leaks, it creatively proposes introduction of privacy computing, data tagging, full process trust, audit traceability, endogenous security and other technologies to achieve security and credibility of computing networking services.

Keywords: Computing Power Network · Network security · Network security computing brain · Atomic security capability · Endogenous security

1 Introduction

Computing power network is "a novel information infrastructure that allocates and flexibly schedules computing resources, storage resources and network resources in cloud, network and edge according to business requirements" [1]. It aims to set up efficient, flexible and agile computing power infrastructure by information exchange carried out with networks as centre stage and information data in processing progress with computing power as kernel.

In order to promote digital economy development, China has successively introduced a number of policies that accelerate construction of a novel infrastructure system with computing power and network as core. In May 2021, the National Development and Reform Commission and other four ministries and commissions jointly issued «The Implementation Plan for Computing Hub of the Collaborative Innovation System of the National Integrated Big Data Center», which clearly proposes to lay out the national hub nodes of the national computing network; opens up the network transmission channels; improves the level of cross regional computing scheduling, accelerates the implementation of the "Mega-projects approved for data clusters", and build a national computing power network system [2].

As an important part of the digital economy, network security affects all over as a slight move in one part may affect the situation as a whole.

2   Analysis of Computing Power Network Security

Computing power network is a novel type of infrastructure that provides deep integration and integrated services of computing power and network. Compared with traditional network security threats, computing power network has characteristics of computing power generalization, computing network symbiosis, flexible connections, etc., therefore, computing power network will generate more assets exposure and higher connection frequency, and corresponding probability of assets being attacked will also increase significantly. As base of computing power network construction and application, network security urgently needs to be improved in network security awareness, monitoring, early warning, disposal and evaluation capabilities in an all-round way. It accelerates security protection level of data resources in the full life cycle, improves computing security monitoring and scientific scheduling support capabilities, and copes with the transformation of network attacks awareness from static analysis to dynamic analysis, post-processing to prevention in advance, single point prevention and control to global joint defense (Fig. 1).

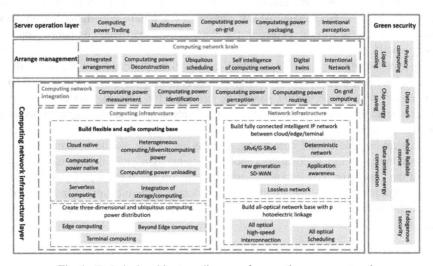

Fig. 1. Technical architecture diagram of computing power network

It is three-layer architecture of computing power network that from bottom to top it is computing infrastructure layer, orchestration management layer and operation service layer [4]. Infrastructure layer consists of computing power infrastructure and network infrastructure to form a new computing network integration infrastructure, which builds a flexible and agile computing base and a fully connected intelligent network from cloud side to edge and terminal side.

The arrangement of orchestration management layer realizes unified layout and intellectualization of computing and network through constructing computing network brain.

Operation service layer creates a new operation service system and business model by using technologies such as computing power trading and computing power grid connection. In this framework, network security runs through the whole process, so improving the network security endogenous ability has become an important development goal. This paper will analyze the related network security issues from the above dimensions.

2.1 Computing Power Infrastructure Security

Computing power infrastructure is the core of computing power network. With the goal of building efficient, flexible and agile computing power infrastructure, it actively introduces cloud native, serverless computing, heterogeneous computing, computing power offloading and other technologies, explores new directions such as computing power native, storage and computing integration, and continues to enhance computing power and release the value of computing power. At the same time, it evolves from cloud to computing, from center to edge and from end to ubiquitous network. Through the development of edge computing, super edge computing and end computing, a more extensive multi-dimensional muti-dimensional computing power layout is formed.

Computing infrastructure includes cloud computing, edge computing and end computing. While providing powerful computing technology support services for upper tier applications, it also faces many risks. It is necessary to build a comprehensive, systematic and three-dimensional protection for cloud computing, edge computing and end computing [5, 6].

In cloud computing, security protection should be provided for physics, virtualization, business, data, operation and maintenance management, etc. In terms of edge computing, security protection should be provided for network services, hardware environment, virtualization, edge computing platform, applications, capacity opening, management, data, etc.

In terms of end-to-end computing, security protection should be carried out for physics, virtualization, application, capacity opening, management, data, etc.

At the same time, it is also necessary to do a good job in the security protection of cloud, edge and end interconnection, including identity authentication, traffic monitoring and audit, interface control, security situation monitoring and other security protection means.

2.2 Network Facility Security

Network infrastructure layer builds a high-quality network infrastructure, optimizes the network structure, expands the network bandwidth, reduces the data rotation delay, and builds a new generation of computing infrastructure and a new system of computing network collaboration through structuring all-optical network with photoelectric linkage and intelligent IP network with full connectivity from cloud to edge.

Facing flexible carrying and scheduling requirements of computing power resources, computing power network needs to build IP network infrastructure centered on computing power. Through the introduction of SRv6/G-SRv6, deterministic network, new generation SD-WAN, application awareness, lossless network and other technologies, a programmable, deterministic, perceptible, business on-demand and intelligent IP network is built to achieve flexible, agile and efficient supply of computing networks [7].

But traditional security solutions do not have the good scalability and programmability of SRv6 and the performance, flexibility or interconnection required for SD-WAN connection. The atomic security capability can support flexibility, interconnection, scalability and programmability, sense the changes of edge connections, and provide consistent policy implementation. This policy can isolate users, applications, workflows, or data based on many parameters to provide security over the entire transaction path. Traffic can be forced to follow specific behaviors, or isolated to specific users or destinations to ensure consistent policy application and execution.

2.3 Arranging and Scheduling Security

Arrangement management layer builds a "computing network brain" concluding integrated orchestration and mixed digital wisdom. Through introduction of integrated scheduling, computing power deconstruction, ubiquitous scheduling and other technologies, resources in various domains of the computing network, it can be coordinated and scheduled. Meanwhile, it is deeply integrated with AI, big data and other technologies to explore new directions such as computing network intelligence, digital twins, and intentional networks, and constantly enhances automation and intelligence capabilities of computing power networks to meet with flexible, dynamic, and diverse business needs of customers, and to provide intelligent closed-loop guarantee capabilities.

Facing the highly complex computing network environment, the arrangement management layer cooperatively schedules the resources of each domain of the computing network according to the diversified and customized computing power requirements. The arrangement management layer perceives and cooperates with the arrangement of computing power users, computing tasks, network resources and computing power resources. The arrangement management shall have the ability to control the security of computing power and solve the problem of computing power abuse. The abuse of computing power includes illegal mining, violent cracking and other acts, which not only encroach on computing power resources, but also may use computing power to launch security attacks. Based on the self-adaptation mode of the computing power network, establish the North-South linkage between security services and computing power, and promote the scheduling of security computing power. Considering the introduction of heterogeneous computing power nodes rather than completely self built, it is necessary to solve the identity and trust problems of computing power nodes, and conduct research and verification on technologies such as differential privacy and homomorphic encryption during the interaction between algorithms and computing power. Carry out the pre research on node collaboration. The computing power is in multiple nodes. The nodes need to have a synchronization mechanism. The nodes need to adopt an adaptive and self-organizing architecture. The "edge by edge collaboration" mechanism is used for local interaction of capability and performance information.

2.4 Operation Service Security

Through construction of operational service technology system that includes computing power trading, computing power integration, computing power packaging, computing power unloading, intention perception, etc.as key technologies, computing power network realizes cultivation of industrial ecology, innovation of computing network services, and integration of social computing power, creating a new computing network integrated operation service system and business model, and reshaping the value chain distribution system of information service industry.

Operation service security mainly ensures the security of computing network services, including three parts such as identity security, operation security and integrated application security. Among them, identity security ensures that identities of computing nodes and users in the computing network can be recognized and verified; Operation security realizes functions of security transaction, security monitoring, security audit, etc.; The integrated application security provides flexible, dynamic and end-to-end business security for diverse application scenarios such as digital life, smart production and digital society.

2.5 Data Security

Data security [3] runs through all levels of the computing power network, mainly including data asset identification, data security protection, data flow security, computing security, etc. which can effectively ensure that the data is in an effective and legitimate use state in the whole life cycle.

Data Asset Identification. Data asset identification combines initiative and passivity to discover assets including servers, relational databases, non-relational databases, interfaces, etc., and complete the completion of data asset attributes through information completion and in-depth scanning. From the perspective of data assets, data is obtained from SMC/SMP and data resource scanning discovery, and the data is classified and managed at different levels. The classification and classification list management function mainly includes data classification and classification list, important data list and sensitive data list. Real time display of classification and classification data information of different dimensions, data sorting of identified asset data, classification and classification mapping of data according to data sensitivity, visual display in the form of charts, and controllable storage of warm and cold data.

According to the data classification and grading rules of countries, industries or enterprises, preset templates can be formed according to AI models, regular matching, keywords, combination rules, etc. you can also configure classification and grading templates according to the needs of the current business.

Data Flow Security. Data flow involves data aggregation, data transmission between providers and users, as well as the use of data out of the control of owners. Data will face greater security risks, including personal information disclosure, data vulnerable to attack and disclosure, illegal over collection, analysis and abuse of data, etc. During the data flow process, the data shall be identified, the data flow node, operation, flow direction and other information shall be recorded, and a unified cross domain and cross system data flow identification shall be established to realize that the data flow direction can be controlled and the data flow can be perceived. In order to monitor the flow of data in real time, it is necessary to strengthen network security monitoring through technical means, especially automated security monitoring, and comprehensively monitor and analyze the data sharing platform and system through traffic, logs, configuration files, etc., so as to facilitate early warning and collaborative defense of network security events, and improve the overall security situation awareness, security decision-making and other capabilities.

3   Atomic Security Capability in Computing Power Network

To provide users with low latency and high reliability computing connectivity and enjoy better computing services, we must build a network security value system in computing networks and provide refined, ubiquitous and native twin security services; Build a ubiquitous security computing network brain, provide a synchronous "pay as you go" security experience, transform application based into task based, achieve a more refined process of differentiated security experience, implement the near source defense mode based on the twin computing power mode, and achieve the ultra edge + near source defense mode.

With the rapid development of computing network technology and the continuous integration with Internet+, industrial Internet, big data, cloud computing and other new technologies, more and more information assets provide services with the help of Internet technology. At the micro security capability implementation level, they build a gradually evolving atomic capability security means to protect network security from all dimensions (Table 1).

Table 1. Atomic security capability table

Name of atomic security capability	Atomic security capacity of corresponding resource pool
Host asset discovery	Security asset management system -> host asset discovery
Software asset identification	Security asset management system -> software asset discovery
Web vulnerability scanning	Web vulnerability scanning
Host vulnerability scanning	Vulnerability scanning
Web page tamper proof	Web page tamper proof
Weak password scanning	Terminal detection and response -> weak password scanning
Webshell scan	Terminal detection and response -> webshell scanning
Baseline configuration check	Terminal detection and response -> safety baseline check
Terminal access control	Terminal detection and response ->host network access isolation
Document monitoring and protection	Terminal detection and response/Web page tamper proof
Access behavior audit	Terminal detection and response -> access behavior audit
Backup recovery	Terminal detection and response -> backup and recovery
Host Forensics	Terminal detection and response -> host certificate
Terminal antivirus	Terminal detection and corresponding -> anti virus
Network access control (combined network attack suppression)	Next generation Firewall -> access control
Network address translation (NAT)	Firewall -> network address translation
Network isolation switching	Firewall -> network isolation switch
Network Intrusion Prevention	Next generation firewall
Denial of service protection	Anti denial of service system -> denial of service protection
Sensitive data leakage prevention	Intrusion protection system -> sensitive data protection

(*continued*)

Table 1. (*continued*)

Name of atomic security capability	Atomic security capacity of corresponding resource pool
Spam protection	Mail Security Gateway -> spam protection
Network virus defense	Network virus defense
Network threat detection	Intrusion detection system
Network data leakage detection	Intrusion detection system -> sensitive data outgoing detection
Web application protection	Web application firewall
Code audit	Code audit system -> code audit
Database audit	Database audit
Log audit	Log audit
Network security audit	Network security audit
Sensitive data identification	Data security system -> sensitive data identification
Desensitization of sensitive data	Data security system -> sensitive data desensitization
information service	Threat Intelligence Platform -> intelligence service
VPN access	VPN
Operation&Management access control	Fortress -> access control
Name of safe atomic capability	Honeypot -> network attack entrapment

4   Secure and Credible Computing Network Service

4.1   Building Enterprise Security Capability Framework (IPDRR) Based on Computing Power Network

With the deepening of social digital transformation, network attacks are increasing and destructive power is gradually enhanced. Computing Power Network deepens active defense system and takes into account internal and external security capabilities. Security methodology evolves from "security defense against threats" to "business-oriented security governance" (IPDRR). Focusing on key segments such as identification, protection, monitoring, response and recovery, the "IPDRR" framework systematically enhances endogenous security capabilities and builds new security capabilities (Fig. 2).

The IPDRR capability framework model includes five capabilities, namely, risk identification, security defense, security detection, security response, and security recovery. From core protection model, it turns into the model with detection and business continuity management, changing from passive method to active method, and finally achieves adaptive security capabilities.

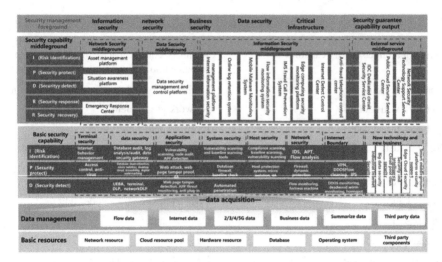

Fig. 2. Panorama of security capability of computing power network

Specifically, IPDRR mainly includes the following five parts:

Risk **Identification** refers to the recognition and confirmation of security risks faced by systems, assets, data and networks. It further improves the compliance database based on the computing power network, integrates security scanning resources, and forms the ecological ability to adapt to multiple manufacturers; It covers identification of sensitive data in all important systems and provides automatic detection.

Security **Protection** refers to the development and implementation of appropriate security measures to ensure provision of critical infrastructure services. It uniformly manages the security protection equipment strategy in computing power network; Comprehensive management, connection with 4 A, desensitization, document authorization, encryption and other security control tools are used to reduce the risk of sensitive data leakage and improve the compliance use of sensitive data.

when attack occurs, Security **Detection** is used to immediately monitor whether the business and protection measures operation normally, it formulates and implement appropriate actions to discover network security incidents. It provides scenario analysis capabilities for overall network threats, asset threats, and user abnormal behaviors; Various monitoring tools for managing data security enable monitoring of sensitive data leakage for abnormal operation, outgoing and cross domain transaction of sensitive data in various domain systems.

Security **Response**&Security **Recovery**, Security response refers to taking appropriate actions against discovered network security incidents. The specific procedures are based on the impact of the incident, including incident investigation, damage assessment, evidence collection, incident reporting and system recovery. Security recovery restores system status to normal state, finds the root caused by the event, prevents and repairs. It establishes the fine linkage disposal capability of computing power network, rely on the combination of IP blocking and other means to achieve the fine disposal of protection ends, builds the security closed-loop capability of data security incidents, and achieves the monitoring of data flow, security management and control and closed-loop disposal of events.

4.2 New Security Concept of Computing Power Network

From cloud computing to edge computing then to distributed cloud computing, the ubiquity of computing power has introduced more security risk points. More open network architecture and wider data flow have led to an increase in uncertain security threats, making computing services face serious security risks such as network attacks and data privacy leaks. The traditional "plug-in" or "patch" security construction model, which focuses on security protection, cannot cope with the above security issues, A new security concept based on endogenous security capability and security credibility emerged as times requires.

In the computing network environment with highly collaborative resources, flexible and open networks and high-speed data circulation, in order to fully respond to dynamic security needs, it introduces privacy computing, data tagging, whole process trustworthiness, audit traceability, endogenous security and other technologies, which can achieve the integrated security protection effect of node stealth "unknown", attack threat "unreachable", and computing network system "uncontrollable", and fulfil computing network security from a single point of control to the whole process trustworthiness [4].

Privacy Computing. It is a technology of Privacy computing that uses secure multiparty computing, homomorphic encryption to analyze and calculate data without disclosing sensitive data. On the premise of providing privacy protection, it is realized for the technical system of data value mining. The introduction of privacy computing into computing power network can rely on multi party computing power, divide and conquer computing tasks, and integrate intermediate data to obtain the final computing results, so as to achieve the "availability and invisibility" of computing power services for data, provide users with secure computing services, break data isolated islands, and better realize data sharing.

Data Marking. Data marking technology is used to build cross system and cross node data flow marking and pre-authorization capabilities by coding and marking data flow nodes, data operations, data flow direction and other information in network layer, so that data can be managed and controlled out of the network and data flow can be perceived. It does not damage data availability, and it can mark the security attributes of data without affecting the normal usage, providing secure and reliable data attribute information support and guarantee for the security management and control of data throughout its life cycle. The introduction of data marking technology can detect data security threats in a timely manner and manage data well.

Full Process Trustworthiness. Full process trustworthiness refers to using the characteristics of blockchain decentralization, multi-party consensus, tamper proof, and full process traces to build trust transfer from physical devices, operating systems, key applications, and key data level by level through the establishment of trusted authentication, so as to ensure reliable business access, secure data transmission, and effective network isolation, improve the ability of the computing network to resist unknown threats, and achieve full process trustworthiness of computing network security, Secure the safety barrier of computing power.

Based on the digital identity of all node elements (including users, terminals, network elements, applications, etc.) in the computing power network, a trusted identifier naming system compatible with the existing network identification naming system is designed [8].

On this basis, it provides the network trusted representation, trust relationship establishment and trust transfer mechanism, and constructs the network trusted communication model and technical framework to meet the trusted management of the identity of the communication end under heterogeneous application scenarios, and achieve end-to-end security transmission of data, active attack prevention, privacy protection and tracking audit (see Fig. 3).

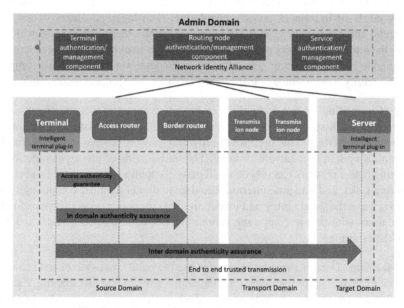

Fig. 3. Implementation of end-to-end trusted network

Audit Traceability. Audit traceability is based on data governance and access control rules, according to a certain security policy, using information such as records, system activities and user activities to check, review and verify the environment and activities of operational events, so as to find intrusion behaviors, track their intrusion source process, and record and audit the access behavior of important data (including system data, configuration parameters, business data and user data) in the computing network, And trace the processing links of the specified data. With the help of block chain smart contracts, multi-party consensus and other technologies, we can achieve audit traceability of behavior in the computing network, which can improve the credibility of the computing network data processing link.

Endogenous Safety. Endogenous security refers to the security function or attribute obtained by using the system architecture, mechanism, scene, law and other internal factors, and by enhancing the internal security capabilities of computer systems and network equipment, the attack is impossible. Have the ability of self-discovery, self-repair and self-balance against general network attacks; It has the ability of automatic prediction, automatic alarm and emergency response against large-scale network attacks; It has the ability to cope with extreme network disasters and ensure uninterrupted key services.

The endogenous security technology framework is mainly divided into two mechanisms: trusted network communication and intelligent cooperative defense, as shown in the figure.

Trusted network communication aims to provide the end-to-end network communication process of the communication party with a safe and reliable capability, specifically involving trusted identity management system, trusted network transmission mechanism, trusted routing guarantee scheme and many other key technical directions, to achieve "cloud edge end" trusted authentication and forwarding in the whole process, as well as end-to-end traffic security (see Fig. 4).

Intelligent cooperative defense is based on the whole network to provide analysis, identification and protection against unknown attacks, realize the detection and defense capability of large-scale network unknown attacks, and improve the attack immunity of the future network.

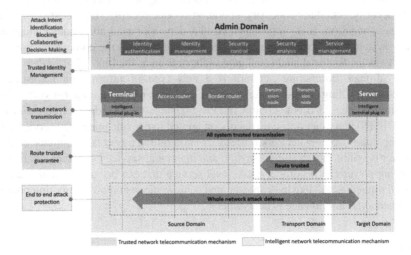

Fig. 4. Computing power network endogenous security technology framework

The endogenous security of the computing network refers to the endogenous security capability that forms active immunity and cooperative elasticity based on the security capability of the computing network itself, intelligent analysis and flexible arrangement, and meets the security needs of predictable network behavior, strong management, and extreme end-to-end differentiation. In the near future, the internal security system of computing power network will be constructed mainly by means of security computing power scheduling technology, high security isolation technology, computing power security countermeasure technology, etc., to achieve the self-immunity of computing power network.

5 Conclusion

The computing network realizes "the network moves with the cloud, and the cloud moves with demand", forming a multi-layer architecture system that includes the computing network collaborative scheduling of the control plane, the network fusion awareness of the data plane, the management and the scheduling of computing resources of the service plane. New security risks may exist in the new architecture, new technology and new services of the Computational Network, which need to be overcome and protected by new security mechanisms. The infrastructure layer has potential complex network risks and computing node security risks. The scheduling management layer involves scheduling security risks and computing power out of control issues. The operation service layer is faced with access to malicious nodes, untrusted transactions, insecure applications and other issues. In addition, the computing network may also have data security risks such as uncontrollable data flow, which need to be strengthened through the integrated whole process trusted mechanism.

This paper makes a comprehensive analysis on the network security problems in the computing power network from the aspects of computing power facility security, network facility security, scheduling security, operation service security, data security, situation awareness and so on. It is proposed to build a network-based ubiquitous endogenous security system with ubiquitous security computing brain as the core, atomic security capability as the foothold, and intelligent orchestration as the link.

The ultimate computing network is a new type of information infrastructure that takes computing as the center, network as the foundation, and network, cloud, data, intelligence, AI/Block chain/Cloud/Big Date/Network/Edge/Terminal/Security (ABCDNETS) and other areas are deeply integrated to provide integrated services. The goal of computing power network is to realize "computing power is ubiquitous, computing power is symbiotic, intelligent layout, and integrated service", gradually realize that computing power can become a social level service that can be "accessed at one point and used immediately" like hydropower, and achieve the vision of "computing power is everywhere, and intelligence is everywhere".

References

1. Reply of the national development and Reform Commission and other departments on Approving the Beijing Tianjin Hebei region to start the construction of the national computing node of the national integrated computing network National Development and Reform Commission document No. (2022) 212

2. Three year action plan for new data center development (2021–2023): Ministry of industry and information technology communication document No. (2021) 76
3. Xuelian, L., Xudong, L., Jinpeng, H.: Research and implementation of XML data security system. J. Beijing Univ. Aeronaut. Astronaut. (04), 82–85 (2003)
4. China Mobile Computing Network Technology White Paper, China Mobile Communication Group Co., Ltd., June 2022
5. Mingxuan, L., Chang, C., Jianjun, Y.: Research on arithmetic scheduling mechanism based on programmable network. ZTE Commun. Technol. **27**((158)03), 22–26 (2021)
6. Yao, H., Lu, L., Duan, X.: Arithmetic perception network architecture and key technologies. ZTE Commun. Technol. **27**((158)03), 11–15 (2021)
7. Duan, X., Yao, H., Fu, Y., Lu, L., Sun, T.: Network computing technology oriented to the evolution of the integration of computing and networking. Telecommun. Sci. **37**(10), 80–89 (2021)
8. White Paper on IP Network Future Evolution Technology, ZTE Communications Co., Ltd., 10 June 2021

In-Band Networking and Fault Adjustment Mechanism of SDN System Based on ONOS and P4

Xu Huang, Wei Niu, Kuo Guo, and Jia Chen[✉]

National Engineering Research Center for Advanced Network Technologies, Beijing Jiaotong University, Beijing, China
{21111024,chenjia}@bjtu.edu.cn

Abstract. With the rapid growth of network traffic and more diversified user requirements, Traditional network is exposing more and more shortcomings. Its closed network equipment has built-in many complex protocols, which increases the difficulty to customize and optimize the network. Based on the Software Defined Network (SDN) architecture, this paper designs and implements a new in-band networking system of SDN with Programming Protocol-independent Packet Processors (P4) and Open Network Operating System (ONOS) for military network communication scenarios. We propose an in-band networking mechanism and an optimal path selection and fault adjustment algorithm for control plane networking in the battlefield environment, which presents a solution for the application of SDN network to military network communication scenarios. The experiment result shows that the system modules can work together well in a coordinated manner to build a control plane in-band network. These modules also can quickly adjust burst faults at a fine-grained level. The system can provide dynamic networking support for major events or emergency tasks. The performance testing shows that the optimal path selection algorithm proposed in this paper can help the network system to complete routing redirection quickly. In addition, in larger networks, the fault adjustment method shows better performance than the OSPF protocol in terms of route convergence time.

Keywords: Software Defined Network · Military network · In-band networking · Programmable network technology · Fault adjustment

1 Introduce

In the military network, the networking system needs to be highly sensitive to network topology and dynamically adjust the networking in the shortest possible time. The networking system should provide a stable and reliable network for nodes. In the face of increasingly complex application, traditional networks, including the military network, are evolving toward Software Defined Network (SDN).

Traditional networking in battlefield includes wired networking protocols and Ad-hoc networking protocols [1]. Traditional wired networking protocols such as Open

W. Quan (Ed.): ICENAT 2022, CCIS 1696, pp. 312–323, 2023.
https://doi.org/10.1007/978-981-19-9697-9_25

Shortest Path First (OSPF) and Routing Information Protocol (RIP) have their own methods to adjust networking. Unfortunately, their own adjustment methods cannot solve the problems about high latency in the process of adjusting networks. Ad-hoc networks routing protocols works for mobile network. Take Ad-hoc On-Demand Distance Vector Routing protocol (AODV) [2] as an example. AODV is essentially a wireless on-demand routing protocol and establishes networking by sending special packets [3]. However, it is not well able to meet the networking requirements of military network environments [4]. As a result, the traditional networking protocols are not suitable to SDN and the separation of control plane and data plane.

In the current military network, the battlefield environment is the main factor affecting warfare [5]. Many combat vehicles are inter connected by Ad-hoc network routing protocols for real-time wartime information transmission [6]. However, the combat vehicles rarely combine with SDN architectures. There is a lack of research on in-band networking for military network scenario.

This paper implements an in-band networking system through SDN. It proposes an in-band networking method and a unified management mechanism in control plane. We also design a path selection algorithm and a networking adjustment strategy, which can get the optimal adjustment path by the real-time topology and help control plane centrally manage the networking. Our works integrate SDN into military network to realize the networking function, giving full use of the advantages of the separation of SDN control plane and data plane.

The rest of this paper is as follows. Section 2 briefly introduces the related work of others. Section 3 is the system design of in-band networking mechanism and fault adjustment method. Section 4 is the implementation of in-band networking mechanism and fault adjustment method. Section 5 shows the system testing and result analysis. Section 6 is the summary and outlook.

2 Related Works

The background of in-band networking in the battlefield is similar to Ad-hoc networks. Both of them face with many network emergencies, high-frequency changes in node status and high network sensitivity.

[7] firstly proposes a slope-based routing algorithm for Ad-hoc networks with holes. They call the algorithm SBRA. SBRA can solve the local minimum problem and avoid the oscillation phenomenon for Ad-hoc networks with holes by using the slope minimum rule. It always detours holes in a clockwise direction, even though there exists much shorter path in a counter-clockwise direction around a hole.

[8] aims towards Vehicle Ad-hoc Networks for connectivity situations such as car-to-car, car-to-Internet, and infrastructure. Since On-demand routing protocols need to find destinations based on request information sent to neighbors, the authors propose a new scheme for Ad-hoc networks based on intelligent AODV. It optimizes the neighbor discovery mechanism and reduces the resource overhead and packet loss rate during neighbor discovery, improving the performance of routing protocols.

In the Ad-hoc network environment where nodes move at high speed, the broadcast storm phenomenon occurs. So, the traditional AODV protocol cannot adapt to the network environment where nodes move fast [9]. To address these problems, in the literature [9], the authors propose an improved AODV protocol. This protocol combines the moving speed of network nodes with the link weights and selects the routing path based on the link weights. It improves the packet delivery rate and shortens the end-to-end transmission delay. It can better work in the network environment where nodes move at high speed. Thanks to [9], it provides a theoretical reference for the fault adjustment method in this paper.

In addition, the performance of RIP protocols and OSPF protocols in SDN networks is also a hot research topic. Deepthi et al. comparatively analyzed the performance of routing protocols in SDN networks and traditional networks [10]. The results show that, in traditional networks, the routing convergence time increases continuously with the increase of topology size. In SDN networks, the routing convergence time does not change much because the control plane separates from the data plane. The control plane makes route convergence instead of the switch updating and maintaining topology information. The study shows the limitations of traditional routing protocols in SDN. Therefore, we design a networking method with SDN architecture in military network scenarios.

According to the above research and problems, this paper designs a new in-band network system of SDN architecture based on P4 and ONOS, including in-band networking mechanism under military network and fault adjustment method by in-band networking.

3   In-Band Networking Mechanism and Fault Adjustment Method System Design

3.1   System Introduce

The designed system is divided into two parts, including the in-band networking mechanism and the fault adjustment method. The in-band networking mechanism is in charge of constructing networking packets and completing networking tasks, while the fault adjustment method ensures normal network connections under complex and changing conditions. The system architecture shows in Fig. 1.

The system adopts a modular design concept and consists of seven functional modules. The previous four modules, including SDN controller deployment module, Connection announcement module, Hop-by-hop route establishment module, and Route maintenance module, which belong to the in-band networking mechanism. The remaining three modules are Path parameters collection module, Path selection module, and Route redirection module, which belong to fault adjustment method.

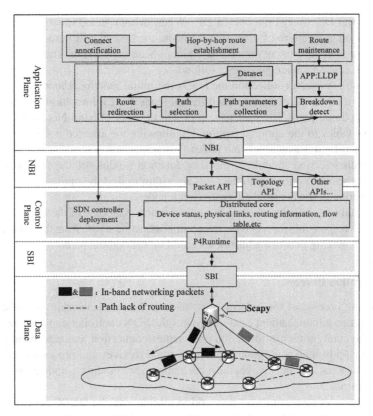

Fig. 1. System architecture of in-band networking mechanism and fault adjustment method

3.2 Module Analysis

This subsection introduces these modules. The SDN controller deployment module is the base of in-band networking system. Its work is deploying ONOS controllers, pushing BMv2 switch devices and basic configuration information to controllers, and enabling basic functions between the control plane and data plane.

The Connection announcement module is the initial functional module of the system establishment. After the system startup, it opens the SDN controller deployment module. At the same time, it will initiate the connection announcement and command the control nodes to construct the connection announcement packets and broadcast these packets.

The Hop-by-hop route establishment module is the core function module of in-band networking. It is responsible for enabling network nodes to receive and process connection announcement packets.

The Routing maintenance module is responsible for analyzing several types of packets. It should add, delete or change the routing entries in the control plane to quickly update and maintain routing information.

The above four modules are in-band networking mechanism modules. After completing in-band networking, the controller collects network topology information using the Link Layer Discovery Protocol (LLDP). When an unexpected situation occurs in the network, such as a failure of a networking node, the system will immediately sense it and start the fault adjustment method based on in-band networking. The modules of the LLDP fault adjustment method are as follows.

The Path parameters collection module is the initial functional module of the fault adjustment method. This module analyzes the node fault information to find out the available optional paths. Then, it generates and delivers In-band Network Telemetry (INT) flow tables to the optional path nodes, allowing the affected nodes to send INT packets to sniff out the optional path nodes.

The Path selection module is the core function module of the fault adjustment method. It uses the optimal path decision algorithm to find the optimal path based on the information of the detected alternative path nodes.

The Routing redirection module is the final function module of the fault adjustment method. It is responsible for receiving the optimal adjustment path from the path selection module and making network adjustments based on the optimal path.

3.3 Operation Process

The working process of the system is as follows. When a networking request arises, the Connection announcement module invokes the SDN controller deployment module to push the configuration information and creates connection announcement packets. Then, the Hop-by-hop route establishment module receives and processes connection announcement packets and invokes the route maintenance module to update and maintain the route entries.

After completing the in-band networking mechanism, the ONOS controller in the controller node will sense the networking status continually. In the event of an unexpected fault, the controller will start the fault adjustment method. First, the Path parameters collection module collects the parameters information of the available alternative paths and stores them in the MySQL database. Afterward, the Path selection module will take out the parameters from the database and input them into the path selection algorithm. The path selection algorithm will output the optimal adjustment path. Once the route redirection module receives the optimal adjustment path information, it will adjust the path information and cooperate with the route maintenance module to complete the route redirection.

4 In-Band Networking Mechanism and Fault Adjustment Method Implementation

4.1 In-Band Networking Mechanism Implementation

In SDN network, in-band networking means that control packets and data packets can share the same physical links. There are control nodes, directly connected nodes (nodes directly connected to the control nodes), and non-directly connected nodes in the network. The non-directly connected nodes communicate with the control nodes through the directly connected nodes. In in-band networking, the control nodes need to construct connection announcement packets and establish connections with the directly connected nodes first. Then the control nodes connect with other non-directly connected nodes through the directly connected nodes by taking the hop-by-hop routing method for networking. Hop-by-hop routing principle is shown in Fig. 2.

The control node forwards the connection announcement packet to the directly connected node and establishes the first-hop route. Then the directly connected nodes send the reverse route packets to the control node, establishing a bidirectional route between the control node and the directly connected node. At the same time, the directly connected nodes modify the connection announcement packets and send them to the non-directly connected nodes through the port. The non-directly connected nodes will establish the second hop route with the directly connected nodes, and complete the entire topology route establishment.

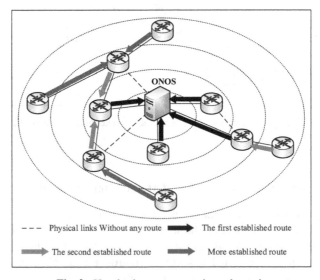

Fig. 2. Hop-by-hop route creation schematic

The implementation of the in-band networking mechanism relies on connection announcement packets and reverse routing packets. The design of these packets shows in Fig. 3. The connection announcement packet adopts the UDP structure. For the control node, the data section of the connection announcement packet is the IP address of the control node port. When the other nodes receive the packet, they will convert the IP to the IP address of this node port and then send it. In the IP header, the source IP is the IP address of the controller node, and the destination IP is the broadcast address. The Ethernet frame header is the hardware address of the corresponding IP address.

In this paper, a route entry established by a connection announcement packet is defined as the reverse route, and similarly, a packet built by a node and returned to the control node along a reverse route is defined as the reverse route packet. For reverse route packets, the structure is similar to that of connection announcement packets. It requires that the IP address of the data portion should be converted to the IP address of the reverse route entry. It should set the source IP of the IP header to the sending port IP address and the destination IP to the control node port IP address. The Ethernet frame header is the hardware address of the corresponding IP address.

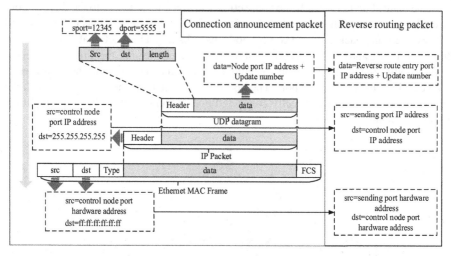

Fig. 3. The design of connection announcement packet and reverse routing packet

4.2   In-Band Network Fault Adjustment Method Implementation

Due to hop-by-hop routing, if a node is out, the nodes will disconnect from the controller node because these nodes connect to the network through the broken one. The disconnect nodes are called the affected nodes. ONOS will search the affected nodes and find all alternative paths from the affected nodes to the controller node. Then ONOS sends INT flow tables to the alternative path nodes, while the affected node sends INT packets to sniff the information of each node on all alternative paths. Finally, the control node receives the INT packets and extracts the useful data.

Table 1. Impact factors and weighting proportions

Impact factor	Quantitative value of each factor in nth link	Weight proportion
Queue depth	$X_{n,1}$	a_1
Hop count	$X_{n,2}$	a_2
Link latency	$X_{n,3}$	a_3
Hop latency	$X_{n,4}$	a_4

Based on the data obtained from INT, the important impact factors will be selected and quantified, including link latency, the number of path nodes (or destination node hops), processing delay, and other factors. They should combine with the weight proportion to generate weight values, as shown in Table 1. According to the formula (1), we can calculate the nth path weight values, and then set the nth path weight values with the corresponding device id into the selection algorithm to get the optimal adjustment path.

$$R_n = \sum_{i=1}^{4} a_i X_{n,i} \tag{1}$$

Based on the optimization of the weight values of the original Floyd algorithm [13], this paper proposes the optimization algorithm. The optimization algorithm pseudo-code shows in Algorithm 1. The algorithm needs to input four types of path parameters to assign weights and we set (a_1, a_2, a_3, a_4) as $(0.1, 0.3, 0.1, 0.5)$, which correspond to the impact factors in Table 1.

Algorithm 1: Weights optimization of the Floyd algorithm

Input: The four impact factors

Output: The optimal adjustment path

---

1. Standardize impact factors, initialize path parameters and assign weights a_j
2. N is the total number of alternative links, i is the number of each link nodes
3. For m=1 to N do
4.   For k=1 to i do
5.   For j=1 to 4 do
6.   Quantize the jth impact factor of kth node in mth alternative path
$$X_{m,k,j}$$
7.   End For
8.   Path parameter weighting value of the kth node in mth alternative path
$$R_{m,k} = \sum_{j=1}^{4} a_j X_{m,k,j}$$
9.   End for
10. End for
11. Replace the initialized node weights with the optimized path weights $R_{m,k}$
12. Invoke the optimization Floyd algorithm
13. Output the optimal adjustment path

---

5 Simulation

5.1 Simulation Environment

This paper tests the in-band networking mechanism and the fault adjustment method respectively. The testing of the in-band networking mechanism uses three Dell servers and one blade machine. The testing environment is Ubuntu 16.04 with P4 and ONOS controller, and the topology of the prototype system shows in Fig. 4.

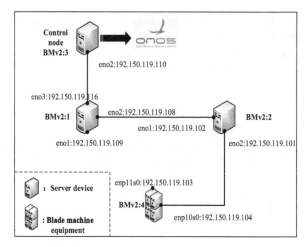

Fig. 4. The topology of the prototype system

5.2 Comparison of Algorithms

This experiment compares the weight optimization Floyd algorithm mentioned in this paper with the weight averaging of the Floyd algorithm (the following are called the weight optimization algorithm and the averaging algorithm, respectively). This experiment took place 30 times. Each test is independent to the other tests and does not affect each other. Each test re-collects the path information, re-determines the optimal adjustment path, and re-analyzes the optimal adjustment path parameters.

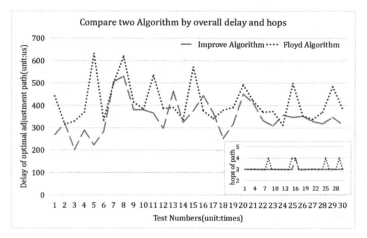

Fig. 5. Comparison of hop counts and overall delay performance of different algorithms

From Fig. 5, it can be seen the following result. For the hop counts, the optimal adjustment path by the decision of the weight optimization algorithm has a smoother trend and mostly stays at three hop counts, while the average algorithm has five times four hop counts. The averaging algorithm is more unstable and its performance is worse than that of the weight optimization algorithm. By comparing the overall latency index, it can obtain that the total processing latency of the weight optimization algorithm is lower than that of the average algorithm, which means that the weight optimization algorithm has a better performance in the overall latency.

Figure 6 shows the comparison between the weight optimization algorithm and the average algorithm in terms of the average hop counts and the overall delay of the optimal adjustment path. As can be seen, for the average of hop counts, the weight optimization algorithm is 3.03 hops, while the average algorithm is 3.17 hops, which is about 4.4% better. For the average of the overall delay, the weight optimization algorithm is 348.57 us, while the average algorithm is 414.44 us, which is about 15.9% better.

Overall, the optimal adjustment path decided by the algorithm of this paper reduces the hop counts and the overall delay of path, meaning that the improved algorithm can better address the actual demand of fault adjustment.

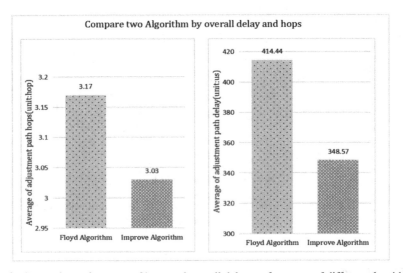

Fig. 6. Comparison of average of hops and overall delay performance of different algorithms

5.3   Comparison of Fault Adjustment Convergence Time

In order to test the convergence time of fault adjustment algorithm mentioned in this paper. This experiment compares the method of this paper with the OSPF protocol, as shown in Fig. 7. The hop counters of affected nodes mean the hop counts of the adjustment path. When the hop counters of affected nodes are one, the convergence time of our method is 90.6 ms, while the convergence time of OSPF protocol is 51.8 ms. When the hop counters are two, the convergence time of this method is 115.5 ms, while the convergence time of OSPF is 97.9 ms. When the hop counters are three, the convergence time of this method is 140.9 ms, while the convergence time of OSPF is

590.8 ms. By comparison, when the number of hops is three, the convergence time of the fault adjustment method proposed in this paper decreases by about 76.2%.

The method we proposed adjusts the routing information of the nodes on the optimal path. The route convergence time is close to the time of adjusting router on a single link. In contrast, the OSPF protocol uses flooding to announce link information and update neighbor relationships to other nodes [11]. When the number of network nodes increases and the topology becomes more complex, the OSPF protocol will require a higher route convergence time and will be prone to the transient loop [12]. It will waste more network resources. In Fig. 7, the convergence time of the fault adjustment method changes smoothly with the increase of topology complexity. It helps the control node to make fast and detailed adjustments for sudden faults in the in-band network.

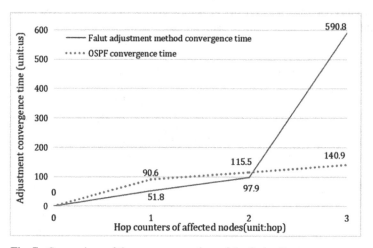

Fig. 7. Comparison of the convergence time of the fault adjustment process

6   Conclusion

This paper proposes a control plane in-band networking mechanism that can meet the requirement in the military network. What's more, the proposed fault adjustment method can realize fine-grained in-band networking fault adjustment by a single node, which can improve the control plane routing convergence efficiency.

The final experiment results show that the fault adjustment method can better address the actual issues by reducing the number of path hops and the overall delay of nodes. What's more, compared with the OSPF protocol, the method is better and more stable.

This experiment has done in a single-controller scenario. As for the multi-controller scenario, how establishing connections between networks governed by different controllers is a problem. At the same time, there is still a very large research space on how to migrate, handover, and restore controller functions to ensure network stability when the control node fails.

Acknowledgment. This research was funded by the fundamental research funds for the central universities under grant no. 2021JBZD003, open research projects of Zhejiang lab under grant no. 2022QA0AB03, nature and science foundation of China under grant no. 61471029, 61972026, 62072030 and 92167204.

References

1. Shi, M.-L., Chun, Y.: Routing protocols for ad hoc neworks: a survey. J. China Inst. Commun. (11), 93–103 (2001)
2. Ari, I., Jethani, N., Rangnekar, A., et al.: Performance analysis and comparison of ah-hoc routing protocols. Project Report (2000)
3. John Wiley & Sons: Mobile ad hoc networking (2004)
4. Niu, D., Zhang, Y., Zhao, Y., Yang, M.: Research on routing protocols in Ad Hoc networks. In: 2009 International Conference on Wireless Networks and Information Systems, pp. 27–30 (2009)
5. Shan, J.: Research on Key Technologies of Dynamic Battlefield Environment Impact Analysis on Military Action. National University of Defense Technology (2019)
6. Zhang, C., Feng, X., Liu, Z., et al.: Performance analysis of multi-frequency and classification structure in mobile Ad Hoc networks based on communications circumstances in battlefield. Fire Control Command Control **S1**, 24–26 (2014)
7. Zhou, J., Lu, J., Huang, S., Fan, Z.: Location-based routing algorithms for mobile Ad Hoc networks with holes. In: 2010 International Conference on Cyber-Enabled Distributed Computing and Knowledge Discovery, pp. 376–379 (2010). https://doi.org/10.1109/CyberC.2010.74
8. Mostajeran, E., Noor, R.M., Keshavarz, H.: A novel improved neighbor discovery method for an Intelligent-AODV in mobile Ad hoc networks. In: 2013 International Conference of Information and Communication Technology (ICoICT), pp. 395–399. IEEE (2013)
9. Kan-Song, C., Hao-Ke, L., Yu-Long, R., et al.: Improved AODV routing protocol based on local neighbor nodes and link weights. J. Softw. **32**(4), 1186–1200 (2021)
10. Gopi, D., Cheng, S., Huck, R.: Comparative analysis of SDN and conventional networks using routing protocols. In: 2017 International Conference on Computer, Information and Telecommunication Systems (CITS), pp. 108–112. IEEE (2017)
11. Sharon, O.: Dissemination of routing information in broadcast networks: OSPF versus IS-IS. IEEE Netw. **15**(1), 56–65 (2001)
12. Arai, Y., Oki, E.: A fast-convergence scheme to update metrics without loop in OSPF networks. In: 2011 1st International Symposium on Access Spaces (ISAS), pp. 213–217. IEEE (2011)
13. Xue, B., Guiqin, Y., Zhanjun, J.: research and application of floyd algorithm based on SDN network. In: 2019 12th International Conference on Intelligent Computation Technology and Automation (ICICTA), pp. 317–320 (2019). https://doi.org/10.1109/ICICTA49267.2019.00073

CNN-CGAN: A New Approach for Intrusion Detection Based on Generative Adversarial Networks

Zhengxia Ji and Xin Gao[✉]

School of Electronic and Information Engineering, Beijing Jiaotong University,
Beijing 100044, China
1048121431@qq.com

Abstract. With malicious traffic occurring all the time, network intrusion detection remains a critical task. However, data imbalance in the network and the increasing number of unknown attack types make the detection difficult. Therefore, in this study, we propose an anomalous traffic detection method named CNN-CGAN, which achieves data equalization by a modified generative adversarial network (GAN) and uses an convolutional neural network (CNN) as the detection model. First, chi-square test is used to extract various types of features from network attack data to accelerate the convergence of the model. Then, we use a improved generative adversarial network to generate data with similar distribution to the small sample data to complete the data equalization. Finally, CNN effectively extracts data features for attack detection and classification. Experiments on the network security dataset NSL-KDD prove that the CNN-GAN model in this paper outperforms the classical detection models in performance indicators such as F1 score, precision and recall. In addition to this, the detection rate of unknown attacks and attack types is also higher with fewer samples.

Keywords: Intrusion detection · Chi-square test · Generative adversarial network

1 Introduction

As modern technology develops by leaps and bounds and the continuous expansion of the network scale to the world, cyberspace has been in an important position as the fifth dimension [1]. However, more and more user devices access the network, which bring huge difficulty to the cyberspace. The emergence of complex and volatile cyber attacks makes the network security situation remains critical. Therefore, how to effectively detect and differentiate various intrusionshas become the key topic of network security researches.

Intrusion detection systems, as an active form of security protection, can carry out real-time monitoring of the network. It can better detect network attacks and provide relevant personnel with important response decisions [2].

In addition, it can also actively defend against network attacks, make corresponding actions before the network is compromised, and effectively maintain network security. In recent years, many new algorithms have been applied in the field of IDS to build relatively stable and high-accuracy intrusion detection systems. However, with the dramatic increase of network data, the bandwidth has enhanced significantly. In addition, the complex features and the diversity of information show an increasing number of new forms of attacks. Shallow machine learning (ML) that relies too much on feature learning is no longer able to handle massive network intrusion data [3]. Deep learning (DL) builds a nonlinear network system containing many hidden layers to learn the underlying laws of sample information. It not only satisfies high-dimensional research, but also has high efficiency. Therefore, deep learning has important value for processing traffic in the network.

In the face of increasingly sophisticated network attacks and massive amounts of high-dimensional data, traditional security techniques are gradually failing, and deep learning algorithms are gradually being applied to the field of network intrusion detection [4]. DL techniques can solve the problems of shallow learning algorithms in detection, effectively extract deep features in network data, and speed up model convergence. In recent years, DL-based intrusion detection methods have made phased progress, but a number of unresolved issues remain. For one thing, the traffic of normal behavior is often significantly larger than the traffic of abnormal behaviors in real network environments. In addition, the number of different attack types is unbalanced, resulting in poor detection of rare data by the model. For another thing, the complexity and diversity means of network attacks makes the existing detection techniques not well adapted to the current changing types of network attacks. Some new types of attacks also pose a major threat to network security, which has become a major problem in the application of deep learning in the field of intrusion detection [5,6].

With the aim of solving the problem of low detection accuracy caused by new types of attacks and data imbalance in the network, this paper proposes an effective network anomaly detection model, CNN-CGAN, which combines the improved GAN with CNN. CNN-CGAN solves the class distribution imbalance problem by data augmentation and extracts the deep features in the network data by CNN, thus effectively improving the accuracy of the model in detecting attack data. The contributions of CNN-CGAN model proposed in the atricle are as follows:

(1) Chi-square test performs feature screening on network data, extracts effective features in the network, and reduces confusion among various attack categories. In addition, feature selection can also accelerate model convergence and improve model training efficiency.
(2) CGAN takes the real data and preset labels in the network as input, and completes data augmentation by generating specific types of attack data, thereby reducing the imbalance of the training set. In addition, synthetic data can be used to simulate unknown cyberattacks, helping to improve the performance of detection models in identifying minority and unknown attacks.

The rest of the study is structured as follows. We present the related work of intrusion detection. Section 3 presents an anomaly detection framework combining GAN and CNN. Section 4 analyzes the experimental results and the performance of the CNN-CGAN model. In Sect. 5, a conclusions is given.

2   Related Works

As machine learning develops by leaps and bounds, its classification techniques have been introduced as detection models for various network security monitoring. The authors in [7] introduced the detection performance and experimental results of various machine learning models including decision trees in intrusion detection. Reference [8] compared the differences between traditional ML and DL in intrusion detection, and showed that traditional methods can no longer effective in dealing with the big data environment, while deep learning can analyze large data and has a good classification effect. In [9], the authors proposed a recurrent neural network-based method for abnormal traffic identification, and investigated the effect of different learning rates on accuracy and training time in binary and multi-classification. Literature [10] realized an intrusion detection model based on gated recurrent unit (GRU) by analyzing the characteristics of intrusion detection data, which achieved detection accuracy comparable to Long short-term memory, and had shorter training and detection time.

However, the data in the network is unbalanced, with significantly more normal behavior traffic than abnormal traffic. This means that the detection model will focus more on normal behavior and less on the correct identification of a small number of samples. To address these issues, the methods used in existing research are generally to increase small number of samples, that is, oversampling technology, such as, random oversampling [11], SMOTE [12] and adaptive synthesis [13]. Reference [14] proposed a small-sample oversampling technique based on Radius-SMOTE, which used a safe radius distance to create synthetic data, reducing the overlapping problem of synthetic data. Besides, the authors of [15] studied an anomaly detection methods based on GAN and RF, and it successfully solved the overfitting problem in traditional oversampling techniques and exhibited good detection performance.

In a conclusion, the researches show that it is vital to obtain good training data to solve the sample imbalance problem, which remains a very challenging job in the current network traffic anomaly identification.

3   Methods

The intrusion detection method combining improved generative adversarial network and CNN proposed in the paper consists of two main parts: data processing and model training. The overall block-diagram is shown in Fig. 1.

3.1   Data Processing

This module consists of three parts, including data standardization, feature selection, sample equalization and data enhancement. The main role of this module is to perform feature selection and data balancing for the dataset used for the training of the model.

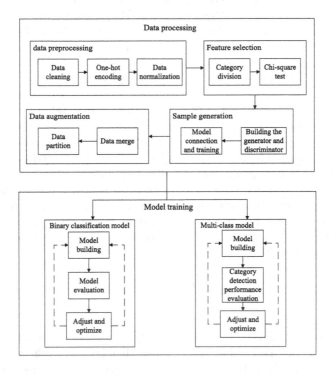

Fig. 1. Overall block diagram of intrusion detection

Data Normalization. Data normalization mainly completes data cleaning, one-hot encoding, and data normalization, thus laying the foundation for later training. First, we remove the missing and invalid values from the dataset. Then, we convert the text types to numeric types since datasets often contain both numeric and string-type features, and machine learning cannot train on string-type data. Finally, some numerical data have large numerical differences, which may lead to problems such as slowing network convergence. Therefore, in order to reduce the influence of inter-indicator dimensions on the data analysis results, the data need to be normalized. The eigenvalues of the data are restricted between [0, 1] by using the max-min normalization method which can be described as follows:

$$D' = \frac{D - D_{\min}}{D_{\max} - D_{\min}} \tag{1}$$

where D is the original data that needs to be normalized, $D_{\max}$ and $D_{\max}$ are the feature minimum and maximum values in the dataset, respectively.

Feature Selection. The second step in data processing part of this paper is feature selection. According to the NSL-KDD dataset selected in the article, the attack data is divided into four types, namely, denial-of-service attack, port monitoring or scanning, unauthorized access from remote host, and privileged access by unauthorized local super users. Each piece of data in the dataset used in this paper consists of 41 features and 1 label.

Feature selection can improve model efficiency and detection accuracy, it removes label-independent features and reduces computational burden. The method chosen in this paper is the chi-square test, which can calculate the degree of deviation between the observed value of the statistical sample and the expected value, and reflect the degree of correlation between the label and the feature, so as to obtain the feature that needs to be retained. As shown in Eq. (2), M means the observed value, and E means the expected value. Features in the sample can correspond to the observed value, and the label category can correspond to the expected value. The stronger the correlation between observed and theoretical values indicates that the feature will have a greater impact on the label and the more important the feature is likely to be. Therefore, feature selection can be performed by calculating the cardinality value between the label and category and ranking them.

$$X_c^2 = \sum \frac{(M_i - E_i)^2}{E_i} \qquad (2)$$

Data Imbalance. Data imbalance is the third step of data processing, which is used to solve the data imbalance problem that normal traffic is larger than abnormal traffic in the network data. In this paper, CGAN is used to generate rare data and to mix synthetic data with real data to disrupt the order for subsequent model training.

Generative Adversarial Network [16] draws on the idea of zero-sum game and consists of generator and discriminator, the specific structure is described in Fig. 2. The discriminator is a binary classifier consisting of a neural network that discriminates whether the input sample is real or fake. Similarly, the generator learns the latent distribution of real samples and is able to generate fake samples that approximate the distribution of real samples.

The G and D of the GAN are trained by minimizing the Jensen-Shannon scatter between the false and true distributions, with the following objective function.

$$\min_{G} \max_{D} V(D, G) = E_{x \sim p_r}[\log D(x)] + E_{\tilde{x} \sim p_g}[\log(1 - D(\tilde{x}))] \qquad (3)$$

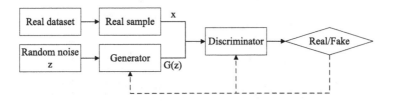

Fig. 2. The network structure of GAN

where $\tilde{x} = G(z)$ is the synthetic data generated by the generator. z denotes the random noise data sampled from $p(z)$. The original data distribution and the data distribution of the generated samples are represented by p_r and p_g respectively. The two neural networks are confronted with each other and iteratively optimized. First, the discriminator D is trained to improve the accuracy of the discriminated true and false data, and generator G is optimized to produce more realistic synthetic dates and deceive the discriminator D.

The generator of GAN can synthesize data based on random noise, but cannot generate specific types of data. Therefore, we add conditional constraints to the generator and discriminator based on GAN, which can use data and corresponding labels for training. As shown in Fig. 3, the generator and discriminator of CGAN add a label to the input, which can be specified to generate the desired type of samples, so the loss function of CGAN can be described as:

$$\min_G \max_D V(D, G) = E_{x \sim p_r}[\log D(x|y)] + E_{z \sim p_z}[\log(1 - D(G(z|y)))] \quad (4)$$

where y is the unique heat coded data for each attack category label in the data.

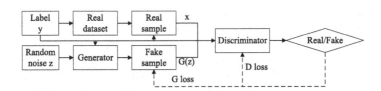

Fig. 3. The network structure of CGAN

The CGAN model is built with keras. First, a generator for synthesizing data and a discriminator for judging the authenticity of the data are constructed, and then the model is connected and trained. Details as follows:

(1) Construction of generator and discriminator: The generator and discriminator in CGAN use fully connected networks, which mainly include Dense, LeakyReLU and BatchNormalization layer. As we can see, Fig. 4(a) is the

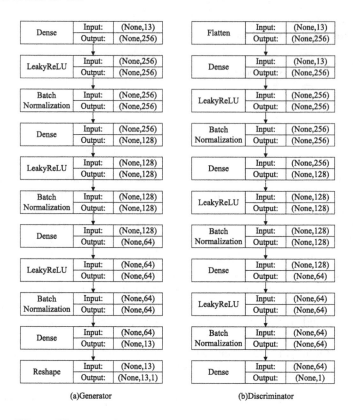

Fig. 4. The network structure of generator and discriminator

network structure of the G, and its output layer uses the tanh function. Meanwhile, Fig. 4(b) is the structure of the discriminator, and its output layer is the sigmoid function. In this paper, random noise and labels are used as inputs to the generator, and synthetic samples are used as outputs. Specifically, it uses the embedding layer to convert the label into a dense vector with the same length as the random noise vector, and then uses the Multiply layer to multiply the label and the random noise vector as the generator's input. The input of discriminator is a sample-label pair, and the output is the probability of whether the sample-label pair is true. The discriminator will take a label, use the Embedding layer to turn the label into a dense vector of sample length, and then use the Multiply layer to multiply the label and the sample as the input to the discriminator.

(2) Model connection and training: The constructed generator and discriminator are trained against each other to build a complete CGAN model. The specific training process is as follows. First, we randomly initialize the model

parameters, and control the generator G to remain unchanged, train the discriminator D, and use the Adam optimization algorithm as the optimizer to update the parameters in the network. Then, the training of the discriminator is suspended and the generator uses the feedback from the loss to the generator to complete the parameter update. Finally, when the loss value and cycle frequency do not reach the set thresholds, the steps of the first two steps are repeated, and the optimization gradient is updated using the Adam optimizer.

3.2   Model Training

This part uses CNN to complete the training of binary-class and multi-class model. The binary classification realizes the classification of normal traffic and abnormal traffic. Multi-classification identifies various attack types, and compares the detection accuracy of small samples before and after data balance. In addition, we continuously tune and optimize for better training results, improving the model's accuracy and generalization ability.

4   Experiments

4.1   Metrics of Performance Evaluation

In order to study the impact of different optimization methods on the classifier, and effectively evaluate the performance of the classifier, we select 4 performance indicators that are widely used in most works, including accuracy, precision, detection rate (DR), F1 score. In addition, the confusion matrix is demonstrate in Table 1.

The accuracy is the most commonly used and most intuitive performance indicator. It represents the ratio of the correct samples predicted by the detection model to all samples. The higher the accuracy of the model classification, the better the classification performance. Its definition is described as Eq. (5):

$$Acc = \frac{TN + TP}{TN + TP + FN + FP} \tag{5}$$

DR or Recall represents the proportion of all actual positive samples that are predicted to be positive. The definition of DR is as Eq. (6):

$$DR = \frac{TP}{FN + TP} \tag{6}$$

The precision rate represents the proportion of all the samples classified as positive examples that are truly positive examples. The higher the accuracy, the better the performance of the classification model. It is described as Eq. (7):

$$Precision = \frac{TP}{FP + TP} \tag{7}$$

F1 score is the recall and precision weighted harmonic average, also known as F-Score. In an imbalanced dataset, F1 can better measure the performance of the model ($F1 \in [0,1]$). F1 is defined as Eq. (8):

$$F - Score = \frac{2 \times TP}{2 \times TP + FN + FP} \qquad (8)$$

Table 1. Various types of data distribution

	Predicted attack	Predicted normal
Actual attack	TP	FN
Actual normal	FP	TN

4.2   Dataset

The dataset selected in the experiment is the NSL-KDD dataset consisting of five categories, and the data distribution of each category is shown in Table 2. We can see that the original testing set and training set are highly unbalanced, with the least category in training set accounting for only 0.04%, and the test set data of R2L and U2R is much larger than the training set data. At the same time, there are many categories that do not emerge in the training set, which places a demand on the generalization ability of the model. The above problems further highlight the role of sample balancing and feature selection.

Table 2. Various types of data distribution

Type of data	Number of training sets	Training set ratio (%)	Number of testing sets	Testing set ratio (%)
Normal	37343	53.46	9710	43.07
DoS	45926	36.45	7636	33.87
Probe	11657	9.26	2423	10.75
R2L	994	0.78	2570	11.41
U2R	53	0.05	203	0.90

4.3   Model Performance Comparison

We split the NSL-KDD dataset into a training set and a test set for training and evaluating the model, respectively. The evaluation metrics of different classifier models on the dataset are shown in Fig. 5. We can see that the CNN-CGAN model proposed in this paper is higher than other intrusion detection systems in terms of accuracy, recall and F1 score. So the detection method proposed in

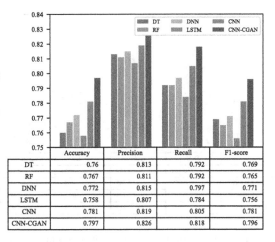

	Accuracy	Precision	Recall	F1-score
DT	0.76	0.813	0.792	0.769
RF	0.767	0.811	0.792	0.765
DNN	0.772	0.815	0.797	0.771
LSTM	0.758	0.807	0.784	0.756
CNN	0.781	0.819	0.805	0.781
CNN-CGAN	0.797	0.826	0.818	0.796

Fig. 5. Performance comparison under different classification

this paper can effectively classify the anomalous traffic in the network and the accuracy of the classification is improved by 3%.

Figure 6 displays the improvement of detection performance by different data enhancement models. It can be seen that data enhancement techniques have improved the detection accuracy and other performance. The detection effect of the model proposed in this paper is significantly improved. The experimental results show that the data equalization effect of CGAN is more effective than other methods.

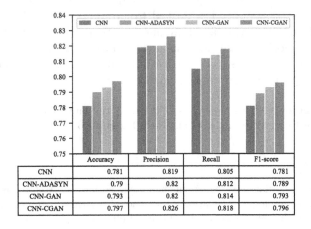

	Accuracy	Precision	Recall	F1-score
CNN	0.781	0.819	0.805	0.781
CNN-ADASYN	0.79	0.82	0.812	0.789
CNN-GAN	0.793	0.82	0.814	0.793
CNN-CGAN	0.797	0.826	0.818	0.796

Fig. 6. Effects comparison of different data enhancement methods for detection.

From Fig. 7, we can see that CGAN has improved detection performance for all four categories. The smaller number of R2L and U2R categories have a larger performance improvement. Therefore, it can be concluded that cGAN has a high improvement in improving the detection accuracy of small samples.

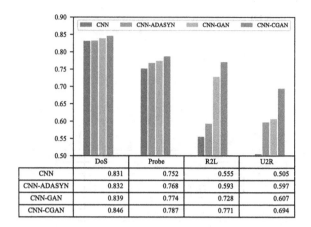

	DoS	Probe	R2L	U2R
CNN	0.831	0.752	0.555	0.505
CNN-ADASYN	0.832	0.768	0.593	0.597
CNN-GAN	0.839	0.774	0.728	0.607
CNN-CGAN	0.846	0.787	0.771	0.694

Fig. 7. Comparison of the detection performance of different models for various types of attacks

5   Conclusion

In this paper, we propose an anomaly identification method based on an improved generative adversarial network, which solves the problem of low attack data detection accuracy caused by data imbalance in existing networks. First, we perform feature screening through the chi-square distribution, which speeds up the training of the model. Then, we use CGAN to generate designated attack data with similar distribution to the original data based on the categories of input labels to achieve data augmentation and reduce training data imbalance. Finally, our detection method is verified to have better detection performance on the NSL-KDD dataset. In addition, our detection method improves detection accuracy for minority classes and unknown attack types more than the other five baseline methods. This method effectively alleviates the problems caused by changes in attack types and data imbalance in the network.

Acknowledgements. This paper is supported by the Fundamental Research Funds for the Central Universities under Grant No. 2020JBM013.

References

1. Zhong-hua, W., Jian-feng, M., Wen-sheng, N., Ya-hui, L.: Architecture of security protection technology for aviation cyberspace. In: 2020 7th International Conference on Dependable Systems and Their Applications (DSA), pp. 21–24 (2020). https://doi.org/10.1109/DSA51864.2020.00009
2. Jamalipour, A., Murali, S.: A taxonomy of machine-learning-based intrusion detection systems for the Internet of Things: a survey. IEEE Internet Things J. **9**(12), 9444–9466 (2022). https://doi.org/10.1109/JIOT.2021.3126811
3. Shone, N., Ngoc, T.N., Phai, V.D., Shi, Q.: A deep learning approach to network intrusion detection. IEEE Trans. Emerg. Top. Comput. Intell. **2**(1), 41–50 (2018). https://doi.org/10.1109/TETCI.2017.2772792

4. Shu, J., Zhou, L., Zhang, W., Du, X., Guizani, M.: Collaborative intrusion detection for VANETs: a deep learning-based distributed SDN approach. IEEE Trans. Intell. Transp. Syst. **22**(7), 4519–4530 (2021). https://doi.org/10.1109/TITS.2020. 3027390
5. Bao, F., Deng, Y., Kong, Y., Ren, Z., Suo, J., Dai, Q.: Learning deep landmarks for imbalanced classification. IEEE Trans. Neural Netw. Learn. Syst. **31**(8), 2691–2704 (2020). https://doi.org/10.1109/TNNLS.2019.2927647
6. Liang, W., Hu, Y., Zhou, X., Pan, Y., Wang, K.I.K.: Variational few-shot learning for microservice-oriented intrusion detection in distributed industrial IoT. IEEE Trans. Ind. Inf. **18**(8), 5087–5095 (2022). https://doi.org/10.1109/TII.2021. 3116085
7. Ahmad, I., Basheri, M., Iqbal, M.J., Rahim, A.: Performance comparison of support vector machine, random forest, and extreme learning machine for intrusion detection. IEEE Access **6**, 33789–33795 (2018). https://doi.org/10.1109/ACCESS. 2018.2841987
8. Dong, B., Wang, X.: Comparison deep learning method to traditional methods using for network intrusion detection. In: 2016 8th IEEE International Conference on Communication Software and Networks (ICCSN), pp. 581–585 (2016). https://doi.org/10.1109/ICCSN.2016.7586590
9. Yin, C., Zhu, Y., Fei, J., He, X.: A deep learning approach for intrusion detection using recurrent neural networks. IEEE Access **5**, 21954–21961 (2017). https://doi.org/10.1109/ACCESS.2017.2762418
10. Javed, A.R., Ur Rehman, S., Khan, M.U., Alazab, M., Reddy, T.: CANintelli-IDS: detecting in-vehicle intrusion attacks on a controller area network using CNN and attention-based GRU. IEEE Trans. Netw. Sci. Eng. **8**(2), 1456–1466 (2021). https://doi.org/10.1109/TNSE.2021.3059881
11. Lemaître, G., Nogueira, F., Aridas, C.K.: Imbalanced-learn: a Python toolbox to tackle the curse of imbalanced datasets in machine learning. J. Mach. Lear. Res. **18**(1), 559–563 (2017)
12. Chawla, N.V., Bowyer, K.W., Hall, L.O., Kegelmeyer, W.P.: Smote: synthetic minority over-sampling technique. J. Artif. Intell. Res. **16**, 321–357 (2002)
13. He, H., Bai, Y., Garcia, E.A., Li, S.: ADASYN: adaptive synthetic sampling approach for imbalanced learning. In: 2008 IEEE International Joint Conference on Neural Networks (IEEE World Congress on Computational Intelligence), pp. 1322–1328. IEEE (2008)
14. Pradipta, G.A., Wardoyo, R., Musdholifah, A., Sanjaya, I.N.H.: Radius-SMOTE: a new oversampling technique of minority samples based on radius distance for learning from imbalanced data. IEEE Access **9**, 74763–74777 (2021). https://doi.org/10.1109/ACCESS.2021.3080316
15. Huang, S., Lei, K.: IGAN-IDS: an imbalanced generative adversarial network towards intrusion detection system in ad-hoc networks. Ad Hoc Netw. **105**, 102177 (2020). https://doi.org/10.1016/j.adhoc.2020.102177. www.sciencedirect.com/science/article/pii/S1570870519311035
16. Zhang, G., Wang, X., Li, R., Song, Y., He, J., Lai, J.: Network intrusion detection based on conditional Wasserstein generative adversarial network and cost-sensitive stacked autoencoder. IEEE Access **8**, 190431–190447 (2020). https://doi.org/10. 1109/ACCESS.2020.3031892

A Lattice-Based Multisignature Scheme for Blockchain-Enabled Systems

Xiao Liang[1], Xiaohui Wang[1], Qianyi Zhang[2(✉)], Shuai Yuan[3], and Zhitao Guan[2]

[1] Artificial Intelligence on Electric Power System
State Grid Corporation Joint Laboratory, State Grid Smart Grid Research Institute Co. Ltd.,
Beijing 102209, China
[2] School of Control and Computer Engineering, North China Electric Power University,
Beijing 102206, China
qianyicheung@163.com
[3] Department of Finance, Operations, and Information Systems (FOIS),
Brock University, St. Catharines, ON, Canada

Abstract. Multisignature scheme enables a class of users to produce a signature interactively on a shared message, thus significantly reducing the signature size. This is especially important in blockchain-enabled systems where a consensus is required to complete a transaction. However, most existing approaches are constructed based upon traditional problems, for example, the integer factoring assumption and the discrete logarithm assumption, which in turn bear the risk of quantum computing attacks. Although lattice-based solutions are considered in some studies, the computational overhead due to high level of interaction becomes a major concern. In this paper, we present a new lattice-based multisignature scheme, which is constructed upon Bimodal Lattice Signature Scheme (BLISS). Next, we apply it to the blockchain-enabled systems through the demonstration of a cryptocurrency transaction. At last, we compare the proposed model with existing works on the performance. The result shows that our work can satisfy the security and efficiency concerns of the blockchain-enabled systems.

Keywords: Blockchain · Multisignature · Lattice cryptography

1 Introduction

As a variant of signature scheme [2], multisignature [1] enables a class of users to sign on a given message to show their agreement on it. Specifically, these users are able to cooperate and generate the joint signature, which can be also verified later by their public keys. By adopting multisignature schemes, merely one short aggregated signature that generated from the entire group is needed, and anyone can check the validity of the aggregated signature simultaneously. Therefore, the length of a multisignature is significantly shorter than the length of the aggregated individual signatures. This characteristic provides a good fit for the blockchain-enabled systems, since the transactions on the blockchain are performed by consensus among participants.

In contrast, lattice-based cryptographic structures have developed into a promising competitor for post-quantum cryptography recently. This is because they are efficient and typically simple on implementation, and also play an important role in resisting quantum computing attacks. Furthermore, the unique security properties provide a reduction from worst-case hardness to average-case instances, i.e., to break the lattice-based cryptographic construction is provably at least as tough as solving several lattice problems in the worst case. Therefore the lattice-based cryptographic schemes provide a solution to guarantee the security and distinguish themselves from established public key cryptosystems. A number of works such as [3, 4] have incorporated well-studied lattice problems. Different from conventional constructions such as large integer decomposition problems or RSA, sub-exponential time attacks on lattice problems haven't been observed yet, thus incentivizing a wider adoption of lattice-based cryptosystems.

Though substantial amount of research has focused on multisignature systems, most studies are built upon the RSA and/or the discrete logarithm assumption [5–11], which in turn bear the risk of quantum computing attacks. Therefore, in this work, we present a brand-new lattice-based multisignature scheme for blockchain-enabled systems to address this challenge, following the Bimodal Lattice Signature Scheme (BLISS) [12].

The remainder of this paper is organized as follows. Section 2 presents the related work on multisignature schemes. Section 3 highlights the mathematical background and notations. In Sect. 4, we develop the multisignature scheme and apply it in the blockchain-based systems by using the demonstration of a cryptocurrency transaction. Performance evaluations have been done in Sect. 5. We conclude with Sect. 6.

2   Related Work

The multisignature scheme [13], which is a modification of digital signature scheme, enables multiple signers to jointly construct a compact signature on a shared message through interactions. It is advantageous for the signers to diminish the size of a multisignature than the case of generating signatures individually, which can make better use of computing resources [31]. We address the research in this area along two dimensions: the traditional multisignature schemes and the post-quantum multisignature schemes.

Since the RSA algorithm provides a foundation to design the underlying cryptosystems, much of the pertinent work in the traditional multisignature schemes literature are developed under RSA assumption. Harn et al. [14] propose the first RSA-based multisignature scheme, where the time of signature generation is related to the number of signers. Itakura and Nakamura [1] develop the first ordered multisignature scheme, while Okamoto [15] solve the problem on efficiency in [1] by using a one-way hash function. Furthermore, Kiesler and Harn [16] present a technique, which can solve the fundamental issue of bit expansion on message blocking in multisignature context. Two enhanced RSA multisignature schemes motivated by [15] and [16] are proposed respectively by Park et al. [17] such that the restriction on signing order has been removed, resulting in an improvement on efficiency. Bellare and Neven [18] develop an identity-based multisignature (IBMS) scheme and subsequently improved by Bagherzandi et al. [19], by reducing the round complexity from three to two.

However, since Shor presents the quantum algorithm [20], the classical constructed schemes start to face the risks of attacks by quantum computers. Therefore, the issue of quantum-resistance on multisignature schemes becomes a primary challenge and focused by the existing literature. As a candidate solution, the lattice-based multisignature schemes are generally classified into two categories: the one based on the hash-and-sign approach [21], and the other based on the Fiat-Shamir technique [22]. We focus solely on the Fait-Shamir related work as follows.

Due to its support for public key aggregation, Ohta and Okamoto [10] propose the first multisignature scheme and demonstrate the security with the random oracle model [23]. Micali et al. [24] develop the Accountable-Subgroup Multisignature (ASM) model, which is the first study of this kind to explicitly incorporate key generation without depending on trusted third parties. Feng et al. [25] present a changeable threshold signature scheme where the signing algorithm is performed successively by each participant. However, the computational overhead due to high level of interaction is a major concern from most of the proposed lattice-based schemes.

3 Preliminaries

3.1 Lattices and Notation

Without loss of generality, given a ring $\mathcal{R}$, the quotient ring is denoted by $\mathcal{R}_q = \mathbb{Z}_q[x]/(x^n + 1)$ (or $\mathcal{R}_{2q} = \mathbb{Z}_{2q}[x]/(x^n + 1)$), where we assume that n is a power of 2 and q is a prime number such that $q = 1(mod\,2n)$. Column vectors are written in boldface lower case, e.g., u, and let u^t denote the transpose of u. Matrices are in capital boldface and I_n stands for the identity matrix of dimension n, in which n is a positive integer.

We define $\|u\|_p = \left(\sum_i |u_i|^p\right)^{1/p}$ as the ℓ_p-norm of a vector u for $p > 0$. By default, $\|.\|$ represents the ℓ_2-norm. We also apply Huffman Coding to derive smaller size of signatures by compressing the highest bits of certain parameters, which is denoted by $\lfloor \cdot \rceil_d$. A lattice is defined by a series of multi-dimensional points with a repeated structure as follows.

Definition 1. Given n linearly independent vectors b_1, b_2, ..., b_n, the lattice generated by them is defined as

$$\mathcal{L}(b_1, b_2, \ldots, b_n) = \left\{\sum x_i b_i | x_i \in \mathbb{Z}\right\}$$

We refer to b_1, b_2, ..., b_n as a basis of the lattice. Equivalently, if B is defined as the $m \times n$ matrix with columns b_1, b_2, ..., b_n, then the lattice generated by B is denoted as

$$\mathcal{L}(B) = \mathcal{L}(b_1, b_2, \ldots, b_n) = \left\{Bx | x \in \mathbb{Z}^n\right\}$$

Let n be the rank and m be the dimension of the lattice, if $n = m$, we call it a full-rank lattice.

In addition, our multisignature scheme is developed on top of the hardness of the ring-based short integer solution (Ring-SIS) problem, which is defined as below.

Definition 2 (Ring-SIS problem). Let $\mathcal{R}$ be a ring. Given $a_1, \ldots, a_\ell \in R_q$ sampled independently and uniformly at random, find $e_1, \ldots, e_\ell \in R_{\{-1,0,1\}}$ such that non-zero polynomial $a_1 e_1 + \cdots + a_\ell e_\ell = 0 \bmod q$.

3.2 Multisignature Scheme

Next, we present the definition of the multisignature as well as its security. A multisignature scheme *MSig* contains a 3-tuple (*KeyGen*, *Sig*, *Ver*). Each signer produces a secret key and a public key with the protocol $KeyGen(1^\lambda)$. Then, all signers collectively issue a signature σ on a message m by processing the multi-party protocol $Sig(PK, sk_i, m)$, in which PK is a collection of the public keys from all users and sk_i is the secret key from the i-th user. The signature σ on a message m can be verified by $Ver(\sigma, PK, m)$ where the output is either 0 (invalid) or 1 (valid), respectively. The detailed descriptions are as follows:

- $KeyGen(1^\lambda)$: The non-interactive key generation algorithm that returns an individual key pair given a security parameter λ.
- $Sig(PK, sk_i, m)$: The interactive protocol that returns a signature σ with a given message m.
- $Ver(\sigma, PK, m)$: The verification algorithm that returns 1 if σ is a valid signature for (PK, m), 0 otherwise.

Completeness. A *multisignature* scheme should meet the completeness property: for any given message m, if $Sig(PK, sk_i, m)$ is carried out by all signers, then each individual should receive a signature σ such that $Ver(\sigma, PK, m) = 1$, where $PK = \{pk_i\}_{i=1}^N$ for N signers.

Security. A multisignature scheme is EUF-CMA (existential unforgeability under adaptively chosen message attacks) secure if for any probabilistic polynomial time adversary $\mathcal{A}$ with known messages and signatures, the probability that $\mathcal{A}$ construct an authentic signature on a different unsigned message is trivial.

3.3 Blockchain Technology

Blockchain is a decentralized and distributed database technology where all the negotiation processes are recorded, validated, and managed securely [26, 27]. In general, blockchain is tamper-resistant and classified into three main categories depending on who can participate in the network: public, consortium and private [28].

In the case of the public blockchain, every user is allowed to enter or quit the network, participate in transactions, and the transaction data on the chain can also be created and viewed accordingly. Each individual is given the delegation of authority equally, rather than a third party in the centralized systems [28, 29]. A typical application is the Bitcoin. In addition, for the consortium blockchain, also known as the industry chain, only those users who are pre-selected to be authorized are capable of validating transactions [30]. A consortium blockchain is considered as a polycentric system, typically represented by Hyperledger Fabric. Finally, all the data is not publicly available in the private blockchain. The consensus is controlled by only one specific organization [28]. However, enterprise-class applications on the private blockchain are still under development.

4 Proposed Scheme

We first introduce BLISS [12] as the fundamentals of our proposed scheme in the following discussion.

For any integer q, use $\mathbb{Z}_q$ to denote a cyclic group with components in $\left[-\frac{q}{2}, \frac{q}{2}\right) \cap \mathbb{Z}$. Elements in $\mathbb{B}$ are binary integers, and $\mathbb{B}_w^n$ denotes a set of binary vectors whose weight is w and length is n. Let H_1 be a random oracle hash function, which output uniformly in $\mathbb{B}_w^n$. A secret/public key pair is denoted by $\left(S \in \mathbb{Z}_{2q}^{m \times n}, P \in \mathbb{Z}_{2q}^{n \times m}\right)$ so that $PS = P(-S) = qI_n (mod\ 2q)$. To jointly sign on a shared message m, all the signers should first samples a bit $b \xleftarrow{\$} \{0, 1\}$ and a vector $y \leftarrow D_\sigma^m$ respectively, where D_σ^m is a discrete Gaussian distribution with m dimension. Then each signer computes $c = H_1(Py\ mod\ 2q, m)$ and $z = y + (-1)^b Sc$, performs rejection sampling, and finally returns the result (z, c) with a $1/\left(M\ exp\left(-\frac{\|Sc\|^2}{2\sigma^2}\right) \cosh\left(\frac{z, Sc}{\sigma^2}\right)\right)$ probability. Details of the rejection sampling are provided in Sect. 3.2 from [12].

4.1 Our Multisignature Scheme

For illustration purposes, we consider N signers with standard parameters $(n, q, d, \delta_1, \delta_2, \sigma)$ as listed in Table 1 [12]. Let H be a homomorphic hash function satisfies $H(A + B) = H(A) + H(B)$ generate two random polynomials. We denote d as the number of dropped bits, and let $p = \lfloor 2q/2^d \rfloor$. Our multisignature scheme is defined as follows:

Table 1. Parameters of the proposed multisignature scheme.

	Security level	0	1	2	3	4
	Optimized for	Fun	Speed	Size	Security	Security
n	Dimension	256	512	512	512	512
q	Modulus	7681	12289	12289	12289	12289
d	Number of dropped bits	5	10	10	9	8
δ_1, δ_2	Secret key densities	.55, .15	.3, 0	.3, 0	.42, .03	.45, .06
σ	Gaussian standard deviation	100	215	107	250	271

Key Generation. The protocol $KeyGen()$ returns a key pair (S, P) such that $SP = q\ mod\ 2q$, which is carried out as follows:

a.   Given densities δ_1 and δ_2, generate two random polynomials f and g who have exactly $d_1 = \lceil \delta_1 n \rceil$ coefficients in $\{\pm 1\}$ and $d_2 = \lceil \delta_2 n \rceil$ coefficients in $\{\pm 2\}$ respectively, while others set to 0.
b. $S = (s_1, s_2)^t \leftarrow (f, 2g + 1)^t$.
c. $a_q = (2g + 1)/f\ mod\ q$ (Restart if f is not invertible).

d. Return (S, P) where $P = (2a_q, q - 2) \bmod 2q$.

Signature Algorithm. Given a set of public keys $PK = \{pk_i\}_{i=1}^N$ and a message m, the algorithm $Sig(PK, sk_i, m)$ returns a signature $\sigma = z_2$ of the message m. Note that $sk_i = (s_{i,1}, s_{i,2})^t \in R_{2q}^{2 \times 1}$, $pk_i = (a_i, q - 2)^t \in R_{2q}^{2 \times 1}$. ζ is defined such that $\zeta \cdot (q - 2) = 1 \bmod 2q$. All signers run $Sig()$ interactively, where each individual with (sk_i, pk_i) carries it out as follows:

a. $y_{i,1}, y_{i,2} \leftarrow D_{\mathbb{Z}^n, \sigma}$, where D_σ^m is a m-dimensional discrete Gaussian distribution.
b. Compute $u_i = \zeta \cdot a_i \cdot y_{i,1} + y_{i,2} \bmod 2q$.
c. Compute $c_i \leftarrow H(\lfloor u_i \rceil_d + m \bmod p)$ and broadcast c_i.
d. Receive $\{c_j\}_{j \in [1,N] \setminus \{i\}}$ from the other signers and broadcast $\lfloor u_i \rceil_d$.
e. Receive $\{\lfloor u_j \rceil_d\}_{j \in [1,N] \setminus \{i\}}$ from the other signers, stop if $\neg (c_j = H(\lfloor u_j \rceil_d + m \bmod p))$ for all $j \in [1, N] \setminus \{i\}$.
f. Choose a random bit b_i.
g. Set $(z_{i,1}, z_{i,2}) = (y_{i,1} + (-1)^{b_i} s_{i,1} \cdot c_i, y_{i,2} + (-1)^{b_i} s_{i,2} \cdot c_i)$.
h. Continue with probability $1 / \left(M \exp\left(-\frac{\|sk_i \cdot c_i\|^2}{2\sigma^2} \right) \cosh\left(\frac{\langle z, sk_i \cdot c_i \rangle}{\sigma^2} \right) \right)$, otherwise restart.
i. Compute $z_{i,2}' = (\lfloor u_i \rceil_d - \lfloor u_i - z_{i,2} \rceil_d) \bmod p$.
j. Broadcast $(z_{i,1}, z_{i,2}')$.
k. Receive $\{(z_{i,1}, z_{j,2}')\}_{j \in [1,N] \setminus \{i\}}$ from the other signers, then compute $z_2 = \sum_{j=1}^N z_{j,2}' \bmod p$.
l. Return $\sigma = z_2$.

Verification Algorithm. The signature is verified by $Ver(\sigma, PK, m)$ if and only if:

$$c = H\left(\sum_{i=1}^N \lfloor \zeta \cdot a_i \cdot z_{i,1} + \zeta \cdot q \cdot c_i \rceil_d + z_2 + N \cdot m \bmod p \right)$$

4.2 Correctness and Security Analysis

Correctness. We now prove that $Ver(\sigma, PK, m)$ always accept the signature for any $i \in [1, N]$, $(sk_i, pk_i) \leftarrow KeyGen()$ and $\sigma \leftarrow Sig(PK, sk_i, m)$, where $PK = \{pk_i\}_{i=1}^N$.

If each signer is behaving honestly to perform the algorithm, we have

$$\zeta(q - 2) = 1 \bmod 2q \tag{1}$$

$$sk_i \cdot pk_i = a_i \cdot s_{i,1} + s_{i,2}(q - 2) = q \bmod 2q \tag{2}$$

$$H(A + B) = H(A) + H(B) \tag{3}$$

Therefore, following Eqs. (1), (2) and $Sig()$, we get

$$u_i - z_{i,2} = \zeta \cdot a_i \cdot y_{i,1} + y_{i,2} - \left(y_{i,2} + (-1)^{b_i} s_{i,2} \cdot c_i\right) \ mod \ 2q$$

$$= \zeta a_i y_{i,1} - (-1)^{b_i} s_{i,2} c_i \ mod \ 2q$$

$$= \zeta a_i y_{i,1} - (-1)^{b_i} s_{i,2} c_i \zeta (q - 2) \ mod \ 2q$$

$$= \zeta a_i y_{i,1} - (-1)^{b_i} c_i \zeta \left(a_i s_{i,1} + s_{i,2}(q - 2)\right)$$
$$+ (-1)^{b_i} c_i \zeta a_i s_{i,1} \ mod \ 2q$$

$$= \zeta a_i y_{i,1} - (-1)^{b_i} c_i \zeta q + (-1)^{b_i} c_i \zeta a_i s_{i,1} \ mod \ 2q$$

$$= \zeta a_i \left(y_{i,1} + (-1)^{b_i} s_{i,1} c_i\right) + \zeta q c_i - \left(\zeta q c_i + (-1)^{b_i} \zeta q c_i\right) \ mod \ 2q$$

$$= \zeta a_i \left(y_{i,1} + (-1)^{b_i} s_{i,1} c_i\right) + \zeta q c_i \ mod \ 2q$$

$$= \zeta a_i z_{i,1} + \zeta q c_i \ mod \ 2q \tag{4}$$

Furthermore, following (3) we get

$$H\left(\sum_{i=1}^{N} (\lfloor \zeta a_i z_{i,1} + \zeta q c_i \rceil_d) + z_2 + N \cdot m \ mod \ p\right)$$

$$= H\left(\sum_{i=1}^{N} \left(\lfloor \zeta a_i z_{i,1} + \zeta q c_i \rceil_d + \lfloor u_i \rceil_d - \lfloor u_i - z_{i,2} \rceil_d + m\right) mod \ p\right)$$

$$= H\left(\sum_{i=1}^{N} \lfloor u_i \rceil_d + m \ mod \ p\right) \tag{5}$$

$$= \sum_{i=1}^{N} H(\lfloor u_i \rceil_d + m \ mod \ ) p$$

$$= \sum_{i=1}^{N} c_i$$

$$= c$$

Hence,

$$c = H\left(\sum_{i=1}^{N} \lfloor \zeta \cdot a_i \cdot z_{i,1} + \zeta \cdot q \cdot c_i \rceil_d + z_2 + N \cdot m \, mod \, p\right) \tag{6}$$

QED.

Security Analysis. Assuming that the attacker can intercept the information during the interactions among the signers, the possible information leaked from the proposed multisignature process includes $\{c_j\}_{j \in [1,N]}$, $\{\lfloor u_j \rceil_d\}_{j \in [1,N]}$, $\left\{\left(z_{i,1}, z'_{j,2}\right)\right\}_{j \in [1,N]}$, and the signature $\sigma = z_2$. If the proposed scheme is followed, c_j is secure since it is encrypted by the homomorphic hash function H, u and $z_{i,1}$ are secure based on the hardness of Ring-SIS problem, $z'_{i,2}$ is secure due to the security of u_i, and therefore the signature σ is secure.

4.3 An Application in Blockchain Systems

A blockchain is a distributed ledger where blocks are linked in a chronological order and can be validated using cryptographic techniques. It was first used in Bitcoin and is now considered one of the most encouraging disruptive technologies in the economic region. With its decentralized nature, it deemphasizes the need for any trusted third-parties in the domains of credit collection, Internet of Things and asset management. However, there are some challenges that must be addressed. In the case of Bitcoin, for example, the blockchain ledger for Bitcoin increased from 319GB to 383GB in 2021 and continues to grow with increasing number of transactions. In other words, the size of data on the blockchain may become one of the many obstacles for future progress in cryptocurrency systems.

Motivated by the issue above, our lattice-based multisignature scheme discussed in Sect. 4.1 can provide certain benefits. Since the signatures from all the users involved in a single transaction are required to be verified on the blockchain, large scale data will possibly incur particularly in the scenario where the fund is owned jointly. Our work serves as an important tool to hedge against such risk by compressing the size of aggregated signatures. Let $U_i(1 \leq i \leq N)$ be the users who jointly own a fund where N denotes the amount of the users, let m be the transaction of the shared fund. The transaction consists of three phases as Fig. 1. Illustrates.

① **Signature phase.** All the users $U_i(1 \leq i \leq N)$ who shared fund interactively perform the algorithm $Sig(PK, sk_i, m)$ from the proposed multisignature scheme and generate a signature σ. Note that each individual key pair (pk_i, sk_i) is generated when joining the network.
② **Verification phase.** A verifier collects the transaction and performs the algorithm $Ver(\sigma, PK, m)$, then the transaction is accepted if $Ver(\sigma, PK, m) = 1$, rejected otherwise.
③ **Upload phase.** If the transaction is verified, it will be packed into a block and uploaded on the blockchain.

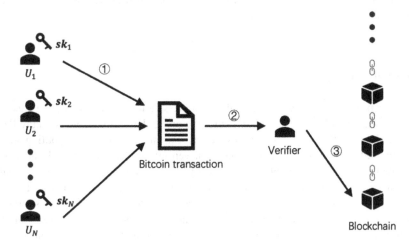

Fig. 1. A transaction of multi-user shared funds on the blockchain

5 Performance Evaluation

We now present a brief evaluation of the multisignature scheme we previously proposed, and a comparison with the existing benchmarks.

The scheme in [2] has been proved to be secure under the PPK (Plain Public Key) and random oracle model with post quantum secure assumptions of Ring SIS and the Decisional Compact Knapsack. Ma and Jiang [3] propose an effective lattice-based multisignature scheme and develop it to allow the process of public key aggregation with acceptable performance. It is also based on the Ring-SIS assumption and has been proved to be secure in the random oracle model.

We obtain the parameters in our scheme following Table 1 [12], then we derive the component size from [2] and [3] accordingly. As shown in Table 2, given the security level, the signature size is smaller than the benchmarks. In addition, as the security level increases where σ increases from 215 to 271, the signature size of our work increases at a slowing pace. This experiment highlights how stable the proposed scheme is on the signature size, given various levels of security requirement.

Table 2. Comparative analysis on the component size with benchmarks.

Scheme	Secret key size	Public key size	Signature size
[2]	$2n\lceil log^{2d}\rceil$	$2n\lceil log^{q+d}\rceil$	$2n\lceil log^{N\cdot2(k-32)+1+160N}\rceil$
[3]	$2n\lceil log^{3}\rceil$	$n\lceil log^{q}\rceil$	$2n\lceil log^{2N\cdot(\alpha-32)+1}\rceil$
Our scheme	$2n\lceil log^{2q}\rceil$	$n\lceil log^{2q}\rceil + q$	$log_2(4.1\sigma)$

$\lceil\bullet\rceil$ indicates upward rounding. n is a power-of-2 positive integer, q is a modulus, chosen as a prime convergent to 1 modulo $2n$. d is a very small integer parameter in the employed commitment scheme. N denotes the number of signers. The boundary k is to maintain the balance of the security and the runtime in [2]. α is the number of basis to generate an exponential number of commitments in [3]. σ is the gaussian standard deviation.

6 Conclusion

This paper proposes a lattice-based multisignature scheme where users can generate a signature interactively on a shared message. We prove that our scheme is secure based on the hardness of Ring-SIS problem, as well as resistant to quantum computing attacks due to the lattice assumption. Furthermore, driven by the need to diminish the size of aggregated signatures, we apply our scheme to blockchain-enabled systems. Finally, we evaluate the efficiency of this work with the existing works, which demonstrates its comparative advantages. Future research may concentrate on more intricate settings to address the trade-off between security requirement and computational overhead. The practitioners would benefit from this research line to effectively control and manage security risks in the quantum computing era.

Acknowledgment. This work is supported by the science and technology project of State Grid Corporation of China "Research on Information Security Supporting and Identity Management Key Technologies for Energy and Power Blockchains" (grant No. 5700-202158411A-0-0-00).

References

1. Itakura, K., Nakamura, K.: A public-key cryptosystem suitable for digital multisignatures. NEC Res. Dev. **71**, 1–8 (1983)
2. Yang, W., Wang, N., Guan, Z., et al.: A practical cross-device federated learning framework over 5G networks. IEEE Wirel. Commun. (2022)
3. Ma, C., Jiang, M.: Practical lattice-based multisignature schemes for blockchains. IEEE Access **7**, 179765–179778 (2019)
4. Damgård, I., Orlandi, C., Takahashi, A., et al.: Two-round n-out-of-n and multi-signatures and trapdoor commitment from lattices. J. Cryptol. **35**(2), 1–56 (2022)
5. Bellare M., Neven G.: Multi-signatures in the plain public-key model and a general forking lemma. In: Proceedings of the 13th ACM Conference on COMPUTER and Communications Security, pp. 390–399 (2006)
6. Bellare, M., Namprempre, C., Neven, G.: Unrestricted aggregate signatures. In: Arge, L., Cachin, C., Jurdziński, T., Tarlecki, A. (eds.) ICALP 2007. LNCS, vol. 4596, pp. 411–422. Springer, Heidelberg (2007). https://doi.org/10.1007/978-3-540-73420-8_37
7. Komano, Y., Ohta, K., Shimbo, A., Kawamura, S.: Formal security model of multisignatures. In: Katsikas, S.K., López, J., Backes, M., Gritzalis, S., Preneel, B. (eds.) ISC 2006. LNCS, vol. 4176, pp. 146–160. Springer, Heidelberg (2006). https://doi.org/10.1007/11836810_11
8. Le, D.-P., Bonnecaze, A., Gabillon, A.: Multisignatures as secure as the Diffie-Hellman problem in the plain public-key model. In: Shacham, H., Waters, B. (eds.) Pairing 2009. LNCS, vol. 5671, pp. 35–51. Springer, Heidelberg (2009). https://doi.org/10.1007/978-3-642-032 98-1_3
9. Steve, L., Ostrovsky, R., Sahai, A., Shacham, H., Waters, B.: Sequential aggregate signatures and multisignatures without random oracles. In: Vaudenay, S. (ed.) EUROCRYPT 2006. LNCS, vol. 4004, pp. 465–485. Springer, Heidelberg (2006). https://doi.org/10.1007/117616 79_28
10. Ohta, K., Okamoto, T.: Multi-signature schemes secure against active insider attacks. IEICE Trans. Fundam. Electron. Commun. Comput. Sci. **82**(1), 21–31 (1999)
11. Yanai, N.: Meeting tight security for multisignatures in the plain public key model. IEICE Trans. Fundam. Electron. Commun. Comput. Sci. **101**(9), 1484–1493 (2018)
12. Ducas, L., Durmus, A., Lepoint, T., Lyubashevsky, V.: Lattice signatures and bimodal Gaussians. In: Canetti, R., Garay, J.A. (eds.) CRYPTO 2013. LNCS, vol. 8042, pp. 40–56. Springer, Heidelberg (2013). https://doi.org/10.1007/978-3-642-40041-4_3
13. Rivest, R.L., Shamir, A., Adleman, L.: A method for obtaining digital signatures and public-key cryptosystems. Commun. ACM **21**(2), 120–126 (1987)
14. Harn, L., Kiesler, T.: New scheme for digital multisignatures. Electron. Lett. **25**(15), 1002–1003 (1989)
15. Okamoto, T.: A digital multisignature scheme using bijective public-key cryptosystems. ACM Trans. Comput. Syst. (TOCS) **6**(4), 432–441 (1988)
16. Kiesler, T., Harn, L.: RSA blocking and multisignature schemes with no bit expansion. Electron. Lett. **18**(26), 1490–1491 (1990)
17. Park, S., Park, S., Kim, K., Won, D.: Two efficient RSA multisignature schemes. In: Han, Y., Okamoto, T., Qing, S. (eds.) ICICS 1997. LNCS, vol. 1334, pp. 217–222. Springer, Heidelberg (1997). https://doi.org/10.1007/BFb0028477

18. Bellare, M., Neven, G.: Identity-based multi-signatures from RSA. In: Abe, M. (ed.) CT-RSA 2007. LNCS, vol. 4377, pp. 145–162. Springer, Heidelberg (2006). https://doi.org/10.1007/11967668_10

19. Bagherzandi, A., Jarecki, S.: Identity-based aggregate and multi-signature schemes based on rsa. In: Nguyen, P.Q., Pointcheval, D. (eds.) PKC 2010. LNCS, vol. 6056, pp. 480–498. Springer, Heidelberg (2010). https://doi.org/10.1007/978-3-642-13013-7_28

20. Shor, P.W.: Polynomial-time algorithms for prime factorization and discrete logarithms on a quantum computer. SIAM Rev. **41**(2), 303–332 (1999)

21. Bellare, M., Rogaway, P.: The exact security of digital signatures-How to sign with RSA and Rabin. In: Maurer, U. (ed.) EUROCRYPT 1996. LNCS, vol. 1070, pp. 399–416. Springer, Heidelberg (1996). https://doi.org/10.1007/3-540-68339-9_34

22. Fiat, A., Shamir, A.: How to prove yourself: practical solutions to identification and signature problems. In: Odlyzko, A.M. (ed.) CRYPTO 1986. LNCS, vol. 263, pp. 186–194. Springer, Heidelberg (1987). https://doi.org/10.1007/3-540-47721-7_12

23. Bellare M., Rogaway P.: Random oracles are practical: a paradigm for designing efficient protocols. In: Proceedings of the 1st ACM Conference on Computer and Communications Security, pp. 62–73. (1993)

24. Micali S., Ohta K., Reyzin L.: Accountable-subgroup multisignatures. In: Proceedings of the 8th ACM Conference on Computer and Communications Security, pp. 245–254. (2001)

25. Feng T., Gao Y., Ma J.: Changeable threshold signature scheme based on lattice theory. In: 2010 International Conference on E-Business and E-Government, pp. 1311–1315. IEEE, (2010)

26. Glaser F.: Pervasive decentralisation of digital infrastructures: a framework for blockchain enabled system and use case analysis. In: Hawaii International Conference on System Sciences (2017)

27. Lin, X., Wu, J., Bashir, A.K., et al.: Blockchain-based incentive energy-knowledge trading in IoT: joint power transfer and AI design. IEEE Internet Things J. **9**(16), 14685–14698 (2020)

28. Xu X., Pautasso C., Zhu L., et al.: The Blockchain as a Software Connector. In 2016 13th Working IEEE/IFIP Conference on Software Architecture (WICSA), pp. 182–191. IEEE (2016)

29. Sankar L. S., Sindhu M., Sethumadhavan M.: Survey of consensus protocols on blockchain applications. In: 2017 4th International Conference on Advanced Computing and Communication Systems (ICACCS), pp. 1–5. IEEE (2017)

30. Zheng, Z., Xie, S., Dai, H.N., et al.: Blockchain challenges and opportunities. Int. J. Web Grid Serv. **14**(4), 352–375 (2018)

31. Liao, S., Wu, J., Mumtaz, S., et al.: Cognitive balance for fog computing resource in Internet of Things: An edge learning approach. IEEE Trans. Mob. Comput. **21**(5), 1596–1608 (2020)

Improvement of AFL's Seed Deterministic Mutation Algorithm

Shitong Wei$^{(\boxtimes)}$, Shujie Yang , and Ping Zou

Beijing University of Posts and Telecommunication, Beijing, China
{stwei,sjyang,2021110917}@bupt.edu.cn

Abstract. With the continuous development of software technology, software vulnerabilities have become one of the focuses of people's attention. More and more methods for mining software vulnerabilities are emerging, and fuzzing technology has become one of the main methods for mining software vulnerabilities. A large number of fuzzing software tools such as AFL, Honggfuzz, and libufuzzer continue to emerge. However, at present, the mutation method of fuzz testing for test cases is inefficient, and it is difficult for a large number of mutated input test cases to trigger the deep logic code of the program. In this paper, we improve the deterministic seed mutation algorithm of AFL. The deterministic seed mutation efficiency of the improved AFL is higher than that of the original AFL, and it can trigger more paths in the same time.

Keywords: Fuzzing test · AFL · Seed mutation

1 Introduction

With the continuous development of software technology, automatic or semi-automatic detection of software vulnerabilities has become one of the directions that people pay attention to. Fuzzing can meet the needs of automated or semi-automated detection of software vulnerabilities. One of the most popular fuzzing software is American fuzzy loop (AFL) developed by Google. AFL has become one of the most advanced fuzzing tools due to its easy-to-use and powerful vulnerability detection capabilities. AFL needs to instrument the program under test before running the program, and then the tester needs to provide some initial seeds as test cases. AFL will run each test case, and then continuously mutate these test cases, run the mutated test cases under the program, and continuously cycle.

At present, one of the shortcomings of AFL is that the efficiency of test case mutation is low. It is difficult for a large number of mutated test cases to trigger a new program path and can only be discarded, which greatly reduces the efficiency of AFL in mining program vulnerabilities. If the program has the danger of loopholes in a certain code segment, but the test case can not reach the code segment no matter how mutated it is, then it is difficult to dig out these loopholes.

© The Author(s), under exclusive license to Springer Nature Singapore Pte Ltd. 2023
W. Quan (Ed.): ICENAT 2022, CCIS 1696, pp. 347–357, 2023.
https://doi.org/10.1007/978-981-19-9697-9_28

This paper first introduces the working principle of AFL, including the principle of instrumentation and the principle of seed mutation. Since there are many seed mutation algorithms in AFL, as many as 6, this article will introduce the principle of some seed mutation algorithm in detail, and then improve the deterministic seed mutation algorithms on the basis of the original version. As a result, in programs that test ffmpeg, the total number of discovering new paths to the program increases in the best case.

2 Background

2.1 Fuzzing Test

Fuzz testing [4,18] is a software testing technology. It usually adopts automatic or semi-automatic technology. The generated data is input into the program as a test case, and then the program is monitored for phenomenon of exceptions such as crashes and assertions. At present, fuzzing, symbolic execution [17] and taint analysis [6,11,15] have become the main technologies for program vulnerability mining.

The main process of fuzzing testing technology is shown in Fig. 1. Test cases are used as input to the program under test, and then AFL execute the program to observe whether an exception occurs in the program. If an exception occurs, then AFL will record the input data at this time. Otherwise AFL continue to generate new test cases. Currently, there are two basic methods for the generation of new test case. One is rule-based generation, and the other is the mutation of test cases. The former requires higher grammatical requirements or semantic requirements [20,23] for the data input by the program, such as the database MySQL program. The latter provides some initial seeds as input at the beginning, and then mutates these seeds continuously to generate new input test cases.

In recent years, fuzzing technology has become one of the most effective methods of mining vulnerabilities, and a large number of fuzzing tools have emerged, such as AFL, Honggfuzz and libufuzzer. The emergence of these tools has greatly lowered the threshold of fuzzing technology, making it easier for testers to get started, and they can perform vulnerability mining on the program under test without knowing the code of the program under test. But if the tester has a certain in-depth understanding of the program, the input data of the generated program under test will be more prepared, and the efficiency of the fuzzing test will be improved. Therefore, no matter whether the tester has an understanding of the program under test or not, fuzzing technology can help the tester to quickly discover the program loopholes.

2.2 American Fuzzy Loop (AFL)

AFL [9,16] (American Fuzzy Lop) is a coverage-guided fuzzing tool developed by security researcher Michał Zalewski (@lcamtuf), which records the code coverage

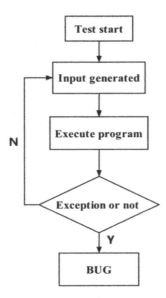

Fig. 1. Fuzz testing flow chart

of input samples and adjusts input samples to improve coverage rate, increasing the probability of finding vulnerabilities. AFL uses the method of mutating test cases to generate the input data of the program under test. AFL can instrument the source code of the program before executing fuzz testing, which can be used to detect the execution path inside the program under the test and generate better test cases.

The execution flow of the overall AFL is shown in Fig. 2 below. AFL mainly uses a genetic algorithm, which provides some seeds as input at the beginning, and then mutates each seed. Mutated seeds are used as the input of the program. If these mutated test cases can trigger a new program path, then these test cases are marked as interesting, added to the seed queue, and saved to the next generation. Otherwise these test cases are discarded and the above process is repeated. If an exception occurs in the program when running the program, AFL will record the test case at this time and output it to the file. The whole process loops back and forth until the tester manually ends the fuzzing.

AFL is based on basic blocks (BB) to count the coverage of the code. When AFL performs instrumentation, it is instrumenting for basic blocks, not for each instruction. According to the features of basic blocks, each divided basic block has only one entry and one exit. Therefore, for a basic block, if the first instruction in BB is executed, all subsequent instructions will also be executed. Code coverage statistics are performed for basic blocks instead of code coverage statistics for each instruction, which reduces the burden of statistical code coverage ratios and speeds up efficiency. AFL uses two-tuples to record jumps between basic blocks, which records information about each edge. The execution of the

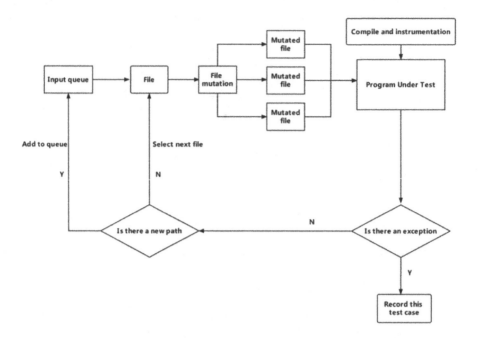

Fig. 2. AFL workflow

entire program can be divided into a control flow graph (CFG), in which each node represents a basic block, and the edge is used to represent the jump between basic blocks, so that the number of executions of each statement in the program can be known. Thereby, the coverage information of the execution path of the input test case is obtained.

AFL divides seed mutation into two categories, one is deterministic variation and the other is non-deterministic variation. Deterministic mutation has no randomness. In this stage, each mutation method is deterministic. Deterministic seed mutation is divided into 4 methods: 1.bitflip, bitwise flip, 1 becomes 0, 0 becomes 1. 2.arithmetic, integer addition/subtraction arithmetic operations. 3.interest, replace some special content into the original file. 4.dictionary, replace/insert automatically generated or user-provided tokens into the original file. Non-deterministic mutation is full of randomness. Non-deterministic seed mutation is divided into 2 major methods: 1. havoc, a large number of random mutations are performed on the original file. 2. splice, a new file is obtained by splicing two files together. AFL will pick a file from the seed queue, mutate deterministically, then mutate non-deterministically, and then AFL will pick the next file from the seed queue to mutate. If all the files in the queue are mutated, then a cycle is complete, and the entire queue is remutated starting from the first file of the new queue. But this time is different from the first time, and no more deterministic mutation is required.

3   Method

AFL will maintain a queue, take out a file from the queue each time, and mutate this file, resulting in a large number of new files. AFL will check whether the mutated test case can cause the program to crash and find a new path for the program. There are a total of 6 kinds: bitflip, arithmetic, interest, dictionary, havoc and splice. Among them, the first four are deterministic mutation, and the latter two are non-deterministic mutation.

3.1   Deterministic Mutation

Arithmetic. When AFL executes arithmetic, it will add and subtract files according to the size of the files. The upper limit of addition and subtraction operations is defined in ARITH_MAX of config.h, and the default is 35. So AFL mutates the target integer by $+1$, $+2$, ..., $+35$, -1, -2, ..., -35.

The default upper bound for adding and subtracting integers is 35, but in many cases this is not the most efficient. The program under test for our experiments is ffmpeg. Our experiments show that if the upper limit of the value is set to 65535, that is, the arithmetic operations of $+1$, $+2$, ..., $+65535$, -1, -2, ..., -65535 are performed, then the converged the speed will be slightly faster than the value set to 35, but the total number of paths that can be detected in the end is the same. The time it takes to converge to the maximum number of detection paths improves the performance by about 4.0% compared to the original version.

After our continuous testing and changing the values, we found that the number of finding paths at the end is the same, but the speed of convergence is slightly different. Setting a larger number will make the convergence speed slightly faster. But this mutation method does not affect the number of paths discovered, because the results of addition and subtraction operations are still close to the input space of the original test case [5]. If original test case is difficult to trigger the new path, then the result after addition and subtraction is also difficult to trigger the new path.

Therefore, at this stage, we will skip the arithmetic or set the value of addition and subtraction to 1. After our test, setting the value of addition and subtraction to 1, or setting these values to 35 and 65535, we finally found that the number of paths discovering is the same, but the convergence speed will be slightly different. These differences are shown in Fig. 3. In short, in this part of the mutation algorithm, it is not useful for us to find more paths, so we quickly skip this stage.

Interest. In the mutation stage of this Interest, AFL will replace the byte, word or dword of each file in the seed queue, and the value used for replacement is a special value preset by AFL. Most of these set values are overflowing. In the source code of AFL, the replacement content will be -128, -1, 0, 1, 16, 32, 64, 100, 127, -32768, -129, 128, 256, 512, 1000, 1024, 4096, 32767 such values.

We delete a lot of these replaced contents, such as -1, 0, 1, leaving a very small number of values that may overflow, and the final result is that these values removed are all is ineffective. It is difficult to discover new paths with these invalid substituted values.

We've made improvements to these replaced values. First, after extensive experiments, we believe that deterministic mutation is difficult to generate interesting test cases. Because the test cases generated by deterministic mutation are all deterministic in the input space. Deterministic mutation can only find new paths under very few or specific test cases, and a large number of interesting test cases are generated by random methods. Therefore, we make the stage of this Interest into random, so that the replaced values are all randomly generated. For the sake of time efficiency, the number of generated replaced values is between 500 and 1000. The more values that are replaced, the more likely it is to generate interesting test cases, the higher the probability of finding new paths, but the more time it takes.

This improved algorithm may not necessarily be able to discover new paths, but it can increase the probability of discovering new paths. Whether a new path can be finally discovered depends not only on the random number generated, but also on the program code itself and the initially provided test case seed. If the code of the program itself has less deep-level logic, or if the test cases provided are better, it is easier to discover new paths.

3.2 Non-deterministic Mutation

There are two methods of non-deterministic mutation: Havoc and Splice. This stage is full of randomness, and any test case may mutate into the input required by the program. In the havoc method, multiple rounds of mutation are performed on the file, and each round is composed of multiple methods. This method includes: randomly deleting a byte, taking a byte and setting it as a random number, etc. The entire original file will be completely revised, full of random and uncontrollable features. Splice will randomly select one from the file seed queue and compare it with the current file seed. If the difference is not significant, then randomly select one again. If the difference between the two is obvious, then the two files will be spliced to form a new test case.

Since the non-deterministic mutation stage is full of random characteristics, the random input test case may become the input required by the program, which is also a powerful feature of the AFL seed mutation algorithm. We learn from the characteristics of randomness and change the method of mutation in the deterministic stage to a non-deterministic method, which will increase the randomness of the overall algorithm. Whether the algorithm of non-random mutation can be more optimized, we will carry out in the follow-up work research, which is also a hot direction in the current research on AFL.

4   Evaluation

Our experiment is to test ffmpeg, an open source computer program that can be used to record, convert digital audio and video, and convert them to streams.

ffmpeg can be installed and used in various operating systems such as Windows, Linux, and Mac OS. In our experiment, the environment is Ubuntu 18.04 and the test case provided is audio downloaded from the network under 10 MB.

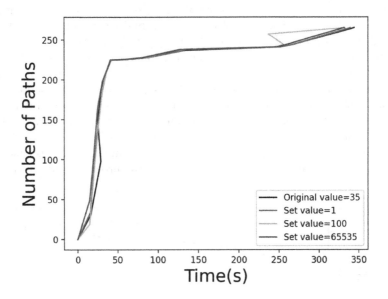

Fig. 3. Results of setting different values in arithmetic

Results of Arithmetic. The results for Arithmetic's mutation are shown in Fig. 3. In our experiment, we changed the value settings to 1, 100, 65535, compared with the original 35, and found that the number of paths detected is the same. However, the convergence situation is different. When the parameter is set to 100, the convergence time is the shortest, while the original version has the longest convergence time. In the end, no matter how many parameters are set, the number of paths found in this experiment is 265. Therefore, the mutation at this stage does not have much significance for finding more paths. It is recommended to set the parameter value to 1, or skip the mutation at this stage, so that AFL spends more time executing other mutation algorithms.

Results of Interest. The result of deleting the replaced value of the Interest method is shown in Fig. 4. The deleted values are all fixed values originally set by AFL such as −128, 1, 0, −32768, −129, etc. These fixed values are difficult to generate interesting test cases. Therefore, after deleting these values, there is no difference in performance compared to the original. The efficiency of the two is almost the same, and the number of paths found is the same. So these removed values are not valid on discovering new paths.

The improved results for the Interest method are shown in Fig. 5. Since this experiment changed the characteristics of non-random into random, we selected the one with the best experimental results for display. In the early stage, the algorithm of the original version of Interest will find more loopholes, but when the number of paths reaches more than 200, it will always be stuck and cannot generate more interesting test cases. Since the improved Interest algorithm generates a large number of random numbers for replacement, in the early stage, the number of paths found will be less, but new paths will always be found and will not get stuck at a certain point. In the best case, the improved Interest will find more paths than the original version, but in general, the improved Interest may not be able to find more paths. Whether the improved Interest can discover more paths depends not only on the number of random substitutions generated, but also on the initial test case seed provided by the program under test itself.

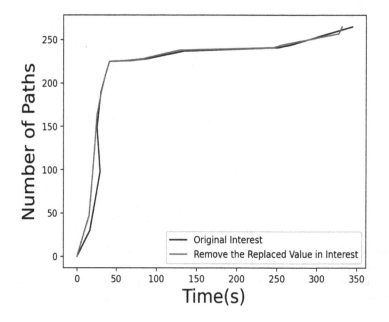

Fig. 4. Result of remove the replaced value in interest

5   Future Work

In AFL, non-deterministic mutation is the most critical mutation method. Therefore, we will focus on the method of non-deterministic mutation and investigate

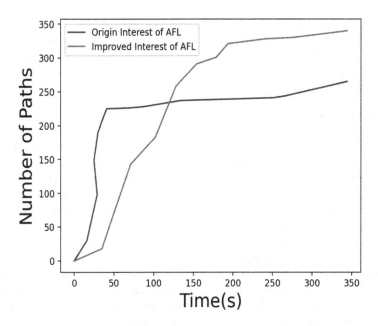

Fig. 5. Result of improved in interest

whether there is a more optimized random algorithm. In addition to the great influence of mutation algorithm on the performance of AFL, another key strategy is how to improve the seed selection strategy. M. Böhme et al. [2] proposed an energy scheduling algorithm to improve the seed strategy. Methods such as CollAFL [10] and ADFL [19] have also been proposed to improve seed selection strategies. Therefore, the seed selection algorithm is also one of the important ways to improve the performance of AFL.

In addition to the improved seed mutation algorithm and seed selection algorithm above, the initial test case also has a great impact on the performance of AFL. If the initial test cases are well selected, then AFL will be greatly improved in terms of performance. Conversely, if the initial seed selection is not very good, even if the algorithm for seed mutation and seed generation is improved, the results of the run may not be as good as the original AFL with a better initial seed. Generally, for large-scale commercial software, some test cases are officially provided as test suites, but most of these test cases are redundant. How to use automated or semi-automated techniques to remove redundant test cases and generate better initial test cases is also a focus of our future work.

AFL is also being combined with other technologies. IJON [1] adopts the mechanism of annotation to deal with more complex programs. It has been proposed to use primitive techniques to improve the performance of fuzzing [22]. Fuzzing based on interaction with injection of misconfigurations [8,12,13,21] is also a focus of future research. Besides, the binary program is applied to fuzzing [7,14]. There is also a combination of fuzzing and deep learning related technologies [3]. All in all, the combination of fuzzing with other techniques is a future research focus.

6   Conclusion

In this paper, we make some improvements based on the existing shortcomings of the AFL seed selection algorithm. We improved the seed selection algorithm for deterministic mutation in AFL. Our experiments show that AFL's deterministic mutation algorithms are very incapable of discovering new program paths, because the input space after mutation of these algorithms is deterministic. We modify or delete the parameters of these deterministic algorithms and find that the number of paths finally found is the same. For this reason, we skip the Arithmetic deterministic mutation algorithm, and introduce the idea of the non-deterministic mutation algorithm into Interest, and modify the value generated in Interest to be randomly generated instead of the original specified value. By adopting such a strategy, these seeds can discover new paths under certain specific conditions. Our experiments show that if the selected test cases are better, more paths will be found than the original version.

In conclusion, we have improved the deterministic mutation algorithm in AFL, so that the non-deterministic mutation algorithm of AFL can occupy a larger proportion, which can increase the probability of generating interesting test cases and discover more paths of the program, thereby improving the possibility of discovering program vulnerabilities.

Acknowledgements. The authors are grateful to the Network Architecture Research Center of Beijing University of Posts and Telecommunications for their help and support.

References

1. Aschermann, C., Schumilo, S., Abbasi, A., Holz, T.: Ijon: exploring deep state spaces via fuzzing. In: 2020 IEEE Symposium on Security and Privacy (SP), pp. 1597–1612. IEEE (2020)
2. Böhme, M., Pham, V.T., Roychoudhury, A.: Coverage-based greybox fuzzing as Markov chain. IEEE Trans. Softw. Eng. **45**(5), 489–506 (2017)
3. Böttinger, K., Godefroid, P., Singh, R.: Deep reinforcement fuzzing. In: 2018 IEEE Security and Privacy Workshops (SPW), pp. 116–122. IEEE (2018)
4. Chen, C., Cui, B., Ma, J., Wu, R., Guo, J., Liu, W.: A systematic review of fuzzing techniques. Comput. Secur. **75**, 118–137 (2018)
5. Chen, J., Chen, J., Guo, D., Towey, D.: An improved fuzzing approach based on adaptive random testing. In: 2020 IEEE International Symposium on Software Reliability Engineering Workshops (ISSREW), pp. 103–108. IEEE (2020)
6. Chen, P., Chen, H.: Angora: efficient fuzzing by principled search. In: 2018 IEEE Symposium on Security and Privacy (SP), pp. 711–725. IEEE (2018)

7. Choi, J., Jang, J., Han, C., Cha, S.K.: Grey-box concolic testing on binary code. In: 2019 IEEE/ACM 41st International Conference on Software Engineering (ICSE), pp. 736–747. IEEE (2019)
8. Dai, H., Murphy, C., Kaiser, G.: Configuration fuzzing for software vulnerability detection. In: 2010 International Conference on Availability, Reliability and Security, pp. 525–530. IEEE (2010)
9. Fioraldi, A., Maier, D., Eißfeldt, H., Heuse, M.: AFL++: combining incremental steps of fuzzing research. In: 14th USENIX Workshop on Offensive Technologies (WOOT 2020) (2020)
10. Gan, S., et al.: CollAFL: path sensitive fuzzing. In: 2018 IEEE Symposium on Security and Privacy (SP), pp. 679–696. IEEE (2018)
11. Ganesh, V., Leek, T., Rinard, M.: Taint-based directed whitebox fuzzing. In: 2009 IEEE 31st International Conference on Software Engineering, pp. 474–484. IEEE (2009)
12. He, H., et al.: Multi-intention-aware configuration selection for performance tuning. In: 2022 IEEE/ACM 44th International Conference on Software Engineering (ICSE), pp. 1431–1442. IEEE (2022)
13. Li, W., et al.: Challenges and opportunities: an in-depth empirical study on configuration error injection testing. In: Proceedings of the 30th ACM SIGSOFT International Symposium on Software Testing and Analysis, pp. 478–490 (2021)
14. Li, Y., Chen, B., Chandramohan, M., Lin, S.W., Liu, Y., Tiu, A.: Steelix: program-state based binary fuzzing. In: Proceedings of the 2017 11th Joint Meeting on Foundations of Software Engineering, pp. 627–637 (2017)
15. Liang, G., Liao, L., Xu, X., Du, J., Li, G., Zhao, H.: Effective fuzzing based on dynamic taint analysis. In: 2013 Ninth International Conference on Computational Intelligence and Security, pp. 615–619. IEEE (2013)
16. Nossum, V., Casasnovas, Q.: Filesystem fuzzing with American fuzzy lop. In: Vault Linux Storage and Filesystems Conference (2016)
17. Peng, H., Shoshitaishvili, Y., Payer, M.: T-Fuzz: fuzzing by program transformation. In: 2018 IEEE Symposium on Security and Privacy (SP), pp. 697–710. IEEE (2018)
18. Takanen, A.: Fuzzing: the past, the present and the future. Actes du, pp. 202–212 (2009)
19. Wang, C., Kang, S.: ADFL: an improved algorithm for American fuzzy lop in fuzz testing. In: Sun, X., Pan, Z., Bertino, E. (eds.) ICCCS 2018. LNCS, vol. 11067, pp. 27–36. Springer, Cham (2018). https://doi.org/10.1007/978-3-030-00018-9_3
20. Wang, J., Chen, B., Wei, L., Liu, Y.: Skyfire: data-driven seed generation for fuzzing. In: 2017 IEEE Symposium on Security and Privacy (SP), pp. 579–594. IEEE (2017)
21. Wang, T., Liu, X., Li, S., Liao, X., Li, W., Liao, Q.: MisconfDoctor: diagnosing misconfiguration via log-based configuration testing. In: 2018 IEEE International Conference on Software Quality, Reliability and Security (QRS), pp. 1–12. IEEE (2018)
22. Xu, W., Kashyap, S., Min, C., Kim, T.: Designing new operating primitives to improve fuzzing performance. In: Proceedings of the 2017 ACM SIGSAC Conference on Computer and Communications Security, pp. 2313–2328 (2017)
23. Zhong, R., Chen, Y., Hu, H., Zhang, H., Lee, W., Wu, D.: SQUIRREL: testing database management systems with language validity and coverage feedback. In: Proceedings of the 2020 ACM SIGSAC Conference on Computer and Communications Security, pp. 955–970 (2020)

Active Detection Path Planning Algorithm and Implementation for SFC Fault Detection

Shang Liu, Kuo Guo, Yu Zhao, and Jia Chen[✉]

National Engineering Research Center for Advanced Network Technologies,
Beijing Jiaotong University, Beijing, China
22115009@bjtu.edu.cn

Abstract. Service Function Chain (SFC) technology is closely integrated with Virtual Network Function (VNF) to improve the efficiency of service deployment and provide high quality network services to users. However, the dynamic changing nature of SFC orchestration increases the difficulty of network management. In order to reduce the SFC telemetry overhead and ensure the real-time requirements of network status monitoring data, this paper proposes an active detection path optimization mechanism in the SFC fault detection scenario. The mechanism uses a depth-first search algorithm to plan a detection path that satisfies the three conditions of length balancing, covering SFC network and no overlapping links at the same time to reduce the network telemetry overhead and telemetry delay difference. The experimental results show that the proposed detection path optimization mechanism can achieve the sensing of the full range of SFC states with a small overhead. Among them, the detection overhead is reduced by about 65.7% compared with the path-tracer detection method, and the delay difference of network sensing is reduced by about 94.4% compared with the SFC passive sensing scheme.

Keywords: Service function chaining · In-band network telemetry · Fault detection

1 Introduce

The "static" and "rigid" characteristics of traditional network architecture make it difficult to respond to user service demands quickly. In order to solve this problem, the Smart Integration Identifier Network (SINET) decouples the service space and network space vertically, and unifies the scheduling and convergence of heterogeneous resources across the network through the "three layers" and "three domains" architecture. SINET constructs a SFC consisting of VNF to improve the efficiency of service deployment and provide fast, flexible, and high-quality network services to users [1]. However, the dynamic change of SFC scheduling in the SINET increases the difficulty of network management. In addition, the mapping relationship between VNFs and underlying physical devices changes dynamically and has complex dependencies [2], making it difficult to establish an accurate failure model to accurately predict failures. Therefore, accurate and efficient SFC fault detection has become the focus of SFC management.

W. Quan (Ed.): ICENAT 2022, CCIS 1696, pp. 358–368, 2023.
https://doi.org/10.1007/978-981-19-9697-9_29

Traditional fault detection methods, such as Simple N-network Management Protocol (SNMP) [3] collect network device operation status information by polling, and NetFlow [4] technology and sFlow [5] technology collects network traffic information with a certain sampling frequency. They all collect network traffic information with a certain sampling frequency, the disadvantages of poor real-time data collection, coarse granularity, low efficiency and high cost, which cannot truly reflect the full network status and increase the probability of network failure misdiagnosis. Although both monitoring technologies can be considered for deployment in the network, this scheme increases the CPU burden of network devices and reducing the service forwarding performance [6]. Therefore, traditional network management techniques can hardly guarantee efficient and accurate identification of complex fault types in SFC and cannot be applied to SFC fault detection scenarios. While the SFC detection method based on active path planning can accurately and efficiently collect the state information of SFCs and better support SFC fault detection [7].

The main contributions of this paper are as follows.

1) Collate the current research status of SFC fault detection problem and analyze the problems faced by SFC state detection.
2) Propose a depth-first search algorithm for SFC detection path planning in fault detection scenarios, and plan telemetry paths with balanced length, no duplicate links and covering SFC topology according to SFC physical forwarding topology to reduce the overhead and delay difference of data collection.
3) Implement the prototype system of SFC for SINET based on BMV2 software switch on the universal server. The impact of the algorithm detection performance is also tested in terms of the number of detections, detection latency, and detection repetition rate.

2   Related Works

Probe based fault detection techniques can be used in active and passive schemes. For the passive probing scheme, the network performance can be detected when and only when the user has service demand, which is less flexible although it avoids the additional overhead caused by active probes. For the active probing scheme, the network administrator can periodically detect the network performance according to the demand, but still needs to consider the overhead problem caused by probes. A common network probing technology is Out-band Network Telemetry (ONT), which injects probing messages similar to ping probes into the network through external monitoring devices. ONT solves the problem of single information collected by SNMP, NetFlow and sFlow technologies mentioned above. However, the ONT method only targets one forwarding path for reachability detection, which is easy to ignore other links, thus causing the problem of missing other link failures. The literature [8] determines whether a link is faulty by injecting multiple probe packets into the SFC network and recording the end-to-end delay of the probe packets transmitted in the network. However, this method does not consider the overhead caused by probes and the impact on normal services. The IETF devised a method to record the time of SFC packets arriving at the forwarding device by adding a timestamp field to the NSH header of SFC packets, and then determine whether SFC has network performance problems by the time delay [9–11]. It solves the problem of additional overhead caused by active injection of probes. However, this method can only probe network performance when providing services to users, which is inflexible.

The existing research on SFC status information detection has the drawbacks of repetitive information data collection, poor flexibility, and poor real-time performance. There is still a lack of a global perspective on SFC resource data detection using active path planning, so as to make fault judgments on SFC. How to realize the sensing of SFC's full range of underlying physical network availability and resource utilization with as little overhead as possible without affecting service delivery is currently the key direction of SFC fault detection research.

3   System Model and Problem Formulation

In the SINET, the SFC heterogeneous resources of the whole network are deployed through the unified orchestration of SINET-I controller. The SINET-I controller not only stores the deployment information of SFC, but also needs to sense the state information of SFC, so as to manage the SFC intelligently.

To address the overhead problem caused by the INT active sensing method in the SINET, this paper proposes a detection path planning algorithm based on Depth First Search (DFS) for SFC fault detection scenarios. The algorithm transforms the overhead problem of minimizing active telemetry into the problem of solving duplication-free telemetry paths. This algorithm ensures that data is collected only once for duplicate network links and enables telemetry of SFC network state information with fewer INT probes, reducing network sensing overhead and reducing the bandwidth usage of probes in the network.

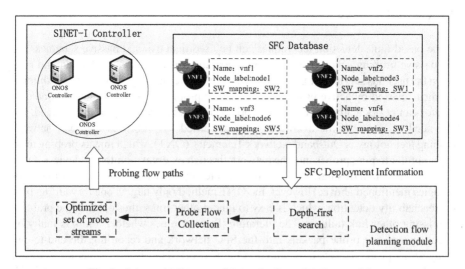

Fig. 1. Schematic diagram of the probe flow planning module

As Fig. 1 shows the workflow of the probe flow path planning algorithm, which reads the SFC deployment information to obtain the physical topology connection relationships. First, the set of all eligible probe flows is found by the DFS method. Then, according to the optimization objective, the set of probe flow number and length is filtered and the optimized result is generated. Finally, the result is given to the controller, which sends the probe flow table to the switch according to the probe path.

As shown in Fig. 2 is a schematic diagram of SFC physical network forwarding, the actual physical network topology consisting of multiple SFCs can be considered as a directed network forwarding graph G (V(G), E(G)). Where V(G) denotes the set of network forwarding nodes, hereafter referred to as nodes, and E(G) denotes the set of links between forwarding nodes, hereafter referred to as edges. Nodes V2, V3, V4, V5, and V8 have multiple inputs and outputs, indicating that the VNFs at that node are shared multiple times. When performing service forwarding, different packets will all pass through the links between nodes V2 and V3, V8 and V4, and V4 and V5, i.e., the packets will pass through e23, e84, and e45 multiple times. When the network service volume increases, the number of VNFs shared among SFCs also will increase, and the number of shared links increases in the process of providing services to users.

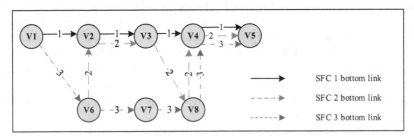

Fig. 2. SFC physical network forwarding diagram

The INT passive status data collection method encapsulates telemetry commands and data in the normal SFC packet load and forwards the status collection with the SFC packet routing. On the one hand, the method has problem that the packet payload is relatively low and the switch has a large delay in processing SFC packets. And on the other hand, there is the problem that the telemetry path cannot be decided on demand, resulting in the link being repeatedly telemetry, thus causing additional overhead.

To solve the above problems, this paper adopts the INT active telemetry algorithm based on Depth First Search, which actively injects telemetry probes into the network to collect real-time, fine-grained network status data of SFCs. To reduce the detection overhead and the detection delay difference of each path, the algorithm designs the detection paths in the fault detection scenario based on the current SFC deployment information. The detection path has a balanced length and covers the SFC topology with no duplicate links. The result is output to the controller, which sends the probe flow table to the forwarding devices in the network, and the forwarding devices will forward telemetry probes according to the probe flow table.

Therefore, these two points need to be fully considered in the active detection path planning algorithm: 1) The number of probes is as small as possible. In this paper, we consider that when passive telemetry is used, the minimum number of detection paths is equal to the number of SFCs. If SFCs are considered as a collection of links composed of each small segment, there are various possibilities for their detection paths. In this paper, we will traverse all SFCs and generate the set of all possible detection streams, and use the number of SFCs as a threshold to select the combination with the least number of probes. 2) The difference in length of each detection path in this set of detection streams should not be too large. In this paper, based on solving the first problem, we will further optimize with the goal of minimizing the delay difference in state data acquisition. In the set of combinations with the minimum number of probes, the path length difference of each possible monitoring stream is calculated.

4   Path Planning Algorithm Design

In this paper, we design the DFS-based probe flow planning algorithm for SFC fault detection scenario, which is further optimized according to the above objectives. Considering that SFC forwarding is directional, the path planning algorithm designed in this paper replaces the search nodes with search edges and evaluates each edge searched to decide whether to continue the search on this basis. During the search process, the current parent edge is recorded by index, and the depth search is performed according to the conditions, and the child edges that meet the conditions are added to the current set of edges at each search. But when the end condition is touched, the parent edge is retraced and a parent edge is selected again for searching. During the search process, all the visited edges are always recorded in a stack fashion. Finally, the optimal set is selected from the set of searched edges according to the optimization conditions and is used as the output of the algorithm.

The flow chart of the designed algorithm is shown in Fig. 3 Let the target set of the search process be M, where a is the set of SFC links and their sub-links, b is the set of SFC link combinations, and c is the set of SFC links. The o1 set stores the better set generated in the optimization process. The algorithm designed in this paper has two retraces.

1)   In the process of searching, a parent edge is selected from the set c, and then a possible case from the set b is selected to search forward, when the result of the selection is found to be wrong, the backtracking re-selects a possible case from the set b, and at the same time, the state is restored to the previous step.
2)   When there is no case satisfying the condition in the set b or the edge s is the last one in the set b, further backtrack and re-select a parent edge from the set c to continue the search. The algorithm search process is as follows.

① Select a parent edge s from the set c, put it into M (m) and remove the edge s from the set c. Judge whether the set c is empty, if not, proceed to the next step, if yes, proceed to ④.
②Select the combination of edges from set b that meet the conditions and add them to M (m), and judge the length of M (m), if the length exceeds the threshold, the first backtracking 2); if the length is not exceeded, proceed to the next step.

③ Judge whether the edge s is the last one in the set b, if yes, put the selected edge into M as the set m, backtrack 1) for the second time, and reselect the parent edge; if not, proceed to 2).

④ Update the data in the set M to produce N sets of unoptimized sets of monitor streams without duplicates.

⑤ Compare the lengths of the subsets of monitor stream sets in set M, and select the subset with the smallest length into set o1.

⑥ Compare the length difference sum of elements in each subset of the set o1, select the subset with the smallest length difference sum, put it into the Optimized set, update the Optimized set, and the subset in this set is the desired one.

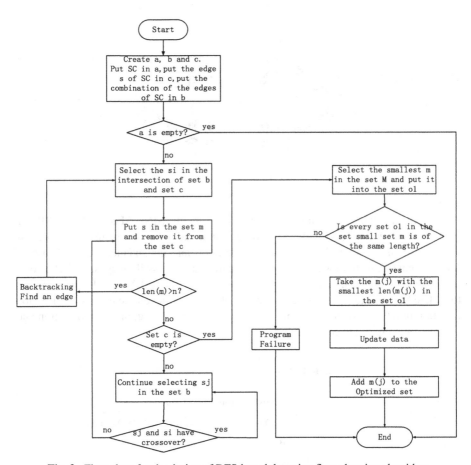

Fig. 3. Flow chart for the design of DFS-based detection flow planning algorithm

5 Experimental Simulation and Performance Analysis

The SFC active detection path planning algorithm designed in this paper is based on the prototype system of the Smart Integration Marking Network, and the network topology is built for system validation. The network topology is shown in Fig. 4 and consists of seven 64-bit x86 general-purpose servers. One of the servers serves as the SINET-I controller at the control layer with an integrated Kubernetes orchestration management system and ONOS controller.

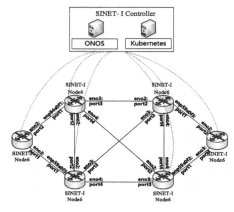

Fig. 4. System topology

Specifically, the SFC is built on seven servers, and the SINET-I controller of SINET completes the unified control of SFC resources. It includes the use of Kubernetes orchestration system for VNF deployment, orchestration and management, and the use of docker container technology to realize the encapsulation of VNF images. SINET-I component integrates Kubernetes work nodes, bearer VNFs and BMv2 software switches to realize SFC packet forwarding and INT probe forwarding and telemetry information insertion into the load, etc. The specific server hardware configuration information and OS version number are shown in Table 1.

Table 1. Server configuration information

Name	Parameters/Version
CPU	Intel(R) Xeon(R) Silver 4210R CPU @ 2.40GHz
Memory	64 GB
OS	Ubuntu18.04.5 LTS
Kubernetes	v1.19.3
ONOS controller	v2.2

Based on the built network topology, this paper deploys 11 VNFs in six working nodes and orchestrates them to form 6 SFCs. Where the VNFs are connected to the docker bridge through the exposed IP addresses, and the cluster uses the macvlan network plug-in to realize the communication of VNFs between different working nodes. The SFC forwarding diagram is shown in Fig. 5.

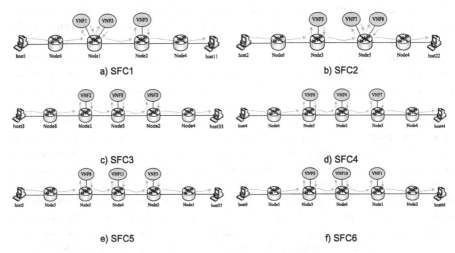

Fig. 5. The forwarding topology of SFC

As shown in Fig. 6, the latency performance graphs for eight tests of the probe flow planning and flow table issuance process are shown. As can be seen in Fig. 6 (a), for the six SFCs deployed in the prototype system, the eight-test delay of the probe flow planning algorithm fluctuates in the range of 130 ms–165 ms, with an average delay of about 146 ms. From Fig. 6 (b), it can be seen that the issuance delay fluctuates in the

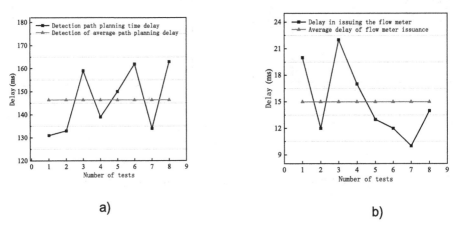

Fig. 6. Performance chart of delay test for each module: a) Detection of flow planning latency; b) Configuration of flow table latency

range of 9 ms–24 ms, with an average delay of about 15 ms. i.e., the total average delay from the start of probe path planning to the controller's distribution of the telemetry flow table is about 0.16 s.

5.1 SFC State Active Awareness Performance Test

First, the usability verification of the DFS-based detection path optimization algorithm designed in this paper is performed. It is ensured that the detection flow generated by the algorithm meets the requirements in the SFC fault detection scenario. As shown in Fig. 7 (a), the SFC link repetition rate statistics are plotted. For the six SFCs built in this paper, if the INT passive probing method is used, the status information of six link segments will be repeatedly collected eight times, resulting in additional overhead. As shown in Fig. 7(b), the number of probes of the probing path strategy obtained from the path planning algorithm designed in this paper is compared with the number of probes of all other probing path strategies. From the figure, it can be seen that the detection strategy finally generated by the algorithm designed in this paper is the best, and the algorithm finally generates the least number of probes for the detection strategy compared to all possible detection strategies. In addition, the algorithm eventually plans a balanced detection path length compared to all the detection strategies with the least number of probes to achieve the goal of minimizing the data acquisition delay difference. The horizontal coordinate ordinate 14 in the figure corresponds to a y-value of 4, indicating the number of probes generated. The set of probe streams with ordinal number 14 is the best telemetry path based on the SFC network topology built by the actual system.

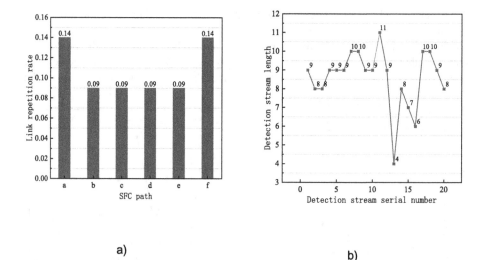

a)   b)

Fig. 7. Detection path planning algorithm usability testing: a) Link repetition rate comparison; b) Comparison of the number of detection streams

Next, the effectiveness of the DFS-based detection path optimization algorithm designed in this paper is verified. As shown in Fig. 8 (a), the eight-test performance plots of the delay of SFC passive sensing method based on INT for collecting SFC state information are shown. The maximum average delay, i.e., the eight-test longest path information acquisition delay, is 61.8 ms, and the minimum average delay, i.e., the eight-test shortest path information acquisition delay, is 24.6 ms. This means that the average delay difference of network state data collection for six SFCs is 37.2 ms. As shown in Fig. 8 (b), the eight-test performance graphs of the delay of SFC state information collection based on INT's SFC active sensing method after probe path optimization are shown. The maximum average delay, i.e., 6.5 ms for the eight-test longest path information collection, and the minimum average delay, i.e., 4.4 ms for the eight-test shortest path information collection, can be seen from the figure. This means that the average delay difference of network state data collection for six SFCs using SF active sensing method is 2.1 ms.

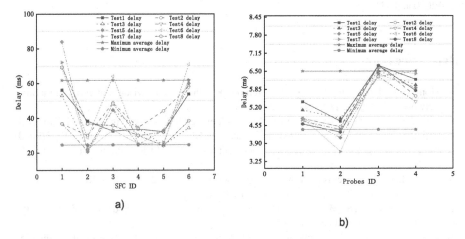

a)

b)

Fig. 8. SFC-aware latency performance test chart: a) Passive method; b) Active method

The experimental results show that the total time delay of the SFC state active sensing method proposed in this paper is about 0.27 s. Compared with SFC passive sensing method, the data collection time of INT probe after path planning is much lower than that of passive detection method. Because it does not need to pass through the VNF, it avoids the problem of repeatedly collecting state data of the same link. In addition, compared with the passive sensing method, the active sensing method reduces the delay difference by about 94.4% for telemetry tasks of all physical links of SFC in the same cycle, meeting the real-time and synchronization requirements of data acquisition in fault detection scenarios.

6 Conclusion

Facing the characteristics of dynamic changes in the service function chain and complex network configuration, the intelligent management of network services ushers in new challenges. Fault detection as the first step of fault management in network intelligence management, its detection efficiency and accuracy directly affect the efficiency of fault recovery, which in turn affects the quality of service for users. In terms of SFC network state sensing, this paper designs and implements an INT active sensing algorithm with minimal overhead. The algorithm solves the problem of low payload rate of SFC normal service flow due to the passive INT detection method and improves the flexibility of data collection. However, in the face of different network-aware requirements of users, packet formats can be further optimized based on programmable techniques in terms of telemetry granularity, packet processing priority and user quality of service to improve customizable network-aware solutions.

Acknowledgement. This research is funded by the fundamental research funds for the central universities under grant no. 2021JBZD003, open research projects of Zhejiang lab under grant no. 2022QA0AB03, nature and science foundation of China under grant no. 61471029, 61972026, 62072030 and 92167204.

References

1. Hongke, Z., Bohao, F., Wei, Q.: Research on the foundation of wisdom integration marking network. J. Electron. **47**(5), 977–982 (2019)
2. Cai, Z., Liu, F., Xiao, N., et al.: Virtual network embedding for evolving networks. In: 2010 IEEE Global Telecommunications Conference GLOBECOM, vol. 2010. pp. 1–5. IEEE (2010)
3. Stallings, W.: SNMPv3: a security enhancement for SNMP. IEEE Commun. Surv. **1**(1), 2–17 (1998)
4. Claise, B.: Cisco systems netflow services export version 9[EB/OL]. IETF RFC3954 (2004). https://www.rfc-editor.org/in-notes/pdfrfc/rfc3954.txt.pdf
5. Phaal, P., Panchen, S., McKee, N.: InMon corporation's sFlow: a method for monitoring traffic in switched and routed networks (2001)
6. Dongfeng, M., Man, J., Xiaoming, H., et al.: Network telemetry technology and its application in network automation operation and maintenance. Telecommun. Sci. **37**(2), 154–163 (2021)
7. Lee, J., Ko, H., Suh, D., et al.: Overload and failure management in service function chaining. In: 2017 IEEE Conference on Network Softwarization (NetSoft), pp. 1–5. IEEE (2017)
8. Oi, A., Endou, D., Moriya, T., et al.: Method for estimating locations of service problem causes in service function chaining. In: 2015 IEEE Global Communications Conference (GLOBECOM), pp. 1–6. IEEE (2015)
9. Mizrahi, T., Moses, Y.: The case for data plane timestamping in SDN. In: 2016 IEEE Conference on Computer Communications Workshops (INFOCOM WKSHPS), pp. 856–861. IEEE (2016)
10. Quinn, P., Elzur, U.: Network service header. internet engineering task force [EB/OL]. Internet-Draft draft-ietf-sfc-nsh-10, 2016. https://datatracker.ietf.org/doc/draft-ietf-sfc-nsh/04/
11. Guichard, J., Smith, M., Kumar, S., et al.: Network service header (NSH) context header allocation (Data Center) [EB/OL]. (2016-02-16) [2016-06-30]. https://datatracker.ietf.org/doc/draft-guichard-sfcnsh-dc-allocation/

A Super-Nash Equilibrium Defense Solution for Client-Side Cache Poisoning Attacks

Qingzhao An$^{(\boxtimes)}$, Shujie Yang, Tengchao Ma, Tan Yang, Yiting Huang, Zhaoyang Liu, and Zhongyi Ding

Beijing University of Posts and Telecommunications, Beijing 100876, China
anqingxhao@bupt.edu.cn

Abstract. A new class of DNS poisoning attacks targeting client-side DNS caches has recently emerged. This attack works with external attackers to poison users' DNS cache through a spy program installed on the client side to induce users to visit the wrong web pages. However, the client-side defenses that can be applied have problems such as difficulty in deployment, the low correct rate of defense detection, and the inability to deal with intelligent attackers effectively. Therefore, we propose a novel double oracle algorithm Neural Online Double Oracle, for defending the client-side against intelligent attackers. The algorithm uses a new way of combining neural networks with reinforcement learning to build a mapping from the environment to the equilibrium solution. The algorithm can be deployed on a lightweight system framework to force the adversary's strategy to an equilibrium point when it does not know the adversary and to find the best strategy when familiar with it. First, we describe the offensive and defensive adversarial scenarios in the language of imperfect information games. Then we design the Neural Online Double Oracle algorithm and prove its convergence for the scenario's limited but rapidly changing state space. Finally, we experimentally verify that the algorithm can converge effectively and has the desired defense success rate.

Keywords: DNS cache poisoning attack · Deep reinforcement learning · Double oracle · Nash equilibrium

1 Introduction

DNS is a core service on the Internet that provides domain name resolution services necessary for Internet access and also undertakes important tasks such as routing and load balancing at the application layer. Commensurate with the central role of DNS on the Internet, attacks that inject malicious information into the DNS resolution system have proliferated. They typically target DNS resolution servers and execute their attacks by poisoning the domain name resolution entries shared by all computing programs. Recently, a new type of DNS cache poisoning attack targeting clients has emerged, which initiates poisoning attacks

W. Quan (Ed.): ICENAT 2022, CCIS 1696, pp. 369–380, 2023.
https://doi.org/10.1007/978-981-19-9697-9_30

on client caches by off-path attackers collaborating with privileged malware to lure clients into interacting with specific web pages [2].

As the number and speed of attacks will grow by several orders of magnitude, the use of intelligent methods for cybersecurity protection is the future trend [17–19]. Gartner [1] predicts that by 2035, 90% of cyber attack detection and 60% of response will be handled by artificial intelligence. It can be argued that the algorithms adopted for defense methods are critical. There have been many effective solutions to DNS poisoning attacks [7]. The defense mechanisms available for client-side DNS cache poisoning attack mitigation can be divided into three categories: encryption schemes, defense mechanisms for traffic monitoring, and moving target defense. However, these solutions suffer from difficulty in deploying, excessive consumption, insufficient accuracy, and defective algorithm design that cannot cope well with intelligent attackers.

Unlike existing approaches, we want to implement a defensive scheme that is easy to deploy and can cope with intelligent attackers. To this end, in this paper, we revisit and build a Markov abstraction model corresponding to the problem, design a new algorithm NODO on a lightweight defense architecture to play against potential attacker algorithms, and experimentally verify the effectiveness of the scheme. Our main contributions are:

1. Rationalize and simplify the offense-defense confrontation problem. The non-necessity of recording all historical behavioural choices of both attackers and defenders and considering the value of a given state in the state transfer matrix is analyzed and justified.
2. Redesigned the NODO algorithm with stronger adversarial capabilities. The algorithm that combines the no-regret idea with the double oracle theory allows the client to obtain gains above the Nash equilibrium in response to any attacker and establishes a mapping from the input to the optimal solution through a neural network.
3. Theoretical derivation of the Nash convergence of the algorithm, which, to our knowledge, is the first real Nash equilibrium in this scenario against an intelligent attacker.
4. Experimentally verify the convergence and effectiveness of the algorithm. The algorithm has a stable convergence property with no weaker performance than Nash equilibrium and achieves an average defense success rate of 90% in the set-up simulation environment.

This paper is organized as follows. We categorize existing ideas for client-side DNS cache poisoning attack defense in Sect. 2. In Sect. 3, we describe our threat model. Section 4 presents the outer neural network dual prediction algorithm. We show the practical results of our solution in Sect. 5 and conclude with Sect. 6.

2   Related Work

This section introduces three ideas that can be applied to defending client-side DNS cache poisoning attacks.

The first category is cryptographic schemes: DNSSEC [15] is a series of DNS security authentication mechanisms provided by the IETF and is considered a suitable solution for defending against cache poisoning attacks [14], but it is often difficult to implement at scale because of its excessively high cost, and although the recent WSEC DNS [13] can be deployed immediately, its overhead is still too large [13], it still suffers from problems such as too much overhead and the need for more lightweight solutions.

The second solutions attempt to detect malicious behavior. These include Kalman filter-based detection of DNS cache poisoning attacks [16] and detection of malicious behavior by analyzing the correlation of messages with a public resolution [9]. Such DNSSEC schemes can provide cryptographic evidence for investigating and detecting attacks [14]. However, research has pointed out that DNSSEC suffers from low detection accuracy [3,5]. There are also mechanisms designed to protect the privacy of DNS traffic [6], but they cannot be widely deployed currently1. The third category of solutions is mechanisms that apply moving target defense: multiple vNIC intelligent mutations [20] force attackers to passively guess real-time NICs by dynamically creating virtual network interface cards. Adaptive defense strategies [10,11] establish a lightweight client-side intelligent defense strategy that intelligently and dynamically selects DNS resolution servers to evade attackers' poisoning attacks through deep reinforcement learning strategies.

However, the previous work suffers from a shortcoming. When the attacker adopts an intelligent approach, the attacker is one-sidedly endowed with the same improved Proximal Policy Optimization (PPO) algorithm as the proposed defense mechanism. During the training process of the PPO algorithm, intelligence that does not receive positive feedback for a long time often fails to achieve the expected training effect, which was ignored in the previous scheme. That result in attackers not being effectively trained for a long time, further leading to a large discrepancy between the defender and the expected performance when responding to an intelligent attacker.

3   System Description and Modeling

3.1   Threat Model

The complete attack flow to satisfy the conditions is shown in the Fig. 1. The successful execution of an attacker's attack is built on the basis that.

1. The attacker needs to know the target domain name requested by the client, which is achieved through message passing between an unprivileged spy program disguised as a normal program and the attacker.
2. The client cannot find the corresponding IP mapping in the local DNS cache and needs to request domain name resolution services from the DNS resolver.
3. Since the existing response mechanism of the client follows the first-come, first-received principle, the attacker's forged mapping needs to reach the client before the normal DNS resolver's response.

4. The forged source IP, source port, TXID, destination IP, and destination port must correspond to the request message.

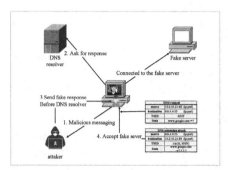

Fig. 1. Client-side cache poisoning attack schematic

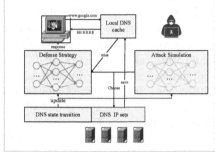

Fig. 2. Intelligent defense strategy

3.2 System Overview

Our defense strategy is based on the analysis and improvement of the previous strategy, and the framework continues to be the same as the previous setup. The schematic diagram of the system architecture is shown in Fig. 2.

The defense architecture consists of an attack simulation module that simulates an attacker conducting an attack, an intelligent defense policy and DNS state transition component responsible for defense decisions, and the IP set and local DNS. The defense philosophy is derived from the moving target defense. The defense policy is located between the DNS resolution server and the local application on which our NODO algorithm is deployed. The algorithm analyzes information from the DNS state transition component when the client initiates a resolution request to guide the client to dynamically select a DNS server, enhancing the uncertainty of its selection. The attack simulation module also simulates an attacker launching an attack during model training to play offense and defense games.

3.3 Scene Modeling

We model the attack and defense scenario as an imperfect information zero-sum game problem. The zero-sum game property of the problem is obvious, where the interests of the attacker and the client are opposed to each other, and both sides gain from the success or failure of the defense. In reality, the attackers and defenders do not know each other's strategies, and they cannot know more information than their own strategies, so the problem is an imperfect information game problem. Finally, it can be considered that the action choices of both sides in this problem are only related to the current state, so we model the problem as a Markov process.

The game problem described in this paper is defined as follows.

- Define $N = n_1, n_2, ..., n_N$ as the action space, i.e., the DNS domain servers to be chosen by the client as well as the attacker, where N can also be expressed as the number of optional servers, which is also the dimension of the action space.
- Define $S = S_1, S_2, ..., S_\infty$ where $S_i = [S_{net}, S_h]$ is the state space of the game. In order to guarantee the generalization of the algorithm, the game space is defined, considering only the necessary external environmental factors. Here we have chosen the Round Trip Time (RTT) of the DNS server, which has a decisive influence on the selection of the DNS server by the client. The choice of this state space is sufficient to represent the overall environment since we can customize the function to take into account the influence of environmental factors, which has the same form as the RTT defined in this paper, and a kernel that characterizes the influence of the environment.S_h denotes the action selection history of both games, which we only record and do not reflect in the defender's training process.
- $Gt = (Nc, Na) \in R^{2 \times N_{TAR}}$ defines the action selection matrix of the defender and attacker at the current time round. N_{TAR} is the number of DNS servers that the defender and attacker can select in a single round given the current technology.

Unlike previous state transfer matrices, our state transfer matrix contains only the RTT of each DNS server. This has the following advantages:

1. It frees up the width of the neural network, which gives us more arithmetic power to extend the depth of the neural network.
2. Our state transfer matrix, i.e., the input to the neural network, maintains a minimum number of data inputs, which makes the algorithm much more scalable, as will be added below to show that these inputs are sufficient and efficient.
3. The historical decisions of the intelligence in the problem no longer impact the current decision, which guarantees the preconditions for using our reinforcement learning algorithm.

Our approach is to solve the best strategy in each scenario and fit it with a neural network. The following section will focus on describing our subgame solution process.

- Define the subgame problem: Given the state space S_i, solve the strategy that the defender should adopt to request the DNS domain name server with the shortest RTT without being caught by the attacker, while the attacker needs to learn to launch a cache poisoning attack on the defender successfully.
- Define the subject of the game in the subgame problem row-player r and column-player c. The two players consist of the strategy Π of the game and the probability π of choosing each strategy. The strategy of the game

$a_i = [N_c, N_a]$ indicates which particular action the attacker and the defender should choose in the subgame.

- Define e (exploitability) as the difference between the rewards obtained by the row player as the attacker and the defender playing against the column player in the subgame problem. e represents the difference between the capabilities of the row player and the column player and decreases as the training process progresses, which means that the algorithm is converging to the Nash equilibrium point.

The reward R for the defender in the subgame process consists of two components: The defender chooses the lower RTT of the DNS name server; The defender's action selection is not captured by the attacker. The calculation formula is as follows.

$$R = \begin{cases} -k_0 S\left[N_a\right] - k, & \text{if } N_a = N_c \\ -k_0 S\left[N_a\right], & \text{if } N_a \neq N_c \end{cases} \tag{1}$$

The attacker's reward is naturally $-R$.

4   Intelligent Reinforcement Learning Algorithms

4.1   The Overall Framework

The complete framework of the algorithm is shown in Fig. 3. With the algorithm NODO, the client can interact with the environment and realize the intelligence of the defense policy. The algorithm pseudo-code is shown in Algorithm 1. Where the strategies $\Pi_{r,0}$, $\Pi_{c,0}$ denote the strategies of the row and list players, respectively, A represents the game matrix, N_{do} is the total number of rounds needed to train the row and column players. Where θ denotes neural network, t denotes the t-th round of strategy update, π_t is the weight of each strategy, and T_i denotes the i-th class of mixed strategies.

Algorithm 1: NODO Algorithm

Input: Action space N

1 initialize θ;
2 **for** $ep \leftarrow 0$ **to** eps **do**
3   initialize $net \in \mathcal{R}^N$, probability $action = \theta([p_1, p_2, ..p_N])$;
4   sample $\Pi_{r,0}$, $\Pi_{c,0}$, calculate A of $\Pi_{r,0} \& \Pi_{c,0}$;
5   **for** $t \leftarrow 0$ **to** N_{do} **do**
6   find best responsea_t, update $\Pi_{t+1} = \Pi_t \cup a_t$;
7   calculate l_t according to $l = A\pi_{c,t}$;
8   update π_t if $\Pi_t = \Pi_{t-1}$ else recalculation π_t;
9   **end**
10     $loss = \Pi - action$, update θ by equation 2;
11 **end**

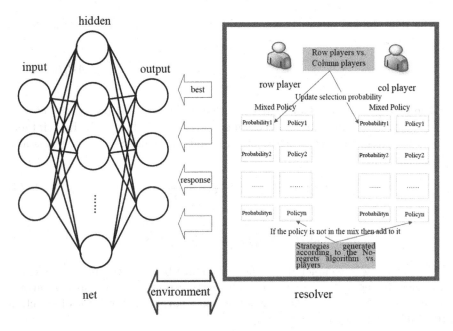

Fig. 3. An overall framework for deep learning combined with reinforcement learning

First, the Nash equilibrium solver solves the Nash equilibrium in the current scenario and outputs the probability of selecting each action of the current optimal policy (optimal hybrid policy). The loss of the neural network is given by the difference between the output of the neural network and the solver action selection. The update method is chosen as the Adam momentum update method, accelerating the descent at the beginning of the descent and reducing the oscillation at the middle and end of the descent. The update formula is as follows.

$$\hat{m}_t = \frac{\beta_1 m_{t-1} + (1 - \beta_1) \frac{1}{m} Z^T (Z_{X_t} - Y),}{1 - \beta_1^t}$$

$$\hat{v}_t = \frac{\beta_2 v_{t-1} + (1 - \beta_2) (\frac{1}{m} Z^T (Z_{X_t} - Y))^2}{1 - \beta_2^t} \qquad (2)$$

$$x_{t+1} = x_t - \frac{\alpha}{\sqrt{\hat{v}_t} + \epsilon} \hat{m}_t$$

Then we describe how the solver obtains the equilibrium solution. The algorithm ODO [8] randomly initializes a mixed strategy consisting of pure strategies according to the incoming parameters. The r and c are trained in turn, and the training process is mainly based on the update of the player's strategy and the update of the selection probability of the player's strategy:

- Calculate the best response strategy for the opponent's strategy and update the number of strategies contained in the player.

- The gain matrix is calculated according to Eq. 3, and the loss function is calculated.

$$r_{i,j} = \sum_{i_1 \in N_1} \sum_{i_2 \in N_2} \cdots \sum_{i_{TAR} \in N_{TAR}} p_1[i_1] p_2[i_2] \ldots p_{TAR}[TAR]\mathbf{R} \qquad (3)$$

- The two players continuously play to update the selection probability of each strategy. The probability of selection is updated according to the Eq. 4 if there is a new best strategy; otherwise, Eq. 5 and the number of strategies is also updated.

$$\pi_{t+1}(i) = \pi_t(i) \frac{e^{-a^{i^T}l}}{\sum_{i=1}^{n} \pi_t(i)e^{-a^{i^T}l}} \qquad (4)$$

$$\pi_{t+1}(i) = \begin{cases} \frac{\pi_t(i)N-1}{N}, & \text{if} \quad i \in [N-1] \\ \frac{1}{N}, & \text{if} \quad i = N \end{cases} \qquad (5)$$

The training is completed to reach a balance between the players, and the strategies are no longer upgraded. The best response for the specific attack strategy in the current scenario is solved and output in the form of selection probabilities for each action.

4.2 Algorithm Convergence Under Dual Prediction

Theorem 1. *The algorithm in this problem converges to a minimum-maximum equilibrium [12].*

Proof. The first is convergence: since the number of optional actions for attackers and defenders in this problem is limited to combinations of DNS name servers. (The final optimal strategy for attackers and defenders may contain all the choice spaces, but pure strategies can linearly tabulate the corresponding linear strategies)

The second is correctness, assuming that convergence is reached at k steps of the algorithm. According to the practice of the dual prediction algorithm, it is known that the best strategy of the row player is no longer updated. This means that the best payoff of the row player under the current strategy of the former player is equal to the best payoff of the column player under the current strategy of the row player. It can be concluded that the current strategy is a maximal optimal solution for the column player. Subsequently, it is only necessary to prove that the current strategy is a min-maximal optimal solution. Since we were given the current strategy, for any row player, the gain is less than the current gain. Moreover, given the row player strategy, the gain under all strategies of the column player will be less than the current gain. Similarly, we can get that the current row player strategy goes to the minimum of the maximum gain of the following player, so the point of convergence is the minimum-maximum equilibrium; that is, the algorithm in this problem can converge to the minimum-maximum equilibrium.

5   Experiment

5.1   Experimental Environment and Parameter Settings

Our simulation environment is run on a physical device with a Core i7-8750H, 2.2 GHz processor, and 16 GB RAM. The simulation environment is set up with network latency fluctuating between 1–100, and the number of optional DNS resolvers is 18, with the client choosing one DNS resolver at a time and the attacker choosing three DNS resolvers at a time. The reward k for a successful attack is given separately in each experiment and k_0 is set to 0.02. The neural network learning rate is set to 0.0005, and the network structure is given separately in each experiment. The neural network is updated with parameters in one round of 40 data sets, and the training lasts 500 sets. The number of rounds updated by the game solver and the learning rate is given by the algorithm corresponding to the formula that requires the solver to find 300 better strategies.

5.2   Convergence Experiment

We first designed experiments to verify the convergence of the algorithm in practice.

When setting k in the reward Eq. 1 to 10, the effect of our subgame solution is shown in Fig. 4. It can be seen that the sum of the exploited values of the row and column players (representing the weakness of the player's mixed strategy) gradually decreases with the number of training rounds and reaches a near minimum for the first time at 50 steps. This shows that our algorithm can effectively solve the Nash equilibrium problem under the zero-sum game and has a stable convergence effect under the setting of strong transitivity [4].

The algorithm fluctuates around 50, 100, and 250 rounds, and the fluctuations become smaller, which reflects the effectiveness of our algorithm design concept. The fluctuation here is because the row players are trained first. After trying multiple strategies, it breaks out of the cycle of mutual restraint of current strategies and finds a better strategy. While the column player has not yet been trained to deal with such strategies effectively, resulting in a sharp increase in the exploitation value of the column player. After training the column player to cope with the new strategy, the exploited value returns to the minimum again. The decrease in the magnitude of fluctuations illustrates that the algorithm is taking stronger and stronger strategies as the training rounds increase. Furthermore, the algorithm can stay without being exploited too much and respond to them quickly even when better strategies appear.

With k set to 20 in the reward Eq. 1, the effect of our subgame solution is shown in Fig. 5. We can see that the fluctuation of the algorithm is the same as when k is set to 10. This is because when the transitivity increases, the phenomenon of first cyclic restraint appears. Nevertheless, after longer iterations, it gradually converges to Nash equilibrium at 100 steps, which shows that our algorithm can effectively solve the Nash equilibrium problem under a zero-sum game and the setting of weaker transitivity with a convergence effect.

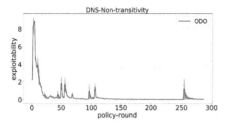

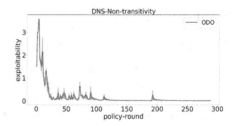

Fig. 4. Convergence under transitivity   **Fig. 5.** Convergence under non-transitivity

5.3   Effect in Simulation Environment

Finally, we examine the performance of the algorithm in a real-world scenario.

The k in the reward Eq. 1 is set to 15, and the previous solver performance analysis shows it has good performance at 50 rounds. Here we ask the subgame solver to find 120 better strategies to ensure that the solver's output is the optimal solution. The algorithm's results are shown in Fig. 6, 7. It can be seen that the deviation of the neural network's output from the solution given by the subgame solver decreases with the number of rounds. This means that the performance of the algorithm increases gradually. The algorithm's performance hardly improves around round 225 and does not improve until round 500, when it is considered to have reached its performance limit. The average deviation of the algorithm represents the gap between the algorithm and the optimal solution, which is 60 at the maximum. The gap shrinks to about 8 as the algorithm is trained, which indicates that our algorithm is effective.

At the same time, the defense success rate of the algorithm gradually increases from 0.83 at the beginning. Finally, it converges to around 0.90 of the defense success rate of the subgame solver, indicating that although our algorithm has a certain gap with the equilibrium solver in terms of action selection, the actual operation effect can reach the level of the solver. We infer that this situation occurs because there is strong non-transitivity under the setup, leading to difficulty defining the advantages and disadvantages between strategies.

We set up three sets of neural networks to explore what network structure is more suitable for fitting the equilibrium solution of this problem. We set up $6 \times 121 \times 6$, $6 \times 100 \times 6$, and $6 \times 61 \times 61 \times 6$, three control groups, respectively, while each group of experiments was done twice under different random seeds to reduce the effect of chance. The experimental results show that in the scenario of this paper, the expansion of the neural network breadth improves the algorithm performance more than the depth expansion.

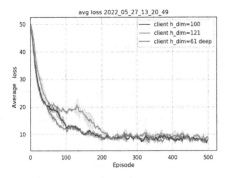

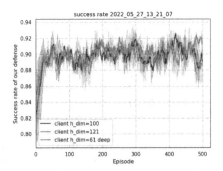

Fig. 6. Algorithm deviation value   **Fig. 7.** Defensive success rate

6   Summary and Outlook

In this paper, we design the NODO algorithm for the unresolved problem of combating intelligent attackers in the client-attacker offense-defense confrontation problem in DNS cache poisoning attacks. Verify the algorithm's convergence and defense success rate in a simulation environment. Convergence of the strategy was obtained in both the strong and weak transferability settings, and timely responses to changing environments were achieved with the help of neural networks.

In the future, we intend to understand the concepts related to deep reinforcement learning and game theory to make theoretical improvements to the algorithm's convergence stability and convergence rate. Furthermore, design an interface to connect the algorithm to the real environment to test the algorithm's operation in the real environment and improve the algorithm parameter settings in a targeted manner.

References

1. Gartner security & risk management summit 2022 national harbor: day 1 highlights. https://www.gartner.com/en/newsroom/press-releases/2022-06-07-gartner-security-and-risk-management-summit-national-harbor-day-1-highlights.html. Accessed 7 June 2022
2. Alharbi, F., Chang, J., Zhou, Y., Qian, F., Qian, Z., Abu-Ghazaleh, N.: Collaborative client-side DNS cache poisoning attack. In: IEEE INFOCOM 2019-IEEE Conference on Computer Communications, pp. 1153–1161. IEEE (2019)
3. Antonakakis, M., Dagon, D., Luo, X., Perdisci, R., Lee, W., Bellmor, J.: A centralized monitoring infrastructure for improving DNS security. In: Jha, S., Sommer, R., Kreibich, C. (eds.) RAID 2010. LNCS, vol. 6307, pp. 18–37. Springer, Heidelberg (2010). https://doi.org/10.1007/978-3-642-15512-3_2
4. Czarnecki, W.M., et al.: Real world games look like spinning tops. Adv. Neural Inf. Process. Syst. **33**, 17443–17454 (2020)

5. Hao, S., Wang, H.: Exploring domain name based features on the effectiveness of DNS caching. ACM SIGCOMM Comput. Commun. Rev. **47**(1), 36–42 (2017)

6. Hu, Z., Zhu, L., Heidemann, J., Mankin, A., Wessels, D., Hoffman, P.: Specification for DNS over transport layer security (TLS). Technical report (2016)

7. Khormali, A., Park, J., Alasmary, H., Anwar, A., Saad, M., Mohaisen, D.: Domain name system security and privacy: a contemporary survey. Comput. Netw. **185**, 107699 (2021)

8. Le Cong Dinh, Y.Y., Tian, Z., Nieves, N.P., Slumbers, O., Mguni, D.H., Ammar, H.B., Wang, J.: Online double oracle (2021)

9. Li, C., Dai, L., Xu, Z., Ding, Y., Han, Y.: A message-based malicious detection scheme of public DNS services. In: 2021 IEEE 23rd International Conference on High Performance Computing & Communications; 7th International Conference on Data Science & Systems; 19th International Conference on Smart City; 7th International Conference on Dependability in Sensor, Cloud & Big Data Systems & Application. HPCC/DSS/SmartCity/DependSys, pp. 733–740. IEEE (2021)

10. Ma, T., et al.: An intelligent proactive defense against the client-side DNS cache poisoning attack via self-checking deep reinforcement learning. Int. J. Intell. Syst. **7**, 8170–8197 (2022)

11. Ma, T., Xu, C., Zhou, Z., Kuang, X., Zhong, L., Grieco, L.A.: Intelligent-driven adapting defense against the client-side DNS cache poisoning in the cloud. In: GLOBECOM 2020–2020 IEEE Global Communications Conference, pp. 1–6. IEEE (2020)

12. McMahan, H.B., Gordon, G.J., Blum, A.: Planning in the presence of cost functions controlled by an adversary. In: Proceedings of the 20th International Conference on Machine Learning (ICML-03), pp. 536–543 (2003)

13. Perdisci, R., Antonakakis, M., Luo, X., Lee, W.: WSEC DNS: protecting recursive DNS resolvers from poisoning attacks. In: 2009 IEEE/IFIP International Conference on Dependable Systems & Networks, pp. 3–12. IEEE (2009)

14. Shulman, H., Waidner, M.: Towards forensic analysis of attacks with DNSSEC. In: 2014 IEEE Security and Privacy Workshops, pp. 69–76. IEEE (2014)

15. Weiler, S., Blacka, D.: Clarifications and implementation notes for DNS security (DNSSEC). Technical report (2013)

16. Wu, H., Dang, X., Zhang, L., Wang, L.: Kalman filter based DNS cache poisoning attack detection. In: 2015 IEEE International Conference on Automation Science and Engineering (CASE), pp. 1594–1600. IEEE (2015)

17. Zhang, T., Xu, C., Zhang, B., Shen, J., Kuang, X., Grieco, L.A.: Toward attack-resistant route mutation for VANETS: an online and adaptive multiagent reinforcement learning approach. IEEE Trans. Intell. Transp. Syst. **23**, 23254–23267 (2022)

18. Zhang, T., et al.: How to mitigate DDOS intelligently in SD-IOV: a moving target defense approach. IEEE Trans. Ind. Inform. **19**, 1097–1106 (2022)

19. Zhou, Z., Kuang, X., Sun, L., Zhong, L., Xu, C.: Endogenous security defense against deductive attack: when artificial intelligence meets active defense for online service. IEEE Commun. Mag. **58**(6), 58–64 (2020)

20. Zhou, Z., Xu, C., Ma, T., Kuang, X.: Multi-vNIC intelligent mutation: a moving target defense to thwart client-side DNS cache attack. In: ICC 2020–2020 IEEE International Conference on Communications (ICC), pp. 1–6. IEEE (2020)

Optimization of TCP Congestion Control Algorithms Loss-Based in Wireless Network

Xiaolin Xing[(✉)], Shujie Yang, Xiang Ji, and Shuai Peng

Beijing University of Posts and Telecommunications, Beijing 100876, China
`xlxing@bupt.edu.cn`

Abstract. With the rapid development of computer network, today's network structure has become very complex. The promotion of Wi-Fi and the widespread use of mobile terminals such as cell phone, laptop and smart watch, have made wireless access become the main way of Internet surfing. Conventional congestion control algorithms are based on packet loss to perceive network congestion like NewReno, CUBIC. On Wi-Fi scenarios, last-mile delivery is wireless, and it may cause random loss. In this case, these congestion control algorithms based on packet loss perception can not distinguish the network congestion correctly and maybe reduce the congestion window when congestion doesn't occur. To solve this problem, we propose optimization of these congestion control algorithms, which can be intelligently aware of packet loss and improve TCP transmission performance. We evaluated TCP transmission performance on wired network and wireless network. The results show that the performance of our method is similar to that of the conventional congestion control algorithms in wired environment, while the bandwidth utilization is significantly improved on wireless network. In addition, our work achieves great competition fairness using logical analysis.

Keywords: TCP · Congestion control algorithm · NewReno · CUBIC · Wireless network

1 Introduction

Transmission Control Protocol (TCP) is a connection-oriented, reliable, byte-stream based transport layer communication protocol. In network transmission, TCP is used for a large amount of traffic transmission [22]. Numerous Hyper Text Transfer Protocol (HTTP) [5] packets are sent to the network which bottom layer is TCP. With the increasing number of users and mobile terminals, today's Internet is becoming more and more congested. Congestion control algorithm is the key mechanism of global network traffic control in TCP and is used to prevent congestion and reduce congestion after it occurs. It can decide sending rate which is the smaller value of the receiver window and the congestion window. At the same time, it can effectively ensure the fairness of network resource allocation among all Internet access users. Congestion control algorithm aims to maximize

© The Author(s), under exclusive license to Springer Nature Singapore Pte Ltd. 2023
W. Quan (Ed.): ICENAT 2022, CCIS 1696, pp. 381–392, 2023.
https://doi.org/10.1007/978-981-19-9697-9_31

transmission performance including high throughput and low delay. However, due to the limitation of the backbone network bandwidth, sending packets too aggressively may cause network congestion, which reduces TCP data transmission performance. Therefore, the design and improvement of congestion control algorithm has always been a major research topic in TCP protocol.

In terms of design and implementation, congestion control algorithms can be divided into four categories and we would give a brief review.

First of all, TCP Tahoe [10], TCP Reno [21], TCP NewReno [8], TCP BIC [26] and TCP CUBIC [7] are packet loss based. They regard packet loss as an indicator of network congestion. It gradually increases the congestion window by slow probe at first, when packet loss occurs, the congestion window decreases in a specific way. This method greedily fills up the whole network resources, causing BufferBloat [6] problem. Secondly, delay-based congestion control, representative algorithms include TCP Vegas [1], FAST TCP [12] and TCP Nice [14], which use delay as indicator of congestion, including one-way delay, queuing delay or round-trip time (RTT). Although there will be noise interference in the measurement process, the delay can roughly show the number of packets in the network. Unfortunately, this kind of method is sensitive to network delay and has poor stability, so it is rarely used in practical deployment. Thirdly, TCP BBR [2] congestion control algorithm proposed by Google in 2016 introduced the bandwidth delay product (BDP) and real-time detection of link capacity, achieving huge increment in optimizing network performance. However, a lot of work has proved that it has serious fairness problems [9,23]. This algorithm is mainly deployed on streaming media servers such as Youtube, Netflix [2,20], but the market occupancy in personal mobile terminals is small. Recently, due to the rise of machine learning [3,13,18], congestion control algorithms based on machine learning are put forward, it has no specific congestion signal. With the aid of training data and evaluation function, it can construct a great control strategy [11,15–17], but these algorithms are relatively complicated, energy-expensive, and difficult to deploy. Worse, the fairness is unsatisfactory [11], so this kind of solution mostly remains in the laboratory up to now.

Although congestion control algorithms loss-based are difficult to adapt to current complex network, they are still the most widely used and deployed on most devices due to its maturity and stability [7]. Fortunately, most of the time, they work fine. The open source operating system Linux [25] compiles Reno(In fact, Reno is NewReno) and CUBIC into the kernel and sets CUBIC as default congestion control algorithm. Hence, it is still of great significance to study the congestion control algorithms loss-based.

There are two types of packet loss in network transmission: a) network congestion, router active packet loss in queue buffer; b) random loss in wireless link. For algorithms loss-based, the cause of packet loss cannot be distinguished. It is worth noting that congestion control by the sender triggered by packet loss in the wireless link will not improve the transmission efficiency of the TCP transmission, but will reduce the size of the sender window due to the incorrect judgment of network congestion, resulting in lower transmission rate and throughput. This means that channel resources, network bandwidth is underutilized. Multiple packets loss in wireless link would result in network jitter, performance decline.

This paper focuses on high packet loss and high bit error rate of wireless network, and improve the throughput, stability of the TCP transmission. Our algorithm works well in wired networks or networks with low packet loss and low bit error rate, while its performance is improved in wireless network.

Overall, this paper analyzes the problems and challenges of current congestion control algorithms. Firstly, the problems of current congestion control algorithm in wireless network are discussed, and this situation is deeply analyzed. Based on the widely used congestion control algorithms TCP NewReno and TCP CUBIC, a heuristic algorithm is proposed, which analyzes data transmission of TCP connection. The last hop of the whole TCP connection from mobile devices such as mobile phones, laptops to the Wireless Access Point(WAP) is simulated. Packet loss rate and bit error rate are closely related to the network signal strength. RTT is taken as an important factor to determine whether the packet loss of the current TCP connection is caused by network congestion or random loss. For the packet loss caused by these two situations, take different measures to make full use of network resources reasonably and improve the throughput and stability of transmission as much as possible. For network congestion perception, the sender adjusts the congestion window to adapt the data transmission rate, which has the same fairness as common TCP New Reno and TCP CUBIC and will not preempt more network resources.

2   Loss-Based Congestion Control Algorithms

TCP NewReno and TCP CUBIC are two the most representative loss-based congestion algorithms. The curve of TCP CUBIC is shown in Fig. 1. I would describe two algorithms below.

2.1   TCP NewReno

TCP NewReno is the extension of TCP Reno, and the Linux kernel uses *Reno* instead of *NewReno* in the name. TCP NewReno improved the fast recovery mechanism based on TCP Reno. If only one packet is lost, the mechanism is the same as Reno. Its advantages come into play when multiple packages are lost at the same time. TCP Reno algorithm consists of three states: slow start, congestion avoidance and fast recovery. In the slow start state, the congestion window grows exponentially. Although it is named slow start, the window grows at a very fast rate. Congestion avoidance state is based on historical experience, a simple prediction of network congestion state is made in advance. When the congestion window grows to a certain *threshold*, the window value is slowly increased to maintain a period of high sending rate transmission. When packet loss occurs, it happened that three repeated acknowledges (ACKs) are received or the timer times out. The former considers it a partial packet loss and enters a fast recovery state, halving the sending window and then slowly increasing it. When the timer times out, it considers that serious network congestion has happened and enters the slow start state.

2.2   TCP CUBIC

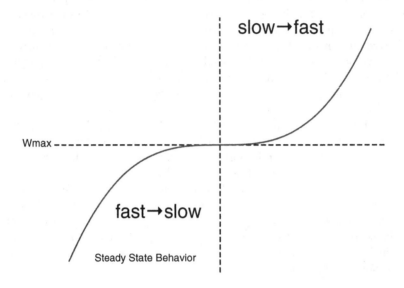

Fig. 1. TCP CUBIC window growth function.

In TCP Reno algorithm, the case of network congestion and packet loss is not considered, and the case of loss of one packet and multiple packets is not subdivided. TCP NewReno algorithm makes up for its second shortcomings. Because our work is related with packet loss situations, we would't go into the details of the TCP NewReno algorithm improvements here.

The implementation details of TCP NewReno algorithm are relatively simple. The congestion window increases exponentially in slow start state and linearly in the congestion avoid state. The congestion window growth curve for TCP CUBIC is a cubic function in mathematics. In slow start state, the window grows fast and is the convex contour of cubic function. When the packet loss event occurs, it records the value of congestion window as W_{max}, then multiplies the congestion window reduction by the multiplier factor β, where β is a window reduction constant, and performs regular TCP fast recovery and retransmission.

The window growth function formula of TCP CUBIC is shown below:

$$W(t) = C(t - K)^3 + W_{max} \tag{1}$$

$$K = \sqrt[3]{\frac{W_{max} * \beta}{C}} \tag{2}$$

where t is the time from last packet loss, $W(t)$ is the congestion window value at time t, and C is the adjustment parameter of growth rate in usual state. On most recent Linux kernel, C is 0.4 and β is 0.3. In the slow start state, the window grows from fast to slow, and in the maximum window, the window grows from slow to fast. Compared with window increasing of TCP NewReno, TCP CUBIC has more time to stay near the maximum value of the window estimate, so it's more stable and has a higher bandwidth utilization in theory.

3 Background and Motivation

3.1 Wireless Access

As the name implies, it is a network that does not use physical transmission (such as optical fiber, twisted-pair), and transmits radio frequency signals through devices. The 4G, 5G and Wi-Fi networks we use are all wireless access. Wireless access has greatly provided convenience for users to access the Internet, users can easily access the Internet anytime and anywhere. However, the biggest disadvantage of wireless network is poor stability, signal strength is greatly affected by the surroundings. The quality of the wireless network depends on whether there's interference around it. The closer you get to the signal source, the better the quality of network transmission.

In computer network architecture, the transmission between user terminals and wireless access points is point-to-point in data link layer. In wired access or wireless access with good signal quality, the packet loss rate is low. By default, the packet loss and retransmission operation is not enabled on the data link layer. The upper layer protocols ensure the reliability of data transmission.

3.2 Motivation

Congestion control algorithm is end-to-end that detects network congestion through sensing data transmission. The biggest disadvantage of the congestion control algorithm loss-based is that it does not distinguish packet loss between wireless access network and routers. When packet loss occurs, network congestion is considered. In the wired network, the performance and fairness are very good, but in the wireless network, the network quality is unstable, random packet loss is easy to happen. Random loss in wireless network does not affect the entire backbone network, but only affects the transmission performance of specific users. It is unwise to switch to congestion avoidance when the network is not congested. Martin et al. believes that there is a weak correlation between delay and network congestion in [19]. Therefore, and we are motivated, we still take packet loss as the indicator of congestion control instead of delay. However, we can decide random loss or network congestion by the perception of some other network parameters including RTT, and then adopt different coping strategies.

4 Proposed Method

4.1 Implementation

After three handshakes and the establishment of TCP connection, the data packets are transmitted in the IP layer which is connectionless. The routing algorithm of the IP layer selecting a path makes the transmission delay of multiple data packets transmitted close. In wired networks, the propagation delay is often much greater than the propagation delay of the last wireless link hop. Taking the minimum transmission delay Round-Trip Time (RTT) as a reference, when packet loss occurs, if the RTT is large, it is considered that the network is congested, and there is a delay on the IP layer. If the RTT is small, and the difference between RTT and the minimum RTT is small, it is considered that the last wireless link hop has lost a packet. At this time, it is determined that the network is not congested.

Heuristically, let f be the parameter to quantify RTT, expressed as:

$$f = 1 - \tau_{\min}/\tau \tag{3}$$

where τ is the RTT and $\tau_{\min}$ is the minimum in all RTTs.

We define one constant F. When packet loss occurs, if $f < F$, it means that data transmission over the network is less affected by BufferBloat [6], the queuing delay in the router is low, and the probability of active packet loss by the router is little. It is considered as random loss at the last hop with large probability.

When packet loss happens in wireless access, the network resources are not fully utilized. The processing methods are as follows:

- Retransmit the two lost packets at a time;
- Do not switch to congestion avoidance state.

Each lost packet is retransmitted twice. For example, if the packet $seq = 15$ is lost, the sender retransmits two packets with $seq = 15$. The core idea is: network is not congested and the network resources do not reach the threshold. Unfortunately, for packet loss in wireless networks, our retransmitted packets may still be lost.

In order to make full use of the bandwidth resources, send two packets at once. This is also to improve the success rate of retransmission. Assuming that the packet loss rate of the wireless hop is r at this time, then the probability of successful retransmission is $1 - r^2$. If $r = 0.3$, the probability of successful retransmission is 0.91.

4.2   Fairness Analysis

The core idea of our method is to distinguish packet loss in wireless networks, and then take specific action when packet loss occurs because of bad quality in wireless network. The basic framework of congestion control algorithm loss-based remains.

In wired networks, our method is compatible with original methods. Because packet loss in wireless networks usually would not occur, we believe that all packet losses are caused by network congestion. In our method, we also regard it as network congestion, and the behavior taken is consistent with the original strategy. Therefore, in wired networks, our proposed method has good fairness. Of course, it is also consistent in wireless networks with good network quality.

In TCP connection, when packet losses in the last wireless link hop, but the RTT is not large, we think that the network resources are not fully utilized. At this time, we do not enter into the congestion avoidance state. On the contrary, we reduce the occurrence of packet loss by increasing the number of packets sent. Because every retransmission packet loss will add a RTT, which has a great reduction on network transmission. With the increment of network congestion and RTT, our method will be transformed into the response actions of conventional congestion control algorithms, so it will not encroach on other TCP flows. This method uses redundant retransmission temporarily to reduce packet loss only when the backbone network bandwidth resources are underutilized.

All in all, our optimization does not affect the fairness of the congestion control algorithms.

5   Simulation and Experiment

In this section, we simulated the proposed method to prove the effectiveness of our proposed method. At first, NS3 [4] tool was used to conduct performance simulation. Then, we implement the proposed method on the Linux kernel and try to evaluate their performance improvement in a real network. Our proposed optimizations of TCP congestion control algorithms are named as TCP NewRenoW (reno_w) and TCP CUBICW (cubic_w) respectively.

5.1   Simulation in NS3

Network simulator NS3 is used to simulate these congestion control algorithms. We have established the network topology, as shown in Fig. 2. The variables that can be set including bottleneck link bandwidth, packet loss rate and delay. Set a higher packet loss rate in the last hop, which can be used to simulate wireless networks. We tested the bandwidth of four congestion control algorithms with a bottleneck bandwidth of 30 Mbps and a delay of 30 ms, as shown in Fig. 3.

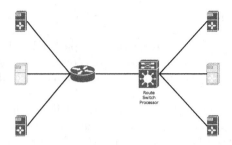

Fig. 2. Network topology for NS3 simulation. The red host is the sender, and orange one is the receiver. (Color figure online)

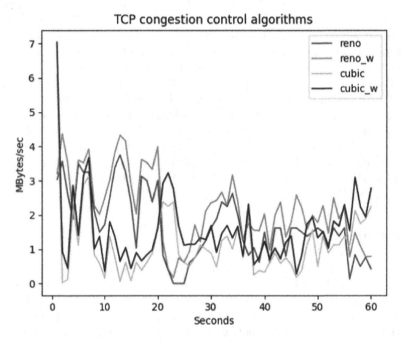

Fig. 3. Throughput of TCP transmission for 60 s. Three clients connect with one server. The window size is 500 KByte and random drop rate is 0.005%. The average throughputs of the four congestion control algorithms are 1.68 MByte/s, 1.74 MByte/s, 1.34 MByte/s, 1.40 MByte/s.

5.2   Simulation in Real Network

Based on TCP NewReno and TCP CUBIC, we implement the proposed congestion control method in Linux kernel 5.4.0. We simulate network throughput and delay in a real network. The sender is a local PC installed with the modified Linux kernel, which supports system switching of the four congestion control algorithms, TCP NewReno, TCP NewRenoW, TCP CUBIC, TCP CUBICW.

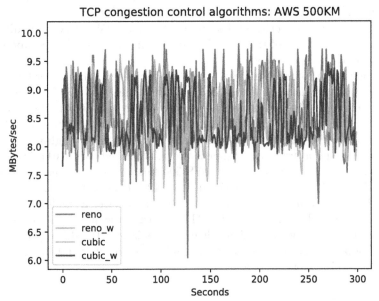

(a) Throughput of TCP connection between my pc and AWS-100km

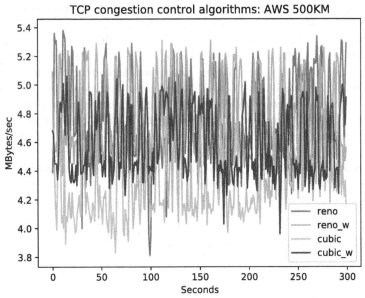

(b) Throughput of TCP connection between my pc and AWS-500km

Fig. 4. Test throughput of four congestion control algorithms in AWS-100 km, AWS-500 km using Iperf. Results show our proposed method have a litter improvement compared with conventional algorithms.

The receiver is AWS server, Ubuntu20.04 with single-core CPU and 2 GB RAM. Test network performance tests using Iperf [24] tools.

We designed two experimental scenarios by using AWS servers at different locations. The distances of the two AWS servers from the sender are about 100 KM and 500 KM respectively.

Our congestion control algorithms are only deployed at the sender host. Iperf tool is used to test network transmission performance, and my personal PC is set as *client* and AWS cloud server as *server*. We do not set parameters on the *server*, all experiments use default parameters. Result are shown in Fig. 4.

We tested 10 times for this experiment and averaged the throughput. In AWS-100 km server, the average throughputs are 8.532 MBytes/s, 8.611 MBypts/s, 8.361 Mbyts/s, 8.502 MBytes/s. In AWS-500 km server, the average throughputs are 4.763 MBytes/s, 4.769 MBypts/s, 4.342 Mbyts/s, 4.604 MBytes/s. We can get the conclusion that our proposed solution achieves a small performance improvement. In addition, when the RTT is large, the performance improvement is greater. We speculate that when RTT is larger, the difference between the delay of packet loss in wireless environment and the overall delay is smaller, and our method is more motivated.

6   Conclusion

In this paper, we briefly describe several kinds of congestion control algorithms, and then focus on congestion control algorithms loss-based such as TCP NewReno, TCP CUBIC. Although they has some disadvantages, such as causing BufferBloat, it is still the most deployed congestion control algorithms due to its good robustness and fairness. This paper analyzes the weakness of the congestion control algorithms loss-based, that is random loss caused by the possible high packet loss rate under wireless access is judged as network congestion. Based on the backbone of the congestion control algorithms loss-based, this paper uses RTT as the indicator and proposes a packet loss discrimination method. Our solution is implemented in Linux kernel, and a simple experiment is carried out. Experimental results show that our algorithm has good adaptability, and for wireless access networks with bad network quality and high packet loss rate, our method has some increment.

Acknowledgements. Thanks to Teacher Shujie Yang for his guidance in this work. I would like to thank Xiang ji for useful discussions.

References

1. Brakmo, L.S., O'Malley, S.W., Peterson, L.L.: TCP Vegas: new techniques for congestion detection and avoidance. In: Proceedings of the Conference on Communications Architectures, Protocols and Applications, pp. 24–35 (1994)
2. Cardwell, N., Cheng, Y., Gunn, C.S., Yeganeh, S.H., Jacobson, V.: BBR: congestion-based congestion control: measuring bottleneck bandwidth and round-trip propagation time. Queue **14**(5), 20–53 (2016)

3. Carleo, G., et al.: Machine learning and the physical sciences. Rev. Mod. Phys. **91**(4), 045002 (2019)
4. Casoni, M., Grazia, C.A., Klapez, M., Patriciello, N.: Implementation and validation of TCP options and congestion control algorithms for ns-3. In: Proceedings of the 2015 Workshop on Ns-3, pp. 112–119 (2015)
5. Fielding, R., et al.: Hypertext transfer protocol-http/1.1. Technical report (1999)
6. Gettys, J.: Bufferbloat: dark buffers in the internet. IEEE Internet Comput. **15**(3), 96 (2011)
7. Ha, S., Rhee, I., Xu, L.: CUBIC: a new TCP-friendly high-speed TCP variant. ACM SIGOPS Oper. Syst. Rev. **42**(5), 64–74 (2008)
8. Henderson, T., Floyd, S., Gurtov, A., Nishida, Y.: The NewReno modification to TCP's fast recovery algorithm. Technical report (2012)
9. Hock, M., Bless, R., Zitterbart, M.: Experimental evaluation of BBR congestion control. In: 2017 IEEE 25th International Conference on Network Protocols (ICNP), pp. 1–10. IEEE (2017)
10. Jacobson, V.: Congestion avoidance and control. ACM SIGCOMM Comput. Commun. Rev. **18**(4), 314–329 (1988)
11. Jay, N., Rotman, N., Godfrey, B., Schapira, M., Tamar, A.: A deep reinforcement learning perspective on internet congestion control. In: International Conference on Machine Learning, pp. 3050–3059. PMLR (2019)
12. Jin, C., Wei, D.X., Low, S.H.: Fast TCP: motivation, architecture, algorithms, performance. In: IEEE INFOCOM 2004, vol. 4, pp. 2490–2501. IEEE (2004)
13. Jordan, M.I., Mitchell, T.M.: Machine learning: trends, perspectives, and prospects. Science **349**(6245), 255–260 (2015)
14. Kokku, R.: {TCP} nice: a mechanism for background transfers. In: 5th Symposium on Operating Systems Design and Implementation (OSDI 2002) (2002)
15. Kong, Y., Zang, H., Ma, X.: Improving TCP congestion control with machine intelligence. In: Proceedings of the 2018 Workshop on Network Meets AI & ML, pp. 60–66 (2018)
16. Lan, D., Tan, X., Lv, J., Jin, Y., Yang, J.: A deep reinforcement learning based congestion control mechanism for NDN. In: ICC 2019–2019 IEEE International Conference on Communications (ICC), pp. 1–7. IEEE (2019)
17. Li, W., Zhou, F., Chowdhury, K.R., Meleis, W.: QTCP: adaptive congestion control with reinforcement learning. IEEE Trans. Netw. Sci. Eng. **6**(3), 445–458 (2018)
18. Mahesh, B.: Machine learning algorithms-a review. Int. J. Sci. Res. (IJSR) **9**, 381–386 (2020)
19. Martin, J., Nilsson, A., Rhee, I.: Delay-based congestion avoidance for TCP. IEEE/ACM Trans. Netw. **11**(3), 356–369 (2003)
20. Mishra, A., Sun, X., Jain, A., Pande, S., Joshi, R., Leong, B.: The great internet TCP congestion control census. In: Proceedings of the ACM on Measurement and Analysis of Computing Systems, vol. 3, no. 3, pp. 1–24 (2019)
21. Padhye, J., Firoiu, V., Towsley, D.F., Kurose, J.F.: Modeling TCP reno performance: a simple model and its empirical validation. IEEE/ACM Trans. Netw. **8**(2), 133–145 (2000)
22. Polese, M., et al.: A survey on recent advances in transport layer protocols. IEEE Commun. Surv. Tutor. **21**(4), 3584–3608 (2019)
23. Sasaki, K., Hanai, M., Miyazawa, K., Kobayashi, A., Oda, N., Yamaguchi, S.: TCP fairness among modern TCP congestion control algorithms including TCP BBR. In: 2018 IEEE 7th International Conference on Cloud Networking (CloudNet), pp. 1–4. IEEE (2018)

24. Tirumala, A.: Iperf: The TCP/UDP bandwidth measurement tool (1999). http://dast.nlanr.net/Projects/Iperf/

25. Torvalds, L., et al.: Linux **2**, 263–297 (2002). http://www.linux.org

26. Xu, L., Harfoush, K., Rhee, I.: Binary increase congestion control (BIC) for fast long-distance networks. In: IEEE INFOCOM 2004, vol. 4, pp. 2514–2524. IEEE (2004)

Priority-Aware Deployment of Multi-objective Service Function Chains

Xue Yu[1,2], Ran Wang[1,2(✉)], Changyan Yi[1,2], and Qiang Wu[1,2]

[1] Nanjing University of Aeronautics and Astronautics, Nanjing, China
{yyuxue,wangran,changyan.yi,wu.qiang}@nuaa.edu.cn
[2] Collaborative Innovation Center of Novel Software Technology
and Industrialization, Nanjing, China

Abstract. 5G is moving from the consumer Internet, where people are connected to people, to the industrial Internet, where humans, machines and objects are connected. In addition to ultra-reliable and low-latency communication (uRLLC), future 5G Advanced and 6G technology needs to further improve metrics such as latency, acceptance rate and cost to support more diverse scenarios, better service experiences, and richer mobile scenarios support and to enable service function chain (SFC) deployments that support multiple optimization targets. To address the challenges of smart and closed-loop SFC deployments in 5G Advanced and 6G, we first adopt the Markov Decision Process (MDP) model as an approach to capture the actual network traffic characteristics in networks. To minimize the latency and maximize the request acceptance rate, we prioritize requests so that requests with high real-time requirements can be processed first. To minimize the latency and deployment cost, we propose a deep reinforcement learning method with prioritization (ASPD) algorithm to effectively deploy and schedule requests with different Quality of Service (QoS) requirements. Extensive experimental results show that compared to FFT and Random algorithms, ASPD always uses the least amount of resources and nodes to obtain the highest payoff, in addition, ASPD reduces latency by 29.5% and 34.75%, respectively.

Keywords: Network function virtualization · Deep reinforcement learning · Service function chain · Markov Decision Process · Priority

1 Introduction

5G [21] is pioneering the process of moving from the consumer Internet with human connections, to the industrial Internet, with connections between

This work is supported by the National Natural Science Foundation of China under grant No. 62171218, and by the Industry-University-Research Cooperation Fund project of ZTE under grant No. 2022ZTE02-07.

humans, machines and objects. 5G advanced communication technologies prioritize the expansion and integration of application scenarios, focusing on new scenarios and new needs in vertical areas to further expand the application boundaries. In addition to ultra-reliable and low-latency communication (uRLLC) [18], future 5G Advanced and 6G still needs to further improve metrics such as latency, acceptance rate and cost expecting to support more diverse scenarios, better service experiences, and richer mobile scenarios. The advent of Network Function Virtualization (NFV) [4] has made network service deployment more flexible and agile by providing a novel way to design, orchestrate, deploy and standardize a variety of mobile services to support increasingly complex and variable customer requests.

In the 4G phase, SFC deployment has a single optimization goal of maximizing resource utilization, and the main mathematical model includes the abstraction and quantitative description of bandwidth, computational resources, storage, and other resources, resulting in a variety of SFCs for improving resource utilization. In the 5G Advanced and 6G phase, the basic development model in mobile communication needs to be changed to enable SFC deployments that support multiple optimization objectives. Among them, ultralow latency, ultrahigh acceptance rate and ultralow cost have become common metrics for integrated human-machine-object interconnections, and these common metrics are the basis for extending the application scenarios of 5G communication technologies and the key to realize the 6G vision [13].

Current SFC deployment approaches focus on optimizing network resource utilization while meeting various Quality of Service (QoS) constraints [20]. However, to meet the ultralow latency, ultrahigh acceptance rate and ultralow cost requirements of latency-sensitive mobile services in 5G Advanced and 6G networks, smart and closed-loop SFC deployment still faces some key challenges: (1) Different network entities may pursue different, or even conflicting, goals, such as lower latency, lower operating cost and higher acceptance rate; (2) The network traffic and state fluctuate over time due to changes in service demand.

Therefore, in this paper, To address the above challenges, we investigate the multi-objective SFC deployment scheduling problem, and we consider three objectives: first, the latency of all requests should be minimized to meet the QoS requirements; second, the deployment cost should be minimized; and third, the acceptance rate of the requests should be improved to deploy the SFC more efficiently. The existing methods of solving the deployment problem are mainly integer linear programming methods, evolutionary algorithms and heuristic algorithms, most of which can solve simple deployment problems well; however, for some more complex problems, such as multi-objective deployment problems, these methods have greater shortcomings. The emergence of deep reinforcement learning (DRL) [12] has changed the shortcomings of traditional algorithms by complementing the advantages of deep learning and reinforcement learning [16] and by being able to learn the policy of control directly from some high-dimensional initial data without human intervention. In this paper, we design a deep reinforcement learning method with prioritization (ASPD) to solve the multi-objective SFC deployment problem.

The contributions of this paper are as follows:

- To capture real-time network changes, we formulate the online SFC deployment problem using the MDP model, where network changes are automatically and continuously represented as MDP state transitions.
- Since physical resources are limited and some requests need to be processed in a timely manner, requests with high real-time should be prioritized, and then low real-time requests can use the remaining resources. In this paper, we define two priority levels - high priority and low priority - and specify that if more than one request arrive at the same time, the high priority request is processed first.
- To better solve the multi-objective SFC deployment problem, we propose a deep reinforcement learning method with prioritization (ASPD) to automatically deploy requests with different QoS requirements.

The rest of this paper is organized as follows: Sect. 2 discusses related works. Section 3 describes the system model and SFC deployment scheduling problem. In Sect. 4, we formally propose a deep reinforcement learning method with prioritization (ASPD). Sect. 5 provides performance analysis and finally, Sect. 6 concludes the paper.

2 Related Work

In recent years, there has been an increasing amount of research on the VNF placement problem. To achieve some specific optimization objectives, e.g., minimizing the number of occupied servers, minimizing the end-to-end delay and maximizing the acceptance rate of requests, some mathematical planning methods such as integer linear programming (ILP) and hybrid ILP (MILP), as well as heuristic algorithms for near-optimal solutions, are usually used. Addis *et al.* [1] proposed a VNF chain and placement model and designed a MILP formulation. Behrooz Farkiani *et al.* [6] studied the problem of deployment and reconfiguration of a set of chains with different priorities, and a MILP formulation of the problem and two solution algorithms were proposed. Li *et al.* [9] first formalized the VNF migration and SFC reconfiguration problem as a mathematical model aiming to minimize the end-to-end delay of all affected services and to guarantee network load balancing after simultaneous migration, and an improved hybrid genetic evolution (IHGE) algorithm was proposed to solve it. Yoshida *et al.* [19] proposed a multi-objective VNF placement method MORSA to minimize physical machine load and traffic within the data center. In [2], a novel fair-weighted affinity-based heuristic algorithm is proposed to deploy SFC to reduce the total turnaround time and the total traffic generated for complete end-to-end services in the service function chain. To solve the VNF placement and service chain allocation problem, Ruiz *et al.* [10] proposed a genetic algorithm that minimizes the service blocking rate and CPU usage considering computational resources and optical network capacity. Akhtar *et al.* [7] used binary integer programming (BIP) to study the placement of SFCs in edge networks with high data rates and ultralow latency.

From the above, it can be seen that there is still little research on solving SFC deployment problems with DRL, and it is worthwhile to study this issue more deeply. In addition, network traffic and state exhibit fluctuations across time due to changes in service demand, which is not considered in most of the literature, so in this paper, we design appropriate model to capture the uncertainty of network transitions and an adaptive dynamic adjustment mechanism to achieve automatic and closed-loop network management.

3   Problem Formulation

In this section, we first introduce the system model, notation and ideas used in this paper. We then formally present the SFC deployment problem formulation with objectives and constraints.

3.1   Network Model

We consider a network of NFV represented by an undirected graph $G = (N \cup S, E)$, where S denotes the set of switches, N and E denote the set of server nodes and physical edges, respectively. More specifically, $N = \{n_i \mid i \in [1, |N|]\}$ and $E = \{e_j \mid j \in [1, |E|]\}$, where n_i denotes the ith server and e_j denotes the jth physical edge. Each server can instantiate multiple VM to support multiple types of VNF. The set of VMs supporting VNFs is $M = \{m_i \mid i \in [1, |M|]\}$. Each switch $s \in S$ is used to forward traffic only.

Each server has a maximum capacity of computing resources, and $C_{n_i} = \{C_{n_i}^{cpu}, C_{n_i}^{mem}\}$ denotes the number of CPU and memory resources. Each physical edge $e_j \in E$ connects two servers. The physical edge e_j is denoted as a quaternion $\{n_{src}, n_{dst}, B_{e_j}, D_{e_j}\}$, where $n_{src}, n_{dst} \in N \cup S$ denotes the source and target nodes of e_j, B_{e_j} is the maximum bandwidth capacity, and D_{e_j} is the inherent propagation delay of edge e_j.

3.2   SFC Request Model

In this subsection, we use $R = \{r_\mu \mid \mu \in [1, |R|]\}$ to denote a set of SFC requests in the network, while r_μ denotes the μ-th SFC request. Any SFC request $r_\mu \in R$ is denoted as $\{f_1^\mu, \ldots, f_v^\mu, \ldots, f_{I_\mu}^\mu, B_\mu, D_\mu^{max}, \lambda_\mu\}$. This means that the SFC requests r_μ are sequentially passed through I_μ VNFs. B_μ, D_μ^{max} denote the minimum bandwidth and the maximum end-to-end delay tolerance. Considering the dynamic nature of the flow, the arrival rate of SFC request r_μ satisfies Poisson distribution with an average arrival rate of $\lambda\mu$.

The VNF set of SFC request r_μ is denoted as $F_\mu = \{f_v^\mu \mid v \in [1, I_\mu]\}$, where f_v^μ is the vth VNF used for request r_μ. For each VNF f_v^μ, we use $C_{f_v^\mu} = \{C_{f_v^\mu}^{cpu}, C_{f_v^\mu}^{mem}\}$ to denote the CPU and memory requirements, respectively.

In addition, we denote the set of virtual edges of SFC request r_μ as $E_\mu = \{e_h^\mu \mid h \in [1, I_\mu - 1]\}$, where e_h^μ is the hth virtual edge connecting VNF f_h^μ and VNF f_{h+1}^μ in SFC request r_μ.

3.3 Mapping Relationship

A VNF can be placed on any node $n_i \in N$ if the server node has sufficient resource capacity. We use a binary variable $x_{f_v^\mu}^{n_i}$ to indicate whether, in the request $r_\mu \in R$, the VNF f_v^μ is deployed on the server node $n_i \in N$ or not (1 or 0). $x_{e_h^\mu}^{e_j}$ indicates whether, in the request $r_\mu \in R$, the virtual link $e_h^\mu \in E_\mu$ is mapped to a physical link $e_j \in E$ (1 or 0).

In addition, to address the real-time network changes due to random arrivals and departures of requests, we introduce the concept of time slots [17]. We define list $R_\tau \in R$ to represent the requests that arrive at time slot τ. In each time slot, if a request arrives alone, it can be processed immediately; if multiple requests arrive at the same time, they are processed according to priority.

We use $\tau_r^s = m \times \Delta$ to denote the request arrival time and $\tau_r = l \times \Delta$ to denote the SFC survival time. In time slot τ, we use the binary $a_{r,\tau}$ to indicate whether the request $r_\mu \in R$ is still in service (1 or 0).

$$\forall r_\mu \in R : a_{r,\tau} = \begin{cases} 1, \tau_r^s \leq \tau < (\tau_r^s + \tau_r), \\ 0, \text{ otherwise.} \end{cases} \tag{1}$$

3.4 SFC Deployment Problem Formulation

Now, we present the mathematical formulation of the SFC deployment scheduling problem. We start with the constraints, followed by the objectives.

Resource constraint: Since multiple service instances of a VNF can be deployed on the same node to handle multiple requests, we use $s_{n_i,\tau}^{f_v^\mu}$ to denote the number of service instances of the VNF $f_v^\mu \in F_\mu$ deployed on the node $n_i \in N$. Thus, we have

$$\forall n_i \in N, f_v^\mu \in F_\mu : s_{n_i,\tau}^{f_v^\mu} = \sum_{r_\mu \in R} \sum_{1 \leq i \leq I_\mu}^{r_\mu(i) = f_v^\mu} x_{f_v^\mu}^{n_i} a_{r,\tau}, \tag{2}$$

where $r_\mu(i)$ represents the i-th VNF in the request.

If a server node has sufficient resources, multiple VNFs can be placed on the same server node, so the resources on the server are constrained to

$$\forall n_i \in N : \sum_{f_v^\mu \in F_\mu} s_{n_i,\tau}^{f_v^\mu} \cdot C_{f_v^\mu} \leq C_{n_i}. \tag{3}$$

Bandwidth constraint: Second, since the bandwidth requirement of all requests passing through the server node cannot exceed its total output bandwidth, the bandwidth constraint is

$$\forall e_j \in E : \sum_{r_\mu \in R} \sum_{e_h^\mu \in E_\mu} x_{e_h^\mu}^{e_j} \cdot a_{r,\tau} \cdot B_\mu \leq B_{e_j}. \tag{4}$$

Latency constraint: Finally, we introduce the latency constraint. We use D_μ to denote the total response latency of a request $r_\mu \in R$, which is the sum of the communication latency on the link, the processing latency on the server node, and the queuing latency. We use T_μ to denote the communication latency on the link.

$$\forall r_\mu \in R : T_\mu = \sum_{e_h^\mu \in E_\mu} \sum_{e_j \in E} x_{e_h^\mu}^{e_j} D_{e_j}, \tag{5}$$

The processing latency of a VNF instance is determined by the computing capacity of the VM and the type of VNF. Therefore, the processing latency may vary from VM to VM. $v_{m_i}^\mu$ indicates the processing rate. P_μ is defined to represent the total processing latency.

$$\forall f_v^\mu \in F_\mu, \forall n_i \in N, \forall r_\mu \in R : P_\mu^{n_i} = x_{f_v^\mu}^{n_i} \cdot \frac{1}{v_{m_i}^\mu - \lambda_\mu}, \tag{6}$$

$$\forall m_i \in M : v_{m_i}^\mu = \frac{\eta_{m_i}^\mu C_{m_i}}{w_{m_i}^\mu}, \tag{7}$$

$$\forall r_\mu \in R : P_\mu = \sum_{f_v^\mu \in F_\mu} \sum_{n_i \in N} P_\mu^{n_i}, \tag{8}$$

where C_{m_i} denotes the maximum aggregated processing capacity of the VM m_i, $w_{m_i}^\mu$ denotes the processing density of the VM m_i for SFC request r_μ, and $\eta_{m_i}^\mu$ denotes the CPU sharing rate on the VM m_i [11].

We define the queuing delay for high priority requests as W_{q1}, low priority as W_{q2}, and the average queuing delay as $\overline{W_q}$, satisfying the following equation.

$$(\lambda_1 + \lambda_2)\overline{W_q} = \lambda_1 W_{q1} + \lambda_2 W_{q2}, \tag{9}$$

In summary, the total response latency is

$$D_\mu = T_\mu + P_\mu + \overline{W_q}, \tag{10}$$

Therefore, the latency constraint is

$$\forall r_\mu \in R : D_\mu \leq D_\mu^{\max}. \tag{11}$$

In this paper, we have three objectives. Objective 1 is to minimize the total response latency, which can be expressed as

$$\min \sum_{r_\mu \in R} D_\mu, \tag{12}$$
$$s.t. \quad (1), (5) - (11).$$

Objective 2 is minimizing deployment cost, which can be expressed as

$$\min \quad C(\tau), \tag{13}$$
$$s.t. \quad (1) - (11), (14).$$

Deployment cost at each time slot τ: Only the operational cost of occupying the servers is considered here, and no other costs are taken into account. The total operation cost $C(\tau)$ in time slot τ thus is the sum of operation costs of all occupied servers, i.e.,

$$C(\tau) = \sum_{n_i \in N} \sum_{f_v^\mu \in F_\mu} x_{f_v^\mu}^{n_i} \zeta_c C_{n_i} + \sum_{e_j \in E} \sum_{e_h^\mu \in E_\mu} x_{e_h^\mu}^{e_j} \zeta_B B_{e_j}, \tag{14}$$

where ζ_c is the unit cost of server resource, while ζ_B is the unit cost of bandwidth.

Objective 3 is maximizing acceptance rate of requests. We find that this is equivalent to maximizing the total throughput of the accepted requests, which can be expressed as

$$\max \sum_{r_\mu \in R} y_{r_\mu} B_\mu \tau_r, \tag{15}$$

$$s.t. \quad (1) - (11), (16).$$

y_{r_μ} indicates whether request r_μ is accepted or not (1 or 0), and if request $r_\mu \in R$ is accepted, its total response delay D_μ cannot exceed its response delay limit D_μ^{max}, which can be expressed as follows:

$$\forall r_\mu \in R, y_{r_\mu} = \begin{cases} 1, & \text{if } D_\mu \leq D_\mu^{max}, \\ 0, & \text{if } D_\mu > D_\mu^{max}. \end{cases} \tag{16}$$

4 Proposed Algorithm

In this section, we present the proposed algorithm. First we capture the dynamic network state transitions with MDP. Then, we propose a deep reinforcement learning method with prioritization (ASPD) to automatically deploy SFCs.

4.1 Agent Design

Here, we detail the state, action, and reward representation of the MDP model. An MDP is usually defined as $<S, A, P, R>$, where S is a discrete set of states, A is a discrete set of actions, P is a set of transfer probability distributions, and R is a reward function.

(1) STATE

We define each state as a set of vectors $(C(t), W(t), R_{new}, R_{old}, I_t)$, where $C(t)$ denotes the remaining resources of nodes, while $W(t)$ denotes the remaining output bandwidth. R_{new} represents the new service requests, and the requests left over from the previous time slot are R_{old}. $I_t = (W_{r_\mu}, T_{r_\mu}^n, C_{f_v^\mu}, T_{r_\mu})$ denotes the characteristics of the VNF currently being processed, where W_{r_μ} is the bandwidth requirement, $T_{r_\mu}^n$ is the remaining latency space, $C_{f_v^\mu}$ denotes the resource requirement of VNF, and T_{r_μ} is the TTL of the request.

(2) ACTION

We denote the action $A = \{0, 1, 2, \ldots, |N|\}$ is the set of server indexes. $a = 0$ means that the VNF cannot be deployed; otherwise, it indicates the index of the server node, which means that we have successfully deployed the VNF on the a-th server node.

(3) REWARD

Since we want to jointly optimize the three objectives, we define the reward function as the weighted total accepted request throughput minus the weighted total deployment costs and the weighted total response latency to deploy the arriving requests, which can be combined with the three objectives.

$$R(s_t, a_t) = B_\mu \tau_r \cdot \varepsilon - C(\tau) \cdot \delta - D(\mu) \cdot \eta. \tag{17}$$

where ε, δ and η are weighting factors for each objective function.
Therefore, the total reward is

$$R_t = \sum_{k=0}^{\infty} \gamma^k R(s_{t+k}, a_{t+k}), \tag{18}$$

where $\gamma \in [0, 1]$ is the discount factor for the future reward.

4.2 Deep Reinforcement Learning Method with Prioritization (ASPD)

To allow adaptive online scheduling and deployment of SFCs, we propose a deep reinforcement learning method with prioritization (ASPD). The architecture of ASPD is illustrated in Fig. 1. In each time slot R_τ, the system first removes the time-out requests, then classifies all current requests R_τ into high and low priority according to real-time requirements, initializes the time slot τ. If the current request set R_τ is empty, the requests are moved to the next time slot; if they are not empty, the requests are deployed in order of priority, and the deployment strategy is to choose the appropriate action in each state to obtain the highest return and then update the network state. If all requests in the time slot τ have been processed, the time slot $\tau + 1$ is entered.

We use a PG-based approach [5] to train ASPD. Using PG, the strategy $\pi|S \times A$ is defined as a multi layer fully connected DNN Q^π based on back propagation network. It has one input layer, one output layer and several hidden layers. The input layer is the state vector and the output layer is the probability distribution of the actions. The number of hidden layers in the DNN and the width of each hidden layer are referenced to [17].

5 Evaluation and Analysis

5.1 Simulation Setup

The simulation is implemented in Python based on TensorFlow, a wider simulation environment for VNF resource allocation with a 2.6 GHz Intel (R) Core

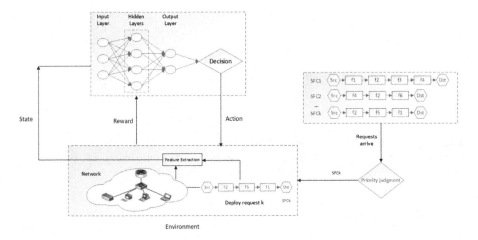

Fig. 1. The architecture of ASPD.

(TM) i5-11400 CPU processor and 16 GB memory. The parameters of network and SFC requests are all generated within the actual range to emulate a realistic environment [14,22]. The related parameters of the simulation are given below.

Network topology. We use a traditional NFV network topology based on the fat-tree architecture [15]. The number of servers is assumed to be between 12 to 100 and the computing power of each server is set to [10, 30] CPU cores and [32, 64] GB of memory [11]. The maximum processing capacity corresponding to each CPU core is 1000 cycles/sec. The output bandwidth of each server is set to [100 M, 100 G] bps, and the propagation delay is [2, 5] ms.

SFC requests. The requests we simulate are based on real-world traces in [4] with 7 VNF types in the network. We simulate between 50 and 300 requests, with the number of VNFs per request set to [1, 6]. We assume that packet arrival rate ranges from 1 to 100 packets/s [3]. The minimum required bandwidth for SFC requests is set to a randomly distributed number within the range (0, 10] Mbps [14]. In addition, the maximum tolerable latency per SFC request is set to [50, 100] ms [14]. Each VNF is considered as a network function requiring a CPU capacity of [1, 2] cores and a memory capacity of [2, 4] GB [16]. For the cost defined in Eq. (14), we set $\zeta_c = 0.2$ and $\zeta_B = 0.006$ [8].

5.2 Performance Evaluation

To evaluate the performance of ASPD, we compared it with two state-of-the-art algorithms, FFT (the VNF-placed nodes are the first ones fitted) and Random (the VNF-placed nodes are selected randomly). We study the comparison of each metric of the three algorithms when the number of requests scales from 50 to 300 with a server node of 12.

First, we compare the latencies of several algorithms. From Fig. 2, it can be seen that the ASPD always has the lowest latency and FFT has the highest

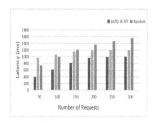
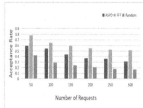
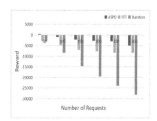

Fig. 2. Shows the latency comparison of three algorithms.

Fig. 3. Shows the acceptance rate comparison of three algorithms.

Fig. 4. Shows the reward comparison of three algorithms.

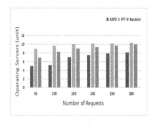
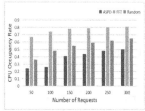
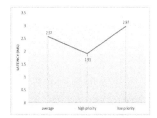

Fig. 5. Shows the mean operating servers comparison of three algorithms

Fig. 6. Shows the mean CPU usage comparison of three algorithms.

Fig. 7. Impact of prioritization and non-prioritization on latency.

latency when the number of requests is less than 100, while Random has the highest latency when the number of requests is greater than 100. We can conclude that the latency of ASPD is 29.5% and 34.75% smaller than the latencies of FFT and Random, respectively.

Figure 3 shows that the acceptance rate of FFT algorithm requests is the highest regardless of the number of requests. This is because FFT deploys VNFs as soon as it finds a suitable server node without considering other factors; therefore, as shown in Fig. 2 and Fig. 4, it sacrifices metrics such as latency and reward. The acceptance rate of Random is always the lowest, while the acceptance rate of ASPD is in the middle; although ASPD's acceptance rate is not as good as FFT's, from the other figures, we know that ASPD's other performance characteristics are far better than those of FFT.

Regarding rewards, as seen from Fig. 4, the reward of ASPD is always the largest. It can be seen that when the number of fixed server nodes is 12, the reward of ASPD is much larger than those of the other two algorithms: it is 65.67% and 86.34% larger than FFT and Random, respectively.

Next, we examine the total number of operating nodes in the service. Fig. 5 shows that ASPD always uses the fewest server nodes, while FFT always uses the most server nodes. It can be seen that ASPD and FFT, Random use 6.8, 9.9 and 8.9 computing nodes on average when the number of nodes is fixed at 12. In addition, we also evaluate the resource usage of the service nodes, as shown in Fig. 6, and we find that ASPD always has the lowest resource usage, using the fewest service nodes and resources regardless of whether the number of requests changes.

We investigate the effect of dividing priorities and not dividing priorities on SFCs. As shown in Fig. 7, the average queuing delay of an SFC is 2.57 ms without prioritization, and the average queuing delay is 1.91 ms for high priority and 2.97 ms for low priority when prioritization is divided. Without prioritization, SFCs with high real-time needs are likely to be queued and processed later, and the average total delay from entry to completion of processing for an SFC is 6.19 ms; this means that the minimum waiting time for an SFC with high real-time needs is at least 6.19 ms, which is likely to result in the SFC being rejected for processing due to exceeding the TTL, thus reducing the acceptance rate of the request. If we divide the priority, the average waiting delay of an SFC with high real-time needs can be reduced by 0.66 ms, and together with the other reductions in delays due to prioritizing, we conclude that it is necessary to divide the priority.

6 Conclusion

In this paper, to satisfy the strict and diverse QoS requirements and rapidly changing network traffic demands in future 5G Advanced and 6G networks, we propose a solution to the multi-objective SFC deployment scheduling problem. We first employ the MDP model as a method of capturing the actual network traffic characteristics in the network. To minimize the latency and maximize the request acceptance rate, we prioritize requests so that requests with high real-time requirements can be processed first; to minimize the latency and deployment cost, we propose a deep reinforcement learning method with prioritization (ASPD) algorithm to effectively deploy and schedule requests with different QoS requirements. Extensive experimental results show that ASPD always uses the fewest resources and nodes to obtain the highest returns compared to FFT and Random algorithms; in addition, ASPD has 29.5% and 34.75% less latency, respectively.

References

1. Addis, B., Belabed, D., Bouet, M., Secci, S.: Virtual network functions placement and routing optimization. In: 2015 IEEE 4th International Conference on Cloud Networking (CloudNet) (2015)
2. Bari, M.F., Chowdhury, S.R., Ahmed, R., Boutaba, R., Duarte, O.C.M.B.: Orchestrating virtualized network functions. IEEE Trans. Netw. Serv. Manag., 1 (2016)
3. Benson, T., Akella, A., Maltz, D.A.: Network traffic characteristics of data centers in the wild. In: ACM SIGCOMM Conference on Internet Measurement (2010)
4. Cui, C., Deng, H., Telekom, D., Michel, U., Damker, H.: Network functions virtualisation: an introduction, benefits, enablers, challenges and call for action (2012)

5. Deng, L., Hinton, G., Kingsbury, B.: New types of deep neural network learning for speech recognition and related applications: an overview. In: IEEE International Conference on Acoustics, Speech, and Signal Processing (ICASSP), May 2013

6. Farkiani, B., Bakhshi, B., Mirhassani, S.A., Wauters, T., Turck, F.D.: Prioritized deployment of dynamic service function chains. IEEE/ACM Trans. Netw. $\mathbf{PP}$(99), 1–15 (2021)

7. Farkiani, B., Bakhshi, B., MirHassani, S.A.: A fast near-optimal approach for energy-aware SFC deployment. IEEE Trans. Netw. Serv. Manag. $\mathbf{16}$(4), 1360–1373 (2019)

8. Huang, M., Liang, W., Ma, Y., Guo, S.: Maximizing throughput of delay-sensitive NFV-enabled request admissions via virtualized network function placement. IEEE Trans. Cloud Comput. $\mathbf{PP}$(99), 1 (2019)

9. Jang, I., Suh, D., Pack, S., Dan, G.: Joint optimization of service function placement and flow distribution for service function chaining. IEEE J. Sel. Areas Commun. $\mathbf{PP}$(11), 1 (2017)

10. Kuo, T.W., Liou, B.H., Lin, C.J., Tsai, M.J.: Deploying chains of virtual network functions: on the relation between link and server usage. IEEE/ACM Trans. Netw. $\mathbf{26}$, 1562–1576 (2018)

11. Li, B., Cheng, B., Liu, X., Wang, M., Chen, J.: Joint resource optimization and delay-aware virtual network function migration in data center networks. IEEE Trans. Netw. Serv. Manag. $\mathbf{PP}$(99), 1 (2021)

12. Liu, Y., Lu, Y., Li, X., Qiao, W., Zhao, D.: SFC embedding meets machine learning: deep reinforcement learning approaches. IEEE Commun. Lett. $\mathbf{PP}$(99), 1 (2021)

13. Nekovee, M.: Transformation from 5G for verticals towards a 6G-enabled internet of verticals. arXiv e-prints (2021)

14. Pei, J., Hong, P., Xue, K., Li, D.: Efficiently embedding service function chains with dynamic virtual network function placement in geo-distributed cloud system. IEEE Trans. Parallel Distrib. Syst. $\mathbf{30}$(10), 2179–2192 (2019)

15. Sun, Y., Chen, J., Liu, Q., Fang, W.: Diamond: An improved fat-tree architecture for large-scale data centers. J. Commun. $\mathbf{9}$(1), 91–98 (2014)

16. Tao, M., Kaibin, H.: Special topic on machine learning at network edges. ZTE Commun. $\mathbf{18}$((70)02), 5+34 (2020)

17. Xiao, Y., Zhang, Q., Liu, F., Wang, J., Zhang, J.: NFVdeep: adaptive online service function chain deployment with deep reinforcement learning. In: The International Symposium (2019)

18. Yang, P., Kong, L., Chen, G.: Spectrum sharing for 5G/6G URLLC: research frontiers and standards. IEEE Commun. Stand. Mag. $\mathbf{PP}$(99), 1–12 (2021)

19. Yoshida, M., Shen, W., Kawabata, T., Minato, K., Imajuku, W.: MORSA: a multi-objective resource scheduling algorithm for NFV infrastructure. In: 2014 16th Asia-Pacific Network Operations and Management Symposium (APNOMS) (2014)

20. Yu, S., Bo, J., Gupta, G.R., Du, X., Lin, Y.: Provably efficient algorithms for joint placement and allocation of virtual network functions. In: IEEE INFOCOM 2017 - IEEE Conference on Computer Communications (2017)

21. Zhang, Y.: Network Function Virtualization: Concepts and Applicability in 5G Networks (Concepts and Applicability in 5G Networks). Network Function Virtualization (2018)

22. Xu, Z., Liang, W., Xia, Q., Xu, W., Galis, A.: Throughput optimization for admitting NFV-enabled requests in cloud networks (2018)

Network Link Status Classification Method Based on Graph Autoencoder

Guoli Feng[1], Ning Wang[1], Run Ma[1], Wenbin Wei[1], Xiaobo Li[1], and Peng Lin[2(✉)]

[1] Information and Telecommunication Company, State Grid Ningxia Electric Power Company, Ningxia, China
[2] Beijing Vectinfo Technologies Co., Ltd., Beijing, China
737662744@qq.com

Abstract. In recent years, with the rapid development of the Internet, the amount of data in the network increases exponentially, and people have higher requirements on the quality of network links, which poses new challenges to network management and analysis. Network link status classification can be used to predict network link status categories by using the current network topology information and feature information, facilitating network management and analysis. However, most of the existing models consider to predict the time sequence information of the link status without considering the topology information and node attributes of the network. Therefore, we design a network link status classification model based on graph autoencoder for computer network scenarios. The attention mechanism is introduced into the encoder, and then the node vector is spliced into edge vector, which is then input into the multi-layer perceptron for classification. Finally, the feasibility and validity of the link status classification model are verified on two datasets.

Keywords: Link prediction · Graph autoencoder · Multilayer perceptron · Node embedding

1 Introduction

For network link status prediction, the network topology information, node attribute information and link status information are used to predict the link status of the network, such as link load, link quality, and link existence, which is convenient for network management and analysis. With the development and popularization of Internet technology, people have higher and higher requirements on network link status. Abnormal link status will have a great impact on the transmission of real-time video and other information. By predicting the status of network links, network administrators can predict the status of network links in advance, thus processing some abnormal link status in advance, and providing a better network environment for users.

Link status data, which contains information about nodes in a network and links between nodes, can be modeled and represented using networks. At present, most of the researches on link status prediction at home and abroad are applied to the prediction of

© The Author(s), under exclusive license to Springer Nature Singapore Pte Ltd. 2023
W. Quan (Ed.): ICENAT 2022, CCIS 1696, pp. 405–416, 2023.
https://doi.org/10.1007/978-981-19-9697-9_33

link existence. These link prediction methods can be roughly divided into similarity based methods, probability and statistics based methods, machine learning based methods and graph embedding based methods [1]. In addition, the existing link status prediction methods focused more on the fitting of link status and time sequence, rather than using network topology information and node attributes to predict link status. For example, Xu et al. proposed a new traffic network status prediction model for freeways based on a generative adversarial framework, which can effectively predict future traffic network status [2].

In this paper, we propose a link status classification method based on graph autoencoder. The main structure of the model is realized based on the basic model of graph autoencoder, in which the attention mechanism is introduced in the encoder part, and the decoder part is replaced by the multilayer perceptron classifier. In this way, the node features and topology information of the network can be extracted, and we can predict the category of a link according to the link status evaluation index proposed in this paper. In this paper, simulation experiments are performed on LT-DATA and Network-DATA, and it is compared with existing algorithms to evaluate the model's performance and prove the effectiveness of LSC-GAE.

2   Related Work

In recent years, graph embedding method has been widely used in graph analysis tasks such as node classification, node clustering, link prediction and product recommendation due to its superior performance. Traditional graph embedding methods fall into three categories. The first is a method of modeling graph structures, such as DeepWalk [3], Node2vec [4]. The second is the method of modeling node features, such as NEU [5] and so on. The next is the method of joint modeling of graph structure and node features, like DNGR [6] et al. However, the methods above do not allow learning of complex graphs.

Graph autoencoder, as a new graph embedding method, performs very well. Kipf et al. proposed a variational graph autoencoder model, which is a framework for unsupervised learning on graph structure data, consisting of a simple encoder-decoder structure, which achieved good results in link prediction tasks [7]. Most graph autoencoders use graph convolutional neural networks as encoders, but Salha et al. used simple linear encoders to replace GCN encoders for training, and proved that simple encoders can also achieve good results [8]. Petar et al. proposed graph attention networks, which does not need to use Laplacian matrix to carry out complex calculation, but only updates node features through the representation of a neighbor node, and does not need to know graph structure in advance [9]. Rayyan et al. Proposed a framework for generating variational graph datasets, which was named epitomic VGAE(EVGAE), and it improved the generative capability of VGAE [10].

3   Link Status Prediction Method Based on Graph Autoencoder

In this section, we describe our proposed LSC-GAE. First, we introduce the overall architecture in Sect. 3.1. Then, we describe node feature extraction module and link status classification module in turn. Finally, we propose a link status evaluation model in Sect. 3.4.

3.1 Overall Architecture

An undirected weighted graph is used to describe a network, and the graph is defined as $G = (V, E)$ with $N = |V|$ nodes. The adjacency matrix A and the feature matrix $X \in R^{N \times d}$ of the graph G is input into the encoder, where d is the dimension of the node's feature matrix. As for the adjacency matrix A, if the value of A_{ij} is zero, it shows that node V_i and node V_j is disconnected. If the value of A_{ij} is not zero, it demonstrates there is a path of chain between V_i and V_j, and A_{ij} is the value of the link status evaluation indicator after 0–1 normalization. The link status evaluation indicator will be introduced in detail in Sect. 3.4.

In this paper, a Link Status Classification Method Based on Graph Autoencoder is proposed, which is called LSC-GAE for short. The main part of the model is based on the original graph autoencoder structure, that can extract the topological information and node information of the network at the same time, and use the extracted node features to classify link status.

The overall framework is shown in Fig. 1, which is divided into two modules: node feature extraction module and link status classification module.

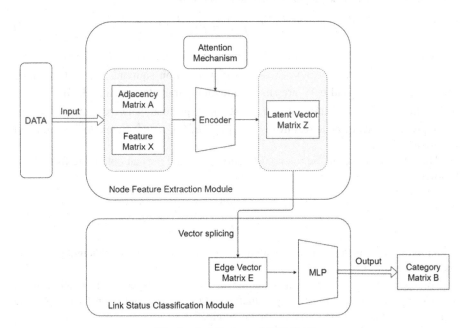

Fig. 1. Architecture of LSC-GAE

The node feature extraction module uses two-layer encoder and introduces attention mechanism to extract node features of the link. The input of the module is the weighted adjacency matrix of the network and the feature matrix of the node, and the hidden layer in the middle is obtained through coding, which contains the extracted feature vector of the node.

The link status classification module uses the information of the middle layer of the link existence prediction module to classify the link status. The input of this module is implicit vector matrix Z. Then we splice the vectors of nodes in pairs to obtain the edge vector matrix E, which is input into multi-layer Perception (MLP) for classification, and finally obtain the category matrix B.

3.2 Node Feature Extraction Module

In the existing graph autoencoder models, graph convolutional neural networks are used to extract node features. In the model of this paper, for the encoder part of the model, attention mechanism is introduced to encode the graph structure and node features into a unified representation, which is used to process the adjacency matrix A and the feature matrix X. And then the middle layer, namely the embedding of nodes, is obtained.

In general, the encoder layer can be defined as:

$$Z = \text{Att}(A, X) \tag{1}$$

$\text{Att}(\cdot)$ adopts a two-layer attention network. For adjacent nodes V_i and V_j, the correlation between the kth layer is calculated as follows:

$$e_{ij}^{(k)} = \sigma\left(p_1^{(k)T} W^{(k)} h_i^{(k-1)} + p_2^{(k)T} W^{(k)} h_j^{(k-1)}\right) \tag{2}$$

wherein, $e_{ij}^{(k)}$ is the attention coefficient, representing the correlation between nodes V_i and V_j at the kth layer. $\sigma(\cdot)$ is the activation function sigmoid, whose formula is $\sigma(x) = \frac{1}{1+e^{-x}}$. $p_1^{(k)}$ and $p_2^{(k)}$ are shared attention parameters of layer k. $W^{(k)}$ is the weight matrix of the kth layer, which is used to apply parameterized linear changes. $h^{(k)}$ represents a set of node features $h^{(k)} = [h_0^{(k)}, h_1^{(k)}, \cdots, h_{n-1}^{(k)}]$, and $h^{(0)}$ is the input feature matrix X.

Then, the softmax function is used to normalize, and we can obtain the formula as follows:

$$\alpha_{ij}^{(k)} = \frac{exp(e_{ij}^{(k)})}{\sum_{u \in N_i} exp(e_{iu}^{(k)})} \tag{3}$$

Among it, $\alpha_{ij}^{(k)}$ is the normalized attention coefficient, and N_i is the neighborhood of node i.

By aggregating the node representation of the $(k-1)^{\text{th}}$ layer in the neighborhood of node i according to the weight parameter and normalized attention coefficient, the expression of node i at the kth layer can be obtained as:

$$h_i^{(k)} = \sum_{j \in N_i} \alpha_{ij}^{(k)} W^{(k)} h_j^{(k-1)} \tag{4}$$

After applying 2-layer attention encoder, we can get the representation matrix of middle layer node $Z = [h_0^{(2)}, h_1^{(2)}, \cdots, h_{n-1}^{(2)}]$.

3.3   Link Status Classification Module

Classifier. The link status classification module uses MLP classifier to classify link status. The input of the module is the implicit vector matrix Z obtained after coding in the node feature extraction module. In the implicit vector matrix, the ith row vector represents the node vector Z_i, which contains the node embedding information of node i. For the vector of each node, splicing operation is performed in pairs to obtain an edge vector, and all the edge vectors form the edge vector matrix. Figure 2 shows the process of node vector splicing.

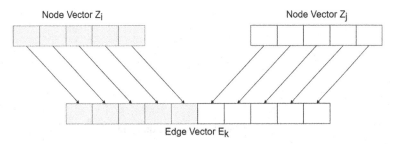

Fig. 2. Splicing diagram of node vector

The training set adjacency matrix and node feature matrix in the network are input into the encoder, and the original data are mapped to the hidden layer space, where each node vector in the hidden layer space fused the node feature information and network structure information. Then two node vectors are spliced, and the spliced vector contains the information of the nodes at both ends, which can be regarded as the edge vector between the two nodes. The subsequent classification and prediction operations can be carried out by using the edge vector.

The structure of the classifier is shown in Fig. 3. Assuming that the number of categories of network link status is n, we first input the edge vector matrix E into the MLP classifier. And the feature representation of the edge are mapped to the sample marker space through two full-connection layers. Next, each edge will generate a score for each category, and then output an N-dimensional vector. Then input the n-dimensional vector into the softmax layer, and a probability value will be generated for each category. The one with the highest probability corresponds to the category to which the front edge belongs.

Loss Function. In this module, the classification loss is calculated by weighted cross entropy. In the calculation of the loss, the correct category label of the link status needs to be one-hot coded first.

In the training set, the adjacency matrix of the network is sparse, and most of them are link-less. In the existing links, the sample number of each link status category is unbalanced, and the number of each category varies greatly. Therefore, it is necessary to assign weight to each category when calculating the loss value. Otherwise, the model will be difficult to obtain accurate results during training, and will prefer the category with more samples, resulting in large errors in the results.

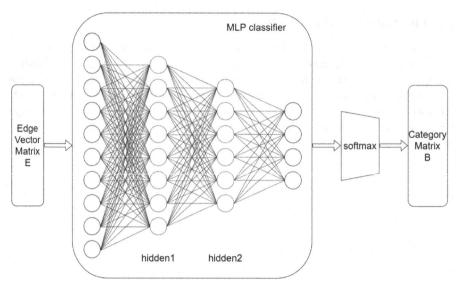

Fig. 3. Classifier structure diagram

The loss function of this module is defined as follows:

$$L = -\sum_{i=1}^{n} y_i \log \widehat{y}_i \tag{5}$$

$$Loss_\beta = mean(Weight_{class} \cdot L) \tag{6}$$

where, L is the cross entropy loss of the classification. y_i Represents the ith value of the actual tag, and $\widehat{y}_i$ represents the value of the ith element in the output vector of softmax. mean(x) Function means you take the mean of x. And $Weight_{class}$ is the weight calculated for each category based on the number of samples in the training set.

3.4   Link Status Evaluation Model

In order to ensure the scientificity and credibility of the link status index in this paper, the index design does not adopt the method of artificial weight, but uses the weight method to objectively assign the attribute. This method measures the weight of each item from the two dimensions of the difference and correlation degree of indicators, and comprehensively considers the comparative strength of indicators and the conflict between indicators. First of all, dimensionless processing is required for each attribute. If it is a positive indicator, it is forward processing; if it is a backward indicator, it is backward processing. Finally, the values of all attributes are in the range of (0,1). Then the standard deviation of each attribute is calculated to measure the variability, and the correlation coefficient between attributes is calculated to measure the conflict. The information amount of each attribute is obtained by multiplying the connected values, and the final weight is calculated by normalization of the information amount.

In this paper, two data sets are used for simulation experiments, which is shown in details in Sect. 4.1. As the link attributes of the two data sets are slightly different, the calculation formulas for the link status indicators of the two data sets are also slightly different, which will be introduced respectively in the following sections.

For LT-DATA, the result of weight calculation of CRITIC is shown in the following table:

Table 1. CRITIC weight calculation results of LT-DATA

Attribute name	Index variability	Index conflict	Information quantity	Weight
Average inbound bandwidth usage, AIBU	0.177	2.427	0.429	32.68%
Average outbound bandwidth usage, AOBU	0.169	2.495	0.423	32.23%
Delay, D	0.107	2.925	0.314	23.94%
Packet loss rate, PL	0.052	2.818	0.146	11.15%

Therefore, in LT-DATA, the calculation formula of the link status comprehensive evaluation index is as follows:

$$\text{Link\_status} = 32.68\% \cdot \text{AIBU} + 32.23\% \cdot \text{OBU} + 23.94\% \cdot \text{D} + 11.15\% \cdot \text{PL} \quad (7)$$

For Network-DATA, the result of weight calculation of CRITIC is shown in the following table:

Table 2. CRITIC weight calculation results of Network-DATA

Attribute name	Index variability	Index conflict	Information quantity	Weight
Link utilization, LU	0.094	1.474	0.139	33.25%
Throughput, T	0.042	1.204	0.050	11.99%
Delay, D	0.123	1.865	0.229	54.77%

Thus, in Network-DATA, the calculation formula of the link status comprehensive evaluation index is as follows:

$$\text{Link\_status} = 33.25\% \cdot \text{LU} + 11.99\% \cdot \text{T} + 54.77\% \cdot \text{D} \quad (8)$$

Based on the link status indicator, the link status between nodes is classified into the following categories in Table 3. A larger number indicates a better link status, that is, a higher link utilization and throughput, and a lower delay and packet loss rate. Based on the value of the link status indicator, the link status is divided into five categories, as shown in the following table:

Table 3. Link status classification table

Link status indicator value	Link status category
$0.7 <$ value ≤ 1.0	Overload
$0.5 <$ value ≤ 0.7	Congestion
$0.3 <$ value ≤ 0.5	Normal
$0.0 <$ value ≤ 0.3	Idle
Value $= 0.0$	No link

4   Experiments

4.1   Datasets

In this paper, we use two datasets to evaluate the validity of the LSC-GAE model. The description of them is shown as follows:

LT-DATA is a dataset that deployed lots of backbone routers in many Chinese cities by a mobile operator. In this data set, the characteristics of nodes include router load, average incoming bytes per second, average outgoing bytes per second and node delay. Link attributes include eleven dimensions, including link bandwidth, average inbound bandwidth usage, average outbound bandwidth growth rate, peak inbound bandwidth usage, peak inbound bandwidth growth rate, delay, and packet loss rate.

Network-DATA is a dataset that was simulated by a laboratory. They use OPNET to build a network, and simulate the packet operation and data flow between nodes. The data in this dataset is extracted from the network structure by summarizing and recording these sampled values. This dataset contains 686 router nodes, 63 switch nodes, and 1 server node, with a total of 756 links. In this data set, node features include node CPU utilization, experiment, node load, bytes of traffic received per second, number of packets received per second, bytes of traffic sent per second and other 12 dimensions. Link attributes include three dimensions: link throughput, link utilization, and delay. Since this topic does not involve time sequence information, the node and link information of one time point are selected for simulation experiment.

4.2   Compare Algorithm and Evaluation Index

Compare Algorithm.   To verify the performance of the improved model, we selected three comparison algorithms to replace the encoder part of the model, and then the experimer representation of a node, and the subsequent link prediction operations.

VGAE [7] is a variant of GAE that maps lower-dimensional vectors of nodes to a distribution (such as a Gaussian distribution), sampling to obtain an implicit vector matrix, and decoding, finally process the link prediction task.

Linear-VGAE [8] is a variant of VGAE that no longer uses GCN as an encoder, but instead replaces GCN with a simple linear model, with an inner product decoder for the decoder part.

Evaluation Index. In the link status classification experiment, we use accuracy, weighted-F1, weighted-precision and weighted-recall to evaluate the experimental results.

4.3 Simulation Results

Among all the models, we selected 0.02 to be the learning rate. The dimensions of each layer of MLP classifier were 16, 8, and 5 respectively. In the actual training, because the LT-data dataset had no node features, it was more difficult to fit, and the epoch number was 5000. The node features of Network-data are rich, and the loss of the model has converged when there are about 1200 epochs, so the number of epochs selected is 2000.

The following figures show the results of the link status classification task. As you can see, LSC-GAE gets the best performance, which means that increasing the attention mechanism on the encoder is effective (Fig. 4).

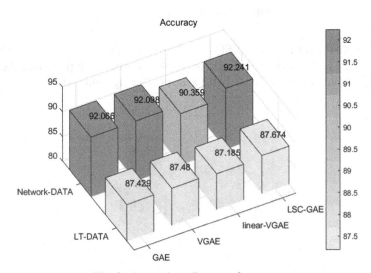

Fig. 4. Comparison diagram of accuracy

In LT-DATA, accuracy of LSC-GAE has improved by 0.175%, 0.143%, 1.882% compared with GAE, VGAE and linear-VGAE, respectively. In Network-DATA, accuracy of LSC-GAE has increased by 0.309% on average (Fig. 5).

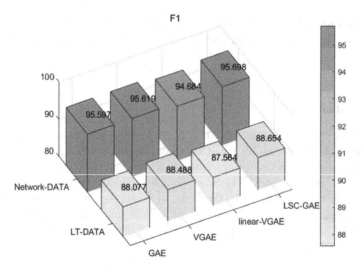

Fig. 5. Comparison diagram of F1

In LT-DATA, the F1 score of LSC-GAE is basically the same as GAE and VGAE, but it's 0.712% higher than linear-GAE. In Network-DATA, GAE performed the worst, with a significant difference of nearly 0.5% from other algorithms (Fig. 6).

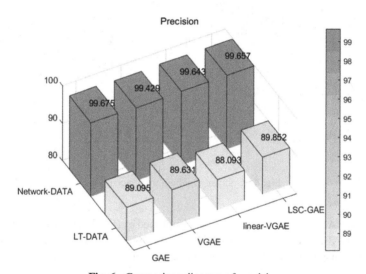

Fig. 6. Comparison diagram of precision

In LT-DATA, the precision of the four models is not much different. In Network-DATA, although GAE is slightly better than LSC-GAE in precision, our method has improved significantly in accuracy, F1 and recall. And linear-VGAE seems to get the worst score in Network-DATA due to its simplified encoder, which is 1.4% lower than other algorithms on average (Fig. 7).

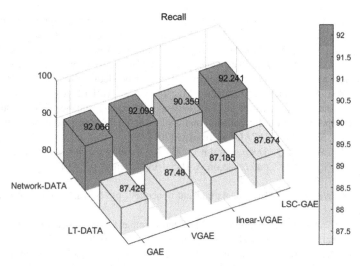

Fig. 7. Comparison diagram of recall

In LT-DATA, the recall score of LSC-GAE performed the best, which is averagely 0.73% higher than the other models. In Network-DATA, LSC-GAE, GAE and VGAE are almost the same, and LSC-GAE got the best score of 87.674%. Compared with other methods, LSC-GAE has certain improvement in the performance of accuracy, F1 and recall indicators. In addition, we propose a link status evaluation model and a method to classify and predict link status, which is generally meaningful.

5   Conclusion

In this paper, a link status classification model based on graph autoencoder is proposed, which can predict the status category of network link and facilitate network analysis and management. In addition, we put forward the evaluation index of link status that can classify the link running status. Experimental results show that LSC-GAE has good performance and can complete the task of link status classification. In the future, new algorithms can be designed to directly predict link attribute values instead of categories.

Acknowledgment. The project was supported by the science and technology project of State Grid Ningxia Electric Power Company "Research and Application of Twin-based Power Communication Superposition Control Network Technology "(5229XT220001)".

References

1. Mutlu, E.C., Oghaz, T., Rajabi, A., et al.: Review on learning and extracting graph features for link prediction. Mach. Learn. Knowl. Extract. **2**(4), 672–704 (2020)
2. Xu, D., Peng, P., Wei, C., et al.: Road traffic network state prediction based on a generative adversarial network. IET Intel. Transport Syst. **14**(10), 1286–1294 (2020)

3. Perozzi, B., Al-Rfou, R., Skiena, S.: Deepwalk: Online learning of social representations. In: Proceedings of the 20th ACM SIGKDD international conference on Knowledge discovery and data mining, pp. 701–710. Association for Computing Machinery, New York (2014)

4. Grover, A., Leskovec, J.: node2vec: Scalable feature learning for networks. In: Proceedings of the 22nd ACM SIGKDD international conference on Knowledge discovery and data mining, pp. 855–864. Association for Computing Machinery, New York (2016)

5. Yang, C., Sun, M., Liu, Z., et al.: Fast network embedding enhancement via high order proximity approximation. In: 26th International Joint Conference on Artificial Intelligence (IJCAI), pp. 3894–3900. IJCAI, FREIBURG (2017)

6. Cao, S., Lu, W., Xu, Q.: Deep neural networks for learning graph representations. In: Proceedings of the AAAI Conference on Artificial Intelligence, pp. 1145–1152. AAAI Press, Phoenix (2016)

7. Kipf, T.N., Welling, M.: Variational graph auto-encoders, pp. 1–3. arXiv preprint arXiv:1611.07308, (2016)

8. Salha, G., Hennequin, R., Vazirgiannis, M.: Keep it simple: Graph autoencoders without graph convolutional networks, pp. 1–8, arXiv preprint arXiv:1910.00942, (2019)

9. Veličković, P., Cucurull, G., Casanova, A., et al.: Graph attention networks, pp. 1–12, arXiv preprint arXiv:1710.10903, (2017)

10. Khan, R.A., Anwaar, M.U., Kleinsteuber, M: Epitomic variational graph autoencoder. In: 2020 25th International Conference on Pattern Recognition (ICPR), pp. 7203–7210. IEEE, Milan (2021)

Deployment of Asynchronous Traffic Shapers in Data Center Networks

Xiaoxi Liu[(⊠)], Wei Su, and Gaofeng Hong

School of Electronics and Information Engineering, Beijing Jiaotong University, Beijing, China
{20120074,wsu,honggf}@bjtu.edu.cn

Abstract. With the proliferation of distributed applications in data centers and the increase in latency-sensitive flows, it has become increasingly important to provide deterministic latency guarantees for business flows. The main component of business flow latency in the data center is queuing latency. Existing congestion control methods work in a passive reaction working approach, which can neither determine the queuing delay nor guarantee zero data loss. In this situation, this paper proposes a mechanism to deploy asynchronous traffic shapers on the Layer 3 switches of the data center network from the network side perspective. This mechanism shapes the data flow at each hop switch, which can prevent buffer overflow and packet loss, thus improving the deterministic performance of the data center network latency guarantee. We built a large Layer 2 data center network for simulation to verify the asynchronous traffic shaping mechanism based on laboratory conditions and we found that the shaping mechanism has deterministic delay guarantee capability, which can improve the delay deterministic performance of the network.

Keywords: Asynchronous Traffic Shaping · Data Center Network · Deterministic Latency

1 Introduction

Data Center is an important Internet infrastructure for storing and computing network resources. The core part of Data Center is Data Center Network (DCN). DCN is responsible for connecting hundreds of thousands or even millions of servers. DCN carries the north-south access traffic and the east-west internal traffic. In the past decade, DCNs have been growing rapidly in terms of both size and link speed. At the same time, the rise of online services in DCNs and the widespread use of distributed technologies have led to more and more extensive communication between servers and an increasing proportion of east-west traffic, resulting in an increasingly severe long-tail effect of packet transmission latency within the network. Therefore, it is particularly important to control the transmission of east-west traffic in the DCN effectively at present.

There are many types of stuff traffic in data center networks, such as web search, remote calls, data mining, distributed user queries, and other application traffic. What they have in common is that they are all interactive user-oriented business flows with

© The Author(s), under exclusive license to Springer Nature Singapore Pte Ltd. 2023
W. Quan (Ed.): ICENAT 2022, CCIS 1696, pp. 417–429, 2023.
https://doi.org/10.1007/978-981-19-9697-9_34

strict requirements on the duration of flow completion time and need flexible and reliable transmission strategy [1]. Their typical working model is based on the branch aggregation workflow model [2]. First, the master node slices and distributes the user requests to the lower-level worker nodes layer by layer. Then, lower-level worker nodes process the received requests and generate partial results. Finally, the results are aggregated layer by layer to the master node and the final result is returned to the user. In this process, the data flow, such as request flows and result flows, have strict latency requirements. If they are not delivered within a specific deadline, they will be discarded, with the result of degrading the network quality of service and wasting the occupied bandwidth [3]. Therefore, deterministic latency is an important performance in data centers today, especially for latency-sensitive applications and microsecond mission-critical requests. Modern data center network hardware provides ultra-low processing latency, so the latency of flows in DCNs is mainly queuing latency. So providing queuing latency guarantee capability will be extremely important for DCNs.

To address the latency assurance capability, the challenge to be faced is the TCP incast phenomenon and the burst cascade effect of traffic. "TCP incast" is common in DCNs, referring to a "many-to-one" communication pattern. This happens when a parent server makes a request to a cluster of servers and all the nodes in the cluster receive the request and respond to it almost simultaneously. A lot of TCP answer flows will be transmitted at the same time, from the child server to the parent server, thus creating a "micro-burst". The buffers in data center switches are relatively shallow, so "Incast" can easily cause the buffers to overflow, resulting in traffic crashes [4]. In addition, in the Ethernet scheduling mechanism, traffic passing through each hop forwarding device will cause the burst size of the flow to grow. This growth in turn affects the burst size of other flows at the next hop. This phenomenon is called cascading of burst traffic, and both it and TCP Incast lead to uncontrollable delay boundary calculations.

Current traffic control strategies for data center networks focus on congestion control, load balancing, routing policies, etc. The control points are generally located on the sending or receiving side, i.e., the network side, with little consideration given to traffic control on the network side, i.e., the per-hop switch.

Therefore, this paper focuses on the network side, deploying traffic shaping mechanisms on switches in data center networks, and describes schemes that help build deterministic latency data center networks.

Traffic shaping is a measure that actively adjusts the output rate of traffic. By limiting traffic with bursts, messages are sent outward at a more uniform rate. Traffic shaping can limit the rate at which micro-burst flows are sent over the link in a data center network. And deploying shaping policies at each hop switch to eliminate the burst cascade effect can effectively reduce the impact of burst traffic and improve the deterministic guarantee of network latency.

In addition, according to the mixed traffic characteristics of the data center network where sporadic and periodic flows coexist and sporadic flows are predominant and periodic flows have irregular cycles, IEEE 802.1Qcr Asynchronous Traffic Shaping (ATS) [5] is adopted. The features of ATS:

- Zero congestion loss without time sync

- A shaper state machine for a set of streams, and the right shaper applied to the packet upfront of the queue
- Smoothen traffic patterns by re-shaping per hop
- Prioritize urgent traffic over relaxed traffic

In summary, ATS operates asynchronously based on the local clock in each bridge. It can improve link utilization for mixed traffic types while effectively reducing the scaling pressure and economic stress associated with clock synchronization. In addition, additional NICs or switching devices are not required by the ATS. The only requirement is to add new software features at the existing switch, so it is easier to have a wide range of deployment and application. In ATS, the interleaving shaper calculates a qualified send time for each flow with assigned priority to achieve the shaping of the output rate of the traffic, thus reducing the send rate of the traffic out of the switch port, reducing the buffer overflow, and mitigating the network incast phenomenon and burst traffic cascade effect.

The rest of this paper is structured as follows: Sect. 2 presents the related work and the basic idea of P4-based network traffic shaping scheduling for data centers. Section 3 describes the module design of the ATS system. In Sect. 4, we make a simple experimental demonstration of the system's delay guarantee capability based on the data center network layer 2 topology. Finally, a short conclusion is given.

2 Related Work

The current traffic control strategies in data centers can be divided into two main types: synchronous and asynchronous.

2.1 Synchronous Scheme

One synchronization scheme is to use centralized control to achieve global optimality. The central arbiter is responsible for assigning time slots and transmission paths to each packet, which theoretically avoids conflicts between scheduled packets. Fastpass was proposed by J. Perry et al. in 2004. All senders in the network establish communication with the central arbiter, which uses fast maximal matching to calculate the transmission rate and transmission path specified by the flow and sends it down to the sender. This traffic control is fine-grained, avoiding conflicts and queuing delays and achieving high bandwidth utilization.

Synchronization schemes also include distributed control, typically using reconfigurable electrical switches and time-division multiplexing mechanisms. RotorNet [6] and Opera [7] are all circuit switching design approaches with distributed control. The allocation of link capacity is achieved through time-varying methods based on fixed scheduling and traffic demand. However, distributed control often creates a bandwidth tax problem. This is path redundancy which is caused by insufficient matching of workflows to the network structure and inadequate network configuration. It results in wasted bandwidth.

2.2 Asynchronous Scheme

Asynchronous solutions can currently be divided into two categories: sender control and receiver control. Sender control means that the scheduling decision is made on the sender side. M. Alizadeh et al. proposed DCTCP [8] in 2010. DCTCP detects the current congestion level by identifying the queue length of the switch and sends an ECN signal to inform the receiver, correspondingly, the receiver will send back an ECN echo to the sender, which receives it and adjusts the sending window. This accomplishes congestion control. DCTCP provides the basis and direction for researching new protocols suitable for data center network transmission. Two years later, M. Alizadeh et al. proposed High-bandwidth Ultra-Low Latency (HULL) [9], an upgraded version of DCTCP. HULL reduces the transmission time of small streams by reserving transmission bandwidth for them through advanced ECN tagging.

The sender control flow scheduling is scalable and reliable and can be fully implemented on the host side. However, blindly scheduling traffic based on shortest flow first (SFF) or shortest remaining traffic first (SRTF) can cause congestion within the data center network. Because the sender cannot have visibility of the traffic information elsewhere. This causes the flow to be sent out but blocked in the intermediate switch or the queue on the receiving side. In addition, sender-driven scheduling can only respond passively after congestion occurs, which becomes impractical in high-speed network environments.

Receiver control means that scheduling decisions are made at the receiver side. Packets are controlled for transmission based on current network state information, mostly belonging to active queue congestion solutions. Typical method is pHost [2] proposed by P. X. Gao in 2015 and ExpressPass [10] proposed by I. Cho et al. in 2017, which is a credit-based congestion control protocol.

Receiver-controlled flow scheduling senses network state changes more quickly than sender-driven flow scheduling. However, implementing receiver-driven scheduling requires modifications to the entire network protocol stack. The receive-side driven approach tends to trigger first RTT wastage due to the presence of ECN send times. In addition, the receive-side control generally assumes that congestion occurs only at the last-hop ToR switch.

In summary, the control point of synchronous and asynchronous traffic control strategies is at the central arbiter, sender, or receiver, which we can collectively refer to as the network side. But there is a certain response time for control at the network side, such as the decision calculation time in the synchronous scheme and the transmission time of ECN in the asynchronous scheme, etc. These determine that the traffic control strategy at the network side will not be synchronized with the network response at the same time. It is not as efficient as scheduling directly within the network.

Therefore, this paper uses direct deployment of traffic shaping at the switches to reshape the traffic inside the network at each hop switch, thus reducing network congestion and providing deterministic delay guarantee capability. It is worth noting that this paper enhances the switch devices of the data center network from the network-side perspective only, and can be used in conjunction with any of the aforementioned traffic scheduling strategies for the network side (Fig. 1).

3 Detailed Design

3.1 Design Overview

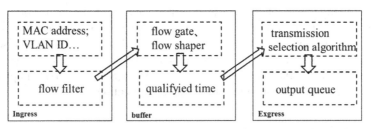

Fig. 1. ATS scheduling architecture

Asynchronous traffic shaper (ATS) is a traffic scheduling strategy proposed by the IEEE802.1Qcr standard that uses per-class queuing and per-flow reshaping to prioritize urgent traffic. ATS scheduling mechanism requires the following components: filter, stream gate, shaping queues, shapers, shared queues, and transport selection algorithms. The overall architecture is shown in the figure above. The procedure of ATS mechanism is:

1. Firstly, the data frame identifies the flow by the source mac address, destination mac address, VLAN ID, and priority fields in the VLAN tag in the data frame header, and matches into the corresponding flow filter, which specifies the subsequent stream gates and shaper for the data frame to pass through.
2. After matching, streams that meet the size requirements go to the specified stream gated controller. The flow gated controller assigns an internal priority to the data frames. This priority differs from VLAN priority in that internal priority is used for the allocation of shared queues inside the switch, while external priority only works outside the switch. This approach allows for a per-class assignment and per-flow shaping policy, improving flexibility in handling data flows.
3. Data frames with assigned internal priority enter the designated shaper for shaping the data frames. The shaping process uses a token bucket-based interleaving shaping algorithm(ISA). Each shaped data frame will be assigned a qualifying time, which is the desired data frame sending time for the subsequent transmission selection algorithm.
4. After passing the shaper, the data frames will be queued in the corresponding shared queue waiting for sending according to the internal priority. The transmission selection algorithm is based on strict priority scheduling, with the transmission in order from highest to lowest priority. If the qualification time of the currently shared queue head data frame is earlier than the current time then send the head data frame directly and re-execute the transmission algorithm from the higher priority, otherwise, send the data frame from the next priority shared queue.

To achieve the above process, we designed and implemented a P4-based asynchronous traffic shaping mechanism, where the control plane holds global information and controls the forwarding behavior of the data plane through the P4 runtime protocol, that is, flow table control forwarding. The advantages of a flow table as a control method are its lightweight configuration information, efficient configuration distribution, and secure configuration change capability. P4, as a nascent SDN architecture solution, provides deep customization capability for network forwarding behavior, making the network programmable and able to provide stronger scalability for future time-sensitive network implementations. In this paper, the multilevel pipeline (Subsect. 3.2), buffer (Subsect. 3.3), and interleaving shaping algorithm (ISA) (Subsect. 3.4) are implemented using the V1model model of p4 technology and its evolution.

3.2 Parser—Multi-stage Pipeline

Filter. After passing through the switching fabric, the data frame headers are first parsed to obtain the key fields used for matching. The stream_handle field is determined by the input port, source MAC address, destination MAC address, VLAN ID, and external priority fields. After matching to the stream_handle field, the flow filter is matched by both the stream_handle and priority fields. When more than one stream filter in the match result, the stream filter with the smallest ID is matched, and if there are no matching data frames, they will be discarded. After entering the matched filter, the flow is specified with a stream gate and shaper for subsequent transmission. In this case, the filter, stream gate, and shaper matching flow tables are issued from the control level.

Stream Gate. It is a time-scheduled gate. Data frames are matched to the stream gate and shaper frames, of which those that meet the service data size requirements are transmitted to the stream gate first, and the gating is opened or closed to limit the traffic sent according to the traffic scheduling timetable. It should be noted that the scheduling mechanism designed in this paper does not require a traffic scheduling timetable to control the transmission of flows to achieve deterministic latency, so all instances of stream gating will always be on. In addition, the stream gate also serves to assign an internal priority value(IPV) to each data frame. IPV determines the shared queue of subsequent data frames and works only inside the switch. When the data frame leaves the switch, the internal priority will be removed and the external priority will be restored. Like filters, stream gate is also implemented at the P4 level. IPV is configured for each stream gate instance at the control level through the flow table, and all data frames passing through flow gating are assigned internal priority values for subsequent scheduling modules.

3.3 Buffers —Shaping Queues, Shared Queues

There are two types of buffer queues in the ATS scheduling mechanism, shaping queues and shared queues.

Shaping Queue. According to the traffic assignment rules, the flows are assigned to different shaping queues to reduce interference between flows, and the traffic in different shaping queues is shaped using ISA. The shared queue aggregates the traffic that has undergone interleaving shaping and sends the data frames according to the transmission selection algorithm. To avoid the header blocking problem between flows in the same queue and to reduce the interference between flows, different flows are assigned to be queued in different shaping queues by the following three rules.

1. Flows from different switches cannot enter the same shaping queue.
2. Flows of different IPVs from the same switch cannot enter the same shaping queue.
3. Flows with different internal priorities cannot enter the same shaping queue.

Rule 1 avoids the impact of malicious traffic sent by one upstream switch on the traffic of other upstream switches; rule 2 ensures that high priority traffic from upstream can bypass low priority traffic to avoid header blocking of high priority traffic; rule 3 ensures that high priority traffic in this switch can bypass low priority traffic. The above three rules will determine which shaping queue the data frame will enter.

Shared Queue. The shared queue will aggregate the traffic in the shaping queue and perform transmission selection algorithm(TSA) on the data frames. Shared queues are highly isolated, with separate queuing policies for frames from different senders, the same sender but different priority, and the same sender and priority but the different priority at the receiver. Queue isolation prevents the propagation of malicious data, ensures that ordinary streams are not disturbed, and enables flexible stream or transporter blocking control through management operations. The minimum number of shared queues is the number of ports minus one, plus more with additional isolation policies. Shared queues are scheduled according to IPV and frames are transmitted on the first-come, first-served(FIFS) principle.

The outgoing queue of the shared queue is transmitted using the transmission selection algorithm(TSA), which is based on strict priority scheduling. It first needs to determine whether a data frame exists in the queue, and if it does not exist, this shared queue is skipped for the next priority shared queue to be sent. If the data frame exists, it is judged whether the data frame is empty or not. If it is empty, it means that the data frame is a data frame used to pass the control signal, and the data frame is directly discarded and the shared queue resources are released to complete the exit of the switch. Otherwise, it will determine whether it is the turn of the current priority shared queue to send, and if it is not to that shared queue to send, it needs to wait for the transmission turn. When it is the turn of that shared queue to send, it will judge whether the eligibility time of data frame binding is less than the current time, which means the frame is qualified earlier, if it is less than the current time then the data frame can be sent directly, otherwise the shared queue will be skipped and sent by the next priority shared queue.

3.4 Interleaving Shaping Algorithm

In the ATS mechanism, the shaping queue head uses an interleaving shaping algorithm(ISA) to assign an eligibility time to the data frame. First, some key time points and time intervals need to be calculated.

- Token recovery time = Data frame length/Token growth rate, which means the time interval to grow the number of tokens required to send the data frame length
- Time required to fill the token bucket from empty to full = Token bucket capacity/Token growth rate, which means the time interval required to fill the token bucket
- Shaper qualification time = The last moment when the token bucket was empty + Token recovery time
- The time when the token bucket is full = The last moment when the token bucket was empty + Time required to fill the token bucket from empty to full

After that, the maximum of the data frame arrival time, shaper combination frame time, and shaper pass time are taken as the passing time of the data frame. When the passing time is greater than the data frame arrival time plus the maximum dwell time, the data frame cannot be sent out within the maximum dwell time (this happens when the data frame arrival rate is too large and the switch processing rate is insufficient), so the data frame is discarded directly. If the frame can be sent within the maximum residence time, the shaper combination eligibility time is set to the frame eligibility time. Afterward, it is determined whether the frame eligibility time is less than the moment when the token bucket is full, and if it is less, the moment when the token bucket is empty is updated to the shaper eligibility time. If not, the shaper pass time is added to

Table 1. Interleaved shaping algorithm

Algorithm 1 Interleaved shaping algorithm		
1.	$lengthRecoveryDuration = Length(frame) / CommittedInformationRate$	
2.	$emptyToFullDuration = CommittedBurstSize / CommittedInformationRate$	
3.	$shaperEligibilityTime = BucketEmptyTime + lengthRecoveryDuration$	
4.	$bucketFullTime = BucketEmptyTime + emptyToFullDuration$	
5.	$eligibilityTime = \max\{arrivalTime(\text{frame}), GroupEligibilityTime, shaperEligibilityTime\}$	
6.	**if** $eligibilityTime \leq (arrivalTime(\text{frame}) + MaxResidenceTime/1.0e9)$ **then**	
7.	$GroupEligibilityTime = eligibilityTime$	
8.	**if** $eligibilityTime < bucketFullTime$ **then**	
9.	$BucketEmptyTime = shaperEligibilityTime$	
10.	**end**	
11.	**else**	
12.	$BucketEmptyTime = shaperEligibilityTime + eligibilityTime - bucketFullTime$	
13.	**end**	
14.	$AssignAndProcessed(\text{frame}, eligibilityTime)$	
15.	**else**	
16.	**else**	
17.	$Discard(\text{frame})$	
18	**end**	

the frame eligibility time and subtracted from the token bucket full time. Finally, the frame eligibility time is bound to the data frame (Table 1).

4 Evaluation

In the previous section, we introduced and designed the overall architecture and components of the asynchronous traffic shaping mechanism. In this section, we first theoretically analyze the single-hop queuing delay bound of ATS, and then experimentally verify the delay guarantee capability of ATS.

4.1 Theoretical Single-Hop Time Latency

In this paper, a similar theoretical analysis of the ATS is performed to obtain Eqs. (2–10), drawing on the analysis of the single-hop delay bound for strict priority scheduling in the literature [11].

$$D_{BU,max}(k,f) = max_{h \in F_s(k,f)} \left\{ \frac{\sum_{g \in F_{H(k,h)} \cup F_{s(k,h)}} b_{max}(k,g) + l_{LP,max}(k,h)}{R(k) - \sum_{g \in F_{H(k,h)}} r_{max}(k,g)} + \frac{l_{max}(h)}{R(k)} \right\} \quad (1)$$

This formula takes into account the worst-case scenario for data frame transmission. A certain priority frame arrives just as a lower priority frame is sent, so the frame first waits for the lower frame to finish sending, and then the higher priority frame will be sent, And this data frame is sent exactly at the end of the frames with the same priority as it. Where,

$F_H(k, h)$ and $F_H(k, f)$ denote the set of all flows with higher priority than flows h and f.
$F_s(k, h)$ and $F_s(k, f)$ denote the set of all streams with priority equal to streams h and f.
$b_{max}(k, g)$ denotes the maximum burst flow size at the k th hop of flow g.
$l_{LP,max}(k, h)$ denotes the maximum frame length in all flows with a priority lower than flow h.
$l_{max}(h)$ denotes the maximum frame length of flow h.
$R(k)$ denotes the maximum transmission rate of the port.
$r_{max}(k, g)$ denotes the maximum transmission rate size at the k th hop of flow g.

The above equation can give the single-hop queuing delay bound under the worst-case condition, and from this, the end-to-end delay bound can be calculated. As can be seen from the equation, the assignment of internal priorities and shaping queues directly determines the delay boundaries of data frames, while in the flow gate component of each hop switch, different internal priorities can be assigned to frames instead of external priorities, thus allowing more flexibility in assigning the service level of frames in switches.

Due to the cascading effect of burst traffic, the SP single-hop queuing delay increases as the hop increases. The ATS queuing delay, on the other hand, eliminates the cascading effect of bursty traffic due to shaping for each hop.

4.2 Experimental Design

We set up a small Layer 2 data center network using six blade switches with a Spirent Traffic Meter. The Spirent traffic meter sends data frames on four ports and receives the forwarded data frames on one port (Fig. 2).

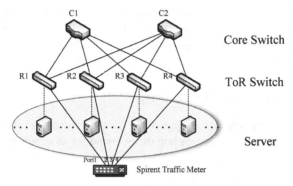

Fig. 2. Layer 2 data center network

By stress testing, we measured a delay of 285.42 ms in addition to the queuing delay, and the limit forwarding capacity of the switch is 398 Mbit/s. To test the worst-case delay boundaries, we punched the limit forwarding rate traffic into the switch in our experiments. We punched the limit forwarding rate traffic into the switch in both Experiment I and II.

Experiment I. Each Flow Passes through Only One ToR Switch. In this case, the fifth port of the traffic meter is enabled as the receiver, and each port sends out 2 high-priority flows and 2 low-priority flows.

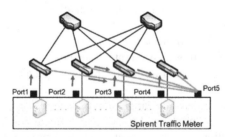

Fig. 3. Each flow passes through only one ToR switches

There are 16 streams in the network whose forwarding path and priority configuration are shown in Fig. 3 and Table2. The end-to-end transmission delay of the flow can be read in the visual interface of the Spirent Traffic Meter. Transmission delay subtracts the processing delay measured in the stress test to get the queuing delay and calculates the theoretical delay boundary of the ATS using Eq. (1) to get a comparison line graph.

Table 2. Experiment 1 16 flows configuration tables.

ToR Switch No.	Forwarding path	Stream No.	Priority
R1	1-R1–5	R1–1	1
		R1–2	1
		R1–3	0
		R1–4	0
R2	2-R2–5	R2–1	1
		R2–2	1
		R2–3	0
		R3–4	0
R3	3-R3–5	R3–1	1
		R3–2	1
		R3–3	0
		R3–4	0
R4	4-R4–5	R4–1	1
		R4–2	1
		R4–3	0
		R4–4	0

Experiment II. Each Flow Passes through Three Hop Switches. Each port sends out $2*4 = 8$ flows, including four high priority and four low priority, through different ToR switches and Core switches respectively. Taking the R1 switch as an example, the flow configuration is shown in Fig. 4 and Table3. The queuing delay is calculated in the same way as Experiment I and draw the comparison graph with the theoretical delay bound.

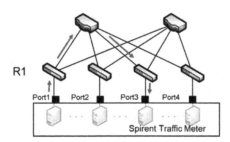

Fig. 4. Each flow passes through three hop switches.

Table 3. Experiment ll R1 flows configuration tables.

ToR Switch No.	Core Switch No.	Forwarding path	Stream No.	Priority
R1	C1	P1-R1-C1-R1-P1	P1–1	1
		P1-R1-C1-R2-P2	P1–2	1
		P1-R1-C1-R3-P3	P1–3	0
		P1-R1-C1-R4-P4	P1–4	0
	C2	P1-R1-C2-R1-P1	P1–5	1
		P1-R1-C2-R2-P2	P1–6	1
		P1-R1-C2-R3-P3	P1–7	0
		P1-R1-C2-R4-P4	P1–8	0

4.3 Experimental Results

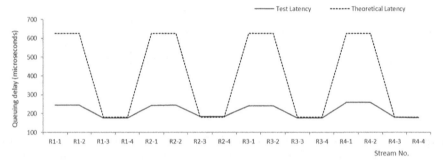

Fig. 5. Experiment I results

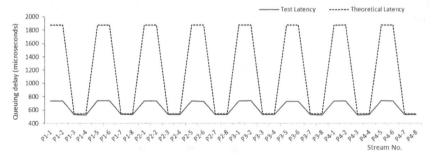

Fig. 6. Experiment II results

The results are shown in Fig. 5 and Fig. 6. As we can see from the figures, after adopting the ATS shaping mechanism, the delay of high priority streams is all smaller than low priority streams, and the delay reduction for high priority streams is better. In addition, the test delay of streams is smaller than the theoretical experiment, which satisfies the strictness of the delay boundary, and the delay drift of streams is significantly reduced, which helps the construction of deterministic delay networks.

5   Conclusion

In this paper, we introduce the asynchronous traffic shaping mechanism (ATS). It is different from previous data center traffic scheduling strategies, implemented on a programmable switch on the network side, requires no clock synchronization, is simple to deploy, and is highly scalable. We use a multi-level pipeline matching mechanism to assign an internal priority to data frames and assign frames to a shaping queue for interleaving shaping based on that priority, enabling class-by-class grouping and flow-by-flow shaping. Finally, we show a simulation experiment based on a data center network. The experimental results show that the ATS mechanism satisfies the stringency characteristics of the delay boundaries and facilitates the construction of deterministic delay data center networks.

References

1. Lizhuang, T., Wei, S., Yanwen, L., Xiaochuan, G., Wei, Z. : DCQUIC: flexible and reli-able software-defined data center transport. In: INFOCOM WKSHPS, pp. 1–8 (2021)
2. Peter, X.G., et al.: pHost: distributed near-optimal data center transport over com-modity network fabric. In: Proceedings of 11th ACM Conference Emerging Network-ing Experiments and Technologies (CoNEXT), pp. 1–12 (2015)
3. Han, F., Wang, M., Cui, Y., et al.: Future data center networking: from low latency to deterministic latency. IEEE Netw. **36**(1), 52–58 (2022)
4. Benson, T., Akella, A., Maltz, D.: Network traffic characteristics of data centers in the wild. In: Proceedings of the ACM Sigcomm Conference on Internet Measurement Conference (IMC), Melbourne, Australia, pp. 267–280 (2010)
5. IEEE standard for local and metropolitan area networks--bridges and bridged net-works amendment 34: asynchronous traffic shaping. IEEE Std 8021Qcr-2020, pp. 1–151 (2020)
6. Mellette, W.M., et al.: RotorNet: a scalable, lowcomplexity, optical data center network. In: Proceedings of ACM SIGCOMM 2017 Conference, pp. 267–80 (2017)
7. Mellette, W.M., et al.: Expanding across time to deliver bandwidth efficiency and low latency. In: Proceedings of 17th USENIX Symposium on Networked Systems Design and Implementation (NSDI 20), pp. 1–18 (2020)
8. Alizadeh, M., Greenberg, A., Maltz, D.A., et al.: Data center tcp (dctcp). In: Proceed-ings of the Special Interest Group on Data Communication (SIGCOMM), New Delhi, India, pp. 63–74 (2010)
9. Mohammad, A., Abdul, K., Tom, E., et al.: Less is more: trading a little bandwidth for ultra-low latency in the data center. In: Proceedings of USENIX Symposium on Net-worked Systems Design and Implementation (NSDI), San Jose, USA, pp. 253–266 (2012)
10. Cho, I., Jang, K., Han, D.: Credit-scheduled delay-bounded congestion control for datacenters. In: Proceedings of the Special Interest Group on Data Communication (SIGCOMM), CA, USA, pp. 239–252 (2017)
11. Grigorjew, A., Metzger, F., Hoßfeld, T., et al.: Technical report on bridge-local guaran-teed latency with strict priority scheduling[R/OL]. 22 Jan 2020, 2 May 2021. https://opus.bibliothek.uni-wuerzburg.de/opus4wuerzburg/frontdoor/deliver/index/dcId/19831/file/Grigorjew_Guaranteed_Latency_Technical_Report.pdf

An Efficient Firewall Application Using Learned Cuckoo Filter

Honglei Peng[1], Deyun Gao[1(✉)], Meiyi Yang[1], and Junfeng Ma[2]

[1] National Engineering Research Center of Advanced Network Technologies,
School of Electronic and Information Engineering, Beijing Jiaotong University,
Beijing 100044, China
gaody@bjtu.edu.cn
[2] China Academy of Information and Communication Technology,
Beijing 100191, China

Abstract. With the development of Software Defined Networking (SDN), the most investigated firewall type is software firewall, running as application on control plane. The main process in firewalls is matching network traffic with stored security policies, that is, packet classification. Although extensive research has been conducted in this area, existing packet classification algorithms still face problems of low classification performance and large storage space. To minimize the impact of the packet classification on the entire network, we propose an efficient firewall using Learned Cuckoo filter (LCF) based packet classification algorithm. This algorithm adopts a hierarchical search strategy. The single-field matching results is obtain first. Then the machine learning model is used as a pre-filter in front of the cuckoo filter, which effectively eliminates unnecessary rule search in the next stage and achieves a memory reduction, as well as an improvement on performance. We implemented a proposed firewall prototype. Extensive simulations verify the superiority of the introduced design in terms of false positive rate, memory consumption and memory access.

Keywords: Firewall · Packet classification · SDN

1 Introduction

Firewall is a key defense component widely used in traditional and future network. It relies on packet classification to match the fields in the packet header with the preset firewall rules, find the matching rules and determine the processing action (allow, deny) of the packet, so as to implement security control over the network [1]. In recent years, with the expansion of network scale and the improvement of people's security awareness, more and more rules are included in the firewall, which greatly affects the packet classification speed and memory usage. Therefore, it is necessary to study how to improve the firewall packet classification performance especially under large scale rule sets.

Packet classification in firewalls is essentially a multi-field classification problem [2], which been the bottleneck of extensive research for many years. Take

© The Author(s), under exclusive license to Springer Nature Singapore Pte Ltd. 2023
W. Quan (Ed.): ICENAT 2022, CCIS 1696, pp. 430–441, 2023.
https://doi.org/10.1007/978-981-19-9697-9_35

advantage of hardware devices, such as Ternary Content Addressable Memory (TCAM) [3] and Field Programmable Gate Array (FPGA) [4] to reach high-performance packet classification is one solution. However, they have inherent disadvantages, for instance, high power consumption and high cost. Therefore, researchers are more active in researching software-based solutions, because they are more flexible, scalable and less expensive.

Current software-based packet classifications can be categorized broadly into two approaches: decision-tree techniques [5] and hash table based algorithms [6]. Decision tree works by recursively separating the searching space until each sub-space contains less than a predefined number of rules. If a rule spans multiple subspaces, there will be a problem of rule duplication, which will cause its classification speed to slow down and memory usage to increase. Tuple Space Search (TSS) builds a hash table for each rule with different prefix lengths. Rules with the same prefix length are stored in the same hash table, that is, tuple space. It does not have the problem of rule duplication and has advantages in fast update. But due to sorting packets requires a thorough search of all hash tables, it sacrifices matching speed. Some improved hash table based schemes improve classification speed by reducing hash table access by combining them with Bloom filters [7] or decision trees [8]. It can be found that there is a lot of potential to improve classification performance by eliminating unnecessary search.

In this paper, to fulfil the needs of the firewall for fast lookup and low memory usage, we present a Learned Cuckoo filter (LCF) based packet classification algorithm. We validate the effectiveness of our algorithm using both simulation and deployment in a software firewall, which is implemented by ONOS controller an P4 switches. Essentially, LCF is a hierarchical search framework, which contains three stages. In the first search stage, we perform single-field matching on the source address (SA) and destination address (DA) in the packet header. No more than five matching results is obtained for each field [9], thereby enabling initially search space narrowing. The second stage uses Learned Cuckoo filter to classify SA-DA pairs which obtained from cross-combining the matched results of above, where may introduce false positive rate. Those address pairs that are grouped for inclusion in a rule will go into the next stage. A salient fact is that after pre-filtering, the number of items which need to be searched in the third stage has been has been significantly reduced. In the third stage we employ a TSS-based algorithm called Priority Sorting Tuple Space Search (PSTSS) [10], check inputs in the order of descending priority, which can ensure the minimum number of searches.

The main contributions of this paper are as follows:

- The proposed LCF-based algorithm adopts combination of LCF and PSTSS to achieve high performance packet classification. The hierarchical search framework makes full use of the ruleset features in pre-filtering.
- A rule insertion algorithm is proposed, so that rulesets can be realized dynamically. A theoretical analysis of LCF false positive rate and memory.

- A proposed firewall prototype is implemented. We evaluate the performance of our proposed algorithm under different parameter settings, and compare the memory usage and memory access performance with existing work.

2   System Design

Figure 1 depicts the overall system architecture. The implementation of our firewall can be divided into two parts: the actual firewall running on the data plane of every assess gateway and the control plane dynamically deploying the security policies on the data plane.

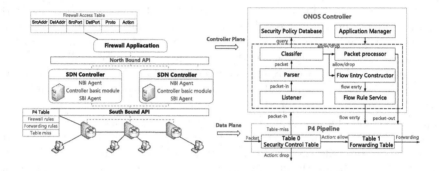

Fig. 1. System architecture and implementation details

Data Plane. In order to improve the flexibility and scalability of the system architecture, we use a switch device that supports P4 programmable language as an access gateway (hereafter P4 gateway) in the data plane. We design a P4 pipeline to combine firewall function and generic forwarding function, as shown in Fig. 1. The Firewall on the data plane uses the flow rules stored inside the P4 gateway as firewall rules. The pipeline consists of two flow tables. The first flow table contains the security control flow entries converted by the firewall rules, and the second flow table contains the forwarding flow entries. For the firewall rule whose action is Allow, the command action of the converted flow entry is enter the next table, the allowed packets are sent to the forwarding table for matching and forwarding. For the firewall rule whose action is Drop, the converted command action is drop flow entry, that is, directly blocking the matched packets. In addition, we set the action of the table-miss flow entry in the security control table to be sent to the controller, that is, to the firewall application in the controller for decision-making.

Control Plane. Figure 1 describes the firewall application that runs on top of the ONOS controller in the control plane. It is responsible for storing security policies, querying security policies, converting security policies into flow rules and delivering them to the data plane. When the firewall service is enabled, the

Listener starts to monitor packet-in messages sent by the data plane to the controller. Then the Parser extracts the original data of the packet from the packet-in message, the packet header information of the second layer to the fourth layer is restored and encapsulated in the form of an object. The Classifier matches the packet header information with the firewall rules stored in the Security Policy Database to find the matching rule with the highest priority and obtain its action. A packet classification algorithm based on the Learned Cuckoo filter is used to achieve efficient matching, and the algorithm will be detailed described in Sect. 4. The flow entry is constructed by the Flow Entry Constructor according to the header information of the packet and the obtained firewall rule action, then sends it to the switch. The Packet Processor re-encapsulates packet into a packet-out message and sending it to the switch.

3   Packet Classification Algorithm Design

Baboescu et al. concluded that the packet classification rule set has the following characteristics: 1) The number of rules obtained by single-field matching of the source address or destination address is at most 5. 2) When a packet is matched in multiple fields, the rules it can match are quite limited. Given the combination of the first two fields, the number of matching rules does not exceed 20 in the worst case. According to the above study, the idea directly perceived is to design a hierarchical search framework to do packet classification in steps. In the following, we first give the structure and composition of the algorithm, then describe rule insertion algorithm and packet classification algorithm, finally analyze the performance of the proposed algorithm theoretically.

3.1   Structure of Proposed Algorithm

We represent our structure in Fig. 2. It mainly includes three parts: single-field matching algorithm data structure, LCF and PSTSS.

Single-Field Matching Algorithm Data Structure. Responsible for implementing prefix matching of IP addresses and reporting all the matched prefixes. Any single-field matching algorithm in the field of packet classification algorithms can be used here to solve PM problem.

LCF. It is used to determine whether a rule exists whose first two dimensions are given address pairs. In order to achieve the goal of improving the filtering accuracy and reducing the memory size it occupies, we propose a Learned Cuckoo filter structure inspired by [11]. Let R denote the packet classification rule set. We define K as a positive set that contains all SA-DA pairs in R, and U as a negative set that contains SA-DA pairs that do not exist in R. A model is first trained with set $G = \{(x_i, y_i = 1)|x_i \in K\} \bigcup \{(x_j, y_j = 0)|x_j \in U\}$, and use a logistic sigmoid function $f(x) = \frac{1}{1+e^{-x}}$ to produce a probability and note its range belongs to $[0, 1]$. Finally achieve the goal of minimizing the loss function

$$L = \sum_{(x,y) \in R} y log(f(x)) + (1 - y)log(1 - f(x)) \tag{1}$$

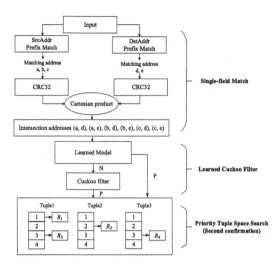

Fig. 2. The framework of our proposed LCF-based packet classification algorithm

We use the learned model to give each input x a score $f(x)$, which is usually positively associated with the odds that $x \in K$. Then uses this score and treats score $f(x)$ higher than a pre-determined threshold τ as the basis for grouping that $x \in K$. If $f(x) \geq \tau$, we consider that x belongs to K. Otherwise, $x \in U$ and this situation may provide a false negative. We need send x to the backup cuckoo filter (BCF) to reconfirm. Since the Cuckoo filter guarantees no false negative, the address pairs which can not be found in BCF are absolutely true negative.

PSTSS. Responsible for storing the ruleset and doing final checks to eliminate false positive rates of LCF. In order to reduce the invalid hash table access as much as possible, we map the rule set to a set of hash tables using the PSTSS algorithm. Each hash table T is associated with a tuple δ. A tuple is a vector of two lengths, for example (30, 16) is a tuple representing the source address is a 30-bit prefix, the destination address is a 16-bit prefix. We define a rule $\widetilde{R}$ maps to tuple $\widetilde{\delta}$ if its fields is specified to exactly $\delta[\cdot]$ bits. Rules with the same tuple are stored in the same hash table. Moreover the hash tables and tuples are sorted in the order of the rules with the highest priority in each hash table. When a search occurs, the address pair is searched in the hash table from high to low according to the priority order of its corresponding tuple.

3.2 Rule Insection Algorithm

Since LCF architecture consists of two layers, the first layer of the learned model will generate false negative which will produce errors in practical application. To ensure overall false negatives is 0, we need insert those false negative records that should be recognized positive in the negative results into backup cuckoo filter. The pseudocode of rule insertion algorithm is shown in Algorithm 1.

Algorithm 1: LCF Insection Algorithm

Input: Rule set R, Threshold τ, Set K, Set U

1   Model=trainModel(K, U);

2   **for** $x \in K$ **do**

3   obtain $f(x)$ from the Model;

4   **if** $f(x) < \tau$ **then**

5         $f = $ fingerprint(x);

6         $i_1 = $ hash(x);

7         $i_2 = i_1 \oplus$ hash(f);

8   **if** $\exists entry$ is $empty$ in $BCF.bucket[i_1]$ or $BCF.bucket[i_2]$ **then**

9   add f to that bucket;

10   **else**

11            $i = $ randomPick(i_1, i_2);

12   **for** $n=1$ to $BCF.MaxNumKicks$ **do**

13   entry $e = $ randomPick(all entries from bucket[i]);

14   kick out the fingerprint f_e stored in entry e;

15   add f to that bucket;

16                $i = i \oplus hash(f_e)$;

17   **if** $\exists entry$ is $empty$ in $BCF.bucket[i]$ **then**

18   add f_e to that bucket;

19   return;

20   **if** $\delta_x = \delta_{T_\theta}$, $T_\theta \in \Gamma$ **then**

21         $T_\theta[x] = R$(SP,DP,Protocol,pri);

22   **else**

23   create a new hash table T_x for R_x with tuple δ_{T_x};

24         $T_x[x] = R$(SP,DP,Protocol,pri);

For the insertion algorithm, the input x is obtained by extracting SA-DA pair of the rule. We feed x into the trained model and check if $f(x) < \tau$. If it happens, x is inserted into the BCF. Otherwise, the rule corresponding to x is defined as R_x and only inserts it into the hash table. Then consider the case where we need to insert a new rule into PSTSS structure. For each table T, R_x is comptible with T if $\delta_x = \delta_{T_\theta}$. The rule will be inserted into this table. Otherwise, we need to create a hash table with tuple for R_x.

3.3 Packet Classification Algorithm

In this subsection, we present our packet classification algorithm. The algorithm can be divided into three steps: single-field matching, LBF filtering and hash table lookup. Algorithm 2 gives the pseudocode of packet classification algorithm.

Upon receiving the object containing the key fields of packet header, we first use the Trie tree to perform prefix matching on SA and DA respectively. In order to better distinguish IP addresses with variable prefix length, CRC is used to obtain different 32 length binary sequence. We obtain the intersection address set

I and associated tuple set δ_I, and process set I based on $\delta_{I*} = \delta_I \bigcap \delta_T$ to get an active intersection address set I^*. Then we sort the elements in set I^* according to the priority order of the integral hash tables. Secondly, in the LCF filtering step, we input each SA-DA pair in the I^* into the learned model in order. If $f(x) < \tau$, the BCF is used to filter out the false negatives, and then send x to the hash table to perform the second confirmation. Otherwise, if $f(x) \geq \tau$, the hash table is only used. In the last step, each pair is looked up in the hash table in order. If the stored rules can be found in the corresponding hash table, we perform the linear match for the last three fields, and then get the matching rule r_x. When the priority of this rule $r_x.pri$ is higher than the priority of the hash table corresponding to the next pair to be confirmed in set I^*, the whole classification algorithm ends and return the action of the matching rule.

Algorithm 2: Packet Classification Algorithm

Input: Object=SA, DA, SP, DP, PT
Output: The action α of the final matching rule
1 $D_1, P_1 = \text{triePM(SA)}$;
2 $D_2, P_2 = \text{triePM(DA)}$;
3 doCRC(D_1) and doCRC(D_2);
4 $I, \delta_I = \text{cartesianProduct}(D_1, D_2; P_1, P_2)$;
5 obtain set I^* corresponding to the tuple set $\delta_{I*} = \delta_I \bigcap \delta_T$;
6 sort I^* and δ_{I*} in descending order;
7 **while** $r_x.pri < T_{next}(max(rule.pri))$ **do**
8   **for** $x \in \{1,...,I^*\}$ **do**
9   obtain $f(x)$ from the learned model;
10   **if** $f(x) < \tau$ **then**
11   check if x in BCF;
12   **if** $BCF[i_1]$ or $BCF[i_2]$ is not empty **then**
13   Value=$T_\theta[x](\delta_x = \delta_{T_\theta})$;
14   **else**
15   x is not a valid address combination;
16   **else**
17   Value=$T_\theta[x](\delta_x = \delta_{T_\theta})$;
18   liner search for the other three fields;
19   get the matching rule r_x;
20 **return** the action α of rule r_x;

3.4   Theoretical Analyze

The accuracy and memory are important indicators to measure the packet classification algorithm, and the false positive rate of LCF is closely related to the accuracy. In this subsection, we will analyze the false positive rate and memory requirement of the entired LCF.

False Positive Rate. Assuming that an input $q \in$ query set Q and $q \notin K$. If the situation that $f(q) \geq \tau$ happens, means it produces a false positive in model.

Otherwise, it produces a false negative in model when meets the condition an input $q \in K$ but via $f(q) < \tau$. In fact, set τ can let the model has the desired FPR, but beware the FPR goes down, the FNR will go up. The BCF remove the false negative rate of the model, but produces a new false positive when $f(q) < \tau$ and BCF checks that $q \in K$.

We donate the FPR of our learned model with given τ by $FPR_\tau(M)$ and $FPR(C)$ represents the FPR of the BCF. Combining our discussion of the situations above, the overall FPR of the LCF can be formulated as follows

$$FPR_{overall} = FPR_\tau(M) + (1 - FPR_\tau(M))FPR(C) \tag{2}$$

where $FPR_\tau(M) = \frac{\sum_1^{|Q-K|} P(f(q)>\tau)}{|Q-K|}$. For a cuckoo filter that uses fingerprints of f bits, the false positive rate can be approximated by $FPR(C) = \frac{8o}{2^f}$ where o is the filter occupancy, defined as $\frac{n}{mb}$, where n is the number of elements stored in the filter, b is the number of entries per bucket, m is the number of buckets.

Memory. In addition, for rule sets of different sizes, the size of the learned model obtained by training is independent. Let S_m be the size of the model, the size of the LCF S_l can be as $S_l = S_m + mbf$. Choosing the right parameters for cuckoo filters can significantly affect space efficiency [12]. Assume that a query is made on BCF, the probability that it returns a false positive rate is at most $1/2^f$. After doing $2b$ queries, we can derive the upper bound of the total FPR using: $1 - (1 - 1/2^f)^{2b} \approx 2b/2^f$. Let γ_τ denote the target false positive rate when the threshold is τ, and FNR_τ^K denote the false negative rate of the learned model on set K when given τ. Note that $\gamma_\tau \leq 2b/2^f$ need to be ensured. We can obtain the minimal f is: $f \geq \lceil log_2(2b/\gamma_\tau) \rceil = \lceil log_2(1/\gamma_\tau) + log_2(2b) \rceil$ bits. Substituting the value of S_l consist, the memory usage of LCF can be expressed as follows

$$S_l \geq S_m + \frac{|K|FNR_\tau^K}{o} \lceil log_2(1/\gamma_\tau) + log_2(2b) \rceil \tag{3}$$

4   Experimental Results

In this section, we evaluate the system from two aspects. Firstly, we deploy a simple system to verify our solution feasibility. A network topology is built using ONOS and BMv2. We will use the proposed firewall to control the external network to access the internal network. Secondly, we test the performance of the packet classification algorithm our system used and compare the performance with existing software algorithms.

4.1   Experiment Setup

As shown in Fig. 3, we have established a simple topology with multiple hosts and 2 switches. The network consists of two regions: 1) Internal network (10.0.1.0/24), contains a host h3. 2) External network, contains one reliable host h1 and one unreliable host h2.

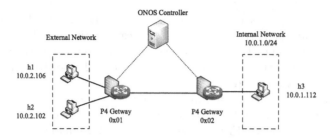

Fig. 3. Experiment topology

Before starting the experiment, we need to establish a connection between the controller and each switch. Then add some security policies, which contains allow reliable hosts to access the intranet and prevent unreliable hosts from accessing the intranet. After that, open the firewall application on the controller. Two operations of h1 initiating a connection to h3 and h2 initiating a connection to h3 were respectively implemented. It can be observed that only h1 can establish a connection and communicate with h3, verifying that the system can improve access control services.

4.2 Performance Evaluation

In our experiments we use a server running ubuntu18.04. The server is equipped with 2 10-Core2.40 GHz Intel Xeon CPU and 62 GB of main memory. The proposed algorithm structure code is implemented by python.

We use the standard benchmark, ClassBench [13], to generate access control list rule sets whose size varies from 10k to 100k. We get the SA-DA pair for each rule in the ruleset, treat them as the positive set. We collect cross combinations of SA and DA that are not presence in the positive set as negative set. Divide the entire dataset into train set (80) and test sets (20), and use cross-validation to ensure the stability and accuracy of the trained model.

False Positive Probability. Our learned cuckoo filter contains a two-layer architecture, we can reduce the false positive rate of the entiored model by setting a reasonable threshold τ in the first layer. As shown in Fig. 4, when model learning rate is 0.01, we compared the impact of threshold on the false positive rate under neural networks with hidden layer sizes ranging from 0 to 32, respectively. When $\tau < 0.5$, the model with more hidden layers has a faster drop in false positive rate, and when $\tau > 0.5$, the false positive rate generated by the five situations is almost equal. Overall it can be seen that the false positive rate decreases as the threshold increases. The reason is $f(x) \in [0, 1]$, the closer the value of τ is set to 1, only inputs whose value produced by $f(x)$ is closer to 1 are considered to belong to set K, thereby lead to the more accurate the output value results of our model in a smaller false positive rate. This result verifies our earlier analysis.

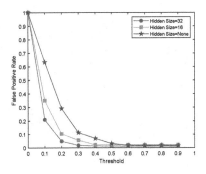

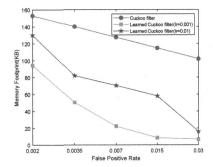

Fig. 4. The influence of threshold selection on false positive rate

Fig. 5. Memory consumption vs False positive rate

Figure 5 further shows the memory consumption to insert 100k rules required by learned cuckoo filter and standard cuckoo filter under the same false positive rate. The learned model in LCF uses a learning rate of 0.01 or 0.001. The memory footprint of LCF = learner size + backup cuckoo filter size, where the size of the learned model is 5.32 KB. When building the cuckoo filter, we use the same load factor. For the spread of false positive rate, we take a three-quarters approach to the learned the model and one-quarter to the cuckoo filter. We can find that this structure setup is effective in that the learned model can be fairly small relative to the size of the data. Furture, the size of the BCF depends on FNR, is much less than cuckoo filter which size depends on the whole data set. We also observe that a learned model with setting $l_r = 0.001$ performs better. To better explain, give the false negative rate of a model with l_r of 0.01 and 0.001 when the false positive rate is 0.7, which are 46 and 13, respectively. By comparing the false positive rate, we can know the model is more effective when $l_r = 0.001$, resulting in a smaller size of the BCF.

Memory Footprint. Figure 6 shows the average memory access of LCF as well as TSP, CutTSS and CutSplit. TSP is the representative Bloom filter-based solution. Cutsplit and CutTSS are excellent improved solutions based on decision tree and tuple space search respectively. We perform simulation when $FPR_{overall}$ and $FPR_{tsp} = 0.1\%$, and $S_m = 5.32$ KB. We experimented by increasing the number of rules in order to see the corresponding memory consumption. As expected, LCF does significantly better than CutTSS and CutSplit since it has no rule replication, show a 23% and 48% mean improvement over them. And our algorithm still has room for improvement. If use a lower false positive rate, the result of our algorithm can continue to decrease. Compared to TSP, LCF has a lower memory footprint and the gap between them increases with the size of the ruleset. We can also find that, there is a potential advantage of LCF is that most of the memory consumption is caused by the inherent memory brought by the ruleset, which makes it well suitable for larger classifiers without adding too much exact memory.

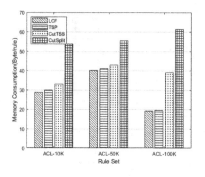

Fig. 6. Memory footprint comparison

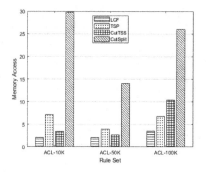

Fig. 7. Memory access comparison

Memory Access. The number of memory accesses is an important dimension to measure the time efficiency of the algorithm. We used trace file generated by ClassBench when it constructs the corresponding rule sets to measure memory access and kept the false positive rate of LCF $= 0.1\%$. Average memory access of LCF and another three algorithms are shown in Fig. 7. For each classification, we consider traversing a decision tree leaf node, a rule or a hash table as one memory access in our experiments. Clearly, LCF produce a better performance regardless of the type and size of rulesets, consuming an average of 2.56 across all of the rule sets, while it requires 5.94, 5.47 and 23.3 in TSP, CutTSS and CutSplit respectively. Separately, we also note that the average number of memory accesses for LCF is close to 2, which shows that almost all elements filtered by LCF can be found in the hash table in order of priority, indicating that our algorithm can effectively reduce the number of unnecessary rule searches.

5 Conclusion

In this paper, we propose a LCF-based packet classification algorithm for achieving more efficient firewall system in SDN, in which the firewall application is deployed in control plane and the security policies is distributed to the switches of the data plane in the form of flow table entries. Our proposed algorithm first uses the Tried tree to obtain the single-field matching result, and cross-combines these matching results. These cross-combination results are input into LCF for filtering to obtain the matching results of the first two domains, and the filtering results are confirmed by TSS. Finally, we perform a linear search on the last three fields of the elements in the resulting small rule set. Compared with Cut-Splits, experimental results show that using ClassBench, our algorithm achieves a memory reduction over 2 times, as well as 11x improvement on performance in terms of the number of memory access on average.

Acknowledgements. This work is supported by the National Key Research and Development Program of China (grant no. 2018YFE0206800) and the National Natural Science Foundation of China (grant no. 61971028).

References

1. James, D., Alex, X.L., Eric, T.: A difference resolution approach to compressing access control lists. IEEE/ACM Trans. Netw. **24**(1), 610–623 (2016)
2. Yuzhu, C., Weipin, W., Jianxin, W.: A fast firewall packet classification algorithm using unit space partitions. Adv. Eng. Sci. **50**(4), 144–152 (2018)
3. Alex, X.L., Chad, R.M., Eric, T.: Packet classification using binary content addressable memory. IEEE/ACM Trans. Netw. **24**(3), 1295–1307 (2016)
4. Li, C., Li, T., Li, J., Shi, Z., Wang, B.: Enabling packet classification with low update latency for SDN switch on FPGA. Sustainability **12**(8), 3068 (2020)
5. Wenjun, L., Xianfeng, L., Hui, L., Gaogang, X.: CutSplit: a decision-tree combining cutting and splitting for scalable packet classification. In: IEEE INFOCOM 2018 - IEEE Conference on Computer Communications, pp. 2645–2653 (2018)
6. James, D.-T.: TupleMerge: fast software packet processing for online packet classification. IEEE/ACM Trans. Netw. **27**(4), 1417–1431 (2019)
7. Jinyuan, Z., Zhigang, H., Bing, X., Keqin, L.: Accelerating packet classification with counting bloom filters for virtual OpenFlow switching. China Commun. **15**(10), 117–128 (2018)
8. Wenjun, L.-L.: Tuple space assisted packet classification with high performance on both search and update. IEEE J. Sel. Areas Commun. **38**(7), 1555–1569 (2020)
9. Baboescu, F., Sumeet, S., Varghese, G.: Packet classification for core routers: is there an alternative to CAMs?. In: IEEE INFOCOM 2003. Twenty-Second Annual Joint Conference of the IEEE Computer and Communications Societies (IEEE Cat. No.03CH37428), pp. 53–63 (2003)
10. Ben, P.-C.: The design and implementation of open vSwitch. In: 12th USENIX Symposium on Networked Systems Design and Implementation (NSDI 2015), pp. 117–130. USENIX Association, Oakland, CA (2015)
11. Tim, K.-P.: The case for learned index structures. In: Proceedings of the 2018 International Conference on Management of Data (SIGMOD 2018), pp. 489–504. Computing Machinery, New York (2018)
12. Bin, F., Dave, G.A., Michael, K., Michael, D.M.: Cuckoo filter: practically better than bloom. In: Proceedings of the 10th ACM International on Conference on Emerging Networking Experiments and Technologies (CoNEXT 2014), pp. 75–88. Computing Machinery, New York (2014)
13. David, E.T., Jonathan, S.T.: ClassBench: a packet classification benchmark. IEEE/ACM Trans. Network. **15**(3), 499–511 (2007)

A Framework of Intrusion Detection Inspired by Artificial Immune System

Haodi Zhang[(✉)], Zeyuan Huang, Shuai Wang, Huamin Jin, and Xiaodong Deng

China Telecom Corp Ltd, Guangdong Research Institute, Guangdong, China
zhanghaodi@chinatelecom.cn

Abstract. The Human Immune System categorizes substances into self and non-self to find intrusions. This idea provides a good model for intrusion detection systems in the computer science field. This model has developed into a research field called Artificial Immune Systems. Such a system uses several algorithms and concepts like Negative Selection, a classical algorithm in this field. This paper takes an overview of the strengths and weaknesses of Negative Selection. It proposes the design of Artificial Immune System(AIS) based Intrusion Detection Systems (IDSs), which consists of three layers to attain accommodative immune response and an improved algorithm to decrease false positives and false negatives. Experiments on the same dataset prove the validity of our proposal and some specific indicator values can achieve the performance of the classical Artificial Intelligence(AI) algorithm.

Keywords: Artificial Immune System · Negative Selection Algorithm · Intrusion Detection

1 Introduction

The Human Immune System (HIS) is highly complex and has two branches: the innate immune system and the adaptive immune system. The innate immune system is the first protector, and can against the entry of microorganisms, called the Barrier Immune System(BIS). Meanwhile, Pathogens that enter the body are handled by the Adaptive Immune System [1]. The body's Adaptive Immune System reacts to unidentified foreign substances by developing a reaction that will persist there for a long period. Figure 1 illustrates the basic processes of the Immune System [2]. In simple terms, either the innate or adaptive immune system has to categorize all cells and molecules in self or non-self substances, or non-dangerous and dangerous, and the system's behavior is decided by matching; the antibodies have to match antigens (but not self). In this way, the body can acquire a defensive effect and thus keep the organism's homeostasis.

W. Quan (Ed.): ICENAT 2022, CCIS 1696, pp. 442–453, 2023.
https://doi.org/10.1007/978-981-19-9697-9_36

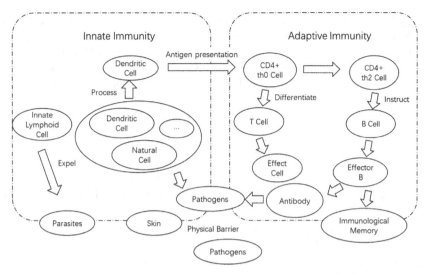

Fig. 1. The basic processes of the immune system: the innate and adaptive immune systems

Researchers acquire some inspiration by studying the resemblance between the immune and network security systems. In recent years, the property in HIS has caused it to become the focal point of computer science. Since then, developing theoretical immunology and applying immune models to computer security has bit by bit grown out of a research field called Artificial Immune Systems(AIS). Paper [3] conducted a study on how AIS solves security issues. Many researchers have conducted in-depth research in this field and made remarkable achievements like the significant algorithms of AIS including the Negative Selection Algorithm (NSA), Clonal Selection, and the Danger Theory (DT) over recent years.

Table 1. Computational immunity based models and specific immunological concepts [4]

Immunological entities	Immunity algorithm	Computer security
Self/Non-Self: T cells recognition	Negative Selection algorithm	Anomaly behavior detection
Immunological memory, B cell	Immune networks theory	Supervised and unsupervised learning
Clonal Expansion, maturation, B cell	Clonal Selection. Algorithm	Search and optimization
Innate Immunity	Danger theory	Defense strategy

In short, in the computer security area, the immense formative AIS research plays a foundation as a reference for IDSs [5]. Specifically, IDSs typically revolve around NSA, an abstract model of biological negative selection. The NSA algorithm randomly generates candidate detectors. If they match any self-set (i.e., if the detector area has overlap with the self-set), they are erased and regenerated till fulfilling the quantity of detectors [6]. Table 2 summaries some major works on AIS for IDS. This classical algorithm shows several drawbacks in practice. The significant problem is that making effective detectors require an enormous amount of computing power. In addition, the issue of holes (the non-self region that any valid detectors cannot cover) is impossible to ignore.

Table 2. Summary of some major works on AIS for IDS

Ref.	AIS models	ID approach	Dataset
[7]	Negative Selection	Network-based intrusion detection	KDD'cup 99 dataset
[8]	Artificial immune system: generation of detectors	Anomaly Detection	
[9]	Cooperative AIS	Malware detection and network based detection	
[10]		Network Intrusion Detection	
[11]	Immune Intrusion Detection Algorithm	Intrusion detection	

Previous research has shown that a difficult difficulty in NSA is choosing the right radius for self-samples. For building and training detectors, these radiuses are employed. The problem of boundary invasion and sample overlap, which raises the false detection rate, can be brought on by the improper selection of a radius. Meanwhile, the exponential growth computational time of generated detectors is also a critical issue.

These years, several optimized NSA has proposed. In the scenario described by [14], the evolution of NSA is divided into four periods. The first phase, according to researchers, involved the representation of detectors as binary strings, whereas the second phase involved the representation of detectors as real values. Later, grid-based representations were proposed by Yang. Considering the performance result of the first two phases, the third phase is aiming at improving NSA accuracy and decreasing computational costs by developing an adaptive methodology. Deals with the shortcomings of constant-size detectors; in the majority of the early NSA iterations, detector initialization was random. Later, researchers experimented with heuristic techniques to initialize the detector position using evolutionary computation-based adaptiveness and pseudorandomness. One illustration is the variable size detector (also known as the V-detector) [12]. In addition, the first three periods are devoted almost entirely to real-valued anomaly detection problems rather than specific scenarios, which brings about high false positives and high false negatives in intrusion detection. As result, the last phase, the current period, concentrates on the NSA algorithm combined with another algorithm in a specific application area.

In this paper, we abide by the fourth period researching train of thought above and propose a framework for intrusion detection. Our focus is more specifically on the systematic design of IDS. The following are this paper's main contributions:

- We proposed a systematic design for intrusion detection. The framework builds three lines of defense against invaders: the barrier layer, the innate layer, and the adaptive layer.
- We introduced Principal Component Analysis (PCA) into intrusion detection to refine the internal structure of detector generation and proposed a tuning value to optimize the training process. The two improvements can help solve the existing drawbacks, produce effective detectors and keep the algorithm's computational complexity within reasonable bounds. Experimental results show specific indicators enough to achieve the performance of the classical AI algorithm.

The rest of the paper is organized as follows. Section 2 illustrates the basic algorithm and how the algorithm worked mathematically, briefly describes the workflow mainly used in intrusion detection, and Sect. 3 introduces the details of the structure and process of the updated algorithm. Then in Sect. 4, the evaluation of experiments is presented. Finally, Sect. 5 concludes the paper.

2 Preliminaries

2.1 Basic Negative Selection Algorithm Used in AIS

The AIS is an approach that uses the HIS as a metaphor for solving computational problems, not modeling the immune system, and not an algorithm we can use directly. It is a model with specific properties and multiple concepts.

The NSA is the most widely used technique in AISs. It is based on the principles of self/non-self discrimination. Given this, the self-set S is a set of genes that characterizes the self, and the antibodies should not match any gene in S. To train the artificial immune system with the self in the first step, we need a test set TS $\in$ S. This set should be a subset of self so we can use negative selection to find antibodies that do not match any $g \in S$.

$$S = \{g_0, \ldots, g_n\} \tag{1}$$

After defining the test set, we move on to AIS's main aspects, which contain encoding, similarity measure, selection, and mutation.

Encoding. The genes, antibodies, and antigens should be represented in the system in a format that can be easily manipulated. Originally this was a binary string that represented a gene. However, based on the current matching rule, such a representation provides inadequate coverage of the problem space from the standpoint of the affinity relation.

In the proposed framework, we use a vector of real-valued genes between 0 and 1.

$$g = \{g_0, \ldots, g_n\} \cap 0 < g_i < 1 \tag{2}$$

Similarity Measure. Detectors bind themselves to non-self with a specific degree of affinity. Similarity or distance measure, the genes' encoding, and the data's properties are closely related to affinity. Hamming distance, euclidean distance, r-continuous bits, r-chunks, and landscape affinity are used to gauge the degree of affinity. Since we are using vectors of real values, the euclidean distance and similarity are appropriate.

Because of this, in the proposed framework, the detector contains gene g and has a binding threshold, and then matching between a detector d and antigen g is defined as.

$$d = \{bt, g\} \cap 0 < bt < 1 \tag{3}$$

$$m_{dg} = 1 \Big/ 1 + \sqrt[2]{\sum_i \sqrt{(d_i - g_i)^2}} \tag{4}$$

Selection. An ais selection can be both positive and negative. The system is empty at the beginning for positive selection, and target data items could be encoded as antigens. Antibodies are created, and each starts with a specific concentration value which decreases over time (death rate), and antibodies below a specific value should be removed from the system. An antibody's concentration is increased when it matches antigens.

A detector d matches a gen g if the matching value m_{dg} is lower than the binding threshold d_{bt} of the detector.

$$match(d, g) = \begin{cases} true \ if \ m_{dg} > d_{bt} \\ false \ if \ m_{dg} < d_{bt} \end{cases} \tag{5}$$

Mutation. In artificial immune systems, the mutation most frequently utilized is similar to genetic algorithms. Bits are switched around in binary strings. In vectors of real numbers or characters, values are changed at random. According to a high-rate mutation mechanism, detectors clone their parents. It is a colony search mechanism in nature, the amount of mutation depends on the closeness of the match, which can increase or decrease the strength of mutation by the type used.

2.2 The Workflow of Basic Negative Selection Algorithm Used in AIS

The detector creation and selection algorithm used in AIS is based on the NSA algorithm. It generates real-valued random detectors, which are then compared with the test set. The basic algorithm works as follows .

Table 3. Basic NSA algorithm

The Workflow of Basic Negative Selection Algorithm
Require: Set a counter n because of the number of detectors

Define an empty set of detectors DS
Determine the training set of self-pattern as S
While DS's size! = n do
Generate detectors d_i randomly
Not Matched;
For g_i belongs to S
If affinity between d_i and g_i is higher than affinity threshold d_{bt} then
Matched;
Break;
end if
end
if not matched then
add d_i to DS;
end
end

According to the pseudo code of NSA in Table 3, the key processes are illustrates as Fig. 2.

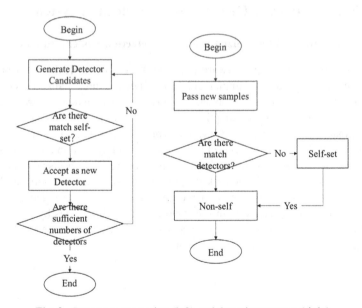

Fig. 2. Detectors generation (left) and detection process (right)

2.3 Intrusion Detection Systems Based on AIS

Most IDS rely on suspicious signatures based on known intrusions. An IDS evaluates a suspected intrusion and signals an alarm once it has occurred. Researchers want IDS to be adaptive and self-organizing. Because of this, immune-inspired algorithms have been used in the past few years to detect abnormal behaviour.

In this paper, we focused on the NSA algorithm. In addition to the drawbacks mentioned in the chapter introduction, two other issues are also involved in algorithm application in the intrusion detection area. At first, along with the extension of the scale, the number of detectors can raise. However, because the system is limited, much like our body, we are unable to produce antibodies indefinitely [11]. Secondly, most current intrusion detection methods cannot handle huge amounts of data by means of an online audit. Beyond that, one thing to note is that the transmission from the roles of self to non-self exists, the legal and dangerous behaviours may exchange, and vice versa. The old and invalid detectors must be eliminated. This counterbalance is crucial for the homeostasis of an immune response. Instead of directly abandoning detectors that match self-samples, [12] suggested introducing dynamical detectors with time. He defines a finite period of time for the detector; later in life, the detectors are going to be removed and a new candidate detector will take their place. Even though researchers like [12] have already optimized the algorithm significantly, there is still room for improvement. As a counter-example, there are a million "hits" on our network daily, and the attack-defence model states dynamically change, so it is difficult to determine the lifetime.

3 Optimized Adaptive Gene Intrusion Detection System

3.1 The Framework of Optimized Intrusion Detection System Based on AIS

Given the above sections, we put forward a hybrid IDS composed of AIS and an optimized NSA algorithm. Firstly, to fully implement AIS in IDS, the three main layers of the HIS are recommended to be indeed modeled. The three layers include the Barrier layer, the Innate Immune Layer, and the Adaptive Immune Layer. The Barrier layer is applied as a preliminary measure to prevent invaders from entering, such as a firewall or other security gateway. The Signature Based IDS, which is widely used in computer security, should be used to represent the Innate Layer. This layer greatly impacts reducing specific detector generation in this framework due to the efficient iteration and rapid feature matching. In short, both layers restrict the generation of detectors and decrease the workload of eliminated detectors, in other words, the preliminaries by the two layers facilitate the dynamic maintenance of detectors to attain Hofmeyr's effects while not increasing algorithms' time and space complexities.

Secondly, the Adaptive Immune System is represented by an optimized NSA. Currently, the emphasis is on including an algorithm to optimize NSA for the particular application area. The thought has been reviewed, [13] analysis of a cooperative immunological approach for detective network anomaly, it defines the communication triple (source, destination IP and Port, and protocol) as a binary vector in self-set. This idea of this thesis shows light on our framework. We introduce Principal Component Analysis (PCA) into intrusion detection to extract the five most relevant features. The step is necessary to make the genes real-valued and keep the algorithm's computational complexity in reasonable bounds. In addition, as mentioned above, when using AIS to solve an intrusion detection problem, it's critical to produce precise and effective detectors. We have made research and simulation to the problems. At first, we align with Forrest's original NSA for randomly generated detectors. Until the required detector set size is reached, new detectors are created. Each detector is checked for matches with the self-set. And then, we pay attention to the exponential growth computational time of generated detectors, on the other hand, we recommended a good detector that has minimal overlap with other detectors apart from the difference between self-spaces. As a result, the detectors in our proposal that match self are not directly removed from the generated detectors. These weak detectors are tuned until they do not match any self-gene. The tuning value reduces the area of the space that is matched by that detector.

3.2 The Workflow of Basic Negative Selection Algorithm Used in AIS

Table 4. The workflow of optimized intrusion detection system based on AIS

Defense	Layer	Preliminary and workflow
The static defense	The barrier layer	Require1: Adopting access control measures to prevent invaders from entering
		Static defense systems use physical isolation such as a firewall or virtual logical isolation to resist external attacks
The dynamic defense	The innate layer	Require2: Drive Dataset or incoming traffic to Signature based IDS
		Provide general intrusion detection and protection means by using intrusion detection, sandbox, and patch technologies to reduce the number of generated detector
	The adaptive layer	Require3: Improved NSA algorithm Set a counter n as the number of detectors

(*continued*)

Table 4. (*continued*)

Defense	Layer	Preliminary and workflow

		Define an empty set of detectors DS
		Determine the training set of self-pattern as S
		While DS's size! $= $ n do
		Generate detectors d_i randomly;
		Not Matched;
		For g_i belongs to S
		distance_list $=$ list(euc_distance(d_i, g_i));
		distance_ bt_{min} $=$ np.min(distance_list);
		distance_ bt $=$ distance_ bt_{min} $-$ distance_ bt;
		If distance_ bt_{min} between d_i and g_i is higher than affinity threshold d_{bt} then
		Matched $=$ true;
		Break;
		end if
		end
		if not matched then
		add d_i to DS;
		end
		end

		Require4: Intrusion detection based on improved NSA

		Require:DS
		Require: test set as T
		Require: A_t alert threshold, such as belong to (0,1)
		
		Require: anomaly$(T_i, \mathrm{V}) = \begin{cases} true \ if \ V > A_t \\ false \ if \ V < A_t \end{cases}$
		
		for g $\in$ T do
		votes $= 0$
		for d $\in$DS do
		if match(d, g) then
		votes $=$ votes $+ 1$
		return vote
		end if
		end for
		if votes $\geq A_t$ then
		Anomaly
		end if
		end for

4   Experimental Results

4.1   Description of Open Source Datasets

Most traffic classification studies use their private traffic datasets for individuals or companies, which affects the reliability of the classification results. So we chose the KDDCUP'99 dataset [14]. The data collection is utilized to create a network intrusion detector, a forecasting model capable of identifying abnormal network traffic (such as intrusions, attacks and etc.) and normal behaviours. In terms of the standard dataset, this dataset contains intrusions simulated in a military network environment, it is easy to be evaluated false positives.

In the dataset, there are 4,900,000 entries which are single connection vectors. The entries consist of 41 features, and each of the entries is labeled as either normal or a specific attack, such as DoS, U2R, R2L, etc.

4.2   Discussion About Experiment Result

In this section, we compare the changed algorithm to classical AI algorithms to see the differences in performance. The algorithms will be evaluated on the same dataset for intrusion detection.

Experiments Setting: For the adaptive algorithm and the experimental settings, We take the power threshold $PT = 0.7$, and the binding threshold for detectors is initialized at $d_{bt} = 0.3$. we mostly keep the two values that the original NSA algorithm has proposed since they have been experimentally evaluated to be effective. For the test set, we take $|TS| = 311029$. The test set TS will contain 311029 values, both normal and intrusions. We take a value as high as possible for the detector generation while still keeping a reasonable running time, which is $|DS| = 6000$, and we use one detector set. Primarily, we introduce the self-tuning factor. Each configuration will be run 20 times, and we will take the average. In the Intrusion Detection phrase, the alert threshold will be $A_t = 1$.

Examples that are classified as non-self are counted as true positives(TP); examples that are classed as self are counted as false negatives(FN). A false positive(FP) is recorded if the example is self and it is determined to be non-self. The performance will be evaluated with precision and recall which are calculated as:

$$\text{Precision rate} = \frac{TP}{TP + FP} \tag{6}$$

$$\text{Recall rate} = \frac{TP}{TP + FN} \tag{7}$$

Classification Experiments: Table 5 presents the results matrix and the performance measures for K Means, Decision Trees, Multi-Level Perceptron, Random Forrest Classifier, K Neighbors, and our proposal. The matrix shows that most samples are predicted accurately. On the other hand, by comparison with the results of these classical algorithms, the results prove the validity of the dynamic self-tuning factor and dimensionality reduction.

For a given specific problem set, by examining the misclassified samples, we found that both classifiers tend to classify those misclassified samples as negative. Applications based on NSA are appropriate for situations involving outlier detection problems where outlier data have fewer representations.

Table 5. Experimental environment parameters.

Category	Precision	Recall
K Means	Attack 0.95 Normal 0.83	Attack 0.96 Normal 0.80
Decision Trees	Attack 1.0 Normal 0.74	Attack 0.91 Normal 0.99
Multi-Level Perceptron	Attack 0.99 Normal 0.73	Attack 0.91 Normal 0.97
Random Forrest Classifier	Attack 1.0 Normal 0.73	Attack 0.91 Normal 0.99
K Neighbors	Attack 1.0 Normal 0.73	Attack 0.91 Normal 0.99
Adaptive NSA	Attack 0.81 Normal 0.78	Attack 0.76 Normal 0.98

5   Conclusion

The majority of AIS-based IDS reviews are summarized from the perspective of the system development or algorithms that were utilized. These theories and methods can act as the foundation for efficient intrusion detection. However, in specific application areas like intrusion detection, more details ought to be considered, such as feature vectors, which might be extracted by adding additional algorithms, besides, efficient detector generation is critical due to computationally expensive. For the above considerations, in our proposal, we put forward a hybrid IDS composed of the Barrier layer, the Innate layer and the Adaptive layer, the preliminaries by the first two layers facilitate the dynamic maintenance of detectors, and then in the third layer, feature selection techniques (PCA)were used to focus intrusion detection field and reduce the data set's dimensionality, in addition, we also introduce the self-tuning factor to produce efficient detectors.

From our analysis, due to the lack of negative data, traditional clustering-based approaches cannot cover some of the negative data space, but the optimal generation of detectors can. It is apparent that our proposal has helped to reduce false positives and increase the true positives. Furthermore, in comparison to other ML, the optimized NSA's dynamic size and generation procedure further shields NSA from the overfitting issue. We also noticed that NSA is just as efficient as other well-known algorithms for classifying outliers.

So far, due to the requirement of real-time detection and much more complicated real-world networks, AIS-based IDS faces many challenges. The majority of current NSA-based innovations are optimization-based and restricted to specific problem domains. In future work, IDSs should make a profound study on important properties in mutation operators for a quick response.

References

1. Forrest, S., et al.: Self-nonself discrimination in a computer. IEEE (1994)
2. Yu, Q., et al.: An immunology-inspired network security architecture. IEEE Wirel. Commun. **27**(5), 168–173 (2020). https://doi.org/10.1109/MWC.001.2000046
3. Yang, H., et al.: A survey of artificial immune system based intrusion detection. The Sci. World J. **2014**, 156790 (2014)
4. Dasgupta, D., Nino, L.F.: Immunological computation, theory and application, Auerbach (2009)
5. Dasgupta, D., Gonzalez, F.: Artificial Immune Systems in Intrusion Detection, chapter 7 of "Enhancing computer security with smart technology" V. Rao Vemuri (2005)
6. Selahshoor, F., Jazayeriy, H., Omranpour, H.: Intrusion detection systems using real-valued negative selection algorithm with optimized detectors. In: 2019 5th Iranian Conference on Signal Processing and Intelligent Systems (ICSPIS), pp. 1–5 (2019). https://doi.org/10.1109/ICSPIS48872.2019.9066040
7. Luther, K., Bye, R., Alpcan, T., Muller, A., Albayrak, S.: A Cooperative AIS Framework for Intrusion Detection. In: IEEE International Conference on Communications, pp. 1409–1416 (2007)
8. Wang, X.: Research of Immune Intrusion Detection Algorithm Based on Semi-supervised Clustering. In: Deng, H., Miao, D., Lei, J. (Eds.) Artificial Intelligence and Computational Intelligence Lecture Notes in Computer Science vol. 7003, pp. 69–74 (2011)
9. Suliman, S.I., Abd Shukor, M.S., Kassim, M., Mohamad, R., Shahbudin, S.: Network Intrusion Detection System Using Artificial Immune System (AIS). In: 2018 3rd International Conference on Computer and Communication Systems (ICCCS), pp. 178–182, (2018). https://doi.org/10.1109/CCOMS.2018.8463274
10. Kumari, K., Jain, A., Jain, A.: An efficient approach to categorize data using improved dendritic cell algorithm with dempster belief theory. In: Kumar V., Bhatele M. (eds.), Proceedings of All India Seminar on Biomedical Engineering, Lecture Notes in Bioengineering, pp. 165–172 (2013)
11. Ji, Z., Dasgupta, D.: V-detector: an efficient negative selection algorithm with 'probably adequate' detector coverage. Inf. Sci. **179**(10), 1390–1406 (2009)
12. Hofmeyr, S.A.: An immunological model of distributed detection and its application to computer security. The University of New Mexico (1999)
13. Gupta, K.D., Dasgupta, D.: Negative Selection Algorithm Research and Applications in the last decade: A Review. (2021)
14. Sobh, T.S., Mostafa, W.M.: A cooperative immunological approach for detecting network anomaly. Appl. Soft Comput. **11**(1), 1275–1283 (2011)
15. KDDCUP99 Homepage. http://kdd.ics.uci.edu/databases/kddcup99/kddcup99.html

Hop-by-Hop Verification Mechanism of Packet Forwarding Path Oriented to Programmable Data Plane

Junsan Zeng[1], Ying Liu[1], Weiting Zhang[1(✉)], Xincheng Yan[2,3], Na Zhou[2,3], and Zhihong Jiang[2,3]

[1] National Engineering Research Center of Advanced Network Technologies, Beijing Jiaotong University, Beijing, China
{21120164,yliu,wtzhang}@bjtu.edu.cn
[2] State Key Laboratory of Mobile Network and Mobile Multimedia Technology, Shenzhen 518055, China
{yan.xincheng,zhou.na,jiang.zhihong}@zte.com.cn
[3] ZTE Corporation, Nanjing 210012, China

Abstract. Attacks against the forwarding path could deviate data packets from the predefined route to achieve ulterior purposes, which has posed a serious threat to the software-defined network. Previous studies attempted to solve this security issue through complex authentication or traffic statistics methods. However, existing schemes have the disadvantages of high bandwidth overhead and high process delay. Hence, this article proposed a lightweight forwarding path verification mechanism based on P4 implementation. First, we deployed inband network telemetry to obtain path information, and then performed the path verification inside each hop in the programmable data plane to ensure that various attacks against forwarding paths could be intercepted. Finally, complete path verification information would convey to the control plane for backup. Corresponding experimental results demonstrate that our mechanism can effectively improve the security of the packet forwarding path with acceptable throughput and delay.

Keywords: Path verification · SDN · P4 · INT

1 Introduction

Source authentication and path authentication in the network are very important security mechanisms [1,2], which can help mitigate various network forwarding-based attacks, such as DDoS, address spoofing, and traffic redirection attacks [3,4]. In traditional networks, the end host cannot control the path taken by its data packets [5]. The receiving end host only knows the information of the switch directly connected to itself, and cannot know the previous forwarding path [6].

Supported by State Key Laboratory of Mobile Network and Mobile Multimedia Technology.

This feature makes the forwarding efficiency in the network low, reduces the security, and hinders the user's perception of the data forwarding path. Therefore, it is of great significance to design an efficient and secure path verification mechanism. There are three main ways to achieve source authentication and path verification in traditional networks: adding labels or signatures to data packets [7], detecting forwarding anomalies through traffic analysis, and using packet detection and message authentication code (MAC) [8]. Most of these methods will bring the extra load to the data packets, and it is difficult to ensure the quality of network forwarding.

Software-Defined Networking (SDN) provides network administrators with a global perspective, which can obtain the connection status of all switches in the network, define network forwarding policies on the control plane, and enforce them on the data plane. This feature enables researchers to propose many source authentication and path authentication mechanisms based on the SDN control plane, but this makes the controller, which has a large overhead, take on more responsibilities. In 2014, the team of Professor Nick Mckeown of Stanford University [9] proposed the programmable protocol-independent packet processor technology (Programming Protocol-independent Packet Processor, P4). The emergence of P4 makes it possible to implement path authentication in the data plane. To solve the problems of excessive overhead and insufficient security of the existing solutions, this paper focuses on the realization of path verification based on P4 to ensure the security of the data plane forwarding path under the SDN architecture. The main contributions of this paper are as follows:

1. A path verification mechanism is designed based on P4. Based on inband telemetry to obtain path status information, hop-by-hop verification is implemented in the data plane, and complete path verification is implemented in the control plane.

2. Reasonable experiments for the performance evaluation are executed. The results show that our scheme brings security enhancement with a little overhead.

The rest of this paper is organized as follows: Sect. 2 presents related work. Section 3 introduces the technical foundation and theoretical background on which this paper is based in detail. Section 4 details the complete flow of our designed mechanism. Section 5 analyzes the security of our proposed mechanism. Section 6 presents the experiments we designed. The Sect. 7 summarizes the full text.

2 Related Work

ICING [10], OPT [11], PPV [12], and ECPI [5] all provide relatively complete path verification mechanisms. ICING first proposed the network primitive of Path Verification Mechanism (PVM). ICING adds 42 bytes to each hop router, which is expensive. OPT is more lightweight, adding 16 bytes per hop and requiring only one MAC per router. PPV implements path verification with a fixed 64-byte overhead, but only implements probabilistic verification, not all packets. EPIC is implemented based on an architecture called a path-aware network

[13], which provides a complete path verification mechanism for inter-AS inter-domain forwarding. EPIC is divided into four levels. The more complete levels, L3 and L4, require a basic overhead of 24 bytes, while adding 5 bytes of overhead per hop. In general, the common disadvantage of such schemes is that the path information verification code is too long, which will lead to unacceptably high communication overhead, but the short and efficient verification code is not secure enough. In addition, there are many path verification mechanisms implemented under the SDN architecture. SDNsec [14] uses the message authentication code MAC to verify whether the flow path is the same as the policy issued by the controller. However, when verifying the flow of multiple packets, SDNsec will bring huge bandwidth overhead in the control channel. The paper [15] based on the rule execution verification REV, proposes a heuristic traffic algorithm to compress the MAC, which greatly reduces the traffic overhead of the switch-to-controller interaction when the controller is used for path verification. The paper [16] proposes DYNAPFV, which is based on the controller monitoring the data packets and traffic statistics in the network and then detects the violation of data packet integrity and forwarding behavior. Similar to the paper [17], the above two schemes both aim to check the correctness of the network policy and do not verify the integrity of the forwarding path.

In contrast, our mechanism is implemented based on P4. Each hop only needs to add 9 bytes, and only calculates the message verification code for the next hop, and implements hop-by-hop verification. On the premise of ensuring low overhead, it can not only do to check the correctness of the network forwarding policy, but it can also effectively defend against attacks on the forwarding path.

3   System Model

This section briefly introduces the characteristics of SDN and P4, as well as some basic assumptions and attacker models of the studied mechanisms.

3.1   SDN and P4

SDN increases the flexibility of traditional networks by decoupling the control and data planes [18]. The emergence of P4 redefines the logic of data plane packet processing, providing a high degree of protocol-independent programmability for the data plane. Using P4, we can redefine the packet header structure, parsing process, and processing logic of data packets [19]. We customize the packet headers that save path status information and verification codes and rewrite the parsing process to generate and verify specific packets. Action that provides path validation services for a specific flow.

3.2   Basic Assumptions

This paper uses in-band telemetry [14] to obtain the forwarding path, and the controller manages and updates the path information uniformly. Compared with traditional network measurement technologies, in-band telemetry can obtain more fine-grained and more real-time network information. We design the verification mechanism assuming that all switches, controllers, and endpoints share the path state information. Furthermore, it is assumed that the interaction between the control plane and the data plane is secure and reliable, which will determine the key security of this mechanism.

3.3 Attacker Model

Assume such an attacker model: in the data plane, an attacker can fully control a switch on the link, intercept, drop, forge or replay packets [16], thereby disrupting the communication between hosts. Based on this attack model, various attacks on the data plane may occur, such as path hijacking, replay attacks, path tampering, etc., which will be analyzed in detail in Sect. 6.

4 Design

This section first introduces the overall framework of the verification mechanism, then introduces the functions implemented by the control plane and data plane respectively, and finally summarizes the complete verification process.

4.1 OverView

Our scheme is divided into three modules, label calculation module, identity verification module and key management module.

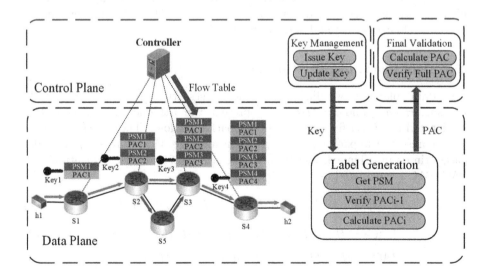

Fig. 1. The overall framework of the path verification mechanism.

As shown in Fig. 1, the control plane implements key management and identity verification, and the data plane implements identity generation and hop-by-hop verification. On the whole, when the switch receives the message from the previous hop switch, it first uses the verification key Key_{i-1} to verify the Path-Authentication-Code PAC_{i-1} of the data packet. If the verification is successful, the Path-State-MessagePSM_i and PAC_i of this hop will be inserted into the data packet and sent to the next hop. If the verification fails, the data packet will be discarded directly. After the data packet passes through the last hop, the controller will verify the complete path status information.

4.2   Control Plane: Identity Verification Module and Key Management Module

The identity verification specifically refers to the verification implemented by the terminal or the controller after the data packet has gone through the complete link. Hop-by-hop verification before the last hop is implemented on the switch and will be covered in the next section. In this paper, we use the controller to verify the complete PAC. This design uses the global perspective of the controller. If the verification is unsuccessful, the controller can further locate the abnormal node and take necessary measures to deal with it. If the verification is unsuccessful The packet is discarded directly.

In addition, the control plane implements the distribution and management of keys. Assuming secure communication between the control plane and the data plane, in a network with hop switches, the controller maintains different keys. Taking the switch S3 in Fig. 1 as an example, the key issuing rule is described. The controller first determines the encryption key Key_3 to be issued and then determines that it may be used as the decryption key of the switch S3, namely Key_2, Key_4, and Key_5, and issues the four keys together. In the key update phase, the four keys are updated together.

4.3   Data Plane: Identity Generation

The data plane forwarding data packet structure is shown in Fig. 2. $EthernetHeader$ and $Ipv4Header$ represent the Ethernet header and IPv4 header and the $Data$ field represents the packet payload. The $VerifyMessage$ field represents the packet path verification message, $VerifyMessage$ includes packet timestamp Timepkt, path status message PSM and path verification code PAC. PAC is calculated as Formulas (1)–(3):

$$PAC_1 = Hash(Time_{pkt}||PSM_1||Key||...)[0:l] \tag{1}$$

$$PAC_2 = Hash(PAC_1||Time_{pkt}||PSM_2||Key||...)[0:l] \tag{2}$$

$$PAC_i = Hash(PAC_{i-1}||Time_{pkt}||PSM_i||Key||...)[0:l] \tag{3}$$

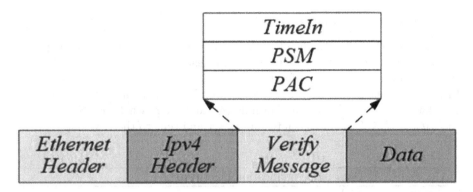

Fig. 2. Verify mechanism packet structure.

Our mechanism can be combined with a variety of hash algorithms. Hash in Formula 2 indicates that the path verification code is obtained using the hash algorithm, such as HashCRC16, HashCRC32, HashMD5, HashSHA2, etc. PSM_i indicates forwarding path status information. For the first hop switch, only the Hash operation is performed on the path status information of this hop. Starting from the second hop, the path verification code of the previous hop is added to the calculation, and the path verification code at the last hop will be related to all the state information on the path. $Time_{pkt}$ in Formulas (1)–(3) represents the time stamp of the data packet, and the time stamp of the data packet entering the switch can be used, and the time stamp of the outgoing port can also be used. The Key is the key saved by the switch, $[0 : l]$which means that it is truncated to bits. In addition, the fields involved in Hash calculation can continue to be expanded to provide more verification functions. In this research, considering the current computing power and overhead of the P4 switch, we use HashCRC32 to calculate the message verification code. HashCRC32 is an algorithm that can quickly generate a 32-bit Hash value, which can be used to quickly verify the data Completeness. The calculation result is truncated to 32 bit, in other words, $l = 31$, in order to minimize the extra overhead when the number of hops is large. The Formula for calculating PAC_i in this paper is as follows

$$PAC_i = Hash\_CRC32(PAC_{i-1}||Time_{in}||PSM_i||Key_i)[0 : 31] \qquad (4)$$

$$PSM_i = (SWID||Port_{in}||Port_{out}) \qquad (5)$$

$Time_{in}$ in Formula (4) represents the time stamp when the data packet enters the switch. Key_i is a 32 bit key saved by the switch. The details is shown in Formula (5), $SWID$ represents the number information of the switch in the path, occupying 8 bits. $Port_{in}$ and $Port_{out}$ represent the ingress port number and egress port number of the switch when the packet is forwarded, respectively. If the length of the Hash operation option in the formula is less than 32 bits, it will be automatically filled to 32 bits, and if the length exceeds 32 bits, it will be truncated to 32 bits.

4.4 Verification Process

As shown in Algorithm 1, when the switch receives a packet, it parses the packet header in the order of Ethernet Header, IPv4 Header, and Verify Message Header. If the packet contains the Verify Message Header, the verification logic is entered. First, obtain the information of PSM_{i-1} and PAC_{i-1} in the data packet, then calculate $VerifyPAC_{i-1}$ using Formula (4), and judge whether PSM_i is equal to PAC_{i-1}. PAC_i is inserted into the packet and sent to the next hop.

Algorithm 1: Data plane verification algorithm

   Input: receive packet
   Output: True or False
1 i represents the i-th hop switch
2 **while** $i \neq n$ **do**
3   **if** *packet have Ethernet IPv4 VerifyMessage* **then**
4        $VerifyPAC_{i-1} =$
       $Hash(Min\|PAC_{i-1}\|Time_{in}\|PSM_{i-1}\|Key_{i-1}\|Max)[0:l]$ **if**
       $VerifyPAC_{i-1} == PAC_{i-1}$ **then**
5   Get this hop PSM and calculate PAC use Formula (3)
6   flag=True
7   break
8   **else**
9   flag=False
10   break
11   **end**
12   **else**
13   flag=False
14   break
15   **end**
16 **end**
17 return flag

When the data packet reaches the last hop switch, the switch reports the path state information and verification information obtained by parsing to the controller and performs verification according to Algorithm 2. The controller verifies the PSM of each hop, in turn, starting from PAC_n, and uses the same Hash as the encryption operation to calculate to obtain $VerifyPAC_n$. The controller will use the forwarding rules saved by itself in the calculation of the path forwarding rules. This provision is to prevent attackers from tampering with the path information during forwarding. If $VerifyPAC_n$ is equal to PAC_n, continue to verify PAC_{n-1}, and directly command the switch to discard the data packet if the verification fails. If all PAC are verified successfully, the command of normal forwarding is issued to the last hop switch, and the destination host will receive the data packet normally.

Algorithm 2: Control Plane Verification Algorithm

Input: $PAC_1 - PAC_n, PSM_1 - PSM_n$

Output: True or False

1 i represents the i-th hop switch

2 $i = n$ flag=Ture

3 **while** $i >= 1$ **do**

4     $VerifyPAC_i =$
   $Hash\_CRC32(Min||PAC_{i-1}||Time_{in}||PSM_i||Key_i||Max)[0:31]$ **if**
   $VerifyPAC_i == PAC_i$ **then**

5        $i--$

6   continue

7   **else**

8   flag=False

9   break

10   **end**

11 **end**

12 **return** flag

---

5 Security Analysis

This section analyzes several possible attackers based on the attacker model introduced in Sect. 3, and analyzes how to defend against these attacks.

Data Packet Tampering Attack: The attacker controls the switch to hijack the data packet and modify various information carried in the data packet so that the receiver receives the wrong information. When calculating the verification information of each hop, our mechanism also takes the verification information of the previous link as input, namely PAC_{i-1} in Formula (5). Once a packet is hijacked, its forwarding path state information will change, PAC_{i-1} will change, and it will be discarded during data plane verification. Even if the attacker completely modifies and forges the path information and bypasses the data plane verification, the final control plane verification cannot be consistent with the path forwarding rules saved by the controller. Such attack packets will be detected by the control plane verification mechanism and discarded.

Packet Replay Attack: The attacker monitors the data packets sent to a certain host, obtains the authentication information that has been successfully authenticated, and then replays the same data packets into the network and sends them to the destination host, to destroy the normal path forwarding verification purpose. Our verification mechanism adds timestamps in the calculation of PAC and sends the timestamps as path state information to the next hop. The timestamps of the replayed packets have expired and will be discarded during the verification of the data plane. In addition, we maintain different authentication keys for different switches, and packets from unreasonable switches will not be authenticated with the correct key.

Path Deviation: Malicious nodes may modify the packet forwarding path, resulting in packets not being forwarded according to predetermined rules. Path detours, out-of-order packets, etc. belong to this type of attack. We maintain different verification keys in data plane verification. Each switch has its verification key and encryption key. Once the path detour occurs, the next hop switch will use the attacker's key for verification, which will not be able to verify success. For out-of-order problems, we add timestamp verification to the verification mechanism, which can effectively prevent out-of-order problems.

6   Simulation and Analysis

In this section, we evaluate the performance of the proposed mechanism, and we will evaluate the actual performance of the mechanism in terms of forwarding delay and communication overhead. In the Ubuntu18.04 virtual environment, we use Mininet to build the topology and use the BMv2 software switch for experiments. The computer hardware configuration we use is Intel(R) Core(TM) i5-7300HQ CPU @ 2.50 GHz, RAM: 16 G.

6.1   Forwarding Delay

Using the direct connection topology of two hosts and two switches to test the forwarding delay, the P4 program can read and record the time stamps of packets entering and leaving the switch, and use the method of subtracting the incoming and outgoing timestamps to calculate the switch forwarding delay.

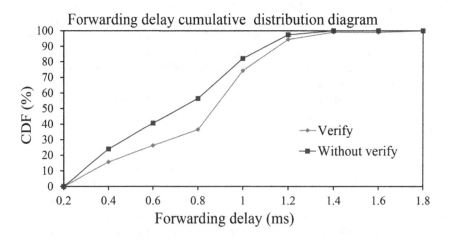

Fig. 3. The cumulative probability distribution of the delay of BMv2 switch processing 1000 packets.

We use a custom packet sending script to send 1000 data packets on the sender side, test the data packets with verification function and the data packets with only telemetry path information, set a 95% confidence interval to remove bad values, and draw out Cumulative distribution graph (CDF) of forwarding delay, evaluating the impact of our mechanism on packet forwarding delay.

As shown in Fig. 3. Overall, the forwarding delay is within 1.8 ms for both packets with validation and only telemetry path information. The delay of packets without verification function is less than 1 ms, accounting for 82.2%, and the delay of packets with verification function is less than 1 ms, accounting for 74.3%, that is, the delay of packets with verification function is an additional 7.9%. The delay is greater than 1 ms. In addition, the average forwarding delay of data packets with verification function is 0.805 ms, and the average forwarding delay of data packets without verification function is 0.710 ms, that is, the average forwarding delay increases by 0.095 ms. It can be seen that although our mechanism adds extra overhead to the data packet, the extra forwarding delay caused is very limited.

6.2   Throughput

We build a topology with two hosts and multiple BMv2 switches directly connected for throughput testing, setting the maximum throughput of all links to 10 Mbps. Use the bandwidth measurement tool D-ITG 2.8.1 to measure the throughput of 2, 3, 4, 5 and 6-hop switches when they are directly connected. Compare the throughput variation of basic IPv4 forwarding (Basic), packet forwarding with telemetry (INT), verify without timestamp (Verify without timestamp), and verify with timestamp (Verify).

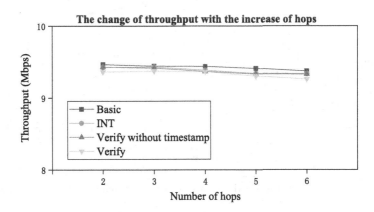

Fig. 4. The change of throughput with the increase of hops.

Figure 4 shows the throughput changes of 2, 3, 4, 5, and 6-hop switches under different forwarding rules, respectively. As the number of hops increases, the throughput of INT, Verify without timestamp and Verify all decrease compared to Basic due to the increase in the length of the data packet, and the throughput of the switch using the verification scheme decreases more significantly. Among the schemes with verification mechanisms, the Verify without timestamp scheme has an average decrease of 0.54% compared with the Basic scheme, and an average decrease of 0.1% compared with the INT scheme. The complete solution with timestamp, Verify, has an average decrease of 0.98% compared to Basic and an average decrease of 0.55% compared to INT. The results show that our mechanism brings very little throughput drop to packet forwarding.

6.3   Goodput Ratio

In addition, we evaluate the goodput ratio. The goodput ratio is defined as the ratio between goodput and throughput, or equivalently as the ratio of payload and total packet size as shown in Formula (6).

$$GR = \frac{p}{p + HD} \tag{6}$$

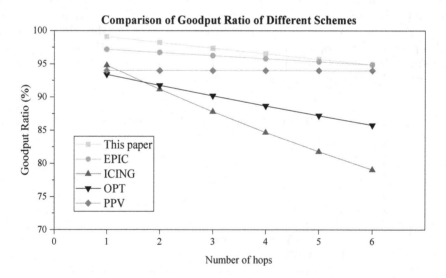

Fig. 5. The variation of the goodput ratio of different schemes with the increase of hops.

HD represents the extra overhead caused by the verification mechanism. We compare the proposed mechanism with the schemes of EPIC, ICING, OPT, and

PPV. Assuming that the payload p is 1000 bytes, plot the goodput ratio as a function of the number of hops as shown in Fig. 5. The green curve in the figure is the mechanism designed for this paper, our mechanism has higher goodput ratio than other mechanisms at 1–6 hops. The goodput ratio rate at 6 hops is still as high as 94.88%, which is the same goodput ratio rate as EPIC and higher than other schemes. In summary, our mechanism can provide highly goodput ratio in most cases.

7   Conclusion

Path verification is a very important network security mechanism. Facing SDN architecture, this paper proposes a lightweight packet forwarding path verification mechanism based on the P4 language. First, we use in-band telemetry to obtain the path state information, and then verify the path of every hop of each packet in the data plane to ensure that all kinds of attacks against the forwarding path are intercepted in the data plane. Finally, the final complete verification message is verified in the control plane. The experimental results show that our mechanism can effectively improve the security of the packet forwarding path on the premise of ensuring acceptable throughput and delay reduction.

Acknowledgements. This work was supported by the ZTE industry-university research cooperation fund project "Research on network identity trusted communication technology architecture", the State Key Laboratory of Mobile Network and Mobile Multimedia Technology and the Fundamental Research Funds under Grant 2021JBZD204.

References

1. Cai, H., Wolf, T.: Source authentication and path validation with orthogonal network capabilities. In: 2015 IEEE Conference on Computer Communications Workshops (INFOCOM WKSHPS), pp. 111–112 (2015). https://doi.org/10.1109/INFOCOMW.2015.7179368
2. Zhang, C., Zhao, M., Zhu, L., Zhang, W., Wu, T., Ni, J.: FRUIT: a blockchain-based efficient and privacy-preserving quality-aware incentive scheme. IEEE J. Sel. Areas Commun. (Early Access, 2022)
3. Yan, Z.J.: Trusted communication technologies for future networks. ZTE Technol. J. **27**(5), 8 (2021)
4. Wang, J., Liu, Y., Zhang, W., Yan, X., Zhou, N., Jiang, Z.: Relfa: resist link flooding attacks via Renyi entropy and deep reinforcement learning in SDN-IoT. China Commun. **19**(7), 157–171 (2022). https://doi.org/10.23919/JCC.2022.07.013
5. Legner, M., Klenze, T., Wyss, M., Sprenger, C., Perrig, A.: EPIC: every packet is checked in the data plane of a path-aware internet. In: 29th USENIX Security Symposium (USENIX Security 2020), pp. 541–558. USENIX Association, August 2020. https://www.usenix.org/conference/usenixsecurity20/presentation/legner

6. Li, Y., et al.: Achieving a blockchain-based privacy-preserving quality-aware knowledge marketplace in crowdsensing. In: Proceedings of IEEE EUC, Wuhan, China, pp. 1–6 (2022)

7. Liu, X., Li, A., Yang, X., Wetherall, D.: Passport: secure and adoptable source authentication. In: Proceedings of the 5th USENIX Symposium on Networked Systems Design and Implementation. NSDI 2008, pp. 365–378. USENIX Association, USA (2008)

8. Yaar, A., Perrig, A., Song, D.: Siff: a stateless internet flow filter to mitigate DDOS flooding attacks. In: IEEE Symposium on Security and Privacy, Proceedings, pp. 130–143 (2004). https://doi.org/10.1109/SECPRI.2004.1301320

9. Bosshart, P., et al.: P4: programming protocol-independent packet processors. SIG-COMM Comput. Commun. Rev. **44**(3), 87–95 (2014). https://doi.org/10.1145/2656877.2656890

10. Naous, J., Walfish, M., Nicolosi, A., Mazières, D., Miller, M., Seehra, A.: Verifying and enforcing network paths with icing. In: Proceedings of the Seventh COnference on Emerging Networking EXperiments and Technologies. CoNEXT 2011. Association for Computing Machinery, New York (2011). https://doi.org/10.1145/2079296.2079326

11. Sengupta, B., Li, Y., Bu, K., Deng, R.H.: Privacy-preserving network path validation. ACM Trans. Internet Technol. **20**(1) (2020). https://doi.org/10.1145/3372046

12. Wu, B., et al.: Enabling efficient source and path verification via probabilistic packet marking. In: 2018 IEEE/ACM 26th International Symposium on Quality of Service (IWQoS), pp. 1–10 (2018). https://doi.org/10.1109/IWQoS.2018.8624169

13. Barrera, D., Chuat, L., Perrig, A., Reischuk, R.M., Szalachowski, P.: The scion internet architecture. Commun. ACM **60**(6), 56–65 (2017). https://doi.org/10.1145/3085591

14. Sasaki, T., Pappas, C., Lee, T., Hoefler, T., Perrig, A.: SDNSec: forwarding accountability for the SDN data plane. In: 2016 25th International Conference on Computer Communication and Networks (ICCCN), pp. 1–10 (2016). https://doi.org/10.1109/ICCCN.2016.7568569

15. Zhang, P., Wu, H., Zhang, D., Li, Q.: Verifying rule enforcement in software defined networks with REV. IEEE/ACM Trans. Netw. **28**(2), 917–929 (2020). https://doi.org/10.1109/TNET.2020.2977006

16. Li, Q., Zou, X., Huang, Q., Zheng, J., Lee, P.P.C.: Dynamic packet forwarding verification in SDN. IEEE Trans. Depend. Secure Comput. **16**(6), 915–929 (2019). https://doi.org/10.1109/TDSC.2018.2810880

17. Zhang, P., et al.: Network-wide forwarding anomaly detection and localization in software defined networks. IEEE/ACM Trans. Netw. **29**(1), 332–345 (2021). https://doi.org/10.1109/TNET.2020.3033588

18. Zhang, S., Cao, C., Tang, X.: Computing power network technology architecture based on SRv6. ZTE Technol. J. **28**(1), 5 (2022)

19. Song, F., Li, L., You, I., Zhang, H.: Enabling heterogeneous deterministic networks with smart collaborative theory. IEEE Netw. **35**(3), 64–71 (2021). https://doi.org/10.1109/MNET.011.2000613

A Reconfigurable and Dynamic Access Control Model in the Programmable Data Plane

Xincheng Yan[1,2(✉)], Na Zhou[1,2], Zhihong Jiang[1,2], Letian Li[3], and Ying Liu[3]

[1] State Key Laboratory of Mobile Network and Mobile Multimedia Technology, Shenzhen 518055, China

[2] ZTE Corporation, Nanjing 210012, China

{yan.xincheng,zhou.na,jiang.zhihong}@zte.com.cn

[3] National Engineering Research Center of Advanced Network Technologies, Beijing Jiaotong University, Beijing, China

{tianll,yliu}@bjtu.edu.cn

Abstract. The explosive growth of various emerging online services has created severe challenges in terms of flexibility and scalability of access control. In order to break through the drawbacks of static and redundancy in traditional access control, we implement an endogenous network access control mechanism based on a reconfigurable decision tree model. First, we explored how to optimize the deployment of access control policies, choosing a decision tree model as the judge based on the network architecture. Second, the authorization decision procedure running on the control plane is migrated to the forwarding device located in the data plane, which can reduce the processing delay. Finally, experiments in the simulation environment show that our scheme can implement access control with less memory overhead, has higher correctness, and has less impact on forwarding than the alternative schemes.

Keywords: P4 · Machine learning · Access control

1 Introduction

Information technology such as artificial intelligence [1], mobile communication [2], and industrial applications [3,4] has spawned ever-changing online services, and the massive traffic growth has introduced new threats to cyberspace security. Attackers inject a variety of malicious traffic into the network through more complex methods to illegally access service resources or hinder the normal services of legitimate businesses. For the purpose of effectively protecting the rights and interests of network users and service providers, access control technologies are often deployed in servers or networks to defend against potential malicious attacks. Access control processes user requests through a unified interface, and determines whether it has the right to access a network or service

Supported by State Key Laboratory of Mobile Network and Mobile Multimedia Technology and ZTE Corporation.

by analyzing packet header fields and flow feature information [5]. Therefore, a reasonable and efficient access control strategy is the key to ensuring business security and service efficiency.

However, with the massive growth of mobile users and emerging services, attackers' increasingly cunning and ever-changing attack modes have brought great challenges to traditional access control strategies. Ensuring the legitimacy of traffic in the distributed Internet is a very complex system engineering. Traditional access networks usually implement role-based access control policies with the help of access control lists (ACLs) to restrict requests from illegal users from reaching servers. However, with the continuous development of technology, it is difficult for a fixed strategy to deal with more complex and flexible attack methods and dynamically changing malicious traffic. Well-planned attack traffic will break through the defense of static and simple ACLs and cause serious consequences.

The software-defined network (SDN) architecture provides the basis for dynamic access control. The forwarding device copies the data packets to the controller. The controller makes authorization decisions based on data analysis technologies such as machine learning and deep learning, then adjusts the action policy of the ACL in the switch by remote control to deal with dynamic attack traffic. However, for the increasingly massive communication requirements, in the traditional SDN architecture, only the OpenFlow protocol can be used to separate control and forwarding, and the data plane is not customizable. On the one hand, the implementation of authorization in the controller leads to unacceptable interaction delay and inefficient concurrency capability, which cannot meet the massive user requests that are difficult to deal with in real networks. On the other hand, the access control far from the user side not only fails to perceive the access environment but also allows malicious traffic to be injected into the network. The current attacker's goal is not limited to illegally accessing network resources, but also trying to interfere with other legitimate users' normal access to services. Therefore, it is necessary to block malicious traffic in a timely manner when it enters the network.

The emergence of the programmable data plane provides a new technical route to solve the above problems. As a representative technology, the programmable protocol independent packet processor (P4) [6] performs flexible and customizable processing of data packets based on a pipeline working mode similar to traditional switches [7]. The emergence of P4 makes it possible to directly complete authorization decisions and ACL changes within the switch, which greatly reduces the delay and bandwidth overhead of traffic access control. The network is divided into a control plane and a data plane. The control plane consists of high-performance servers, which are responsible for mapping advanced network application requirements into data plane action policies, and delivering them to the data plane switches through the southbound interface in time. The data plane is currently divided into three types: programmable switches that support P4, switches that support Openflow, and traditional switches. The P4 switch itself has the key features of scalability and real-time reconfiguration, which can offload the simple computing and storage requirements of the control plane to the P4 switch.

For access control, lightweight and flexibility are promising goals. Flowfence [9] should be an access control method to analyze the application flow context, which is faster than traditional encryption methods. Poise [10] proposed a method to directly implement context-based access control within the network but did not consider the impact of redundant and huge matching tables on device storage overhead. Qin, et al. [11] focused on the design of an attack detection mechanism based on data flow characteristics and considered the convolution neural network method, but its authorization process still occurs in the control plane. Xavier, et al. [12] implemented the intra-network traffic classification method based on the decision tree, but its model cannot be directly configured remotely during forwarding, and the characteristics adopted are also fixed. Above all, proposed reconfigurable and dynamic access control in this article provided unprecedented flexibility and implemented improvements for actual requirements.

Currently, the key problem that needs to be solved urgently is how to efficiently and flexibly deploy the analysis technology of traffic legitimacy and access control strategy to P4 switches. Artificial intelligence technologies such as neural networks [8] are deployed in the P4 switch domain for network security applications such as traffic classification and attack detection, but there is still a lack of specific technical solutions for implementing traffic access control, and they are insufficient in flexibility and dynamics. Therefore, this paper proposes a lightweight and efficient dynamic access control mechanism. The network will have the ability to customize the extraction of various characteristics of data flow or data packets. Switches could process packets in real-time based on the reconfigurable decision tree model. Actions include alerting, diverting, and discarding malicious data flow, and pre-checking and re-authorizing legitimate data flow. It ensures the normal operation of communication services between terminals and reduces the computing overhead and communication load on the user side. It solves the three important problems of high computational overhead, high processing delay, and difficulty in real-time configuration in access authorization. The specific contributions are as follows:

- Discuss machine learning-based lightweight user authorization methods and design key components for converting decision trees into P4 program statements.
- For the programmable data plane supporting P4, it realizes dynamic access control by combining condition judgment and state register.
- Reproducible experimental evaluations show that our scheme can be executed at wire speed inside the switch with high accuracy.

The remainder of this paper is organized as follows. Section 2 provided a description of the considered network model and Sect 3 introduced the proposed access control mechanism. Then, we analysed the simulation results and demonstrated the advantages of our method. Finally, conclusions of this paper was presented.

2   System Model

The mechanism design in this paper is implemented based on the programmable network architecture. In order to facilitate the organization and management of networks, the software-defined networking paradigm has been widely used in wide area networks, data centers, and private networks. It logically divides the network into a control plane and a data plane. The former is responsible for the centralized management and scheduling of the network, and complex computing functions such as routing, load balancing, and network security. The latter focuses on transferring massive amounts of data reliably at high speeds. With the development of in-network computing research, the programmability of the data plane has gradually received attention. Specifically, the system model considered in this paper includes the following three components.

Control plane entities: undertake relatively expensive tasks such as storage and computing. Storage nodes should maintain key data within the network, such as the fine-grained state of the entire network, forwarding tables of switches, operation records of flow tables, and access request logs. Compute nodes are responsible for complex decision-making tasks. The easiest-to-understand example is to dynamically route packets based on the real-time status of the network to improve the quality of service transmitted. Usually, the control plane entity is composed of distributed high-performance servers, which complete the network management tasks through the southbound interface and the data plane.

Data plane entity: It is a necessary entity to interconnect the terminals at the edge. These entities determine their behavior based on the execution logic and matching set of operational rules received from the control plane. These devices can be divided into two categories: access devices and core forwarding devices according to their main functions. Access aggregation equipment supports the connection of heterogeneous terminals. In order to prevent malicious traffic, mechanisms such as intrusion detection and firewall are usually deployed in such equipment. The core forwarding equipment has a powerful switching array, which can realize high-speed transmission of massive data. Since most of the resources are used for querying and forwarding, complex advanced computing functions are difficult to implement directly on the data plane.

End Entity: Includes terminals that communicate with each other via TCP/IP or other network protocols. In the actual transmission process, the terminal is usually divided into client and server. Sever is a provider of data resources, providing clients with a variety of information services, such as online games, streaming media, and social platforms. In order to ensure the security of the service, the provider usually filters malicious access requests with the help of network security technologies such as intrusion detection, firewall, and access control, which usually requires setting up an independent security monitoring node at the entrance of the server network.

The above components describe the programmable network scenario considered in this paper, next, we will introduce how the dynamic access control mechanism we designed optimizes the existing access control scheme.

3   Dynamic Request Access Control

The goal of this section is to describe the steps necessary to lightweight deploy an access control model that supports dynamic configuration into programmable forwarding. To more clearly explain the limitations of our solution breakthrough, we first introduce the overall framework and highlight its technical advantages in the next subsection. In the next two subsections, the key implementation steps in the control plane and data plane will be described respectively.

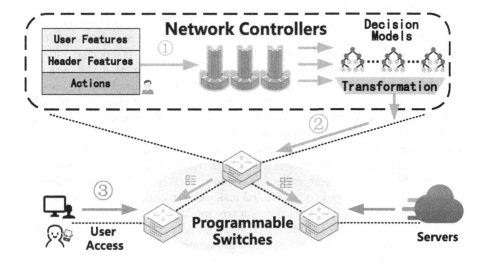

Fig. 1. Dynamic request access control

Overview. In order to enhance the flexibility and intelligence of service access control in the network, a user access authorization method in the network is implemented in the programmable data plane, and the legitimacy of the terminal request is directly completed by the decision tree model located in the switch. An overview of the scheme is shown in Fig. 1, and the basic functions of the network controller and programmable switch have been described in Sect. 2.

Overall, first, the controller generates an accurate machine learning model on demand. This process needs to convert prior knowledge such as access log records and security management policies into data sets that can be understood by machine learning libraries. Considering the limited computing power of the programmable data plane, the Dynamic Request Access Control (DRAC) mechanism adopts a lightweight decision tree model as a judge. Due to the existence of multiple heterogeneous user domains in the network (such as wired terminals, mobile terminals, IoT devices, etc.), a single decision tree cannot meet various access control requirements. Control nodes need to fit different features and generate a set of differentiated decision tree models with corresponding actions.

Secondly, in order to map the control plane policy and data plane actions, the model conversion component of the control plane maps the trained model to the conditional judgment logic given the switch hardware architecture (x86/FPGA/ASIC, etc.), and combines it with the P4 switch Recognized matching action rules and register read and write commands generate core code. The program code also needs to generate a recognizable file format for the specific target hardware through the compiler, and then distribute and install it into the forwarding device. Next, the controller sends the corresponding match-action rules and registers read and write commands to the data plane through the southbound interface.

Finally, in the data plane, the access switch installation receives the access control executive, matching operation rule set and register read and write command set from the control plane. When user-side traffic is injected into the network, the node performing access control determines whether the data flow has been authorized based on the access control list. If it has been authorized, it will be processed according to the corresponding action. Otherwise, the judge model will complete the real-time authorization decision according to the key characteristics of the data packet, and add the entry of the access control list. In summary, DRAC has the following advantages over popular candidates.

Lightweight: DRAC compresses a large number of ACL rules into a condensed set of conditional judgment statements, which greatly reduces the number of matching tables that need to be enabled inside the switch. Under the premise of providing high accuracy, a set of decision tree models can perform access control at wire speed inside the switch, which introduces low computational load and processing delay, and is friendly to high-throughput networks.

Online configurable: DRAC allows the control plane to adjust the characteristic parameters of the decision tree model in real time according to the dynamic traffic patterns and security requirements in the network, and the stateful register structure allows the switch to select the packet characteristics that need to be considered at any time in the running state, deploy or revocation of specific trees gives network managers the ability to deal with complex attacks.

Scalability: DRAC's highly customizable performance provides on-demand access control services for heterogeneous networks and service providers. Through the feature pool, any feature in the data packet can be extracted, and the user authorization decision can be completed within the network. This feature can prevent invalid requests from reaching the server, block malicious requests directly inside the network, and avoid the bad impact of request flooding attacks on legitimate requests.

Model Generation and Transformation. In order to build and maintain decision models that can be deployed directly on the data plane, key methods for data processing, algorithm selection, data fitting, and model transformation need to be clarified on the control plane.

Most fundamentally, what to do with the original access authorization rules. In traditional access control scenarios, experienced network administrators formulate complex policies for user attributes to determine whether a user is qualified to access the network. The continuous expansion of the network, not only poses a huge challenge to the formulation of rules but also requires a large number of policies to occupy large storage space. For hardware-constrained forwarding devices, it may not be reasonable to store massive access control policies in flow tables, so a more lightweight and accurate processing method is required. A popular idea is to extract key features from a large number of policies based on machine learning technology, and establish an appropriate algorithm model to fit access control policies. Therefore, it is necessary to convert access authorization rules and records into tabular data sets for the training of machine learning models according to different access control requirements.

Once the dataset is ready, the next step is to select an appropriate classification algorithm model. A large number of supervised learning techniques exist, but not all of them are suitable for execution in the programmable data plane. In addition to considering the accuracy and generalization of the algorithm itself, the key point is that the data structure of the model can be implemented by P4, and it is easy to adjust online to deal with dynamically changing access requests. For any target hardware, the processing latency should be on the order of the forwarding latency. Therefore, for our framework, we decided to use decision trees to try to satisfy both properties. The advantages of the decision tree itself in terms of accuracy, enforceability, and interpretability make it easier to deploy in P4-enabled switches. In order to fit the decision tree model and access control policy, the training and validation procedures of the model need to be performed. We use the widely used sklearn algorithm library and use the CART algorithm to build each decision tree. For homogeneous access requirements, multiple cross-entropy data verifications are required to select the optimal decision tree suitable for the corresponding access strategy. For heterogeneous requirements, a brand new decision tree needs to be trained.

Model transformation components are the core elements of the DRAC control plane. The core idea is to convert the features and feature thresholds stored in the leaf nodes of the trained decision tree model into assignment, register read and condition judgment statements that can be read by the P4 switch. The schematic diagram of the core code is shown in Fig. 2. In order to be able to modify the features considered by leaf nodes without changing the switch executor, the potential feature parameters need to be collected into feature pool variables at the data plane. Assuming that a tree model has k features, the index in the feature pool of the required feature that should be read by each leaf node is indicated by the ordered register Regindex. This requires the decision tree model to maintain a fixed structure D when it is generated. It is formulated as:

$$D = \{Reg_{index}(i_1, i_2, \cdots, i_k) \mid Reg_{thre}(t_1, t_2, \cdots, t_k)\} \tag{1}$$

For leaf nodes deleted due to pruning, they are reserved by padding with zeros on the data plane. The feature thresholds are also stored through another set of separate ordered registers, Regthre, so that the controller can update the model parameters at any time. An example of the core code is shown in Figure

X. Finally, the controller sends the compiled execution file to the P4 switch and installs it, and then changes the value of the specified index of the switch register based on the P4runtime or Thrift protocol to complete the deployment of the dynamic decision tree model. Considering the needs of dynamic changes, the control node needs to update the data set by observing the real-time state of the network, and periodically train and update the model.

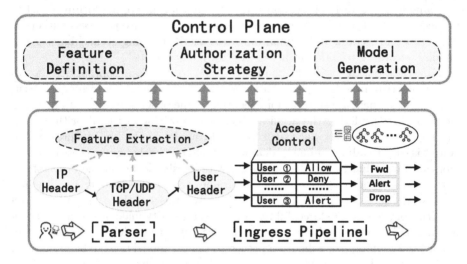

Fig. 2. Access control procedures inside switch

In-network Access Control Deployment. The execution of flow access control in DRAC is only implemented inside the P4 switch without the involvement of any other entity. After the switch has installed the forwarding program delivered by the control plane, it should execute the corresponding processing flow in a fixed pipeline sequence. The key lies in how to determine whether the data access is authorized, and then forward, alarm, or discard according to the result. As shown in Fig. 2, after the data packet enters the switch processing pipeline, the corresponding execution steps in the switch are as follows:

1) In the packet header parsing process of the switch, the fields of the corresponding packet headers are extracted as features according to predefined rules. Corresponding to the previous section, after the header is parsed, the P4 switch temporarily stores the header field in multiple hdr structures. User attribute fields, etc.) are assigned to feature pool variables.

2) In order to judge whether the data access is legal, there are two available ways to establish an access control list. On the one hand, in the entry pipeline, according to the IP quintuple (source address, destination address, source port, destination port and protocol number) of the data packet, the user to which the data packet belongs is determined, and the quintuple hash value is used as the query element to construct with registers. The access control list is used

to determine the actions to be performed by the current data packet, including reauthorization, normal forwarding, discarding, or alarming to the control plane. On the other hand, the authorization action will change the meta.identification of the packet defined in the switch, and the different values indicated by this attribute can be matched in the matching table to determine whether the packet can access the network.

3) If the corresponding entry cannot be queried in the access control list, the authorization needs to be executed, then the features defined by the control plane are extracted from the feature pool and input into the decision tree model D composed of conditional judgment statements and register read statements. Depending on the type of access or security level, appropriate models are used to evaluate authorization.

4) In the case of adopting the first method in 2), according to the decision result returned by the decision tree, add the entry of the data stream to which the current data packet belongs to the access control list, and use the hash value of the five-tuple of the data packet as the key, The authorization result is stored as a value. If the second method is adopted, there is no need to add entries, and each data packet entering the switch needs to go through the authorization step 3).

The implementation of DRAC differs from the standard match-action paradigm in software-defined networking. Actions in P4 are usually driven by table matching, which can range from matching using only MAC addresses to multivariate matching rules. However, due to the limitation of the hardware structure, the cost of enabling multiple tables on most platforms is a decrease in throughput. Therefore, we try to avoid adding the "Match-action" process in the switch to reduce the impact on forwarding performance.

In this section, we provide a comprehensive introduction to DRAC. We illustrate our contribution in the next section by demonstrating the classification accuracy and communication overhead of the proposed method through experiments in a simulated environment.

4 Evaluation

In this section, we will demonstrate a user access control scenario to verify the performance of the DRAC. We first describe the dataset and experimental setup we use, with guidance from real-world real-world scenarios. Next, the effect of the proposed method on the forwarding performance is evaluated in a simulation environment. The results show that DRAC can be executed at wire speed inside the switch, and the latency and throughput are acceptable.

4.1 Experiment Setup

The simulation is executed on a laptop with Intel Core i5 10400F CPU and 16 GB memory. The operating system is Linux with a kernel version of 4.15. The experiment topology is a mesh network initialed by mininet, including 4 switches. Popular software switch BMv2 is used to carry out the P4 process workflow. All links are set to 5 ms delay and 10 Mbps bandwidth. The functions in the control plane are implemented based on the Python language. All decision tree models are generated through the sklearn codebase. The network controller is connected to the separated switches directly.

In the actual access scenario, employees access the enterprise network through various applications. It is assumed that employees with the same role will access the same or similar resources. Typically, supervisors are required to grant the required access to overcome access barriers manually. This way empowers wastes a lot of time and money as employees move around in the company. Therefore, we place the authorization behavior at the network entrance to run automatically. The dataset used in the simulation is Amazon Employee Access Records. Terminals are able to join the network through any access switches, all packets should carry the attributes of users. The random traffic generator is utilized to simulate generating employee requests.

4.2   Results

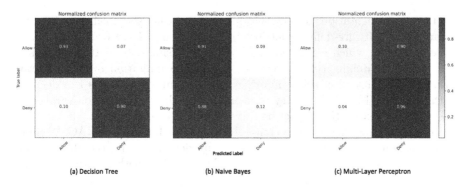

Fig. 3. Confusion matrix

The first evaluation is the performance of the machine learning model. We compare the performance widely used machine learning algorithms (including Naive Bayes and Multilayer Perceptrons). User attributes are embedded in the data packet, the DRAC performs the classification directly on the data plane, while other algorithms process the summary information passed to the controller. The performance results are shown in Figs. 3 and 4. Figure 3 is the confusion matrix of the final decision results of the three algorithms, which is mainly used to compare the classification results and the actual measured values. The results show that the decision tree algorithm used by DRAC has obvious advantages. Naive Bayes and multilayer perceptrons can hardly fit complex authorization rules. The same result can be found in the ROC curve in Fig. 4. The decision tree is the algorithm closest to the upper left corner of the ROC space, and its classification effect is the best in this experiment.

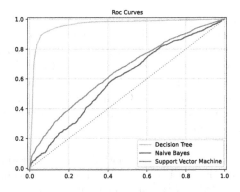

Fig. 4. Roc curves

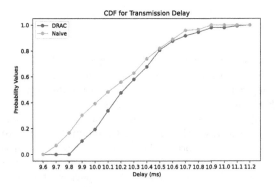

Fig. 5. Transmission delay

Second, we analyze the impact of access control on packet forwarding delay. This is a crucial metric. If the DRAC needs to consume a lot of time, it will reduce the data capacity that the network can carry, which is unacceptable to the network service provider. Figure 5 demonstrates the cumulative distribution function of the transmission delay of the data packet when only the IP forwarding function is implemented and the DRAC exists. Note that the horizontal axis of the coordinates represents the end-to-end delay in milliseconds. For basic forwarding scenarios, the forwarding delay of 100% of the data packets is less than 10.9 ms. The deployment of DRAC increased this value by 2.75%, which is clearly an acceptable overhead.

5   Conclusion

Access control technology has always been a hot topic in the field of network security research. For a long time, rigid forwarding devices could not handle multi-dimensional access requests, and the network only relied on inflexible tools such as firewalls or access control lists to deal with various attacks. However, as attack methods become more complex and dynamic, existing methods can no longer prevent attackers from reaching their goals. Combining mature machine learning technology with emerging programmable data plane technology, this paper proposes a remotely configurable access control model DRAC that converts complex authorization rules running on the control plane into an executable decision tree model on the data plane. Compared with other schemes, DRAC can obtain better correctness and low forwarding delay. In the future, improvement of the model generalization is in need.

Acknowledgements. This work was supported by ZTE industry-university research cooperation fund project "Research on network identity trusted communication technology architecture" and State Key Laboratory of Mobile Network and Mobile Multimedia Technology.

References

1. Yang, D., et al.: TC-flow: chain flow scheduling for advanced industrial applications in time-sensitive networks. IEEE Netw. **36**(2), 16–24 (2022)
2. Yan, X.C., et al.: Study on security of 5G and satellite converged communication network. ZTE Commun. **19**(4), 79–89 (2021)
3. Zhang, W., et al.: Optimizing federated learning in distributed industrial IoT: a multi-agent approach. IEEE J. Sel. Areas Commun. **39**(12), 3688–3703 (2021)
4. Song, F., et al.: Smart collaborative balancing for dependable network components in cyber-physical systems. IEEE Trans. Industr. Inform. **17**(10), 6916–6924 (2021)
5. Cao, J.H., et al.: Integrating coarse granularity part-level features with supervised global-level features for person re-identification ZTE Commun. **19**(1), 72–81 (2021)
6. Bosshart, P., et al.: P4: programming protocol independent packet processors. SIG-COMM Comput. Commun. Rev. **44**(3), 875 (2014)
7. Song, F., et al.: Enabling heterogeneous deterministic networks with smart collaborative theory. IEEE Netw. **35**(3), 64–71 (2021)
8. Qin, Q., et al.: Line-speed and scalable intrusion detection at the network edge via federated learning. In: IFIP Networking Conference (Networking) 2020, pp. 352–360 (2020)
9. Fernandes, E., et al.: Flowfence: practical data protection for emerging IoT application frameworks In: 25th USENIX Security Symposium, pp. 531–548 (2016)
10. Kang, Q., et al.: Programmable in-network security for context aware BYOD policies. In: 29th USENIX Security Symposium, pp. 595–612 (2020)
11. Qin, Q., et al.: A learning approach with programmable data plane towards IoT security. In: 2020 IEEE 40th International Conference on Distributed Computing Systems (ICDCS), pp. 410–420 (2020)
12. Xavier, B.M., et al.: Programmable switches for in-networking classification. In: IEEE INFOCOM 2021 - IEEE Conference on Computer Communications, pp. 1–10 (2021)

A Correlation Analysis-Based Mobile Core Network KPI Anomaly Detection Method via Ensemble Learning

Li Wang[1], Ying Liu[1], Weiting Zhang[1(✉)], Xincheng Yan[2,3], Na Zhou[2,3], and Zhihong Jiang[2,3]

[1] National Engineering Research Center of Advanced Network Technologies, Beijing Jiaotong University, Beijing, China
{liwang0716,yliu,wtzhang}@bjtu.edu.cn
[2] State Key Laboratory of Mobile Network and Mobile Multimedia Technology, Shenzhen 518055, China
[3] ZTE Corporation, Nanjing 210012, China
{yan.xincheng,zhou.na,jiang.zhihong}@zte.com.cn

Abstract. With the development of new networks, applications in mobile communication networks, such as mobile payment and online classes, have become an indispensable part of people's lives. The core network is one of the most important components of the mobile communication network, which is not only essential but also complex. If the core network fails, it will cause a substantial economic loss. To ensure the reliability and stability of the mobile core network, operators need to detect abnormalities in Key Performance Indicators (KPI,e.g., average response time). Datasets of KPI are usually unbalanced and have a wide range of features. Therefore, we propose a correlation analysis-based KPI anomaly detection via an ensemble learning frame. This frame first performs data augmentation on the dataset using SMOTE oversampling algorithm and uses the Pearson correlation coefficient method for feature selection, then construct an ensemble learning XGBoost-based anomaly detection method for KPI. Finally, we evaluate our scheme with the confusion matrix. The results show that our scheme obtained a high accuracy and recall rate. The training and testing dataset we collected is a KPI dataset of a Chinese operator for the first three months of 2020. It is worth noting that no relevant studies used this dataset before.

Keywords: Anomaly detection · Ensemble learning · Feature selection · Data augmentation

Supported by organization ZTE industry-university research cooperation fund project "Research on network identity trusted communication technology architecture," and State Key Laboratory of Mobile Network and Mobile Multimedia Technology, and Fundamental Research Funds under Grant 2021JBZD204.

1   Introduction

The emergence of COVID-19 in recent years has made mobile network activities, such as online offices and online classes, more deeply embedded in people's lives than usual. Data show that in 2019, users of Tencent classrooms using the mobile terminal for learning accounted for 54%, exceeding the PC terminal for the first time. For the payment terminal, the number of users who choose to pay by the mobile terminal is as high as 79.8% [1]. Seeing the big picture in a small way, mobile business has proliferated in the past five years and has become a future trend. People's lives will become increasingly inseparable from the mobile network.

As the most critical part of the mobile communication network, the core network is responsible for call reception, individual service processing, and other functions. The significance of a core network is reflected in two aspects: on the one hand, a mobile core network contains a large capacity of network elements and a wide range of fault impacts, which directly affects the revenue of operators; On the other hand, the core network becomes more complex with the acceleration of VoLTE commercialization. These two significance leads to the introduction of more fault-prone points. The core metric to evaluate the performance of the mobile core network is the Key Performance Indicator (KPI), which is a set of time series data that can reflect the performance and quality of the network [2].

As the key to guaranteeing the service quality of the mobile core network, KPI anomaly detection becomes a highly challenging task in today's practical application environment. Once the mobile core network fails, it will have a massive impact on the quality of service of the whole network and cause considerable losses in economic and other aspects. Therefore, KPI anomaly detection techniques put higher demands on the algorithms' performance in processing massive amounts of data, selecting features for datasets, and expanding homogeneous classes of datasets [3].

To address the above challenges, researchers have proposed several KPI anomaly detection methods in recent years, mainly including traditional statistical and supervised, semi-supervised machine learning methods. Each method has its advantages and disadvantages in a particular scenario. The statistical-based methods have the advantage of simplicity but are increasingly unsuitable for natural OM environments due to the lack of self-adaptability. The supervised machine learning method has a certain degree of adaptiveness. However, it relies heavily on labels, and the results are not as satisfactory in the face of unbalanced data sets. While unsupervised machine learning methods have lower labeling requirements and better classification results, they often require enormous datasets for training support and a long training time.

Hence, this paper aims to design a new anomaly detection system that can rapidly detect mobile core network KPI anomalies and mitigate the negative consequences of anomalies. The system faces the following three main challenges:

(1) Different forms of KPI anomaly data: the characteristics of KPI data and the location of detected network elements affect their data forms.

(2) Unbalanced dataset: Since abnormalities are rare in natural network environments, the data set will have the problem of extreme imbalance between abnormal and normal data, which in turn affects the detection results.

(3) Time efficiency problem: The data scale and overhead in online operation and maintenance scenarios are significant, and it is challenging to apply inefficient anomaly detection models to large-scale data detection.

In this paper, we propose an effective KPI anomaly detection method to analyze the quality of communication networks with full consideration of the data set imbalance problem, the accuracy of detection results, and the time overhead. Our method first adopts SMOTE oversampling to expand the initial imbalance dataset, then use the Pearson correlation coefficient feature selection method to reduce overhead while improving the accuracy. After that, XGBoost with high performance in ensemble learning is used for classification. Finally, we use a confusion matrix to evaluate the detection results.

The rest of this paper is organized as follows. We first present the related work of this paper in Sect. 2. Then we design the general framework in Sect. 3, introduce the dataset used in this paper and perform dataset analysis in Sect. 4. Finally, in Sect. 5, we evaluate our method by experimentally testing and confusing matrices.

2 Related Work

KPI are time series, so the existing anomaly detection algorithms are basically focused on time series algorithms. According to the development history, KPI anomaly detection methods can be broadly classified into statistical-based, supervised machine learning-based, and deep learning-based detection algorithms.

2.1 Statistical-Based Anomaly Detection Methods

Due to the mathematical nature of the anomaly detection problem, researchers realized in the early days that statistical principles could be used to distinguish normal samples from abnormal samples. ARIMA [4] uses difference, autoregressive, and moving average models to achieve prediction by historical values uniquely current values. SPOT [5] uses extreme value theory to detect sudden changes in time series. FluxEV [6] uses the method of moments based on SPOT to improve the speed of automatic threshold estimation further. Literature [7,8] uses the time series decomposition (TSD) method to construct a base model of the time series, thus completing the data prediction.

The performance of these anomaly detection models is generally inferior. Statistical-based methods assume that the KPI sequences obey a specific probability distribution, but the data in real scenarios are haphazard. In addition, probabilistic statistics-based methods require a large amount of parameter tuning, yet inefficient manual tuning methods are difficult to adapt to the needs of massive data.

2.2   Machine Learning-Based Anomaly Detection Methods

To improve the accuracy and robustness of anomaly detection, researchers consider automatic learning of patterns or laws from massive amounts of data [9]. Therefore machine learning methods have become the focus of research on KPI anomaly detection. Supervised learning was the earliest applied machine learning anomaly detection method. It can integrate supervised global features [10]. Opprentice [11], proposed in 2015, applies machine learning for the first time in a KPI anomaly detection framework, using a random forest algorithm to train the model. Yahoo proposed an automatic anomaly detection framework EGADS [12], which used multiple traditional anomaly detection models for feature extraction of KPIs and used labels to train anomaly classifiers to determine anomalies, achieving more desirable results. However, supervised learning algorithms rely excessively on anomaly labeling. They also have a high training and detection overhead, making them difficult to apply to large-scale Internet services.

As a result, there have been unsupervised learning-based anomaly detection methods. They do not require labels and can handle imbalanced datasets to reduce labeling overhead. DDCOL [13] used density-based parametric adaptive clustering as the core technique and higher-order difference and subsampling techniques to perform online anomaly detection for various KPI time series mutations. The literature [14] used the PCA algorithm for characterization learning of data and performed cluster analysis and unsupervised training based on the One-Class SVM algorithm for anomaly detection of KPI sequences.

2.3   Deep Learning-Based Anomaly Detection Methods

Deep learning is widely used in anomaly detection because of its powerful ability to extract high-dimensional features from data using multilayer neural networks, which have a high degree of abstraction and discover intrinsic connections in the data. Deep learning can not only make classification judgments on the time series but also achieve the purpose of detecting and judging through the flow characteristics of a period of time [15,16]. Donut [17] used a variational autoencoder (VAE) for unsupervised anomaly detection against periodic KPI time series. Buzz [18] performed anomaly detection against complex KPIs at the machine level based on the adversarial training side of the VAE. Literature [19,20] optimizes the federated learning performance. It introduces a three-layer cooperative neural network architecture to support deep neural network (DNN) training. Faster convergence is achieved while effectively saving energy on the device. Literature [21,22] introduces a cloud-based architecture and proposes a deep reinforcement learning-based resource management scheme that enables real-time optimal resource allocation decisions. These deep learning algorithms further reduce the annotation cost and significantly improve the application performance, which is important for anomaly detection.

In summary, each anomaly detection method has its advantages and disadvantages in a particular scenario. In this paper, we propose a method for KPI anomaly detection using XGBoost for a practical application scenario of mobile core networks. We also use data augmentation and feature selection to overcome the disadvantages of supervised learning and to provide a general framework capable of detecting most anomalies.

3 Method

Before elaborating on our scheme, we need to reiterate the research scenario of our research. In this paper, we do anomaly detection on Key Performance Indicators.KPI is a set of time series data that can reflect the performance and quality of the network [2], generally containing answered traffic, called a response rate, average response time, and so forth. It consists of values and timestamps, and each KPI time series has a fixed time interval. Different KPI time series have different data patterns.

As shown in Fig. 1, we propose a general framework based on feature selection and ensemble learning. It is divided into the following modules: Data Collection module, Data Pre-processing module, and adaptive Anomaly Detection module. Specifically, the first module is used to collect data in the mobile core network. In this paper, we used the dataset from the existing database for subsequent detection. The second module is used for data pre-processing, which consists of data augmentation and feature selection. Due to the small percentage of abnormal KPI in the mobile core network, the data set has unbalanced characteristics. If the unprocessed datasets are directly used for classification training, the detection results will be unsatisfactory. Therefore, in the data augmentation module, we chose the SMOTE oversampling algorithm to expand the data set before anomaly detection. Feature selection can select features that strongly correlate with labels from the unprocessed KPI dataset and discard weak features, thus reducing training overhead and obtaining better detection results. In our scheme, we finally chose the Pearson correlation coefficient method for feature selection.

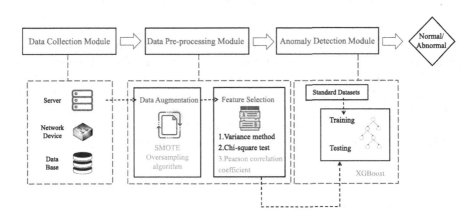

Fig. 1. A framework diagram for correlation analysis-based mobile core network KPI anomaly detection via ensemble learning.

The last part is the anomaly detection module. It uses ensemble learning based on a voting mechanism to output anomaly detection results. The following subsections will describe these modules in detail.

3.1   Data Collection Module

Usually, the operations and maintenance personnel need to analyze each KPI comprehensively to ensure different application services operate normally. Therefore, they need to collect the crucial parameters of each key indicator with the help of detecting tools. The mainstream detecting systems currently in use are Zabbix, Nagios, etc. These detecting systems can sample the system state to get KPI data.

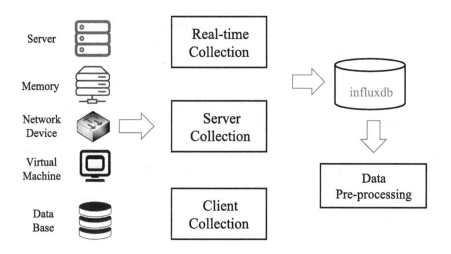

Fig. 2. The framework diagram of the data collection module.

As shown in Fig. 2, operations collect detecting data from the underlying physical devices such as servers, storage, and virtual machines. Then we store these data in a real-time database. In this way, subsequent studies can obtain the collected KPI data from the database for anomaly detection. Usually, it is difficult to deploy new devices in the mobile core network. Due to this reason, we get unprocessed KPI sequences from Simple Network Management Protocol (SNMP), system logs, web access logs, and other data sources [11].

3.2   Data Pre-processing Module

Data Augmentation. In the real mobile core network scenario, anomalies are in the minority. This leads to a class imbalance characteristic between abnormal data and normal data. Therefore, we need to use data augmentation on the initial dataset to balance both classes. Data augmentation can simplify the problem to a traditional binary classification problem and facilitate subsequent anomaly detection.

Oversampling and undersampling are commonly used data augmentation methods. Undersampling can balance class distribution by removing the number of majority class instances. Since the number of minority class data in the mobile core network KPI scenario is already deficient, deleting the majority class data may lose important sample information. Moreover, the classification results will be unstable. Therefore, we adopt SMOTE oversampling algorithm [23]to solve the imbalance problem by adding new minority class instances to achieve a rebalancing of the original biased data [24].

Feature Selection. In this module, we perform feature selection on the original mobile core network KPI data, extract the features and select the KPI with solid features. Thereby, feature selection improves the model's accuracy and reduces the overhead. Feature selection is not only for data dimensionality reduction but also to eliminate redundant and irrelevant features [25]. Commonly used correlation feature selection methods include variance feature selection, chi-square feature selection, and Pearson correlation coefficient feature selection.

Pearson correlation coefficient can measure the relationship between features and their corresponding variable. Our method can measure the correlation between KPI indicators and labels. The Pearson correlation coefficient takes the value interval $[-1, 1]$, with 1 representing a perfectly positive correlation, 0 indicating no linear relationship, and -1 representing a perfectly negative correlation. The closer the correlation coefficient is to 0, the weaker the correlation is [26]. When a correlation coefficient higher than 0.8 represents, two characteristics are very strongly correlated.

3.3   Anomaly Detection Module

Mobile core network KPI anomaly detection can be abstracted as a binary problem. SMOTE oversampling algorithms are used in conjunction with ensemble learning methods to improve accuracy. Thus we choose XGBoost from Boosting algorithm to do anomaly detection. XGBoost is an extension of the gradient boosting algorithm. Multiple CART trees integrate it, and the various classifiers must be serial. Equation 1 explains the principle of XGBoost algorithm for generating new models based on the past models [27].

$$\hat{y}_i^{(t)} = \sum_{k=1}^{t} f_k(x_i) = \hat{y}_i^{(t-1)} + f_t(x_i) \tag{1}$$

In this equation, t means the new round, and t−1 means the previous round. f is a new function. Nodes in CART trees use values instead of categories, which can improve the running speed of XGboost. It also has built-in cross-validation. Since SMOTE oversampling algorithm selects all minority class samples to generate new samples, there is certain blindness in the selection of nearest neighbors. The built-in cross-validation of XGBoost can prevent overfitting. Therefore, XGBoost is suitable for anomaly detection of mobile core network KPI.

SMOTE-Pearson-XGboost algorithm flows as follows:

Algorithm: SMOTE-Pearson-XGboost anomaly detection algorithm

Input:

1. 48 KPI time-series data sequences as feature sequences, features=[x1,x2,...,xt]

2. The sequence of labels corresponding to each data, label=[y1,y2,...,yt], the value of yi is 0/1

Output:

Anomaly detection result sequence, pred label=[a1,a2.,...,at], the value of ai is 0/1

Step1: count the number of 0 and 1 in the labels, Use the SMOTE algorithm to expand data label1 to the same number as label0. New features sequence X sos=[X1,X2,...,Xt], new labels sequence Y sos=[Y1,Y2,...,Yt].

Step2: Using Pearsonr algorithm for each feature in X sos with Y sos, select the feature sequence with high correlation coefficient, X final=[X1',X2',...,Xm']

Step3: Input X final, Y sos into XGBoost classification model, get the predicted values according to cross-validation, pred label=[a1,a2,... ,at]

Step4: End for

---

4 Dataset

This section will detail the using dataset in this paper. We also perform waveform analysis on all 144 KPIs of VoLTE application server network elements at three different locations.

4.1 Dataset Overview

This paper uses 48 KPI data collected by an operator for a total of 78 days from January 14, 2020, to March 31, 2020. This dataset collects data at three different VoLTE application server network elements in Nanjing, Jiangsu Province. The collection frequency was hourly and uninterrupted over 78 days. We collect 5614 samples during this period. Label0 means normal data has 5563, and label1 means abnormal data has 51, accounting for 0.91% of the overall data. The specific data set is shown in Table 1.

As can be seen from the table, the most important characteristic of this dataset is that the proportion of abnormal in all samples is small. Thus, selecting a targeted method for this characteristic is necessary, and combining some existing algorithms to obtain the ideal scheme. We design an anomaly detection scheme based on correlation feature selection and ensemble learning.

Table 1. Details of the dataset.

	VoLTE AS11	VoLTE AS12	VoLTE AS11	Total
Label 0 (normal)	1850	1854	1859	5563
Label 1 (abnormal)	22	16	13	51
Total	1872	1870	1872	5614
Abnormal ratio	1.18%	0.86%	0.96%	0.91%

4.2 Waveform Analysis

The types of KPI vary, and different indicators may affect the subsequent classification results. We first analyze the waveforms of 48 KPI at three network elements. Waveform analysis provides a visual understanding of the dataset's characteristics and allows for the classification of KPI. This paper only shows a few representative waveforms of VoLTE AS11. As shown in Fig. 3, they are representatives of different types of KPIs. The horizontal coordinate is the time, the vertical coordinate is KPI, and the red triangle is abnormal data.

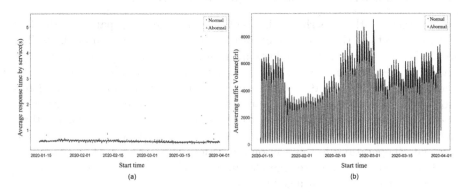

Fig. 3. (a) Waveforms of average response time by service over time. (b) Waveforms of answering traffic volume over time.

By comparing the waveform graphs of 48 KPIs for all network elements, the KPIs can be classified into 22 periodic, 25 discrete, and one monotonic. Therefore, the first two KPI types should be considered in the feature selection, and the monotonic KPI can be discarded because they are not representative. Through comparison, the waveform of VoLTE AS13 has a big difference from VoLTE AS11 and VoLTE AS12. Therefore, the experiments in Sect. 5 will separate the three network elements for anomaly detection.

Since the results of waveform analysis cannot intuitively determine outliers as anomalies. Also, there is no linear relationship between features and classifier performance. If the number of features is too large, it does not make the classification better but leads to a worse performance [28] or causes wasted overhead.

Therefore, feature selection methods must be used for correlation analysis. The specific experimental simulations are illustrated in Sect. 5.

5   Experimental Results

In this section, we first introduce the experimental environment and select the confusion matrix as the evaluation criterion for the model. Then we chose the dataset in Sect. 4 to evaluate our proposed scheme in Sect. 3. The results verify the feasibility and high performance of the method.

5.1   Experimental Environment

The experimental environment selected for this experiment is specified as follows: We use Intel(R) Core(TM) i7 7700HQ CPU @ 2.80 GHz 2.81 GHz. The graphics card is NVIDIA GeForce GTX 1050, the editor is Pycharm, and the language we use is Python 3.8.0.

5.2   Comparative Analysis of Experimental Results

In this section, the experiment is divided into three main parts. In the first part, we select the threshold values for the three feature selection methods. The methods are variance feature selection, chi-square test, and Pearson correlation coefficient. We try to reduce the overhead based on guaranteeing accuracy. In the second part, we use different feature selection methods for anomaly detection for VoLTE AS11. The third part respectively uses the Pearson correlation coefficient feature selection method to perform anomaly detection for the three network elements VoLTE AS11, VoLTE AS12, and VoLTE AS13. It is worth noting that all operations in this section are performed after SMOTE oversampling of the dataset. Furthermore, the classification algorithm we used is XGBoost from ensemble learning during this section.

The Threshold of Feature Selection Method Selection. We selected three feature selection methods: variance feature selection, chi-square feature selection, and Pearson correlation coefficient selection for the 48 KPIs. We compare the principle and application scenarios of the three feature selection methods. The variance method feature selection uses an autocorrelation algorithm that cannot derive the relationship between KPI features and label values. Although chi-square feature selection is a kind of mutual correlation, it only applies to discrete features, making it more challenging to select threshold values.

The selection criteria for the threshold, which is the key to feature selection, are as follows: As the threshold value decreases, the number of selected KPIs increases, which leads to an increase in detection accuracy. However, after the number of selected KPIs increases to a certain level, the accuracy no longer changes significantly. Therefore, the threshold should choose the number of KPIs corresponding to the inflection point. Figure 4 shows the trend of threshold versus accuracy using the Pearson correlation coefficient feature selection method. With the increase of the threshold value, the detection accuracy does improve. However, when the percentage of KPI is chosen to be 40% (19 KPIs), the accuracy does not change much. In order to reduce the complexity of the model, we chose to leave 40% of the KPIs (19 KPIs). The distribution of the number of specifically selected features and KPI indicator types are shown in Table 2.

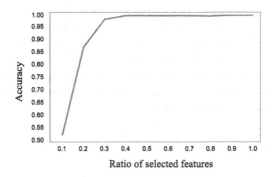

Fig. 4. The trend of accuracy with the ratio of selected features using the Pearson correlation coefficient.

Table 2. Feature selection result.

	Variance selection	Chi-square test	Pearson correlation coefficient
Total number	22	20	19
Discrete KPI	8	7	13
Continuous KPI	14	13	6

Performance Comparison Between Different Feature Selection Methods. We use features obtained from these three feature selections to train separately for VoLTE AS11. Moreover, compare the three methods by confusion matrix [29] and the evaluation index. The specific analysis is as follows: As shown in Fig. 5, (a) is the confusion matrix of variance feature selection, (b) is the confusion matrix of chi-square test feature selection, (c) is the confusion matrix of Pearson correlation coefficient method.

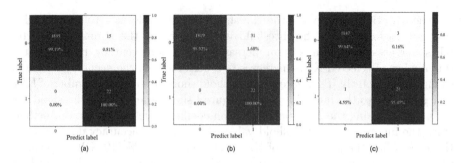

Fig. 5. (a) The confusion matrix of variance feature selection under XGBoost. (b) The confusion matrix of chi-square test feature selection under XGBoost. (c) The confusion matrix of the Pearson correlation coefficient method under XGBoost.

We apply evaluation indexes such as Accuracy and Recall to evaluate and analyze the data obtained by the above three feature selection methods. The results are shown in Table 3. We find a slight difference between the three feature selection methods' results by comparing the evaluation metrics. However, the Pearson correlation coefficient has the highest accuracy on balance, which is consistent with our theoretical analysis.

Table 3. Different methods to evaluate index values under XGBoost.

Method	Accuracy	Recall	Precision	F score
Variance selection	0.992	0.992	1.00	0.996
Chi-square test	0.983	0.983	1.00	0.992
Pearson correlation coefficient	0.997	0.998	0.999	0.999

Performance Comparison Between Different Network Elements. We use Pearson correlation coefficient feature selection for anomaly detection of three different network elements. The confusion matrix and evaluation metrics compare the three network elements. The specific analysis is as follows: As shown in Fig. 6, (a) is the confusion matrix of VoLTE AS11, (b) is the confusion matrix of VoLTE AS12, and (c) is the confusion matrix of VoLTE AS13. We evaluate and analyze the results of these three confusion matrices using evaluation metrics such as accuracy and recall. The results are as shown in Table 4.

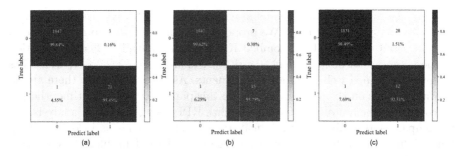

Fig. 6. (a)The confusion matrix of VoLTE AS11 using Pearson correlation coefficient and XGBoost. (b)The confusion matrix of VoLTE AS12 using Pearson correlation coefficient and XGBoost. (c) The confusion matrix of VoLTE AS13 using Pearson correlation coefficient and XGBoost.

Table 4. Evaluation index values for the different network elements.

Network element	Accuracy	Recall	Precision	F score
VoLTE AS11	0.997	0.998	0.999	0.999
VoLTE AS12	0.995	0.996	0.999	0.997
VoLTE AS13	0.984	0.993	0.999	0.992

We analyzed and found that due to the small dataset used in this paper. Although in Sect. 4.2 we get the conclusion that VoLTE AS13 is not quite the same as the other two network elements based on waveform. In real experiments, all evaluation metrics were high for either network element, with F scores basically at 100%. In order to reduce overfitting, the three network elements can be combined together for anomaly detection to improve the feature richness of the dataset. The results show the accuracy is 0.984, recall is 0.993, and F score is 0.996.

Experimental results show that our scheme solves the problem of unbalanced KPI anomaly data sets in mobile core networks and obtains better detection results. In addition, this method can be ported to other real unbalanced datasets to obtain better performance. However, there may be some suspicion of overfitting in our scheme. We believe the possible overfitting result may be due to the Aggregation of the new anomaly samples generated by the SMOTE oversampling algorithm. Therefore, future studies can use modified oversampling algorithms to avoid overgeneralization, such as SSCMIO [30] or SMOM [31].

6   Conclusion

With the popularity of the mobile network, its operation closely affects people's production life. The core network KPI can reflect the network operation and quality in real-time. In this paper, we have conducted a brief survey on the existing anomaly detection schemes for core network KPIs and explored the detection process, algorithm logic, and model of mobile core network KPI anomaly detection based on previous studies. We proposed a complete KPI anomaly detection scheme based on a waveform combed KPI system, multiplied feature selection methods, and data enhancement algorithms, finally using XGBoost, which has recently performed well in major tournaments. As far as we know, there are no relevant studies on the dataset selected in this paper. At the same time, there is no complete scheme to classify and visualize KPIs using waveform analysis and to compare and analyze multiple feature selection schemes as in our method. Our method solves the unbalanced KPI anomaly dataset problem and achieves high performance.

References

1. China Education Times. http://www.edu-gov.cn/edu/6547.html. Accessed 17 Jan 2020
2. Pei, D.: A study on KPI anomaly detection of cloud data center servers based on machine learning, Zhengzhou University (2020)
3. Sun, Y.Q., et al.: Evaluation of KPI anomaly detection methods. Front. Data Comput. Dev. **4**(03), 46–65 (2022)
4. Zhang, Y., et al.: Network anomography. In: Proceedings of the 5th ACM SIG-COMM Conference on Internet Measurement, p. 30 (2005)
5. Siffer, A., et al.: Anomaly detection in streams with extreme value theory. In: Proceedings of the 23rd ACM SIGKDD International Conference on Knowledge Discovery and Data Mining, pp. 1067–1075 (2017)
6. Li, J., et al.: FluxEV: a fast and effective unsupervised framework for time-series anomaly detection. In: Proceedings of the 14th ACM International Conference on Web Search and Data Mining, pp. 824–832 (2021)
7. Chen, Y., et al.: A provider-side view of web search response time. ACM SIG-COMM Comput. Commun. Rev. **43**(4), 243–254 (2013)
8. Vallis, O., et al.: A novel technique for long-term anomaly detection in the cloud. In: 6th USENIX Workshop on Hot Topics in Cloud Computing (HotCloud 2014), Philadelphia, USA, pp. 534–537 (2014)
9. Pei, D., et al.: Intelligent operation and maintenance based on machine learning. Commun. Chin. Comput. Soc. **13**(12), 68–72 (2017)
10. Liu, W.C., et al.: Artificial intelligence rehabilitation evaluation and training system for the degeneration of joint disease. ZTE Commun. **19**(3), 46–55 (2021). https://doi.org/10.12142/ZTECOM.202103006
11. Liu, D.P., et al.: Opprentice: towards practical and automatic anomaly detection through machine learning. In: Proceedings of the Internet Measurement Conference 2015, pp. 211–224 (2015)
12. Laptev, N., et al.: Generic and scalable framework for automated time-series anomaly detection. In: Proceedings of the 21st ACM SIGKDD International Conference on Knowledge Discovery and Data Mining, New York, USA, pp. 1939–1947 (2015)
13. Yu, G., et al.: Unsupervised online anomaly detection with parameter adaptation for KPI abrupt changes. IEEE Trans. Netw. Serv. Manag. **17**(3), 1294–1308 (2020)
14. Hu, M., et al.: Detecting anomalies in time series data via a meta-feature based approach. IEEE Access **6**, 27760–27776 (2018)

15. Jia, M., et al.: DDoS attack detection method for space-based network based on SDN architecture. ZTE Commun. **18**(4), 18–25 (2020). https://doi.org/10.12142/ZTECOM.202004004

16. Li, Y., et al.: IEEE EUC. Achieving a Blockchain-Based Privacy-Preserving Quality-Aware Knowledge Marketplace in Crowdsensing. Wuhan, China (2022)

17. Xu, H.W., et al.: Unsupervised anomaly detection via variational autoencoder for seasonal KPIs in web applications In: Proceedings of the 2018 World Wide Web Conference (2018)

18. Chen, W., et al.: Unsupervised anomaly detection for intricate KPIs via adversarial training of VAE. In: IEEE INFOCOM 2019-IEEE Conference on Computer Communications. IEEE, pp. 891–1899 (2019)

19. Zhang, W., et al.: Optimizing federated learning in distributed industrial IoT: a multi-agent approach. IEEE J. Sel. Areas Commun. **39**(12), 3688–3703 (2021). https://doi.org/10.1109/JSAC.2021.3118352

20. Zhang, C., et al.: FRUIT: a blockchain-based efficient and privacy-preserving quality-aware incentive scheme. IEEE J. Sel. Areas Commun. Early Access (2022)

21. Zhang, W., et al.: Deep reinforcement learning based resource management for DNN inference in industrial IoT. IEEE Trans. Veh. Technol. 1 (2021)

22. Wang, J.S., et al.: ReLFA: resist link flooding attacks via Renyi entropy and deep reinforcement learning in SDN-IoT. China Commun. **19**(7), 15 (2022)

23. Chawla, N.V., et al.: SMOTE: synthetic minority over-sampling technique. J. Artif. Intell. Res. **16**, 321–357 (2002)

24. Abdi, L., Hashemi, S.: To combat multi-class imbalanced problems by means of over-sampling techniques. IEEE Trans. Knowl. Data Eng. **28**(1), 238–251 (2015)

25. Chen, R., et al.: Looseness diagnosis method for a connecting bolt of fan foundation based on sensitive mixed-domain features of excitation-response and manifold learning. Neurocomputing, p. S0925231216310694 (2016)

26. Xue, X., Zhou, J.: A hybrid fault diagnosis approach based on mixed-domain state features for rotating machinery. ISA Trans. **66**, 284–295 (2016)

27. Chen, T.C., Guestrin, C. XGBoost: a scalable tree boosting system. In: The 22nd ACM SIGKDD International Conference (2016)

28. Wang, J., et al.: A review of feature selection methods. Comput. Eng. Sci. **12**, 72–75 (2005)

29. Yıldız, O.T., Aslan, Ö., Alpaydın, E.: Multivariate statistical tests for comparing classification algorithms. In: Coello, C.A.C. (ed.) LION 2011. LNCS, vol. 6683, pp. 1–15. Springer, Heidelberg (2011). https://doi.org/10.1007/978-3-642-25566-3_1

30. Dong, M.G., et al.: A multi-class unbalanced oversampling algorithm using sampling safety factor. Comput. Scie. Explor. **14**(10), 1776–1786 (2020)

31. Zhu, T.F., et al.: Synthetic minority oversampling technique for multiclass imbalance problems. Pattern Recogn. J. Pattern Recogn. Soc. **72**, 327–340 (2017)

An Efficient BGP Anomaly Detection Scheme with Hybrid Graph Features

Jian Sun[1], Ying Liu[1], Weiting Zhang[1(✉)], Yikun Li[1], Xincheng Yan[2,3],
Na Zhou[2,3], and Zhihong Jiang[2,3]

[1] National Engineering Research Center of Advanced Network Technologies,
Beijing Jiaotong University, Beijing, China
{jiansun,yliu,wtzhang,liyikun}@bjtu.edu.cn
[2] State Key Laboratory of Mobile Network and Mobile Multimedia Technology,
Shenzhen 518055, China
[3] ZTE Corporation, Nanjing 210012, China
{yan.xincheng,zhou.na,jiang.zhihong}@zte.com.cn

Abstract. Border Gateway Protocol (BGP) is responsible for managing connectivity and reachability information between autonomous systems, and plays a critical role in the overall efficiency and reliability of the Internet. Due to anomalies caused by misconfiguration or hijacking, etc. there can be a significant impact on the Internet. Neural network-based detection methods provide high accuracy, but their complex structure increases network latency and storage overhead. In addition, small-scale anomalies such as prefix hijacking and path hijacking are difficult to detect due to their small propagation range. We implement a lightweight BGP anomaly detection using a binary neural network (BNN) in this paper, achieving similar results to full-precision neural networks with reduced computation and storage. In addition, we use a mixture of BGP attribute features and graph features to detect small-scale anomalous events, and the results show that the detection accuracy of our proposed method is significantly improved compared to BGP attribute features.

Keywords: BGP · Anomaly detection · BNN · Graph features

1 Introduction

The Internet is a decentralized network consisting of tens of thousands of autonomous systems. Autonomous systems (ASes) are loosely defined as networks operated by an independent governing body using its own network routing policies. The routing information exchanged between ASes is controlled by BGP (Border Gateway Protocol). BGP is the most widely used inter-domain routing

Supported by ZTE industry-university research cooperation fund project "Research on network identity trusted communication technology architecture" and State Key Laboratory of Mobile Network and Mobile Multimedia Technology and Fundamental Research Funds under Grant 2021JBZD204.

protocol in the Internet today, and is a global The BGP is the most widely used inter-domain routing protocol in the Internet today. It is a fundamental component of the global routing system and plays a vital role in the overall efficiency and reliability of the Internet [1,2]. However, BGP was designed with a focus on how to forward data quickly and efficiently, without fully considering the security issues, and there is a huge security risk [3].

There are two main approaches to deal with routing security risks, namely routing trusted authentication technology and anomaly detection technology. The routing trusted authentication technique is to enhance the security of BGP protocol by RPKI (Resource Public Key Infrastructure) to ensure the authenticity of source AS and the integrity of AS path [4]. However, RPKI's trust infrastructure is centralized and complex to manage. Although related technologies combined with blockchain enable decentralization and simple certificate management [5–7], the high cost of deploying routing trusted authentication technologies in general makes their deployment painful. The dominant technique to deal with routing security issues before is the BGP anomaly detection technique. The goal of anomaly detection technology is to effectively and quickly identify anomalous route announcement attacks such as prefix hijacking, path forgery, and route leakage. It helps network administrators gain insight into the true state of BGP security issues in the Internet and respond quickly to anomaly route announcement attacks to reduce the damage of the attacks on inter-domain routing systems. The most popular anomaly detection methods are machine learning methods [8–10]. Among them, neural network is one of the best and most popular methods for detection accuracy [11–13].

But there are two problems facing machine learning and neural networks. One is the problem of feature selection. There are two types of features selected for BGP anomaly detection based on machine learning: BGP attribute features and graph features, both of which have their advantages and disadvantages. The advantage of BGP attribute features is that they are easy to obtain and have low training costs, but it is difficult to detect small-scale hidden anomalous events such as prefix hijacking and path hijacking. The graph features have unique advantages for detecting small-scale anomaly events [14], but the feature extraction process is more complicated [15], and the training cost is expensive with long detection time. The second problem is that the neural network model is complex, and the sophisticated weight parameters occupy a huge memory space and cannot be detected in real time at the second level [16]. And anomaly detection requires extremely high real-time performance for detection; research has shown that anomalous events such as hijacking and misconfiguration can pollute 90% of the Internet within two minutes [17].

We propose an efficient BGP anomaly detection method using hybrid graph features. It solves the two main problems mentioned above and achieves efficient, high accuracy and low-overhead BGP anomaly detection. The main contributions of this paper are two: first, we design a two-stage detection task based on hybrid graphical features. The method combines the advantages of BGP attribute features and graphical features. Compared with the detection method using only BGP attribute features, the detection accuracy is significantly improved for small-scale anomalies. Second, we propose a BNN-based lightweight BGP anomaly detection method. This method significantly reduces the storage and computation overheads while offering advantages in accuracy over traditional methods such as decision trees.

This paper is structured as follows: in Sect. 2, we provide an introduction to the background, graph features of BGP anomaly detection, and binary neural networks. In Sect. 3, we introduce the anomaly classification for BGP. In Sect. 4, we present the designed system model. Section 5 focuses on designing experiments to evaluate the anomaly detection accuracy of BNN as well as hybrid graph features. In Sect. 6 a summary is given as well as an outlook for future work is described.

2   Related Works

BGP routing information is a prerequisite for BGP data analysis and anomaly detection. The source of most anomaly detection data is BGP data collected and stored by the RouteViews and RIPE RIS projects' BGP collectors deployed around the world. By extracting valuable information from the BGP control plane, different types of BGP attribute features can be obtained. AS_PATH and BGP volume seem to be the two most common types of BGP attribute features. Most machine learning algorithms use these features for BGP anomaly detection and achieve excellent performance in detecting large-scale anomalous events such as misconfigurations, worm proliferation, and link failures. However, for small-scale anomalies, its performance is only slightly better than that of the random classifier.

Graph Theory is a branch of mathematics. It takes graphs as its object of study. A graph in graph theory is a figure consisting of a number of given points and a line connecting the two points. Such graphs are usually used to describe a particular relationship between certain things. A point represents a thing, and a line connecting two points indicates that the corresponding two things have this relationship. Graph has advantages in handling unstructured data, making it a new breakthrough in network data analysis. Since BGP update messages are often noisy and bursty, and graph features can capture dynamic changes in network topology more intuitively, better performance may be obtained by using relatively more robust graph features to detect BGP anomalies. Some researchers have used dynamic graphical representations of BGP to study BGP topology and further argue the applicability of graphical representations for BGP anomaly detection [15]. Metrics such as clustering in graph theory are uniquely advantageous for detecting small-scale events.

The essence of anomaly detection problem is classification problem, machine learning has significant advantages in classification detection. With the support of large data sets such as RIPE RCC [18] and RouteViews [19], it has become the mainstream method for BGP anomaly detection. Currently, the more widely used are traditional machine learning algorithms, such as Decision trees [9,10],

Naive Bayes classifier [8,9], etc. Neural networks have the advantages of high classification accuracy and strong generalization ability compared with traditional algorithms.

Courbariaux et al. [20] proposed a binary neural network (BNN), in which the middle layer of the network is characterized by the original accuracy, and only the network weights are binarized. Compared with the traditional neural network (NN), the multiplication operation of the binarized neural network in the forward and backward propagation is changed to an additive operation. During training, binary weights are used for gradient calculation in forward and backward propagation, while full-precision weights are used to update the weights; when the full-precision weights cross the threshold, the corresponding binary weights are changed. In the test, only binary weights are kept and used, and each weight occupies only 1 bit of space, with 32–64 times compression for 32-bit or 64-bit floating-point numbers; and the network operation efficiency is greatly improved by replacing multiplication with accumulation. The multiplication of two floating-point numbers becomes a 1-bit operation. This reduces the capacity requirements of the host device in terms of parameter occupation and computation, making the model easier to port to embedded devices. Thus the BNN binarizes all the heavy parameters and has less computational and memory requirements for inference compared to the NN. This not only increases the computational speed but also saves memory space significantly.

3   BGP Anomaly Considerations

Depending on the scale of impact and the complexity of detection, BGP anomalies can be divided into two categories, namely large-scale anomalies and small-scale anomalies.

Large-scale anomalies are characterized by a large impact on the Internet, rapid propagation, and also the easiest to detect, specifically events such as misconfiguration, routing leak, and link failures. Misconfiguration is a security risk caused artificially by the network administrator. Link failure is an interruption of a physical link. Route leak is the propagation of route announcements beyond their expected scope, and is a security problem caused by system vulnerabilities in the BGP routing system. If an autonomous system (AS) propagates route announcements that violate the routing policy to neighboring autonomous systems, it can lead to a route leak security event.

Small-scale anomalies include prefix hijacking and path hijacking [21]. Compared with large-scale anomalies, the process of their occurrence is more hidden, and the scale of impact mostly involves only a few ASes, which has a smaller impact on the whole Internet. Prefix hijacking is caused by the inability of the BGP protocol to confirm the authenticity of Network Layer Reachability Information (NLRI) declared by an AS. The basic principle is that an autonomous system initiates a reachable route announcement for a prefix that is not owned by the system in its own autonomous domain (i.e., NLRI is not true). Specifically, in the normal case of an inter-domain routing system, the legitimate owner of an

IP prefix, AS, announces this prefix to its neighbors. This routing information is propagated over the Internet, and each AS obtains the path information to reach this prefix and indicates the route AS in its routing table with the AS_PATH attribute. However, for reasons such as configuration error or malicious attack, an AS that does not own an IP prefix illegally announces this prefix, which triggers a BGP prefix hijack event. Path hijacking refers to the propagation of non-true route announcements of AS_PATH path attributes from one autonomous system to neighboring autonomous systems. Specifically, the AS_PATH attribute affects the routing decision. So the attacker in path hijacking falsifies, removes, or maliciously adds to the AS_PATH to influence the path decision of subsequent routers thus achieving traffic hijacking. Unlike prefix hijacking, has the same origin AS as in the legitimate case. While maintaining the victim's connectivity, the attacker is introducing an inter-domain link in the AS path that does not actually exist or has not yet been observed.

4   Proposed Methodology

In this section, we describe the architectural design of the proposed lightweight anomaly detection system, as shown in Fig. 1. The system mainly consists of a hybrid graph feature extraction module and an efficient anomaly detection module. The hybrid graph feature extraction module first performs the extraction of two different types of features, BGP attribute features and graph features from the BGP update message. And then detects them using our proposed lightweight anomaly detection algorithm. The detection process is a two-stage task. First, a fast light-weight detection is performed using attribute features, and then further detection is performed using graph features on top of that, saving overhead and improving detection accuracy at the same time.

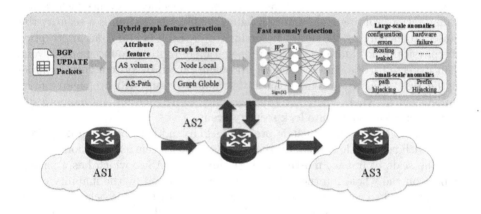

Fig. 1. Lightweight anomaly detection system.

4.1   Hybrid Graph Feature Extraction

The module is divided into two stages. The first stage uses BGP attribute features for fast detection, taking advantage of the fast detection speed and low acquisition cost of attribute features. The second stage uses graph features for accurate detection. Further improve the accuracy based on the first stage and reduce the overhead of using graphical features alone. The traffic of BGP update messages is extracted from the control platform to extract BGP attribute features and graph feature information. Then each packet feature data sample is parsed into four types of features: BGP volume features, AS path features, node-level features and graph-level features. BGP volume features and AS path features indicate the announcements and withdrawals of route stability changes and the path of route update information. The volume features include the number of route announcements and withdrawals, the number of origin changes, the average number of announcements per AS and inter-arrival. The AS path features include the number of announcements to a shorter or to a longer AS-path and the AS path edit-distance and 17 other features. The graph features are divided into Node level metrics and Graph level metrics. Node level metrics are used to describe the properties of each node in the graph and are locally defined. We selected 16 Node level metrics, which have clustering coefficient, eccentricity and the connectivity of a node, etc. Graph level metrics are globally defined for individual attributes of the entire graph. And we selected 15 Graph level metrics, among which are algebraic connectivity, the weighted spectrum and the percolation limit etc. The details are shown in Table 1.

4.2   Efficient Anomaly Detection

This module consists of a batch normalizationlayer (BN), a binary neural network model and a classifier. We take the feature-extracted BGP packet sample x_i as input. First, x_i is normalized to $BN(x_i)$ by the BN layer, and then $BN(x_i)$ is fed into the BNN model to obtain the output representation sequence x_o. Finally, we send these redistributed representation sequences to a classifier consisting of a fully connected layer and a Softmax layer to obtain the probability of each anomaly and identify the classified anomalies.

Neural networks are one of the most commonly used methods for anomaly detection. Nevertheless, it requires a large number of dot product operations on real-valued vectors, as well as a usually nonlinear activation function. Routers were originally designed for network interconnection, routing and forwarding. Most devices cannot meet the high computational and memory requirements for neural network training and deployment. To overcome this difficulty, we deploy binary-valued neural networks with weights of only binary (+1 or −1) values and symbolic activation functions. More specifically, we consider a neural network with L fully connected layers. We denote the neuron weights of layer l by the

Table 1. The extracted BGP attribute features and graph features.

Type	Feature	Description	Type	Feature	Description
Volume feature	Announcements	Total number of announcements per prefix	Local node feature	Clustering coefficient	Measure of the degree to which nodes in a graph tend to cluster together
	Withdrawals	Total number of withdrawals per prefix		Node eccentricity	The length of a longest shortest path starting at that node
	Inter arrival time	Inter arrival time of BGP updates		Node connectivity	The minimum number of nodes that must be removed to disconnect G or render it trivial
	NLRI	Total number of Network Layer Reachability Information per prefixes	Global Graph feature	Eigenvector centrality	A way to measure the impact of nodes on the network
AS-path feature	Max AS-PATH length	The maximum length of AS-PATHs of all BGP update messages		Algebraic connectivity	The second-smallest eigenvalue of the Laplacian matrix of G
	Avg Edit distance	The average number of is required to switch from one AS-path to another		Betweenness centrality	One of the measures based on the shortest path against the centrality of the network graph
	Announcement to the shorter path	Announcement to the shorter AS-Path length		Weighted spectrum	The properties of a graph in relationship to the characteristic polynomial, eigenvalues, and eigenvectors of matrices.
	Origin change	Reannouncement with new origin attributes		Percolation limit	The formation of long-range connectivity in random systems

2-dimensional vector W_l^b and the inputs of that layer by x_{l-1}. The output of layer l is

$$x_l = sign(x_{l-1}, W_l^b) \tag{1}$$

where

$$sign = \begin{cases} 1, & x \geq 0, \\ -1, & x < 0. \end{cases} \tag{2}$$

Compared with the full-precision neural network, BNN binarizes all weight parameters and has smaller computational and memory requirements for inference, which not only improves the computational speed but also saves memory space significantly. Meanwhile, BNN, as a neural network method, has significantly improved performance such as accuracy compared to traditional neural networks.

5   Evaluation

5.1   Experiment Setup

We collected 24 anomalous events as a dataset using the BML tool [22], including four large-scale anomalies such as misconfigurations and link failures and nine small-scale anomalies such as prefix hijacking events and 11 path hijack-ing events. These include the origin and path hijacking events used for anomaly classification in the article [21], while the large-scale events in [15] were used to detect BGP anomalies using graphical features. These events have been manu-ally reviewed and can be considered as accurate and real events. We normalize all features using Z-score normalization. The features are transformed into the form of 0-mean and unit variance distributions. While assigning reasonable weights to various features, in order to prepare for the next step of anomaly detection.

We set up a binary neural network containing a fully connected hidden layer, 16 neurons and two neurons for the output. Different machine learning algo-rithms can be applied to the same classification task, yielding different results and performance. Using the scikit-learn library, we have selected Naive Bayes (NB) classifier, a Decision Tree (DT) and K-Nearest Neighbors (KNN) classifier. A comparison is made with our BNN algorithm. We propose a cross-validation approach where, for n events contained in the dataset, data from n-1 of the events are used as the training set and the remaining samples are used as the training set. Each event can be used as a test set and the accuracy of the model is evaluated by averaging over n iterations to reduce the error. To filter out features with low weights and prevent overfitting, we use Principal Component Analysis (PCA) to reduce the dimensionality of the feature space. The features are mapped into a two-dimensional space and redundant and irrelevant elements are filtered out.

We used the standard metrics of binary classification for performance evalu-ation, including accuracy (ACC), precision, recall and F1-score which are calcu-lated based on the true positives (TP), false positives (FP), true negatives (TN) and false negatives (FN) in the confusion matrix. Accuracy is used as a mea-sure of the percentage of the total sample that is predicted correctly; precision indicates the accuracy of the prediction of positive sample outcomes; recall indi-cates the probability of an actual positive sample being predicted as a positive sample; and F1score is a balanced measure between precision and recall. These indicators are calculated as follows.

$$Accuracy = \frac{TP + TN}{TP + FP + TN + FP} \tag{3}$$

$$Precision = \frac{TP}{TP + FP} \tag{4}$$

$$Recall = \frac{TP}{TP + FN} \tag{5}$$

$$F1score = 2 * \frac{Precision * Recall}{Precision + Recall} \tag{6}$$

To find the best combination of parameters for each machine learning algo-rithm, we perform parameter tuning using scikit-learn's GridSearchCV function, which exhaustively searches for specified parameter values of the estimator, such as the maximum depth of the DT and the number of adjacencies of the KNN.

5.2 Performance of Different Features

In this subsection, we design comparative experiments to compare the performance of the same dataset for different selected features. The types of events in the dataset include a total of 4 large-scale anomalies, 11 path hijacking anomalies and 9 prefix hijacking events. The selected dataset features are BGP attribute features, graphical features and a combination of both hybrid features. We use the BNN algorithm proposed in this paper for testing, and the accuracy metric is selected to measure the detection results. As shown in Fig. 2, the results indicate that the accuracy of all three features remains high for large-scale anomalous events, with a slight advantage for BGP attribute features. The reason for this is that mass hijacking events such as misconfigurations and link failures are more obvious and can have a greater impact on the network, making them easier to detect. However, in the detection of small-scale anomalies, including source and path hijacking events, the detection result using BGP attribute features is around 55%, which is only slightly higher than the random classifier, because the scope and scale of small-scale anomalies are relatively small and do not have a real-time impact on the network.

BNN detection methods using graphical features have an accuracy of over 65%, with a 10% to 15% performance improvement over BGP attribute features. The reason for this may be that measuring the grouping factor (e.g., clustering coefficient, cliques, triangles) are more likely to detect small-scale incidents. In contrast, BGP attribute features are cheap to train and fast to detect, so we devised a two-stage detection method that mixes the two features. The first stage uses BGP attribute features for fast detection, and the second stage uses graphical features to further predict anomalies based on the first stage detection results. Experimental results show that the hybrid approach can achieve an accuracy rate of over 70%, which is a more desirable result for small-scale anomalies that are difficult to detect.

In addition, Table 2 demonstrates the same conditions. The runtime of hybrid features compared to graphical features and BGP attribute features, and the results show that the runtime results of our proposed hybrid approach are similar to those of BGP attribute features, but significantly faster than the detection time using only graphical features. Thus the fast nature of hybrid features is proved.

Table 2. Program runtime for different features

Feature	BGP attribute features	Graph features	Hybrid features
Runtime	0.4925 s	0.7776 s	0.5219 s

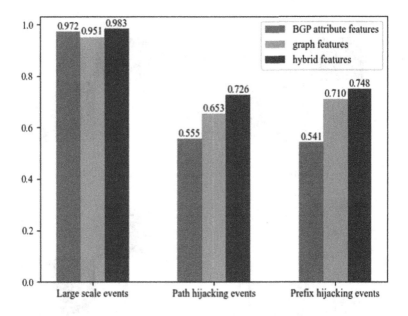

Fig. 2. Accuracy of different features.

5.3   Performance of Lightweight Detection Models

Figure 3 shows the confusion matrices using the different methods, allowing a more visualization of the true positive (TP), false positive (FP), true negative (TN) and false negative (FN) values.

Table 3 shows the results of our accuracy, precision, recall and F1-score measurements on the dataset using the BGP attribute features. The results show that BNN has the best performance among the four methods. The reason is that neural networks are more capable of generalization and better than traditional machine learning. The prediction performance of BNN is slightly higher than that of NB, DT, and KNN prediction methods. In addition, it should be noted that the accuracy rates are all around 70% because most of the data sets we used are small-scale source hijacking and path hijacking events with obscure and difficult features to detect.

In summary, our experiments lead to two conclusions: first, anomaly detection using hybrid graph features has a significant improvement in accuracy compared to BGP attribute features when detecting small-scale anomalies. It also has a slight improvement compared to using only graph features. However, its overhead is smaller and its real-time performance is better than using only graph features. Second, BNN as a neural network has higher detection accuracy than traditional machine learning algorithms such as DT, NB, and KNN.

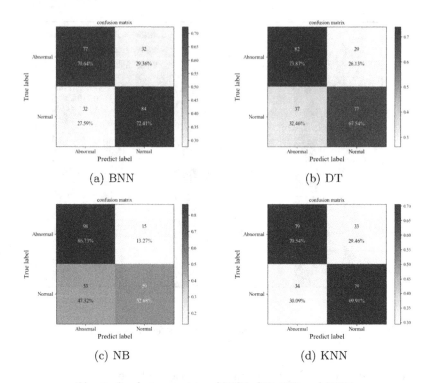

Fig. 3. Confusion matrix of BNN, DT, NB and KNN.

Table 3. Performance indicators of ML models

Method	Accuracy	Precision	Recall	F1-score
BNN	0.716	0.706	0.706	0.706
NB	0.698	0.867	0.649	0.742
DT	0.707	0.709	0.689	0.699
KNN	0.702	0.705	0.699	0.702

6   Conclusion

In this paper, we have proposed a lightweight BGP anomaly detection method
using hybrid features. First, we have compared the performance of BGP anomaly
detection using BGP attribute features, graphical features, and hybrid features.
The results show that all three achieve satisfactory performance for large-scale
anomalies. For small-scale anomalies, such as source hijacking and path hijacking, the performance of using BGP attribute features is only slightly better than
that of the random classifier. The accuracy of graphical features has a small
improvement compared to BGP attribute features. However, graph features have
the disadvantage of high training cost and high overhead. Therefore, we have

designed a two-stage hybrid approach that combines the two features and provides significant improvement in the accuracy of small-scale anomaly detection. Second, we experimentally compared BNN with other traditional machine learning algorithms such as decision trees. The results show that the accuracy of BNN has a slight advantage over other machine learning algorithms. It proved that it has high application value as it can still guarantee the reliability of accuracy with small overhead of small memory consumption and fast running speed. It can be applied to hardware such as P4 programmable switches and FPGAs.

In our future work, we will further investigate the practical deployment of BNN. Deployment in P4 programmable switches will be evaluated for network latency and actual overhead. In addition, we conjecture that the packet factor is more suitable for detecting small-scale anomalous events. We will do further validation and experiments to prove the most suitable graphical features for BGP anomaly detection to further reduce the cost.

References

1. Rekhter, Y., Li, T., Hares, S.: RFC 4271: a border gateway protocol 4 (BGP-4). In: Internet Engineering Task Force, Fremont, CA, USA (2006)
2. Sun, C.H., Yin, B., Li, X.D., et al.: Adaptability analysis of IP routing protocol in broadband LEO constellation systems. ZTE Commun. **18**(4), 34–44(2020). https://doi.org/10.12142/ZTECOM.202004006
3. Li, S., Zhuge, J., Li, X.: Study on BGP security: study on BGP security. J. Softw. **24**, 121–138 (2014)
4. Huston, G., Michaelson, G.: RFC 6483: validation of route originationusing the resource certificate public key infrastructure (PKI) androute origin authorizations (ROAs). In: Internet Engineering Task Force, Fremont, CA, USA, RFC 6483 (Informational), February 2012
5. Wang, J., Li, M., He, Y., Li, H., Xiao, K., Wang, C.: A blockchain based privacy-preserving incentive mechanism in crowdsensing applications. IEEE Access **6**, 17545–17556 (2018). https://doi.org/10.1109/ACCESS.2018.2805837
6. Zhang, C., Zhao, M., Zhu, L., Zhang, W., Wu, T., Ni, J.: A blockchain-based efficient and privacy-preserving quality-aware incentive scheme. IEEE J. Sel. Areas Commun. Early Access (2022)
7. Li, Y., et al.: Achieving a blockchain-based privacy-preserving quality-aware knowledge marketplace in crowdsensing. In: Proceedings of IEEE EUC, pp. 1–6 (2022)
8. Ding, Q., Li, Z., Batta, P., Trajković, L.: Detecting BGP anomalies using machine learning techniques. In: 2016 IEEE International Conference on Systems Man and Cybernetics (SMC), pp. 003:352–003:355, October 2016
9. de Urbina Cazenave, I.O., Köşlük, E., Ganiz, M.C.: An anomaly detection framework for BGP. In: 2011 International Symposium on Innovations in Intelligent Systems and Applications, pp. 107–111, June 2011
10. Li, Y., et al.: Classification of BGP anomalies using decision trees and fuzzy rough sets. In: 2014 IEEE International Conference on Systems Man and Cybernetics (SMC), pp. 1312–1317, October 2014
11. Zhang, W., et al.: Deep reinforcement learning based resource management for DNN inference in industrial IoT. IEEE Trans. Veh. Technol. **70**(8), 7605–7618 (2021). https://doi.org/10.1109/TVT.2021.3068255

12. Dong, Y., Li, Q., Sinnott, R.O., Jiang, Y., Xia, S.: ISP self-operated BGP anomaly detection based on weakly supervised learning. In: 2021 IEEE 29th International Conference on Network Protocols (ICNP), pp. 1–11 (2021). https://doi.org/10.1109/ICNP52444.2021.9651957

13. Jia, M., Shu, Y.J., Guo, Q., et al.: DDoS attack detection method for space-based net-work based on SDN architecture. ZTE Commun. **18**(4), 18–25, December 2020. https://doi.org/10.12142/ZTECOM.202004004

14. Hoarau, K., Tournoux, P.U., Razafindralambo, T.: Suitability of graph representation for BGP anomaly detection. In: 2021 IEEE 46th Conference on Local Computer Networks (LCN), pp. 305–310 (2021). https://doi.org/10.1109/LCN52139.2021.9524941

15. Sanchez, O.R., Oliveira, S.F., Pelsser, C., Bush, R.: Com-paring machine learning algorithms for BGP anomaly detection using graph features. In: Proceedings of the 3rd ACM CoNEXT Workshop on Big DAta, Machine Learning and Artificial Intelligence for Data Communication Networks (2019)

16. Qin, Q., Poularakis, K., Leung, K.K., Tassiulas, L.: Line-speed and scalable intrusion detection at the network edge via federated learning. In: IFIP Networking Conference (Networking) 2020, pp. 352–360 (2020)

17. Murphy, S.: BGP security vulnerabilities analysis (2006). https://tools.ietf.org/html/rfc4272

18. Routing information service (RIS). https://www.ripe.net/analyse/internet-measurements/routing-information-service-ris/routing-information-service-ris

19. Routeviews - university of oregon route views project. https://www.routeviews.org/routeviews/

20. Hubara, I., Courbariaux, M., Soudry, D., Yaniv, R., Bengio, Y.: Binarized neural networks. In: Proceedings of the Advances in Neural Information Processing Systems, vol. 29, pp. 4107–4115 (2016)

21. Cho, S., Fontugne, R., Cho, K., Dainotti, A., Gill, P.: BGP hijacking classification. In: 2019 Network Traffic Measurement and Analysis Conference (TMA), pp. 25–32 (2019)

22. Hoarau, K., Tournoux, P.U., Razafindralambo, T.: BML: an efficient and versatile tool for BGP dataset collection. In: IEEE International Conference on Communications Workshops (ICC Workshops) 2021, pp. 1–6 (2021). https://doi.org/10.1109/ICCWorkshops50388.2021.9473737

Generating Network Security Defense Strategy Based on Cyber Threat Intelligence Knowledge Graph

Shuqin Zhang[✉] [iD], Shuhan Li[iD], Peng Chen[iD], Shijie Wang[iD], and Chunxia Zhao[iD]

Zhongyuan University of Technology, Zhengzhou, China
zhangsq@zut.edu.cn

Abstract. Network systems are composed of thousands of devices connected in complex network topologies. The diversity and complexity of these devices increase the security risks of network systems. Cyber Threat Intelligence (CTI) contains rich information about devices, cyber, and defenses. However, due to the lack of correlation among security knowledge, some advanced reasoning tasks cannot be performed, such as device attack information and defense strategies. We construct the CTI ontology and knowledge graph, and propose a defense strategy inference model consisting of knowledge graph embedding algorithms CTI-KGE and reasoning rules. CTI-KGE is based on knowledge representation learning, and link prediction tasks can infer the tail entities that have any relationship with the head entity automatically, completing the threat information. Rule reasoning is interpretable, which can generate defense strategies automatically. Finally, we evaluate the effectiveness of the model and demonstrate its feasibility using actual network system scenarios.

Keywords: Network security · Cyber threat intelligence · Knowledge graph · Defense strategy

1 Introduction

With the continuous expansion of informatization and network technology, the methods of network attack are gradually becoming more complex, showing the characteristics of long persistence, high concealment, and cross-system. To respond to cybersecurity incidents more accurately and timely, security teams need to comprehensively analyze multi-channel data. Traditional defense methods such as Intrusion Detection System (IDS) and Intrusion Prevention System (IPS) are slightly insufficient in the face of large-scale network systems. Expert knowledge hidden in network security reports has become a very important breakthrough to solve the above problems. Therefore, Cyber Threat Intelligence (CTI) [1] emerges as a comprehensive defense method.

Network attack and defense are carried out in a dynamic and complex environment. When defenders face constantly updated vulnerabilities and attack patterns, they cannot master the latest attack techniques and vulnerability information to formulate corresponding defense strategies. Network security knowledge base can provide a reliable

W. Quan (Ed.): ICENAT 2022, CCIS 1696, pp. 507–519, 2023.
https://doi.org/10.1007/978-981-19-9697-9_41

defense scheme for network systems. However, with the large increase in CTI, the effective use of security knowledge is challenged by horizontal expansion. Building a CTI knowledge graph can effectively solve this challenge. Knowledge graph visualizes threat information in a structured way [2], which helps security teams respond to threats faster. Due to the heterogeneity of intelligence sources, the simple integration of CTI lacks the correlation between entities, and it is difficult to provide complete attack information and defense strategies only by using rule-based reasoning. An important issue is how to use large-scale CTI to build a reliable knowledge base to improve the standardization and availability of security knowledge. In recent years, knowledge graphs have been widely used in the field of network security, such as, device anomaly detection [3], software defect reasoning [4], device state prediction [5], network attack attribution [6], and attack strategy generation [7].

This paper focuses on making better use of CTI to enhance the security of network systems. Our contributions are as follows:

- We proposed a new ontology and integrated multi-source data to build a CTI knowledge graph.
- We proposed a CTI-KGE model that can model semantic-level features and relational mapping properties of entities to complement threat information.
- According to the characteristics of CTI, we designed the corresponding reasoning rules, which can automatically generate defense strategies.

2 Related Works

Network attack can gain access to users' private information and have an impact on the security of critical information infrastructure [8, 9]. CTI provides guidance on defending, identifying, analyzing, and mitigating the risk of network attack.

Generally, CTI is composed of security projects, network entities, hacker organizations, and attack information. In order to solve the information explosion problem of human-readable threat intelligence (PRTI), Ming Du et al. [10] proposed a human-readable threat intelligence recommendation knowledge graph, which integrated the knowledge graph representation method into the PRTI recommendation system. To automatically extract security information from continuously updated cybersecurity reports, Injy Sarhan et al. [11] developed an open CTI knowledge graph framework—OpenCyKG, which was built using an attention-based neural open information extraction model. OIE can extract valuable network threat information from unstructured Advanced Persistent Threat (APT) report. CTI about malware is accessible in a variety of formats, but the scarcity and inaccuracy of threat information might result in incomplete or incorrect triples. Nidhi Rastogi et al. developed a malware ontology that can extract structured information and generate knowledge graph -- MALOnt [12]. They proposed an end-to-end method to generate malware knowledge graph (MalKG) [13], which can generate structured and contextual threat intelligence in unstructured threat reports. Hongbin Zhang et al. [14] developed a stochastic game-based situational awareness model and used CTI to situational awareness. The model can properly predict attack behaviors and precisely reflect changes in network security settings.

Indeed, many existing approaches have attempted to solve cybersecurity problems using knowledge graph. Weilin Wang et al. [15] constructed a network attack knowledge using the entities and relationships in the network security knowledge base, which provided supplements and guidelines for attack prediction and network situational awareness. Traditional attack scenario detection approaches based on alerts are prone to massive redundancy and false positives. Yan Wang et al. [16] proposed a Knowledge Graph-based Network Security Situational Awareness (KG-NSSA) model, which solves the two traditional problems of network attack scene discovery and situational understanding. Through similarity estimation and attribute graph mining methods, KG-NSSA effectively simulates network attack scenarios of asset nodes. In order to solve the difficulty of attack prediction caused by 0-day vulnerability, Cheng Sun et al. [17] proposed a 0-day attack path prediction method based on network defense knowledge graph. This method transforms the attack prediction task into the link prediction problem of knowledge graph. Kiesling et al. [18] illustrated how to connect alerts from a Network Intrusion Detection System (NIDS) to the SEPSES network security knowledge graph to gain a better understanding of potential threats and ongoing attacks.

It can be seen that threat intelligence and security knowledge graph are important in solving network security problems. The majority of existing research focuses on attack detection and situational awareness, with less focus on defense. This paper mainly studies the combination of CTI and knowledge graph, and applies the reasoning technology of knowledge graph to generate defense strategies.

3   CTI Knowledge Graph

As attack groups and cyber threats become more sophisticated, security teams are struggling to find useful information in hundreds of pages of threat reports. Constructing multi-source heterogeneous CTI into a knowledge graph can improve search engine capability and security personnel search quality.

3.1   CTI Knowledge Graph Construction Method

The CTI knowledge graph provides an intuitive modeling method for displaying various attack and defense scenarios in real network systems. Knowledge graph is a structured semantic knowledge base that describes concepts and their relationships in the physical world in a symbolic form.

Figure 1 describes the framework for constructing CTI knowledge graph. The framework is divided into four sections: data sources, information extraction, ontology creation, and knowledge storage. Firstly, we analyzed the public network security knowledge base, extracted the concepts and relationships of network security field, and constructed the CTI ontology. On this basis, we carried out the knowledge extraction and fusion with reference to the knowledge mode defined by the ontology. In the process of information extraction, the framework uses the D2R (relational database to RDF) [19] tool for the structured data provided by the security knowledge base. For unstructured security reports, the framework uses the Open Information Extraction (OIE) model [11] for information extraction. Finally, we use neo4j for knowledge storage and data visualization.

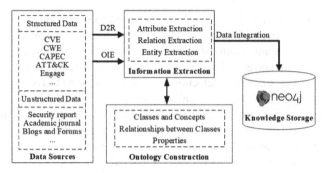

Fig. 1. Construction framework of CTI knowledge graph

3.2 CTI Ontology Construction

An ontology is a set of terms used to describe a domain. It can serve as the knowledge base's skeleton and foundation. The goal of constructing a CTI ontology is to capture, describe, and represent knowledge in the field of network security. It can provide a common understanding of network security knowledge. Figure 2 shows the entities and relationships in our CTI ontology.

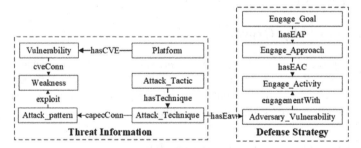

Fig. 2. CTI ontology

To eliminate the discrete and independent multi-source heterogeneous cybersecurity data, we collect security datasets widely used in the cybersecurity domain and refer to their experimental environments. First, we constructed the concepts required for the CTI model, which are divided into two modules: threat information and defense strategy. Threat information includes attack pattern, weakness, vulnerability, platform, attack technique, and attack tactic. Defense strategy includes adversary vulnerability, engage activity, engage activity, and engage goal. As shown in Table 1, we provide a detailed description of each top-level class concept. Finally, by mapping the formatted security data to the ontology model, we add the generated instances to the CTI knowledge graph to describe the relationships between network security entities.

Table 1. Top-level classes and descriptions

Classes	Descriptions
Platform	Threat carriers in network systems are defined as platforms, including hardware, software, and firmware
Vulnerability	Flaws or bugs in the platform that can be exploited by attackers
Weakness	Exploiting certain security weaknesses for a certain period of time can have both short- and long-term negative effects on the system
Attack_Pattern	Attacks are divided into different categories based on the attacker's exploitation of the weakness
Attack_Tactic	Attack purpose during attack, planning and tracking of short-term tactical targets
Attack_Technique	A specific operation by an attacker to achieve a tactical objective
Adversary_Vulnerability	The limitations that attackers have when attacking the platform
Engage_Goal	Staged goals for the platform to reduce or eliminate security risks
Engage_Approach	A range of approaches to advancing safety goals
Engage_Activity	Specific operations or actions performed by security personnel

4   Generating Defense Strategy Based on CTI Knowledge Graph

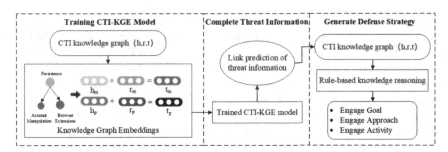

Fig. 3. Defense strategy generation models

Knowledge reasoning based on knowledge graph can obtain new knowledge and conclusions from existing data [20]. Rule-based reasoning is interpretable, and its essence is to define the logic and constraints of relational reasoning. Knowledge representation-based reasoning projects knowledge graphs into continuous low-dimensional vector spaces, which can effectively predict missing relationships and entities. As shown in Fig. 3, this section introduces the design of an effective combinatorial reasoning model. The model uses KGE algorithm to predict missing relationships to complete threat information, and then uses rule reasoning to create new relationships to generate effective defense strategies.

4.1 Cti-Kge

The purpose of KGE is to map the knowledge graph into a dense, low-level feature space that preserves as much structural and property information of the graph as possible and facilitates computations about entities and relationships. Given a set of triples $CTIKG = \{< h, r, t >\}$ of the CTI knowledge graph, and a predefined embedding space d, KGE represents each entity $h \in E$ and relation $r \in R$ in a continuous vector space of dimension d, where E and R represent sets of entities and relations, respectively.

The Hierarchy-Aware Knowledge Graph Embedding (HAKE [21]) model maps entities to a polar coordinate system, and represents entities with the same semantic level as vectors with the same modulus (i.e., concentric circles). Based on HAKE, we propose CTI-KGE. CTI-KGE can model the semantic-level features and relational mapping properties of entities, and it consists of two parts: modulus and phase. The modulus part is designed to model entities at different classes of entities (e.g., CWE-119, CVE-2005–0879), the vectors of h, r, and t are represented as h_m, r_m, and t_m, and the modulus part is represented as:

$$h_m \circ r_m = t_m \tag{1}$$

$$d_{r,m}(h_m, t_m) = w_r \| h_m \circ r_m - t_m \|_2 \tag{2}$$

$$w_r = \frac{1}{\log(ht_r + th_r)} \tag{3}$$

where $h_m, t_m \in \mathbb{R}^k$, and $r_m \in \mathbb{R}_+^k$. $\circ$ represents the Hadamard product. $d_{r,m}$ is the distance function of the modulus part. Due to the high proportion of instances of Many-To-Many relationships in the CTI knowledge graph, we must consider the degree of relationship mapping. We designed the formula 3 to measure the relationship mapping degree, where ht_r is the number of head entities corresponding to the tail entity, and th_r is the number of tail entities corresponding to the head entity.

Entities with the same class will have the same modulus if only the modulus part is used to model the entity. Assuming that r is a relation that reflects the same semantic level, then $[r]$ will tend to 1, and it is difficult to distinguish entities of the same type. The phase part can distinguish entities in the same class (e.g., CWE-119, CWE-787). Specifically, the phase part considers entities on the same semantic level as nodes on different phases on the same circle. The phase part formula is as follows:

$$(h_p + r_p) \bmod 2\pi = t_p \tag{4}$$

$$d_{r,p}(h_p, t_p) = \| \frac{\sin(h_p \circ r_p - t_p)}{2} \|_1 \tag{5}$$

where $h_p, r_p, t_p \in [0, 2\pi]^k$. Because the phase is periodic, we use the sine function $sin(\bullet)$ to calculate the distance between angles. $d_{r,p}$ is the distance function of the phase part.

Combining the modulo and phase parts, CTI-KGE maps the entity to the polar coordinate system, where the radial and angular coordinates correspond to the modulus and phase parts, respectively. The formulas of the CTI-KGE scoring function are as follows:

$$f_r(h, t) = -d_r(h, t) = -w_r \|h_m \circ r_m - t_m\|_2 - \lambda \| \frac{\sin(h_p \circ r_p - t_p)}{2} \|_1 \qquad (6)$$

where $\lambda \in R$ is the parameter learned by the model. For better training results, we use the negative sampling loss function and self-adversarial training method in the RotatE [22] model for training.

By training the CTI-KGE model, the initial CTI knowledge graph can be mapped to vector space. The threat information is completed by performing the link prediction task, which predicts the sparse and missing relationships in the knowledge graph.

4.2 Reasoning Rules for Defense Strategy

This paper's final task is to provide specific defense strategies based on threat information. As in Sect. 3.2, we divide defense strategies into four levels: adversary vulnerability, engage goal, engage approach, and engage activity. Generate defense strategies according to different scenarios, which can adapt to multiple use cases or security goals.

The reasoning rules we designed are as follows:

1. If the platform P has a vulnerability V, and the vulnerability V is related to the vulnerability W, it can be inferred that the platform P has a vulnerability W.

$$hasCVE(P, V) \cap cveConn(V, W) \rightarrow hasCWE(P, W)$$

2. If the attack pattern AP uses the weakness W and the platform P has the weakness W, it can be inferred that the platform P may be affected by the attack mode AP.

$$exploit(AP, W) \cap hasCWE(P, W) \rightarrow hasAttackPattern(P, AP)$$

3. If the attack technique T is related to the attack pattern AP and the platform P may be affected by the attack pattern AP, it can be inferred that the platform P may be attacked by the attack technique T.

$$capecConnT, AP \cap hasAttackPattern(P, AP) \rightarrow isDamaged(P, T)$$

4. If the attacker uses the attack technique T, there is an adversary vulnerability AV, and the engage activity EA can counter the adversary vulnerability AV, it can be inferred that the Engage activity EA can counter the attack technique T.

$$hasEav(T, AV) \cap engagementWith(AV, EA) \rightarrow hasEngage(EA, T)$$

5. If the platform P is likely to be attacked by the attack technique T and the engage activity EA can counter the attack technique T, it can be inferred that the platform P can use the engage activity EA to reduce the attack risk.

$$hasDamage(T, P) \cap hasEngage(EA, T) \rightarrow hasDefend(P, EA)$$

6. If the defender uses engage approach *EAP* can achieve the engage goal *EG*. The specific engage activity of *EAP* is *EA*, and the platform *P* can use *EA* to reduce the attack risk. It can be inferred that the engage goal *EG* needs to implement the engage activity *EA*, and the platform *P* can complete the engage goal *EG*.

$$hasEAP(EG, EAP) \cap hasEAC(EAP, EA) \rightarrow hasImplement(EG, EA)$$

$$hasImplement(EG, EA) \cap hasDefend(P, EA) \rightarrow hasDefend(P, EG)$$

Due to the complexity of attack scenarios and the diversity of network systems configurations, security experts usually need to design defense strategies according to the actual situation. The process of developing a defense strategy is divided into three steps:

Step 1. Determine the topology of the current system, and build an asset description table, which includes name, type, supplier, and version.

Step 2. Export all threat information related to assets from the CTI knowledge graph.

Step 3. Create a set of defense strategies according to the above reasoning rules, including engage goals, engage approaches, and engage activities.

5   Experiment

In this section, we empirically study and evaluate the proposed defense strategy generation. We first evaluate CTI-KGE, and then use a real-world network system scenario to demonstrate the efficacy and feasibility of our proposed method.

5.1   Evaluation of CTI-KGE

We constructed the CTI knowledge graph, which includes 224,430 entities, 9 relation types, and 408,885 triples. Based on the CTI knowledge graph, we constructed the dataset CTIKG for KGE. We randomly selected 5000 triples as test set and validation set, respectively, and the remaining triples were used as training set to train our model.

The link prediction is a hot topic in the field of knowledge graphs, which completes triples for missing entities such as $(?, r, t)$ or $(h, r, ?)$ or missing relations $(h, ?, t)$. For each triple (h, r, t) in the test dataset, we replace the head entity or tail entity of each candidate triple, and then sort the candidate triples in descending order of scores. To evaluate experimental results, we employ two evaluation metrics: MRR and Hit@n.

Table 2 shows the evaluation results of the CTI-KGE, HAKE model on our dataset. Our model achieves the best performance in both categories of evaluation metrics.

Table 2. CTI-KGE evaluation results

Model	MRR	Hits@1	Hits@3	Hits@10
HAKE	0.415	0.358	0.430	0.478
CTI-KGE	0.515	0.476	0.493	0.499

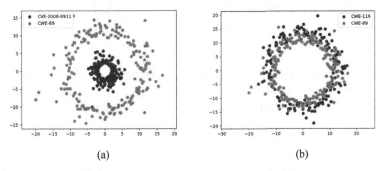

(a)   (b)

Fig. 4. Visualization of three entities' embeddings

Figure 4 shows the visualization results for three entities of the CTIKG dataset. We can clearly find that in Fig. 4(a), entities 'cwe-89' and 'cve-2008–6911' at different semantic levels are located in different circular regions, and in Fig. 4(b), the entities 'cwe-119' and 'cwe-89' of the same semantic level are located in the same circular region. This shows that our model can effectively discriminate different semantic levels.

5.2 Case Study of Defense Strategy Generation

We test our method through an Intelligent Transmission Pipeline system (ITP). The ITP includes a Master Control Center (Master CC), a Remote Terminal Unit (RTU), and sensors. When ITP is running, the sensors installed on the pipes will send pressure and flow information to the RTU, which sends this information to the Master CC. According to the information, Master CC instructs the RTU to open or close the valve (or pump) to regulate the pipeline pressure (or flow) to ensure that the pressure in the pipeline does not exceed the specified threshold. Attacker may intercept and manipulate the communication from the pressure sensor to the PLC, resulting in malfunction of the valve operation. This will lead to an abnormal increase in pipeline pressure, exceeding the safety threshold.

Table 3. Asset description of ITP

Name	Cpe(2.3)
s14_firmware	cpe:2.3:o:mobotix:s14_firmware:mx-v4.2.1.61:*:*:*:*:*:*:*
DL 8000	cpe:2.3:h:emerson:dl_8000_remote_terminal_unit:-:*:*:*:*:*:
DeltaV	cpe:2.3:a:emerson:deltav:9.3.1:*:*:*:*:*:*:*
IDS Sensor Software	cpe:2.3:a:cisco:ids_sensor_software:4.0\(1\)e0:*:*:*:*:*:*:*
Linux	cpe:2.3:o:linux:acrn:2018w49.5-140000p:*:*:*:*:*:*:*

According to the system architecture, we can get the asset description table as shown in Table 3. Taking 's14_firmware' as an example, by querying the CTI knowledge graph and using the CTI-KGE model to complete the threat information, the knowledge graph is obtained as shown in Fig. 5.

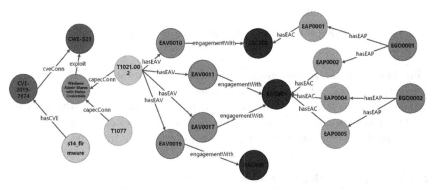

Fig. 5. 's14_firmware' related threat information

According to Fig. 5, 's14_firmware' has vulnerability 'CVE-2019–7674' and weakness 'CWE-521'. The weakness 'CWE-521' is at risk of being attacked by attack pattern 'Windows Admin Shares with Stolen Credentials' and attack technique 'SMB/Windows Admin Shares' (T1021.002). When attacker uses attack technique 'T1021.002', the adversary vulnerabilities 'EAV0010', 'EAV0011', 'EAV0017', and 'EAV0019' will be generated.

We can infer effective defense strategies for's14 firmware' using defense strategy reasoning rules, as shown in Fig. 6. Table 4 shows the specifics and explanations for the defense strategies. Referring to the listed defense strategies, when ITP detects an abnormality, the security team can quickly make decisions and implement defense strategies for the device, reducing the risk of attack significantly.

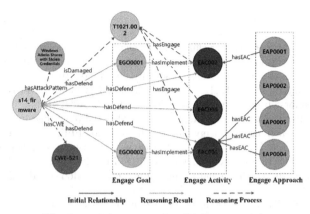

Fig. 6. 's14_firmware' related defense strategies

Table 4. 's14_firmware' related defense strategies specific information

Steps	Defense strategies
Engage Goal	EG0001(Expose): Reveal the presence of ongoing adversary operations EG0002(Affect): Negatively impact the adversary operations
Engage Approach	EAP0001(Collect): Gather adversary tools, observe tactics, and collect other raw intelligence about the adversary's activity EAP0002(Detect): Establish or maintain awareness regarding adversary activity EAP0005(Disrupt): Impair an adversary's ability to conduct their operation as intended EAP0004(Direct): Encourage or discourage the adversary from conducting their operation as intended
Engage Activity	EAC002(Network Monitoring): Monitor network traffic in order to detect adversary activity EAC005(Lures): Deceptive systems and artifacts intended to serve as decoys, breadcrumbs, or bait to elicit a specific response from the adversary EAC006(Application Diversity): Present the adversary with a variety of installed applications and services

6   Conclusion

This paper proposes a defense strategy for generating CTI-based knowledge graphs. We use the cybersecurity knowledge base and security reports to build the CTI knowledge graph. The CTI-KGE algorithm is used to fill in the missing entities in the CTI knowledge graph. We also design reason rules to generate CTI-based knowledge graphs for effective defense strategies and display them graphically. In the future, we will expand the CTI knowledge base to consider more factors when choosing defense strategies, such as attack probability, vulnerability severity, and asset cost.

References

1. Burger, E.W., Goodman, M.D., Kampanakis, P., Zhu, K.A.: Taxonomy model for cyber threat intelligence information exchange technologies. In: Proceedings of the 2014 ACM Workshop on Information Sharing & Collaborative Security, pp. 51–60 (2014)
2. Noel, S., Harley, E., Tam, K.H., Limiero, M., Share, M.: CyGraph: graph-based analytics and visualization for cybersecurity. Handbook Statist. **35**, 117–167 (2016)
3. Cui, B.: Electric device abnormal detection based on IoT and knowledge graph. In: 2019 IEEE International Conference on Energy Internet, pp. 217–220. IEEE, Nanjing, China (2019)
4. Han, Z., Li, X., Liu, H., Xing, Z., Feng, Z.: Deepweak: Reasoning common software weaknesses via knowledge graph embedding. In: 2018 IEEE 25th International Conference on Software Analysis, Evolution and Reengineering, pp. 456–466. IEEE. Campobasso, Italy (2018)
5. You, S., Li, X., Chen, W.: Intelligent Prediction for Device Status Based on IoT Temporal Knowledge Graph. In: 2020 IEEE/CIC International Conference on Communications in China, pp. 560–565. IEEE. Chongqing, China (2020)
6. Zhu, Z., Jiang, R., Jia, Y., Xu, J., Li, A.: Cyber security knowledge graph based cyber attack attribution framework for space-ground integration information network. In: 2018 IEEE 18th International Conference on Communication Technology, pp. 870–874. IEEE. Chongqing, China (2018)
7. Chen, X., Shen, W., Yang, G.: Automatic Generation of Attack Strategy for Multiple Vulnerabilities Based on Domain Knowledge Graph. In: IECON 2021–47th Annual Conference of the IEEE Industrial Electronics Society, pp. 1–6. IEEE. Toronto, ON, Canada (2021)
8. Y u, S., Liu, M., Dou, W., Liu, X., Zhou, S.: Networking for big data: a survey. IEEE Commun.Surv. Tutor. **19**(1), 531–549 (2017)
9. Feng, C., Zhou, B., Zhang, H., et al.: HetNet: a flexible architecture for heterogeneous satelliteterrestrial networks. IEEE Network **31**(6), 86–92 (2017)
10. Du, M., Jiang, J., Jiang, Z., Lu, Z., Du,: X.: PRTIRG: a knowledge graph for people-readable threat intelligence recommendation. In: International Conference on Knowledge Science. Engineering and Management, pp. 47–59. Springer, Cham (2019)
11. Sarhan, I., Spruit, M.: Open-cykg: An open cyber threat intelligence knowledge graph. Knowl.-Based Syst. **233**, 107524 (2021)
12. Rastogi, N., Dutta, S., Zaki, M.J., Gittens, A., Aggarwal, C.: Malont: An ontology for malware threat intelligence. In: Wang, G., Ciptadi, A., Ahmadzadeh, A. (eds.) MLHat 2020. CCIS, vol. 1271, pp. 28–44. Springer, Cham (2020). https://doi.org/10.1007/978-3-030-59621-7_2
13. Rastogi, N., Dutta, S., Christian, R., Zaki, M., Gittens, A., Aggarwal, C.: Information prediction using knowledge graphs for contextual malware threat intelligence. arXiv preprint arXiv: 2102.05571 (2021)
14. Zhang, H., Yin, Y., Zhao, D., Liu, B.: Network security situational awareness model based on threat intelligence. Journal on Communications **42**(6), 182–194 (2021)
15. Wang, W., Zhou, H., Li, K., Zhe, Tu., Liu, F.: Cyber-Attack Behavior Knowledge Graph Based on CAPEC and CWE Towards 6G. In: You, I., Kim, H., Youn, T.-Y., Palmieri, F., Kotenko, I. (eds.) MobiSec 2021. CCIS, vol. 1544, pp. 352–364. Springer, Singapore (2022). https://doi.org/10.1007/978-981-16-9576-6_24
16. Wang, Y., Li, Y., Chen, X., Luo, Y.: Implementing Network Attack Detection with a Novel NSSA Model Based on Knowledge Graphs. In: 2020 IEEE 19th International Conference on Trust, Security and Privacy in: Computing and Communications, pp. 1727–1732). IEEE. Guangzhou, China (2020)
17. Sun, C., Hu, H., Yang, Y., Zhang, H.: Prediction method of 0day attack path based on cyber defense knowledge graph (Chinese). Chinese Journal of Network and Information Security **8**(1), 151–166 (2022)

18. Kiesling, E., Ekelhart, A., Kurniawan, K., Ekaputra, F.: The SEPSES Knowledge Graph: An Integrated Resource for Cybersecurity. In: Ghidini, C., et al. (eds.) ISWC 2019. LNCS, vol. 11779, pp. 198–214. Springer, Cham (2019). https://doi.org/10.1007/978-3-030-30796-7_13
19. Sahoo, S.S., Halb, W., Hellmann, S. et al.: A survey of current approaches for mapping of relational databases to RDF. W3C RDB2RDF Incubator Group Report, 1, pp. 113–130 (2009)
20. Chen, X., Jia, S., Xiang, Y.: A review: Knowledge reasoning over knowledge graph. Expert Syst. Appl. **141**, 112948 (2020)
21. Zhang, Z., Cai, J., Zhang, Y., Wang, J.: Learning hierarchy-aware knowledge graph embeddings for link prediction. Proceedings of the AAAI Conference on Artificial Intelligence **34**(03), 3065–3072 (2020)
22. Sun, Z., Deng, Z. H., Nie, J. Y., Tang, J.: Rotate: Knowledge graph embedding by relational rotation in complex space. arXiv preprint arXiv:1902.10197 (2019)

A Computing Efficient Algorithm Specialized for Pseudo-Constant Metrics

Mingxia Wang[1]([✉]), Yongxiang Zhao[1], Chunxi Li[1], Weidong Wang[2], Yue Wang[2], and ChengWei Liu[2]

[1] Beijing Jiaotong University, Beijing, China
{20120119,yxzhao,chxli1}@bjtu.edu.cn
[2] Beijing Baolande Software Corporation, Beijing, China
{weidong.wang,yue.wang,chengwei.liu}@bessystem.com

Abstract. AIOps (Artificial Intelligence for IT Operations) improve operation and maintenance efficiency of complex IT systems by quickly locating the root causes of failures through machine learning methods. The key of AIOps is to quickly locate anomaly in huge amount of monitoring metric time series. In this paper, we show that there are a considerable number of Pseudo-Constant metrics in actual large systems, whose values vary little or occasionally change violently. Based on feature of this kind of metric, we propose a Binary Mixed Detection algorithm for Pseudo-Constant metric. We build a model to evaluate its detection time and also analyze its false negative and false positive probability. Finally, we show the performance of BMD on actual data set. The experimental results show that BMD can save 85% of the detection time.

Keywords: Anomaly detection · AIOps · Time series

1 Introduction

In order to monitor system operation state, existed IT systems generate large amounts of monitoring data. Using traditional methods, it is impossible to find out major events such as root causes of failures from these monitoring data. AIOps (Artificial Intelligence for IT Operations) can quickly locate root causes of failures by artificial intelligence methods to improve operation and maintenance efficiency of complex IT systems, and has been a research hotspot in recent years.

Anomaly detection is one of the core technologies of AIOps [11]. In order to locate anomaly in IT system, management system sample hardware and software state regularly and these sample data form metric time series(we use metric time series and metric interchangeably in this paper). A distributed IT system usually produces more than 10000 measurement metric values per time interval, e.g., every minute or second. AIOps applies anomaly detection to detect these measurement metrics to find anomalous metric signals, and then discover the real failure causes through root cause localization algorithm. The key of anomaly detection algorithm is to locate anomaly quickly and correctly.

W. Quan (Ed.): ICENAT 2022, CCIS 1696, pp. 520–532, 2023.
https://doi.org/10.1007/978-981-19-9697-9_42

The research on anomaly detection in AIOps can be divided into the following three categories: statistical, supervised learning and unsupervised methods.

Statistical methods ignores the sequence of the time series and regards the points in the time series as statistical sample points [1,3,9,12]. This method assumes that the data obey a certain model (such as Gaussian distribution or arma model [10]), and the data point deviating from model is considered to be anomalous point.

Supervised learning-based anomaly detection methods utilize labeled data to train models to detect anomalies. Ref [8] applies multiple existing detectors to extract anomalous features and the extracted features are used to train a random forest classifier to detect anomalies. Ref [13] detects anomalies with Spectral Residual (SR) and then uses the detection result as label to train a CNN network. This type method also includes EGADS [5], ensemble classifiers [16], etc.

Unsupervised learning methods detect anomalies without labeling data. Ref [6] converts non-extreme anomalies to extreme values by two-step smoothing and then uses SPOT [14] algorithm to detect anomalies. Ref [7] uses MCMC-based method to obtain time series reconstructions and use reconstruction error to detect anomalies. This type method also includes SeqVL [2], and GAN [15], etc.

The above works are devoted to finding anomaly points in dynamically changing metric. Their difference lies in the definition and understanding of anomalies. However, this paper observes that about 20% of the metric in the actual large-scale distributed system, either do not vary with time or vary very little except apparent spike like anomaly points. This paper calls this kind of metric as Pseudo-Constant metric whose anomaly points are easy to identify. For Pseudo-Constant metrics, the key is to design a detection algorithm to detect anomaly quickly which means it can save computing power as much as possible so that more computer power can be used for highly dynamically metric detection.

Based on this observation, the paper proposes an anomaly detection algorithm called Binary Mixed Detection (BMD) which is specifically designed for Pseudo-Constant metrics. BMD combines multiple Pseudo-Constant metric time series into an aggregated time series and a detection algorithm will be used on it. If there is no anomaly in aggregated time series, there is no anomaly in all combined Pseudo-Constant metrics. Otherwise, the dichotomy method is used to search for anomalous metrics. Since anomaly happened in Pseudo-Constant metric with rather small probability, the algorithm can reduce the detection number greatly. The time cost of BMD algorithm is consisted by detection time and metric aggregation time. This paper also models BMD's detection time, the false positive and false negative probability. Experimental results show that BMD algorithm reduces the time cost by 85% under actual data set.

The organization of this paper is as follows. Section 2 shows the motivation and proposes Binary Mixed Detection. Section 3 shows the details of BMD algorithm and models its detection time. Section 4 analyzes the probability of false positive and false negative of BMD. Section 5 presents experimental results on actual data set. Section 6 concludes this paper.

2   Motivation and Basic Idea

This section first introduces the concept of Pseudo-Constant metric and shows the non-negligible proportion in real dataset and then proposes BMD algorithm.

2.1   Motivation

This subsection investigates the real data set and introduces the concept of Pseudo-Constant metric.

The dataset analyzed in this paper is Exathlon dataset [4]. Exathlon dataset is constructed based on real data traces from around 100 repeated executions of large-scale stream processing jobs on an Apache Spark cluster. Each trace contains thousands of metric time series.

For a time series, first use the standard deviation method to determine the anomalies, and remove the anomalies from the time series to obtain a new time series; if the anomalies are greater than (or less than) k times the mean of the new time series (k is 6 in this paper), and the standard deviation of the new time series is less than a certain threshold (1.93 in this paper), then we call this time series a Pseudo-Constant metric. Figure 1 shows six Pseudo-Constant metrics examples. It can be seen that three time series in Fig. 1(a) and two time series in Fig. 1(c) almost remain constant and one time series in Fig. 1(c) fluctuates rather small except few large spikes.

This paper screens 202,239 metric in the Exathlon dataset [11] and finds that 45,858 metrics are classified as Pseudo-Constant metrics according to the definition of Pseudo-Constant metric, accounting for 22.7% of the total dataset. Therefore, in the actual data set, the Pseudo-Constant metric accounts for a non-negligible proportion of the whole data set.

By Fig. 1, the difference between abnormal and normal points of Pseudo-Constant metric is obvious, and it is easy to detect anomaly points of Pseudo-Constant metric using statistical methods. For such metrics, it is more important to shorten the detection time under the condition of ensuring detection performance, so as to leave more time to other highly dynamic time series' detection.

2.2   Basic Idea of BMD

This subsection proposes BMD algorithm and discusses its feasibility.

This paper proposes BMD to optimize Pseudo-Constant metric detection time. Its basic idea can be shown in Fig. 1(b) and Fig. 1(d). By default, this paper adopts the method of three-time standard deviation [12] to detect anomalous points. We refer to the following method as Traditional Method in this paper: each metric is detected individually by three-time standard deviation detection. In Traditional Method, we perform three detections in Fig. 1(a) and Fig. 1(c) respectively since each time series needs to do one detection.

We first consider the detection of time series in Fig. 1(a). We perform vector addition(i.e. metric aggregation) operation on these time series by treating each time series as a vector and the result is shown in Fig. 1(b), which is a constant

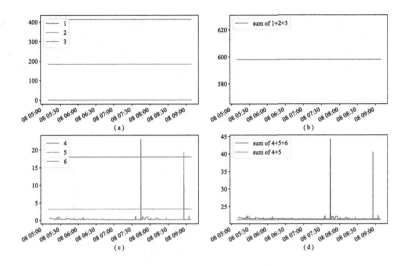

Fig. 1. An example of Pseudo-Constant metrics.

curve. We will see no anomaly point on this resulting time series if we perform three-time standard deviation detection on curve in Fig. 1(b). This means that we only need to do one detection for three time series in Fig. 1(a).

Then we consider the detection of time series in Fig. 1(c). First, we perform vector addition operation on three time series in Fig. 1(c) and the result is shown in Fig. 1(d), labeled as "sum of 4+5+6". After applying three-time standard deviation detection to the curve "sum of curve 4+5+6", it is found that the curve contains anomalous points. In this case, the metric set(4,5,6) will be divided into two set: set(4,5) and set(6). Time series of 4 and 5 in former set are added up and the resulting curve is named as "sum of 4+5" which is shown in Fig. 1(d). Apparently, there is no anomaly point in "sum of 4+5". We further detect curve 6 in latter set and can finally locate the anomalous points. Consequently, we need three times of detection to locate anomalous points in Fig. 1(c) beside we perform two times of vector addition.

The feasibility of BMD is explored by following experiments in which there are 2000 metrics and each metric is consisted by 1440 fixed data points. We use Traditional Method as baseline. In first case, the 2000 metrics are detected by Traditional Method, and the sum of their detection time is recorded. This experiment is repeated 10000 times. In second case, the 2000 metrics are detected by BMD algorithm that perform a vector addition of 2000 metrics and one detection. Because the value of each metric is fixed, there is no anomaly point in these metrics. This experiment is also repeated 10000 times. The experimental results are shown in Fig. 2.

According to the Fig. 2, BMD's time cost is far less than that of Traditional Method when there is no anomaly point in Pseudo-Constant metrics, which shows the benefit of BMD algorithm. This means that time cost of vector addition is far less than that of three-time standard deviation detection which is due to vector addition can be paralleled and detection algorithm can't.

Thus, BMD can greatly reduce the number of detections when the number of time series with anomalies in the dataset is very small, which is precisely the characteristic of Pseudo-Constant metric.

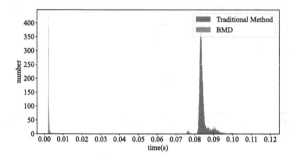

Fig. 2. Detection time comparision between BMD and Traditional Method when metric number is fixed to 2000.

3   Binary Mixed Detection and Model Evaluation

This section presents the details of the BMD and models its detection time.

3.1   BMD Algorithm

The details of BMD are shown in Algorithm 1. The input of the algorithm is a matrix of N rows and M columns which is called *Input_Data* and each column represents a metric and each metric consists N time instants. For simplicity, this paper assumes that N is a fixed constant (1440 by default). All metrics are numbered from 0 to M-1 in sequence. *check_list* stores the metric intervals to be detected and each metric interval is represented by a pair of numbers that represent the left and right endpoints of metric interval. It is initialized with an interval [0, M]. Line 3 takes one metric interval from *check_list*, and line 4 filters the data from the left endpoint column to the right endpoint column of this interval from Input_Data, denoted as *test_data*. Line 5 mixes test_data by performing *Vector_Addition*, where each column in the test_data set is treated as a vector, and vector summation is performed on these vectors, that is, the elements in the same position of each vector are added, and finally a vector is formed. Line 6 uses function *Anomaly_Detection* to detect the resulting metric vector and this paper adopts the standard deviation method as anomaly detection method. If line 6 detects anomaly points and there is only one metric in the detection interval, line 11 outputs the metric number and anomalous positions. Otherwise, lines 13 to 15 split the detection interval into two intervals and add them to the *check_list*.

3.2   Model BMD

This subsection models vector addition's time and the number, detection's time and the number, then validates the model with experiment.

In the BDM algorithm, most execution time of BDM is spent on 5th line of metric vector addition and 6th line of detection. We will build a model to analyze two part time in this subsection.

Suppose there are M metrics, of which Q metrics contain anomalous points. Let $q = \frac{Q}{M}$ be probability that a metric contains anomalous points. When BMD works on this data set, it will take out one interval from $check\_list$ successively, denoted as $1^{th}, 2^{th}, \ldots, K^{th}$, until $check\_list$ is empty. For i^{th} interval, BMD will perform a detection and $M_i = end\_ptr\_i - start\_ptr\_i$ vector addition, where $start\_ptr\_i$ and end_ptr_i are left and right end of ith interval. Define $D(M, Q)$ and $A(M, Q)$ as detection number which is K and vector addition which is $\sum_{i=0}^{K} M_i$ respectively, where M represents metric number and Q represents anomalous metrics number. Obviously, when $M = 1$, no matter whether the metric is anomalous or not, it needs to be detected once, that is, $D(1, 1) = 1, A(1, 1) = 0, D(1, 0) = 1, A(1, 0) = 0$. When $M > 1$ and $Q = 0, D(M, 0) = 1, A(M, 0) = M$. When $M > 1$ and $Q > 0$, the M metrics will be divided into left and right subsets of size $L = \lceil \frac{M}{2} \rceil$ and $R = \lfloor \frac{M}{2} \rfloor$ respectively. Therefore,

---

Algorithm 1. Binary Mixed Detection

Input: Input_Data [N,M]
Output: Id of col and Row of anomaly
1: Initialize:$check\_list = [[0,M]]$
2: **while** $check\_list$ is not empty **do**
3:     $start\_ptr\_i, end\_ptr\_i = i^{th}$ interval for i^{th} interval in $check\_list$
4:     test_data = Input_Data$[:, start\_ptr\_i: end\_ptr\_i]$
5:     mixed_data = $Vector\_Addition$(test_data)
6:     pos = $Anomaly\_Detection$(mixed_data)
7:     **if** pos is empty **then**
8:        continue
9:     **end if**
10:    **if** pos is not empty and $(start\_ptr\_i + 1)$ equals end_ptr_i **then**
11:       Output $start\_ptr\_i$ and pos
12:    **else**
13:       middle = $(end\_ptr\_i - start\_ptr\_i)/2$
14:       add $[start\_ptr\_i, start\_ptr\_i+$middle$]$ to $check\_list$
15:       add $[start\_ptr\_i+$middle$, end\_ptr\_i]$ to $check\_list$
16:    **end if**
17: **end while**

---

if there are Q anomalous metrics among M metrics, the probability p_i that the left subset contains i anomalous metrics is

$p_i = P(i$ anomalous metrics in left set$|Q$ anomalous metrics in M metrics)

$$= \frac{P(i \text{ anomalous metrics in left set}) * P(Q - i \text{ anomalous metrics in right set})}{P(Q \text{ anomalous metrics in } M \text{ metrics})}$$

$$= \frac{C_L^i * q^i * (1 - q)^{L-i} * C_R^{Q-i} * q^{Q-i} * (1 - q)^{R-(L-i)}}{C_M^Q * q^Q * (1 - q)^{M-Q}}$$

$$(1)$$

Thus, the number of vector additions to detect M metrics containing Q anomalous metrics is

$$A(M, Q) = M + \sum_{i=0}^{Q} p_i * (A(L, i) + A(R, Q - i)) \tag{2}$$

The first term M on the right side of Equation(2) indicates the vector addition of M metrics, and the second term represents the expected sum of the number of vector additions after the M metrics are divided into left and right sets.

Similarly, the number of detections to detect M metrics containing Q anomalous metrics is

$$D(M, Q) = 1 + \sum_{i=0}^{Q} p_i * (D(L, i) + D(R, Q - i)) \tag{3}$$

where the first item 1 in the right side of Eq. (3) indicates one detection on the aggregated metric of M metrics.

Finally, functions $F_a(A(M, Q))$ and $F_d(D(M, Q))$ are used to map vector addition $A(M, Q)$ and detection number $D(M, Q)$ to their corresponding time, so the time for detecting M metrics containing Q anomalous metrics is

$$T(M, Q) = F_a(A(M, Q)) + F_d(D(M, Q)) \tag{4}$$

To find the specific expressions of $F_a(A(M, Q))$ and $F_d(D(M, Q))$, we do the following experiments: M is fixed 2000 and Q is varies from 1 to 40 and the step size is 1. We also set the following combinations of M and Q: 1) M is one of the set[10, 20, 50, 100] and Q is [1, 2]; 2) M is one of the set [200, 300, ...,1300] and Q is one of the set [1, ..., (M*0.02)]. For each combination of M and Q, the experiment is repeated 5000 times and each experiment randomly set Q positions in data [N, M] as anomalous points that are much larger than other data points. In each experiment, $F_a(A(M, Q))$, $F_d(D(M, Q))$, $A(M, Q)$ and $D(M, Q)$ are collected.

The experiment machine in this paper is equipped with Intel(R) Core (TM) i7-1065G7 CPU @1.30GHz and 8GB of RAM. The programming language used is Python.

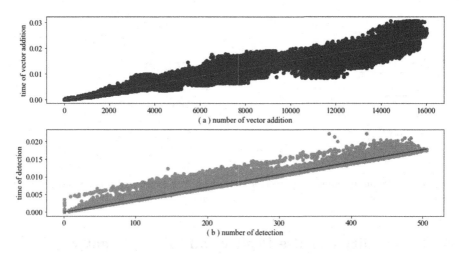

Fig. 3. Modeling detections and vector additions's time.

Figure 3(a) and Fig. 3(b) show scatter plot of $F_a(A(M,Q))$ and $A(M,Q)$, and $F_d(D(M,Q))$ and $D(M,Q)$. It is clear that $F_a(A(M,Q))$ and $F_d(D(M,Q))$ can be fitted as linear function.

The average number of experiments for $A(M,Q)$ and $D(M,Q)$ under different Q are represented in Fig. 4(a) and Fig. 4(b). The corresponding result calculated by equation (2) and equation (3) are also represented in this figure. From Fig. 4, it can be observed that the experimental results for the number of vector additions and detections are consistent with the results calculated by the model, which proves the accuracy of the model.

Figure 5 shows the BMD's model time under different value of Q, labeled as 'model all time', which is calculated by Eq. (4). Figure 5 also shows vector addition time, labeled as 'model add time', and detection time, labeled as 'model detect time', which correspond to two components of Eq. (4). Figure 5 also shows corresponding experiment time. As a comparison, this figure shows the Traditional Method's detection time, labeled as 'experiment individual time'.

This figure shows: as the number of anomalous metrics increases, so does the time of BMD. When the number of anomalous metrics in the 2000 metrics less than 40, the time of BMD is always less than that of Traditional Method.

In addition, Fig. 5 shows that modeled result and experimental result fit very well under different number of anomalous metrics.

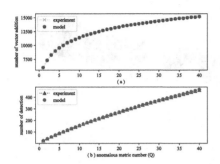
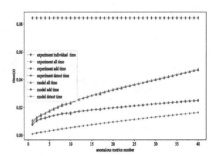

Fig. 4. Modeling number of detections and vector additions.

Fig. 5. Experimental time and Modeling time.

4   Probability of False Positive and False Negative

This section studies the probability of false positive and false negative for BMD and analyzes their numerical results.

Metric set is represented by $\{m_1, m_2, m_3, \cdots, m_M\}$, where each metric is a time series contained N points, i.e., $m_i = \{x_i^1, x_i^2, x_i^3, \cdots, x_i^N\}$. Because this paper uses standard deviation rule as the detection of anomalies, the mean has no effect on the detection algorithm. For brevity, this paper assumes that the mean of the time series is 0. By its definition, the standard deviation of a Pseudo-Constant metric is less than a fixed value. Therefore, this paper assumes that the standard deviation of the time series is σ.

4.1   False Positive

Firstly, the situation of false positive at time t_0 is studied. A false positive event happened if following happed: At time t_0, there is no anomaly point in M metrics in fact, but BMD reports an anomaly point on the aggregated metric of M metrics. This paper assumes that the detection algorithm uses k-time standard deviation. At time t_0, the probability of false positive which is $p_{FP,t}$ is as follows.

$$p_{FP,t} = P(|\sum_{i=1}^{M} x_i^{t_0}| > k * \sigma_t \quad | \quad |x_1^{t_0}| < k * \sigma, |x_2^{t_0}| < k * \sigma, \ldots, |x_M^{t_0}| < k * \sigma)$$

$$= \frac{P(|\sum_{i=1}^{M} x_i^{t_0}| > k * \sigma_t, |x_1^{t_0}| < k * \sigma, |x_2^{t_0}| < k * \sigma, \ldots, |x_M^{t_0}| < k * \sigma)}{P(|x_1^{t_0}| < k * \sigma)^M}$$

$$< \frac{P(|\sum_{i=1}^{M} x_i^{t_0}| > k * \sigma_t)}{P(|x_1^{t_0}| < k * \sigma)^M} = \frac{2 * Q(k)}{(1 - 2 * Q(k))^M}$$

$$(5)$$

where $x_i^{t_0}$ represents the value of the ith metric at time t_0, σ_t represents the standard deviation of the aggregation metric of M metrics and it is $M * \sigma$, and $Q(x) = \int_x^{\infty} \frac{1}{\sqrt{2\pi}} * e^{-\frac{t^2}{2}} dt$.

It is further inferred that the probability of true positive at time t_0 is $1 - p_{FP,t}$, then the probability of true positive in whole time series is $(1 - p_{FP,t})^N$, and the probability of false positive in the entire time series is P_{FP}, given by the following formula.

$$P_{FP} = 1 - (1 - p_{FP,t})^N \qquad (6)$$

4.2 False Negative

Then we study false negative for BMD. A false negative event happened if following happed: At time t_0, at least one of the M metrics is anomalous, but BMD reports that there is no anomaly point on the aggregated metric of M metrics. Similarly, a true negative event happened if following happed: At time t_0, BMD reports that there is no anomaly point on the aggregated metric of M metrics, and none of the M metrics are anomalous in fact. Thence, at time t_0, the probability of true negative which is $p_{TN,t}$ is as follows.

$$
\begin{aligned}
p_{TN,t} &= P(|x_1^{t_0}| < k * \sigma, |x_2^{t_0}| < k * \sigma, \ldots, |x_M^{t_0}| < k * \sigma \quad | \quad |\sum_{i=1}^{M} x_i^{t_0}| < k * \sigma_t) \\
&= \frac{P(|\sum_{i=1}^{M} x_i^{t_0}| < k * \sigma_t, |x_1^{t_0}| < k * \sigma, |x_2^{t_0}| < k * \sigma, \ldots, |x_M^{t_0}| < k * \sigma)}{P(|\sum_{i=1}^{M} x_i^{t_0}| < k * \sigma_t)} \\
&< \frac{P(|x_1^{t_0}| < k * \sigma)^M}{P(|\sum_{i=1}^{M} x_i^{t_0}| < k * \sigma_t)} = (1 - 2 * Q(k))^{M-1}
\end{aligned}
$$

$$(7)$$

It is further inferred that at time t_0, the probability of false negative which is $p_{FN,t}$ is

$$p_{FN,t} = 1 - p_{TN,t} = 1 - (1 - 2 * Q(k))^{M-1} \qquad (8)$$

Then the probability of true negative in whole time series is $p_{TN,t}^N$, the probability of a false negative in the entire time series is P_{FN}, given by the following formula.

$$p_{FN} = 1 - p_{TN,t}^N \qquad (9)$$

4.3 Numerical Result

We show the numerical result of P_{FP} and P_{FN} calculated by Equation(6) and (9). We fixed N to 1440 and vary M from 5 to 2000. Figure 6 (a), (c), (e), (g) show the P_{FP} under different M when detection algorithm uses three, four, five or six-time standard deviation in BMD algorithm. Figure 6 (b), (d), (f), (h) show the P_{FN} under same setting.

First, we analyze the probability of false positive. As shown in Fig. 6 (a), (c), (e), (g), when detection algorithm is three-time standard deviation, false positive rate exceeds 0.98, and even reaches 1 when the number of metrics is about 250. When detection algorithm is four, five or six-time standard deviation, the false positive rate is small and grows slowly. This means BMD works well only when detection algorithm uses four, five or six-time standard deviation. Thus, BMD requires that the anomaly point is different apparently from other normal values.

Then we analyze the probability of false negative. As shown in Fig. 6(b), (d), (f), (h), when the number of metrics is 10, the false negative rate of three-time standard deviation is already 1. The false negative rate of four-time standard deviation increases rapidly as the number of metrics increases, and when the number of metrics is 60, the false negative rate is 1. When the number of metrics is 140, the false negative rate of five-time standard deviation is 0.1, so BMD can apply the five-time standard deviation detection algorithm only when the number of metrics does not exceed 140. The false negative rate of six-time standard deviation is very small, and it is suitable for thousands of metrics.

From above analysis, BMD requires that detection algorithm uses five or six-time standard deviation to locate anomaly. Fortunately, the anomaly point in Pseudo-Constant metric is apparently different from other normal values and can satisfy this requirement.

5   Experimental Results

This section compares the time cost and anomalous results of Traditional Method and BMD algorithm on real Exathlon dataset. Both detection algorithm in Traditional Method and BMD is five-time standard deviation criterion.

The Pseudo-Constant metric dataset is divided into 38 groups according to the principle of grouping metric time series with the same time index into one group. The BMD and the Traditional Method are called for each group, and the result is shown in Fig. 7. In this figure, x-axis is id of group and y-axis is ratio

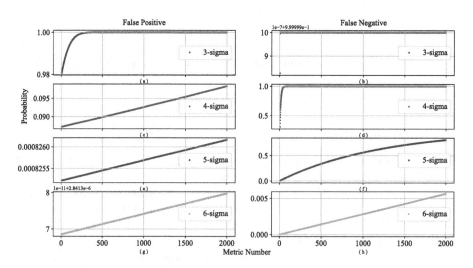

Fig. 6. The probability of False Positive and False Negative under different metric numbers.

between BMD' time and Traditional Method' time. As shown in Fig. 7, ratio is always bellow 0.5 and average ratio is about 15% (as shown in the red line).

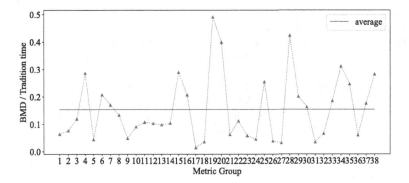

Fig. 7. The ratio between BMD' time and Traditional Method' time. (Color figure online)

According to Traditional Method, there are 479 anomalous metrics, including 2082 anomaly points. BMD finds 479 anomalous metrics, in which there are 2049 anomaly points. Traditional Method can completely detect anomaly points of Pseudo-Constant metric due to the characteristics of Pseudo-Constant metric. Thus, we regard the results of Traditional Method as ground-truth. The number of FN, FP, TP are 33, 0, 2049, respectively. Thence, precision and recall are 1 and 98.41% respectively where $Precison = \frac{TP}{TP+FP}$ and $Recall = \frac{TP}{TP+FN}$.

6   Conclusion

In this paper, we show that there are a considerable number of Pseudo-Constant metrics in actual large systems, whose values vary little or occasionally change violently. We propose Binary Mixed Detection algorithm for Pseudo-Constant metric. We build a model to evaluate the detection time of BMD. We also analyze the false positive and false negative of BMD to show the usage requirement of BMD. Finally, we also show the performance of BMD on actual data set.

Acknowledgements. This work was supported in part by National Natural Science Foundation of China under Grants 61872031.

References

1. Breunig, M.M., Kriegel, H.P., Ng, R.T., Sander, J.: LoF: identifying density-based local outliers. In: Proceedings of the 2000 ACM SIGMOD International Conference on Management of Data, pp. 93–104 (2000)
2. Chen, R.Q., Shi, G.H., Zhao, W.L., Liang, C.H.: Sequential vae-LSTM for anomaly detection on time series. arXiv preprint arXiv:1910.03818 (2019)

3. Chou, J.S., Telaga, A.S.: Real-time detection of anomalous power consumption. Renew. Sustain. Energy Rev. **33**, 400–411 (2014)
4. Jacob, V., Song, F., Stiegler, A., Rad, B., Diao, Y., Tatbul, N.: Exathlon: a benchmark for explainable anomaly detection over time series. arXiv preprint arXiv:2010.05073 (2020)
5. Laptev, N., Amizadeh, S., Flint, I.: Generic and scalable framework for automated time-series anomaly detection. In: Proceedings of the 21th ACM SIGKDD International Conference on Knowledge Discovery and Data Mining, pp. 1939–1947 (2015)
6. Li, J., Di, S., Shen, Y., Chen, L.: Fluxev: a fast and effective unsupervised framework for time-series anomaly detection. In: Proceedings of the 14th ACM International Conference on Web Search and Data Mining, pp. 824–832 (2021)
7. Li, Z., et al.: Multivariate time series anomaly detection and interpretation using hierarchical inter-metric and temporal embedding. In: Proceedings of the 27th ACM SIGKDD Conference on Knowledge Discovery & Data Mining, pp. 3220–3230 (2021)
8. Liu, D., et al.: Opprentice: towards practical and automatic anomaly detection through machine learning. In: Proceedings of the 2015 Internet Measurement Conference, pp. 211–224 (2015)
9. Marathe, A.P.: LRZ convolution: an algorithm for automatic anomaly detection in time-series data. In: 32nd International Conference on Scientific and Statistical Database Management, pp. 1–12 (2020)
10. Pincombe, B.: Anomaly detection in time series of graphs using ARMA processes. Asor Bulletin **24**(4), 2 (2005)
11. Prasad, P., Rich, C.: Market guide for AIOPS platforms (2018). Accessed 12 Mar 2020
12. Pukelsheim, F.: The three sigma rule. Am. Stat. **48**(2), 88–91 (1994)
13. Ren, H., et al.: Time-series anomaly detection service at Microsoft. In: Proceedings of the 25th ACM SIGKDD International Conference on Knowledge Discovery & Data Mining, pp. 3009–3017 (2019)
14. Siffer, A., Fouque, P.A., Termier, A., Largouet, C.: Anomaly detection in streams with extreme value theory. In: Proceedings of the 23rd ACM SIGKDD International Conference on Knowledge Discovery and Data Mining, pp. 1067–1075 (2017)
15. Su, H., He, Q., Guo, B.: KPI anomaly detection method for data center AIOps based on GRU-GAN. In: 2021 10th International Conference on Internet Computing for Science and Engineering, pp. 23–29 (2021)
16. Timčenko, V., Gajin, S.: Ensemble classifiers for supervised anomaly based network intrusion detection. In: 2017 13th IEEE International Conference on Intelligent Computer Communication and Processing (ICCP), pp. 13–19. IEEE (2017)

Research and Implementation of Cycle Control Technology for Time Sensitive Networking

Pengfei Cao, Jintao Peng, Maowen Wu, Yinhan Sun, and Zhigang Sun[✉]

National University of Defense Technology, Changsha, China
sunzhigang@263.net

Abstract. Time Sensitive Networking (TSN) is a deterministic network technology with wide application prospects. As a part of TSN, the function of cycle control is to keep the beginning time of the scheduling period of each switch node in the TSN network synchronized, which is the premise of implementing the TSN Time Aware Shaper (TAS). The IEEE 802.1Qbv specification describes the principle of cycle control, but there is a lack of relevant research on how to implement high-precision cycle control in TSN switch devices. In this paper, an accurate cycle control method called Cycle Synchronization Algorithm (CSA) is proposed. The algorithm generates a beginning signal (cycle_start) for each cycle on the basis of Precision Time Protocol (PTP). The paper proves that the cycle synchronization deviation is not greater than the PTP clock synchronization deviation. In a six-node TSN network based on a FPGA array, the effectiveness and stability of the CSA algorithm is verified.

Keywords: Time Sensitive Networking · Cycle control · Cycle synchronization deviation · PTP clock synchronization deviation

1 Introduction

With the data exchange services' types and quantity continuously expanding in industrial control networks, sophisticated equipment and other distributed real-time scenarios, the traditional Ethernet has been unable to meet increasing data and distributed network requirements. As a result, Time-Sensitive Networking (TSN) came into being, which uses traditional Ethernet technology to increase time synchronization, time-aware shaper and other functions, so that it can inherit the traditional Ethernet's good compatibility, high bandwidth and provides high-precision deterministic services.

The IEEE 802.1Qbv standard is the core standard for the TSN data plane, which defines three state machines for accurately describing the behavior of key operations, such as gate control configuration, cycle control, and gate control execution in the gate control implementation of the TSN output interface. The function of cycle control is to keep the beginning of the scheduling cycle of each switching node in the TSN network synchronized, which is the premise for realizing TSN time-aware shaping. However, there is a lack of relevant research on how to achieve high-precision cycle control in

© The Author(s), under exclusive license to Springer Nature Singapore Pte Ltd. 2023
W. Quan (Ed.): ICENAT 2022, CCIS 1696, pp. 533–544, 2023.
https://doi.org/10.1007/978-981-19-9697-9_43

TSN switching devices, which poses a challenge to the implementation of TSN traffic scheduling in the data plane.

This paper proposes an accurate cycle control method called Cycle Synchronization Algorithm (CSA), which generates the beginning signal of the scheduling cycle (cycle_start) for each cycle on the basis of Precision Time Protocol (PTP), and proves that the cycle synchronization deviation is not greater than the PTP clock synchronization deviation through theoretical analysis and experiments.

This article has three contributions:

1   We propose a CSA algorithm, which uses PTP clock synchronization to generate a cycle_start signal at the beginning of each scheduling cycle, thus achieves a high-precision cycle control;
2   We achieved a performance analysis of the CSA algorithm, which demonstrated that the cycle synchronization deviation of each node cycle does not exceed the PTP clock synchronization deviation;
3   We verified the effectiveness and stability of the CSA in the six-node topology network based on a FPGA array.

2   Background

The IEEE 802.1Qbv standard is one of the core standards of TSN, and includes three state machines for describing the gate control mechanism of the output interface of TSN devices. Among them, the gated configuration state machine is mainly responsible for calculating the configuration switching time and realizing the configuration task. The cycle control state machine is mainly responsible for calculating the beginning time of each scheduling cycle, and generating the scheduling cycle's beginning signal. Finally, the gate control execution state machine is responsible for reading the gate control list when the cycle start signal is valid. Among them, the cycle control state machine calculates the beginning time of each gate control execution state machine by comparing the beginning time of each cycle with the current global synchronization time, referring to the initial time of the cycle, the relationship between the configuration switching time and the current global synchronization time, and whether it is in the configuration switching state, and generates a cycle start signal to trigger the gate control execution state machine. The specific implementation is as follows:

(1)   When the global clock is synchronized, we set a cycle start time, and when the global synchronization time reaches that time, the first cycle_start signal is generated.
(2)   After the start of the first scheduling cycle, whenever the global synchronization time reaches the beginning of a scheduling cycle, the length of the scheduling cycle is increased and is calculated as the start of the next cycle, and when the global synchronization time reaches the beginning of the next cycle, the next cycle_start signal is generated.
(3)   For the situation in which the operation configuration parameters in the gated configuration state machine are about to be switched to the new configuration, after the global clock's synchronization, we set an initial moment of the cycle. If the current

global clock's synchronization time is more than one scheduling cycle time from the configuration switching time, then we continue to follow the step 2, whenever the global synchronization time reaches the beginning of the next cycle, the next cycle_start signal is generated.

(4) For the situation in which the operation configuration parameters in the gate configuration state machine are about to be switched to the new configuration, after the global clock's synchronization, if the current global clock's synchronization time distance from the configuration switching time is within a scheduling cycle time length range, the new cycle start time is the configuration switching time, meaning that when the global synchronization time reaches the moment, the next cycle_start signal is generated.

3   Problem Description

In this section, we describe a model we created that shows the gate control implementation of TSN devices. Then we emphasize the importance of the cycle control by introducing the function of each module in the model. Finally, we described the problems in the implementation of gate control by analyzing the generation of global clock's synchronization deviation and cycle synchronization deviation.

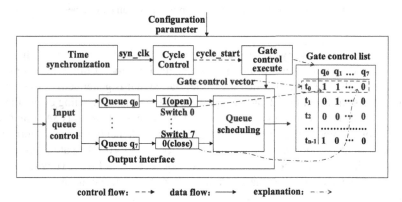

Fig. 1. Gate implementation model

As shown in Fig. 1, the gate control implementation model includes a time synchronization module that provides a global synchronization time (syn_clk), a cycle control module that ensures the periodic synchronization of each node and provides a cycle start signal (cycle_start) for the gate control execution module, a gate control execution module that reads the gate control table content to provide a gate control vector for the output interface, and an output interface 1 that performs gate control operations, which contains inbound control, eight queues, eight gate control switches, and queue scheduling. The process of gate control implementation in TSN device is as follows: first, according to the input configuration parameter information, the time synchronization module sends the global synchronization time to the cycle control module, after which the cycle control module calculates the beginning time of each scheduling cycle and sends the generated cycle start signal to the gate control execution module. The gate control execution module then reads the contents of the gate control list, and calculates and generates the gate control vector (including the gate control status of the slot and eight queues) according to the global time, the slot length and the cycle start signal from the cycle control module, and then sends gate control vector to the output interface 1. The inbound control module sends the traffic to the corresponding queue according to the priority, for example, when the slot is t0, according to the gate control vector, the gate control switches of queue 0 and 1 are open, and the gate control switch of queue 7 is closed.

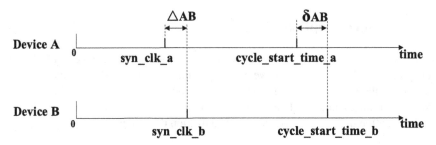

Fig. 2. Analysis of time deviation at the beginning of the same cycle between devices

Due to the different crystal oscillator frequencies of different devices, the timing between devices is different, resulting in the beginning time of different equipment's scheduling cycle (the time at which the cycle_start signal is generated) not being synchronized. As shown in Fig. 2, at the beginning of the same scheduling cycle, the time deviation of devices A and device B in generating cycle_start signal is δAB, and when the deviation becomes large, the result of gate control implementation cannot correspond with the planning result. For example, when device A performs the gate control vector 1 in Fig. 1, device B may perform the gate control vector 2 in Fig. 1. How to maintain high-precision cycle control is the key to the realization of gate control.

4   Cycle Synchronization Algorithm

4.1   Algorithm Description

To achieve high-precision cycle control in TSN devices, we propose an accurate cycle control method called CSA. The algorithm generates a scheduling cycle's beginning signal for each cycle on the basis of PTP clock synchronization, and the logic of the CSA is shown in Algorithm 1.

Algorithm1. CSA

Input: global synchronized time: *syn_clk*, scheduling cycle: *oper_cycle_time*,
         the moment when the first cycle begins: *oper_base_time*
         PTP clock synchronization signal: *syn_ok*

Output: cycle start signal: *cycle_start*

① CYCLE_INIT
②   **if**(syn_ok==1)**then**
③   *cycle_start*←0, *cycle_start_time*←*oper_base_time*;
④   next_state←SET_CYCLE_START_TIME;
⑤   **end if**
⑥ SET_CYCLE_START_TIME
⑦   *cycle_start*←0;
⑧   **if**(*cycle_start_time*>*syn_clk*)**then**
⑨   next_state←SET_CYCLE_START_TIME;
⑩   **else**
⑪   *cycle_start_time*←*cycle_start_time*+oper_*cycle_time*;
⑫   next_state←START_CYCLE;
⑬   **end if**
⑭ START_CYCLE
⑮   *cycle_start*←1;
⑯   next_state←SET_CYCLE_START_TIME;

Pseudocode description: First, in the CYCLE_INIT state, when the global time is synchronized, the scheduling cycle's beginnings with a signal setting of 0, setting the beginning time of the first scheduling cycle, and then entering the state of SET_CYCLE_START_TIME (lines 2 and 4). In this state, if the beginning time of cycle is greater than the current time, it remains in this state (lines 7 to 9). If not, the current beginning time of cycle is increased by one cycle length on top of the original and counted as the next beginning time of cycle (line 11), and then the algorithm enters the START_CYCLE state (line 12). In this state, the cycle_start signal is set to 1 (line 15), indicating the beginning of a new scheduling cycle, after which it returns to the SET_CYCLE_START_TIME state to wait for the next cycle (line 16).

4.2 Algorithm Performance Analysis

According to the IEEE 1588 standard and the CSA algorithm designed in this paper, the main terms used in this paper are defined as follows.

Definition 1. PTP clock synchronization deviation.

PTP clock synchronization deviation refers to the time difference between the clocks of any two devices in the network at any time after the global clock's synchronization. $\triangle$ is the synchronization deviation threshold, and $\triangle 12$ is the synchronization deviation of devices 1 and 2 at a certain time.

As shown in Fig. 2, after the global clock is synchronized, the PTP clock synchronization deviation $\triangle AB$ of TSN devices A and B at a certain time is satisfied:

$$\triangle AB <= \triangle \tag{1}$$

Definition 2. Periodic synchronization bias.

Cycle synchronization bias refers to the time difference between any two devices in the network at the beginning of the same cycle after it begins. δ is the period synchronization deviation threshold, and δ12 is the synchronization deviation of devices 1 and 2 in a certain period.

As shown in Fig. 2, TSN devices A and B at the beginning of a scheduling cycle, the cycle synchronization deviation δAB of the two is satisfied:

$$\delta AB <= \delta \qquad (2)$$

Theorem 1. After at least one clock cycle, the cycle synchronization deviation of each node is not greater than the synchronization deviation of the PTP clock in the network topology. The proof of the pass is as follows:

As shown in Fig. 3, it is a three-node topology diagram. SW1 is the master node of PTP clock synchronization, and NIC1 and NIC2 are slave nodes.

Fig. 3. Star topology with three nodes

After global clock's synchronization, we set the time of NIC1, SW1, and NIC2 in the current clock cycle to tsyn1, tsyn2, and tsyn3 respectively, and the time of NIC1, SW1, and NIC2 after global clock's synchronization in the next clock cycle are t'syn1, t'syn2, t'syn3, and the start time of the current scheduling cycle of NIC1, SW1 and NIC2 is tstart1, tstart2, tstart3 respectively, the next scheduling cycle's beginning time of NIC1, SW1 and NIC2 is t'start1, t'start2, t'start3 respectively, the clock cycle size is Tsyn, the scheduling cycle size is Tcycle, the cycle start time is toper, and the new beginning time of clock cycle's global synchronization time is t'. Suppose that the timing speed of SW1 is slower than NIC2, and is faster than NIC1.

1. When the scheduling cycle is less than the clock cycle

(1) As shown ① in Fig. 3, if the clock cycle's synchronization time is earlier than the scheduling cycle's beginning time, i.e. t' < = tstart1, t' < = tstart2, t' < = tstart3. When the global clock of the 3 nodes reach the beginning of the scheduling cycle,then:

$$tstart1 = t'syn1, tstart2 = t'syn2, tstart3 = t'syn3 \qquad (3)$$

When the global clock of the 3 nodes reach the end of the scheduling cycle (the start of the next scheduling cycle):

$$t'start1 = t'syn1, t'start2 = t'syn2, t'start3 = t'syn3 \qquad (4)$$

(2) As shown ② in Fig. 3, if the clock cycle's global synchronization time is in the scheduling cycle, i.e. tstart1 < = t' < = t'start1, tstart2 < = t' < = t'start2,

tstart3 < = t' < = t'start3.then:

$$tstart1 = tsyn1, tstart2 = tsyn2, tstart3 = tsyn3 \qquad (5)$$

When the global clocks of the 3 nodes reach the end of the scheduling cycle (the start of the next scheduling cycle):

$$t'start1 = t'syn1, t'start2 = t'syn2, t'start3 = t'syn3 \qquad (6)$$

(3) As shown ③ in Fig. 4, if the clock cycle's global synchronization time is after the end of the scheduling cycle, i.e. t' > = t'start1, t' > = t'start2, t' > = t'start3, then:

$$tstart1 = tsyn1, tstart2 = tsyn2, tstart3 = tsyn3 \qquad (7)$$

$$t'start1 = tsyn1, t'start2 = tsyn2, t'start3 = tsyn3 \qquad (8)$$

Obviously, the periodic synchronization deviation of each node at this time is equal to the PTP clock synchronization deviation.

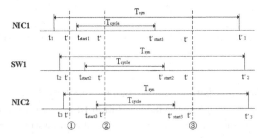

Fig. 4. Global synchronization time distribution when the scheduling period is shorter than the clock period

2. When the scheduling cycle is equal to the clock cycle size

The global synchronization time may be before the end of the scheduling cycle that crosses the clock cycle, or it may after the scheduling cycle within a clock cycle.

(1) As shown ① in Fig. 5, if the global synchronization time is before the end of the scheduling cycle, when it reaches the beginning of the next scheduling cycle, i.e. tstart1 < = t' < = t'start1, tstart2 < = t' < = t'start2, tstart3 < = t' < = t'start3, then:

$$tstart1 = tsyn1, tstart2 = tsyn2, tstart3 = tsyn3 \qquad (9)$$

$$t'start1 = t'syn1, t'start2 = t'syn2, t'start3 = t'syn3 \qquad (10)$$

(2) As shown in ② in Fig. 5, if the global synchronization time is after the end of the scheduling cycle, the beginning time and the end time of the scheduling cycle are both equal to the global synchronization time of the previous clock cycle, i.e. t' > = t'start1, t' > = t'start2, t' > = t'start3, then:

$$tstart1 = tsyn1, tstart2 = tsyn2, tstart3 = tsyn3 \qquad (11)$$

$$t'start1 = tsyn1, t'start2 = tsyn2, t'start3 = tsyn3 \qquad (12)$$

Obviously, the periodic synchronization deviation of each node at this time is equal to the PTP clock synchronization deviation.

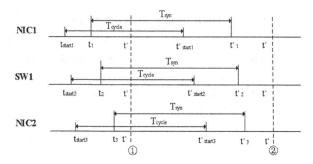

Fig. 5. Global synchronization time distribution when the scheduling period is equal to the clock period

3. When the scheduling period is more than the clock cycle
As shown in Fig. 6, the global synchronization time is within the clock cycle. i.e. tstart1 < = t' < = t'start1, tstart2 < = t' < = t'start2, tstart3 < = t' < = t'start3, then:

$$tstart1 = tsyn1, tstart2 = tsyn2, tstart3 = tsyn3 \qquad (13)$$

$$t'start1 = t'syn1, t'start2 = t'syn2, t'start3 = t'syn3 \qquad (14)$$

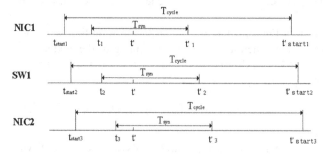

Fig. 6. Global time distribution when the scheduling period is longer than the clock period

Obviously, the periodic synchronization deviation of each node at this time is equal to the PTP clock synchronization deviation.

Combining the three types of situations 1, 2 and 3, we can conclude that after at least one clock cycle, the cycle synchronization deviation of each node in the network topology is equal to the PTP clock synchronization deviation. Considering that clock synchronisation deviations are continuous and cycle synchronisation deviations are non-continuous, thresholds for clock synchronisation deviations may occur in the middle of a cycle. We can find that the cycle synchronization deviation of each node in the network topology is not greater than the PTP clock synchronization deviation.

5 Experiment

5.1 Setup

To verify the effect of the algorithm, we verified the prototype system using the FPGA-based reconfigurable TSN network verification environment provided by the Fenglin open-source TSN and OpenTSN open-source projects, and the experimental environment is shown in Fig. 7.

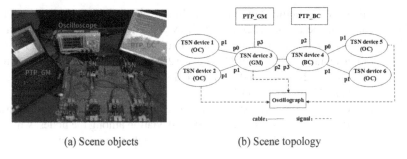

(a) Scene objects   (b) Scene topology

Fig. 7. Dumbbell topology scenario

The experimental environment consists of six TSN devices, two parallel controllers and one oscilloscope. Among them, the controller PTP_GM connects to TSN device 3 and configures it as the PTP master clock node, the parallel controller PTP_BC connects to TSN device 4 and configures it as a PTP boundary clock node. Due to the use of parallel control, the time of TSN devices 1 and 2 is equivalent, and that of TSN devices 5 and 6 is also equivalent. Therefore, when verifying the periodic synchronization performance of six nodes in the topology, we select TSN devices 2, 3 and 5 to test and generate the corresponding data for analysis and verification.

5.2 Experiment Results

To verify the effectiveness and stability of the CSA algorithm, we compare the distribution of PTP time synchronization deviation and the period synchronization deviation under the same clock cycle. In addition, we chose to test 1000 sets of data at different clock cycles to compare the distribution of cycle synchronization deviations.

(1) Comparison of cycle synchronization deviation and time synchronization deviation under the same clock cycle.

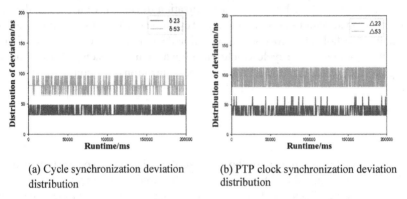

(a) Cycle synchronization deviation distribution

(b) PTP clock synchronization deviation distribution

Fig. 8. Accuracy of PTP and CSA at the same clock cycle

We set the first beginning time of scheduling cycle to 2 min, set the scheduling cycle to 1 ms, and the clock synchronization cycle to 100 ms, then we made a test. As shown in Fig. 8, a and b, we can conclude that: After 2000 clock cycles, the clock synchronization deviation $\delta 23$, $\delta 53$ of TSN device 2, 5 and TSN device 3 are concentrated in the distribution of 32–48 ns, 64–96 ns, period synchronization deviation $\Delta 23$, $\Delta 53$ are concentrated in 32–48 ns, 80–112 ns.

We can conclude that the cycle_start pulse signal time synchronization deviation does not exceed the PTP global clock synchronization deviation among the nodes, which can ensure the high precision cycle control in the TSN switching equipment.

(2) Cycle synchronization effects at different clock cycles.

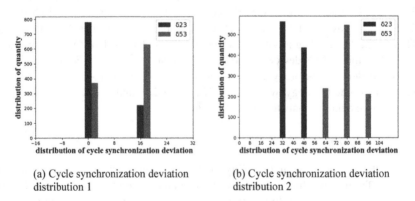

(a) Cycle synchronization deviation distribution 1

(b) Cycle synchronization deviation distribution 2

Fig. 9. Accuracy of CSA at different clock cycles

First, we set the clock synchronization period to 10 ms and the scheduling period to 1ms, then we then run a 1000 sample test. As can be seen from Fig. 9, a, the period synchronization deviation δ23 and δ53 of TSN device 2 and 5 and TSN device 3 are both concentrated in 0–16 ns; we set the clock synchronization period to 100 ms and the scheduling period to 1ms, then we then run a 1000 sample test. As can be seen from Fig. 9, b, the period synchronization deviation δ23 and δ53 of TSN device 2 and 5 and TSN device 3 are concentrated in 32–48 ns and 64–96 ns respectively. We can conclude that the increase in deviation is in the nanosecond range and has no impact on the actual TSN traffic scheduling results.

It can be concluded that the time synchronization deviation of the cycle_start pulse signal generated by the CSA, proposed by this paper does not exceed the PTP global clock's synchronization deviation, and that the CSA ensures the periodic synchronization of each node in the topology.

6 Related Work

The goal of the TSN Working Group is to standardize "deterministic Ethernet" technology to meet the needs of the Industrial Internet. Among them, the EEE 1588 PTP standard is used to distribute an accurate reference time synchronization mechanism between devices and switches in the network. Time synchronization is a prerequisite for the implementation of other features of TSN.

For the time deviation algorithm of time synchronization, the gPTP performance has been simulated and measured in the literature [11], and it is found that in Gigabit Ethernet, the communication time synchronization accuracy is maintained within 500 ns. Previous work [12] has proposed a method for adjusting the optimal synchronization message period for high-precision time synchronization in the vehicle network, and it automatically adjusts the number of synchronization messages sent from the master node according to the traffic state or the state of the slave node in the vehicle network to minimize the traffic of the entire network and optimally maintain the synchronization performance of the node. However, the above methods either only solve the problem of local synchronization or require additional hardware support. To further improve the time synchronization accuracy of gPTP, previous literature [13] has proposed a time marker processing scheme based on DP83640, which improves the synchronization accuracy through high-precision hardware timestamping.

TSN devices not only need precise time synchronization, but also need to achieve accurate coordination in the time domain when forwarding frames. The circular control function defined in the EEE 802.1Qbv specification aims to synchronize the scheduling cycles of each switching node in the TSN network at all times. However, there is a lack of relevant research on how to achieve high-precision cycle control in TSN switching equipment. Therefore, the industry urgently needs a high-precision cycle control method.

7 Conclusion

We propose an accurate cycle control algorithm called CSA. Based on PTP clock synchronization, the algorithm generates a scheduling cycle's beginning signal for each cycle, which ensures the high-precision cycle control in the TSN switching equipment. This paper carried out performance analysis of the algorithm and proved that the cycle synchronization deviation between nodes generated by the proposed algorithm is not greater than the PTP clock synchronization deviation.

References

1. Alliance of Industrial Internet. Time sensitive network (TSN) industry white paper v1.0 [OL]. [2021–03–10]. http://www.aii-alliance.org/staticupload/202009/0901_165010_961.pdf
2. Peizhuang, C., Ye, T., Xiangyang, G., et al.: A survey of key protocol and application scenario of time-sensitive network. Telecommun. Sci. **35**(10), 1–42 (2019)
3. Time-Sensitive Networking Task Group. IEEE Std 1588 -2019(evision of IEEE Std 1588 -2008) IEEE Standard for a Precision Clock Synchronization Protocol for Networked Measurement and Control Systems . Piscataway, NJ, IEEE (2020)
4. Time-Sensitive Networking Task Group. IEEE Std 802.1Qbv-2015 (Amendment to IEEE Std 802.1Q) IEEE Standard for Local and Metropolitan Area Networks - Bridges and Bridged Networks - Amendment 25: Enhancements for Scheduled Traffic. Piscataway, NJ, IEEE (2016)
5. Oliver, R.S., Craciunas, S.S., Steiner, W.: IEEE 802.1 Qbv gate control list synthesis using array theory encoding. In: Proceedings of the 24th IEEE Real-Time and Embedded Technology and Applications Symp (RTAS). Los Alamitos, CA, IEEE Computer Society, pp. 13–24 (2018)
6. Craciunas S.S., Oliver R.S., Chmelík, M., et al. Scheduling real-time communication in IEEE 802.1 Qbv time sensitive networks. In: Proceedings of the 24th International Conference on Real-Time Networks and Systems. New York, ACM, pp. 183–192 (2016)
7. Quan, W., Wenwen, F., Zhigang, S., et al.: Fenglin one: a low-power time-sensitive network chip customized for high-end equipment. J. Comput. Res. Develop., **58**(6), 1242–1245 (2021)
8. Quan, W., Wenwen, F., Jinli, Y., et al.: OpenTSN: an open-source project for time-sensitive networking system development. CCF In: Trans. Netw. **3**(1), 51–65
9. Xiangrui, Y., Jinli, Y., Bo, C., et al.: FlexTSN: A Flexible TSN Switching Implementation Model. J. Comput. Res. Develop. **58**(1), 153–163 (2021)
10. Wenwen, F., Jinli, Y., Wei, Q., et al.: Fenglin-I: an Open-source TSN Chip for Scenario-Driven Customization. In: Proceedings of the ACM SIGCOMM. Conference Posters and Demos. **2020**, 1–2 (2020)
11. Garner, G.M.,Gelter, A.,Teener, M.J.: New situation and test results for IEEE 802.1AS timing performance. In: Intertional Symposium on Precision Clock Synccchronization for Measurement.IEEE (2009)
12. Kim, Y.J., Cheon, B.M., Kim, J.H., et al.: Time synchronization method of IEEE 802.1AS through automatic optimal sync message period adjustment for in-car network. IEEE In: International Conference on Information & Automation.IEEE (2015)
13. Yafeng, C., Yuan, C.: IEEE 1588-based node hardware timestamp implementation method study. J. Zhongyuan Softw. (2015)

Network Traffic Classification Based on LSTM+CNN and Attention Mechanism

Kaixuan Liu⬤, Yuyang Zhang$^{(\boxtimes)}$ ⬤, Xiaoya Zhang⬤, Wenxuan Qiao⬤,
and Ping Dong⬤

School of Electronic and Information Engineering, Beijing Jiaotong University, Beijing 10004,
China
{zhyy,18111040,19111033,pdong}@bjtu.edu.cn

Abstract. Nowadays, the Internet is characterized by diversification, large scale, and high public dependence. The static and rigid traditional network is increasingly showing its limitations. In order to better meet the public's requirements for an efficient and secure Internet, the intelligent collaborative identification network shows its strong vitality. But at the same time, the new network also puts forward higher requirements for the classification of network traffic. To this end, based on deep learning theory, this paper constructs a traffic classification model that combines CNN and LSTM. To solve the problem of traffic data imbalance and temporal correlation, the model introduces Squeeze & Excitation and Data Augmentation, and finally, three sets of experiments are used to verify that the CNN + LSTM model has better performance than the ordinary single model, and it has excellent performance when dealing with classification problems with different granularities and different traffic representation.

Keywords: Traffic classification · Deep learning · The intelligent identification network · Imbalanced dataset

1 Introduction

1.1 Background and Problem

The intelligent identification network proposed in paper[1] realizes efficient network management through flexible and controllable connections, but the network traffic generated in it also has different characteristics from traditional networks. At the same time, the Internet continues to accelerate the integration of public services and infrastructure, and the public is increasingly reliant on the Internet. The China Internet Network Information Center (CNNIC) released the 49th China Internet Development Statistical Report [2] in Beijing, which showed that as of December 2021, the public's dependence on the Internet was as high as 73.0%, especially for instant messaging.

The application is the most popular and the fastest-growing areas include online medical care, online office, online consumption, etc. The number of people using the Internet reached 1.032 billion, an increase of 12.6% over the same period last year.

W. Quan (Ed.): ICENAT 2022, CCIS 1696, pp. 545–556, 2023.
https://doi.org/10.1007/978-981-19-9697-9_44

The proposal of the intelligent identification network architecture and the increasing dependence of the public on the network have put forward stricter requirements for the efficient utilization of the network, operation and maintenance management, and network security. Among them, the traffic identification and classification technology plays a crucial role.

However, traditional traffic classification methods are all inadequate in the current network environment. Based on the fixed port number, network traffic is classified by detecting the source port number and destination port number of data packets. With the emergence of new applications, port numbers are dynamic and random, and the method based on port is no longer applicable. The method based on both port and load information, and relies on the limited number of existing traffic features in the signature database. In the face of sudden unknown traffic, the signature database will not be able to cope with, so it is not suitable for the current complex and changeable network environment. The classification method based on machine learning first requires experts to analyze network traffic features, and then input the labeled traffic features into the neural network. After training, the network can achieve the purpose of distinguishing different feature traffic. It can be seen that this method extremely relies on the expert team to deal with the network traffic in the early stage, and the labor cost is high.

In contrast, deep learning not only has end-to-end learning ability but also can automatically specialize features. Therefore, designing a deep learning traffic classification method is a problem worthy of study. Deep learning-based classification methods mainly face two problems:

1. Traffic data distribution is unbalanced. The imbalance between small-class traffic and large-class traffic makes the classification results naturally tend to large-class traffic. In many specific scenarios in the real world, small classes of data are often the object of concern, such as malicious traffic in large amounts of normal data.

2. The emergence of new types of traffic makes data distribution time-variant. In order to avoid the model only supporting a certain distribution of data classification, it has become an urgent problem to update the model by using the correlation between old and new data.

1.2 Related Research

In the direction of the imbalance of network traffic classification, paper [3] firstly convert the load of traffic into a two-dimensional gray image, and then put them into a deep learning model which can automatically learns relevant features and has certain advantages in classification accuracy compared with traditional methods. Paper [4] collect network traffic from Open Network Operating System platform, and use deep neural network for classification. The research confirmed that not only the data packets that are intended to be delivered but also data packets required to maintain networks should be considered when use DNN for real network traffic classification. Paper [5] propose a deep learning based model for traffic classification with just a few packets. The main method is to use five meaningful statistics from the flow as hand-crafted features. Such features when combined with deep learning features, improve the classification accuracy significantly.

In order to cope with the emerging new types of traffic, paper [6] proposes a tCLD-Net model that combines transfer learning and deep learning. It can be trained on a small amount of labeled data to distinguish network encrypted traffic with a high accuracy. Paper [7] propose a transfer-learning network flow generation framework for intrusion detection. The model uses invariant extraction and sequence to sequence generation, to extract the attack invariant of the existing attack data set and transfer the knowledge to the target network system. It is proved that this method can generate effective anomaly traffic as well as improve the accuracy of intrusion detection. However, in practical applications, transfer learning has two limitations that make it unable to be promoted effectively. One is that it needs a large amount of computing resources and the other is that it needs a large amount of storage space to store the original data for a long time.

In order to solve the shortcomings of the above methods, this study uses the advantages of CNN in extracting advanced features of images [8] and LSTM in predicting the long-term dependence relationship of sequences [9] to construct a network traffic classification model based on CNN + LSTM [10]. Experimental results show that the algorithm has better classification performance.

2 DataSet

2.1 Data Analysis

The traffic generated by intelligent cooperative identification network mainly has the following two characteristics, which also bring new problems to traffic classification: **(1) The distribution of traffic data is unbalanced. (2) The emergence of a large number of new network traffic makes the data distribution time-differentiated.**

Based on the above requirement analysis, the ISCX VPN-nonVPN 2016 dataset [11] released by UNB (University of Brunswick) is used in this design. The data set has rich traffic categories, multi-granularity and no processing, which strictly conforms to the traffic characteristics of intelligent collaborative identification network. The following table describes the seven service types of traffic contained in the data set and the applications contained therein. Figures 1 and 2 show the size and duration of the data sets, which can visually show the imbalance of the data distribution.

According to Fig. 1, the proportion of nonVPN sessions is significantly higher than VPN. There is also a serious imbalance among service types. That's because File-transfer

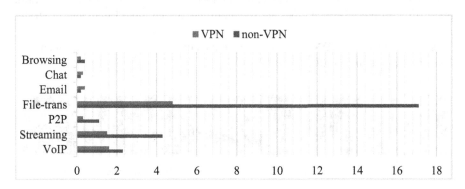

Fig. 1. Traffic size distribution statistical chart.

and Streaming data are mainly used to send and receive continuous multimedia data such as audio and video, while Browsing, Chat, Email data only contain simple text. According to Fig. 2, the flow is also unbalanced in duration. This is because long time traffic is mainly VoIP, streaming, and browsing, while short burst traffic is mainly chat and Email.

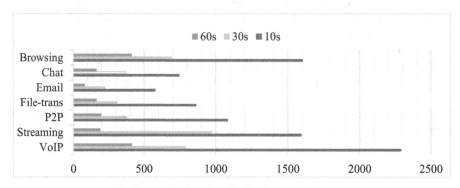

Fig. 2. Traffic duration distribution statistics chart.

2.2 Data Processing

Processing the original traffic data into image data that can be directly input into the deep learning model is the key to data processing, which mainly includes the following five steps.

Step. 1. Traffic Segmentation and Uniform Length. Divide the original traffic based on pcap files with the same "source IP address, source port, destination IP address, destination port, and protocol".And then unify the traffic to the same length by means of zero-padding and interception. That's because the data input to the convolution neural network needs to be of uniform size.

Step. 2. Pixel Mapping. The input specification of CNN based on image processing is generally a picture of 28*28, including 784 pixels, and the grayscale range is [0,255], corresponding to the two-digit hexadecimal number in the message. The generated traffic graphs of 7 different service types are shown in Fig. 3, and more Email and Ftp traffic graphs are shown in Fig. 4.

Step. 3. Convert to IDX. Convert the generated image to IDX format, and then input the deep learning model for training.

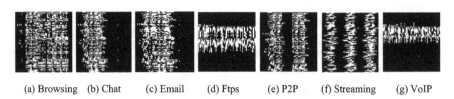

(a) Browsing   (b) Chat   (c) Email   (d) Ftps   (e) P2P   (f) Streaming   (g) VoIP

Fig. 3. Traffic graph for 7 different service types.

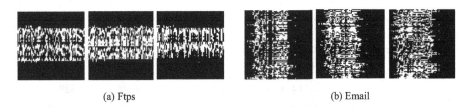

(a) Ftps   (b) Email

Fig. 4. Ftps and Email traffic graph.

3   CNN+LSTM Classification Model

This paper proposes a traffic classification model based on the combination of CNN and LSTM. In this section, we will introduce the design, optimization and implementation of each sub-model, and finally give the connection method and classification steps of the overall model.

3.1   Sub-model I: CNN for Data Imbalance Problem

The parameter configuration of the network structure of sub-model I is shown in Table 1.In order to solve the problems caused by imbalanced datasets, the following two mechanisms are introduced to CNN.

Data Augmentation

Optimize at the data set level consisting of traffic graphs, the traffic map will be flipped, intercepted, and noise introduced. After Data Augment, the distribution of the data set is artificially changed to balance it.

Squeeze and Excitation

Regarding the way of introducing weight coefficients into the CNN model, the literature [12] introduced an attention mechanism for CNN. The main idea is to assign different weights to the high-dimensional information of the image extracted by the CNN, strengthen the information that needs special attention, and weaken the less important information, this method achieves the purpose of balancing the dataset. There are various implementation forms of the attention mechanism. This design selects the channel attention mechanism (Squeeze and Excitation, SE) [13]. The mechanism consists of the following two phases.

1   Squeeze: Compress the input features and input the compressed data into the subsampling layer.

$$z_c = \frac{1}{w \cdot h} \sum_{i=1}^{w} \sum_{j=1}^{w} d_c(i,j) \tag{1}$$

2   Excitation: The weight matrix S acts on the activation function between layers, and the final weight of the sample is generated in the fully connected layer of the network terminal.

$$S = \sigma[W\delta(Wz)] \tag{2}$$

Table 1. Network architecture and parameter configuration of sub-model I CNN

Layer	Operate	Input	Kernel	Stride	Padding	Output
1	C1 + ReLU	28*28*8	5*5*32	1	Half	14*14*8
2	P1	14*14*8	2*2*1	3	Half	32*32*8
3	C2 + ReLU	32*32*8	5*5*64	1	Half	16*16*8
4	P2	16*16*8	2*2*1	3	Half	8*8*8
5	F1	8*8*8			None	1024
6	F2	1024			None	2048
7	Softmax	2048			None	14
Dropout		0.2				
Parameter update		Adam				

where Z_c is the *cth* output of compression matrix, d_c is the *cth* input traffic feature map, w is width of d_c, h is height of d_c, i is width serial number of d_c, j is height serial number of d_c, σ represents *Relu* function, S is weight matrix, δ represents *Sigmoid* function, z is the output of Squeeze.

3.2 Sub-model II: LSTM for Temporal Correlation Problem

Aiming at the problem that the classifier cannot make full use of the temporal correlation of traffic caused by the emergence of new network traffic, this section introduces LSTM model.

Network traffic data can be viewed not only as a 2D image, but also as a time series when viewed longitudinally. In the current network environment, the emergence of new types of traffic makes the distribution characteristics of network traffic different in time, which is manifested in the different change rules and distribution methods of the protocols, source ports, and destination ports corresponding to the traffic. This kind of distribution-specific data classification can take full advantage of the temporal correlation of novel traffic and further utilize LSTM classification. In the LSTM model, there is temporal continuity within a single data stream, and temporal correlation between multiple data streams. The connection between CNN and LSTM is shown in Fig. 5.

LSTM has a memory cell with the state s_t at time t. The memory cell will be controlled by three gates: forget gate f_t, input gate i_t and output gate o_t. The parameter learning principle of LSTM is as follows:

$$f_t = \sigma(w_f[h_{t-1}; x_t] + b_f) \tag{3}$$

$$i_t = \sigma(w_i[h_{t-1}; x_t] + b_i) \tag{4}$$

$$o_t = \sigma(w_o[h_{t-1}; x_t] + b_o) \tag{5}$$

$$s_t = f_t \cdot s_{t-1} + i_t \cdot \tanh(w_s[h_{t-1}; x_t] + b_s) \tag{6}$$

$$h_t = o_t \cdot \tanh(s_t) \tag{7}$$

where x_t is the current input, h_{t-1} is the previous hidden state, w_t, w_i, w_o, w_s and b_f, b_i, b_o, b_t are parameters to learn,σ is *Sigmoid* function.

The performance of the LSTM on the test set is shown in Fig. 6. When steps < 200, the model is in the convergence stage and the convergence speed is fast. After convergence, the model accuracy fluctuates around 96% with good stability.

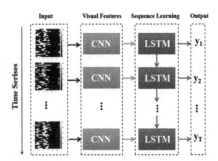

Fig. 5. CNN + LSTM overall model.   **Fig. 6.** Model accuracy of LSTM.

3.3 Overall Model CNN + LSTM and Classification Steps

In order to solve the problem of traffic imbalance and data correlation at the same time, this section integrates CNN and LSTM to form an end-to-end deep learning model, which can completely address the traffic classification problem in the intelligent identification network. The specific classification steps of the model are summarized as follows:

Step. 1. Process the original traffic data to obtain a traffic map as input data.

Step. 2. Sub-modelI-CNN. ① Optimize the dataset: Introduce Data Augmentation to artificially change the distribution of small-class data and large-class data to balance the distribution. ② Optimize the model: Introduce an attention mechanism Squeeze and Excitation to assign different weights to the feature information extracted by CNN, assign larger weights to small-class samples, and assign smaller weights to large-class samples to design classifiers more accurately.

Step. 3. Sub-model II-LSTM. Regards network traffic as a time series, and obtains the time characteristic information in it.

Step. 4. Obtain traffic classification results.

4 Experiment

This section first introduces the classification model evaluation metrics, and then sets up three experiments to evaluate the performance of Data Augment, Squeeze & Excitation and Overall Model.

4.1 Evaluation Metrics

The evaluation Metrics of this design is based on the following three standards [14]: Accuracy, Precision and Recall. The above evaluation criteria have good performance in multi-classification problems, which can help to test and evaluate the comprehensive performance of the designed model. The definitions are as follows.

Accuracy is used to evaluate the overall classification ability of the model.

$$A = \frac{TP + TN}{TP + FP + FN + TN} \tag{8}$$

Precision represents the proportion of the actual positive samples among the samples judged to be positive, and is used to evaluate the scenarios that do not accept false positives.

$$P = \frac{TP}{TP + FP} \tag{9}$$

Recall represents the proportion of the actual positive samples that are judged to be positive, and is used to evaluate scenarios that do not accept missed judgments.

$$R = \frac{TP}{TP + FN} \tag{10}$$

TP is the correct number of positive samples, TN is the correct number of negative samples, FP is the number of errors in positive samples, FN is the number of errors in negative samples.

4.2 Experiment I: Data Augment Performance

Data Augmentation is introduced to the original data set to artificially balance the distribution of small-class samples and large-class samples. The data set information before and after Data Augmentation is introduced as shown in Table 2.

As shown in Fig. 7, with the deepening of training, the data set after Data Augmentation enables the model to converge faster and with higher accuracy. As shown by the green line in the figure, the accuracy suddenly drops when the batch is 1400 and 2800. This is the problem of excessive classification randomness caused by the unbalanced data set. However, the classifier trained with the augmented data set (red line) eliminates the above phenomenon.

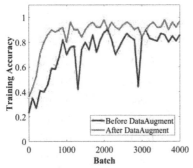
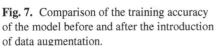

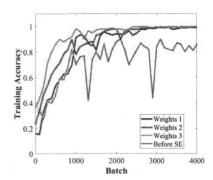

Fig. 7. Comparison of the training accuracy of the model before and after the introduction of data augmentation.

Fig. 8. Comparison of model training accuracy by introducing different weight matrices to SE mechanism

Table 2. Comparison table of the number of datasets before and after data augmentation

Label	Service	Before data augmentation		After data augmentation	
		Training set	Test set	Training set	Test Set
1	P2P	492	326	5000	2000
2	VoIP	736	459	5000	2000
3	Streaming	3749	1506	5000	2000
4	Chat	634	367	5000	2000
5	Email	1200	603	5000	2000
6	Browsing	201	107	5000	2000
7	Ftps	4065	1760	5000	2000

4.3 Experiment II: Squeeze and Excitation Performance

The attention mechanism SE is introduced to 2D-CNN, and different coefficient combinations are assigned to the weight matrix. According to the statistics of the original data set, three groups of more reasonable weight combinations are given here, as shown in Table 3 below.

As shown in Fig. 8, the green line represents the unweighted model. The convergence speed from fast to slow are: Weights 3, Weights 2, and Weights 1. The stability of the model with weighted coefficients is obviously higher than that of the model without weights, and stability from strong to weak are: Weights 3, Weights 1, Weights 2. Comprehensive analysis, Weights 3 has the best performance in both convergence speed and model stability.

Table 3. Weight coefficient combination table

Label	Service	Wights 1	Wights 2	Wights 3
1	P2P	0 0612	0 0714	0 0816
2	VoIP	0.0363	0.0424	0.0484
3	Streaming	0.0081	0.0094	0.0108
4	Chat	0.0462	0.0539	0.0616
5	Email	0.0222	0.0259	0.0296
6	Browsing	0. 1191	0. 1389	0. 1588
7	Ftps	0.0069	0.0081	0.0092

4.4 Experiment III: Overall Model Performance

On the premise of the same dataset and traffic representation, the performance comparison between the CNN model and the CNN + LSTM fusion model in the classification tasks of seven service types is shown in Fig. 9.

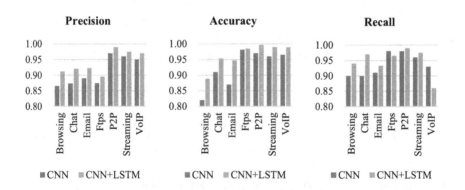

Fig. 9. Comparison of model precision, accuracy, recall between CNN and CNN + LSTM when the classification granularity is 7 service types

Table 4. Model performance comparison between CNN and CNN + LSTM when the classification granularity is 7 service types and the improvement of the fusion model

Model	Non - VPN			VPN		
	Precision	Accuracy	Recall	Precision	Accuracy	Recall
CNN	0.790	0.847	0.783	0.853	0.937	0.950
CNN + LSTM	0.811	0.883	0.804	0.869	0.938	0.950
Improvement	0.021	0.036	0.021	0.016	0.001	0

The overall performance comparison of the fusion model is shown in Table 4. in the non-VPN classification task, CNN + LSTM has improved accuracy, accuracy and recall rate than CNN, and the improvement range is 2.1%–3.6%. In the classification task of VPN, the improvement in precision and accuracy is slightly lower, ranging from 0.1%–1.6%, and the recall rate is the same. Overall, CNN + LSTM shows better classification performance because it makes full use of the temporal correlation of traffic sequences, and improves the randomness of small-class traffic classification.

5 Conclusion

Based on the wide application of intelligent collaborative identification network system and the rising Internet penetration rate, this paper constructs a CNN + LSTM traffic classification model, and combines data augmentation and attention mechanism to solve the problem of unbalanced traffic data distribution and the emergence of new types of traffic. For the problem of large differences in data distribution time, the model has excellent performance in fine-grained traffic classification tasks.

Aiming at the future development trend of the Internet and the problems in this design, the 2D-CNN and LSTM cascade fusion model proposed in this paper based on data amplification and attention mechanism still needs to be improved in the following aspects:

(1) The complex and changeable network environment brings many endogenous security problems. How to achieve the extraction, classification and identification of traffic characteristics on the premise of ensuring traffic security is an urgent problem to be solved [15].
(2) The emergence of malicious traffic brings threats to personal information security and public infrastructure. How to identify malicious traffic with low cost and high accuracy is also an important issue that needs to be extended urgently.
(3) With the improvement of public awareness of personal privacy protection, users' personal information is involved in network traffic,

Contents such as property transaction information will be encrypted [16], which also brings optimization space to the current method.

Acknowledgement. This work was supported in part by the Fundamental Research Funds for the Central Universities under grant 2021RC247, and in part by the China Postdoctoral Science Foundation under grant 2021M690343, and in part by the National Natural Science Foundation of China (NSFC) under grant 92167204, 62072030.

References

1. 张宏科,罗洪斌.智慧协同网络体系基础研究[J]. 电子学报,2013,41(07):1249- 1252+ 1254
2. 中 国 互 联 网 络 信 息 中 心 . 第 44 次《 中 国 互 联 网 络 发 展 状 况 统 计 报 告 》[EB/OL]. http://www.cac.gov.cn/2019-08/30/c_1124938750.htmweb-traffic-will-bee ncrypted-by-2019/.2019-08-31

3. Wei, G.: Deep learning model under complex network and its application in traffic detection and analysis. In: 2020 IEEE 2nd International Conference on Civil Aviation Safety and Information Technology (2020)

4. J. Kwon, J. Lee, M. Yu and H. Park. Automatic Classification of Network Traffic Data based on Deep Learning in ONOS Platform[C]. 2020 International Conference on Information and Communication Technology Convergence (ICTC), 2020

5. Gupta, A., Gupta, H.P., Dutta, T.: A deep learning based traffic flow classification with just a few packets. In: IEEE INFOCOM 2021 - IEEE Conference on Computer Communications Workshops (INFOCOM WKSHPS) (2021)

6. Hu, X., Gu, C., Chen, Y., Wei, F.: tCLD-Net: a transfer learning internet encrypted traffic classification scheme based on convolution neural network and long short-term memory network. In: 2021 International Conference on Communications, Computing, Cybersecurity, and Informatics (CCCI) (2021)

7. Li, Y., Liu, T., Jiang, D., Meng, T.: Transfer-learning-based Network traffic automatic generation framework. In: 2021 6th International Conference on Intelligent Computing and Signal Processing (ICSP) (2021)

8. Wang, W., et al.: HAST-IDS: learning hierarchical spatial-temporal features using deep neural networks to improve intrusion detection. IEEE Access 6, 1792–1806 (2018)

9. Torres, P., Catania, C., Garcia, S., et al.: An analysis of Recurrent Neural Networks for Botnet detection behavior. IEEE biennial Congress of Argentina, pp. 1–6 (2016)

10. Wang, Z.: The applications of deep learning on traffic identification. BlackHat USA, p. 24 (2015)

11. https://www.unb.ca/cic/datasets/vpn.html

12. He, W., Wu, Y., Li, X.: Attention mechanism for neural machine translation: a survey. In: IEEE 5th Information Technology, Networking, Electronic and Automation Control Conference (ITNEC), pp. 1485–1489 (2021)

13. Hu, J., Shen, L., Albanie, S., et al.: Squeeze-and-excitation networks. IEEE Trans. Pattern Anal. Mach. Intell., 7132–7141 (2018)

14. Kwon, J., Jung, D., Park, H.: Traffic data classification using machine learning algorithms in SDN networks. In: 2020 International Conference on Information and Communication Technology Convergence (ICTC), pp. 1031–1033 (2020)

15. Sepasgozar, S.S., Pierre, S.: Network traffic prediction model considering road traffic parameters using artificial intelligence methods in VANET. IEEE Access, 8227–8242 (2022)

16. Zerey, F., Şamil Fidan, M., Uslu, E.: Detection and classification of traffic signs with deep morphological networks. In: Innovations in Intelligent Systems and Applications Conference (ASYU), pp. 1–6 (2021)

CQCF: A Cyclic Queuing Cluster Forwarding Based Transmission Mechanism for Large-Scale Deterministic Network

Xu Huang, Jia Chen[✉], Kuo Guo, and Deyun Gao

National Engineering Research Center for Advanced Network Technologies, Beijing Jiaotong University, Beijing, China
{21111024,chenjia,19111017,gaody}@bjtu.edu.cn

Abstract. With the increase of time-sensitive applications, the traditional networks using Best Effort approach can no longer meet the needs of the network applications. For satisfying the demand for high-quality, low delay, and low jitter transmission, IETF establishes the TSN and DetNet Working Group. However, there is no DetNet mechanism specifically designed for time synchronization scenarios. In this paper, we propose a time synchronization cross-domain transmission mechanism for a large-scale Deterministic Network, which is named CQCF (Cyclic Queuing Cluster Forwarding). CQCF adopts the queuing cluster module to cache and forward time-sensitive traffic, making sure that packets can be received at the specified time. Meanwhile, we propose the mapping principle on the Cycle and Hypercycle between access networks and core networks to improve the feasibility of cross-domain transmission. The experimental results show that the CQCF mechanism can schedule more flows than DIP under the time synchronization scenario. The runtime of the scheduling algorithm using CQCF improves by 27.9% compared with the algorithm using DIP under scheduling 2000 flows.

Keywords: Time sensitive network · Deterministic network · Quality of service · Queuing clusters

1 Introduction

With the diversified requirements of traffic demands induced by different network applications, such as Industry Internet, Compute First Networking, and military network, time-sensitive businesses increasingly emerge. Traditional networks adopt Best-Effort (BE) approach to meet Quality of Service (QoS) demands [1]. However, the BE approach can not address the micro-burst existing in the networks [2], resulting in difficulties to achieve deterministic transmission for traditional networks.

To provide deterministic delay and jitters for the networks, IETF has established the Time-Sensitive Network (TSN) Task Group, which aims to achieve deterministic transmission in the field of Industrial Internet, Mobile Communication, and Vehicles [3]. But TSN does not consider deterministic transmission in large-scale networks. Therefore, Deterministic Networking (DetNet) Task Group is founded. The DetNet combines

© The Author(s), under exclusive license to Springer Nature Singapore Pte Ltd. 2023
W. Quan (Ed.): ICENAT 2022, CCIS 1696, pp. 557–569, 2023.
https://doi.org/10.1007/978-981-19-9697-9_45

routing protocols to achieve deterministic forwarding at the routing level, extending deterministic networks to Wide Area Networks [4]. Many research institutions have proposed cross-domain transmission mechanisms. The DetNet proposes the CSQF (Cycle Specified Queuing and Forwarding) to achieve cross-domain deterministic transmission, which specifies the cycles and queues of time-sensitive traffic by source routing. The DIP (Deterministic IP) proposed by Huawei achieves large-scale deterministic transmission by cycles and queues mapping.

Meanwhile, the military network urgently needs deterministic transmission because time-sensitive traffic is required in military networks [5]. For example, the military controller center needs to ensure that the fighting orders reach all combat objectives within a certain time period. However, CSQF and DIP both adopt the strategy of frequency synchronization scenarios, which are both designed for Industry Networks. The military networks can guarantee time synchronization over the whole networks. However, the existing mechanisms are not suitable for the military environment, which motivates us to design a transmission mechanism for military networks. The challenges of deterministic transmission in time synchronization scenarios are as below. 1) how to choose the core network mechanism that matches access network mechanisms. 2) how to design the Cycle transfer in cross-domains.

This paper proposes the Cyclic Queuing Cluster Forwarding (CQCF) mechanism, which adopts time synchronization and can achieve deterministic transmission in large-scale and long-distance networks. The innovations of this paper are as follows.

(1) We propose a new cross-domain deterministic transmission mechanism CQCF, which adopts queuing clusters to make sure cross-domain deterministic transmission;
(2) We propose a mapping principle on Cycle and Hypercycle between access networks and core networks, which clarifies the Cycle and Hypercycle relationship in different domains. What's more, we have designed a cross-domain transmission model combining CQF and CQCF.
(3) The simulation is performed for the proposed CQCF mechanism and performances are compared with the DIP mechanism.

Our work is structured as follows: Sect. 2 introduces related works. Section 3 introduces the details of the proposed method. Section 4 briefly introduces the algorithm design of the method. Simulations are performed in Sect. 5. Section 6 concludes the paper.

2   Related Works

Many existing mechanisms have provided valuable experience in realizing deterministic transmission in large-scale networks.

Literature [6] has proposed a traffic shaping and forwarding mechanism CSQF based on CQF (Cyclic Queuing and Forwarding) [7]. [6] analyzes the reason why CQF can't achieve deterministic transmission in large-scale networks. CQF cannot guarantee that packets cross domains to be transmitted within one Cycle. CSQF adds more queues for caching and forwarding packets, in which three queues are designed for forwarding TT (Time Triggered) Flows. In a cycle, only one queue is allowed to send packets, while the others are allowed to cache packets.

Literature [8, 9] propose a deterministic transmission mechanism DIP. DIP adopts three or more queues and Segment Routing (SR) protocol is usually used, which provides better robustness in cross-domain than CSQF. Literature [10] realizes the first large-scale network by DIP. The data centers are set up in several cities in China for testing, with an overall transmission distance of 2000 km. Experimental results show that DIP can achieve deterministic transmission with a delay size of milliseconds and almost zero jitters.

Literature [11] proposes the Flexible-DIP mechanism based on DIP. Since the DIP cannot simultaneously satisfy diverse QoS requirements, FDIP is proposed by classifying the queues into multiple groups. Each group is formed as a DIP pattern which operates with different cycles size. Then FDIP can provide deterministic transmission with different QoS. Experimental results show that FDIP significantly outperforms the standard DIP in terms of both throughput and latency.

Literature [12] adopts CQF in access networks while DIP in core networks, and designs a compensation algorithm for cross-domain. It successfully solves the problem of inconsistency of cycles and Hypercycles between CQF and DIP. But this algorithm brings additional computational consumption, which accounts for a large proportion of large-scale network scheduling.

3 Architecture and Working Flow of CQCF

In this section, we propose the architecture and working flow of Cyclic Queuing Cluster Forwarding (CQCF). CQCF is specially designed for large-scale transmission in time synchronization scenarios. When using CQCF to achieve deterministic transmission, core networks should adopt the CQCF mechanism, and access networks should adopt the CQF mechanism for matching CQCF.

3.1 The Architecture of CQCF

CQCF adopts four or more priority queues and divides them into two clusters. Each queue cluster has the same number of queues and the number of queues is at least greater than 2 (generally set to 2), as shown in Fig. 1. Figure 1 shows the basic architecture of CQCF.

The two clusters are named as Odd queuing cluster and the Even queuing cluster, respectively. The Parser module is used for extracting the information from packets. The information includes the Priority label, Cycle label, and so on. The Mapping module can identify the packet information and map them to the specified queue. The Queue module and Gate Control List (GCL) module work together. The GCL is a list of the states of queues, where each column represents one cycle number and corresponding gate states, and each row represents all queues' states under the current cycle. The Mapping module can push the packets to cache in the queue corresponding Cycle label. And the GCL will make sure the packets pop the queue during the scheduling Cycle. The deparser module changes the Cycle label with the current Cycle number.

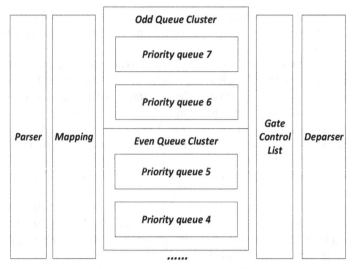

Fig. 1. Architecture of the CQCF

When CQCF works, the node will extract the cycle label and caches the packet in the corresponding queue. The TT (Time-Triggered) flow will cache in the priority queues 7–4, while others will be cached in priority queues 3–0, which can make sure TT flow to be transmitted first than other traffic.

3.2 Routing and Forwarding of CQCF

CQCF is designed for core networks, and for large-scale transmission, it should choose a mechanism working in access networks. We set the same Cycle size in CQF and CQCF, which means CQCF will shift queues with CQF simultaneously.

Since the transmission time (one cycle) between CQF nodes cannot support large-scale transmission. CQCF adopts queuing cluster to solve the problem of the limitation of transmission time. In CQCF, packets are sent from one node to the next node through two or more Cycles. When the network environment is unchanged, the allowed transmission time of packets is increased by one Cycle at least, which is sufficient to guarantee packets for long-distance transmission.

In this paper, we adopt SR for routing and forwarding. The packet with the Cycle label will enter the specified queue. Suppose the transmission time in CQCF domains is two Cycles and the transmission time in CQF domains is one Cycle. The forwarding between CQF and CQCF is shown in Fig. 2.

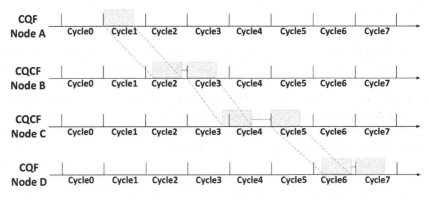

Fig. 2. Example of forwarding between CQF and CQCF

3.3 Cross-Domain Transfer of CQF and CQCF

(1) From CQF to CQCF

In this scenario, packets will enter the core network from the access network. The nodes maintain time synchronization, so the start time of Hypercycle is the same in each domain. Assuming that the current case is in Cycle 1, packets are sent from the Odd Queue of CQF into CQCF, as shown in Fig. 3 below.

In Cycle 1, in the Odd Queuing Cluster of CQCF, priority queue 7 sends packets, and priority queue 6 will send packets after queue 7 finishing sending. The lasting time of sending is one Cycle, which means that priority queue 6 will send packets in Cycle 2. In the Even Queuing Cluster of CQCF, all queues can receive packets, and packets will enter the queue corresponding to the Cycle label.

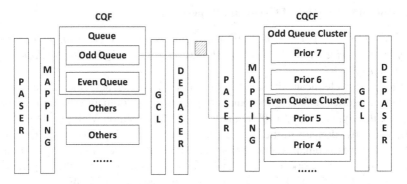

Fig. 3. Scenario of CQF to CQCF cross-domain transmission in Cycle 1

(2) From CQCF to CQF

After the packets are transmitted in the core network, they need to enter a new access network. Suppose Even Queue Cluster of CQCF is transmitting packets in Cycle 3, as shown in Fig. 4 below.

In Cycle 3, the packet enters the Odd Queue of CQF from priority queue 5 of CQCF. The cross-domain transmission time will cost two Cycles. In Cycle 4, packets in prior queue 4 of CQCF will enter the Even Queue of CQF. It means that all packets in Even Queue Cluster can enter the odd-even queue of CQF.

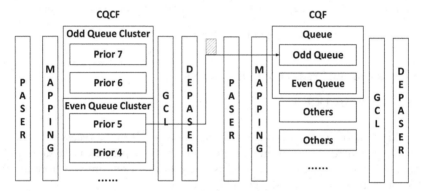

Fig. 4. Scenario of CQCF to CQF cross-domain transmission in Cycle 3

4   Algorithm Design of CQCF

4.1   Mapping Principle of Cycle and Hypercycle

Definition 1: The Hypercycle of CQF and CQCF is the least common multiple of the set of traffic periods in each domain. The Hypercycle of CQF is the multiple of the Hypercycle of CQCF.

The Hypercycle means the set of Cycles. In a large-scale network, traffic is divided into two categories including in-domain traffic and cross-domain traffic. In the access network, the Hypercycle of CQF is the LCM (Least Common Multiple) of in-domain traffic and cross-domain traffic. In the core network, the Hypercycle of CQCF is the LCM of the cross-domain traffic. Since the traffic in the access network includes the traffic in the core network, the Hypercycle of CQCF is a divisor of the Hypercycle of CQF. We set the Hypercycle of CQCF to the Hypercycle size of CQF.

Definition 2: Choose the Cycle of CQF as the standard Cycle and split the Cycle of CQCF into the Cycle of CQF.

The cycle is the transmission time between two neighboring nodes. The minimum Cycle should ensure that MTU can be transmitted between any two nodes. The maximum Cycle should be the Greatest Common Divisor (GCD) of all traffic periods. The maximum Cycle of CQF is the GCD of in-domain traffic and cross-domain traffic periods, and the maximum cycle of CQCF is the GCD of cross-domain traffic periods. So, the Cycle of CQCF is a multiple of the Cycle of CQF. We set the Cycle of CQF as the standard Cycle size and split the Cycle of CQCF into the Cycle of CQF.

4.2 Scheduling Constraints of CQCF

In large-scale deterministic networks, the controller node needs the topology of the network and TT flow information in advance. The flow information is shown in Table 1 below.

Table 1. The parameters of TT flow

Parameter	Description
flownum	The number label of the TT flow
src	Source IP address
dst	Destination IP address
period	The period of TT flow
length	The packet length of the TT flow
starttime	The start time for sending
deadline	Maximum end-to-end time
prior	The priority of TT flow
offset	The offset of TT flow
path	The scheduling path of TT flow

(1) Cycle Constraint

In CQF, the packet needs to be forwarded from the upstream node to the downstream node in one cycle. So, the cycle needs to include all the delays, i.e., sending delay, propagation delay, processing delay, queuing delay, and also the delay compensation brought by time synchronization. Therefore, the minimum cycle is:

$$MinCycle = \max_{f\,inF} f.length/Bandwidth + link\_delay + Sync \qquad (1)$$

link_delay is the sum of propagation delay, processing delay, queuing delay, and test packet delivery delay; *Sync* is synchronous time; $\max_{f\,inF} length/Bandwidth$ is the maximum sending delay.

The maximum Cycle is the maximum convention division of periods of all traffic periods. The maximum Cycle is:

$$MaxCycle = GCD(F.period) \qquad (2)$$

The value range of the Cycle is:

$$MinCycle \leq Cycle \leq MaxCycle \tag{3}$$

What's more, the Cycle needs to be a common divisor of $F.period$.

$$Cycle \in U = CD(F.period) \tag{4}$$

(2) Hypercycle Constraint

The minimum Hypercycle should be the LCM of all traffic periods.

$$MinHypercycle = LCM\,(F.period) \tag{5}$$

We use four queues in CQCF. Then, the Hypercycle should be a multiple of 4:

$$MinHypercycle = LCM\,(F.period, 4) \tag{6}$$

The relationship between the Hypercycle and cycle:

$$Hypercycle = 4n * Cycle, n \in N^+ \tag{7}$$

(3) Offset Constraint

The offset aims to solve the problem of scheduling failure caused by multiple packets entering one switch at the same time. When traffic enters a new domain, it needs to set a new offset. The range of offset is as follow.

$$0 \leq f.offset \leq f.period/Cycle - 1 \tag{8}$$

(4) Deadline Constraint

The whole network is divided into core networks and access networks. The end-to-end delay of each domain needs to be summed. The formula is shown below.

$$\begin{cases} CQF\_delay = Cycle * (cqf\_offset + hop(f.cqf\_path) + 1) \\ CQCF\_delay = Cycle * (lcqf\_offset + 2 * (hop(f.lcqf\_path) + 1)) \\ e2e\_delay = \sum CQF\_delay + \sum CQCF\_delay \\ e2e\_delay \leq f.deadline \end{cases} \tag{9}$$

CQF_delay represents the end-to-end delay of access network, $CQCF\_delay$ represents the end-to-end delay of core network. $e2e\_delay$ represents the overall delay. If $e2e\_delay$ is less than deadline of flow, it means this flow can be scheduled.

(5) Queue Constraint

$O(i, j, m, n, t)$ Is the state of the j th packet of flow i located at port n of switch m at cycle t. $O(i, j, m, n, t) = 1$ means the packet exists, while $O(i, j, m, n, t) = 0$ means the packet does not exist.

In CQF, the relationship of (i, j, m, n, t) is as follows:

$$t = fi.offset + (j - 1) * fi.period / Cycle + hop(fi, S_{mn}) \qquad (10)$$

In CQCF, the relationship of (i, j, m, n, t) is as follows:

$$t = fi.offset + (j - 1) * fi.period / Cycle + 2 * hop(fi, S_{mn}) \qquad (11)$$

$hop(fi, S_{mn})$ indicates the number of hops to S_{mn}.

(6) Transmission Constraint

Usually, we assume that the transmission time between CQF nodes is one Cycle and the time between CQCF nodes is two Cycles. The Cycle label of CQF should add one and the Cycle label of CQCF should add two when deparsing packets.

4.3 The Design of Algorithm

The pseudo-code of the designed algorithm is shown in Algorithm 1. F is the set of all flows. G represents network information. The output is the scheduling matrix H, a three-dimensional matrix whose three dimensions are Cycle t, switch m, and port n. The elements in H are P_{ij}, which means jth packet of flow i.

Algorithm 1 The scheduling of CQCF with the greedy algorithm

$Input : F, \ G$
$Output : H$

---

1. Schedule the shortest path and sort all flows with prior
2. $F \leftarrow Sort\_values(fi.prior)$
3. $F.path \leftarrow Dijkstra(fi)$
4. According to constraints 1 and 2, calculate the Hypercycle and Cycle
5. $Hypercycle = LCM(F.period, 4)$
6. $Cycle = GCD(F.period)$
7. According to constraint 3, calculate the max offset
8. $F.maxoffset \leftarrow Constraint\_offset(F.deadline, Cycle)$
9. According to constraints 4 and 5, calculate end-to-end time
10. $CQF\_delay = Cycle * (cqf\_offset + hop(f.cqf\_path) + 1)$
11. $CQCF\_delay = Cycle * \big(lcqf\_offset + 2 * (hop(f.lcqf\_path) + 1)\big)$
12. $e2e\_delay = \sum CQF\_delay + \sum CQCF\_delay$
13. $If \ e2e\_delay <= fi.deadline \ and \ Constraint\_queue(fi)$
14. $\quad H.add(fi)$
15. $return \ H$

---

5   Simulation

5.1   Experimental Environment

In this paper, we adopt Networkx, which is a Python language package for creating, and manipulating the structure and functionality of complex networks for simulation topology [13]. And the proposed algorithm is simulated using Python. In the experiment, 10 switches are divided into three domains as shown in Fig. 5. The switches in the 192.168.1 segment are the core network nodes, the switches in the 10.0.0 segment are the nodes in the access network 1, and the switches in the 10.0.1 segment are the nodes in the access network 2. In Fig. 5, the switches in the access network use CQF, and the switches in the core network use CQCF. We compare our proposed CQCF algorithm with the DIP algorithm in time synchronization scenarios. By adjusting the startup time of HyperCycle to be the same across all nodes, the DIP algorithm is adapted to time synchronization. All algorithms adopt the Greedy to get results. And the network flows include inner-domain flows and cross-domain flows, which are known before scheduling in this experiment.

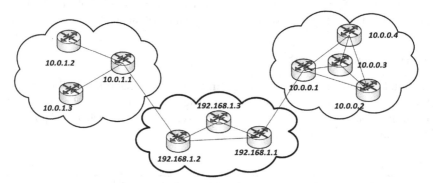

Fig. 5. The topology of the experimental network

5.2   Analysis of Results

The simulation results on successfully scheduled probability and scheduled time are presented under different flow numbers. And the results of CQCF and DIP are compared with the same settings of Cycle size.

Figure 6 shows the number of successfully scheduled traffic under different flow numbers of CQCF and DIP. The CQCF can successfully schedule more traffic because CQCF can utilize Cycles more fine-grained. When the total traffic is 2000, CQCF can schedule about 1600 flows, while DIP can schedule about 900 flows. The CQCF is improved by about 83% compared to DIP in time synchronization scenarios.

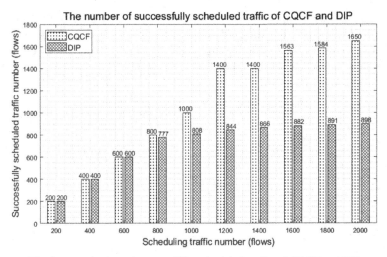

Fig. 6. The number of successfully scheduled traffic of CQCF and DIP

Transmission is affected by cache resources and bandwidth resources. Therefore, the successful scheduling probability will decrease when the resources are exhausted. From Fig. 7, we can know that the successful scheduling probability of CQCF decreases more slowly than that of DIP. It means that CQCF outperforms DIP in terms of the number of successfully scheduled flows and CQCF can utilize network resources more efficiently in time synchronization scenarios.

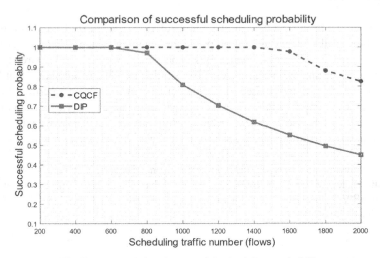

Fig. 7. Comparison of successful scheduling probability

We compare the scheduling time of CQCF and DIP by using Greedy algorithm under different traffic numbers, as shown in Fig. 8. When the traffic is small, the difference in scheduling time is not sharp. When the traffic is large, DIP consumes more time because it needs to consider compensation for inconsistent Cycle size. Under the number of traffic is 2000, the scheduling time of DIP is 1.728 s, while the time of CQCF is 1.246 s. The CQCF optimizes the scheduling algorithm runtime by about 27.9% compared to DIP in time synchronization scenarios.

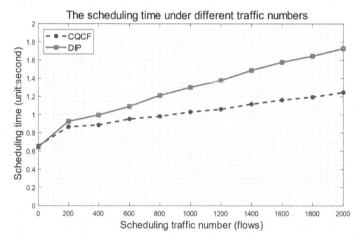

Fig. 8. The scheduling time under different traffic numbers

6 Conclusion

In this paper, we propose a deterministic transmission mechanism CQCF in time synchronization. At the same time, we proposed the mapping principle between cycle and Hypercycle across different domains. Based on which, we proposed a Greedy based scheduling algorithm and perform extensive simulations. The result shows that CQCF outperforms DIP in terms of successful scheduling probability and algorithm runtime. It means CQCF is more suitable for the time synchronization scenario and can improve the efficiency of large-scale deterministic transmission. In the future, we will research on the dynamic scheduling mechanisms of CQCF across different domains.

Acknowledgment. This research was funded by the fundamental research funds for the central universities under grant no. 2021JBZD003, open research projects of Zhejiang lab under grant no. 2022QA0AB03, nature and science foundation of China under grant no. 61471029, 61972026, 62072030 and 92167204.

References

1. Wu, Y., Dai, H.-N., Wang, H., Xiong, Z., Guo, S.: A survey of intelligent network slicing management for industrial IoT: integrated approaches for smart transportation, smart energy, and smart factory. In: IEEE Communications Surveys & Tutorials, vol. 24, no. 2, pp. 1175–1211, Secondquarter 2022, https://doi.org/10.1109/COMST.2022.3158270

2. Shan, D., Ren, F., Cheng, P., Shu, R., Guo, C.: Observing and mitigating micro-burst traffic in data center networks. IEEE/ACM Trans. Networking **28**(1), 98–111 (2020). https://doi.org/10.1109/TNET.2019.2953793

3. Finn, N.: Introduction to time-sensitive networking. IEEE Commun. Stand. Magaz. **2**(2), 22–28 (2018). https://doi.org/10.1109/MCOMSTD.2018.1700076

4. Nasrallah, A., et al.: Ultra-Low Latency (ULL) networks: the IEEE TSN and IETF Det-Net standards and related 5G ULL research. IEEE Commun. Surv. Tutorials **21**(1), 88–145, Firstquarter 2019. https://doi.org/10.1109/COMST.2018.2869350

5. Łubkowski, P., Bednarczyk, M., Maślanka, K., Amanowicz, M.: QoS-aware end-to-end connectivity provision in a heterogenous military environment. In: 2013 Military Communications and Information Systems Conference, pp. 1–8 (2013)

6. Nasrallah, A., Balasubramanian, V., Thyagaturu, A., et al.: Cyclic Queuing and Forwarding for Large Scale Deterministic Networks: A Survey (2019)

7. "IEEE Standard for Local and metropolitan area networks--Bridges and Bridged Networks--Amendment 29: Cyclic Queuing and Forwarding," in IEEE 802.1Qch-2017 (Amendment to IEEE Std 802.1Q-2014 as amended by IEEE Std 802.1Qca-2015, IEEE Std 802.1Qcd(TM)-2015, IEEE Std 802.1Q-2014/Cor 1-2015, IEEE Std 802.1Qbv-2015, IEEE Std 802.1Qbu-2016, IEEE Std 802.1Qbz-2016, and IEEE Std 802.1Qci-2017), pp. 1–30, 28 June 2017. https://doi.org/10.1109/IEEESTD.2017.7961303

8. Qiang, L., Liu, B., Yu, D., Wang, C.: Large-scale deterministic network forwarding technology. Telecommun. Sci. **35**(9), 12–19 (2019)

9. Qiang, L., Geng, X., Liu, B., Eckert, T., Geng, L.: Large-scale Deterministic IP network. Internet Engineering Task Force Internet-Draft draft-qiang-detnet-large-scale-detnet-05, March 2020. https://datatracker.ietf.org/doc/html/draft-qiang-detnet-large-scale-detnet-05

10. Wang, S., Wu, B., Zhang, C., Huang, Y., Huang, T., Liu, Y.: Large-Scale Deterministic IP Networks on CENI. In: IEEE INFOCOM 2021 - IEEE Conference on Computer Communications Workshops (INFOCOM WKSHPS), 2021, pp. 1–6 (2021). https://doi.org/10.1109/INFOCOMWKSHPS51825.2021.9484627

11. Wu, B., Wang, S., Wang, J., Tan, W., Liu, Y.: Flexible design on deterministic IP networking for mixed traffic transmission. In: ICC 2022 - IEEE International Conference on Communications, pp. 4360–4365 (2022). https://doi.org/10.1109/ICC45855.2022.9839201

12. Tan, W., Wu, B.: Long-distance deterministic transmission among TSN Networks: converging CQF and DIP. In: 2021 IEEE 29th International Conference on Network Protocols (ICNP), 2021, pp. 1–6 (2021). https://doi.org/10.1109/ICNP52444.2021.9651955

13. Akhtar, N.: Social network analysis tools. In: 2014 Fourth International Conference on Communication Systems and Network Technologies, pp. 388–392 (2014). https://doi.org/10.1109/CSNT.2014.83

Information Centric Networking (ICN)

Information Centric Networking (ICN)

A Task-Resource Joint Optimization Model in Distributed Computing

Shi Su[1], Hongwen Hui[2]([⊠]), and Wenjie Wei[2]

[1] The Experimental High School Attached to Beijing Normal University, No.14, XiCheng District, Beijing 100032, People's Republic of China
billsu@tom.com
[2] School of Computer and Communication Engineering, University of Science and Technology Beijing, No. 30, Xueyuan District, Beijing 100083, People's Republic of China
hhw21788712@163.com

Abstract. Distributed computing decomposes the user tasks into many small tasks and distributes them to multiple servers for processing to save the overall computing time. There is an important challenge that how to efficiently divide the tasks to achieve the goal. In this paper, aiming at solving the complex relationship between multiple tasks and multiple servers, we propose a resource-task joint optimization model in a distributed computing environment. The optimization goal of this model is to minimize the total computation time, while considering the transmission time and execution time of task data. Based on the task size, intensity, and computing power of the server, we propose a task-resource joint optimization algorithm to solve the proposed model. Numerical simulation verified the feasibility of the model and the correctness of the algorithm.

Keywords: Distributed computing · Resource-task joint optimization · Computation time

1 Introduction

Distributed computing is to connect a group of computers to each other through a network to form a decentralized system, and then disperse the data to be processed into multiple parts, hand it over to a group of computers scattered in the system to calculate at the same time, and finally merge the results to obtain the final result. It provides hardware support for solving large-scale computing problems. In the supercomputer program, artificial intelligence technology has been listed as the core application of future machines to co-design chip architecture and organization. With the increasing scale of users and the popularization of computer technology, a large amount of unstructured or structured data from all walks of life has become an important source of information. Therefore, running machine learning algorithms on a single computing resource cannot meet its huge demand for data processing capabilities, and traditional models have been unable to ensure the reliable completion of ultra-large-scale deep learning tasks. In the next-generation supercomputing system manufacturing plan, it is clearly pointed out that deep learning and distributed computing are the goals of key support [1].

W. Quan (Ed.): ICENAT 2022, CCIS 1696, pp. 573–584, 2023.
https://doi.org/10.1007/978-981-19-9697-9_46

As machine learning methods are widely used in various fields, including image recognition [2], machine translation [3], speech recognition [4], spam filtering [5] and so on. Deep learning has gradually formed a large-scale computing load: first, complex algorithms, such as deep neural networks and deep reinforcement learning can obtain large-scale models through training, which can effectively improve the accuracy of the model. The second is a large amount of heterogeneous training data [6]. Due to the characteristics of uniformity, cheapness, horizontal expansion and distribution of distributed computing systems [7], using its parallel computing resources has become the best choice to solve the above problems. In [8], Li et al. propose a reliability-based offload strategy that maps the task flow to resources that meet high reliability time constraints by considering task attributes, resource status, completion time, and reliability.

However, the physical resources of a distributed computing system are usually divided into discrete subsystems such as computing, storage, and network. Computing resources include central processing units, graphics processors, and tensor processors. They are usually configured on one or more servers, and it is difficult to communicate and coordinate with each other. This makes the utilization efficiency of resources low and is not conducive to the performance optimization of applications based on resource conditions. And it is easy to cause a multi-resource unbalanced resource waste due to interdependence and interference of various resources [9]. Facing the heterogeneous scenarios of multi-queue, multi-cluster, and cloud-edge-device collaboration, this situation will be more difficult to deal with.

In large-scale deep learning model training, due to the distributed computing system has a large number of heterogeneous systems, heterogeneous processors, complex communication links, and differences between user task requirements, there is uneven resource allocation, and it needs to face resource requests from multiple nodes. Especially for parallel or distributed tasks, the communication capabilities between nodes have strict bandwidth requirements, and parallel and distributed tasks usually have many subtasks running on hundreds or thousands of nodes at the same time, so the execution of any node Slowness or glitches affects the overall result of the entire job. Distributed jobs usually strive to ensure the completion of each subtask while achieving a high degree of parallelism. In [10], an intelligent computing offload scheme based on Internet of Things Dependent Applications (CODIA) is proposed, which decouples the performance enhancement problem into two processes: scheduling and offloading. However, due to the complex functional interaction and data dependencies among the subtasks, it is difficult to achieve the average division, scheduling and optimization of parallel jobs. Therefore, it is an urgent problem to study how to design resources and task scheduling algorithms that can ensure task execution, and improve resource utilization and delay.

2   Related Work

The existing research work on cluster resource allocation and scheduling can be divided into methods based on artificial heuristics and methods based on reinforcement learning. This kind of work studies how to reasonably assign each task to each computing resource according to the load status of computing resources and the computing demand of the task. The goal is to ensure load balancing and improve the utilization of computing resources. Therefore, designing an efficient scheduling model to utilize these computing resources more reasonably is the key to improving the system scheduling capability.

The early cluster resource schedulers Yarn [11] and Borg [12] were designed based on the master/slave architecture. The master is mainly responsible for global resource allocation, and the slave node is mainly responsible for the information collection and distribution of this node. Brog is matching resources for tasks. It will filter out some resources for task selection based on soft and hard constraints. Yarn, on the other hand, matches tasks for resources. It chooses the appropriate framework or task to assign when the slave node sends heartbeat information.

The computing resources of the cluster report the availability of their resources to the resource manager every few seconds. The resource manager assigns tasks to idle computing resources based on this information. There are two problems with this centralized scheduler. On the one hand, for large-scale clusters, the resource manager making scheduling decisions for all tasks arriving at the cluster is a processing bottleneck. The completion time of tasks has been increased. On the other hand, for tasks with a small amount of computation that are completed quickly, the idle computing resources can only be used in the next scheduling cycle after a few seconds. Cluster resource usage is reduced.

To solve the above problems, Yaq-d [13] and Sparrow [14] use multiple distributed schedulers to perform task scheduling. Jobs arriving at the cluster are first randomly distributed to a scheduler. On the scheduler, each task of the job is assigned to a certain computing resource. If the computing resource is free, the task is executed immediately. If the resource is occupied, the task is queued on the computing resource until the previous task is completed. This guarantees high resource usage.

If based on the queuing criterion of First-Come-First-Serve (FCFS), the "Join the Shortest Queue (JSQ)" algorithm [15, 16] can theoretically minimize the average task completion time load balancing algorithm. Reference [15] uses a birth-death Markov process to model the evolution of the total number of jobs in the system. This paper proposes an iterative procedure to estimate the average service rate in different states, and then obtain the average job response time to evaluate the performance of the JSQ strategy. Reference [16] analyzes JSQ routing in PS servers for the first time, providing a method to calculate the approximate steady-state distribution of queue lengths (number of jobs in the system) on any server. Under the above algorithm, when assigning a task, the scheduler first sends a probe message through the cluster network to inquire about the total number of tasks carried out by each computing resource. After receiving the reply from the computing resource, the scheduler allocates the task to the computing resource that currently carries the least number of tasks.

For large-scale clusters, the "join the shortest queue" algorithm not only causes a large amount of information overhead in the network, but also introduces a non-negligible detection delay before assigning each task. Therefore, the "Power-of-two-choices" load balancing algorithm is widely adopted by distributed schedulers [17, 18]. Reference [17] demonstrates that in a simple dynamic load balancing model, allowing clients to choose the shortest path between two servers is an order of magnitude improvement over randomly distributing clients uniformly. Aiming at the problem of large communication load in large-scale distributed systems, literature [18] randomly selects two computing resources from the available node list, and selects the node with the lowest load as the selected node. This method is not only simple to operate (completed directly by querying the host), but also achieves better results on cached load data. The above algorithm not only significantly reduces the information overhead and detection delay, but also has a significantly lower average task completion time than the algorithm that assigns tasks randomly without the overhead. However, the ideal "join the shortest queue" algorithm of this method still has a large performance difference [14].

In order to minimize the queuing delay, researchers proposed the "Batch-filling" load balancing algorithm [19] to reduce the number of sampling queues. The algorithm batch samples computational resources equal to the number of tasks for each task of a job arriving at the cluster at the same time, asks for their load, and assigns each task to those resources that carry fewer tasks among these computational resources. This bulk sampling is equivalent to sampling only one computational resource for one task on average, thus reducing information overhead. In addition, since the sampled computational resource load information is shared among tasks, each task is informed of a more comprehensive cluster load situation, and thus the algorithm can achieve better performance than the "Power-of-two-choices" algorithm.

Some cluster jobs have sequential dependencies between subtasks, such that some subtasks must be scheduled after other subtasks are completed. Such clustered jobs with inter-sub-task dependencies are usually represented as a Directed Acyclic Graph (DAG), where nodes represent subtasks and edges represent inter-sub-task data dependencies. An early approach to scheduling the various subtasks of a DAG is the critical path method [20]. The literature [21] improves the runtime and resource utilization of the whole cluster by focusing on long jobs to exploit the potential parallelism in the DAG. For a series of dependent tasks, the whole scheduling process is divided into two parts: offline analysis for Offline and online scheduling for Online. Firstly, find out the set of troublesome tasks (tasks with long running time and high resource consumption) in the whole job set and package other tasks, Then place the different task sets T, P, C and S in the space of time-resources and choose four orders: TSCP, TSPC, TPSC or TCSP. Online scheduling is performed at the end of the simulation placement of jobs in the offline case. Ultimately, the resource utilization is improved and the execution time of the job is shortened by the parallelism of jobs. Another study [22] proposed an altruistic and delayed scheduling strategy that is oriented to long-term task scheduling and can satisfy multidimensional metric requirements such as fairness, resource utilization, and average task completion time. For inter-task scheduling the main concern is to maximize the remaining resources, the transient scheduling strategy prolongs the task completion time but helps to enforce the altruistic strategy, and the fairness of the scheduling uses the Dominant Resource Fairness (DRF) approach. For intra-task scheduling, the amount of remaining resources is first calculated, followed by an altruistic strategy to allocate the excess resources by delayed scheduling to shorten the average task completion time. However, the above manual heuristic-based DAG scheduling strategy usually fails to achieve near-optimal job completion time performance.

Recent research [23] proposed to use Graph Neural Network (GNN) and Reinforcement Learning (RL) to schedule DAG jobs to solve the scheduling problem of multiple directed acyclic graph (DAG) tasks when running on multiple Executor. For tasks with dependencies, RL is used to train the scheduling algorithm: decima, and scalable GNN is used to represent the scheduling strategy, so as to deal with DAG-like tasks of arbitrary shape and size. This method selectively focuses servers on certain small tasks while leaving no resources idle. To reduce unnecessary IO overhead, an appropriate number of servers are allocated for each job. However, the Decima completes small tasks particularly fast and tends to assign more servers to small tasks [23], no experimental analysis has been made for large tasks. Research [24] proposed a deep reinforcement learning (DRL) method based on Monte Carlo tree search (MCTS) to schedule DAG jobs, taking into account task dependency and heterogeneous resource requirements. The problem framework is first mapped to MCTS, after which the default random policy is replaced by the DRL model to guide the search for more meaningful nodes. By utilizing DRL, the search space can be explored more efficiently without increasing the running time of MCTS, thus efficiently solving the scheduling of task-dependent complex jobs. However, this method selects tasks along the critical path in DAG, which cannot deploy all tasks at once, and the resource utilization is not very high [25].

3   System Model

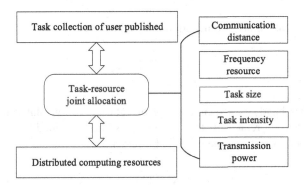

Fig. 1. System model of task-resource joint allocation.

In this section, we will establish a joint allocation system model between user task requests and server distributed resources, as shown in Fig. 1. In this model, we will comprehensively consider the data size, task intensity, server frequency resources, transmission distance between tasks and servers, and transmission power of each user's published tasks. Specifically, it is assumed that there are m users publishing tasks in a distributed computing system, and there are n servers providing computing services at the same time. The set of m users is represented as $U = \{U_1, U_2, \cdots U_m\}$, T_i represents the task of user U_i, and $T_i = \{D_i, C_i\}$, where D_i represents the size of the task data in bit, and C_i represents the task intensity, that is, the number of CPU cycles required to calculate a 1bit task. The set of n servers is denoted as $S = \{S_1, S_j, \cdots S_n\}$, and F_j is the maximum frequency resource that server S_j can provide.

Assuming that the task T_i of each user can be divided arbitrarily, and the channel bandwidth sent to each server is B, the signal power is S and the noise power is $N = N_0B$, then according to Shannon's formula, the data transmission power (unit is bit/s) of U_i is [7].

$$R_i = B \log_2(1 + \frac{S}{N}).$$ (1)

Suppose user U_i's data D_i is split into $d_{i1}, d_{i2}, \cdots d_{in}$, of which $d_{ij} \geq 0$. The completion of each task T_i requires transmission time and execution time. The transmission time of data d_{ij} can be expressed as:

$$t_{ij} = \frac{d_{ij}f(x_{ij})}{R_i}.$$ (2)

where x_{ij} represents the communication distance between the node and the server, and $f(x_{ij})$ is a positive correlation function of x_{ij}. Therefore, the transmission time required for data U_i of user D_i is

$$\sum_{j=1}^{n} \frac{d_{ij}f(x_{ij})}{R_i}.$$ (3)

And the total task transfer time required by all users is

$$\sum_{i=1}^{m} \sum_{j=1}^{n} \frac{d_{ij}f(x_{ij})}{R_i}.$$ (4)

On the other hand, the execution time of data d_{ij} we calculated on server S_j is $\tilde{t}_{ij} = d_{ij}C_i/f_{ij}$, where f_{ij} represents the frequency resource provided by server S_j to user U_i. Then the total execution time required by server S_j is

$$\sum_{i=1}^{m} \frac{d_{ij}C_i}{f_{ij}}.$$ (5)

And the total execution time required for all servers to complete the task is

$$\sum_{j=1}^{n} \sum_{i=1}^{m} \frac{d_{ij}C_i}{f_{ij}}.$$ (6)

Based on the above analysis, it is necessary to find a task segmentation scheme that minimizes the total computation time. This problem can be represented by the following optimization model:

$$\min_{\{d_{ij}, f(x_{ij}), C_i, f_{ij}, R_i\}} \sum_{i=1}^{m} \sum_{j=1}^{n} \frac{d_{ij}f(x_{ij})}{R_i} + \sum_{j=1}^{n} \sum_{i=1}^{m} \frac{d_{ij}C_i}{f_{ij}}$$ (7)

$$s.t. \sum_{j=1}^{n} d_{ij} = D_i, \ d_{ij} \geq 0, \tag{8}$$

$$\sum_{i=1}^{m} f_{ij} \leq F_j, f_{ij} > 0. \tag{9}$$

In the above formula, formula (7) is the objective function of the problem, that is, the total time required to complete the task. Constraint (8) means that all users' tasks can be assigned and completed. Constraint (9) means that the sum of the frequency resources allocated by the server to the user cannot exceed its own maximum frequency resources. d_{ij} is about the splitting of tasks, f_{ij} is about resource allocation, model (7–9) are called task-resource joint optimization model.

4 Algorithm Design

In this section, we will propose a Task-Resource Joint Optimization (TRJO) algorithm to solve model (7–9). Note that there are five variables $d_{ij}, f(x_{ij})$, C_i, f_{ij} and R_i in model (2-1). When the network mechanism is stable, it can be considered that the value of C_i, $f(x_{ij})$ and R_i represents the topology of the network and can be regarded as a constant. The division of tasks d_{ij} and the allocation of resource f_{ij} are two key variables that determine the total computing time of tasks.

In fact, for the execution time, the transmission time has little effect on the objective function. Therefore, we only need to focus on the size of the execution time. Note that the total execution time is $\sum_{j=1}^{n} \sum_{i=1}^{m} d_{ij} C_i / f_{ij}$. Obviously, dividing computing tasks with high task intensity to servers with the largest frequency resources can minimize the total execution time. Assume that the m tasks are sorted by task intensity as $T_{\alpha_1} \geq T_{\alpha_2} \geq \cdots \geq T_{\alpha_m}$. The n servers can be sorted according to the size of their frequency resources as $S_{\beta_1} \leq S_{\beta_2} \leq \cdots \leq S_{\beta_3}$.

Our allocation principle should not only meet the matching of task intensity and frequency resources, but also ensure that all servers are fully utilized. Such an allocation method can minimize the total time. Based on the above analysis, we propose the following TRJO algorithm:

Algorithm 1: TRJO algorithm

Input: the number of users m, the number of servers n, D_i, C_i, F_j, B, h_i,

p_i, N, $f\left(x_{ij}\right)$,

Output: the value of formula (7)

1. the m tasks are sorted by task intensity C_i as $T_{\alpha_1} \geq T_{\alpha_2} \geq \cdots \geq T_{\alpha_m}$

2. the n servers can be sorted according to the size of their frequency resource F_j as $S_{\beta_1} \leq S_{\beta_2} \leq \cdots \leq S_{\beta_3}$

3. calculate the total amount of data for all tasks $\displaystyle\sum_{i=1}^{m} D_i$

4. calculate the sum of all frequency resources $\displaystyle\sum_{j=1}^{n} F_j$

5. calculate the amount of data that should be allocated by U_j is

$$\tilde{D}_j = \sum_{i=1}^{m} D_i\left(F_j / \sum_{j=1}^{n} F_j \right)$$

6. if $D_{\alpha_1} \leq \tilde{D}_{\alpha_1}$, task T_{α_1} does not need to be divided and all tasks are executed by server U_{β_1}; and the split task $d_{\alpha_2,\beta_1} = \tilde{D}_{\alpha_1} - D_{\alpha_1}$ in D_{α_2} is executed by server U_{β_1}, and T_{α_1} is excluded from the task set

7. if $D_{\alpha_1} > \tilde{D}_{\alpha_1}$, split $d_{\alpha_1,\beta_1} = \tilde{D}_{\alpha_1}$ in D_{α_1} is executed by server U_{β_1}, and U_{β_1} is excluded from the server set

8. perform steps 6-7 for the remaining and tasks

9. record d_{ij} and calculate $f_{ij} = C_i x_{ij} / \left(\displaystyle\sum_{i=1}^{m} x_{ij} C_i \right)$

10、 Calculation formula (7)

---

5 Numerical Experiment

In this Section, we verify the performance of the proposed algorithm 1. It was assumed that 10 users and 10 servers are distributed in a 200 m * 200 m area according to the characteristics of local tightness and partial looseness. Some parameters in the experiment are given in Table 1. We designed two groups of comparative experiments. In the first group of comparative experiments, we controlled other parameters unchanged and increased the amount of task data to verify the effectiveness of the proposed algorithm; In the second group of experiments, the user's task intensity increased continuously by controlling other parameters to verify the effectiveness of the proposed algorithm.

Table 1. Simulation parameter settings

Parameter	Value
Channel bandwidth β	$5*10^6$ Hz
Signal transmission power	0.25 W
Channel gain	2 dB
Noise spectral density N_0	10^{-14} W/Hz

Experiment 1

In this experiment, the total amount of task data was assumed to increase from 500 kb to 1000 kb for 10 users (total delay is calculated for every 100 kb increase, 6 experiments), and the amount of data for each user was taken randomly. The user's task intensity is $[C_1, C_2, \cdots, C_{10}] = [3000, 3500, \cdots, 7500]$(cycles/bit). The computational frequency resources of the server were $[F_1, F_2, \cdots, F_{10}] = [5, 5.5, \cdots, 9.5] * 10^{10}$(cycles/s). Distance x_{ij} was calculated from the relative positions of the two nodes for each experiment, $x_{ij} \in (0, 200]$, $f(x_{ij}) = x_{ij}$, where $\delta = 1$ m^{-1} was a relative quantity.

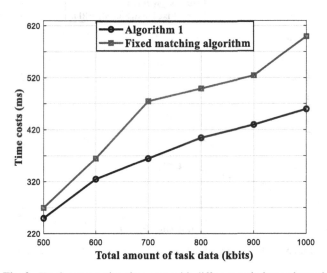

Fig. 2. Total computation time cost with different task data volumes2

As shown in Fig. 2, the black line indicates the total time cost required for the server to complete the task under Algorithm 1. The total time cost tends to increase as the volume of tasks increases. The time growth trend is slower because the algorithm optimizes the order of task completion. When the total number of tasks is 500 kb, the total time cost is about 250 ms, and when the total number of tasks completed is 1000 kb, the total time cost is less than about 460 ms. The fixed matching algorithm performs tasks sequentially according to the order of the user and server numbers. Clearly, the total time cost of the fixed matching algorithm is greater than that of Algorithm 1, and the total time cost of this algorithm increases rapidly with the number of tasks.

Experiment 2
In this experiment, the total amount of data was fixed at 500 kb, and the task intensity for each user in each of the six experiments was given by the following matrix.

$$C = \begin{bmatrix} 3000 & 3500 & \cdots & 7000 & 7500 \\ 3500 & 4000 & \cdots & 7500 & 8000 \\ \vdots & \vdots & \vdots & \vdots & \vdots \\ 5000 & 5500 & \cdots & 9000 & 9500 \\ 5500 & 6000 & \cdots & 9500 & 10000 \end{bmatrix}$$

The rows in matrix C represent the task intensities corresponding to each of the 10 users in each experiment, and the columns in matrix C represent the task intensities corresponding to one user in each of the six experiments, respectively, represented by vector $A_1, A_2, \cdots, A_6$. The computing frequency resources of the server, distance x_{ij}, and the values of $f(x_{ij})$ are the same as in Experiment 1.

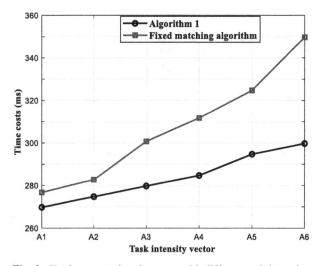

Fig. 3. Total computation time cost with different task intensity.

As shown in Fig. 3, as the intensity of the task increases, the total time cost also tends to increase. When the task intensity vector is A_1, the total time cost is about 270 ms; when the task intensity vector is A_6, the total time cost is when the task intensity vector is A_6, the total time cost is about 300 ms. Similarly, we use the fixed matching algorithm as a comparison, and its total time cost is obviously greater than that of Algorithm 1. When the task intensity vector is A_6, the time cost of the fixed matching algorithm is about 350 ms.

The feasibility of the joint resource-task optimization model proposed in this paper is verified by comparing two sets of experiments.

6 Conclusion

Distributed computing makes efficient use of free computing resources by moderately decomposing large amounts of complex data and distributing these decomposed smaller computational pieces to multiple computer resources for piecemeal computation and finally computing the final result. In this paper, we focus on the tasks partitioning and resource allocation problems in a distributed computing environment, and we jointly optimize the tasks partitioning and resource allocation problems to minimize the total time cost. Firstly, we propose a joint task-resource optimization model with total time cost as the optimization objective. Additionally, we propose Algorithm 1 to solve the joint task-resource optimization model. Finally, numerical simulations verify the feasibility of the proposed joint task-resource optimization model and the effectiveness of the algorithm. The approach in this paper provides an effective solution for task partitioning and resource allocation in distributed computing environments.

References

1. Lu, Y., Qian, D., Fu, H., et al.: Will supercomputers be super-data and super-AI machines? Commun. ACM **61**(11), 82–87 (2018)
2. He, K., Zhang, X., Ren, S., et al.: Deep residual learning for image recognition. In: Proceedings of the IEEE Conference on Computer Vision and Pattern Recognition, pp. 770–778 (2016)
3. Bahdanau, D., Cho, K., Bengio, Y.: Neural machine translation by jointly learning to align and translate. arXiv preprint arXiv:1409.0473 (2014)
4. Chan, W., Jaitly, N., Le, Q., et al.: Listen, attend and spell: a neural network for large vocabulary conversational speech recognition. In: 2016 IEEE International Conference on Acoustics, Speech and Signal Processing (ICASSP), pp. 4960–4964. IEEE (2016)
5. Thomas, K., Grier, C., Ma, J., et al.: Design and evaluation of a real-time url spam filtering service. In: 2011 IEEE Symposium on Security and Privacy, pp. 447–462. IEEE (2011)
6. Diaz-Montes, J., Diaz-Granados, M., Zou, M., et al.: Supporting data-intensive workflows in software-defined federated multi-clouds. IEEE Trans. Cloud Comput. **6**(1), 250–263 (2015)
7. Samal, A.K., Parida, A.K., Pani, S.K., et al.: A novel fault-tolerant scheduling of real-time tasks on multiprocessor using discrete-elitist multi-ACO. In: 2015 International Conference on Communications and Signal Processing (ICCSP), pp. 1939–1945. IEEE (2015)
8. Li, B., Li, K., Jin, S., et al.: Reliability based offloading strategy for deadline constrained taskflows in vehicular edge computing environments. Trans. Emerging Telecommun. Technol. e4615 (2022)
9. Nedic, A., Ozdaglar, A.: Distributed subgradient methods for multi-agent optimization. IEEE Trans. Autom. Control **54**(1), 48–61 (2009)
10. Xiao, H., Xu, C., Ma, Y., et al.: Edge Intelligence: a computational task offloading scheme for dependent IoT application. IEEE Trans. Wirel. Commun. (2022)
11. Vavilapalli, V.K., Murthy, A.C., Douglas, C., et al.: Apache hadoop yarn: Yet another resource negotiator. In: Proceedings of the 4th annual Symposium on Cloud Computing, pp. 1–16 (2013)
12. Verma, A., Pedrosa, L., Korupolu, M., et al.: Large-scale cluster management at Google with Borg. In: Proceedings of the Tenth European Conference on Computer Systems, pp. 1–17 (2015)
13. Rasley, J., Karanasos, K., Kandula, S., et al.: Efficient queue management for cluster scheduling. In: Proceedings of the Eleventh European Conference on Computer Systems, pp. 1–15 (2016)

14. Ousterhout, K., Wendell, P., Zaharia, M., et al.: Sparrow: distributed, low latency scheduling. In: Proceedings of the Twenty-Fourth ACM Symposium on Operating Systems Principles, pp. 69–84 (2013)
15. Lin, H.C., Raghavendra, C.S.: An approximate analysis of the join the shortest queue (JSQ) policy. IEEE Trans. Parallel Distrib. Syst. 7(3), 301–307 (1996)
16. Gupta, V., Balter, M.H., Sigman, K., et al.: Analysis of join-the-shortest-queue routing for web server farms. Perform. Eval. 64(9–12), 1062–1081 (2007)
17. Mitzenmacher, M.: The power of two choices in randomized load balancing. IEEE Trans. Parallel Distrib. Syst. 12(10), 1094–1104 (2001)
18. Richa, A.W., Mitzenmacher, M., Sitaraman, R.: The power of two random choices: a survey of techniques and results. Comb. Optim. 9, 255–304 (2001)
19. Ying, L., Srikant, R., Kang, X.: The power of slightly more than one sample in randomized load balancing. Math. Oper. Res. 42(3), 692–722 (2017)
20. Kelley, J.E.: The critical-path method: resource planning and scheduling. Industrial scheduling (1963)
21. Grandl, R., Kandula, S., Rao, S., et al.: GRAPHENE: packing and dependency-aware scheduling for data-parallel clusters. In: 12th USENIX Symposium on Operating Systems Design and Implementation (OSDI 2016), pp. 81–97 (2016)
22. Grandl, R., Chowdhury, M., Akella, A., et al.: Altruistic scheduling in multi-resource clusters. In: 12th USENIX Symposium on Operating Systems Design and Implementation (OSDI 2016), pp. 65–80 (2016)
23. Mao, H., Schwarzkopf, M., Venkatakrishnan, S.B., et al.: Learning scheduling algorithms for data processing clusters. In: Proceedings of the ACM Special Interest Group on Data Communication, pp. 270–288 (2019)
24. Hu, Z., Tu, J., Li, B.: Spear: optimized dependency-aware task scheduling with deep reinforcement learning. In: 2019 IEEE 39th International Conference on Distributed Computing Systems (ICDCS), pp. 2037–2046. IEEE (2019)
25. Awada, U., Zhang, J., Chen, S., et al.: AirEdge: a dependency-aware multi-task orchestration in federated aerial computing. IEEE Trans. Veh. Technol. 71(1), 805–819 (2021)
26. Prothero, J.: The Shannon Law for non-periodic channels. Technical ReportR-2012-1, Astrapi Corporation, Washington, DC, pp.1–31 (2012)

Cache Strategy for Information Center Satellite Networks Based on Node Importance

Dejun Zhu, Rui Xu, Xiaoqiang Di$^{(\boxtimes)}$, Haowei Wang, Hao Luo, Jing Chen, Juping Sun, and Yuchen Zhu

School of Computer Science and Technology, Changchun University of Science and Technology, Changchun 130022, China
dixiaoqiang@cust.edu.cn

Abstract. For low earth orbit (LEO) satellite networks, the high-speed movement of satellites makes the inter-satellite links time-varying, resulting in increased user content access delay. In this paper, we introduce information-centric networking (ICN) architecture in satellite networks, reasonably distribute data content cache on different nodes to improve inter-satellite data transmission, and propose a caching strategy for information center satellite networks based on the importance of nodes (CSNI). By preserving stable inter-satellite links, the LEO satellite network is modeled as a series of steady-state topological graphs. Local clustering coefficients, closeness centrality, and betweenness centrality are calculated for each node in the steady-state topology graph. And the content with high popularity is cached in the appropriate nodes by these three metrics, which improves the data transmission efficiency. Simulation results show that the strategy proposed in this paper can effectively improve the cached content hit ratio ate and reduce average user request delay compared with the LCE, LCD, Prob, and Betw.

Keywords: Satellite networks · Information-centric network · Cache nodes · Node importance

1 Introduction

In recent years, satellite networks are gaining more and more attention as the demand for communications in areas such as global data communications, emergency relief, and defense and security continues to grow. Compared with terrestrial communication networks, satellite networks have the characteristics of global coverage, long information dissemination distance, and are not restricted by the geographical environment, and are widely used in mobile communication, broadcast access, weather forecasting, environment and disaster monitoring, resource detection, and positioning, etc. Compared with high earth orbit satellite (GEO) and medium orbit earth satellite (MEO), LEO has gained

This research was funded by the National Natural Science Foundation of China under grant No. U21A20451, and the China University Industry-Academia-Research Innovation Fund under grant No. 2021FNA01003.

widespread attention for their excellent characteristics such as lower time delay, lower signal fading, and lower operation and maintenance costs [1].

However, satellite network topology changes dynamically and the inter-satellite links environment is complex, leading to problems such as large propagation delay, round-trip links asymmetry, and intermittent connection of information transmission during communication. ICN has excellent data forwarding strategies and content distribution caching mechanisms within the network [2, 3]. In this paper, we introduce ICN architecture in a satellite network, which greatly reduces the distance of users' access to resources by caching them on routing nodes with cache space.

However, when satellites move around the Earth at high speed, the connectivity and transmission paths of inter-satellite links change. Traditional caching strategies create problems such as slow or mismatched data matching, so traditional ICN caching strategies are not suitable for dynamic satellite networks. For the above problems, this paper proposes a caching strategy applicable to satellite networks.

1. In steady-state processing of satellite network topology, three different node metrics are selected in the steady-state topology graph, local clustering coefficients that efficiently aggregate nodes from local clustering coefficient, and closeness centrality and betweenness centrality that effectively characterize the information dissemination influence from a global perspective, and these three factors are taken into account to effectively distinguish the importance degree of each node in the steady-state graph to filter out the appropriate nodes as cache nodes.
2. The caching strategy for information center satellite networks based on node importance to cache high popularity data in caching nodes to improve data transmission impact is proposed. The effectiveness of the strategy is demonstrated through ndnSIM simulation experiments.

2   Related Work

The in-network caching mechanism has received extensive attention in ICN. Caching decision strategies refer to the efficient utilization of caching resources in the network through cooperation among nodes. The existing research on caching decision strategies be classified into non-collaborative caching, explicit collaborative caching, and implicit collaborative caching based on the degree of cache cooperation [4].

Non-collaborative caching strategies make caching decisions independently, without requiring nodes to cooperate with others without taking into account other information factors of the network. Leave copy everywhere (LCE) is a classical non-collaborative caching strategy for ICN [5], that requires caching the content on all nodes along the data packet return path. The non-collaborative caching strategy is simple to operate and does not consider the overall layout of the network, but it repeatedly caches the same content and reduces the diversity of cached content.

Explicit collaborative caching strategies use global controllers to calculate cache locations, increasing the effectiveness of data transfer and reducing the complexity of router operations. Implicit collaborative caching strategies rely on some additional information to make caching decisions. In terms of implicit collaborative caching strategies, when a cache hits, Leave copy down (LCD) [6] cache content copies at the next-hop node of the hit node. Therefore, with each identical request, the distance between the user and the content copy decreases with one hop. Probabilistic caching (Prob) [7] requires all routing nodes on data packets to return paths to cache objects of fixed probability p. The effectiveness of the above implicit collaborative caching strategy has been demonstrated in static networks. However, satellite networks are time-varying and periodic, and the continuity of inter-satellite links changes, resulting in inconsistent transmission paths of user requests and packet return paths. Therefore, the cache placement strategy in static topologies is less applicable in satellite time-varying networks.

About the caching strategy for satellite networks. In [8], proposed an on-satellite caching strategy called SatCache, which exploits the broadcast characteristics of satellite communication to estimate the content preferences of satellite coverage users and improve the cache hit ratio. In [9], proposed cache allocation for satellite-assisted network emergencies, and showed that end-to-end transmission delay is effectively reduced by introducing an ICN architecture with caching capabilities. In [8, 9] that does not consider subsequent user requests, adversely affecting the global user request hit ratio while increasing the convergence time of the solution process. In [10] propose to deploy intra-network caching techniques in a multi-layer satellite network and established a three-layer satellite network model. Probabilistic caching strategies based on satellite cache capacity size and content popularity are proposed, and better results on average content access delay are derived in simulations. The strategy is compared with traditional IP protocols, no-cache strategy, and LCE, and achieves better results in terms of average content access delay, but it does not consider different users' different demands for popular files. The above approach verifies the feasibility of onboard deployment of ICN cache, but it does not consider the current status of on-star computing power and the benefits of deploying cache for the whole network cycle of the satellite.

In this paper, the satellite network topology is steady-state processed to obtain a collection of stable topological graphs. For the present problem of limited on-star data processing capacity, local clustering coefficients, closeness centrality, and betweenness centrality are fused to evaluate the importance of nodes within each steady-state topology graph and filter out suitable cache nodes for efficient data forwarding. Simulation experiments demonstrate this strategy reduces user request delay and improves the cache hit ratio.

3 System Model

In terrestrial networks, data transmission follows a fixed path. However, the topology of the satellite network keeps changing with inter-satellite links breaking, when the network topology changes, the transmission path of the request and return path of the data packet be inconsistent. Satellites move according to a fixed orbit and also have periodicity, this indicates topologies of satellite networks have an upper limit and a regular number, which provides a reference for our subsequent research.

The model proposed in this paper combines the advantages of high accuracy of contact sequence graph representation and low storage complexity of aggregation graph model. The satellite network model is represented as $G = \{V, E, T\}$, $v \in V$, $e \in E$, where V denotes the set of nodes, E denotes the set of inter-satellite links, and T denotes the satellite operation period. The contact sequence graph is a more accurate description of the time-varying network characteristics, and the state of any node at any moment be visualized. The transmission of contacts and changes in weights be seen through the links between nodes and the identified variables. Therefore, in the present paper, the integration of nodes and links between nodes of a satellite time-varying network is characterized as a contact sequence graph. The contact sequence graph is sliced isochronously, and the time size of each time slice after slicing is $t = \sqrt{T}$. The contact sequence graph after slicing is shown in Fig. 1, representing contact sequence graphs of the entire operation cycle of the network, black markings on the line represent contact moments of edge-connected nodes, and numbers between nodes numbers marked to indicate the times the two nodes have link links at the time.

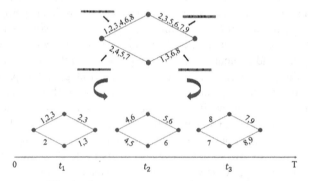

Fig. 1. Contact sequence graph segmentation

Converting contact sequence graphs into aggregation graphs through aggregation representation of resources, aggregating links identify between nodes of process contact sequence graphs as weight edges, and obtaining weight aggregation graphs identifying links between nodes in terms of importance. Therefore, the average weight edges of each graph are calculated, links greater than or equal to weight averages are retained in aggregation graphs, and unweight aggregation graphs with slicing characteristics are obtained, reducing the storage complexity of time-varying models. As shown in Fig. 2 screening out inter-satellite links are important in satellite networks by inter-satellite links with higher than average weights, and at the same time, ensures satellite network integrity is not affected.

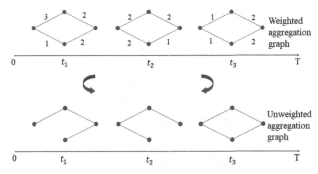

Fig. 2. Polymerization graph steady state processing

4 Method

4.1 Node Importance Index

The steady-state topology diagram is obtained from the time-varying network processing of the satellites in Subsect. 3. The satellite nodes are abstracted as points and the inter-satellite links are abstracted as edges to account for the important assessment of their nodes, at which point the topology is modeled as a complex network. In complex network theory, centrality is a core metric. Which is usually used to reflect the importance of nodes in network topology. The larger the centrality metric, the more important the node is in the network topology.

In this subsection, the problem is to select the high-impact satellite nodes from the network topology. Considering the limited storage resources of the satellite nodes, the content cache is placed on the more influential satellite nodes. The average content acquisition delay of users is reduced and the hit rate of user-requested content is increased. Complex networks are represented by an undirected graph $G = (V, E)$, assuming that G has n nodes and m edges, and denoting the set of vertices of G by $V = \{v_1, v_2, ..., v_n\}$ and the set of edges of G by $E = \{e_1, e_2, ..., e_m\}$.

The local clustering coefficient is a measure of the structural hole theory. Structural hole theory is an important theory proposed by Burt to analyze social networks [11]. If neighbors of nodes in the network are connected, but sometimes expected connections between neighbors do not exist, then these disappearing connections are called structural holes, in the overall view, the network structure then appears as caves. The structure hole graph is shown in Fig. 3, the relationship constituted by node E and its neighboring node pairs AB and AC is a structural hole, the relationship constituted by node E with its neighboring node pair BC is not a structural hole, node B and node C are directly connected, i.e., there are redundant connections.

Local clustering coefficients indicate the ability of nodes' neighboring nodes to aggregate into clusters. The smaller the local clustering coefficient of the node, the more likely node is the node at the structural hole. The expression of the local clustering coefficient is as follows.

$$C_C(v_i) = \frac{2E(v_i)}{k(v_i)[k(v_i) - 1]} \tag{1}$$

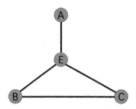

Fig. 3. Structure hole graph

where $C_C(v_i)$ represents the clustering coefficient of node v_i, $E(v_i)$ is the actual number of edges directly connected to node v_i, and $k(v_i)$ is the degree of node v_i and the possible number of edges directly connected to node v_i.

The closeness centrality of a node reflects the closeness between a certain node along with other nodes in the network [12]. The closeness centrality $C_C(v_i)$ of node v_i can be described by the reciprocal of the sum of the shortest distances from node v_i to the rest of the nodes, which is expressed as follows.

$$C_B(v_i) = \frac{1}{\sum\limits_{j=1, j \neq i}^{n} d(v_i, v_j)} \tag{2}$$

where n denotes the network size for node v_i and $d(v_i, v_j)$ denotes the shortest distance from node v_i to node v_j. Closeness centrality eliminates the interference of special values by calculating the average distances between nodes along with other nodes in the network. The smaller the average distance between a node and other nodes in the network, the greater the closeness centrality of that node.

Betweenness centrality portrays control of nodes to network flow transmitted along the shortest path in the network and is a measure of the importance of nodes to the propagation of information within the entire network. For an undirected graph $G = (V, E)$ with n nodes, the betweenness centrality of node v_i is calculated as follows.

$$C_A(v_i) = \sum_{s \neq v_i \neq t \in V} \frac{\sigma_{st}(v_i)}{\sigma_{st}} \tag{3}$$

where $C_A(v_i)$ represents the betweenness centrality of node v_i, σ_{st} denotes the number of all paths between node s and node t, and $\sigma_{st}(v_i)$ denotes the number of paths between node v_s and node v_t that pass through node v_i. It is known that the more the shortest paths through the node among all node pairs in the network, the more important the node is.

4.2 Cache Node Selection

The selection of cache nodes is based on the principle of reasonable distribution of content objects in different nodes, such as caching content with high popularity in nodes with high node importance with low popularity in nodes with low node importance. According to the definition of node importance, nodes with high node importance are more easily accessed by other nodes of the network, so content cached in such nodes is more likely to be accessed by other nodes, which improves the hit ratio of cache to reduce invalid cache.

The prevalence of content x in a steady-state topological graph within a cycle is calculated as follows.

$$Popu(x) = \frac{R(x)}{R(X)} \tag{4}$$

where $R(x)$ is the number of user requests for content x in the cycle, $R(X)$ is the number of times all content is requested by users in the cycle, and $Popu(x)$ is the popularity of content x in the cycle. The popularity of content is more reflective of user interest, and caching content according to the popularity of content is more conducive to making content cached by satellite nodes reasonable in-network topology.

Due to different mechanisms of different metrics, different metrics have different defects, different results are often obtained when different metrics are used for node importance assessment for the same network. In this paper, the importance of nodes is calculated in the steady-state satellite network topology obtained in Subsect. 3, as shown in the following equation.

$$S(v_i) = \alpha C_C(v_i) + \beta C_B(v_i) + \gamma C_A(v_i) \tag{5}$$

where $S(v_i)$ represents the importance of node v_i. The values of the three indicators have been normalized, α, β and γ are weight coefficients, and the weight coefficients of all three metrics are determined to be 1/3. Considering the centrality metric of each node comprehensively and not favoring any node centrality metric.

$$S_T(v_i) = \sum_{T=1}^{n} S(v_i) \tag{6}$$

where $S_T(v_i)$ represents the importance of node v_i in the whole satellite network cycle.

The importance ranking of all nodes in the network is evaluated, and when the importance of a node is high, that node is more helpful for data transmission. Therefore, the satellite nodes with the top 10% of node importance ranking are selected as the highly popular cache nodes, verifying the caching effect of this paper's scheme in satellite networks.

4.3 Caching Strategy

Satellite network communication is driven through data consumers, i.e. user terminals, exchanging two types of packets: interest packets and data packets. To perform interest packets and data packets forwarding functions, each satellite node needs to maintain three data structures: pending interest table (PIT), forwarding information base (FIB), and content store (CS), as well as a forwarding strategy module that determines when and where to forward each interest packets. PIT stores all interest packets that have been forwarded by satellite nodes but have not yet been satisfied, each PIT entry records names of data carried in these interest packets together with interfaces where interest packets are transmitted to as well as from the satellite node.

In this paper, the content cache locations are selected on nodes of high importance in the network topology, which have a high local clustering coefficient, closeness centrality, and betweenness centrality concerning other nodes. The caching mechanism of this paper is described in detail below.

1. Interest packet processing: When users want to obtain certain content, they send interest packets requesting such content to the network. Satellite nodes in the network forward interest packets along the route of the user's content request to cache nodes of the highest importance. When the cache node receives the interest packet, the satellite node first checks whether it has corresponding cached content in its own CS table. If there is, the satellite node returns a matching data copy from the interface reached by the interest packet by discarding the interest packet; if not, it finds whether there is a request record about this content in the PIT. Add a new message in the PIT and find the forwarding port recorded in the FIB to forward the interest packet to the next-hop node with the update of related record information. In process of interest packet forwarding, the global controller collects satellite network topology information together with the user's content request information, the content popularity and satellite node importance are calculated based on the collected related information.

2. Data packet forwarding: The interest packet gets a response at the content service node, content service node returns a data packet containing corresponding request content. The data packet is backhauled along the path opposite to the forwarding path of the interest packet, and based on the records in the interest packet, if the content of the data packet is more popular, the data packet is cached on the satellite node with the highest importance on the shortest path between the interest packet request node and the data packet service node.

3. Cache Cancellation: To cache newly arrived content resources when cache space is insufficient, the content on the node needs to replace cached content resources using the cache replacement algorithm last recently used (LRU) [13].

5   Experiment

5.1 Parameter Setting

In this paper, the experiments are performed on the network simulation platforms NS-3 [14], and ndnSIM [14]. NS-3 software is a discrete-time simulation software for network systems, and ndnSIM is a simulation platform for ICN architecture. The network structure of the Iridium constellation is used in the simulation [15]. The orbital altitude of the LEO satellite is 780 km, the number of orbital planes is 6, and there are 11 satellites per orbital plane. The topology graph containing 66 satellite nodes is constructed for the experiments. We select one node as the data producer node, 22 satellite nodes as the data request nodes, and 7 satellite nodes as the cache nodes. The number of cache nodes has been shown to have little effect on the experimental results. The request pattern of users obeys Zipf distribution, the replacement policy of all nodes is LRU strategy, and the specific parameters are set as follows during the experiments:

Table 1. Experimental parameter setting

Parameter	Value
Number of Users	22
Default Cache Capacity	30
Zipf Parameter α	0.7–1.3
Default Parameter α	1.0
Request Rate/(req·s^{-1})	50–350
Default Request Rate/(req·s^{-1})	200
Number of Content	500–3500
Default Number of Content	1000

5.2 Evaluation Metrics

For evaluating the performance of the proposed caching strategy in this paper, the average cache hit ratio and the average request delay are used as evaluation metrics.

1. Cache hit ratio

The cache hit ratio (CHR) is the ratio of the number of times a data-requesting node obtains data from a cache node to the total number of requests in all selected time slots. The higher the cache hit ratio, the fewer data request nodes get data from data producer nodes, the less load pressure on data producer nodes, and the more efficient data request nodes get data.

$$CHR = \frac{r}{F} \tag{7}$$

where r denotes the number of responses obtained by the data request node at the cache node during all time slots, F denotes the number of all content requests sent by the data request node.

2. Average content request delay

Average content request delay (ARD) is the average delay elapsed between the time a data request node sends a data request and the time it receives a data packet. It reflects the response speed of the request. Caching nodes receive the request and return data faster than data producer nodes, and therefore have better response speed. The faster the response speed, the more caching strategy plays a role.

$$ARD = \frac{\sum_{i=1}^{F} d_i}{F} \tag{8}$$

where the d_i indicates the delay of each data request node to receive the packet.

5.3 Experiment Results

The subsection focuses on two metrics, cache hit ratio and average content request delay, to evaluate this CSNI against LCE, LCD, Prob (0.3), Prob (0.5), Prob (0.7), and Betw strategy. By changing the parameters such as Zipf value, sending frequency, and the number of contents to observe the performance of different cache placement strategies on the two evaluation metrics. To better analyze the effect of a parameter on cache performance, this paper only changes a single variable while keeping other parameters fixed for the experiments, and the default values of other parameters are set as shown in Table 1.

5.3.1 Zipf Distribution Parameter Impact Analysis

In this section, we study the performance of seven caching strategies on two evaluation metrics, cache hit ratio and average request delay, under different values of the Zipf distribution parameter. In this set of experiments, the Zipf parameter takes values in the range of 0.7–1.3.

As shown in Fig. 4, the cache hit ratio of each caching method gradually increases as the Zipf value increases. The reason for this is that as the Zipf value gradually increases, user requests for data become concentrated and the differences between data begin to manifest. Prob randomly caches data with fixed probability, and when the cache capacity of satellite nodes is full, the data in satellite nodes are randomly replaced. Its cache hit ratio is higher than that of LCE, and the hit ratio of the low-probability caching strategy is better than that of the high-probability caching strategy. Throughout the cycle, the satellite nodes keep changing and LCD will experience constant wavering when caching content, so the hit ratio effect is the worst. Betw caches on the satellite nodes that pass through more shortest paths, its cache hit ratio is better than other strategies, but it does not consider the importance of adjacent nodes and its average content request delay is the highest.

Except for Betw, when the Zipf value gradually increases, the rest of the strategies involve all satellite nodes, and the data in the cache nodes can already satisfy most of the

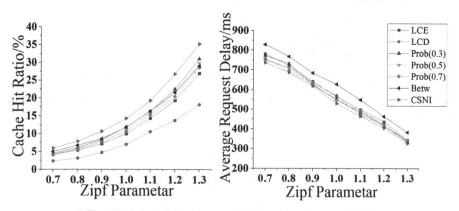

Fig. 4. Zipf value impact on cache hit ratio and request delay

requests, and the results obtained are more average. The LCE, LCD, and Prob strategies cache data closer to the node than the data request node, and their average content request delay is higher than the strategy proposed in this paper. CSNI caches data on satellite nodes with high importance in the cycle, and interest packets are maximally satisfied during propagation without having to request from data producer nodes, so the cache hit ratio and user request delay effects are better than other strategies.

5.3.2 Content Total Impact on Cache Performance

This section studies the performance of seven caching strategies on two evaluation metrics, cache hit ratio, and average request delay, for the different total numbers of cached contents. In this set of experiments, the total number of cached contents is taken in the range of 500–3500.

As shown in Fig. 5, the overall cache hit ratio of each caching strategy shows a decreasing trend as the amount of content in the network increases. The reason is that as the number of user-requested content in the network increases, the number of content blocks to be cached increases and the cache space of the nodes is limited, the probability of hitting a content request in the cache node decreases, resulting in weaker cache performance. CSNI considers the importance of cache node locations in the network structure. Cache nodes residing in more important impact locations have a higher probability of cache access, thus CSNI has a better cache hit ratio than other strategies.

Since as the total number of cached contents increases, the cached contents are continuously replaced. The data-requesting node needs to go to a distant cache node to get it when it initiates another request, and the average content request delay increases. Betw caches data content at nodes with high medium values, ignoring the importance of neighboring nodes, and has the worst effect on the average content request delay. LCE, LCD, and Prob strategies show a tendency to entangle with each other, with little difference in effect. When the total number of contents increases to 3500, the average request delay of CSNI increases to 585/ms, which is better than Betw (645/ms) by 6%.

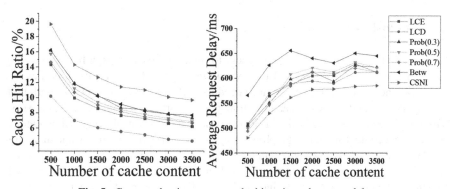

Fig. 5. Cun m value impact on cache hit ratio and request delay

5.3.3 Frequency of Requests on Cache Performance

This section studies the performance of seven caching strategies on two evaluation metrics, cache hit ratio and average request delay, at different request frequencies. In this set of experiments, the request frequency is taken in the range of 50–350.

As shown in Fig. 6, as the content request frequency increases, the average cache hit ratio of all caching strategies shows a decreasing trend. The reason is that when the content request frequency gradually increases, the number of requests sent by user nodes per second increases. At this time, the cached data in the cache nodes cannot meet the demand, the cache hit ratio gradually decreases, and the user request delay gradually increases. The cache hit ratio of the proposed caching strategy is better than several other caching strategies, followed by Betw, Prob, and LCE, and the worst performance is LCD. Betw has the highest request delay, the request delays of other strategies are relatively similar, and CSNI slightly outperforms the other strategies.

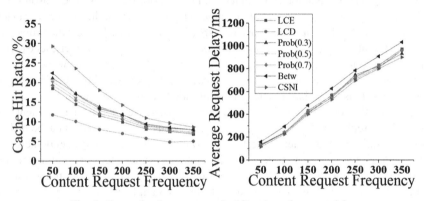

Fig. 6. Freq value impact on cache hit ratio and request delay

6   Conclusion

ICN could provide users with faster access to requested data through built-in caching functions, to reduce the impact of time variability on the data transmission efficiency of satellite networks. In this paper, we introduce ICN into satellite networks with high time-variability and propose a caching strategy for information center satellite networks based on the importance of nodes. The steady-state topology is obtained using a model combining a contact sequence graph with high characterization accuracy and an aggregation graph with low storage complexity. The local clustering coefficients, closeness centrality, and betweenness centrality of each content router are calculated and normalized under the steady-state graph, and then the total metric score of each content router is derived using weighting, and the cache is performed considering the heat of the cached content. Simulation experiments show that the proposed policy in this paper effectively improves the cache hit ratio and reduces the average request delay compared with LCE, LCD, Betw, and Prob.

References

1. Jia, X., Tao, L., Feng, H., et al.: Collaborative data downloading by using inter-satellite links in LEO satellite networks. IEEE Trans. Wireless Commun. **16**(3), 1523–1532 (2017)
2. Jing, R., Wen, Q., Westphal, C., et al.: MAGIC: a distributed MAx-Gain In-network Caching strategy in information-centric networks. In: IEEE INFOCOM 2014 - IEEE Conference on Computer Communications Workshops (INFOCOM WKSHPS). IEEE (2014)
3. Carvalho, I., Ishimori, A., Abelém, A.: A MultiCriteria Caching Decision for information-centric networks. In: International Conference on Information Networking. IEEE (2016)
4. Duan, J., Xing, Y., Zhao, G.: Survey for caching technologies in information-centric networking. Comput. Eng. Appl. **54**(2), 1–10 (2018)
5. Laoutaris, N., Syntila, S., Stavrakakis, I.: Meta algorithms for hierarchical Web caches. In: IEEE International Conference on Performance, Computing, and Communications. IEEE (2005)
6. Bernardini, C., Silverston, T., Festor, O.: A comparison of caching strategies for content-centric networking. In: Global Communications Conference. IEEE (2015)
7. Psaras, I., Chai, W.K., Pavlou, G.: Probabilistic in-network caching for information-centric networks. In: ACM SIGCOMM Workshop ICN, pp. 55–60 (2012)
8. Salvatore, D'Oro, Giacomo, et al.: SatCache: a profile-aware caching strategy for information-centric satellite networks. European Transactions on Telecommunications (2014)
9. Cola, T D., Gonzalez, G., Mujica, V.: Applicability of ICN-based network architectures to satellite-assisted emergency communications. In: Global Communications Conference. IEEE (2017)
10. Ji, X., Tian, S., Yating, Y., et al.: Research on data caching technology for multilayer satellite network. Manned Space **025**(004), 461–467 (2019)
11. Burt, R.S., Kilduff, M., Tasselli, S.: Social network analysis: foundations and frontiers on advantage. Annu. Rev. Psychol. **64**(1), 527–547 (2013)
12. Latora, V., Marchiori, M.: Efficient behavior of small-world networks. Phys. Rev. Lett. **87**(19), 198701 (2001)
13. Podlipnig, S., Boeszoermenyi, L.: A survey of Web cache replacement strategies. ACM Comput. Surv. **35**(4), 374–398 (2003)
14. Mastorakis, S., Afanasyev, A., Zhang, L.: On the evolution of ndnSIM: an open-source simulator for NDN experimentation. ACM SIGCOMM Comput. Commun. Rev. **47**(3), 19–33 (2017)
15. Paradells, J.: On the Energy Performance of Iridium Satellite IoT Technology. Sensors, 21 (2021)
16. Xiao, H., et al.: A Transcoding-Enabled 360° VR Video Caching and Delivery Framework for Edge-Enhanced Next-Generation Wireless Networks. IEEE J. Sel. Areas Commun. **40**(5), 1615–1631 (2022)
17. Zhang, W., et al.: Deep reinforcement learning based resource management for DNN inference in industrial IoT.IEEE Trans. Vehicular Technol. **70**(8), 7605–7618 (2021)
18. Basir, R., et al.: Energy efficient resource allocation in cache-enabled fog networks. Trans. Emerging Telecommun. Technol. **32**(11), e4343 (2021)
19. Cui, E., et al.: Learning-based deep neural network inference task offloading in multi-device and multi-server collaborative edge computing. Trans. Emerging Telecommun. Technol. **33**, e4485 (2022)

Intelligent Online Traffic Optimization Based on Deep Reinforcement Learning for Information-Centric Networks

Hongzhi Yu, Xingxin Qian, Guangyi Qin, Jing Ren, and Xiong Wang[✉]

University of Electronic Science and Technology of China, Chengdu, China
{202122010725,202122010713,202122010727}@std.uestc.edu.cn,
{renjing,wangxiong}@uestc.edu.cn

Abstract. The inherent features of the ICN architecture, such as in-network caching and content-awareness, facilitate traffic optimization. In the meantime, the maturity of deep learning and programmable networking technologies has paved the way for implementing intelligent and fine-grained online traffic optimization in ICN networks. In the paper, we first design an intelligent Online Traffic Optimization (iOTO) system for ICN networks, and then, based on the system, we propose an iOTO scheme, which consists of a deep reinforcement learning-based content-aware routing algorithm and a collaborative caching strategy. The simulation results show that our proposals significantly improve network performance in terms of average content fetching delay and load balance.

Keywords: Information centric networks · Traffic optimization · Deep reinforcement learning

1 Introduction

The current Internet was originally designed to share resources among network nodes. Therefore, it uses a host-centric network architecture, where a dedicated session is required to be established between resource consumer and provider, and each node in the network is identified by a unique IP address. The host-centric communication paradigm of the current Internet makes it very simple to connect new networks to the Internet, enabling a tremendous growth in its size over the past decades. However, the development of network technologies and the emergence of new applications pose new requirements for the Internet architecture, such as support for efficient content distribution, mobility, security, and so on. In order to fulfill these requirements, various patches have been developed for the Internet. However, those patches not only increase the complexity of the network, but also many emerging requirements cannot be fulfilled.

To adequately address the problems of the current Internet, several new architectures and paradigms are proposed for the future Internet. Among these proposals, Information-Centric Networking (ICN) [1,2] is a promising candidate

© The Author(s), under exclusive license to Springer Nature Singapore Pte Ltd. 2023
W. Quan (Ed.): ICENAT 2022, CCIS 1696, pp. 598–613, 2023.
https://doi.org/10.1007/978-981-19-9697-9_48

for the architecture of the future Internet. The communication paradigm of ICN shifts from a host-centric paradigm to a content-centric paradigm. In ICN networks, each content has a unique name, and the content consumers request the desired contents by their names. By naming content at the network layer, ICN enables the deployment of in-network caching and multicast mechanisms, thus significantly improving the content delivery efficiency of networks.

On the other hand, with the development of mobile devices and applications, such as smartphones, IoT devices, and popular multimedia applications (e.g., TikTok, Youtube, Netflix, and Wechat), the volume of network traffic has also been growing exponentially over the last decade. Moreover, future video and computer visualization advances (e.g., high-definition encoding, Augmented Reality, and Virtual Reality) will further increase the amount of traffic data [3]. To accommodate the rapidly increasing data traffic, one approach is to increase network capacity by replacing or upgrading network devices. However, this approach is constrained by limited capital expenditure (CAPEX), operational expenditure (OPEX), and spectrum resources. Therefore, increasing network capacity alone is insufficient to handle growing traffic data, and thus traffic optimization approaches running at the control plane also should be used.

Traffic optimization approaches can efficiently improve network resource utilization and guarantee the QoS of applications by optimizing traffic distribution in networks according to current network status and traffic patterns. In traditional networks, the traffic optimization objectives are realized by optimizing the routing strategies for traffic demands with various requirements. Due to the traffic uncertainty and practical network constraints, the traffic optimization problems are usually very hard to model and solve [4]. In ICN networks, the contents can be cached and evicted dynamically from network nodes, and the content requests can be forwarded to the original content provider or any of the cache nodes that store the content. This means that the network behaviors of ICN networks are more complex than current IP-based networks, which makes the traffic optimization problem in ICN networks more challenging.

Fortunately, with the breakthroughs of machine learning and the dramatic increase in computing power, Deep Reinforcement Learning (DRL) has been shown to be a promising way to handle dynamic and complicated non-linear modeling and optimization problems, such as caching optimization [5] and routing optimization [6]. As mentioned above, traffic optimization in ICN networks is a complex combinatorial optimization problem, which is hard to be modeled accurately as an optimization problem. Furthermore, traditional traffic optimization approaches rely on accurate traffic information, which varies dramatically over time and is hard to predict. On the other hand, DRL-based solution can learn optimal/suboptimal strategies from the varying environments. Moreover, DRL can make decisions timely so that DRL is suitable to online strategies. Therefore, in this paper, we propose an intelligent traffic optimization approach based on Deep Reinforcement Learning (DRL) for ICN networks. In addition, due to the architectural differences between ICN and the current network, the current network devices developed with ASICs cannot be seamlessly extended to support ICN data-plane functions. The emergence of fully programmable networking technologies, along with the availability of high-level programming languages such as P4 [7], now enables us to easily deploy new network architectures and network protocols. More importantly, the centralized control and global view of network status provided by the programmable control plane enable the timely collection of network status and traffic demands as the training or input data for AI-based control algorithms. Thus, the programmable networking technology paves the way for implementing AI-based traffic optimization. The main contributions of this paper are summarized as:

(1) We design an Intelligent Online Traffic Optimization (iOTO) system for ICN networks, which consists of network telemetry, routing decision, and caching decision modules, by leveraging the fine-grained and flexible control capabilities of programmable networks.
(2) We propose an intelligent online traffic optimization scheme that includes a DRL-based content-aware routing algorithm and a collaborative caching strategy to optimize traffic distribution under dynamic traffic patterns.
(3) To evaluate the performance of our proposed system and algorithm for the traffic optimization problem, we conduct extensive simulations in a variety of scenarios. The simulation results show that the proposed system and algorithm can achieve promising performance in terms of content fetching delay and load balance.

2   Related Work and Motivations

Traffic optimization is an important problem since it can improve network resource utilization efficiency and guarantee the QoS of applications without extra capital expenditure. In traditional IP networks, the traffic optimization objectives are mainly achieved by optimizing the routing strategies. Different from IP networks, the ICN networks can optimize the traffic distribution by implementing caching and routing optimization strategies.

Deploying efficient caching strategies can significantly reduce the traffic load and content fetching delays. Thus, the caching optimization problem in ICN has attracted much attention, and many well-known caching strategies, such as LCE [8], LCD [8], WAVE [9], RDM [10], PropCache [11], and so on, are proposed. LCE [8] copies the content at every node along the path. LCD [8] and WAVE [9] gradually move the frequently requested contents to the nodes closer to the content consumers. RDM [RDM] caches contents at a node with a fixed probability, and PropCache [11] improves it by computing a probability according to the available cache resource on the path. To improve caching performance, the authors in [12] propose several collaborative caching strategies. However, the communication and computation overheads are very high.

In ICN networks, content may be cached in multiple nodes. Therefore, content fetching delays and traffic congestion can be reduced by choosing optimal content sources and content delivery paths. This problem is also called the content-aware routing optimization problem. In some early works [13–15], the authors only considered the path selection problem with the knowledge of content metadata (e.g., content size and transmission rate). In these papers, the path selection problems are formulated as mathematical programming problems, and heuristic algorithms are proposed to solve them. The content-aware routing problem was first studied in [16], where the authors proposed a distributed routing algorithm based on reinforcement learning to discover alternative paths towards volatile copies of the requested content. Since the routing decision is made by each node independently, the performance of the proposed algorithm is unsatisfactory. Recently, a DRL-based algorithm for the content-aware routing problem is proposed in [17], where the authors assume that a content consumer can fetch content from multiple cache nodes simultaneously and arbitrary flow splitting is allowed. However, these assumptions may be hard to maintain in real networks.

In addition, the work in [18] also investigated the joint caching and routing problem, which is also called the cache-aware routing problem. In [18], the content placement schemes and routing strategies are jointly considered according to the exact known locations and sizes of contents. However, these approaches are considered unscalable due to their extremely high complexity. Therefore, [19] simplify the problem, and try to allocate resources at the service level, which inevitably causes performance losses.

In summary, the ICN networks provide a better handle to perform the traffic optimization problem. However, it also makes the traffic optimization problem more challenging. Traffic optimization in ICN networks is hard to be modeled accurately as a well-defined optimization problem due to traffic uncertainty. Fortunately, the breakthroughs in machine learning approaches and the emergence of programmable networking technology facilitate the implementation of finer-grained and online traffic optimization schemes in ICN networks. Specifically, DRL can adapt to varying environments and make decisions timely. Therefore, we investigate DRL-based online traffic optimization in programmable ICN networks in this paper. Compared with existing work, our work mainly has the following differences: (1) We design an online traffic optimization system based on programmable networking technology, which includes network telemetry, routing decision, and caching decision modules; (2) We propose a DRL-based content-aware routing algorithm, which can jointly optimize content source and path selections based on dynamic network status and traffic demands; and (3) To reduce complexity, we consider the caching optimization problem separately.

3 The Network Model and the Intelligent Online Traffic Optimization System

3.1 The Network Model

We consider an ICN network built on programmable hardware switches or Network Function Virtualization (NFV) entities, where the ICN-specific operations and components can be described in high-level programming languages (e.g., P4) [7]. In the control plane, there is a logically centralized network controller, which

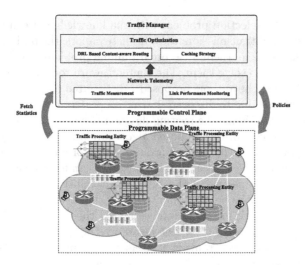

Fig. 1. The intelligent online traffic optimization system

is responsible for issuing runtime instructions and collecting network statistics using standard control protocols. The ICN network can be modeled as a graph $G(V, E)$, where $V = V_n \cup V_p$, V_n is the set of ICN nodes (either programmable hardware switches or virtualized NFV entities), and V_p is the set of content providers that are usually located in data centers. The cache capacity of an ICN node $v_n^i \in V_n$ is K_i. The E is the set of network links, and the bandwidth of the each link $l \in E$ is C_l. Let $O = \{o_1, o_2, ..., o_N\}$ denote the set of contents. We assume that each content provider has a subset of contents, and a content can reside at multiple content providers. Moreover, the contents can be cached at any of the nodes along the content delivery paths. Therefore, there might be multiple sources for each content o_i, each of which is capable of serving requests for the residing contents. We assume that the exact bandwidth requirement of each content is unknown and may vary over time. However, we can roughly divide the bandwidth requirement of a content into three categories: small, medium, and large according to the metadata of the content [22].

In this paper, we consider the online traffic optimization problem in programmable ICN networks, where the content requests arrive dynamically, and the network controllers need to select an appropriate source and calculate the content delivery path as well as the caching strategies when a content request arrives at the network. The optimization objective is to minimize the content fetching delay and balance the traffic loads on links. Since the traffic pattern is unknown and varies over time, the online traffic optimization problem is hardly formulated as a well-defined problem.

3.2 The Intelligent Online Traffic Optimization System

As shown in Fig. 1, the intelligent online traffic optimization system consists of a traffic manager and traffic processing entities, which are implemented on the control and data planes, respectively. The traffic manager runs on a logically centralized network controller and is responsible for calculating traffic optimization strategies according to the varying network status. There are two modules in the traffic manager: the network telemetry and traffic optimization modules. The network telemetry module provides the traffic measurements (e.g., content request frequencies, link loads, and flow sizes) and link performance metrics (link delays and loss rates) information for the traffic optimization module. The traffic optimization module mainly calculates the content-aware routing and caching strategies based on the information provided by the network telemetry module. In the next section, we will introduce the algorithms used in the traffic optimization module in detail.

Network telemetry is important for intelligent traffic optimization since it provides the necessary input information for traffic optimization. In the intelligent online traffic optimization system, the network telemetry module mainly performs the following tasks: generating telemetry strategies, sending telemetry configurations to traffic processing entities, and collecting telemetry results from programmable network nodes. To measure the traffic, we use the Count-Min Sketch (CM-Sketch) [20]. The CM-Sketch is a compact data structure consisting of $d \times w$ counters and d independent hash functions, each of which is associated with a row. When a request/data packet arrives, the CM-sketch performs an update operation, i.e., it computes d independent hash values using the content name extracted from the packet and updates the d counters corresponding to the hash values. The CM-Sketch only performs hashing and addition operations, so it can be easily implemented on programmable switches. The telemetry module periodically collects the CM-Sketch sketch data from network nodes and performs a query operation to get the required measurement results. The query operation first gets values of the d counters according to the hash values of the content name and then returns the minimum one. In addition, we use the link metric monitoring scheme proposed in our previous work to get the real-time link performance metrics [21]. The link metric monitoring scheme can also be easily implemented in programmable networks with low overhead. In this work, we mainly use it to monitor the real-time delays of links.

The traffic processing entity is actually a collection of runtime logic and rules, which are running on a programmable node. The CM-Sketch used to measure traffic and the rules used in the link performance metric monitor scheme are implemented in the traffic processing entities.

3.3   The Intelligent Online Traffic Optimization Scheme

In ICN networks, the traffic distribution is jointly determined by content source selection, routing, and caching strategies. However, jointly optimizing the content source selection, routing, and caching strategies makes the problem very complicated and hard to solve. Therefore, we first consider the joint optimization problem of content source selection and routing, which is also called the content-aware routing problem, and then, based on the obtained content-aware routing solution, we consider the caching strategy for each requested content. In this section, we will introduce algorithms for solving the two problems.

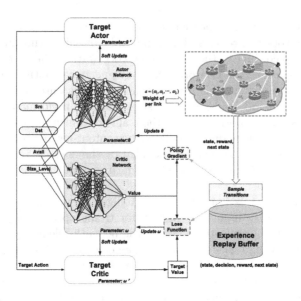

Fig. 2. The DRL-based content-aware routing algorithm

(1) The DRL-Based Content-Aware Routing Algorithm. Under the online traffic optimization scenario, the content-aware routing problem cannot be formulated as a well-defined problem due to the uncertainty factors of traffic and network status, and hence it cannot be solved by using traditional optimization tools. On the other hand, the RL has shown its effectiveness in complicated and real-time decision-making problems. RL can learn optimal behaviors/actions from the process of interacting with a dynamic and stochastic environment. Specifically, a RL learns the value function from experienced states and selects an action for the current state so as to maximize cumulative reward in the long term. The advent of deep learning significantly accelerates the progress in RL, with the use of deep learning techniques within RL defining the field of DRL. The DRL dramatically improves the state of the art in online decision-making problems, such as traffic control, caching optimization, and routing. In this work, we propose a DRL-based content-aware routing algorithm for ICN networks.

The content-aware routing problem jointly optimizes the content source and path selections, and it can also be viewed as a problem that calculates an appropriate path from the content consumer to any of the content sources in the network such that the traffic control objective is achieved. We first assume that content consumers usually fetch contents from the nearest content sources. Under this assumption, we can also adjust the content source and path selections by changing the link weights. It implies that the online content-aware routing problem can be converted to the online link weight optimization problem. Clearly, if we use a DRL-based algorithm to solve the problem, each action is a weight vector $W = (w_1, w_2, ..., w_L)$. Since the weight of a link is a positive real number, we apply the Deep Deterministic Policy Gradient (DDPG) learning algorithm.

As shown in Fig. 2, the DDPG is an actor-critic (AC) algorithm for deterministic policies. Four networks are embedded in the DDPG algorithm: Actor,

---

Algorithm 1. The DRL-based Content-aware Routing Algorithm

Input: The current state $s = (src, dst, avail, size)$

Output: Link weights $a = (\omega_1, \omega_2, \cdots, \omega_L)$ and $Q_{(s,a)}$

1: Randomly initialize critic network $Q(s, a|\theta^Q)$ and actor network $\mu(s|\omega^\mu)$ with weights θ^Q and ω^μ.

2: Initialize target network Q' and ω' with weights $\theta^{Q'} \leftarrow \theta^Q$, $\omega^{\mu'} \leftarrow \omega^\mu$

3: Initialize replay buffer

4: **for** episode=1,P **do**

5:    Initialize observation state $s_1 = (src_1, dst_1, avail_1, size_1)$

6:    **for** step=1,T **do**

7:       Select $a_t = (\omega_1, \omega_2, \cdots, \omega_L)$ according to the current policy and exploration noise

8:       Execute action a_t, and use the shortest path algorithm to acquire the routing strategy, then use **Algorithm 2** to optimize caching

9:       Calculate reward r_t and observe new state s_{t+1}
         $r_t = \eta_1 \cdot r_u + \eta_2 \cdot r_d$
         where, $r_u = -(a \cdot U_{\max})^2 + b$,
         $r_d = -C_1 \cdot \frac{\sum_{i=1}^M delay_f(i)}{M} + C_2$

10:      Store transition(s_t, a_t, r_t, s_{t+1}) in replay buffer

11:      Sample a random mini-batch of B transitions (s_i, a_i, r_i, s_{i+1}) from replay buffer
         Set $y_i = r_i + \gamma Q'(s_{i+1}, \mu'(s_{i+1} \mid \omega^{\mu'}) \mid \theta^{Q'})$

12:      Update the critic network by minimizing the loss:
         $Loss = \frac{1}{B} \sum_i \left(y_i - Q\left(s_i, a_i|\theta^Q\right)\right)^2$

13:      Update the actor network using the sampled policy gradient:
         $\nabla_{\omega^\mu} J \approx \frac{1}{B} \sum_i \nabla_a Q(s, a|\theta^Q)|_{s=s_i, a=\mu(s_i)} \nabla_{\omega^\mu} \mu(s|\omega^\mu)|_{s_i}$

14:      Update the target networks:
         $\theta^{Q'} \leftarrow \tau\theta^Q + (1-\tau)\theta^{Q'}$
         $\omega^{\mu'} \leftarrow \tau\omega^\mu + (1-\tau)\omega^{\mu'}$

15:   **end for**

16: **end for**

Target Actor, Critic, and Target Critic. The actor is the decision maker, and it will output an action at each step. And the critic will evaluate the return that the action obtains from the environment. The target networks are copies of the actor and critic networks. Training with the target networks will constrain the target value to change slowly so as to improve the stability of learning.

We leverage DDPG to generate an optimal content-aware routing strategy. As shown in Algorithm 1, the DDPG agent observes a state s_t at each step t. Based on the current state, we use actor network to generate the action a_t such that the critic network can calculate the action value $Q(s_t, a_t|\theta^Q)$. The environment executes the action a_t to obtain the next state s_{t+1} and the reward r_t. The transition tuple (s_t, a_t, r_t, s_{t+1}) will be stored in the replay buffer, and by sampling a random mini-batch of transitions, the loss function can be constructed. Since there is no terminal state for the online traffic optimization problem, we update the parameters after T content requests. T can not be too small otherwise the samples in the reply buffer will be sampled repeatedly many times. It also can not be too large, which will increase the training time. Using Bellman equation, we can get the formula:

$$y_t = r_t + \gamma Q'(s_{t+1}, \omega^{u'})|\theta^{Q'})$$ (1)

And the critic loss function is defined as:

$$Loss = \frac{1}{B}\Sigma_i\left(y_i - Q(s_i, a_i|\theta^Q)\right)$$ (2)

The critic network is updated by minimizing the critic loss. The actor is updated following the policy gradient:

$$\nabla_{\omega^\mu}J \approx \frac{1}{B}\sum_i \nabla_a Q(s_i, a_i|\theta^Q)|_{s=s_i, a=\mu(s_i)}\nabla_{\omega^\mu}\mu(s|\omega^\mu)|_{s_i}$$ (3)

As shown in Algorithm 1, the target actor network and the target critic network are the copies of the actor and critic networks, and the target network is updated by the soft update method:

$$\theta^Q \leftarrow \tau\theta^Q + (1 - \tau)\theta^{Q'}$$ (4)

$$\omega^\mu \leftarrow \tau\omega^\mu + (1 - \tau)\omega^{\mu'}$$ (5)

Input the loss value that is acquired by the below two formulas into the optimizer and fed back to the feed-forward neural network, the estimated action value will get closer to the target action value. In this way, the problem of content-aware routing is solved and the accuracy of training is improved.

We designed the state, action, and reward functions to enable the DDPG agent to perform content-aware routing optimization.

State: The state is composed of four components: the content consumer, the content sources, the link utilization, and the bandwidth requirement. The values of a state are set to the same order of magnitude to accelerate the convergence of the neural network. Formally, we define $s = (src, dst, avail, size)$ as the state vector. The src is a one-hot vector which represents the content consumer. The dst represents the content sources that have the requested content. And due to the caching capability of ICN networks, the sources for each requested content may not be unique. The $avail = (\mu_1, \mu_2, ... \mu_L)$ denotes the link utilization in the network. The $size$ denotes the bandwidth requirement of each content. As the exact bandwidth requirement of each content is unknown and may vary over time, we roughly divide bandwidth requirements into three categories and use 1, 2, 3 to represent small, medium and large bandwidth requirements.

Action: In our circumstance, the agent uses the state given by the environment to make routing decisions. As mentioned above, we convert the online content-aware routing problem into an online link weight optimization problem. Therefore, we can simply adjust the path selections by changing the link weights. Hence, we adopt the link weights as the output of the actor neural networks such that the shortest path algorithm can be applied to acquire the routing strategies. The action is defined as:

$$a = (\omega_1, \omega_2, \cdots, \omega_L) \tag{6}$$

where ω_l represents the l-th link weight, $l = 1, 2, \cdots, L$, and L represents the number of links in the network.

Reward: In this paper, two factors are taken into consideration when the reward is designed. The first factor is load balance, and the reward is defined as follows:

$$r_u = -(a \cdot U_{max})^2 + b \tag{7}$$

where U_{max} represents the maximum link utilization in the network and a, b are constants. The second factor is the content fetching delay. According to the M/M/1 queuing theory [23], the estimated theoretical delay of the l-th link can be calculated as:

$$D_l = \frac{1}{(\mu_l - \lambda_l)} = \frac{1}{\mu_l} \cdot \frac{1}{1 - \sigma_l} \tag{8}$$

where D_l represents the delay of l-th link, μ_l represents the service rate of l-th link, and σ_l is the link utilization.

The delay of the i-th request in the network is:

$$delay_f(i) = \sum_{l \in path_i}^{p} D_l \tag{9}$$

The average delay in the network is:

$$delay_n = \frac{\sum_{i=1}^{M} delay_f(i)}{M} \tag{10}$$

where M is the number of requests in the network at the current moment. And the reward aimed at improving the performance in term of delay is defined as follows:

$$r_d = -C_1 \cdot delay_n + C_2 \tag{11}$$

where C_1, C_2 are constants.

From what has been mentioned above, the reward used in the DDPG is a combination of the two rewards defined above.

$$r = \eta_1 \cdot \gamma_u + \eta_2 \cdot \gamma_d \tag{12}$$

where η_1, η_2 are constants.

Algorithm 2. The MCG Caching Strategy

Input: The set of nodes $(A = \{v_n^1 = s, v_n^2, ..., v_n^k = d\})$ on the path $p(s,d)$ of the requested content o_j, and the content request rates received by the nodes in set A

Output: The caching strategy for the requested content o_j

1: Let $h_j = 1$

2: **for** each node $v_n^i \in A$

3:    **if** the cache of node v_n^i is not full **then**

4:       Cache content o_j at node v_n^i

5:       Let $h_j = 1$

6:    **else**

7:       Calculate the gain of caching the content o_j at node v_n^i, $G_j = h_j \cdot q_j$, and the cost of replacing each content o_r from node v_n^i, $Cost_r = h_r \cdot q_r$

8:       Let $Cost_{min}$ be the minimum cost of replacing a content from node v_n^i

9:    **if** $G_j \geq Cost_{min}$ **then**

10:       Replace content o_r with o_j

11:       Let $h_j = 1$

12:    **else**

13:       Let $h_j = h_j + 1$

14: **end for**

---

(2) The Collaborative Caching Strategy. In addition to optimizing the content-aware routing, the network performance can be further improved by using efficient caching strategies. Therefore, based on the global information provided by programmable networking technology, we propose a collaborative in-network caching algorithm called Maximizing Caching Gain (MCG), which tries to cache the contents with the largest gains. The MCG strategy is calculated by the controller when the content-aware routing solution $p(s,d)$ is obtained, where s and d are the consumer and source of the requested content o_j, respectively. For ease of description, we let $A = \{v_n^1 = s, v_n^2, ..., v_n^k = d\}$ denote the set of nodes on the path $p(s,d)$.

The detailed procedures of MCG are shown in Algorithm 2. MCG examines each node in set A in the order v_n^{k-1} to v_n^1. For a node $v_n^i \in A$, MCG will directly store content o_j in v_n^i if it has available space, otherwise, MCG will make caching decision based on the gain of caching o_j at v_n^i and the minimum loss of replacing a content that is currently cached at v_n^i. Let h_j be the distance from current node v_n^i to the nearest upstream node caching the content o_j. Then the gain of caching o_j at node v_n^i is defined as $G_j = h_j \cdot q_j$, where q_j is the request rate for content o_j at node v_n^i. Similarly, the cost of replacing a content o_r from a node v_n^i is defined as $Cost_r = h_r \cdot q_r$, where h_r is the distance between the node v_n^i and the nearest content provider. Then MCG will choose the content with the least cost to replace if $G_j \geq Cost_{min}$.

4 The Performance Evaluation

4.1 Simulation Settings

To evaluate the performance of the proposed online traffic optimization algorithms, we develop an even-driven network simulator with Python 3.6.15 and PyTorch 1.10.2. All the simulations run on a server with two A5000 GPUs, two CPUs, and 256 GB of memory. We use the GEANT topology (40 nodes and 61 edges), and the capacity of each link is randomly set from 50 Mbps to 100 Mbps.

In our simulations, the number of contents is set to 10^4, and the contents are originally hosted on three providers located in datacenters. The content requests arrive and leave the network dynamically, and both inter arrival time and service time follows the negative exponential distribution. We assume that the popularity of contents follows the Zipf distribution with the skewness parameter $\alpha = 1$. Each ICN node can cache up to 1% of all contents, i.e., 100 contents. The bandwidth requirement of each content is a random value between 1Mbps and 20Mbps, and the bandwidth requirement of each content is divided into three categories: small (1–5 Mbps), medium (5–15 Mbps), and large (15–20 Mbps) according to the metadata of the content [22].

As shown in Fig. 2, the DDPG model has an actor network and a critic network, and the input of the two networks is a 4-tuple $(Src, Dst, Avail, Size)$. The input layer of the actor and critic networks is connected to two fully-connected hidden layers, each of which has 256 neurons. In the hidden layer, we use the ReLU as the activation function in the critic and actor networks. Besides, the Sigmoid activation function is used in the output layer of the actor network. Based on empirical studies, discount factors, learning rates, and batch sizes for training two networks are set to 0.9, 5×10^{-5}, and 256, respectively.

In the simulations, we generate content requests dynamically and use the algorithms to make decisions as requests arrive. We compare the performance of different algorithms in terms of the maximum link utilization and the average content fetching delay.

4.2   Simulation Results

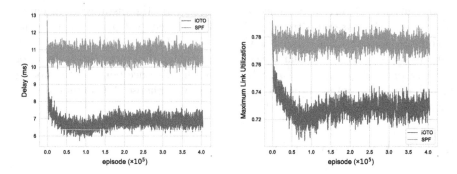

Fig. 3. The performance of iOTO and SPF in terms of delay and load balance

We compared our proposed iOTO scheme with the widely used Shortest Path First (SPF) scheme. The SPF selects the nearest content source to fetch content and uses the shortest path to deliver content. To fairly compare, we assume both iOTO and SPF use the MCG caching strategy. We evaluate the performance of iOTO and SPF under different traffic loads. Figure 3 shows the performance of iOTO and SPF in terms of average content fetching delay (delay for short) and Maximum Link Utilization (MLU) under heavy traffic load. The MLU is a widely used metric for traffic load balancing. We can observe that as the number of episodes increases, the MLU and delay of iOTO decrease quickly. It means that the iOTO can efficiently learn optimal online traffic optimization strategies from the interactions with varying network environments. We can also note that when iOTO converges, iOTO performs much better than SPF in terms of delay and MLU. Specifically, compared with SPF, iOTO can reduce the delay by more than 40%. Moreover, we can see that the delay and MLU are fluctuating over time. This is because the state of the network is constantly varying. When the traffic load is low, the performance gap between iOTO and SPF will be reduced, but iOTO still performs significantly better than SPF. Due to space limitations, we do not show the result here.

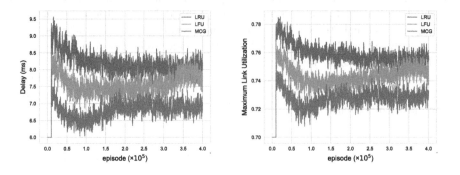

Fig. 4. The performance of iOTO under different caching strategies

Figure 4 shows the performance of iOTO under different caching strategies, including LRU, LFU, and MCG. From Fig. 4, we can see that MCG's performance is significantly better than traditional LRU and LFU. For example, the performance gain of MCG over LRU in the aspect of delay can be up to 20%. The reason is that MCG makes optimal caching decisions based on the global information provided by programming network technology. The results in Fig. 4 also show that the caching strategies of ICN have a great impact on the traffic optimization performance.

To evaluate the performance of iOTO under varying traffic loads, we compare the iOTO scheme with SPF under a 24-h traffic varying model [24] in Fig. 5. The results in Fig. 5 verify that the iOTO can capture the traffic variations and adaptively adjust the traffic optimization strategies according to them. We also observe that the iOTO also significantly outperforms the SPF under all traffic loads.

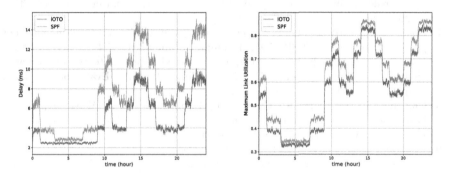

Fig. 5. The performance of iOTO under different traffic loads

5   Conclusion

In this work, we studied the iOTO problem in ICN networks. Specifically, we designed an iOTO system based on the programmable networking technology and propose an iOTO scheme, which can learn optimal content-aware routing strategies and calculate collaborative caching strategy according to the varying network state and traffic pattern. The simulation results demonstrate that the proposed iOTO system and scheme can efficiently optimize the traffic distribution and improve network performance in terms of average content fetching delay and load balance.

Acknowledgement. This work is supported by the Open Research Projects of Zhejiang Lab (No. 2022QA0AB01) and NSFC Fund (62072079, 62001087, U20A20156).

References

1. Zhang, L., Afanasyev, A., Burke, J., et al.: Named data networking. **44**(3), 66–73 (2014)
2. Raychaudhuri, D., Nagraja, K., Venkataramani, A.: MobilityFirst: a robust and trustworthy mobility-centric architecture for the future Internet. ACM SIGMO-BILE Mob. Comput. Commun. Rev. **16**(3), 2–13 (2012)
3. Index, C.V.N.: Global mobile data traffic forecast update, 2016–2022 White paper. Cisco, San Jose (2021)
4. Li, J., Luo, H., Zhang, S., Yu, S., Wolf, T.: Traffic engineering in information-centric networking: opportunities, solutions and challenges. IEEE Commun. Mag. **56**(11), 124–130 (2018)
5. Sadeghi, A., Sheikholeslami, F., Giannakis, G.B.: Optimal and scalable caching for 5G using reinforcement learning of space-time popularities. IEEE J. Sel. Top. Sig. Process. **12**(1), 180–190 (2017)
6. Chen, Y., Rezapour, A., Tzeng, W., Tsai, S.: RL-routing: an SDN routing algorithm based on deep reinforcement learning. IEEE Trans. Netw. Sci. Eng. **7**(4), 3185–3199 (2020)
7. Bosshart, P., Daly, D., Gibb, G., et al.: P4: programming protocol-independent packet processors. ACM SIGCOMM Comput. Commun. Rev. **44**(3), 87–95 (2014)
8. Garetto, M., Leonardi, E., Martina, V.: A unified approach to the performance analysis of caching systems. ACM Trans. Model. Perform. Eval. Comput. Syst. **1**(3), 1–28 (2016)
9. Cho, K., Lee, M., Park, K., Kwon, T.T., Choi, Y., Pack, S.: Wave: popularity-based and collaborative in-network caching for content-oriented networks. In: IEEE INFOCOM Workshops, pp. 316–321 (2012)
10. Chai, W.K., He, D., Psaras, I., Pavlou, G.: Cache "less for more" in information-centric networks. In: International Conference on Research in Networking 2012, pp. 27–40 (2012)
11. Chai Psaras, W.K., Pavlou, G.: Probabilistic in-network caching for information-centric networks. In: ACM SIGCOMM Workshop on ICN (2012)
12. Sourlas, V., Gkatzikis, L., Flegkas, P., Tassiulas, L.: Distributed cache management in Information-centric networks. IEEE Trans. Netw. Serv. Mang. **10**(3), 286–299 (2013)
13. Su, K., Westphal, C.: On the benefits of information centric networks for traffic engineering. In: IEEE ICC (2014)
14. Chanda, A., Westphal, C., Raychaudhuri, D.: Content based traffic engineering in software defined information centric Networks. In: IEEE INFOCOM 2013 Workshop on Emerging Design Choices in Name-Oriented Networking, pp. 357–62 (2013)
15. Avci, S.N., Westphal, C.: A content-based traffic engineering policy for information-centric networks. In: IEEE CCNC (2016)
16. Bastos, I.V., Moraes, I.M.: A forwarding strategy based on reinforcement learning for content-centric networking. IN: International Conference on the Network of Future (2016)
17. Zhang, Q., Wang, X., Lv, J., Huang, M.: Intelligent content-aware traffic engineering for SDN: an AI driven approach. IEEE Netw. **34**(3), 186–193 (2020)
18. Sourlas, V., Flegkas, P., Georgatsos, P., Tassiulas, L.: Cache-aware traffic engineering in information centric networks. In: IEEE CAMAD (2014)
19. Zhang, S., Ravindran, R., Wang, G., Mukherjee, B.: Service-centric traffic engineering and cache orchestration in an ICN-enabled network. In: IEEE CCNC (2014)

20. Cormode, G., Muthukrishnan, S.: An improved data stream summary: the count-min sketch and its applications. J. Algorithms **55**(1), 58–75 (2005)
21. Wang, X., Malboubi, M., Pan, Z., et al.: ProgLIMI: programmable link metric identification in software-defined networks. IEEE/ACM Trans. Netw. **26**(5), 2376–2389 (2018)
22. Luo, H., Xu, Y., Xie, W., et al.: A framework for integrating content characteristics into the future Internet architecture. IEEE Netw. **31**(3), 21–28 (2017)
23. Pioro, M., Mehdi, D.: Routing, Flow, and Capacity Design in Communication and Computer Networks. Morgan Kaufmann, Burlington (2004)
24. Traffic statistics collected by Baidu. https://mr.baidu.com/r/LKeZhqDJ3a?f=cp&u=bbe741d5389b05c3

Detection and Defense Schemes for Cache Pollution Attack in Content-Centric Network

Yang Cao[1]($\boxtimes$), Disheng Wu[1], Mingrui Hu[1], and Shu Chen[2]

[1] School of Electronic Information and Communication, Huazhong University of Science and Technology, Wuhan, Hubei, China
{ycao,dishengwu}@hust.edu.cn
[2] Department of Cardiovascular, Union Hospital, Tongji Medical College, Huangzhong University of Science and Technology, Wuhan, Hubei, China
shu_chen@hust.edu.cn

Abstract. Cache pollution attack is a security problem of cache in Content-Centric Network (CCN). Cache pollution attacks include False Locality Attack (FLA) and Location Disruption Attack (LDA). This paper mainly considers FLA attacks, and cache pollution attacks mentioned in this paper are also referred to FLA attacks. Cache pollution attack mainly refers to the malicious user by a large number of requests for some unpopular content, mislead the network cache node to cache these unpopular content, seriously affect the cache efficiency of CCN. In actual network applications, there may be a large amount of content accessed in a short time, that is, Flash Crowd event. Such legitimate events may also be blocked by the defense system. Therefore, it is necessary to design effective attack detection and defense schemes against cache pollution attack. This paper is mainly carried out from the following aspects: firstly, the difference between FLA attack and Flash Crowd event is discussed, and then attack detection and defense schemes based on user behavior and network parameters is introduced. Finally, ndnSIM is used for simulation experiment, and compared with other algorithms.

Keywords: CCN · FLA · Attack detection · Attack defense

1 Introduction

Content-Centric Network (CCN) is an emerging networking paradigm being considered as a possible replacement for the current IP-based host-centric Internet infrastructure. CCN focuses on content distribution, which is arguably not well served by IP. However, its unique network architecture is prone to security problems, such as cache-based Distributed Denial of Service (DDoS) attacks. Cache-based DDoS attack refers to that malicious user sends a large number of interest packets to the network in a short period of time to request the unpopular content, which makes the content appear to be popular, thus deceiving the CCN routing node to cache the unpopular content and destroying the cache balance.

W. Quan (Ed.): ICENAT 2022, CCIS 1696, pp. 614–629, 2023.
https://doi.org/10.1007/978-981-19-9697-9_49

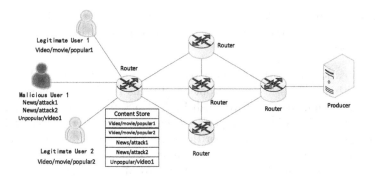

Fig. 1. FLA attack scenario.

There are two types of cache-based DDoS attacks in CCN networks [1]: Location Disruption Attack (LDA) and False Locality Attack (FLA).

FLA attack is caused by malicious users accessing a certain type of network resources with low popularity in large quantities, as shown in Fig. 1. According to the working mechanism of CCN routing node, when a large number of requests are made for these low-popularity content in a short time, the routing node will mistake these requests from malicious users as popular content and cache them in Content Store (CS) for a long time, while the really popular content cannot be cached. The impact of the attack is as follows: limited cache resources are occupied, the cache hit ratio of legitimate users is reduced, the latency of content acquisition is increased, and user experience is affected. Unlike FLA attacks, Flash Crowd events are caused by legitimate users suddenly accessing a large amount of content in a short period of time, so the sudden change in traffic seen by users does not necessarily represent a cyber attack. The mechanism of cache and route aggregation in CCN network itself is helpful to alleviate the impact of Flash Crowd event on the network. However, due to the similarity between FLA attack and Flash Crowd event, the existing research schemes do not consider Flash Crowd event when detecting FLA attack. Therefore, blindly taking measures to cope with the emergent event flow will cause the request of legitimate users to be affected. For example, LMDA scheme adopts traditional statistical strategy to detect attacks according to the change of content request rate [2]. The DDCPC scheme considers two time-dependent characteristics: the same content request rate and the same content request interval [3].

This paper will focus on the following two research questions:

(1) How to distinguish FLA attack from Flash Crowd event in attack detection?
(2) How to design an efficient FLA attack detection scheme to maintain a good detection performance in the presence of Flash Crowd events?

In order to accurately detect FLA attacks, it is necessary to distinguish FLA attacks and Flash Crowd events. and the following contributions are proposed in this paper:

(1) Investigation shows that support vector machine (SVM) algorithm performs well in binary classification problems. In this paper, SVM is selected as a computational tool, to distinguish FLA attack from Flash Crowd event. It is known that SVM is a supervised learning model, which classifies data through relevant learning algorithms, and is widely used in many fields, such as medicine, industry and communication.
(2) Under the premise of considering Flash Crowd event, in order to accurately detect FLA attack, this paper designs a cache pollution attack detection scheme based on user behavior and network parameters by using the difference between user request behavior and network parameters, and takes defense measures against the detection results.

The reminder of this paper is organized as follows: Sect. 2 reviews the related work presented in previous papers. In Sect. 3, we describe the system design. In Sect. 4, the detection and defense schemes of cache pollution attack are introduced. Section 5 presents the results of the system simulation. Finally, the paper is concluded in Sect. 6.

2   Related Work

Literature [4] believes that content requests from legitimate users generally obey power-law distribution (Mandelbrot Zipf, MZipf), and CCN routing will cache content with high popularity. In view of the FLA attack, existing research strategies are mainly based on the interest packet request difference between legitimate users and attacking users to detect and defend against FLA attack, such as request prefix difference, request rate change, request path diversity and popularity difference. Literature [5] proposes a cache placement strategy based on content popularity and node location. Nodes in the network only cache popular content, but this strategy does not have a good effect on FLA attack mitigation. In literature [6], a cache placement strategy is proposed, which uses the output results of neural network and fuzzy inference system to judge whether the request is legitimate, but the algorithm complexity is very high. Literature [7] uses the prefix of interest packet name to detect attacks, considering that malicious users send the same prefix of interest packet, and uses the difference between attack traffic and normal traffic to detect attacks. It is pointed out in literature [8] that although malicious users can send the same number of requests as normal users in a short period of time, they cannot be distributed in each location of the network like normal users. An FLA attack detection and defense scheme based on the diversity of interest packet forwarding paths is proposed. In literature [9] and [10], malicious requests are detected by calculating the average request rate change of each prefix. However, in literature [9], only attacks can be detected and no defense measures are taken. In literature [11], the author selects nodes close to users as monitoring nodes, and uses the monitoring nodes to calculate the request rate and cache hit rate to detect attacks. In literature [12], the author extracted four parameters related to node state to establish a fuzzy hierarchical structure model, and set the threshold of attack detection by observing the impact degree of attacks. In literature [13], gray level prediction is proposed to solve FLA attack, and the predicted popularity is compared with the real popularity of the network, and FLA attack is detected by the difference between them. In literature [14], the author proposed an FLA attack defense scheme based on reinforcement learning, which uses the trained agent to determine whether to cache data packets according to the data request delay, and the agent can adapt to the network state. Literature [3] proposes a scheme based on the popularity of content requests, which uses the same content request rate and the interval of two consecutive requests to detect attacks according to the clustering results. However, this scheme has a high misjudgment in the face of Flash Crowd events.

3   System Design

Before designing the system, we have two observations as follows.

Observation(1): It is difficult for malicious users to be as ubiquitous as normal users in almost every interface of edge routing nodes.

Taking Code Red, a virus with fast transmission speed and wide range as an example, it is found by simulation verification that the infection probability of this virus is very low, which is maintained at 8.4×10^{-5}, and 3.6×10^5 hosts can be controlled among 2^{32} hosts from different locations. By analogy with this virus, it can be seen that because the attacker needs a certain cost to launch an attack, it is generally believed that the attacker cannot control the host in the entire network within the range of its computing and control capabilities.

Observation(2): There are no geographic differences in user requests for popular content.

Users from different countries or different cultural backgrounds have obvious differences in their requests for popular content, but users with the same cultural background have virtually no differences in their requests for popular content. The results show that when users in one community request a certain kind of popular content, the popular content will also be requested in other communities. Users' requests for the truly popular content come from all over the network, so there is no local regional difference in users' requests for popular content.

Flash Crowd events and FLA attacks both increase the number of interest packets requested in the network. However, from Observation(1), it can be seen that the number of malicious FLA attackers is limited, and it is difficult to cover almost every interface of edge routing nodes like legitimate users. In

Table 1. The difference between an FLA attack and a Flash Crowd event

Difference	FLA attack	Flash crowd event
Number of interest packets in the network	Increase	Increase
Number of requesters	Less	More
Distribution of requesters	Small part interface	Almost every interface
Core network traffic	Increase	Remain
Cache hit ratio of legitimate users	Less	More

CCN network, the same interest packet requests from different interfaces will be aggregated by Pending Interest Table (PIT) of edge routing nodes. Each routing node only forwards one interest packet request upstream before PIT entry expires, and the response packet is cached in the edge routing node during the return process to respond to subsequent interest packet requests. In Flash Crowd event, the cache space of the routing node is occupied by popular content, and a large number of interest packets from legitimate users will be hit at the edge side routing node, thus reducing the core network traffic. In the FLA attack, however, the routing node cache space is occupied by a low popularity of content, from attacking side of legitimate users interested in package request cannot cache node to obtain the required content, from the edges of the cache hit ratio is reduced, at the edge of the routing node legitimate users interested in package request are forwarded to the upstream node, which resulted in increased core network flow.

To sum up, the difference between FLA attack and Flash Crowd event is shown in Table 1. It can be seen from Table 1 that there are differences in user request behavior and network parameters between FLA attack and Flash Crowd event.

Based on the analysis of the difference between FLA attack and Flash Crowd event request, we design a system that classifies the received interest packet request by SVM based on the behavior of user request interest packet and the change of network parameters before and after the attack, detects malicious interest request, and defends based on the detection result.

The designed system in this paper aims to detect cache pollution attacks more accurately (maintaining a high detection rate even when Flash Crowd events are encountered), and immediately initiate defense measures to mitigate the impact of attacks on the basis of detected attack requests. As shown in Fig. 2, the proposed detection and defense framework mainly consists of two modules: cache pollution attack detection module and defense module. In the detection phase, for the received interest packets, the standard deviation of the request rate of the same content, the distribution of interface requests of the same content and the change of cache hit ratio of edge routing nodes are calculated. The trained SVM model is used to make binary prediction for the received interest packets to judge whether it is a legitimate request or a suspicious request. In the defense phase, if the content c_k is judged as suspicious for consecutive ε time slots, the interest packet of request content c_k is considered as an attack request,

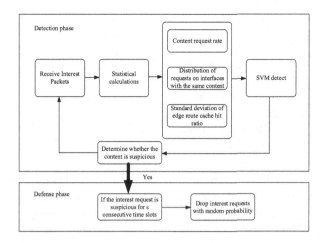

Fig. 2. Cache pollution attack detection and defense framework.

and then defense measures are taken to add content c_k to the blacklist. And in the following several time slots, the interest packet of the requested content c_k is discarded with a certain probability.

In CCN network, interest packet requests from legitimate users follow the MZipf distribution. It is generally believed that the popularity of content increases with the increase of the requested frequency. In this paper, MZipf distribution modeling is used to analyze the popularity of requested content in the network. In the MZipf distribution model, if the popularity ranking of a certain content is r, $p(r)$ represents the occurrence frequency of the content ranked as r, which mostly refers to the popularity of the content, and $p(r)$ represents as

$$p(r) = \frac{\dfrac{1}{(r+q)^s}}{\sum_i \dfrac{1}{(r+q)^s}} \tag{1}$$

q indicates the popularity of top content, and the value of q is greater than 0. s represents the decay rate of content popularity as the ranking increases, and s is greater than 0. When s is larger, the curve will be steeper, indicating that the distribution of popular content is more concentrated. The larger the q, the flatter the curve. The main notations covered in this paper are shown in Table 2.

4   Detection and Defense Schemes

4.1   Characteristic Parameter Calculation

In this subsection, three features, namely request rate of the same content, request distribution of each interface of the same content and standard deviation of cache hit ratio variation of edge routing node, are considered. This section mainly explains and calculates the selected feature parameters.

Table 2. Important symbols and descriptions

Symbols	Descriptions
C	Collection of requested content
c_k	The k'th content block
M	Number of interfaces
N	Number of edge routing nodes
j	The j'th routing interface
n	The n'th edge routing node
τ	Time slot
$n_j(c_k)$	Number of content c_k requested by the j'th interface of route n
$n(c_k)$	The total number of content c_k requested by all interfaces
$E(n(c_k))$	The average number of requests for content c_k across all interfaces
$E(h(\tau))$	Mean value of hit ratio change of all edge routing nodes
$p_\tau(c_k)$	The request rate for content c_k
$q_\tau(c_k)$	Variance of the amount of content c_k requested by each interface
$h(\tau)$	Standard deviation of cache hit ratio change of edge routing node

(1) Description of Characteristic Parameters

Regardless of FLA attack or Flash Crowd event, the number of requested content c_k in the current time slot will increase sharply, and the content c_k request rate will increase. In contrast, Flash Crowd events are caused by some sudden events caused by a large number of requests from legitimate users across the network. This situation causes a sharp increase in traffic to all edge routing nodes across the network, and this content is secure and popular. However, in FLA attack, malicious interest packet requests are sent by malicious users. Although malicious users can send interest packets similar to the number of popular content requested by normal users by increasing the sending rate of interest packets, the number of malicious users is small, and it is impossible for them to be almost everywhere in every interface of the whole network like legitimate users. Therefore, this paper introduces the feature of interface request distribution of the same content in the entire network to distinguish FLA attack from Flash Crowd event.

In addition, due to the special in-network caching and routing forwarding mechanism of CCN network, the content requested by high frequency in the network will be cached in the edge routing nodes. When Flash Crowd event occurs, the cache hit ratio in all edge nodes will be increased. However, when FLA attack occurs, only the cache hit ratio of edge nodes on the attack side will be improved. Therefore, this paper introduces the standard deviation of the cache hit ratio of edge nodes to distinguish FLA attack from Flash Crowd event.

(2) Calculation of characteristic parameters

① Request rate of the same content

Within a time slot τ, the content c_k request rate is denoted as $p_\tau(c_k)$, $p_\tau(c_k)$ represents the proportion of the total number of contents c_k requested by all interfaces $n(c_k)$ to the total number of requested contents in the time slot, which reflects the popularity of content requests. The higher the request rate, the higher the popularity of content. $p_\tau(c_k)$ is expressed as

$$p_\tau(c_k) = \frac{n(c_k)}{\sum_{k \in C} n(c_k)} \tag{2}$$

where C represents the content set requested by users within time slot τ. The total number of contents c_k requested by all interfaces is denoted as $n(c_k)$, $n(c_k)$ is expressed as

$$n(c_k) = \sum_{j=1}^{M} n_j(c_k) \tag{3}$$

where M represents the total number of interfaces, and $n_j(c_k)$ represents the number of requested content c_k by interface j.

② Distribution of requests on interfaces with the same content

The distribution of interface requests for the same content is represented by the variance of c_k quantity of interface requests. Within a time slot τ, the variance of the quantity of c_k requested by each interface is denoted as $q_\tau(c_k)$, which reflects the difference of the quantity of c_k requested by each interface. The larger its value is, the more obvious the difference of the quantity of c_k requested by each interface is. $q_\tau(c_k)$ are represented as

$$q_\tau(c_k) = \sum_{j=1}^{M} (n_j(c_k) - E(n(c_k)))^2 \tag{4}$$

M indicates the number of interfaces. $E(n(c_k))$ is the mean value of the number of contents c_k requested by M interfaces, and $E(n(c_k))$ is

$$E(n(c_k)) = \frac{1}{M} \sum_{j=1}^{M} n_j(c_k) \tag{5}$$

③ Standard deviation of cache hit ratio change of edge routing node

Between time slot $\tau - 1$ and τ, the standard deviation of cache hit ratio change of edge routing node is denoted as $h(\tau)$, which reflects the attack degree. The larger its value is, the more serious the attack is. $h(\tau)$ is expressed as

$$h(\tau) = \sqrt{\frac{1}{N} \sum_{n=1}^{N} (h_n(\tau) - h_n(\tau - 1) - E(h(\tau)))^2} \tag{6}$$

where N indicates the number of edge routing nodes. $h_n(\tau)$ and $h_n(\tau - 1)$ represent the legitimate user cache hit ratio of routing node n in time slot τ and $\tau - 1$, respectively. $E(h(\tau))$ is the mean value of hit ratio change of N edge routes between time slot $\tau - 1$ and τ, and $E(h(\tau))$ is

$$E(h(\tau)) = \frac{1}{N} \sum_{n=1}^{N} (h_n(\tau) - h_n(\tau - 1)) \qquad (7)$$

4.2 Detection Scheme

The principle of the attack detection scheme proposed in this paper is described as follows:

(1) Once receive interest packet which is requested by a user, routing node starts to make statistical calculation on the interest packet. The statistical content includes: the total number of interest packets requested by all users within the time slot, the request rate of the same content, the difference of the requests number of each interface and edge routing nodes cache hit ratio change.
(2) Based on the three characteristic parameters of request rate of the same content, request distribution of each interface of the same content, and standard deviation of cache hit rate change of edge routing node, the trained SVM model was used to periodically predict the binary classification of all the received interest content.
(3) When the prediction result is 1, the content can be judged as suspicious and added to the suspicious list S_τ; Otherwise, the request is considered normal.
(4) If content c_k is judged as suspicious for ε consecutive time slots, content c_k is considered as attack content and is added to blacklist B_τ.

4.3 Defense Scheme

Because FLA detection scheme has a certain false detection rate, if the detected content is discarded directly, the experience quality of legitimate users will be reduced. In this subsection, the random discarding strategy is considered. If the discarding probability is too small, it may not be able to produce effective defense against attacks. Therefore, random probability values ranging from 0.5 to 1.0 are used for discarding.

Once blacklist B_τ is obtained, the request of interest packet arriving in each time slot is processed as follows: Firstly, check whether the content name already exists on the blacklist B_τ. If it exists, it is directly discarded with random probability. If it does not exist, interest requests are allowed to enter the network, and analyzed and processed according to the normal process.

It is worth mentioning that existing research works only add the attack content to the suspicious list after detecting it. Therefore, regardless of legitimate content or attack content, in its corresponding scheme, each interest packet will be forwarded, but the attacked content will not be cached in the return process. In this case, the popular content requested by the user is easily judged as attack content, so the real popular content can not be cached, and finally the advantage of CCN cache can not be highlighted. Therefore, it is important to consider the impact of Flash Crowd event on the network when designing cache pollution attack detection and defense scheme. At the beginning of the design, the scheme in this paper has fully considered the Flash Crowd event. Even in the face of Flash Crowd event, the scheme in this paper can still maintain a good effect.

5   Simulation and Analysis

This section is mainly carried out from the following aspects: First, the simulation environment and simulation parameters are introduced. Then, the detection performance of cache pollution attack is compared from various aspects and the robustness of the proposed scheme in dealing with Flash Crowd events is verified.

5.1   Simulation Environment

In order to evaluate the performance of the proposed scheme, ndnSIM is used to carry out experiments. In the simulation experiment, the link bandwidth is set to 10 Mbps, the number of requested content types is set to 10000, and the volume size of each content is 1 MB. The size of CS is 100 MB, which means that it can cache up to 100 packets, and PIT can cache up to 11,000 entries of interest packets. The interest packet request rate of legitimate users is 3000 interest packets/s, and user requests follow the MZipf distribution, and set $q = 10$ and $s = 0.7$. The link delay between nodes is 5 ms. When the cache space of the routing node is full, the classical Least Recently Used (LRU) cache replacement strategy is used.

For a more realistic network, the common topology XC (XY-complex) and DFN (German Research Network) are used in this paper. XC and DFN topology have been widely used in numerous CCN/NDN related studies, which can provide a basis for evaluating the performance of the proposed scheme in this subsection. XC stands for small network with 19 network nodes, while DFN stands for medium network with 52 network nodes. There are five types of nodes in the topology: legitimate users, malicious users, content providers, edge routing nodes and core routing nodes. The DFN topology is shown in Fig. 3.

5.2   Evaluation Indicators

In order to verify the performance, the proposed scheme is compared with the classical scheme LMDA based on request rate variation and DDCPC based on clustering. The comparison scheme is described as follows:

(1) LMDA: This scheme is a traditional statistics-based scheme, which detects attacks through changes in content request rate.
(2) DDCPC: This scheme uses the characteristics of the same content request rate and the time interval between two consecutive requests for the same content to detect attacks by clustering algorithm.

In the simulation, the evaluation indicators used in this paper mainly include correct detection rate and false detection rate, which are introduced as follows:

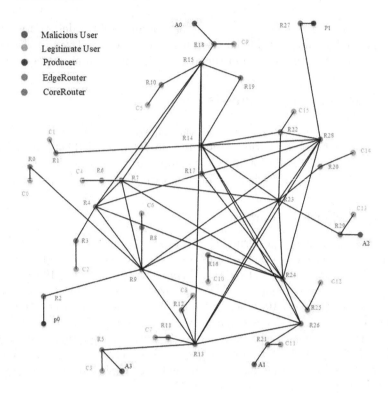

Fig. 3. DFN topology.

(1) Correct detection rate: The proportion of correctly detected requests (including legitimate interest packet requests and malicious interest packet requests) to all data requests.

(2) False detection rate: The proportion of the number of legitimate interest packet requests that are detected as malicious interest packet requests to the number of all legitimate interest packet requests.

(3) Attack intensity: the ratio of the rate at which malicious users send interest packets to legitimate users. In this paper, the request rate of legitimate users is 3000 interest packets/s. The request rate of malicious users can be determined according to the attack intensity value of malicious users.

(4) Attack range: Specifies the number of types of content attacked by malicious users.

5.3   Cache Pollution Attack Detection Experiment and Analysis

In this subsection, in order to verify the detection performance, the proposed scheme is compared with DDCPC and LMDA schemes, and the evaluation indexes are correct detection rate and false detection rate. This subsection will verify the detection performance of the proposed scheme from two aspects:

(1) Consider only FLA attack, that is, a small number of users in the network launch FLA attack maliciously.

(2) Consider the coexistence of FLA attack and Flash Crowd event, that is, the network faces both FLA attack and Flash Crowd event.

In the following, the detection performance of the proposed scheme will be verified from these two aspects.

① Consider only FLA attacks.

The XC and DFN topologies are used to compare the change of the correct detection rate with the attack intensity and attack range under different schemes. The attack intensity values are 0.3, 0.6, 0.9, 1.2, 1.5 and 1.8, corresponding to the request rates of malicious users are 900, 1800, 2700, 3600, 4500 and 5400 interest packets/s, respectively. There are 10,000 kinds of content in the experiment. Malicious users request a small part of content, and the value of attack range is 40, 50, 60, 70, 80, 90, which represents the number of non-popular content types requested by malicious users. The experimental results are shown in Fig. 4 and Fig. 5.

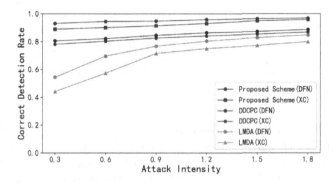

Fig. 4. Comparison of the change of correct detection rate with attack intensity under different schemes.

Figure 4 shows the comparison of the correct detection rate of different schemes with the change of attack intensity under the two topologies. The abscissa represents the attack intensity, and the interest packet sending rate of malicious users is 900, 1800, 2700, 3600, 4500, and 5400 interest packets/s, respectively. The ordinate represents the correct detection rate. As can be seen from the figure, the correct detection rate increases with the increase of attack intensity. This is because as the attack intensity increases, the attacker sends more quickly, the number of attack content increases, and the request rate of attack content changes more, so the detection performance becomes better and better. In addition, it can be seen from Fig. 4 that compared with LMDA and DDCPC, the proposed scheme can achieve better performance and higher correct detection rate. The reason is as follows: LMDA only considers the change of user request rate, which is the worst performance. Compared with LMDA, DDCPC has the second best performance considering the same content request rate and the time interval between two consecutive requests for the same content. However, the proposed scheme based on user behavior and network parameters comprehensively considers three indexes: the request rate of the same content, the difference in the number of interface requests for the same content, and the hit rate change of edge routes. These three indexes can fully reflect the difference between legitimate requests and malicious requests, so the performance is optimal.

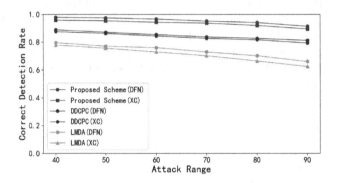

Fig. 5. Comparison of the correct detection rate with the change of attack range under different schemes.

Figure 5 shows the comparison of the correct detection rate of different schemes with the change of attack range under the two topologies. The abscissa represents the attack range, and the types of unpopular content requested by malicious users are 40, 50, 60, 70, 80, 90, and the ordinate represents the correct detection rate. As can be seen from Fig. 5, the correct detection rate decreases as the attack range increases. This is because as the attack range increases, the types of content used by the attacker increase, and the number of each content requested decreases at the same request rate, so the detection performance becomes worse. In addition, it can be seen from Fig. 5 that compared with LMDA and DDCPC, the proposed scheme can achieve better performance with the highest correct detection rate.

② Consider the coexistence of an FLA attack with a Flash Crowd event.

To further demonstrate the robustness of the proposed scheme, it is also confirmed that the proposed scheme can still maintain good performance when faced with Flash Crowd events. In the simulation of Flash Crowd event, legitimate users start to request some content at a high rate, the request rate is 4000 interest packets/s, and the content requested at a high rate is not popular in the last time interval. FLA attacks with a request rate of 4000 interest packets/s, and the attack range is 100 kinds of content. Using XC and DFN topology, considering the coexistence of FLA attack and Flash Crowd event, the detection performance of the proposed scheme when dealing with Flash Crowd event is verified from two aspects: correct detection rate and false detection rate. The experimental results are shown in Fig. 6 and Fig. 7.

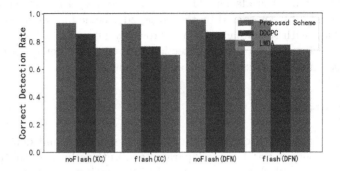

Fig. 6. Comparison of correct detection rate of different schemes in the coexistence environment of Flash Crowd and FLA.

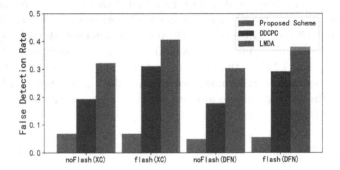

Fig. 7. Comparison of false detection rate of different schemes in the coexistence environment of Flash Crowd and FLA.

Figure 6 and Fig. 7 show the comparison of correct detection rate and false detection rate of two network topologies with or without Flash Crowd event, respectively. As we can see from the figures, the correct detection rate and false detection rate of the proposed scheme basically remain unchanged when Flash Crowd events occur, while both the LMDA and DDCPC schemes show significant performance degradation. The reason is that when a Flash Crowd event occurs, legitimate users suddenly flood the network with requests for something that was not popular at the previous moment, so the request rate for that content varies considerably. However, the LMDA scheme detects attacks only according to the change of content request rate. In this case, the legitimate requests are mostly detected as attack requests, so the correct detection rate is significantly decreased and the false detection rate is significantly increased, resulting in the worst performance. Although the DDCPC scheme considers two characteristics, content request rate and the time interval between two consecutive requests for the same content, these two characteristics will also misjudge legitimate content requests as attack content in the face of Flash Crowd events, resulting in the overall performance degradation. The difference between FLA attack and Flash Crowd event is fully considered by the proposed scheme in this paper, so it can effectively deal with the impact of Flash Crowd event on the network. As can be seen from the figures, the correct detection rate and false detection rate of the proposed scheme are basically stable and unchanged.

6   Conclusion

This paper introduces a cache pollution attack detection and defense scheme based on user behavior and network parameters. In the scheme of this paper, the difference between Flash Crowd event and FLA attack is considered. According to the difference of request behavior between attacking users and legitimate users and the network influence caused by them, three characteristics are considered: The request rate of the same content, the request distribution of each interface of the same content, and the standard deviation of cache hit ratio change of edge routing node, the trained SVM model is used to periodically detect the request packets in the network. Once the attack content is detected, the defense strategy is immediately launched. ndnSIM was used to carry out experiments. Compared with DDCPC and LMDA, the proposed scheme is proved to be more effective in detecting attacks. Furthermore, considering the coexistence of FLA attack and Flash Crowd event, the performance of the proposed scheme is better than DDCPC and LMDA.

References

1. Gao, Y., Deng, L., Kuzmanovic, A., et al.: Internet cache pollution attacks and countermeasures. In: Proceedings of the 2006 IEEE International Conference on Network Protocols, pp. 54–64. IEEE (2006)
2. Conti, M., Gasti, P., Teoli, M.: A lightweight mechanism for detection of cache pollution attacks in named data networking. Comput. Networks 57(16), 3178–3191 (2013)
3. Yao, L., Fan, Z., Deng, J., Fan, X.: Detection and defense of cache pollution attacks using clustering in named data networks. IEEE Trans. Depend. Secure Comput. 17(6), 1310–1321 (2018)
4. Laoutaris, N., Che, H., Stavrakakis, I.: The LCD interconnection of LRU caches and its analysis. Perform. Eval. 63(7), 609–634 (2006)
5. Zhang, G., Liu, J., Chnag, X., et al.: Combining popularity and locality to enhance in-network caching performance and mitigate pollution attacks in content-centric networking. IEEE Access 5, 19012–19022 (2017)
6. Karami, A., Guerrero-Zapata, M.: An Anfis-based cache replacement method for mitigating cache pollution attacks in named data networking. Comput. Netw. 80, 51–65 (2015)

7. Xu, Z., Chen, B., Wang, N., et al.: Elda: towards efficient and lightweight detection of cache pollution attacks in NDN. In: 2015 IEEE 40th Conference on Local Computer Networks (LCN), pp. 82–90. IEEE (2015)
8. Guo, H., Wang, X., Chang, K., et al.: Exploiting path diversity for thwarting pollution attacks in named data networking. IEEE Trans. Inf. Forensics Secur. **11**(9), 2077–2090 (2016)
9. Conti, M., Gasti, P., Teoli, M.: A lightweight mechanism for detection of cache pollution attacks in named data networking. Comput. Netw. **57**(16), 3178–3191 (2013)
10. Kamimoto, T., Mori, K., Umeda, S.,, et al.: Cache protection method based on prefix hierarchy for content-oriented network. In: 2016 13th IEEE Annual Consumer Communications & Networking Conference (CCNC), pp. 417–422. IEEE (2016)
11. Salah, H., Alfatafta, M., SayedAhmed, S., et al.: CoMon++: preventing cache pollution in NDN efficiently and effectively. In: 2017 IEEE 42nd Conference on Local Computer Networks (LCN), pp. 43–51. IEEE (2017)
12. Liu, Q., Li, J.: Multi-parameter cache pollution attack detection algorithm in content-centric network. Comput. Eng. Appl. **55**(4), 130–136 (2019)
13. Yao, L., Zeng, Y., Wang, X., et al.: Detection and defense of cache pollution based on popularity prediction in named data networking. IEEE Trans. Dependable Secure Comput. **18**(6), 2848–2860 (2020)
14. Zhou, J., Luo, J., Wang, J., et al.: Cache pollution prevention mechanism based on deep reinforcement learning in NDN. J. Commun. Inf. Networks **6**(1), 91–100 (2021)

SPOF-NDN: A POF-Based NDN Forwarding Scheme

Wei Guo[1](✉), Yu Zhang[1,2], and Binxing Fang[1,2]

[1] Harbin Institute of Technology, Harbin, China
21B903067@stu.hit.edu.cn, yuzhang@hit.edu.cn, fangbx@cae.cn
[2] Peng Cheng Laboratory, Shenzhen, China

Abstract. Named data networking (NDN) is an instance of information-centric networking (ICN) architecture that delivers data based on the data's name. NDN uses variable-length names to identify data and uses stateful forwarding to deliver packets, which makes NDN forwarders difficult to design on existing programmable data planes. In this paper, we introduce an NDN forwarding scheme based on Protocol-Oblivious Forwarding (POF). This scheme extends a stateful module in the POF architecture to implement stateful forwarding and forward NDN packets with a programmed data plane and a controller application. Packets are forwarded in a forwarder together by a POF switch, a stateful module, and a POF controller. The POF switch implements the stateless forwarding functions of NDN, such as the Forwarding Information Base (FIB) by flow tables. The stateful module implements the stateful forwarding functions, such as the Pending Interest Table (PIT) and the Content Store (CS). The POF controller implements the control functions, such as NDN routing mechanisms. We implemented a prototype by extending a POF software switch. Experimental results show that the prototype can forward NDN packets correctly and can support applications such as live video streaming.

Keywords: Named data networking · Software defined networking · Protocol oblivious forwarding · Network packet forwarding

1 Introduction

Named data networking (NDN) [20] is a new Internet architecture and an instance of information-centric networking (ICN) [2]. The communication of NDN is different from IP (the end-to-end data transfer) in that its users request and receive the content they need from the network. NDN uses hierarchical names to identify data in the network. A consumer (data user) sends an Interest packet with a data name to the NDN network and later receives a Data packet containing the requested data. To complete a communication, the NDN network transmits an Interest packet to the data producer according to its name and then transmits a Data packet back the same way as the Interest packet.

ⓒ The Author(s), under exclusive license to Springer Nature Singapore Pte Ltd. 2023
W. Quan (Ed.): ICENAT 2022, CCIS 1696, pp. 630–644, 2023.
https://doi.org/10.1007/978-981-19-9697-9_50

Forwarders are the basic elements of the NDN network and are used to forward NDN packets. Today's most widely used NDN forwarder is NDN Forwarding Daemon (NFD) [1], a software forwarder that runs on commodity hardware. Hardware forwarders have advantages in performance and deployment, but it is difficult to design and implement an NDN hardware forwarder, and there is less research work on it. Using software-defined networking (SDN) [8] to implement NDN forwarders is a popular idea. Signorello's NDN.p4 [17] is an NDN forwarder based on P4 [3], and Takemasa designed a Tofino-based forwarder [19] that achieved 10 Tbps bandwidth. Additionally, SDN can also be used to enhance NDN functions, such as ENDN [7] and Ma's source routing scheme [9].

In this paper, we present the design of SPOF-NDN. It is an NDN forwarding scheme based on Protocol-oblivious forwarding (POF) [18], running in the POF environment extended with a stateful module that enables POF to forward packets statefully. SPOF-NDN divides the NDN forwarding functions into stateless forwarding, stateful forwarding, and control functions. SPOF-NDN uses a stateful module, a POF switch, and a POF controller to implement these functions respectively in a forwarder. In addition, SPOF-NDN uses a special packet format called SPOF-NDN packet, which has a fixed-length SPOF header that contains all the information required for forwarding (such as the name and the packet type) and can be parsed by the flow table pipeline of the POF switch easily. The forwarding scheme includes the interconversion of NDN packets and SPOF-NDN packets, which occurs at the edge of the SPOF-NDN network.

The main contributions of this paper are as follows:

- We design an NDN forwarding scheme, which divides the NDN forwarding functions into stateless forwarding (including the Forwarding Information Base), stateful forwarding (including the Pending Interest Table and the Content Store), and control functions (including NDN routing mechanisms, such as KITE [21]).
- We design a special packet format to make it easier for the POF switch to parse NDN forwarding information. Some fields of NDN packets in the TLV format are parsed and set into a fixed-length header, which can be matched in flow tables.
- We verify this scheme on a POF software switch. The experimental results demonstrate that the scheme can forward NDN packets correctly and can support applications such as live video streaming.

2 Background

SPOF-NDN is based on two research areas: networking programmability and Named Data Networking. POF is the specific technology of networking programmability which we used to implement SPOF-NDN.

2.1 Protocol-Oblivious Forwarding

Common network hardware devices handle network packets in a fixed process, so network administrators or researchers cannot configure network hardware devices to change their function significantly. Most network hardware devices support TCP/IP, but if the packets of other network layer protocols need to be forwarded, custom hardware devices are required.

SDN [8] is a network programmability technology. In the SDN architecture, the control plane and the data plane of network devices are separated, and the control plane of each device is centrally integrated into a programmable controller. Thus, the software on the controller can define the forwarding method of SDN devices.

OpenFlow [10] is an SDN technology that allows network administrators to define the processing flow of network packets on a network device by programming software. So, OpenFlow can be used to implement custom packet forwarding methods. However, OpenFlow is protocol-dependent, which means that the devices can only handle the packets of some specific network protocols included in the OpenFlow specification. Therefore, OpenFlow is difficult to forward the packets of other network protocols, such as NDN.

POF [18] is a modification of OpenFlow. POF designs a set of protocol-oblivious data plane instructions and a corresponding southbound protocol, thus making the data plane forwarding process independent of the specific network protocols. POF enhances the programmability of the data plane to support the packet forwarding of new network protocols. Specifically, POF uses (offset, length, value) triples to match a field in a packet, so users can implement specific protocol packet processing rules by setting the parameters of the triples.

2.2 Named Data Networking

NDN [20] is an Internet architecture that communicates by transmitting named data. In an NDN communication, the consumer sends an Interest packet with the name of the requested data to the network and then receives a Data packet containing the requested data from the network. The NDN network transmits an Interest packet to the data producer according to its name and later transmits a Data packet back in the same path of the Interest packet (in the reversed direction). This means that each NDN forwarder on the forwarding path should record the forwarding information of the Interest packet until the corresponding Data packet arrives and is forwarded. This kind of forwarding, where the forwarder needs to record additional information, is called stateful forwarding.

A part of the NDN forwarding functions can be classified as a stateful forwarding function, including the Pending Interest Table (PIT) and the Content Store (CS). The PIT is a data structure that stores the forwarding information of Interest packets. The PIT records which interface(s) the forwarder receives an Interest packet from, and it has an index for finding these interface records by NDN names. Once it receives a Data packet, the forwarder will query the interface information stored in the PIT and forward the Data packet towards this interface(s), and finally delete this PIT entry. The CS is an in-network cache mechanism that stores the forwarded Data packets locally to satisfy the corresponding Interest packets directly in the future.

Another part of the NDN forwarding functions can be classified as a stateless forwarding function, including the Forwarding Information Base (FIB). The FIB is a data structure that stores the relationships between a name prefix and the interfaces to which the Interest packets with this name prefix should be forwarded. When a forwarder receives an Interest packet, it queries the FIB and forwards the Interest packet according to the query result. In addition, NDN allows administrators to set routing mechanisms on forwarders, which is a control function.

The NDN packet is in the TLV (Type-Length-Value) format [12], and each field has a variable length and position. This flexible format well supports the NDN hierarchical names with no limit on the number of components and the length of each component. But it also increases the complexity of packet parsing.

3   SPOF-NDN Design

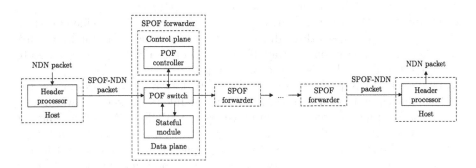

Fig. 1. The overview of the SPOF-NDN architecture

SPOF-NDN is a POF-based NDN forwarding scheme, and Fig. 1 shows the architecture of SPOF-NDN. SPOF-NDN consists of three main parts: header processor, data plane, and control plane.

The header processor implements the interconversion of the NDN packet and the SPOF-NDN packet (a SPOF-NDN-specific packet format). It is deployed on the edge of the SPOF-NDN network, where it could be a border gateway or a host running NDN network applications. When an NDN packet enters a SPOF-NDN network, the header processor converts the NDN packet to a SPOF-NDN packet so that it can be processed and forwarded by SPOF forwarders. When a SPOF-NDN packet leaves a SPOF-NDN network, the header processor converts it to an NDN packet. Therefore, SPOF-NDN is transparent to the NDN network.

The data plane implements some NDN packet forwarding functions, including the PIT, FIB, and CS. The data plane consists of POF switches and stateful modules. The POF switch is the original data plane device of POF and mainly consists of a flow table pipeline. The flow table pipeline contains multiple flow tables, and users can edit these flow tables to build different packet processing flows. SPOF-NDN implements the FIB in the POF switch by building a flow table pipeline. The stateful module runs on commodity hardware and implements the PIT and the CS.

The control plane controls the data plane's forwarding process and implements POF's controller functions, such as initiating flow tables and NDN routing mechanisms (e.g., self-learning and KITE). The control plane is based on the POF controller, which implements the SDN controller functions of POF and provides some application programming interfaces for users to define their forwarder's behavior. SPOF-NDN implements NDN routing mechanisms by developing NDN controller applications in the POF controller.

The process of forwarding an NDN packet in a SPOF-NDN network is divided into the following six steps:

1. A header processor receives an NDN packet from the network or a local application (typically from NFD). It performs the forward conversion to convert the NDN packet to a SPOF-NDN packet and sends the SPOF-NDN packet to the SPOF-NDN network consisting of SPOF forwarders.
2. The SPOF-NDN network routes the SPOF-NDN packet as specified in NDN. The route path passes through several SPOF forwarders and finally reaches a host or terminates on the way. If the next hop is a SPOF forwarder, go to step 3. If the next hop is a host, go to step 6.
3. The SPOF-NDN packet entering the SPOF forwarder is processed by the POF switch and forwarded to the stateful module in the same forwarder.
4. The stateful module receives and processes the SPOF-NDN packet. Then, it forwards a SPOF-NDN packet to the POF switch in the same forwarder.
5. The POF switch receives the SPOF-NDN packet, processes it, and finally sends it to the SPOF-NDN network. If the next hop is a SPOF forwarder, go to step 3. If the next hop is a host, go to step 6.
6. The header processor processes the SPOF-NDN packet entering the host. It performs the backward conversion to convert the SPOF-NDN packet to an NDN packet and sends the NDN packet to the network or a local application (typically to NFD).

A POF switch may communicate with the POF controller in the same forwarder during the forwarding process to obtain new flow table entries. The POF controller implements NDN routing mechanisms such as self-learning and KITE [21] by modifying the flow table entries of the POF switch.

3.1 SPOF-NDN Packet and Header Processor

The SPOF-NDN packet is the packet in the specific format of SPOF-NDN. Figure 2 shows its structure. A SPOF-NDN packet contains a SPOF header between the Ethernet frame header and the NDN packet to implement two functions:

– The SPOF header provides an NDN forwarding information format that can be easily matched and processed by the flow table pipeline of the POF switch to avoid the large overhead caused by parsing the TLV format.

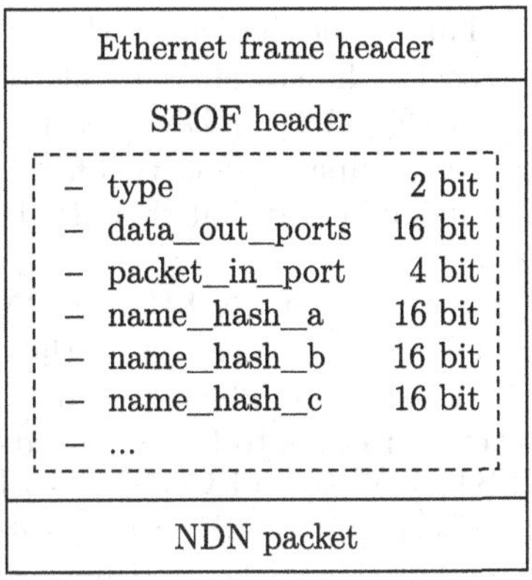

```
┌─────────────────────────────────────┐
│      Ethernet frame header          │
├─────────────────────────────────────┤
│          SPOF header                │
│ ┌ ─ ─ ─ ─ ─ ─ ─ ─ ─ ─ ─ ─ ─ ─ ─ ┐   │
│ │  − type              2 bit    │   │
│ │  − data_out_ports   16 bit    │   │
│ │  − packet_in_port    4 bit    │   │
│ │  − name_hash_a      16 bit    │   │
│ │  − name_hash_b      16 bit    │   │
│ │  − name_hash_c      16 bit    │   │
│ │  − ...                        │   │
│ └ ─ ─ ─ ─ ─ ─ ─ ─ ─ ─ ─ ─ ─ ─ ─ ┘   │
├─────────────────────────────────────┤
│          NDN packet                 │
└─────────────────────────────────────┘
```

Fig. 2. The SPOF-NDN packet structure

– The SPOF header contains some fields that can be read and written by both the POF switch and the stateful module. Thus, the SPOF header can be a container to store and transfer information between modules. It eliminates the need for the POF switch and the stateful module in the same forwarder to keep the session state for communications between them. It simplifies design and improves efficiency.

NDN packets use TLV format, which is characterized by its variable length fields and variable number components. Specifically, a TLV structure consists of some nested TLV substructures containing Type, Length, and Value. The type and length of a field in an NDN packet depend on the values of the Type part and the Length part of the TLV substructure, and its position (the relative position of the first bit of the field from the beginning of the packet) depends on the specifics of other TLV substructures.

The flow table pipeline processes packets in the match-action mode, which can only match fixed-length fields at fixed locations. Specifically, the processing flow of the flow table pipeline consists of several match-action operations. Each match-action operation performs some specific actions (or instructions) when the content of the packet header matches the expected condition, where the match condition is defined by an (offset, match length, expected value) triplet, i.e., the match is successful when the content of the packet has the same bit string in the match length with the expected value at the position of the offset. Therefore, the flow table pipeline cannot directly parse NDN packets in the TLV format.

The SPOF header contains the following fields:

– type: This field is used to distinguish the different processing stages of the SPOF-NDN packet in a forwarding process and to pass the NDN packet's type information, which is parsed by the stateful module, to the flow table pipeline. Its value indicates the type of this SPOF-NDN packet and is one of four enumeration values (expressed as a 2-bit enumeration number):

- UNPROCESSED: This value indicates that this SPOF-NDN packet hasn't been processed by the stateful module of the current SPOF forwarder. It means that this SPOF-NDN packet is being processed by the flow table pipeline for the first time in this forwarding.
- INTEREST: This value indicates that this SPOF-NDN packet is an NDN Interest packet.
- DATA: This value indicates that this SPOF-NDN packet is an NDN Data packet and doesn't need to be processed by the control plane.
- CONTROL_DATA: This value indicates that the SPOF-NDN packet is an NDN Data packet and needs to be processed by the control plane.

Additionally, INTEREST, DATA, and CONTROL_DATA indicate that the SPOF-NDN packet has been processed by the stateful module of the current forwarder. It means that this packet is being processed by the flow table pipeline for the second time in this forwarding. This field is set to one of INTEREST, DATA, or CONTROL_DATA by the stateful module after parsing the NDN packet and is reset to UNPROCESSED by the flow table pipeline during the second time processing.

- data_out_ports: This field is set by the stateful module and used to bring the stateful module's forwarding decision to the flow table pipeline. If the SPOF-NDN packet is a Data packet, the field value indicates a port set (expressed as a 16-bit binary mask) containing several ports to which this packet should be forwarded. Else in the Interest packet case, it is of no use.
- packet_in_port: This field indicates the port (expressed as a 4-bit port ID) from which the forwarder receives the packet. It is set by the flow table pipeline and used in the stateful module.
- name_hash: The SPOF header contains multiple name_hash fields (e.g., eight fields as name_hash_a to name_hash_h), which are used to store the hash values (expressed as a 16-bit code) of name components. The flow table pipeline uses these fields to implement the longest prefix match algorithm on the FIB. Each name_hash field stores the hash value of a name component, and all name_hash fields in the SPOF header store the first few components of the NDN name. The number of name_hash fields is a network parameter, and its value is decided on the network design requirements. More name_hash fields result in longer SPOF headers and higher forwarding costs, but the SPOF forwarders can make more accurate forwarding decisions.

The header processor is a program that interconverts the NDN packet and the SPOF-NDN packet. The forward conversion function converts an NDN packet to a SPOF-NDN packet, and its main process is adding a SPOF header between the Ethernet frame header and the NDN packet. Then, the header processor parses the NDN packet and sets all name_hash fields. The type field is initialized to UNPROCESSED. The backward conversion function converts a SPOF-NDN packet to an NDN packet, and its main action is removing the SPOF header.

Header processors run on the edge of the SPOF-NDN network, thus connecting the SPOF-NDN network and the NDN network. When an NDN packet enters the SPOF-NDN network, a header processor performs the forward conversion and sends the SPOF-NDN packet to the SPOF-NDN network. When a

SPOF-NDN packet leaves the SPOF-NDN network, another header processor performs the backward conversion and sends the NDN packet to the NDN network. Hosts in the SPOF-NDN network can use NDN applications by running a header processor locally and connecting it to an NDN packet forwarder such as NFD.

3.2   Data Plane

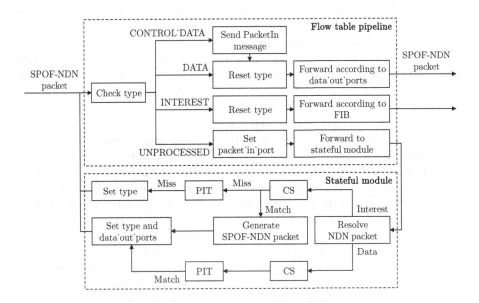

Fig. 3. The forwarding process of the data plane

The SPOF forwarder's data plane implements the input and output of SPOF-NDN packets and the PIT, FIB, and CS functions. The data plane of a SPOF forwarder consists of a POF switch and a stateful module, where the POF switch mainly includes a flow table pipeline. The POF switch implements the stateless forwarding functions, including the input and the output of SPOF-NDN packets, the FIB, and the communications with the control plane by the POF message mechanism. The stateful module implements the NDN packet parsing and the stateful forwarding functions, including the PIT and the CS.

The Flow table pipeline is a module of the POF switch to implement the packet forwarding, which consists of a set of flow tables. Each flow table performs a match-action process on packets, i.e., it matches some specified fields in a packet and performs a set of predefined actions according to the match result. The match conditions in flow tables are defined by (offset, match length, expected value) triplets, where the offset refers to the relative position of the packet header pointer, the length refers to the field's size, and the value refers to the expected content of the field. If the packet's content has the same bit string in the match length with the expected value at the position of offset, the POF switch will execute a set of predefined actions.

A match condition set and an action set constitute a flow table entry, and the match conditions of different entries in a flow table must be the same except for the expected value. POF provides some actions to jump the process flow between different flow tables, which allows multiple flow tables to link to each other to form a flow table pipeline. The packet entering the POF switch is processed step by step along the flow table pipeline and eventually forwarded or dropped.

The FIB is implemented in the flow table pipeline of the POF switch. Because the number, position, and length of the matched fields in POF flow tables need to be predetermined, SPOF forwarders cannot support NDN's variable length names. So, the forwarders consider only the first few components of an NDN name and use the hash value of each component. These hash values are stored in the name_hash fields of the SPOF header. The following examples assume that the SPOF header contains three name_hash fields.

SPOF-NDN implements the longest prefix matching algorithm of the FIB by POF flow table entries' priority. POF allows specifying priority orders for different entries in a flow table. If a packet matches multiple entries in a flow table, POF will execute the actions corresponding to the matched entry with the highest priority. SPOF-NDN sets the priority of a FIB table entry to the number of its prefix's name components. For example, if there is a FIB table entry: prefix /A/B/C to port #1, the corresponding flow table entry's matching condition will be: name_hash_a equals A (hash value), name_hash_b equals B (hash value), name_hash_c equals C (hash value), and the priority will be 3.

When the prefix's components are less than the name_hash fields in the SPOF header, the expected value of the uncovered flow table entries will be set to ANY. For example, if there is a FIB table entry: prefix /A/B to port #2, the corresponding flow table entry's matching condition will be: name_hash_a equals A (hash value), name_hash_b equals B (hash value), name_hash_c matches ANY content, and the priority will be 2.

If a flow table contains the above entries, the packet named /A/B/C/D will match both two entries, and finally be forwarded to port #1 according to the priority order. The packet named /A/B/E will only match the second entry, and finally be forwarded to port #2. Similarly, an NDN FIB table can be converted to a flow table entry by entry.

The stateful module runs on commodity hardware and communicates with the flow table pipeline via network interfaces. The stateful module uses the ndn-cxx library to implement the NDN packet parsing, the CS, and the PIT.

The SPOF forwarder's forwarding process for a SPOF-NDN packet consists of three stages:

1. First, the POF switch receives a SPOF-NDN packet from the network and uses the flow table pipeline to process the packet. This stage performs the packet input function and forwards the packet to the stateful module.

2. Then, the stateful module receives the SPOF-NDN packet from the flow table pipeline and processes it. This stage parses the NDN packet and performs the stateful forwarding functions such as the PIT and the CS. After processing, the stateful module sends a SPOF-NDN packet to the flow table pipeline or drops the received packet only.

3. Finally, the flow table pipeline receives the SPOF-NDN packet from the stateful module and processes it. This stage performs the routing mechanisms together with the control plane and performs the FIB function and the packet output function.

A SPOF-NDN packet enters the flow table pipeline twice during the one-hop forwarding process, and the flow table pipeline uses the same process in these two entries. SPOF-NDN uses the type field of the SPOF header to distinguish these two entries. When the SPOF-NDN packet enters the flow table pipeline for the first time, its type field must be UNPROCESSED, which is ensured by the initialization of the type field by the header processor and the modification of the type field by the SPOF forwarder at the last hop. When the SPOF-NDN packet enters the flow table pipeline for the second time, its type field must be one of INTEREST, DATA, or CONTROL_DATA, which is ensured by the modification of the type field by the stateful module.

When the flow table pipeline receives a SPOF-NDN packet, it first checks the type field to know whether the SPOF-NDN packet is entering the flow table pipeline for the first time. If the type field equals UNPROCESSED, the SPOF-NDN packet is entering the flow table pipeline for the first time, and the POF switch will set the packet_in_port field to the ID of the port from which the POF switch received the packet.

When the stateful module receives a SPOF-NDN packet, it first parses the NDN packet behind the SPOF header. The stateful module runs on commodity hardware, so it doesn't have the same difficulty in parsing the TLV format as the POF switch. The stateful module parses the NDN packet to get its name, type (Interest or Data), and whether it should be processed by the control plane (according to the routing mechanisms). SPOF-NDN currently supports the self-learning mechanism and KITE, which use only Data packets to bring routing information. Therefore, SPOF-NDN distinguishes all NDN packets into INTEREST, DATA, and CONTROL_DATA. Data packets that contain the identification token belonging to the self-learning mechanism or KITE will be classified as CONTROL_DATA, and other Data packets will be classified as DATA. The stateful module sets the classification result to the type field of the SPOF header, which will be used in the flow table pipeline.

The stateful module can get the full NDN name in an NDN packet, so it uses the full name in the PIT and the CS. If the packet is an Interest packet, the stateful module first searches the CS to get a Data packet that can satisfy this Interest. If the search is successful, the stateful module will generate a SPOF-NDN packet corresponding to this Data packet and forward it to the flow table pipeline. The data_out_ports field of this packet will be set to a port set, which only contains the port stored in the packet_in_port field of the corresponding

Interest packet. If the search is failed, the stateful module then searches the PIT to get an entry corresponding to the Interest packet. If the search is successful, the packet_in_port field value of the Interest packet will be added to the port set of the PIT entry, and the Interest packet will be dropped. If the search is failed, a new PIT entry will be created, which is corresponding to the Interest packet. Then, the stateful module will forward the Interest packet to the flow table pipeline.

If the packet is a Data packet, the stateful module will store it in the CS and search the PIT to get an entry corresponding to the Data packet. If the search is successful, the stateful module will set the data_out_ports field to the port set stored in the PIT entry, and then removes this entry. Finally, the stateful module forwards the Data packet to the flow table pipeline. If the search is failed, the stateful module will drop the Data packet.

If the SPOF-NDN packet is entering the flow table pipeline for the second time, its type field must be one of INTEREST, DATA, or CONTROL_DATA. The flow table pipeline processes these packets in different ways:

- For packets in INTEREST type, the POF switch first resets the type field to UNPROCESSED so that this packet can be processed correctly after entering the SPOF forwarder at the next hop for the first time. Then the FIB flow table performs the match-action process on the packet and determines which ports to forward. Finally, the packet is forwarded to the chosen ports.
- For packets in DATA type, the POF switch first resets the type field to UNPROCESSED, which is the same as INTEREST. Then, the POF switch forwards the packet to the ports stored in the data_out_ports field.
- For packets in CONTROL_DATA type, the POF switch first sends a PacketIn message to the control plane. This PacketIn message will be received by the POF controller in the control plane. The controller will parse the packet and other information stored in the PacketIn message, and process them according to the routing mechanisms running in the control plane. The flow table pipeline will then process the packet in the same way as a packet in DATA type.

3.3   Control Plane

The control plane of SPOF-NDN implements the flow table initiation and management, as well as the NDN routing mechanisms such as self-learning and KITE. The control plane includes a POF controller that implements the flow table initiation and management. There are several POF controllers that can meet the functional requirements of SPOF-NDN. To simplify the programming works, we use the Protocol Oblivious Programming (POP) [5] environment and its POF controller application to develop our controller.

The flow table pipeline of the POF switch contains no flow table after startup. The POF controller initiates and updates flow tables in advance or during the processing of the packet, which fills the flow table pipeline with the flow table structure described in Sect. 3.2.

SPOF-NDN implements the NDN routing mechanisms on the control plane. These NDN routing mechanisms may need to process the Data packets associated with them to gather information to make routing decisions. When the stateful module on the data plane recognizes these Data packets, it sets their type fields to CONTROL_DATA. When a SPOF-NDN packet in CONTROL_DATA type enters the flow table pipeline, the POF switch sends a PacketIn message to the POF controller, which carries the whole packet and other information such as the input port ID. When the POF controller receives this message, the NDN routing mechanisms obtain and analyze it. Finally, the routing mechanisms may change the routing rules of the data plane by updating the flow tables.

For example, if a Trace Data (TD) of KITE enters a SPOF forwarder, the stateful module will recognize the KITE flag in the TD's name and set the type field of the packet to CONTROL_DATA. After that, the POF switch checks that the packet is in CONTROL_DATA type and sends a PacketIn message to the POF controller. Then, the KITE mechanism will analyze the PacketIn message, extract its name and the input port ID, and decide to create a new route based on this information. Finally, the KITE mechanism uses the POF controller to create a new entry in the FIB flow table to add the new route.

4   Evaluation

We implemented a prototype of SPOF-NDN by extending the POF software switch and programming in the POP environment. We implemented the stateful module as a Linux TAP device using the ndn-cxx library and developed a POP network policy to implement the function of the flow table pipeline. The POP controller will generate flow tables according to the network policy to implement the function of the SPOF forwarder.

We conducted evaluation experiments on the prototype in two scenarios to verify the function of the forwarding scheme. The experimental environment consists of four servers (Lenovo SR650 server equipped with a single Intel Xeon 3106 8-core CPU, 32 GB memory, and 1 Gbps Ethernet card).

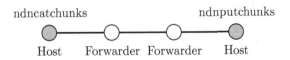

Fig. 4. The topology of the first scenario

In the first scenario, we use NDN Essential Tools' ndnputchunks and ndncatchunks programs [11] to transfer some files and measure the performance. The topology of the experiment is shown in Fig. 4. Two hosts are connected to each other through two forwarders. One host runs ndnputchunks to publish a test file, and the other host runs ndncatchunks to request the test file. We transfer a 64 MB random file by several 1000B chunks in our experiments. Each group of experiments transfers this file 50 times and records the average value of the performance. We conducted two groups of experiments. The first group used SPOF-NDN as the forwarders and the second group used NFD as the forwarders. The results are shown in Table 1.

Table 1. Performances of SPOF-NDN and NFD in file transfer

Forwarder	Time elapsed (s)	Segment received	Goodput (Mbps)	Timeout count	Retransmitted segments	RTT average (ms)
SPOF-NDN	50.22	67109	10.76	1319.64	1286.12	15.23
NFD	4.49	67109	119.71	1645.36	1644.08	5.15

The experimental result shows that the SPOF forwarder can forward NDN packets to the right ports, which indicates that the forwarding scheme is designed correctly. However, the performance of this prototype forwarder has a large gap with NFD. In our opinion, the main reason is that the prototype forwarder is based on the POF software switch. The software switch simulates the behavior of the programmable hardware switch, so its forwarding actions cannot achieve the expected performance. Besides, this prototype program can be further optimized. We think that we can learn from the data structure design of NDN-DPDK [16] and the multi-threading scheme of MW-NFD [4].

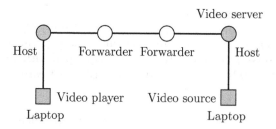

Fig. 5. The topology of the second scenario

In the second scenario, we deployed NDNts-video [13] (a live video streaming system based on NDNts [14] and Shaka Player [15]) in the experimental environment. The topology of the experiment is shown in Fig. 5. One laptop pushes a video stream to the video server by the RTMP protocol. The other laptop connects to the NFD forwarder running on a host by WebSocket and pulls the live video stream. Two hosts are connected to each other through two SPOF forwarders. We observe the playback quality and the performance continuously. Finally, with the adaptive bit rate mechanism, the video plays smoothly at 1200×720 resolution and 5859 Kbps bit rate, with a predicted bandwidth of about 7600 Kbps.

The experimental result shows that the SPOF-NDN network can not only forward test data but also support applications such as live video streaming, which is practical. With the rapid development of new network technologies such as PINet [6], we believe that SPOF-NDN is expected to become a forwarding scheme that can be widely deployed and support real applications.

5   Conclusion

In this paper, we introduced SPOF-NDN, an NDN forwarding scheme based on POF. SPOF-NDN extends the POF architecture with a stateful module to implement the stateful forwarding functions of NDN. The stateless forwarding functions are implemented by the POF switch, and the control functions are implemented by the POF controller. We designed the SPOF-NDN packet format, whose SPOF header is fixed-length and contains all the information required for forwarding. SPOF-NDN uses this packet format to make it easier for the flow table pipeline of the POF switch to parse and handle packets. Experimental results show that SPOF-NDN can forward NDN packets correctly and support applications such as live video streaming, which is practical.

Acknowledgements. This work was supported by National Key Research and Deployment Program of China (Grant No. 2020YFB1806402), STS Planned Project of the Chinese Academy of Sciences (Grant No. E1X0061105).

References

1. Afanasyev, A., et al.: NFD developer's guide. Dept. Comput. Sci., Univ. California, Los Angeles, Los Angeles, CA, USA, Technical report NDN-0021 (2014)
2. Ahlgren, B., Dannewitz, C., Imbrenda, C., Kutscher, D., Ohlman, B.: A survey of information-centric networking. IEEE Commun. Mag. **50**(7), 26–36 (2012). https://doi.org/10.1109/MCOM.2012.6231276
3. Bosshart, P., et al.: P4: programming protocol-independent packet processors. SIGCOMM Comput. Commun. Rev. **44**(3), 87–95 (2014). https://doi.org/10.1145/2656877.2656890
4. Byun, S.H., Lee, J., Sul, D.M., Ko, N.: Multi-worker NFD: an NFD-compatible high-speed NDN forwarder. In: Proceedings of the 7th ACM Conference on Information-Centric Networking, pp. 166–168. ICN 2020, Association for Computing Machinery, New York, NY, USA (2020). https://doi.org/10.1145/3405656.3420233
5. He, C., Feng, X.: POMP: protocol oblivious SDN programming with automatic multi-table pipelining. In: IEEE INFOCOM 2018 - IEEE Conference on Computer Communications, pp. 998–1006 (2018). https://doi.org/10.1109/INFOCOM.2018.8485848
6. Hu, Y., Li, D., Sun, P., Yi, P., Wu, J.: Polymorphic smart network: an open, flexible and universal architecture for future heterogeneous networks. IEEE Trans. Network Sci. Eng. **7**(4), 2515–2525 (2020). https://doi.org/10.1109/TNSE.2020.3006249

7. Karrakchou, O., Samaan, N., Karmouch, A.: ENDN: an enhanced NDN architecture with a P4-programmabie data plane. In: Proceedings of the 7th ACM Conference on Information-Centric Networking. ICN 2020, New York, NY, USA, pp. 1–11. Association for Computing Machinery (2020). https://doi.org/10.1145/3405656.3418720

8. Kreutz, D., Ramos, F.M.V., Veríssimo, P.E., Rothenberg, C.E., Azodolmolky, S., Uhlig, S.: Software-defined networking: a comprehensive survey. Proc. IEEE **103**(1), 14–76 (2015). https://doi.org/10.1109/JPROC.2014.2371999

9. Ma, P., You, J., Wang, L., Wang, J.: Source routing over protocol-oblivious forwarding for named data networking. J. Netw. Syst. Manage. **26**(4), 857–877 (2017). https://doi.org/10.1007/s10922-017-9445-9

10. McKeown, N., et al.: OpenFlow: enabling innovation in campus networks. SIGCOMM Comput. Commun. Rev. **38**(2), 69–74 (2008). https://doi.org/10.1145/1355734.1355746

11. NDN Essential Tools. https://github.com/named-data/ndn-tools. Accessed 16 Aug 2022

12. NDN Packet Format Specification version 0.3. https://named-data.net/doc/NDN-packet-spec/current/. Accessed 4 Aug 2022

13. NDNts Adaptive Video. https://github.com/yoursunny/NDNts-video. Accessed 18 Aug 2022

14. NDNts: Named Data Networking libraries for the Modern Web. https://yoursunny.com/p/NDNts/. Accessed 18 Aug 2022

15. Shaka Player. https://github.com/shaka-project/shaka-player. Accessed 18 Aug 2022

16. Shi, J., Pesavento, D., Benmohamed, L.: NDN-DPDK: NDN forwarding at 100 Gbps on commodity hardware. In: Proceedings of the 7th ACM Conference on Information-Centric Networking. ICN 2020, New York, NY, USA, pp. 30–40. Association for Computing Machinery (2020). https://doi.org/10.1145/3405656.3418715

17. Signorello, S., State, R., François, J., Festor, O.: NDN.p4: programming information-centric data-planes. In: 2016 IEEE NetSoft Conference and Workshops (NetSoft), pp. 384–389 (2016). https://doi.org/10.1109/NETSOFT.2016.7502472

18. Song, H.: Protocol-oblivious forwarding: unleash the power of SDN through a future-proof forwarding plane. In: Proceedings of the Second ACM SIGCOMM Workshop on Hot Topics in Software Defined Networking. HotSDN 2013, New York, NY, USA, pp. 127–132. Association for Computing Machinery (2013). https://doi.org/10.1145/2491185.2491190

19. Takemasa, J., Koizumi, Y., Hasegawa, T.: Vision: toward 10 Tbps NDN forwarding with billion prefixes by programmable switches. In: Proceedings of the 8th ACM Conference on Information-Centric Networking. ICN 2021, New York, NY, USA, pp. 13–19. Association for Computing Machinery (2021). https://doi.org/10.1145/3460417.3482973

20. Zhang, L., et al.: Named data networking. SIGCOMM Comput. Commun. Rev. **44**(3), 66–73 (2014). https://doi.org/10.1145/2656877.2656887

21. Zhang, Y., Xia, Z., Mastorakis, S., Zhang, L.: KITE: producer mobility support in named data networking. In: Proceedings of the 5th ACM Conference on Information-Centric Networking. ICN 2018, New York, NY, USA, pp. 125–136. Association for Computing Machinery (2018). https://doi.org/10.1145/3267955.3267959

Author Index

Printed in the United States
by Baker & Taylor Publisher Services